RACE AND RELIGION
IN EARLY NINETEENTH CENTURY
AMERICA
1800-1850

CONSTITUTION, CONSCIENCE,
AND CALVINIST COMPROMISE

Volume I

RACE AND RELIGION
IN EARLY NINETEENTH CENTURY
AMERICA
1800-1850

CONSTITUTION, CONSCIENCE,
AND CALVINIST COMPROMISE

Joseph R. Washington, Jr.

Studies in American Religion
Volume 39
Two Volume Set

The Edwin Mellen Press
Lewiston•Queenston
Lampeter

Library of Congress Cataloging-in-Publication Data

Washington, Joseph R.
    Race and religion in early nineteenth century America, 1800-1850 :
Constitution, conscience, and Calvinist compromise / Joseph R.
Washington, Jr.
      p. cm. -- (Studies in American religion ; v. 39)
    Bibliography: p.
    Includes index.
    ISBN 0-88946-682-3
    1. Slavery and the church--United States. 2. Racism--United
States--Religious aspects--Christianity--History of doctrines.
3. Calvinism--United States--History--19th century. 4. United
States--Constitutional history. 5. United States--Race relations.
6. United States--Church history--19 century. I. Title.
II. Series.
E446.W27 1989
241'.675'0973--dc19   88-32752
                                                         CIP

This is volume 39 in the continuing series
Studies in American Religion
Volume 39 ISBN 0-88946-682-3
SAR Series ISBN 0-88946-992-X

To the memory of Susie and Joseph R. Washington, Sr.

For Sophia and our sons David and Bryan

My realized past, present, and future hope

CONTENTS

Volume I

Volume II

AUTHOR TO READER

This is an American Christian social ethics essay set in an experimental theological interpretive process. In this pilot project, the ethicist essays to explore the prime rate of Protestant philanthropist prototypes' primary race (reason) and religion (revelation) real interests. These premiums, of a preferred policy and portfolio produced by positively placed prized principle, are no less productive for being selectively denied disincentives and/or affirmed incentives.

One outcome of acceptance following reflection upon this reality is the critical approach of this exercise in examining the charity of the collective conscious class and caste conscience in the civil culture and church. In this treament of the frequently more highly valued than valuable values of victors and vanquishers, the forementioned publicly disclosed preferences are disengaged as actualized intentions and engaged as realized consequences.

The focus is fixed flexible upon the results of the public promise and performance a chosen few power people, paradigmatic parson and parishioner philanthropists, and either self-identified or otherwise identifiable English/Puritan race-specific and British/Protestant ethnic-specific (un-English Scotch, Irish, and Welsh) churchman. Of course, the theological ethics motive and method of this search for the meaning of the public ethics promulgated by Protestant ethicists means it is no more a social science than it is a natural science approach to the subject and object.

The examination is an endeavor within the humanities division of the American Christian social ethics discipline. It is designed and employed neither to develop either a traditional academic analytical methodology or an innovative knowledge retrieving system nor to search for and contribute new data. The essay develops out of a fully developed appreciation of the historical and current secular and religious race relations information, and accepts the solid facts and figures generated by earlier and contemporary productive scholars.

Exactly because their theoretical and experiential empirical evidence are not disputed but their interpretations are probed, their conclusions can be scrutinized without calling into question their significant analysis of the critical factors contributing to rational and relevant class and caste values and disvalues. The primary objective of my writing project is to reflect upon the race/ethnic rules and regulations of the Black race in managed reality competing profane and sacred relative and absolute truth cultural determiners critically imposed upon American society.

In addition to drawing broadly on the wide-ranging philosophical and theological traditions underpinning Western Christian social ethics in North America, I adopt and adapt elementary elements of a probative and deconstructionist analysis. It functions as an interdisciplinary methodological process of reflection upon American establishment Protestant churchmen and their church, state, and race relations.

Common sense suggests it is unnecessary to document the well-known details and statistics related in this critique, since they are readily accessible in the published works of the selected exemplary men, movements, and institutions. I choose to focus on the power agencies they perfectly reflect mainstream social ethics thought and action. I assume the commonsensical commonplace that their highly representative moral models concentrate the mind. But their strengths and weaknesses are delimited in this context to a few of the results issuing forth from their descriptive facts and value judgments that engender the American White race-ethnic and Black race groups' corresponding and competing legitimate claims, interests, desires.

Competitors of the major moral moderates stood out not only in the mainstream and from the establishmentarians but also as adversaries of pro-White race/ethnic interests advocates and protectionists, immediately before and after the birth of the nation. Outstanding Protestant proponents of mutual respect between Black and White race groups formed a minority who particularly distinguished themselves as pro-White race and pro-Black race equalitarians. Howbeit their goal exceeded their grasp, these egalitarians reached the conclusion that the one human species is composed of several mutually fertile races, and to assert the equal ethical value of Black and White races, by extending broadscoped liberating values as traditionalists exercised themselves in expanding narrow-scoped interpretations of natural laws and natural rights.

Largely standard deviations from the norm established by fellow English race representatives, this creative corps within the White Anglo-Saxon Protestant race-ethnic minorities forming the American majority sharpened their fairness and equity principle at the historic race/ethnic transitional stage in the American experiment. At this turning point, new waves of European immigrants disembarking in the East, and old emigrants relocating in the West, were evolving from powerless masses into a critical mass of politically potent British and Continental ethnics.

A singular sectarian development accelerated as a result of these major migrations and changes in the culture: Evangelical Calvinist English-race and British-ethnic cousins forged a formidable church and state confluence which contributed to the dynamic convergence from divergence of their secular relatives. The resulting relative ascendancy of White-ethnic newcomers--compared to the paralleling descendancy of Black-race indigenous North Americans--was accelerated by their utilitarian value no less real than their pro-White race/ethnic and anti-Black race interest values.

This Second Great Awakening White race/ethnic connective linkage expanded the old links New England Congregationalist and Presbyterian leaders fashioned and the current ones they formed with the new masses of Scotch-Irish Reformed churchmen. Thus previously diametrically opposed advantaged and disadvantaged groups formed a race and religion class leverage that placed all the pressure on the perceived undifferentiated whole body of free Black and slave Americans. Quite in line with the elimination of all Black male competition cause and effect of their merged White-ethnic oppressive offensive and White-race repressive defensive or positive negation of the Black-race champion and contender, the alternately affirmed and denied direct outcome from this essentially income-securing middle-class and lower-class coordinated color caste/captive strategy and tactic was the predictable upward and downward spiraling fortunes of White and Black folk.

Lower-class immigrants displayed in their public exhibitions they possessed far less curiosity and accurate information about the past than interest in the opportunity generated in previous North American history. As fortunes-amassing ethnic immigrants--during America's early national years and/or rapidly developing industrialization and expanding wealth initial stages--they followed as the labor class the knowledgeable upper-and middle-class to the point of repeating their secular and religious race/ethnic-specific mistakes more precisely than history.

English-race and British-ethnic slavemasters of multiform Black African-eth-

nic peoples led the other Occidental (and few if any compeer Oriental) immigrant slaveowners in orchestrating and arranging the development of the inces-
sant deethnicization and deculturalization of Black African ethnicity, which experimental method and program English race-specific Quaker-Puritan no less effectively at first than Anglican-Puritan and Calvinist-Puritan settlers initiated
as conscious or unconscious imitators of rival Continental Catholic powers in
the New World. By means of this systematic and systemic process the White
race (Puritan patricians and Cavalier aristocrats) upper-class and middle-class,
together with the White ethnic lower-class and middle-class, separated themselves permanently from Black (as wittingly or unwittingly as these eighteenth-
century Calvinists embraced fellow Dutch Afrikaner or White race-specific)
African ethnics, and fundamentally arrested their development.

Essentially English-race and British-ethnic "*freemen*" and indentured servants,
and their descendants especially, succeeded in the system (at least as well as
other ethnic groups) they managed for the unique multi-ethnic African people to
fail as determinatively as they arranged their deethnicization and deculturalization. The Anglo/American-race power elite and British/American-ethnic powerless masses formed a more ideal than real classless collective conscious and
forged a state of war against the caste class. They shared values and interests
in at once including and excluding the entirely unique and distinct multi-ethnic
African peoples: whom Europeans forced to be both a race-only group, slave
class in perpetuity, and body deprived of basic citizenship rights, responsibilities, opportunities, and privileges.

Such special interests and rationalized real interests were the power people's
highly prized possessions, expressly espoused equivalencies of the general interest, and unquestionably critical impositions. No one questions the commonsensical actuality that these were realized natural needs of the advantaged.

Whether like these security measures the power possessors were par for the
course, or whether these power elite were raised above the norm of peer powerhouses, what is plain to all reasonable ratiocinators resonates and requires no
argumentation: Power corrupts and absolute power corrupts absolutely as certainly as the powerful were so possessed by the absolute power they possessed
until they possessed the powerless absolutely. Equally evidently, few serious citizens doubt either the existence of an elective affinity between having and
holding precious property, or that this positive feedback between possessing and
protecting principal prompted the power people to possesss pariah people.

First and foremost, if not always and everywhere at once, the American system of class over caste originated as predeliberate intentions and consequences
in the color caste chances-cancelling undivided mind and will of the alterna-
tingly contentious and collective consciences controlling community concerns.
Specifically, they were the risk-intensive rational sons of the patrician and
aristocrat creators of the onetime two most powerful North American cultures--
that is, the consistently complementary and competitive hegemonic Puritan/Nor-
theastern and Anglican/Southeastern ecclesiastical and civil powers.

Demonstrable superior English and inferior African power loomed large with
the capacious capacity of exordinary European men (1) to realize their will and
reason with impunity; (2) to form either licit or illicit liaisons and to enjoy
respectable social relations and questionable intimate intercourse with African
women, while preempting the Black male of the power and possibility no less
than the right and responsibility to exercise manhood or to protect his wife (to
say little of his woman and children) from all enemies foreign and domestic; and

(3) to fashion a genetic and cultural formation whereby they re-created the Af-
rican-Europeans a rejected Black-race kith and kin group.

As a result of selective affirmation and disaffirmation of real kin-group relations and responsibility (let alone accepting accountability and culpability or liability), American culture codes conceivers and conductors created *de novo* a
race-specific group, formed in the image of God and man less intentionally and
positively from in the loins of the lions: one at once spiritually *"born-again"*
and cultural reborn a color caste/captive class, stripped of Black African ethnic
elementary constituent elements, and deprived of a viable whole way of life
(ethnic-specific real alternative essence in existence).

White progenitors preempted their cultural kin-group of their natural or
complete, valued, and valuable ethnicity roots,shoots, and branches which are
indispensable for maximum competition and contribution in a society composed
of race/ethnic-specific minorities They fashioned a foreshortened and limited
peoplehood or not an ethnic-specific Black body, whose also single and singular
race constituent element subsists of severed basic formations and therefore severely restricted cultural resources.

Their extraordinarily excessive caste class limitation deters proper nurture of
nature, natural gifts and graces, and each Black female and male. These realities are not disproved but proved by exceptional performers who achieve in the
face of adversity, since it is nonsensical to promote the canard that their success rather failure argues the color caste cultural condition is an existence devoutly to be wished! As a result of the deethnicization and color caste culture-
conditioned handicap, the race-minority competes with the race/ethnic-minorities
forming the American majority at a decided disadvantage.

This Black-race or color caste versus White (Brown, Yellow, Red) race-class
clash generates the unique dynamic race/ethnic and static race-only cultural ka-
leidoscope. What is distinguishable can be denominated the distinctive nature
and condition of Black Americans, form and function of *"the spirit"* of national
anti-Black race values, and the American standard of anti-Black race virtue and
vice.

It is axiomatic and self-evident, of course, that the political, economic, and
social sources together with the anti-Black race virtue they empower spring
from the culture's pivotal secular and sacred doctrine of the sacrosanct individual. Individualism is the principle of elementary efficiency whose interallied ecclesiastical and civil components are structured and directed by profane and religious bureaucrats and technocrats. Inarguably, the asserted equivalency of the
White-ethnic individual and the American individual comprises the constituent
element of both republican democracy and Protestant Evangelicalism (which begins with the new being or *"born again"* person and ends in *"American Civil Religion"*).

Electing not to accept their Black-race kinspeople, because their preferred
acquiesence to the overwhelming White race/ethnic demanding desire for color
caste total rejection, proved a more expedient and convenient or exciting choice
in the early national period.

Primarily White Old Abolitionist churchmen formed an establishment Protestant ecclesiastical and civil confluence, chose to escape the inherited Black
caste versus White class dilemma rather to solve it at the new beginning of the
North American experiment in liberty and justice with freedom for all inhabitants. On the even of the American Revolution, Independence and Union, leading churchmen elected regressive imperialism rather than progressive experimen-

talism, and first attempted to deport the whole body of Black-race indigenous North Americans.

This Evangelical Calvinist experimentation in human beings emanated as a rational Puritan design in the 1770s-mind of Samuel Hopkins--the premier Calvinist philosophical theologian, Congregationalist ethicist, and New England-clergyman Old Abolitionist. Nearly a decade and a half after he died--and Old Abolitionism in establishment Calvinism and New England was buried with him--the pre-democracy and early national innovative Hopkinsian scheme was rediscovered, revitalized, and revised by the Puritan parson's Yankee descendants in English-race Congregationalist (Orthodoxy) and British-ethnic Presbyterian (Reformed) traditions. They constituted not dependent but interlinked indepen-dent and interdependent churches in one Calvinist denomination.

Thus it was neither accidental nor incidental that during the post-theocracy and pre-slavocracy period of embryonic democracy Northeastern Congregationalists and Northern and Southern Presbyterians nationally organized, institutionalized, and developed rapidly the underdeveloped Hopkintonian formula on the eve of the Congressional debate over the Missouri Bill.

The argument resulting in the Missouri Compromise was joined by Yankee Senator Rufus King, one of the few surviving Yankees who remained determined despite being defeated Old Abolitionists, was an elected representative from Massachusetts to the Continental Congresses nearly a half century earlier, and relocated in New York whose adopted state he currently represented in the U-nited Senate.

Fifty years after the ratification of the American Constitution (actualizable as a result of the Republic's initial "*Compromise*" of principle or so-called first "*White Christian Gentlemen's Agreement*" and Act of "*Original Sin*"), but no later than the Missouri Bill or the second negotiated Compromise of principles and the interests of Black Americans, the new antislavery-conscious but anti-abolitionist rather than Old Abolitionist Yankees produced as the first generation born in the Union the American Colonization Society.

Their sacred-profane phalanx possessed the motive, means, and opportunity to banish benevolently all free Black Americans (and slaves manumitted to the care of the American Colonizationists for this purpose). The Society's Black race deportation and denationalization policy, process, and program was an up-to-date reinterpretation of the inspired gospel according to Samuel Hopkins.

The Congregational-Presbyterian Union formed at the beginning of the nine-teenth century from the first Protestant establishment power denomination, composed of equally enterprising and surprising interlocking directorates. Fifteen years after their Alliance was formalized there sprang forth from their formation the Society, which Northeastern and Southeastern Calvinist patricians and aristocrats led the other major Evangelical churches who joined them in endorsing the hierocratic enterprise as their own para-denominational antislavery organization.

The all-White American Colonizationists dominating the Society's corporate board instantly created the pro-White race/ethnic-interest Society the antiBlack race-interest Protestant standard and the perfect parochial, private, and public partnership model.

Finally, then, after two hundred years of granting new ethnic immigrants citizenship rights instantly upon their arrival, and denying the franchise to their indigenous North American Black race kin-group, a minority of nontradi-tionalists emerged in power during the brief but bright fifteen years of the

Civil War and Reconstruction eras; managed to confer citizenship status on Black males; and proceeded to enfranchise Black citizens despite the apparent reluctant consent and replete dissent of Northern and Southern traditionalists.

What these sons of wayward worldly saints (better known to history as the Radical Reconstruction Yankees) demonstrated is equally revealing and relevant: *"Consistent Calvinist"* capitalists were selectively permissive and flexible Puritans, intolerant and rigid Yankees, and pro-political and anti-political parsons. They proved compared to the 1840s relatively praiseworthy when they decided during the mid-1860s not contest the powers who were determined to facilitate a statistically significant increase in the number of Black males granted the privilege of exercising the franchise.

Concurrently Radical Reconstruction Yankees, during the brief period they were formally in command and control and denominated by Evangelical Calvinist traditionalists the instituted powers and authorities ordained by God, documented unwittingly the historic Puritan-Yankee rule of exceptionalism was confirmed and not overturned by selecting and electing Black professionals the exceptions.

Just as publicly, parsons and parishioners disclosed in their roles as parochial and private persons that permitting the competent to compete proved the norm which admits no exceptions to the rule--that is, the Black race can be neither liked nor loved because the Black body is an inferior member of the human species and therefore an unacceptable alien group.

These enduring virtues and lasting values are the dynamic realities and underlying certainties underpinning this probative and deconstructionist critique of secular and sacred race religion. The interpretative essay elucidates the structural (but not inflexible) anti-Black race values in the public sector, as these permanent cultural factors are instrumentalized by the harmonious interplay of profane private and parochial cultural thought and action of professional clergy and lay ministers.

Organization man apposite juxtaposed ecclesiastical bureaucrats and technocrats triumphed in the new Protestant churches (whose structural rationalization and institutionalization marked them off from their forerunners); formation of national and international denominations; and development of multinational missionary bureaucracies and eleemosynary sectarian corporations.

Adopting the Calvinist capitalist management techniques pioneered by Protestant captains of industry and chairmen of corporate boards, New England churchmen and benevolent hierocracies emerged after the death of the (Congregationalist-Puritan) Reverend Jonathan Edwards (1703-58). Edwards developed as the chief challenger of the Arminians and into the premier architect of Evangelical Calvinist theoretical principles and experiential practices.

As a nonesuch Edwards evolved the peerless intellectual exponent of rational, rapid, and radical religious and social structural change induced by the Millennial "Ultimate Revolution" which he specifically detailed and chiefly prayed for diligently. He remained Orthodoxy's premier standard of truth and error until near the end of the long life of his best student and friend, and Orthodoxy's prototypal procolonizationist and Old Abolitionist, the (Congregationalist-Puritan) Reverend Samuel Hopkins (1721-1803).

Contemporary advocates and adversaries credited Edwards and Hopkins with being the two most influential Calvinist dogma (faith) and pragma (ethics) theologians during their successive careers. Some colleagues argued persuasively that the two unsurpassed systematic theologians produced positive good and negative good possibilities and impossibilities, values and disvalues, and virtue and vice devices.

The masterful rationalists intended their Evangelical logic to further nothing so little "*American Civil Religion*," but their faith and ethics productive labor advanced no greater in secular cause and effect. They generated theories as well as theses and hypotheses, which, whether unconsciously or whether unintentionally no less effectively, fashioned precipitating moral principles and practices whose sharp points contributed to the expansion of the Black individual hurt-pervasive and Black race harm-intensive deterrence-benevolence ethic. Anti-Black race interests-specific ideas and ideals, like the deterrence-benevolence ethic they were cause and effect of, scarely limited the capacity of the power elite.

Deterrence-benevolence was cloaked in charity and merely rendered impossible any serious will and reason to advance the best known possible good and right interest of their Black race. These rational faith and ethics principles of dogmatic theological millennialism, and those of the doctrinaire secular-ideological ecclesiastical and civil powers, were underpinned by the social conservative *Great Chain of Being* philosophy.

Their arguable social conservative philosophy and theology was primarily argued from silence, and based on the accepted logical but unexamined premise of fixed human groups possessing natural order-derived natural rights of greater and lesser worth, and existing permanently within a predominant/subdominant ascendancy/descendancy hierarchy.

Far more post-Edwardseans and revisionist descendants of Edwards than of Hopkins added new logics and methodologies by which they transformed these old Calvinistical faith and ethics systems into new schools. In these revisionist systems, Puritan masters of mystery and mystical were transfigured by such wise Yankees sons who dedicated themselves to the process of institutionalizing the Puritans' great ambition and commission.

Pre-antebellum Calvinist-establishmentarian rhetoricians and logicians proved to their entire satisfaction that the peculiar mission of the saints was the opposite of a fool's "*Errand into the Wilderness*" of North America. They were able to make their point stick among the "New Light" (Congregationalist) and "Old School" and "New School" (Presbyterian) Calvinists as a result of the evolving power of their strong Orthodoxy/Reformed interregional denomination.

This bi-Calvinist denomination quickly appeared to be not only exploding, expanding, and proliferating sectarian bodies but developing an ecumenical "*American Civil Religion*." At the commencement of their Congregational/Presbyterian Union, the Calvinists rarely and then discriminately exercised real influence within the profane-directed private and public spheres of the civil sector, social order, and political economy.

Given absolutely persistent but relatively inconsistent public sector interconnections of the ecclesiastical and civil powers, the inquiry investigates this irresistible magnetic moral force field for the Black race, attracting and repelling the Black body, which was created as a result of the antebellum convergence from divergence of old-evolving Puritan-Anglican English race representatives and new-emerging European ethnic-immigrants.

In direct proportion to the swelling trans-Atlantic migrants, and their need and demand for new Evangelical churches generated and supplied by evangelists, largely members of the Calvinist and Arminian leadership class organized national denominations as official legislative bodies of the establishment churches.

Forthwith predominantly English and British sons of the original settlers, cousins, or brethren united with Continental emigrants to form Evangelical rival spiritual and moral pincers which they closed in the Black body, to at once proselytize the Black race and to make anti-Black race values the national virtue and treasure.

A further premise of this social ethics exploration is articulated in this context to clarify the comparative race and religion cultural analysis. By definition of their unmatched access to superior intellectual and educational, political and economic, and legal and social resources, the establishment denominations are the Yankee-Puritan pro-Calvinist (Evangelical Trinitarian) Congregationalists (forming the revised continuum of Orthodoxy); Yankee-Puritan (anti-Calvinist) Unitarian Congregationalists; and the British-American Presbyterians (preponderantly Reformed Scotch-Irish ethnics).

They comprised pre-antebellum members of the five estates whose congregants were Protestant industrialists and Puritan captains of industry, inclusive of Evangelical denominations who spawned foreign and domestic proselytizing or missionizing societies and humanitarian organizations underwritten by Calvinist capitalists, and are understood here as antebellum political and economic ecclesiastical power institutions no less than no less than spiritual and moral forces.

As potent *realpolitik* bodies exercising their power more capriciously than reliably, they are thereby dis-tinguished from the relatively national civil power-deficient Evangelical denominations, expressly, Baptist Calvinist cousins of the Congregationalists and Presbyterians, and, prior to their organization as the Protestant Episcopal Church and the Methodist Episcopal Church, the Latitudinarian Anglicans dominating the traditionalist wing and the Arminian Methodists forming the Evangelical wing of the Church of England.

This elucidation incorporates reflection upon the cooperation and conflict between these major Evangelical denominations, White and Black Old Abolition-ist and New abolitionist churchmen, pro-Evangelical and anti-Evangelical Protestants, and pro-political and anti-political churchmen.

White establishment Protestants were irreconcilably divided into extreme radical/liberal and conservative/reactionary from middle-of-road moderate antislavery strategists, on the one hand, and, on the other hand, internally split as Moral Reformers between the radical/liberal direct actionists who elected the dual civil spiritual and moral plus power politics and the radical/liberal who joined with the conservative/reactionary antislavery agencies who endorsed pure spiritual and moral force only.

Evangelical pacifist moralists and elitist liberal ethicists united as adversaries of all political abolition save for the pressure of petitions, and advocates of abolishing slavery by persuading slavocrats to adopt antislavocrat high principles.

Thus sincere and serious Black and White radical New Abolitionists were "one as the hand" as proponents of immediatism, and "separate as the fingers" as pro-political and anti-political proabolitionists. Scissored New Abolitionist Ombudsmen were a disconnected pair of sharp shears finely honed to cut the ties of bondage, dysfunctional independent rather than functional interdependent blades working at cross-purposes because they were unable to coordinate their means in spite of common motives and objectives, and irretrievably disengaged which was a perfect prescription for diminishing their limited minority force which they directed to secure freedom in liberty for Black non-bondsman and liberation from human bondage for Black slaves.

Yet in pledging minds and bodies to ensure North America-native Black folk would realize in their homeland universal and unconditional immediate deliverance from color caste/captive constraints, the radical New Abolitionists were quite unlike their liberal, moderate, conservative, and reactionary lay and clerical antislavery brethren who were establishmentarians at loggerheads over (A) the morality far less than the fiscal feasibility of the Black American people's deportation to Africa principal antislavery principle of the Protestant power elite churchmen; and (B) the ethical responsibility of White and Black Christian liberationists for removing anti-Black race repression from free Black Americans in the North, to whose safe houses fugitives from legal injustice were fleeing via the Underground Railroad at an ever-increasing rate.

Beleaguered antebellum Black Northerners, struggling to free their slave sisters and brothers in the South, were impaired by brutal benevolence and apartheid apparitors whose difficulties were compounded by increasing varieties of complex discrimination and segregation codes imposed by prototypes of Ku Klux Klan apparatchiki.

When measured according to predictable long term effects of empirically verifiable lasting consequences, what was clearly not the least debilitating pattern of Northeastern prohibition for Black American Patriots of the Revolution (and clerical progenies of English-race and British-ethnic Calvinist masters) was the refusal by Yankee (Northern no less than Cavalier Southern) sons of the White Anglo-Saxon Protestant Daughters of the American Revolution to confer upon them as Freedom Fighters the citizenship rights automatically granted to newarriving ethnic immigrants.

This mortification inflicted upon Black Calvinist parsons and parishioners was a singular one among the precipitating reasons why the large plurality of Black Northeasterners centered their hopes and activity in independent Black societies and institutions.

Evidently a group survival stratagem as well as both a group management mechanism and an individual psychic self-esteem reinforcement technique, autonomous Black community action was a choice preferred by the Black New Abolitionist majority which the Boston-centered White New Abolitionists failed to appreciate as adequately as did the New York-based White New Abolitionists.

Evangelical New Abolitionist New Yorkers enhanced and promoted dramatically, relative to correspondent Bostonians, Black male initiatives, aggressiveness, organizations, leaders, and politics. Progressive understanding and support of Black Protestants in independent organizations was advanced less by Bostonian and more by Manhattan White New Abolitionists primarily because of the New Yorkers' involvement in Evangelical religion and churches.

White New Abolitionists/Evangelical Protestants in Boston who followed William Lloyd Garrison emerged denominational disestablishmentarians. In this deviation from the churchman role, they differed remarkably from compeer Manhattanites who evolved as committed churchmen and formative antiestablishmentarian and revolved around Arthur Tappan. A distinguishing feature of the New Yorkers consisted of advancing politics-intensive private faith-coordinated public interest-ethics.

These Evangelical Calvinist churchmen's pro-politics premium value seemed to approach the verity test and to be validated as a certified higher priority than protecting or promoting traditional schools of theology and ecclesiology. By contrast, guarding the tradition was a major matter dominating and distorting the social ethics vision of the pre-antebellum and early antebellum protectionists at the helm of the prestigious national denominations.

The White New Abolitionist host-minority in New York were joined by a clerical leadership cadre of Black New Abolitionist Manhattanites. For these Black New Yorkers Evangelical religion was also a central commitment, and meant the tandem centermost faith and ethics empowering Protestant churchmen and churches engaged in politics for civil progress. Contrariwise, Boston New Abolitionists, who were resisted by establishmentarian Protestants who followed the pace set by antiabolitionist Presbyterians and Trinitarian and Unitarian Congregationalists, essentially comprised an elite corps of White leaders led by Garrison who was little given to embrace independent Black leadership.

This stance was scarely a spinoff of establishmentarian, but the posture resulted from their reaction to total rejection by pro-Calvinist and anti-Calvinist Protestant establishment clergy at the outset of New Abolitionism. As a result of this rift, Bostonian New Abolitionists persisted during the antebellum decades outside of Orthodoxy; consisted of a very few independent-minded Trinitarian clergymen; and was directed and dominated by Evangelical layman Garrison.

Because after the total rejection by the New Englander leadership of the clerical class Garrison was constitutionally unable to move beyond anticlericalism, though his anti-denominationalism was not all-encompassing but a selective full course press supported by individual clergymen among whom were a statistically insignificant number of non-Unitarians who squared their shoulders with him, Boston New Abolitionists who identified with the New England Anti-Slavery Society were also riveted in opposition to mainstream ministers.

The majority of Black New Abolitionist leaders appreciated the clerical criticism. But they did not find satisfaction in the flailing of Evangelical churchmen, as if all clergymen and laymen (or even churches) were antiabolitionists simply because all the major denominations were.

One reason for this balanced perspective was universally understood: They were clergymen whose Black laymen and churches were abolitionists. Concomitant, being professional lititators and legislators as well as jurists of ecclesiastical law and order enactments, they professed (rather than protested) the parochial profit and pleasure inherent in the rigorously examined whole American public-proselytizing (without regard to race, ethnic, sex, national origin, previous voluntary or involuntary condition of servitude) process (philanthropic income and outcome) and program.

In this persuaded and persuasive posture, proceeding as principals of the peculiar persuasion whose principal purpose pertained to their pumping and planting plain and plump both primary and primed Protestant principles, they discerned, by turns, the secular and sacred sectarians' dissimilar faith forms dividing and similar social ethics uniting them as the nation-wide (whether or not the truly national) White Protestant Churches; the competitive Churches' complementary and contrary distinctive differences and spiritual and material power-seeking difference that made no difference in the chances of the color caste and captive congregants; the conspicuous absence of abolitionism from the plethora of prescriptive principles promulgated by each and every one of the major mainstream (central church governance Communions or) Evangelical Denominations for parsons and parishioners to preach and practice; and the distinguishable presence of pro-abolitionism among a creative minority of White Southern and Northern clergymen, laymen, and churches located in the Northeast and the West.

New York-based New Abolitionist Black clergymen were a sharp contrast in substance rather less than in profession and style, when compared to the Boston-based Black New Abolitionist lecturers. Black New Abolitionist associates of the New England (renamed) Massachussetts Antislavery Society direct actionists were all non-clerical inactive churchmen or nonchurchmen. Similar to the majority membership of the parent body, Black antislavery lecturers for the Society were viewed by indiscriminate friends and foes as undifferentiated secular humanist rather than religious humanitarian agencies.

Frederick Douglass (1817-95) was the most famous and notorious of these stellar Black achievers and antislavery agents who managed magnificent gifts and graces, to be effective in their role as lay prophet and preacher of the gospel according to abolition, and to provide arch-champions and arch-enemies who were deficient of discriminating judgment with arguable but insufficient reasons to adjudge all Black paid lecturers of the New England Anti-Slavery Society God-less, Christ-less, and Grace-less.

They formed in their imagination and current reality for the antiabolitionist mainstream denominations a counter-moving proabolitionist body bent on changing the antislavery direction of the Protestant power elite, and in this counter-culture mode the Black prophets understandably could not get a fair hearing but were stoned because the recipients did not like the message they delivered.

Yet among these exquisite forthtellers who were unfairly accused of being in essence and manifestation the laity rule or anti-churchman norm Douglass stood out as the universally acclaimed first among equals, and unacknowledged exception either to the debatable rule or who proved the rule.

Douglass was the son a captor and captive created in one of their close encounters of the most intimate kind, who revealed the African-Anglo paradox and positive attraction/positive negation for pursuit of happiness (hedonism) Anglo-Americans who proved the hedonist paradox (happiness eludes pursuit or is not an objective but an objective effect a realized subjective objective): Black folk were productive unemployed and unemployable males and females, and/or partly because the people-property materialized far more pure profit and pleasure than pain the Black body was highly prized and despised by White employers and employees (an absolute for the preponderance compared to their relative indifference to the Black soul and mind).

He evolved from this master/bondwoman union of polar opposites a precocious pupil of his Christianity/civility-confessing slavemistress and slave/free brothers and sisters who surpassed these White and Black Methodist preceptors in preaching and practicing Protestant private and parochial principles in public, emerged one runaway who tried and failed to escape before his final flight attempt from Maryland resulted in the slave reaching New York and residing during his initial fugitive years in Rhode Island.

In the long tradition of outlaw Rhode Islanders from the Reverend Roger Williams (c.1603-83), who purchased the land from the Narragansett Indians to secure his escape from Massachusetts legal injustice, to pirates for whom Block Island was a haven from law and order, Douglass came out of the closet as a lawbreaker in New Bedford outlaw.

There he issued his first public antislavery protests and homilies as an African Methodist Episcopal Zion Church (A.M.E.Z.) exhorter (lay preacher). Subsequently, he moved to Massachusetts following his discovery by members of the Massachusetts Anti-Slavery Society, including founder Garrison--the Boston New Abolitionist ruling elder whom his bold brahmin friends called their leader.

But after his bitter dispute with Garrison, Douglass relocated in New York and cooperated with the Manhattan-centered New York Anti-Slavery Society. Whence he synchronously from Massachusetts and Garrison's Boston-headquartered anti-politics orbit of influence to the pro-partisan party power politics abolitionism advocated by the Black brethren of the cloth.

Antebellum Black Northerners labored to advance the race in all-Black and all-White societies and associations because (A) the Black ones were essential to the health and welfare of the Black community; and (B) the highly valuable and valued access to opportunities provided by White bodies were not only arbitrary and selective but few in number and limited to a fixed range of advancement possibilities. What is equally relevant and decisive adds clarity to their valor.

Unlike fellow White agents of the antislavery counterintelligence agencies that the maverick munificence messengers organized to undermine and overthrow the proslavery institutions, few of whom were professionals either paid or called and chosen by the Black communities, Black counteragents of status quo stabilization soldiers for *Christ and Culture* were active participants in the majority and minority groups of both the subdominant Black community and the predominant White society.

After the schism of the Massachusetts and New York Anti-Slavery Societies which divided the united American Anti-Slavery Society, seven years before Douglass relocated his residence in New York, arrived in Black New Abolitionist New Yorkers were Tappanites in conflict with Black and White New Abolitionist Bostonians who were Garrisonians over pro-political versus anti-political antislavery tactics and strategies; the efficiency and sufficiency of pure spiritual and moral force plus strictly enforced single-permissive politics and limited to petition-related as well as generated and engineered political pressure; and the validity of self-defense in the struggle for self-determination.

Cooperation and conciliation with White New York New Abolitionists dominated the relations of the Black New Abolitionist ex-Garrisonians and pro-Tappanites, comprising the younger contemporaries of the few Old Abolitionist Black Patriots and Black warriors for Christ and conscience who lived long enough to become converts to New Abolitionism.

Still, their internal argument over the proper amount of force Moral Reformers can appropriate and apply appropriate was not the only tension between Black and White Garrisonians and Tappanites--in command and control of the three major (Boston and New York followed by Philadelphia) mid-antebellum antislavery centers of the national immediatism movement.

They were undivided in their opposition to the antiabolitionist establishment denominations, and equally irrefutably divided proabolitionists between the Manhattanites who remained engaged with and committed to change the denominations and the Bostonians who made it perfectly clear they were determined to eliminate the churches because they believed them to be not only obsolete but the obstacle to linear moral progress.

The proslavocrat works of these formidable foes of the friends of bondage and caste abolition at the helm of antiabolitionist and procolonizationist antislavery denominations constitute the chief subject and object of this study. These advocates rejected as forcefully as adversaries accepted the conclusion drawn from the analysis of the data which asserts that their affirmative action resulted in considerable contributions to the preservation of the proslavocracy doctrine and anti-Black race ideology.

Whether they were actualized or whether they were realized is a question explored in depth in this examination of stalwarts Lyman Beecher, William Ellery Channing, and Moses Stuart--the representative men of the establishment Presbyterian, Unitarian, and Congre- gational denominations. Their landmark published works are the major documents evaluated in this examination of these ethical excellence ethicists for the power elite.

They are my major subject and object primarily because their cautious moderation has been widely interpreted by secular and religious scholars, who set the Golden Mean above the Golden Rule, to mean these master moralists' antislavery (A) sentiment was in nature and purpose the best known possible high Christian faith and ethics because it argued elitist rational religion and morality principles; (B) thought and action approached the truth and avoided error as explicitly as they equated earnest and honest concern with civil progress; (C) labors escaped entirely the failure of slavocrats who succeeded in positively promulgating anti-Black interests-specific premises and principles, politics and policies processes and programs; and (D) intentions were free and clear of negative extensions and pretensions, and of unloading positive harm as great as their sincerity upon Black people.

Personally partisan politics-reticence spokesmen for sometime nation-wide denominations, if not for as well as to and with Protestants throughout the Union, are appraised because these archetypal Yankee-Puritans illustrate the demanding issues precipitating the New England establishment clergy's (A) re-entrance in the *realpolitik* realm that the sons of the Federalist Party partisan parsons disengaged predeliberately following their Congregationalist/Presbyterian Plan of Union or predominantly between 1800 and 1850; (B) return from disengaging to re-engaging power politics over time, after the schism in the Presbyterian Denomination precipitated dissolution of their Union and the formation of the national Congregationalist Denomination out of the New England-bound Consociations; and (C) previous withdrawal into absolute antislavery/pro-slavery neutrality, the most revealing moment of whose delicate antislavocracy and proslavocrat balance occurred with their dramatic performance of closing their churches (which edifices doubled for townspeople as their New England town halls) to New Abolitionist public meetings.

This antiabolitionist Congregationalist policy established and enforced by professional protectionists of the Calvinist faith and Colonizationist ethics not only involved driving abolitionists from the Temple doors--which clergymen closed in their faces so that White Finneyite revivalists in their role as pro-- Black race evangelists would be shut out and God would be protected in the sanctuary--was an anti-Black race program; an attack upon Free Speech and Freedom of Assembly; and a massive assault upon the Puritan tradition of the local Church of Christ hosting any town meeting the townsfolk chose to convene.

Even their ancillary result produced a no less egregious effect. While not intending to vindicate the slavocracy but apparently bent on appeasing the slavocrats in general and Southern presbyters and presbyteries within their one and only Presbyterian General Assembly in the United States in particular--as they implemented their complemental policy of arbitrarily closing Congregational churches (public meetinghouses) to selective (private and parochial) controversial concerns of the citizenry--Yankee sons who like their Puritan fathers were not known to exude flattery most certainly imitated the slavocracy strategy of preemptively striking abolitionist dissent.

In this unbecoming deferential posture, Yankee clergymen advocates of democracy paid the sincerest compliment New Englanders were capable of extending to Cavalier slavocrats and the slavocracy. Predictably their fellow clerical and lay Calvinist churchmen in the South, some of whom were also influential United States Senators and Congressmen, did not forget this deployment of deterrence-benevolence by Yankees in the early antebellum period and slavocracy era. Straightaway slavocrats took full advantage of this conciliatory and cooperative demonstrable attitudinal and behavioral modification process.

Specifically, Southern proslavocrats demonstrated they were not fatuous but equally clever and dangerous hardball politics players in the midst of treating the enforced Yankee ecclesiastical law and order as a symbol and a sign that signaled civil capitulation to their antiabolitionist and anti-Black race values.

But overconfident Cavalier-slavocrats eventually carelessly stepped beyond the definite limits of firm but not rigid Yankee-Puritans' only seemingly boundless range of non-rigidity, and disclosed in this instance the reckless propensity that would end in making the fatal error of mistaking the Yankee-Puritan capacity for flexibility for an infinitely bending nature.

In sum and substance, slavocrats profoundly misapprehended and relentlessly misinterpreted Northern proslavocrats' indiscriminate indifference to the color caste/captive class' condition as an indicator of Yankees being willing and able to submit unconditionally to seductive slavocrat powers sooner or later; to suffer gladly the aggressive slavocrat offensive forever if properly motivated; and to surrender to the slavocracy's policy of limitless political and economic expansion.

North American Black race and human bondage existence in perpetuity were as far from principles that are unconscionable to compromise and near to negotiable values for selectively anti-political conservative, moderate, and liberal traditionalists Congregationalist clergymen. Nevertheless, while their civil virtues and secular values were subject to pragmatic compromise and negotiable arrangements, Northeastern capitalists would not tolerate forever the perpetual loss to the Southeastern planters of their real political and economic interests in the West.

Protestant parson and parishioner philanthropists learned from the Calvinist capitalists that West subsisted of valuable land, rich marable trading goods, and splendid raw materials whose natural resources Northeastern industrial capitalism investors and industrial manufacturers coveted no less voraciously than did the Southeastern planters and merchants, as certainly as they knew that their respective aggressive Evangelical representatives were rolling and clashing on that marvelous Frontier for God, gold, and glory.

At another level of communicating my point of view, I examine indirectly the personal power of choice possessed and exercised as the right choice in the color caste/captive cultural crisis by the Protestant champions of the resource-laden denominations--which were emerging with the maturing democracy and slavocracy--and the enduring impact of the social consequences resulting from their rational thoughts and actions. The centermost concern is the effect of the Northern Protestant establishment's apparent and real reinforcement of the Southern Protestant establishment's determination to perpetuate slavery.

The functional and dysfunctional factors inherent in this approach are as obvious as the people management skills displayed by the professionals guiding the powerful denominations. Just as clearly, they were no less real ethical instruments wielded by moral and immoral moralists for being expertly sharpened deadly weapons. They most certainly were deployed to manage the cost of the Black race first, to minimize the pain of the caste/captive class second, and primarily to maximize the profit and pleasure of the Black body that the historic rival Puritan and Anglican theocracies united in defining chattel property.

Colonizationists chastised with informed speculations and learned knowledge of history and current realities contemporaries who spurned their solution, and it would have been within the range of their powers of prophecy to predict that the continuum from the English settlement of "*the spirit*" of Black race dehumanization would survive and thrive in American future, as surely as the phenomenon possessed life after death of the theocracy in the new democracy and slavocracy.

Rulers of the anti-Black race rule ruled might makes right in order, but, challengers of the Colonizations also asserted, instead of the dead hand of the past burying its dead rules and regulations they were advanced in their present by means of sophisticated and logical rationalizations, which the evidence cited proved no less callous for being candid justifications rationalists derived from the basic Western Christian principles of the God-ordained Moral Law, divine right, natural law, and natural rights.

With greater intensity than previously known in the history of the Union, antebellum secular humanists and religious humanitarians argued the "*states' rights*" case for the generalizability and universalizability of Black race-specific slavery being the God-granted prerogative of the privileged White Christian individual, who, by definition of existence as the will of God in essence and manifestation, possessed the capacity to effect his intentions and to enjoy the consequences of his actions.

Approaching through the natural and necessary power field generated by the ecclesiastical and civil powers this complex subject, of interracial and interreligious relations during the first half of the nineteenth century, places in perspective the biotic and critical albeit not "missing link" between White Northern and Southern Evangelicals. Slavocrat churchmen who were often human bondage owners as well as not infrequently ecclesiastical and civil powers-authorized preachers to slaves. As managers and/or masters doubling as ministers of Christian bondmen and bondwomen, church and state sponsored clergymen-slavemasters appeared as a class to command and control the destiny in history and eternity of more Black captives, snared by the Constitution-legitimated national system of dehumanization and the "peculiar institution" of democracy's slavocracy, than any other civil-religious authorities.

Antebellum proselytizing Northern and Southern sectarians were predominantly Calvinists and Arminians, whose foundational private and parochial public faith and ethics connection was Evangelical antiblack white-ethnic virtue: Evangelism and revivalism directed and millennialism energized spiritual and moral power discharged to run the "Devil" and evil as well as to drive all black and immoral desires out of the human heart and world, so that therein God could establish His Kingdom.

Antiblack white-ethnic virtue was (A) a fundamental Evangelical ethical principle and practice for Jonathan Edwards and John Wesley; (B) crystallized rather than derived in the First Great Awakening by these masters of philosophy and psychology no less than of theology who were organized to beat the devil; (C) an aggressive defensive principle perverted by professionals into a sheerly offensive one to the Black race; (D) reversed and turned into a Black race positive negation or rejection spiritual and moral measure of puritanicalism; and (E) evolved for the best and brightest into diminished moral capacity and turned out the propensity to equate negative good with the highest ethical standard, and to promote negative good over positive good or efficacious love of God, man, and oneself in the same thought and action.

Eliminating the positive good and accenting the negative good facilitated the perversion of antiblack white-ethnic virtue (evil being repulsion) into anti-Black race virtue (Black human being group rejection). Pro-White race advocates assert this power exercise to be the White Protestant race/ethnic's natural tendency and inevitable destiny. It is examined in this analysis as a public ethics matter of real substance, and not only as a simple question of affairs which begin and end in personal preferences, namely, parochial moralities and manners, private style and individual taste.

Transforming strong opposition to evil into positive negation of the Black race was the public pogrom and published purpose of the American Colonization Society. The Society functioned effectively as the American Evangelical Protestant denominations' original private and parochial antislavery organization. Noteworthy for anticipated successes surpassed only by unexpected failures, prior to the mid-1840s the para-denominational Society and ecumenical enterprise was the surrogate for the churches; substitute for ecclesiastical endeavors and formations; and the only antislavery special-interest and single-issue corporation supported fully by Northern denominations and their executive officials or local congregations.

The ACS was an ecclesiastical and civil multinational eleemosynary corporation, and thus the necessary cause and effect of antiabolitionist interlocking directorates of Evangelical church corporations. In their post as chairman and officers of parochial and private boards, these corporate directors demonstrated conclusively they neither knew and appreciated nor respected and protected nor either loved or liked their Black race; and their love for each encountered individual slave, fugitive, and free Black American whom they did not pretend to like but intended to propel from America to Africa.

This self-determined heart and sole purpose of the American Colonization is definitive deterrence-benevolence, brutal benevolence, and benevolent paternalism.

Doubtless (1) their denied ill-will and affirmed goodwill American Colonizationists delivered with honorable motives; (2) their intentions were as earnest as their honest to God and man pretensions were publicly paraded with pride and prejudice; their open operation was disclosed in their original declaration upon incorporation wherein American Colonizationists announced high principles of Christianity and civility certified Black folk an excludable people from their homeland and their benevolent expulsion Christian charity, commandment, and duty; (3) their word was their bond when they swore their procedural deculturalization principle, denaturalization process, and deportation program was neither a nefarious scheme of deception nor a Machiavellian conspiracy of managed misdirection but demonstrable fair return of their North America-indigenous Black race to the motherland and on Africa's interest; (4) their seriousness and sincerity searched and found their expatriation means and ends served impartially and evenhandedly the best interests of Black African race/ethnic groups, White race/ethnic groups, and the Black-race American group or all three parties to the conflict of interests; and (5) their invincible ignorance of the true and real interests of the Black body resulted in the Colonizationists' corrupt Christian values, which they called great virtues rather than vices, whose worse consequence for their Black-race cultural kin-group was to curtail sharply equal access to opportunity and equity in their fatherland.

Churchmen commanding national influence, in civil and social secular power spheres as well as the interconnected ecclesiastical legislative circles of central church governments, first delayed justice, then denied fairness, and finally raised as the standard of moral American excellence the custom of positively rejecting and repelling their Black-race genetic and cultural kin-group. The ways in which, as well as how and why, these vice-specific descriptive facts and value judgments were rationalized and correlated with virtues are elucidated in this investigation.

I approach these ideas and ideals of great Protestant personalities and seminal minds shaping American culture by comparing the knowledge and information productive Congregationalist and Presbyterian powerhouses related to the relevant facts and values they professed openly, promoted for the public to espouse, and proclaimed vice-free virtues of enduring worth.

Yankee-Evangelical establishmentarians' far less confusing than convoluted insistence upon unconditional and universal immediate religious (faith and ethics) and secular (civil) moral rebirth of the individual--and resistance of rational and rapid radical social structural change--persisted as self-evident Half-way Piety, a contradiction of authentic Puritan Piety, and collective class versus color caste consciousness that neither incidentally nor accidentally increased until the ultimate conflict of Yankee and Cavalier real interests precipitated the Civil War.

Thuswise my appraisal of Yankee determination to be the hegemonic power presence of Calvinist Christianity and culture in North America, and thereby realize the great Puritan ambition, proceeds from a probative and deconstructionist analysis of what may be the far less obvious critical matter than it appears--that is, the race and religion realities driving the color caste/bondage class social ethics intentions of establishment Evangelical Yankees revolving around a results-oriented litmus or effects test, whose immediate negative good cancellation of positive good successes were exceeded only by the long range consequences of their equally cautious and cost-effective actions.

The critique of these managers of reality, and their Christian social ethics interpretations of the class and caste warfare, begins with the Union-commencing national formation of the major denominations, and concludes with the watershed second Fugitive Slave Act. This anti-Black race interest-specific 1850 national law and order, superimposed upon free and slave states alike, united in partisan politics-intensive action antislavocrat versus proslavocrat parties of Yankee religious humanitarians and secular humanists who were previously divided in their opposite immediatism and gradualism camps as anti-political and pro-political antislavery direct actionists and indirect reactionaries.

The national "*Black Code*" made one thing crystal clear to the post-1837 bisected Evangelical denominations who divided into antislavery and proslavery bodies whose distinctive experience was the factor distinguishing them from the Protestant Episcopal Church--which escaped antislavery schisms during antebellum era and mandated silence regarding all abolitionist thoughts in official denominational legislatures as the price of proslavocracy/antislavocracy neutralism: The Northern and Southern severed denominations might reunite either without Black congregants and/or both with bondage and caste constituents--but not until the economically overreaching and politically overbearing slavocracy was either overthwarted or overmastered by overwrought and overpowering Northern interests.

Prior to the inevitable resolution of their intolerable Yankee and Cavalier conflict of real interests rather than values, the mutually fertile basic secular-civil democratic doctrine (individual liberty and freedom) and Evangelical dogma (individual regeneration) interrelated so effectively the combination ap- peared an equally efficient and sufficient universal imperative for White ethnic minorities.

Among the most sanguine of whom emerged the English/Puritan race repre-sentatives in the Northeast who were explicitly unrepentant and uncompromising proponents of "*states' rights*," entirely oblivious to the fact that this negotiated compact with hell they honored as a contract with heaven was appropriated by slavocrats as the driving rational organization principle of the slavocracy, and heedless or careless of the unmistakable evidence indicating the relative advan-tage of the slave states and disadvantage of the slave-free states proceeded apace their error in judgment and compromise of truth.

Slavocrats not only increasingly claimed their rival slave-based political e-conomy produced the legitimate power and authority inherent in autonomous slaveholding states (whose uniqueness meant they were separate and distinct from their sister partially dependent and independent yet always interdependent sovereign states of the Union) but also that they existed primarily as a collec-tive slavocracy whose dual purpose entailed simultaneously competing with de-mocracy and securing a new theocracy.

Once the unaware Protestant power elite were shocked into conscious aware-ness of the serious threat to their perceived vital interests by apperceptive compeers, Northeasterners suspended their overreligious individualism and united in reconstituting the historic New England Confederacy (1649). Thanks to Jethro Willett, the faithful Plymouth slave and first Black American hero, who escaped from Indian captors and returned to his masters with strategic information con-cerning the planned Indian military extermination of the English people and cul-ture, saint and sinner crusaders for Christ and the New England colonies were enabled to execute a surprise survival assault whose attack had the effect of a preemptive strike of the Indian ethnic enemies of the English/Puritan-race's representatives.

The colonists who were victorious in King Philip's War (1675-76), over the Wampanoag, Nipmuck, and Narragansett Indians, vanquished and banished from indigenous Native Americans' prime lands the defeated who were not driven onto to the New England reservations and boundaries, or beyond the margins toward the hinterlands of the region. One unexpected outcome of this critical triumph and defeat was the parallel sharp rise in African-ethnic human bondage residents and income which turned into windfall profits for wealth producing and acquiring Puritans.

The first significant body of Black chattel property were purchased by the saints and "chosen people of God" in the British West Indies--following the vic-tory of the "Elect" and their extermination of their permanent enemies and the formidable foes of their truly coveted Indian friends in the Pequot War (1637)--partly in exhange for the few surviving fierce and feared captive Pequots.

These were among the factors why the New England Confederacy was effec-tively remembered reverently for its demonstrated capacity, and most especially approximately each one hundred thereafter when it was apparently reinstated by the Puritans in the War of Independence and by the Yankees in the Civil War to secure, protect, and defend the interests of their Commonwealth (they iden-tified with the national interests) no less than those of the Disunited States and the United States against the encroaching British Army and the Northern democracy opposing Southern Confederacy.

Hence secular and sacred Puritans were engaged as idealists-checking realists over time and through time coming to terms in time with the necessity of e-ventually settling the Yankee and Cavalier conflict of real interests. But "Con-sistent Calvinists" not only followed suit but continued to ignore the business of settling the conflict of true values, which proved their peculiar problem and one they refused to admit they had on their hands.

Their non-denial denial of their special responsibility in the color caste/captive cultural crisis was one thing; their mental manipulation and management of the problem by not mentioning the moral dilemma dimension of the caste condition in Christian churches and institutions was another thing; their pletho-ra of choice options was yet another thing; and their free choice of neither acceptance nor aggression but only avoidance of conscious class versus caste values was an altogether different thing.

The White-ethnic individual constituent element of republican democracy and Protestant Evangelicalism, and the ecclesiastical and civil powers' sacrosanct criterion of value, was inapplicable to the Black body and applicable to the White individual, ethnic community, and race group--the competent and competi-tive Black male existing without status in an elevated station to the contrary notwithstanding.

This failure to endeavor seriously to raise the faith and ethics standard from exclusion to inclusion of their color and caste bound congregants proved the true measure of Protestant establishmentarians' public ethical concern for their Black race. The relevance of this reality can be stated succinctly: The tension remained and increased between the rejected Black race group and the select "*Reprobate*" or "*Elect*" Black male whom secular or sectarian Yankees chose to approve and to confer privileges upon. The exception repeated in a thousand instances did not overturn but confirmed the rule that the Black race is an un-acceptable people, which fact followed in logic and life.

The Protestant power elite revitalized the national race and religion disval-ues rather than contributed social redeeming values in the process of superim-posing on the public their highly rational social ethics. This sectarian American-ization of secular values and sacred vices developed into a dangerous device de-signed by the divines--for whom achieving the ends of Evangelicalism was their driving desire--and one that transmuted and translated their transcendent time and space mission into unspeakable secular treasures and religious virtues.

Forward from their rules and regulations accelerated the escalating Black male exception and deescalating Black race national standard of fairness and equity, which argued that individual Black female or male enlivened with suf-ficient self-respect to regulate any ineradicable insecurity and unsecurity resid-uals by the millions may be elevated above poverty, ignorance, and disease and join the White race and ethnic confluence.

What is not ironical but paradoxical upsprings from this faulty premise and false principle: the recurring gradual expansion and contraction cycle of access to opportunity for the twice blessed and favored minority of the minority per-sists as an unquestionable process of self-improvement that is not self-defeating but race-defeating.

There exists no real or reasonable alternative to the Black-race competitor seeking a competitive edge on a par with his/her race/ethnic rivals. But the pe-culiar problem of the productive pariah person in the American competitive class system inheres in the seductive nature of its inextricable productivity and profitability motive--that is, just as the person/people enrichment point of life is advanced by avoiding being engaged in a self-defeating process, just so inerrantly possibility is being productive and impossibility is escaping entirely the fantasy that attaining the elusive status of an individual is not fanciful for a competitive Black-race citizen.

True theory and experience reveals the reality that inalienable statuslessness is not an illusion but the peramenent condition of ineradicable Black-race minority existence in a culture where the race/ethnic majority rules class over caste the right of might. In essence and manifestation, Black-race existence is a deethnicized and non-individual being.

Black existence at advantage (relative to the disadvantaged Black person and White individual) remains at risk because s/he continues as a member of the discredited Black race. While fully being neither the beneficiary nor the victim of personal achievement, the Black race's life-enhancing chances, like its death-enhancing chances, are not either retarded or advanced by the achievements of successful individuals.

The "*American Civil Religion*" rule and "*Dilemma*" turn on the culture's pivotal custom law: However far the Black individual rises in a functional or market-place station above marginal existence, the real estate and wealth or value s/he accrues redounds neither to grant s/he status nor to benefit the Black race. The asserted equivalence of statuslessness and denigration is the manifest essence of Black race existence that places an artificial cap on his/her rise. This double damnation White race (and other) ethnic groups do not experience, and therefore their individual members escape scot-free from being eclipsed by the color caste factor.

Contemporary effects form the continuum with these earlier modern consequences and compelling forces, which were generated and/or secured disproportionately by the peerless power elite Yankee sons of the Quaker-, Anglican-, and Calvinist-Puritan fathers. Their sources of virtue and vice are the roots and branches of the currently flowering Moral Majority and its tenacious device of rationalization.

Quite on par with their Calvinist fathers, their apparatus also withstands successively the charge of hypocrisy and impotency by escaping from social realism into individualism and pragmatism. Opportunism, the apparent functional approach of entrepreneurial competitiveness, and realism, the necessary ways and means of imaginative individual existence in American pragmatism and reality and above both fantasy and the disadvantaged, are keys to success in a high-technology (productive) and low-technology (service) political economy.

But although nothing less than the empirically verifiable exquisite efficient methods of the ecclesiastical and civil entrepreneur, neither opportunism nor realism are either sufficiently solid or right and good enough means to advance the best known possible good interests of the Black-race minority and the White (and other) race/ethnic minorities forming the American majority.

Yankee sons of the wayward worldly saints, like their Puritan fathers, understood as comprehensively as they argued the merits and relevance of these great realities they bequeathed and transmitted as cultural certainties.

Inarguably, therefore, continuous endeavors to deepen the question in the quest for deeper appreciation of the enduring meaning and lasting values resulting from their determination to affirm the dehumanization of their Black race serve the general interest.

This is the case insofar as the explorations contribute a modicum of perspective to the egalitarians, who are concerned with more than survival and know from historical and current evidence the inadequacy of simple solutions to complex conflicts of real interests and values.

The appraisal will be considered useful if it supports the efforts of one egalitarian seeking in the present ways and means for future generations to prevent further transmission of the centuries-long color caste class legacy of national harm.

Joseph R. Washington, Jr.
University of Pennsylvania
Philadelphia, Pennsylvania
1 September 1988

1

OVERVIEW OF THE NEW COLOR-CONSCIOUS CONSTITUTION, CHURCHES AND CHURCHMEN

In the British Isles, concurrent with the American Revolution, English Evangelical Members of Parliament and the Church of England discovered in the abolition of African slavery a rational organizing Christian faith and ethics standard of virtue; formed the British Abolition Society; and emerged as partisan party power politics Evangelicals the loyal opposition of church and state powers.

These Evangelical Anglican and Independent churchmen evolved as idealists, fashioned abolitionism into a religious and secular instrument for rational and radical rapid civil structural change, and pressed upon the sacred and profane realists (as well as competitive opportunists and pragmatists) their British Abolition power point. They were convinced it was sharp enough to bear the weight of their audacious demand that Parliament abolish slavery by any means necessary, including restructuring the political economy.

The men in mission emerged submerged giant figures who appeared a chosen people when they finally surfaced and soared as paradigmatic modern moralist models. They strode forth most strikingly in their dual capacities as churchmen selected or appointed by Parliament emissaries of the state, and politicians elected by their constituencies to represent them as Members of Parliament.

At once independent-minded and Evangelical churchmen, the British Abolitionists distinguished themselves as self-acting parishioners and priests of the Church of England and the Independent churches. They were establishmentarians seeking to change rather than to end the establishment, and considered too sincere and serious or too unrealistic and visionary by status quo stabilization-demanding British intellectuals and professionals. Resisting the challengers of conservative cultural conventions and conditions, the champions of convenience and experience snubbed less effectively than they dubbed their counter-culture contemporaries "*the Saints*," that is, British Abolitionists who preferred to peerage prestige the power of principle and principle of power promoted by their antislavery "*Clapham Sect*."

The facts and figures this pro-Black race interest-specific corps of radical establishmentarian ethicists and public servants compiled to narrow the promise and performance gap argued their case for the national security, interest, and values being defended/expanded best by translating high principle-premised pro-abolitionist power politics and ethics into public policy, program, and process.

Thuswise, despite being accused of demanding preferential treatment and elevating special interests above the general interest, the nontraditional observant Protestants elected to deescalate expedience and convenience, to escalate risk in fiscal and momentary matters, and to advance antislavery in the civil sector as the right and the good policy, and to declare abolition not only a public interest securing principle but also a national value accruing program.

These responsible revolutionists were effective *realpolitik* professionals, maintained spiritual and moral force in company with sustained political pressure over two generations while withstanding vigorous Machiavellian opposition, and produced sufficient power to force Parliament to make England the first sovereign power in history to choose to formulate legislation enacting abolition as the empire-wide law and order.

English Abolitionists' origin, development, and expansion of abolition as a public interest ethic featured a dynamic integration of historic polarities that heretofore appeared irreversible private, parochial, and public conflicts of rights and interests.

British Abolitionists turned the moral corner on history-long plagued human bondage by uniting (A) the Christian *agape*-love ethic (rethinking repentance or forgiveness of the neighbor actualized in advancing the best known possible good interest of the enemy); (B) the sacred Judaism and Christendom plus profane Western justice principle (aiding each individual and group to obtain their legitimate claim); (C) the Enlightenment-derived secular and religious civil fairness and equity moral values; and (D) partisan party power politics, distinguished from sectarian and church-specific complementary politics.

Evangelical English Abolitionists entered the political sector to exact the enactment into law of statutes guaranteeing universal self-determination, liberation from dehumanization, freedom in liberty.

Oddly enough, these Evangelical political means and ends were the undeveloped and underdeveloped undercurrents of authentic Puritan Piety. They surfaced with Cotton Mather, submerged in the First Great Awakening as a result of forceful Jonathan Edwards, re-emerged in the American Revolution, and were rejected out of hand by Second Great Awakening New England Evangelicals.

Post-Edwardseans were pro-political parsons who reversed themselves and returned to anti-political Edwardsean Halfway Piety, following the unanticipated defeat but thereafter predictable demise of their dearly loved Federalist Party. This reaction of Evangelical Calvinist parsons appeared a strange reversal of values, since they previously rejected Edwards anti-political theology and e-merged with the new nation partisan party politics parsons.

They re-surfaced in the civil sector as the antislavery American Colonizationists. Save for the tragic failure to translate and communicate effectively the English Abolitionists' critical political connection--and the loss of the underlying philosophical premises of universal and immediate abolition espoused by English and American Old Abolitionists--the British Evangelicals' national antislavery message, method, medium, and mission American Colonizationists transmitted from *Old* to *New England* where it was severely revised and localized.

Self-determination leaped from custom to positive law in England as a result of the 1772 precedent setting and celebrated case won by litigator Granville Sharp. In this class action civil suit, English jurisprudence ruled against the plaintiff slavemaster of James Sommerset, in favor of the defendant's lawyer, and human bondage out of order in the British Isles. Five years later in the Disunited States, the Vermont Constitution (1777) abolished slavery and thereby became the first slave-free state operating under the Articles of Confederation (1781-89).

However, the Constitution was ratified by the Green Mountain colony in 1791 and by the Bay State in 1788, whereby with its Constitution (1780) mandating the abolition of slavery Massachusetts entered the Union as the first slave-free state in the United States. But between ratification of the Constitution (or their *White Gentlemen's Agreement* making slavery a legal matter of *"states' rights"*) and the War of 1812 Massachusetts suspended the ethical standard and surrendered to the rule of law.

Puritan-Yankee ecclesiastical and civil institutions and officials honored the compact above conscience; accepted dehumanization as a *fait accompli* to be preserved like the human bondage condition by White Christian gentlemen slavocrats, into whose courteous and courtly care they delivered for safekeeping and salvation the abandoned Black body and soul; and turned deaf, dumb, and blind along with their backs to the caste and bondage continuum.

Concurrently chattel property and color prejudice existence were unconscionable conditions protested by Quakers and other concerned Christian citizens who followed the Friends' antislavery leadership; resided outside New England; and joined the mid-1770s Friends-originating Old Abolition Societies.

Quakers played a major role in establishing and sustaining the Societies nationally, whose success was a study in contrast with their failure in New England, where the absence of adult-led Old Abolitionist So-cieties was scarcely compensated by the presence in Massachusetts of the only two in the region which were the late-organized (after the formation of the ACS) student Societies at Williams College and Andover Seminary. Grand relief is the additive provided the Quakers between the creation of the nation and the American Colonization Society, when it is recalled that during this period the Religious Society of Friends was the only organized Protestant communion maintaining her own official antislavery society.

As a result of churchmen and nonchurchmen White Christians' *compromise* of their *Constitution and Conscience* and of the civic virtues--along with widespread misplaced values and priorities--incorrectly prioritized ethical principles proliferated together with Christianity and civility exemplars' suspension of the public ethics standard.

For these reasons when, in the mid-1810s, hegemonic Northeastern Evangelical denominations initially experienced a heightened human bondage consciousness they failed to reinstituted the New England Old Abolition tradition; emerged antiabolitionist and procolonizationist types of antislavery Protestant parishes, parishioners, and parsons; and established the ACS as their surrogate antislavery executive action corporation.

Compared to earlier and contemporary English and American Old Abolitionist Societies, the ACS' conservative initiative is evidenced in the leadership deliberately evolving the Society into a truncated anti-slavery body overcharged with the overweening belief that the Colonizationists alone possessed the superior rational antislavery means and ends and all other antislavery operations were inferior; knew the question(s) and had the answer(s); and did not need to learn from the experience of the continuously active English Evangelical and American Quaker abolitionists.

The ACS went beyond assigning blame for the national anti-Black race stream of consciousness to blaming and declaring the victim the source and mouth of the color-intensive cultural river. Instead of the ACS's head group being a failure to communicate they gained the attention of Protestantism's decision-making body when Colonizationists concluded that the "*White Man's Burden*" is the Negro only, neither the human bondage condition nor the color caste condition, and one which ought not to be shouldered or suffered gladly.

From this definition it was easy for Colonizationists to decide Black folk are the American problem, and to choose not to solve but to escape the problem by cutting ties absolutely rather less precisely than by cutting losses through cutting and running--that is, by committing the Colonizationists' considerable resources only to the ACS' final solution, which entailed eliminating the problem by eradicating the Black presence in North America.

Exactly due to these pride and prejudice preferences promoted by principled ACS Protestants, whose desires deleted the desirable alternatives, the American Quaker Old Abolition Societies were not engaged seriously by the ACS; and from the selectively translated Evangelical English Abolitionists' antislavery blue-print the ACS chiefly adopted and adapted the British Abolition Society's Civilization, Christianization, and Colonization components.

Thuswise, in spite of nearly continuous correspondence between Old and New World Evangelical Englishmen as well as British and American Old Abolitionists, something was lost in the translation that was significant because the Colonizationists promoted the ACS as the American counterpart of the British Abolition Society.

Antislavery and abolition were interchangeable terms for the Old Abolitionists in England and America. And the perversion of the non-identical antislavery/abolition twins into the identical antislavery/antiabolition twins by the ACS issued forth as the distortion which became the authorized revised standard version for the establishment mind of the American Evangelical American clergy and laity.

The Evangelical Colonizationists expunged from the antiabolitionist soul of the ACS the abolitionist heart and critical principle of the British Abolition Society, and incorporated Evangelical English Abolitionists' strategic and tactical missionary ministry (of Civilization, Christianization, and Colonization) because the motive and measure fit hand in glove with the driving foreign and domestic missionary dynamic of the ACS' underpinned Evangelical Protestant denominations.

For this last reason at the very least, the basic flaw in the design of the ACS was its failure to appreciate the difference in degree so great as to be tantamount to a difference in kind of English and American color caste/captive task-responsibility.

This distinction subsisted of the color chattel/caste class in its separate and distinct form and function as the unique slavocrats' need and demand, they generated and supplied, object and subject of the Northern and Southern American Colonizationists' an-tislavery mission, whereby, being valued by the sla-vocrats and disvalued by the Colonizationist, these native North American Black millions inhabiting the Southeastern and Atlantic states were distinguished from the British West Indies and other New World slaves of the European powers.

The numerical density and demographic extensity of Black folk in the Cotton Kingdom transparently constituted a different accountability demand for English and American antislavery Protestants, when their population and popularity among the slavocrats are compared to the sparse and unpopular population among the White populous of fellow free Black and slave residents in "Old" and "New" England.

Certainly anti- and pro-Calvinist Anglo-American capitalists in New England, unlike and like their English compeers in the British Isles, could care less about the Black mind and spirit yet could care about nothing more than their investment in the Black body save for the human capital's interest-generating and real estate-appreciating value.

Linear moral progress appeared determinative to the optimistic and predeterminationist Northern Protestant proslavocrats and evidenced as the antebellum era progressed by the increasing number of market-conscious aristocrat and bourgeois masters of large plantations developing into professional people mangers, who, as efficiency experts and skilled disciplinarians, advanced as progressive transformationists committed to ever-improving their capacity to social engineer disciplined, reliable, and predictable slaves.

Slavocrat-slavemaster churchmen and nonchurchmen interested in the souls of Black bondmen and bondwomen being saved were concerned with the future performance in eternity rather less than in history and the market of their slaves --whom they valued on a par with their cattle as well as land and gold or other highly negotiable mediums of exchange--as profit or pleasure producing chattel property.

Southern Protestant secular dogmatic pragmatists and religious pragmatic dogmatists were willing and able realists and managers of reality. Their equally competent and credible competitive Northern proslavocrat brethren were determined to make a difference by hurling flat in the teeth of the slavocrats tortured misinterpretations, that were directly opposite to the unmistakable meaning of their published proslavocracy intentions and consequences.

Thus it is not surprising to discover that the proslavocrat Yankees, who knew that spiritual and moral forces are powerless when divorced from political clout, were bent on directing their driving middle-class morality and respectability to override the conflicts of interests and values no less than perspectives and preferences inherent in (A) the relative absence in *"Old and New England"* and presence in the British West Indies and the American slave states of Black folk; (B) the existence of nothing so great as psychological and physical distance between Black and White people in both *"Old and New England,"* and of nothing so great as psycho-physical intimacy between Black and White folk in the slavocracy; and (C) the endeavor to deprive slavocrats of their slaves, and most highly prized possessions, despite knowing the ultimate pleasure and profit value their Black bodies were for Christian and non-Christian slavocrats.

The upshot of this misconstruction was the transformation of the British Abolition Society's ecclesiastical and civil political power coordinates, empowering Evangelical English Abolitionists' radical structural change rational organization principle and practice, into three conflicting American antislavery moods and modes, namely, the American Convention of Old Abolitionist Societies, the American Colonization Society, and the American Anti-Slavery Society.

These three major American antislavery organizations existed by 1833, engaged in sharp conflict and stiff competition for the American *soul* and body politic, and generated spin-offs which took the form of a measurable yet seemingly infinite number of American antislavery motivations.

Albeit necessarily foreshortened in this context, the forementioned pregnant relations are juxtaposed at this juncture to underscore the fact that they form the relevant connective linkage of this exploratory endeavor.

This luminous indicator is illuminative regarding the pertinent point: The private and parochial intentions far less than the public consequences of the Protestant ethicists who produced this momentum comprise the pertinent subject and object of the deconstructionist and probative analysis employed in this American Christian Social Ethics interpretive essay to examine the color caste/ captive faith and ethics of major modern moralists.

The representative paradigmatic powerhouse approach works because the dominant emphases of the most influential antebellum varieties of Moral Reform race and religion relations, like their immediatism and gradualism variables and variations on the antislavery theme, were often the cause and effect of color-intensive compromise and consciousness of conscience (at different times) in the same cultural crisis and change manager.

JEREMY BELKNAP'S BRIEF REPRESENTATION
OF THE BEST AND BRIGHTEST MODEL MORAL

Secular humanist and religious humanitarian Protestant Americans surfaced during the pre-Revolution and post-Revolution years who believed self-determination, or the Enlightenment's touchstone principle of individual liberty upspringing from the American War of Independence and the French Revolution, was the everywhere at once and near-instantly applicable irreversible, unconditional, and universal categorical imperative.

There is little reason to resist the testimony of the Friends that this beautiful truth inspired pre-Independence "*inner light*" Quakers' immaculate conception of immmediate, unconditional, and universal abolition in the sacred womb of the Religious Society of Friends, new born abolition's post-Independence secular development in the civil sector, and the expectation among the Old Abolitionists that the eradication of human bondage could be accomplished in short order through an appeal to common sense.

This one-step-at-a-time approach to respect for the Black race was realized hope (eschatology), and as such no less optimistic idealism and realism than either its self-determination premises or the Independence spirit of the era. Aggressive New England idealists asserted as realists that once abolition became the rule of the Union there would be time enough to embark upon the second stage of granting free Black New Englanders equal fairness and equity, participatory democracy rights and responsibilities, and access to competitive opportunity and the pursuit of happiness in their American society.

"*New Light*" (Evangelical revisionist) Congregationalists reemerged secular civil sector servants in this very bright and brief moment of demonstrably less realized than realizable pro-White race and pro-Black race true interests and values.

From these fellow Anglo-American Puritans the Reverend Jeremy Belknap (1744-98) distinguished himself as a Boston "*Old Light*" (theological liberal) Congregationalist, an intellectual history specialist, and a divine who fostered the Massachusetts Historical Society (the first historical organization in the United States) and answered in its *Proceedings* Virginian St. George Tucker's (1752--1827) queries on the nature and destiny of human bondage.

Belknap was not the advocate but an adversary of Orthodoxy, and one of the few anti-Calvinist intellectuals prepared to argue in print his serious reflections on the unconscionable terror and error inherent in the perpetuity of the color caste/captive class condition.

He set the precedent for the rationalists who followed the impeccable logic of his rational argument to accept the incorrect conclusion Belknap drew from his accurate analysis. Belknap thought the issue was resolved and that the only remaining question was whether immediately or whether eventually the state of liberty would confer equity and status automatically upon Black and White Americans alike.

The unexpected protracted rage of the resistance and war waged against American abolition, perpetrated by Constitution-wielding warriors for slaveholding rights, blind-sided men of goodwill and consumed the waning time, interest, and thought of the aging ethically-solid and power-oriented Old Abolitionists.

These Old Abolitionist Founding Fathers' debated whether or not as framers and ratifiers of the Constitution they made the bad mistake of compromising their principles that turned into the worse error of cancelling their consciences.

But few of even the partisan party power politics parsons determined this difficulty would be compounded by complexity if clerical social ethicists failed to subject their compromised conscience and constitution to corrective action; refused to secure their Old Abolitionism legitimate claims by not any means necessary but the only means possible in the system of pragmatism they created; and/or declined to direct their natural talent for politics in the mastery of the new American art of politics.

Old Abolitionist "Massachusetts Puritan" parsons entered the dying stages as a class when Belknap entered the throes of death and died with the internment of "Connecticut Puritan" parson Samuel Hopkins. Between these two events, and effective end of the Puritan partisan/Old Abolitionist parson era, their dearly loved Federalist Party commenced its irreversible slide into oblivion.

The Party's dissolution was visited with absolution when the rather more embarrassed than harassed political Puritan survivors and their Yankee sons abandoned the Party, disengaged from partisan party power politics, and leaped from the morality of politics to the politics of morality.

Thus, as a result of lack of interest rather than ability, Yankees left Cavaliers to dominate the profession and the Three Branches of Government.

This incredible reversal of reason and revelation was the unexpected end of Belknap's Puritan competitors and compeers. At the outset of Union they were partisan Federalist Party power parsons, but, after Thomas Jefferson created the Democratic Party and it succeed in precipitating the rapid decline into obscurity of their Federalist Party, Yankee sons of Calvinist Puritan parsons exited the political arena.

In this retraction from political competition the clergy class followed the precedent established during the French and Indian Wars by Quaker Puritans, who withdrew the Religious Society of Friends as a body permanently from hegemony of the Pennsylvania Province Legislature and power politics. Establishment Yankee parsons uniformly argued high principles were instituted by Providence, inimical to professional politicians and politics and the exclusive province of professional ministers and ministries, and distanced themselves from partisan politics between the War of 1812 and the Fugitive Slave Act of 1850 as completely as the clerical Boston rationalists increasingly removed their principles and practices from antislavery activity between 1788 and 1816.

Succinctly stated, the post-Belknap Boston theological liberal Calvinists or anti-Calvinist liberals and Evangelical Calvinist revisionists rapidly turned social conservative Congregationalists. Wherefrom their potentially significant consideration of and contribution to the civil advance of free Black fellow New Englanders was an overt potency overruled by a covert stubborn will to the contrary.

As Black Northeasterners and Southeasterners, together with their problems and prospects, were banished from the concerns of Boston theological "liberals" and "conservatives" increasingly, they vanished from the influenceable political power circles that only the few and far between (if not as rare and hard to find as hens' teeth) powerhouse Protestants challenged with their superior principles.

This positive neglect and negative charge impacted fully and disproportionately free Black Northerners, howbeit a consequence of omission rather more than commission. The near absence in Massachsetts of direct actionist Old Abolitionists, at the beginning of the nineteenth century, did not reflect a corresponding decreasing Black population.

On the contrary, whether like Vermont Massachusetts never established an Old Abolition Society because state abolition obviated the need in the minds of secular and sacred Puritans, or whether the Massachusetts antislavery movement was dead and buried and nearly forgotten, its imperceptible presence contrasted sharply with the numerical increase of free and fugitive Black residents that paralleled the absolute growth of slave and free Black Americans throughout the nation. New England indifference to native and other free Black residents was a baffling development, made all the more enigmatic in light of English Abolitionism by the regional concern withheld from Black Southerners in the slavocracy.

Black Americans at liberty in New England were seeking freedom and finding anti-Black race repression in Massachusetts and Connecticut. Conversely, slaves in the Northeast and the Southeast scarcely possessed a fully developed appreciation of the frustration endured by free Black brethren who were condemned to pursue the elusive freedom they struggled ceaselessly but unsuccessfully to secure.

Slaves enjoyed relative freedom or license and leeway as bondmen and bondwomen, focused on prospects of liberty rather than problems of freedom, and were aided and abetted in this concentration by free-born, freed, and fugitive sisters and brothers who spent less energy managing the mysteries of freedom than they expended in engineering their liberation from bondage.

In the Independence era proliferating liberty formed the platform for the ascendancy of self-determination as the generally accepted precondition for each solitary individual and sovereign state. This appropriated and modified political principle of republican democracy converged with the economic principle of free market mercantilism, currently emerging as free enterprise capitalism and fueling the new industrial economy, and excited the secular humanist and religious humanitarian mix of Northern and Southern Old Abolitionist Protestants.

The Old Abolitionism persuasion gripped the consciences of Northern and Southern men and women, notwithstanding the regional, institutional, and personal variations in cultural customs, tastes and manners, and preferred fashions and life styles.

In both regions this Enlightenment-sparked and Independence-stimulated impressive minority responded by immediately manumitting their slaves. In a pattern pioneered by the Religious Society of Friends, freed slaves frequently remained in the household as hired domestic servants or were the recipients of modest economic grants provided to set them on their feet. Life-long slaves, and perpetual victims of a social system arranged to stabilize preferred anti-- Black race priorities, were released in a society which nowhere provided a sound basis for the preponderancy of Black-race emigrants to secure gradually the wherewithal necessary to compete on an equal footing with White-ethnic immigrants.

Perchance a creative social policy could have evolved in due course, but the possibility was not evident in either the Vermont Constitution or the Massachusetts Constitution that the Bay State citizenry-ratified--which were noteworthy for their pacesetting legal proscription of slavery and lack of precedent-setting public assistance provisions enacted to enable the disadvantaged to compete with the advantaged--to say little of the other Northeastern states which enacted gradual manumission statutes.

Certainly contending Constitution scholars and students in the antebellum revisionist era, no more or less than engaged aggressive antislavery and equally offensive and defensive proslavery agents, both interpreted and argued the same facts differently to make their disperate plaintiff and defendant cases, and specifically the undisputable facts making it unmistakable that even the most liberal manumission policies enacted and enforced--during the first decades following the formation of the Union--by the slaveholding states were bereft of the slightest suggestion support for free Black race residents to gain access to competitiveness was a remote possibility.

This obvious matter of importance was the natural result of the manumission measures of the slave states--unlike the gradual but definite abolition legislation in the Northeastern states--were enacted into law not to end slavery but to secure and to prevent the slave system from breaking: by bending the rules to improve the rule apropos permitting exceptions to prove the rule, standard deviations from the norm, or individualistic slavemasters to manumit their private property. Contemporary comparative culture analysts who either believed or speculated that slavocrats would produce voluntarily a solid plan for gradual manumission of the slave masses--not to mention one promulgated to assist their equal access to political and economic competitiveness--were predictable rational romanticists rather than realists.

THE KINGDOM OF GOD AND MAN AT YALE

IN THE COTTON KINGDOM OF THE OLD SOUTH

At this turning point when a minority among the American power elite collectively possessed the motive, means, and opportunity to design a process for the gradual end of exclusion and beginning of inclusion in the Union of their Black-race cultural kin-group, exactly the opposite initiative transpired which guaranteed the continuation of the retrogression rather than progression in fortune.

Eli Whitney (1765-1825), a "Massachusetts Yankee" who choose a "Connecticut Yankee" education, upon graduation (1792) from Yale accepted an offer to tutor on a South Carolina plantation: in a pattern followed several years later by eighteen year-old William Ellery Channing, after the "Rhode Island Yankee" graduated from Harvard in 1798.

Whitney unwittingly but fortuitously booked passage on the same ship selected by another Yankee journeying south to secure her fortune, yet could not like her descendants who ventured in the South to become rich be caricatured by the poor Cavaliers in "ruin finery" a prototype "carpetbagger" co-conspirator with "scalawags," General Nathaniel Greene's (1742-86) widow.

The native Rhode Islander was traveling from her home to take charge of the Mulberry Grove plantation, near Savannah, that the grateful planter class in the state of Georgia bestowed upon the wealthy and well-respected but post-War impoverished Revolutionary Patriot. Upon disembarking at his destination and discovering he would earn less than his contract stipulated, Whitney departed forthwith to accept his New Eng-land companion's invitation to visit Mulberry Grove.

During the winter of his discontent he enjoyed the Southern hospitality extended by his new-found slavocrat hosts, and responded in kind when Georgians communicated their desire for a mechanical device that would enable planters to separate the fiber of short-staple cotton from the seed rapidly and efficiently. By the spring he had invented the cotton gin (1793).

The inventor's device contributed the missing link in the chain of technological change, which functioned as the vital connective linkage facilitating the development of the Southern agrarian economy, and accelerating the advancement of Cotton Kingdom agronomy from a manual to an industrial society.

His invention revitalized the post-War depressed and pre-industrial cotton economy, enabled it to become economically viable if not competitive with Northern industrial capitalism, and rejuvenated the slave system that Northeasterners had written off as non-competitive but most Southeasterners had not given up on.

Slavocrats followed the rational analysis published by emissaries of mercantilists fast becoming manufacturers to its conclusion, but rejected the advice offered by the intellectuals whom Northern industrial capitalists convinced that the slave-based economy was the worse imaginable one--and the free market-manipulated free enterprise system energized by free entrepreneur and free labor competitors the best efficient and cost-effective productive wealth device ever devised by the mind of man.

Theory and experience dictated the premise that the Southern political economy was a disincentive-replete agrarian, and evolved as Northeastern conventional wisdom with the nascent industrial revolution prior to risk capital discovering incentives for investing in Southern slaves and plantations. The ethic of capitalism was successfully marketed and sold to the Old Abolitionist minority among the Founding Fathers--who appropriated the facts and figures to make their point, albeit they lost their antislavery case and acquiesced to majority rule.

Old Abolitionists argued the economic arguments of the Church and state united religious humanitarians and secular humanists in the Northeast to urge the planters to abolish slavery and the plantations, asserted that their agrarian and slave-based economy was a labor-intensive and consumer-oriented rather than capital-intensive and wealth-producing system, and concluded that the political and economic system of the Old South in the new United States minimized efficiency and maximized costs which diminished the capacity of the devoutly wished for Cotton Kingdom to produce a competitive ever-expanding economy.

Slaveholders heard but did not heed the counsel, opted to go public with their regional interest, and engaged Whitney to whom they made a personal plea to meet the master planters' private need for a machine that would minimize costs and maximize efficiency.

Ironically, in creating the first efficient and productive "cotton picking" machine, Whitney matched his promise with performance, went beyond passing the acid test of meeting the basic need to fulfilling the flightiest fancies of the planter class, and delivered not only a utilitarian invention but also a systems-changing machine. Whitney's cotton gin self-generated a demanding need for mass production that he was unable to supply, and the opportunity for more enterprising entrepreneurs whose competitive edge he could match.

Truth to tell, the better inventor than businessman simultaneously bolstered the slavocracy, failed to meet the stiff competition, and did not succeed in reaping the profits from his technological innovation and advancement of the "peculiar institution."

The "cotton-picking" machine facilitated the movers and shakers who hammered the nails in the closed lid that permanently sealed shut the Southern coffin of voluntary liberation. It intensified the hurt and harm suffered by the Black body, rather than provided help and hope to human bondage. And quite as decidedly as it brought great wealth to Northern industrialists and investment capitalists along with the Southern plantation owners and slavetraders.

To the collective mind of the Southern aristocrat and planter class, that Northern patrician realists and Old Abolitionist rationalists challenged with incontrovertible logic, this early national era and nineteenth-century turn around in economic affairs refuted conclusively the predictive power-deficient theory whose thesis hypothesized that the slave-based political economy was non-competitive, and therefore the system-laborsystem was obsolete because it was founded on a disincentive-intensive and incentive-economic principle.

Thus reared a "Massachusetts Yankee" and educated a "Connecticut Yankee," Whitney emerged in his majority a solid Northern proslavocrat, whether or not he evolved into an antislavocracy/proslavocracy ambivalent. In the characteristic pattern of his deceased Puritan and con-temporary Yankee antislavery/proslavery rerelations--the New England English race and British ethnic Calvinist kin of Cavaliers and Anglicans--Whitney wittingly and unwittingly contributed economic assets to the political clut possessed by professionals, who as aristocrats played hardball politics and beat the patricians in the *states' rights* power game.

The Yankee classmate of Cavalier Yalies managed reality by not examining seriously whether or not his fiscal and monetary assistance added possibilities including the power of choice to these formidable foes of the friends of Black folk. This Northern gift of grace and reason constributed singularly solid substance to style, and enabled Southern antiabolitionists to counter the ideas and to reject the ideals of Northern abolitionists even more effectively.

Whitney's virtue of necessity was at once an argument for necessity being the mother of invention, prototypical profitable Protestant philanthrophy, and classic instance of charity transformed benevolence for White folk and deterrence-benevolence for Black folk. Howbeit an unconscious or conscious intention and consequence effect, the vice and virtue device of utilitarian value facilitated the transition from the old foreign to the new domestic slavemaking and slavetrading process.

Complementing the present-generating future (post-1808) domestic slavetrading and slavebreeding cultural change event, the Whitney apparatus transfigurated the slave overnight from a one-dimensional pleasure-producing creature into a two-dimensional pleasure-producing and profit-making property--albeit a not entirely new convention for the slaveowning classes.

The relatively more productive nineteenth-century Cotton Kingdom plantations than those of the eighteenth-century Old South generated immense economic, political, social, religious, cultural, legal, and personal benefits for the slavocrats. These accrued assets increased the worth of real interests and values, in which narrow sense a fundamental change occurred, and excited slavocrats to generate a new logic for the defense and expansion of the Southern Way of Life.

The new opportunity and logic produced new principles which inevitably overwhelmed previous premises. Foremost among them was the universal self-determination vision of eighteenth-century Northern and Southern Old Abolitionists, who proclaimed to the public that it made good moral, economic, political, and social sense to end slavery.

Liberation from human bondage was so far from a matter of common sense to the nineteenth-century mind of the original New South, that the secular and sectarian slavocrats managed with impunity to dismiss the Old Abolitionist principle of universal and unconditional immediate liberty as perfect nonsense.

Post-cotton gin slavocrats turned Jeffersonians or Democratic Party power politics partisans in 1880, and in the face of *"Old and New England"* slave-free states possessed a real alternative to either admitting abolition as a good or tolerating antislavery as a right.

Slavocrats chose a viable option and elected aggressive promotion of the slavocracy, equated slavocracy with democracy, and proclaimed their "states' rights" exercise of preferred choice the right choice as well as the moral model of freedom of choice.

EVANGELICAL INSTRUMENTS OF SOUTHERN PRESERVATION

These secular proslavery dynamics realigning the Southern political economy appeared no more new than the parallel Second Great Awakening that reshaped the American cultural landscape equally profoundly, and burst forth fifty years after the outbreak of the First Great Awakening. The Evangelicals dominating the Second Great Awakening revival trails along the East Coast generally, and within the slave states particulary, were Methodist (Arminian) and Baptist (Calvinist) rivals challenged by a strong contingent of Presbyterians (Calvinist emissaries for the Congregationalists) and a few Anglicans (Latitudinarians).

Commencing with and as an aftereffect of the 1822 Missouri Bill debate in Congress, and Denmark Vesey's squashed insurrection in South Carolina, Black independent clergymen and churches were outlawed by the enacted and enforced new *"Black Codes."* All the exceptions to the rule were proscribed immediately after the 1831 Nat Turner insurrection, wherefrom the only autonomous church and state authorized evangelists and ministers among Black free and slave Southerners in the slavocracy were White race/ethnic revivalists committed to making, keeping, and improving the human bondage condition. Official ecclesiastical and civil command and control of Black folk was the first official church and state duty of clergymen.

The complementary second and secondary sectarian responsibility entailed evangelizing bondmen and bondwomen. These priorities had the effect of only the odd and even peculiar antebellum deviants being engaged in the Civilization, Christianization, and Colonization of Black Southerners.

Black and White Southern men and women constituted a creative minority who placed conscience above the rule of law and obeyed its dictates to break the law proscribing instructing Black folks. Some of the bold and brave who defiant ones were successful in their endeavors to provide both free and enslaved Black Southerners with rudimentary instruction at a minimum. But the stark norm for church- and state-authorized evangelists and revivalists was to save Black and White souls. Irrespective of the intentions, the consequence of the Evangelicalism was the security of the social order, culture, and slavocracy.

Between the 1776-emerging Old Abolitionists and the 1830-erupting New Abolitionists the mainstream denominations initially became engaged and ecumenical Protestant officialdom established the antiabolitionist ACS as the antislavery agency of the Evangelical churches. Halfway Piety faith and ethics engendered by the Second Great Awakening were powerful factors causing hegemonic antiabolitionist Yankee Colonizationists to sever the Puritan Old Abolitionist connection.

Yankee Congregationalists suddenly surfaced as advocates for the preservation of revisionist Calvinism and the advancement of an authorized revision of Puritan Old Abolitionism, and claimed their progressive transformation means guaranteed linear progression rather than positive regression of values and reversal of roles.

34   CONSTITUTION, CONSCIENCE, AND CALVINIST COMPROMISE

Denominational leaders brought the major Protestant bodies into the antislavery/proslavery struggle ostensibly as proponents of neither party to the conflict, neutral agencies fixed on the straight and narrow fine dividing line between the antagonists, and exponents of a separate and distinct Evangelical Protestant solution to the American dilemma produced and promoted by middle-of-the-road churchman.

Antislavery denominationalists demonstrated they lacked the capacity to admit it made a world a difference to Black Christians that the establishment Evangelical White Christian churchmen and churches were antislavery advocates of Colonizationism, gradualism, antiabolitionism, and the adversaries of Black and White Evangelical clerical and laity agents of immediatism, Old Abolitionism, and New Abolitionism. Rigid establishmentarians drew a line in the dirt and in this inflexible posture guaranteed the generation of their antiestablishment denominations Evangelical denominationalist opposition, declared the New Abolitionists deadly dangerous extremists, and defined the immediatists radicals promoting a prescription for the destabilization of the civil consensus and the status quo Union as indisputably as they were determined to renege on the *White Gentlemen's Agreement* and change the Constitution conservatives honored as a sacred and inviolable sacrosanct social contract.

Prior to churchmen being born again Colonizationists their late First Great Awakening, and early Second Great Awakening, Northern Baptist Calvinist cousins embarked upon an Evangelical mission in the South as evangelists and revivalists to Black and White Southerners.

Initiative was evidenced in their instrumental role as the catalytic agents in the original organization of Evangelical Southern Baptists, their positive integration of moral and political force whose power they directed to pressure the ecclesiastical and civil powers to change from the union to the separation of church and state, and their failure to secure immediately a new policy from Yankees in charge of their onetime Northeastern Puritan establishment but near instant successful in winning a secular and sacred political reversal from the Virginians at the helm of the sometime Southeastern Anglican establishment.

From the Virginians Thomas Jefferson and James Madison led in forming the Virginia State Constitution, these primarily Northern leaders of aggressive Revolutionary War Patriots and Freedom Fighters, politics-intensive Old Abolitionists, and English race and British ethnic Calvinist Baptists won religious freedom and liberty of conscience.

Nearly all these Calvinist Baptist leaders were natives of the abolitionist state of Massachusetts or gradual manumission state of Connecticut, and emerged Northern engaged with Southern Old Abolitionists or at least antislavery advocates who were serious exponents of universal and unconditional immediate private manumission. Synchronically during the mid-1820s the slavocracy was developing, apparently more imperceptibly or less transparently a formidable concentration in the mysterious way an iceberg forms beneath the surface, but surging before the full-fledged tip surfaced in 1822 as an aftereffect of the Missouri Compromise.

In the aftermath the few remaining members of this Northeastern Baptist leadership class departed the South, and the last antislavery Baptist (Presbyterian, Methodist and compeer manumissionist) Southerners were driven out of the slavocracy by the slavocrats.

By 1833, several lay churchmen managed (A) to be the only surviving mainstream Protestant Old Abolitionists; (B) to tarry connected with the Quaker-led

Old Abolitionist Societies that were declining as rapidly as the major denominations and their antiabolitionist ACS were inclining as the hegemonic American antislavery power; and (C) to shoulder the leadership alone and unsupported by professional parsons since the clerical class of New England Old Abolitionists had deceased.

Because the antiabolitionist ACS had replaced the Old Abolitionist Societies Quakers led as the American antislavery standardbearer, and New Abolitionists had erupted out of the ACS to form the American Anti-Slavery Society (AAS), mainstream churchmen committed to join the organization that could abolish human bondage most efficiently were compelled to chose between the ACS (antiabolitionist/procolonizationist antislavery proponents of gradualism) and the AAS (proabolitionist/anticolonizationist architects of immediatism).

Howbeit not entirely obvious why, it is patently clear that at the commencement of the AAS Evangelical Calvinists (primarily along with their Protestant compeers) dominated the ACS (gradualists) and the AAS (immediatists). The plump fact is particularly plain when the Unitarian/Congregationalists-concentrated Boston (New England) Anti-Slavery is compared with the statistically significant numerically superior host constituted by the other member individuals and bodies of the AAS.

Unbridgeable diametrically opposite color caste/captive condition-solving motives, means, and ends predetermined their existence as antiabolitionist and proabolitionist permanent enemies determined to prove they were not the foes but the friends of Black folk.

When the immediatists broke with gradualists and bolted from the ACS to form the AAS, the Moral Reformers remained united spiritual and moral power-only advocates in their competing antislavery organizations for a period, and divided as the Colonizationists totally immersed the ACS in the *realpolitik* realm and the proabolitionists directed the AAS to advance entirely circumspect of politics and above political save for the barest minimum involvement through supporting political petitions.

William Garrison and Arthur Tappan at the helm of the New England Anti-Slavery Society and the New York Anti-Slavery Society guided the two most influential wings of the AAS, but a division in the house of immediatism occurred when the Garrisonians remained unrepentant rigid moralists who would tolerate only anti-political abolitionism, and the Tappanites added pro-political power to pure spiritual and simple moral abolitionist force.

The Tappanites evolved into partisan party power politics parishioners and parsons, and the chief competitors with Colonizationists for the title of the champion American Civil Religion realists, opportunists, and pragmatists. What abides as no less real and relevant for being either more or less obvious than it seems is consequence-laden: All three competitive agencies were equally firm proponents of nonviolence and Temperance.

Fractionalization in the ACS and AAS American antislavery body developed into an advanced stage during this early antebellum period time, primarily as a result of their polar opposite gradualism and immediatism faith and ethics competition and conflict producing, by turns, Halfway Piety and authentic Puritan Piety mutually exclusive Yankee extremes of Evangelical Calvinism, a steady trickle of slaves legally and privately manumitted by parishioner and parson slavemasters to the Africa deportation-specific ACS, and a mid-antebellum era forward ever-expanding stream of illegal self-liberationists in flight as fugitives from the slavocracy.

The steadily growing numbers of runaways from legal injustice did not in their conspicuous preponderancy head for Africa but beat a path to the "*Promised Land.*" Lawless new immigrant and old emigrant intensive White ethnic minorities, who in their role as defenders were joined by the White race representatives, delivered a black lash and front lash in the Frontier Midwest and settled Northeast.

The conscious collective class punishers of the outcast color caste did not let up on striking terror in the hearts and inflicting stripes on the backs of Black folk--whose necks they did not stretch--until American leaders were sensitized by their jaundiced caricature of the Black race as the "*White man's burden.*"

White capital and management tolerated if they neither permitted nor encouraged White labor to thrust themselves viscerally and viciously upon in the hopes of eliminating their competition. Depending upon the extent to which their slavemasters trained and developed them into skilled craftsmen, as a means of guaranteeing productivity and efficiency in their performance of market-oriented task-responsibilities, their Black competitors were quite prepared or unprepared to enter directly into the developing industrialized economy.

White ethnic protectionists not only verbally and physically abused the Black body violently but excluded the color caste from the American labor unions they controlled, and thus prevented competitive Black males from becoming apprentices.

New England Congregationalist clergy who closed out of their churches (town meetinghouses) Finneyite New Abolitionist evangelists--in the mid-antebellum--naturally did not speak up for Black brethren who were frozen out of the competitive economy, and the political participation without access to representation equally solidly. Doubtless Congregationalists considered their charitable contributions to individual Black slaves, fugitives, and free-born natives balanced the scales of injustice weighing down the Black race.

Their spacious justification by faith in reason expanded their capacious powers of rationalization which enabled them to believe the incredible: the combined benevolence amassed and given by their local churches, regional associations, and national denominations amounted to unmatchable effective ameliorative acts because these selective relief deeds were purely voluntary contributions.

The Protestant Episcopal Church and the Methodist Episcopal Church, which formed as American denominations in the mid-1780s when they severed their ties as the Latitudinarian-traditionalist and Evangelical-Arminian wings of the Mother Church of England, were like the later-organized Baptist Denomination less resourceful than the early 1800s-allied Congregation-alist (Orthodoxy) and Presbyterian (Reformed) Calvinist traditions.

But even the Congregationalist/Pres-byterian Union's embryonic Domestic Missions produced programs that were not equal to the challenge the oppressed bondage and repressed caste class of Black thousands presented.

One among the many factors contributing to the limited general interest enrichment utility value of the Congregationalist clergy's social ethics, which were restricted to a fixed set of single-issues and range of special interests ends secured through narrow-scoped means, was a singular perplexity compounded by complexity: Evangelical Calvinist First Great Awakening indiscriminate civil indifference was the direct effect desired and designed by Puritan rationalists at the helm of Orthodoxy (pre-Congregationalism), who engineered the spiritual force and moral power potential generated by the kinetic religious phenomenon to be concentrated dogmatics (faith) consecrated to secure the Churchocracy for Christocracy amid the dying sacred theocracy and borning secular democracy, and source recovered by Yankee organizers of the Congregationalist Churches of Christ in the post-Independence and Second Great Awakening era which diminished the capacity of their pragmatics (ethics).

Forthwith New England divines' public service like their role as public servants appeared choked authentic Puritan Piety, and released Halfway Piety faith and deterrence-benevolence ethics, throttled by their centermost missionary method and rational organizing millennial doctrine which logicians and rhetoricians developed not merely to realize their chief objective (the millennium) but also to actualize this "Ultimate Revolution" and end of history in eternity.

Followers of the Harvard "Old Light" and the Yale "New Light" Calvinist Puritan antagonists from the eastern and western edges of Massachusetts, led by the Reverend Charles Chauncy (1705-87) in Boston and Jonathan Edwards in Northampton, majored in minors such as theological disputes during the First Great Awakening.

These brilliant divines--and better Calvinist faith than Chrisitan ethics thinkers and actors--publicly proclaimed and published in the parochial press their rational reflections on their objective subjective participation and objective participant observer race and religion field reseach findings for the Congregationalist churches and churchmen, who imitated their great faith efforts for race/ethnic minorities and poor ethics promise and performance for the race-only minority.

Thus their public service-limiting internal disputes dominated the era between the death of public servant and genuine Puritan Piety faith and ethics standardbearer Cotton Mather. It ended neither with a bang nor a whimper nor through any fault of their own but with their caste/captive class-specific Calvinist (comparatively grreater dogma than pragma) relative successes and failures being checked and suspended by the energy expended in the all-consuming American Revolution.

The Independence movement gave birth to democracy, slavocracy, and the Evangelical Second Great Awakening. The later spiritual phenomenon initially burst forth in New England, spread throughout the South and the West, and reverberated. The Evangelical faith and ethics dynamics created the opportunity for enterprising ecclesiastical entrepreneurs: whose combination aggressive Protestant proselytism and innovative voluntarism produced new churches, the rational organizations to supply the demand and need generated by proliferating congregations they formed, and the national denominations which as supreme legislative and judicatory ecclesiastical bodies instantly created Foreign Mission Societies.

Evangelical Calvinist and Arminian clergy emerged with the early national years and Victorian Age imperialistic missionaries and millennarians, who as competitive Protestant builders of the Kingdom of the Christ were rival sectarians dedicated to guaranteeing the Gospel would be preached in every culture of the world according to their authorized revised standard version of the "Rule of Scripture, Rational Truth, and Moral Law.

Straightaway Orthodoxy and Reformed clergy united, substituted the surrogate single parochial-specific commitment for the simultaneously eliminated dual ecclesiastical and civil general interest means and ends of the millennial-driven faith and ethics Calvinist Puritan fathers promulgated.

The English race-conscious saints and sinners determined their American Calvinist Puritan version was a real improvement and neither either a revision or a reversal nor a repudiation of genuine Calvinism. Classic Catholicism as communicated by selected Church Fathers formed the connective linkage between the Early Christian and original Calvinism. It constituted a Protestant continuum of the tradition, a rational anti-millenniarian faith and ethics religion revolving around the union of church and state, and an establishmentarian middle-class systematic theology set forth in his *Institutes of the Christian Religion* (1536) by the founding father, the Reverend John Calvin (1509-64).

What argued the English-American race of "chosen people's" was the argument that the New Englanders' church and state or Calvinist-Puritan theocracy--as distinguished from the saints' peculiar ecclesiastical and civil *Errand into the Wilderness* mission--paralleled Calvin's hierocracy in Geneva as a sacred/ secular civil government.

But Edwards burst forth as a counter-culture Puritan majority of one, specifically as a re-revisionist of the theocratic Puritan revision of hierocrat Calvin, and challenged the tradition with his millennium-intensive *"Ultimate Revolution."*

Edwards' mastery of White magic (Western empirical logic and rationalism), combined with his masterful mystical and mystery powers, enabled him to turn the authentic Puritan Piety faith and ethics tradition advanced by elder contemporary Cotton Mather into a Halfway Piety faith and ethics dream state: in which Churchocracy for Christocracy fantasy Edwards attempted to live, move, and find both meaning and his being in deterrence-benevolence.

Edwards believed all polar extremes created by man and culture--no less than those existing between history and eternity or human being and God Being--are predominantly negative rather than equally real or potential positive dimensions of existence, diametrically antithetical far more destructive than creative points of tension, and but contradictions that not only can be but should be solved through union of two anti-podes in a third cruciform.

What remains bracketed and outside of the parameters of this examination is whether or not Edwards' prototypic dialectical faith and ethics either consciously or unconsciously entailed the suppositional dialects of theocracy (thesis), democracy (antithesis), and Christocracy (synthesis).

But the millennialism-intensive evangelist's un-divided empirical rationalist mind and Calvinistical revivalist will most certainly asserted the binary ecclesiastical (thesis) and civil (antithesis) power contraries were resolved by the churchocracy (synthesis) he was engaged in developing.

Churchocracy was fashioned in his peerless logic and forming in his rational imagination as the superstructure and infrastructure of what Edwards the new *"City on a Hill."* This Edwardsean spiritual and material deconstruction and reconstruction was constructed as the revised Puritan subjective purpose and objective mission.

To this peculiar *"Errand into the Wilderness"* he called the "chosen few" saints and other "Elect of God" to be engaged in parochial benevolence as a means of surviving rather than saving the secular culture and civil order; primed for the Second Coming of Christ by preparing the landing space for the imminently arriving millennium to surface initially in New England; and to be certain that following the one thousand year millennial reign and final triumph of eternity over history the Kingdom of Christ or Kingdom of God would be established.

Whereas Calvin treated the church and state as not contrary but complementary entities whose distinctive natures are to be at once preserved and united in civil matters of the common good, Edwards treated the church and state contraries with invincible indifference and as if they could be resolved in the fusion of ecclesiastical and civil powers in the Churchocracy for Christocracy. In the process of establishing the principle of spiritual and moral disregard of secular politics and civil order Edwards created parochial and private philanthropy for the sake of the millennium rather than the public interest.

From this bare essence and manifestation of deterrence-benevolence Edwards effectively established Halfway Piety faith and deterrence-benevolence ethics, and his re-revision post-Edwardseans revised and crystallized as the up-to-date surrogate for authentic Puritan Piety Evangelical faith and parochial/private/public good-maximizing and evil-minimizing ethics.

Edwards' disciple, Samuel Hopkins, initially systematically and systemically developed his mentor's militant millenniarian theology, and millennium-dynamized superior estate. It proved to be of far greater utilitarian value as parochial faith than public ethics. Edwards' inherent strong dogma and weak pragma was the major cause of Hopkins, a true disciple and the original Edwardsean, (1) becoming in the post-Edwards years a better manager of crisis and change than ambiguity; (2) fostering alternately Halfway Piety de-terrence-benevolence and genuine Puritan Piety faith and ethics; (3) orchestrating Hopkinsianism as the standard of Edwardsean Orthodoxy (that post-Edwardseans up-dated and re-named "New Light" and "New School") or "New Divinity;" and (4) distinguishing himself as the best and brightest and worst and woeful wisehead American Christian social ethicist, who was celebrated as a Calvinist expert ethicist in deterrence-benevolence public ethics and the first complete Puritan-Yankee Old Abolitionist clergyman.

ESTABLISHMENT MISSIONARY AND COLONIZATION
SOCIETIES' PRIORITIES

The Congregationalist/Presbyterian Alliance formed prior to the Churches of Christ in New England organizing as the ecumenical agencies of their Orthodoxy and Reformed traditions the American Board of Commissioners for Foreign Missions (1810) and the American Home Mission Society (1826); the schism (1837) in the Presbyterian Denomination--precipitating the deliberate speed with which the Congregationalist Consociations finalized their Congregationalist Denomination in the mid-1840s--wherein the "Old School" and Princeton-centered majority ejected the "New School" and Yale-revolving minority, as an aftereffect of whose division the Reformed "New School" and Orthodoxy "New Light" clergy remained interlocking directorates of the Con-gregationalism-derived foreign and domestic Evangelical bureaucracies and the "Old School" established the Presbyterian Board of Foreign Missions (1837); the American Baptist Missionary Union (1814); the Missionary Society of the Methodist Episcopal Church (1819); and the Domestic and Foreign Society of the Protestant Episcopal Church (1820).

During the early national years Northern and Southern Evangelical (faith) and abolitionist (social ethics) coordinateness as complementaries rather than conflict as contraries existed in theory and experience. In the view of a measurable corps of published observant and nonobservant contemporaries, the dogma and pragma principles succeeded less frequently than they failed to work well together in practice because of the competing preferred priorities exercised as

prerogatives of privilege by establishmentarians. Consequently, Evangelical faith
and ethics appeared to offer consternation in stead of counterdemands to the
exigency presented by free Blacks and slaves in the North and the South. Absolutely certain they were rightheaded Protestant Moral Reformers, influential
missionaries and ministers ministering to the ministering Congregationalist/Pres-
byterian Church proposed and produced for the major denominations their para-
eccle-siastical antislavery American Colonization Society (December-1816--Jan-
uary 1817).

Several days after the architects designed and the framers voted the ACS
the official antislavery agency of power elite Protestantism, the African Methodist Episcopal Church (A.M.E.) exercised her authority as the first and then
only Black denomination to convene and speak for the Black community to the
White community in no uncertain terms. The minority informed the majority
that Colonizationists were worse than wrongheaded in overriding the counterclaims of Black Protestant Americans because in establishing their counterdemanding ACS a church and state antislavery agency they struck a sacred compact to reinforce the secular *White Christian Gentlemen Agreement* to defend
and to secure the American anti-Black race spirit.

The ACS is the universally empirically verifiable evidence that the most resourceful post-Hopkinsian and pre-Colonizationist era establishment denominations considered the well being of their Black-race constituency a matter of enduring insignificance; indicator of the potence rather than impotence of the
sacred and secular saints' public (no less than private and parochial) antiblack
white-ethnic virtue or social ethic inheritance accepted rather than rejected by
the English-race Congregationalists and British-ethnic Presbyterians affirming
themselves the Yankee sons of these Puritan fathers; and capacity of Calvinist
engineers to take their ecclesiastical engine off automatic pilot, to assume
hands-on command of the controls, and to commence to switch on to the dead-
head track (at the very least if not also to derail) the runaway pro-White race
train of Black race harm-in-tensive attitudinal and behavioral mechanisms.

Hence clergymen who turned professional civil engineers and engineered on
the intersecting public and private political and economic tracks their preferred
parochial moralisms, which powerful Orthodoxy fiscally sustained and charged
with ethical energy, disclosed their resources could have been differently directed to positively help rather than hurt the chances of a peo-ple in clear sight
and need of elevation.

Samuel Hopkins managed the Puritan Piety Old Abolitionism and Halfway
Piety deterrence-benevolence deportation Colonizationism ethical exercise as if
it were in accord with the natural law of alternation, carried in this color cas-
te/captive class positive good and negative good or positive negation posture
the New England Standing Order to the initial Puritan Piety public interest-ethics pinnacle of moral principle, and reverted from progression to retrogression
at the power point when he determined to direct organized Congregationalist
charities to advance at once the advantage and disadvantage of Black Calvinists
indigenous to the region.

Hopkins struggled to secure Edwardseanism and lost the war for the hearts
and mind of Evangelical Congregationalism to the younger post-Edwardseans,
some years before he entered into the irreversible stages of death and dying.
The moment after he died and the last rites were administered, final respect for
the venerable crusader for Christ and civility was buried with his body.

Near instantly, Congregationalist churches swiftly fell into sharp decline from the height of Puritan principle he elevated through his clerical advancement of Calvinist Puritanism from antislavetrade to proabolitionist faith and ethics. Irresistible exciting parochial possibilities seduced the Protestant principals whose engagement of enticing denominational organizing priorities resulted in their non-development of Black Congregationalists, though these preferences never exhausted the capacity for moral energy of establishment Puritan Yankees and Anglican Cavaliers.

Corresponding post-Hopkins secular factors contributed to the mounting religious unconcern with free Black and slave sisterhood and brotherhood in the North and the South. First and foremost among the cultural realities capturing the ethical earnestness of the Northeastern and Southeastern religious forces were the new political and economic interests and opportunites, that commenced with the Northwest Territory Ordinance (1787) and increased after the Missouri Compromise (1820-21).

The relevant connecting point of the church and state in secular American Civil Religion consists of this significant profane and sacred formation: Less than fifteen years after Samuel Hopkins died the Congregationalist/Presbyterian establishment memorialized the exemplary Old Abolitionist by jettisoning his practiced abolitionist principles and embracing his 1776-emerging Evangelical missionizing scheme.

This initiative Hopkins pressed in New England revolved around benevolent paternalists affirming their deportation of native Black Americans to Africa to be a critical imposition, identifying the scheme as Christianizing-Civilizing-Colonizing Evangelicalism and inviting the Protestant denominations to adopt the millennialistic mission, and declaring it was neither a brutal benevolence nor a deterrence-benevolence but an Affirmative Action and Equal Opportunity program.

Hopkins' failure to advance his positive abolitionist endeavors on behalf of the Black race over his Evangelical negative initiatives illuminates objective reality: The ecclesiastical powers' non-redeeming reactions to the Black presence were conscious choices, evidence of real resources and selective rather than limited capacities, and not the result of overpowering either internal religious weakness or external secular demands.

Power Protestants who were pro-Colonizationists predeliberately elevated minor moral values to major moral principles, and superimposed as the Christian ethics standard of distinction selective engagement and disengagement with Black Christian brothers and sisters.

Their social ethics involved concentrating church philanthropy in a consecrated eleemosynary program for spiritual rather than material salvation, and marketing blind benevolence in the Black community as the Black race's one and only moral value and directive. Forthwith charity-imbued White folk aggressively marketed in the Black community their unilaterally determined best good of Black folk. Their self-styled altruism entailed incurring the costs of providing Black folk set or born free a pre-paid, all expense-free, and one-way trip to Africa, exclaimed their God helps those who help themselves, and explained that Black people served their own best interests by accepting the only offer of assistance White Protestantism would afford them and voluntarily removing themselves from America.

Demonstrable Halfway Piety faith and deterrence-benevolence or private-parochial-public ethics in essence and manifestation, procolonizationistic morality sprang naturally from "*the spirit*" of the culture.

This so-called American dilemma phenomenon was generated by the convergence of the philosophical and theological confluence, composed of underpinning principles developing over time and through time as derivatives of centuries-long social conservative *Great Chain of Being* philosophy constituting the foundation of hierarchal races, ethnic groups, and classes; the superior cast superimposing hyperexclusivity upon inferior caste; and the demotion of the positive and promotion of the negative dynamic to pervert antiblack white-ethnic virtue into pro-White race/ethnic virtue or anti-Black race virtue.

Orthodoxy thuswise predictably but neither necessarily nor inevitably furthered the Edwardsean Evangelical tradition of color caste/captive class-limiting Halfway Piety faith and deterrence-benevolence--that is, parochial faith and private ethics grounded in personal security and social status quo stability, and severed from Puritan Piety direct actionist (constructive structural social change) ethics of ethicists engaged in advancing the whole public or general (as distinguished from the special) interest.

Edwardseans like Hopkins earned respect for at-tempting even though they failed to overbalance Half-way Piety with authentic Puritan Piety: whose undeveloped potential Puritan Cotton Mather of Massachusetts and Harvard and Puritan Hopkins of Connecticut and Yale successively both advanced and left underdeveloped. But their successors, known to history as the Yale-centered and New Haven-oriented post-Edwardseans, treated the color caste/captive class-conscious Puritan Piety as irrelevant and inconsequential personal faith and public ethics.

Due to these contiguous English-American Puritan race factors and other more or less apparent reasons, Black Congregationalists were as real and important to Puritan Piety slavemaster Mather and Halfway Piety/Puritan Piety slaveholder Hopkins as they were unreal and unimportant to Halfway Piety slaveowner Jonathan Edwards and the post-Edwardseans who emerged the Yankee masters of Evangelical Calvinist faith and ethics. Mather's and Hopkins' model of Orthodoxy turned on parsons of local congregations pastoring Black Calvinist congregants whose ministry included providing their Black parishioners with at least the rudimentary edu-cation elements of Christianization.

But even though elementary command of at least one of the Three R's was a prerequisite for admittance to Evangelical Calvinism's lowest entry level, this assistance for converts Mather and Hopkins delivered was not forthcoming from the post-Edwardseans: who imitated Mather's propensity for associating Black-race Congregationalists with black and evil signs as candidly as he associated the English Puritan race of saints and "chosen people of God" with white and good symbols. Yet, dissimilar from the post-Edwardseans, Mather's pro-Black race public performance was stronger than his private and parochial anti-Black race rhetoric.

Evidently the diminished pro-Black race concernment of the post-Edwardseans did not broaden and deepen as a consequence of declining need, dwindling resources, or lack of opportunity and motive. The fathers bequeathed Puritan tribalism and other cultural customs but neither necessity nor inevitability which their Yankee sons proved when they were selectively rejected human bondage and accepted color caste to perpetuate their definite disregard for the Black race.

Thus Yankee internal resolve was the essential cause of Congregationalists' disastrous religious indifference to their Calvinist color caste/captive class and not the inherited Puritan normative cultural vices and theological virtues.

YALE/NEW HAVEN: CENTERS OF NORTHERN
ORTHODOXY AND SOUTHERN ARISTOCRACY

Post-abolitionist Massachusetts Orthodoxy formed the establishment continuum of Puritanism and declined to undergird the loins of Black men as a matter of expedience and convenience as certainly as Northern and Southern Anglicanism necessarily failed to provide Black folk support.

But this free choice was no more predetermined for pro-Calvinist or anti-Calvinist Yankees than William Ellery Channing (who identified himself as a Puritan shorn of Calvinistic principles) was fated not to embrace in public Old Abolitionist elder contemporary Samuel Hopkins until a half century after Hopkins died; to approach increasingly the abolitionist standardbearer's criterion of authentic antislavery action until his long antiabolitionist life was almost completed; and to affirm the virtue of New Abolitionism and vice of American Colonizationism only as his own career of moderate moral mediation between antislavery Northern and proslavery Southern friends came to a close.

It was an understandable but not an inescapable act for Channing to release his unfettered elitist optimism in the service of fundamental social conservatism even in his late course correction of his career-long cautious leadership. Channing's misexplication of emancipation, and new Orthodoxy's misguided pro-Colonizationism whose ASC principles he found praiseworthy while rejecting its policy as a cost-prohibitive process and objective, evolved from the same curative and lethal Calvinist Puritan Piety and Halfway Piety faith and ethics.

In order to appreciate the theological liberal and conservative Calvinists in their role as persuaded Puritan moralists, and commitment to unabated disrespect for their Black-race converts, it is useful to set in this context their alternative to advancing the Matherean Black race-concernment continuum by forging the Hopkinsian humanistic linkage with Black Congregationalists in a more favorable period.

The perspective of New England Congregationalists and Presbyterians is clarified when set beside Southeastern Reformed friends, Evangelical Pietists, and Calvinist Puritan lineage (however remote) descendants who chose a different live option and kept a vital interest in Black Protestants alive.

Outstanding among these social ethicists were the Southern expatriate Evangelicals in the West, who, joining with their Northern peers in the line of march led by Quaker Old Abolitionists, formed the earliest Evangelical Protestant sustained opposition to the Northeast-headquartered antiabolitionism-defensive and procolonizationism-offensive mainstream denominations.

Their adversaries included the Protestant Episcopal Church and the Methodist Episcopal Church, whose common elements included Manhattan national headquarters and a congregant constituency concentrated south of New York City along the East Cost, and who were (A) the post-Revolution American Anglican and Arminian denominations springing from the Church of England; (B) perceived by Patriots to be an unreliable mixed breed of British Loyalists harboring hidden Tory Persuasions beneath Patriot professions; (C) forced Anglican theocracy descendants specifically to surrender hegemonic status as a result of being heirs of suspect Independence era Tories; and (D) compelled Southern Anglicanism in the post-Independence Old South to share ecclesiastical power and authority with Evangelical Baptists, Methodists, and Presbyterians.

Plausibly before but doubtless as early as the turn of the century after the

American people took charge of their own destiny, and in the newly constituted sov-ereign nation fashioned a body politic governed by republican rules and embodying Christian values, the remarkable progression in democracy from theocracy of mutually reinforcing separate ecclesiastical and civil powers guaranteed the permanency of disestablishmentarianism as the formal relation between church and state in the Union of the South and the North.

This appreciably altered state of conscience and consciousness instituted a new governance principle and rule of law process that was more than a procedural change, from an English race-predominant religious civil political economy to a British (and other) ethnic groups-in-clusive secular civil-religious state. But as a change in fortune for ethnic individuals, republican democracy also marked a transition from old to new religious establishment alignments--and patterns of operation.

Following the Revolution and during the first few national years, partisan Federalist Party political power parsons were at the helm of Connecticut and Massachusetts Congregationalists. They united their efforts to secure the survivable residuals of the former Puritan theocracy, and to preserve Orthodoxy by more vigorous and rigorous than imaginative revisionist ideas and ideals. But these Puritan Patriots were succeeded a different breed of aggressive command and control Evangelical clergy, who as anti-political Moral Reformers promoted alternative systems and consolidated the leadership reins of Orthodoxy and the Reformed churchmen between the late-1700s and early-1800s.

This new hegemonic corps, and the first generation of leaders born in the nascent Union, were forceful figures, dominated by "Connecticut Yankees," and the first evangelists and revivalists to cut the new political ties between traditional ecclesiastical and civil power lawmakers of the political economy.

Positive political reformation preceded the change from manual to industrial technology, and the conversion from mercantilism to capitalism, whose revolution produced the cotton gin that precipitated the economic transformation of the Old South into the Cotton Kingdom.

With little delay prior to the expansive slavocracy the Southeastern plantation and agrarian economy turned into one that increased wealth as a result of the efficient production of crops and natural resources; the supply of raw materials purchased by Northern industrial capitalists and manufactured in Northeastern industrial centers like New Haven; and the number of finished goods sold in the South.

Northeastern bondmen-related shipping, commercial trade in raw materials, and manufactured marketable products free enterprises controlled the Federal government-dependent free market system; supply and demand forces driving the competing and cooperating Northern industrial democracy and Southern agricultural slavocracy; and the cultural certainties in which managed reality the materiality inevitably partially subsidized by slave labor included entrepreneurs, industrial capitalists, plantation owners, wealth-acquiring patricians in the North and aristocrats in the South, and an expansive interdependent political economy.

Hence transpired, albeit far less apparent to current churchmen cultural determiners than it appeared obvious to their critics, the mutually fertile rather than mutually exclusive swift growth from Calvinist mercantilism and theocracy of Protestant capitalism and disestablishmentarianism in the elitist class of Boston--or the certified "hub of the universe" and the old Puritan and new Yankee patrician class--and the rapid development between the slavocrats' conception and "quickening" of the slavocracy whose life after birth was parented by the

peer groups forming the Anglican planter and aristocratic class.
Coincidentally, Yale produced revisionist Evangelical Calvinist Congregation-alists and Presbyterians, from whom she evolved the national capital of the es-tablishmentarian "New Light" Orthodoxy and "New School" Reformed traditions, and New Haven emerged a favorite summer recreation community for Northern patricians and Southern aristocrats.

Whether or not an accident of history it was scarcely a factor of incidental symbolical significance in the cultural crisis that Yale--where concurrently the millenialistic-pervasive systematic faith and ethics of Jonathan Edwards and Samuel Hopkins were revered required texts subject to continuous revisions and honored in the breach--became the Northern academic mecca for a statistically significant number of young Southern gentlemen, who, before the birth of the nation, preferred private tutoring and/or studying in England and on the Con-tinent to an American college education.[1]

ORTHODOXY'S AND SLAVOCRACY'S REORGANIZATION

The nexus between New Haven Orthodoxy-updating Calvinists and Black for-tunes, at the turning point of Northern church-oriented Moral Reform revivalism and Southern human bondage revitalism or the two new es-tablishment "peculiar institutions," consists of a philsophical/theological social conservative value sys-tem and functional correlation connecting political, economic, and legal intellec-tual complements.

The post-Revolution "New Light" Congregationalist parsons and "New School" Presbyterian presbyters followed President John Witherspoon of Princeton and President Timothy Dwight of Yale into the Federalist Party, in which partisan party power politics direct action Dwight was directed by the New England Federalist Party leadership initiatives of his "Connecticut Wit" and Congressman (1806) brother Theodore Dwight (1764-1846).

Timothy Dwight waxed as Samuel Hopkins waned, took charge of the "New Divinity" ("New Haven Theology") school of post-Edwardseans at Yale, and led the predominantly English race/Orthodoxy-conscious Congregationalists. Dwight simultaneously advanced the social conservative morals, reversed the a-political or anti-political civil power indifferent values, and checked the advancement of the philosophical and psychological principles promulgated by his grandfather Jonathan Edwards.

These progressive and regressive concurrences proceeded apace as Dwight switched from Edwards' British logical rationalism/empiricism-grounded and idealism-pervasive philosophical and psychological faith and ethics to the Scot-tish Common Sense philosophy underpinning the Reformed theology expounded by Princeton President John Witherspoon, and preferred by British-ethnic "Old School" Presbyterians.

Just as Congregationalist remained in New England and Presbyterians ad-vanced on the frontier in a tandem instrumentalization of a rational division of Evangelical Calvinist labor, Orthodoxy/Reformed logicians and rhetoricians proved to be like Edwards and Witherspoon in the vanguard of evolving psy-chology (individual-restricted rational thought and action or attitudinal and be-havioral modification) and the rearguard of emerging social psychology or so-ciology (community rights and responsibilities or constructive structural develop-ment and change).

Denominational leaders of Orthodoxy and the Reformed traditions shared civil

conservative rather than social redeeming values as "New Light" Congregationalists, and "New School" and "Old School" Presbyterians, and demonstrated superior private faith and inferior public ethics will and reason in their advancement of Calvinist theology and ecclesiology.

The establishmentarians' competitive Second Great Awakening unlettered, untutored, and uninitiated Calvinists and Arminians also wielded razor sharp rationalism, evenly divided reality and fantasy, and produced a bewildering variety
of sophistic and simplistic but beguilingly simple and literal biblical interpretations of millennialism. They satisfied the masses frustrated by poor fortune, and
the apparent religious dictatorship of the Evangelical proletariat. The latter
Protestant elite leadership corps of evangelists and revivalists appeared less out
of or beyond control than unable to deliver on their promise to micro-manage
social complexities, in a state of real frustration rather than deep despair anx-
iously searching for a American Civil Religion social engineering instrument, and
to key on British realism as the best means and ends to achieve their ultimate
millennialism-specific objective while abandoning both English idealism and the
hard reality of the color caste/captive class condition, social system, and cultural crisis.

In this strident antislavery/proslavery-ambivalent posture, Evangelical Calvinist rationalists seared the indelible impression in the appearances of the apperceptive that millennialists were more interested in the dogmatic certainties and
pragmatic subtleties engendered by millennialism than in its real dehumanization
risks and dangerous double damnation consequences.

Evangelical Calvinist reason could support but not prevent a religious concern for competing individual and community health, wealth, and welfare.

Traditionalist pre-sociology and pre-antebellum (or at least pre-slavocracy)
Evangelical Calvinism narrowly focused on individual psychology to the virtual
exclusion of social psychology; naturally intertied with "rugged individualism"
principles churchmen and non-churchmen captains of industry with emerging
Calvinist capitalists and Christian entrepreneurs turned Protestant philanthropists; and inevitably induced an exaggerated concern with private salvation and
security.

Establishment Evangelical clergymen surfaced in command and control of ecclesiastical ethical resources by cornering the market on highly marketable
moral dogma and pragma, and promptly supplying the demanding desire for social stability with their guaranteed absolute risk-free social change method of
gradualism. This insatiable need for social security and civil status quo stability
Calvinist masters of psychology propagated through preying on fears, praying
for time, offering prayers for preyers.

Evangelical Calvinism survived in the interstices between the periods when
madding crowds dominated the massive mass evangelistic meetings and region-
wide revival because pastors (1) sustained the persuaded through church-centered mini-revivals; and (2) placed primary emphasis upon two special among other
security-specific demands, desires, and interests.

First evangelists focused on millennialism-intensive Evangelicalism whose dynamics stressed, at once, the future (eternity) as the one and only guaranteed
time and space for the Black race to secure equal real power and wealth or social status, and realization of material wealth and spiritual salvation in the
present (history) or realized hope (eschatology) as the guaranteed future of
White race/ethnic peoples.

Evangelists and revivalists fashioned the logical implication and left the inference to be drawn that the future of the White race/ethnic groups was secured best by protecting their investment property in chattel slaves through preserving the physical body of human bondage first and foremost.

They proved to their entire satisfaction that the Black body was more profitable and pleasurable to the White male in history than the God-endowed "*alien dignity*" of every bondman and bondwoman, and source of the ineradicable worth of each person, or authentic human being essence in existence.

Strange to say, establishment evangelists were antiabolitionists and better realists than idealists, their White Western reason coincidentally passed the litmus test for *white magic* and outran their logic.

The evidence validating this assertion subsists of the universally accessible first-hand knowledge: the majestic liberty and freedom that they flaunted and flouted could not be managerially arranged forever to secure the White Christian males' pursuit of happiness exclusively. Between the Puritan theocracy and Yankee democracy Jonathan Edwards had argued the case for "self-determining power" being the *sine qua non* prerequisite for a solid Evangelical Calvinist, to say little of a "real" as distinguished from merely a "presumptive" saint.

The specific secular "self-determination" term and idea that the Independence-era forces of the Enlightenment advanced from a White race-only into a human race-wide categorical imperative ignited an unquenchable spirit. Irresistible self-determination enabled the Black slave-born and free-born indigenous North Americans to drive their essence in existence, while attracting this repelling power of slavemaster resistance.

Certainly self-liberating fugitives surfaced as a real threat antiabolitionist Calvinists feared as clearly as the compelling counter-culture force was a whirlwind of proabolitionism that reasonable proslavocrat men and women simultaneously counterchecked, denied they were ensnared in self-defeating action, and rejected reality whereby their endeavors to prevent self-liberation in particular and self-determination in general *ipso facto* intensified abolitionism and guaranteed the escalation of Black folks' escape from self-destruction which were the diametrically opposite results from their real intentions and consequences.

Antiabolitionism loomed as cherished social wrongheadedness and seemed fairly characterized by righteaded contemporary Black and White Protestant critics who defined the movement the cause and effect of an error of private conception, error of parochial deception, and error of public perception. Yet logic-laced establishmentarian Evangelical dogma and pragma made a singular contribution to the emotional fervor of the rival sectarian revivals.

Its theoretical and technical utilitarian principles produced indiscriminate individual rebirth as the Black and White regenerated Americans' common denominator, whereby directly experienced reality and hope was uniformly articulated, appreciated, and approved by White-ethnic immigrants and native American free-born and slave-born Black Evangelicals.

Individuals known to have undergone a religious and moral change were testaments to the fact that Evangelicalism spawned optimism. It also engendered pessimism, since the parochial *élan vital* produced equally discernible numbers of evangelists who not only excited awareness of personal morality and instructed the converted in private responsibility but also heightened social ethical-consciousness while providing comparatively imperceptible constructive means/ends guidelines.

The transformed individual whom the traditional revivalist called to spiritual consciousness and moral conscience was left alone to determine whether s/he was either bound to change society or the society was bound not to change.

This celebrated Second Great Awakening Evangelicalism, or wedding of Halfway Piety individual faith and individual ethics, was a special service Orthodoxy/Reformed revivalists especially contributed as rationalists to the nation.

As public salvation equated with private moralism, establishmentarian Evangelicalism emerged Evangelical Calvinists' own single issue and special parochial interest that scarcely advanced the general interest. Initially the politics-intensive post-Edwardseans' best and brightest ideas and ideals were related to parochial regeneration and private benevolence, because the new-style Calvinists concentrated upon the individual braced in a parochial community or private sector corporation.

The public spheres and civil social change realms were not addressed with comparable bold and brave rational thoughts and actions, and far more selectively attended with the same enthusiastic rapid and radical personal character transformation middle axioms and ultimate objective. This was true even for the Federalist Party power partisan "New Light" and "New School" parsons.

The Orthodoxy/Reformed Denomination's bureaucrats and technocrats were social conservative establishmentarians who argued that vexing public issues and social problems are the single or multiple effect caused singularly by individual transgressions of the eternal Moral Law. Calvinist establishmentarian evangelists averred, accordingly, that all private and personal mistakes their new Second Great Awakening revivals and revivalists would deter, curb, or cure with strong injections of moralisms. They guaranteed the public well-being external effects of which internal stimuli would take effect automatically if not immediately.

Calvinist denominational establishmentarians were all social conservatives, whether competing rigid reactionary and traditionalist compeers, or whether theological liberals and radicals. Brilliant modern moralist ministers, among the Trinitarian and Unitarian Congregationalists, neither intended nor pretended either to examine carefully or to address directly the compounded errors produced primarily by generations of civil communities or social systems and of which individuals are not the cause but the innocent victims. Social causes and consequences of disvalues, unlike similarly celebrated values, apogees of Orthodoxy/-Reformed national churches avoided with the studied irreverence they fixed upon the Black race. Rational and revised Orthodoxy was promulgated in Massachusetts by Congregationalist parsons and parishes who were state tax-supported as late as 1833.

Being officers and offices of the church and state, paid by the Bay State to be the guardians of the morals of each individual and community member of the Commonwealth, was translated by clergy to mean they were responsible and accountable agencies whose official duty entailed ensuring the protection, defense, preservation of the secular sector. The beauty of this task-responsibility inhered in its being neither an onerous burden nor an arduous liability but a privilege and an unmixed blessing redounding to a double benefit, since the social security of the civil order stabilized the ecclesiastical power and therewith the parochial interests of the churches.

Thus the church and state compact was a sacrosanct social contract that the Yankee (self-styled traditionalists as) inheritors of the Puritan old Standing Order and public servant role equated with the public interest.

Professionals who acceded to the clerical post in new-revised Orthodoxy were as unnecessarily unknowingly the questionable beneficiary as much as the certified Black free and slave cultural kinsfolk were the necessary victim of the color caste condition held invio-lable and dear by the Calvinist status quo protectionists. Orthodoxy was also an influential sphere whose Calvinist sacred and profane rule was more rigid than the governance of the Commonwealth, whose legislators were remarkably flexible in their preservation of selected Puritan order patterns.

Color caste/captive class indiscriminate indifference was a moral difficulty compound the complexity of deterrence-benevolence ethics that Evangelical Orthodoxy so far from finding outrageous rationalized as right and righteous, and this power of rationalism directed by consummate Calvinist logicians and rhetoricians formed the realistic and idealistic combination positive negation potential which made the parochial body a formidable private and public promise and threat.

Orthodoxy was New England bound and pervasive, or the evincement of no race-respecting rational faith and color-conscious deterrence-benevolence ethics, for which reason with New Haven at the helm she had a profound impact on contemporaries and subsequent generations.

The demanding agency, and her directive agents, unconsciously and consciously reinforced nationally influential moral men and society agencies engaged in deflating the positive and inflating the negative dynamics of antiblack white-ethnic virtue in order to pervert the power ethic into anti-Black race vice, and thus establish a secular offense and religious defense to secure the alternating personal faith-specific conversion and public ethics aversion national standard of civility style and Christian substance of moral action in the cultural crisis recommended by establishmentarians.

And at the same time, Evangelical Orthodoxy affirmed proselytizing revivals; organized zealous Foreign and Domestic Missions; generated proliferating academic colleges and seminaries and other positive public interest-advancing humanitarian institutions; created moral improvement societies; and evinced charitable regard increasingly for Protestant philanthropists and approved organized eleemosynary philanthropies.

RELIGIOUS RETENTION OF BONDMEN AND

INATTENTION TO FREE BLACK CALVINISTS

This rational articulation of religious advice and counsel, offered Northeastern academies during the first quarter of the nineteenth century, prepared in the same spiritual and social soil of civil Christianity and secular civility corruption the parson and parishioner private and public sector hegemonic confluences for penetration of the Black body and mind (in the name of sharing love and giving life to the soul); dominance of sacred and profane institutions; and individual and community complete unconcernment with the best interests of the Black race (proclaimed by the Black leadership).

In the era following the Northwest Treaty, deeply rooted anti-Black race desire in the South and the North instantly arrived from the East with the im--migrants and emigrants in the Northwest escape territory--where anti-Black race values encountered far greater resistance than leaders in the Northeast and Southeast mounted. Slavocrats' bid for boundless proliferation of Black Christian or non-Christian bondmen and bondwomen was an interest in competition with their rational knowledge, experience in reality, and ethical religion.

Still, their ultimate concern with keeping Black Americans in human bondage in perpetuity evolved into an established religion, and a complementary secular national and Southern Way of Life, whose slavocrat "*true believers*" and Northern proslavocrat supporters avoided obsession by being faithful attenders of the rational defense of orthodox Evangelical doctrines.

The underpinning logic of biblically-based sacred and secular civil beliefs and dogma, forming the faith and ethics foundational premises of Calvinist capital and caste principles and American Civil Religion, was egregiously wrought by New England minds. Their rationalization of Anglo-American centuries-old English culture-specific values and custom law was widely adopted in free translation and adapted by the New South.

Northeastern race and revelation reason was de-veloped by proslavocrats to disclose objective reality, apprehended by slavocrats to further their subjective reality, and utilized by Southeastern rationalists to compile the evidence from history and current reality lending itself to their self-serving and results-oriented argument: Slavocrats' human experimentation in human bondage merits respect because (1) it is not a dysfunctional precious value but an invaluable slavocracy functional process; (2) social conservative classic Catholics and Calvinists followed St. Paul who followed the precedent established by Moses, and pontificated fulfillment of the Christian commandment to be faithful to the will and law of God and man is being a Christian engaged in involuntary servitude and voluntary slaveownership; and (3) the Churchman captor and captive relation persists in history as a Jewish-Synagogue/Christian-Church ecclesiastical and civil moral, legal, political, economic, and social virtue--whether more frequently in practice than principle or whether less in theory than in experience and reality.

Cautious common sense and the commonage consistently consider this anti-Christian/*agape*-love "friend of my enemy is my enemy" viewpoint of the more vindictive than vindicated vanquisher conventional wisdom. This cost-conscious conscience also takes it for granted and a commonplace matter that these proslavocrat Northeastern and slavocrat Southeastern high principled rationalizations were powerful reinforcements of the North-to-South big church, big government, big labor, and big business establishment connections.

Just as transparently the profane and sacred Northeasterners' theoretical exercises in color-conscious and color-blind Constitution conflicts-avoiding class and caste analysis froze the sensibilities of the intellectual communities within the frostbelt, and their compeer secular and sectarian intellectuals behind the cotton curtain and beneath the magnolias were caught in the thicket of color caste/captive experience, where Black and White flesh and blood issues forced conscience-stricken fathers and sons of slaves and their friends to choose either compulsion or expulsion.

Permanent and permeating questions about the meaning and value of Black co-inhabitants saturated the South, and were translocated with Southerners to the Northwest Territory--to which frontier of opportunity for volunteers slavocrats succeeded in banishing antislavery sons of the slavocracy. Doubtless relocated Southerners comprised a multiform body of transmigrants who were neither only antislavery/proslavery advocates and adversaries nor just frontiersmen.

Some of the venturesome were driven by religious and secular opportunity, the profit motive and the pleasure-maximizing and pain-minimizing principle, and the search for relief from crowded cities on a stretch of land large enough to satisfy their restlessness, sense of unsecurity and insecurity, and wealth-accumulating priorities.

Without question, the slaveholding world in the South and the West included assertive *"born-again"* slavocrats who took their Evangelical Calvinist or Arminian religion and Black property seriously. Whether in their preponderancy they were Christians or whether or not in their plurality they were nonchurchmen more or less consistently respectful of churchmen, the slavocracy's Southern slavocrat Northern proslavocrat constituents were crusaders for Christ and warriors for Providence-ordered and nature-arranged institutional human bondage of the Black race only, entirely, and everywhere at once.

White race/ethnic Northeastern rationalists removed all reasonable doubt concerning their power of concentration and rational powers competing with their worship of reason and love of rationalization when they drove the distinctions between the measurable classes and ethnic groups comprising the several races of the one human species to the *reductio ad absurdum* point of arguing from silence that logic demonstrated conclusively that Black folk lacked rational capacity or knowledge; their Black body and White body are not mutually fertile but mutually exclusive derivatives of diametrically opposite gene pool; and, therefore, White folk rejected on reasonable grounds Black folk kith and kin, their Black race genetic and/or cultural kin-group, and the truth as the error of conception, perception, and deception.

Of course, for perfectly predictable reasons, this distortion of reality did not cause theoretically oriented Northern seers, sages, saints and sinners to hold Orthodoxy in high regard and to disregard the Black race simultaneously.

At this conjunctive point the arguable meaning of these imperial rationalists, apropos their interpretation of the empirical facts and verifiable figures, is the self-evident self-revelation that looms large merely by recalling to mind the opportunity to make a difference that resided consciously in the will and reason of the slavocrats' more permissive if less pernicious proslaveholding brethren in the North.

As the eighteenth century gave way to the nineteenth century, the sister Northern slave states of slave-free Vermont and Massachusetts joined them after gradually abolishing slavery in the Northeast in upholding human bondage as a right of the Southeast; believing a loyal American and true Christian honors the Union by setting the "states' rights" law of the Constitution about the self-determination law of the enlightened conscience; and equating high Christian and civil citizenship with mutual respect for democracy and slavocracy.

Just as the last gradual manumission statutes enacted to legalize the extension of slavery in the Northeastern states ran their all deliberate speed course, and with their expired inspired time slavery was finally outlawed slavery in the region, this 1820s-abrogation left sensitive and sensible Northeasterners looking askance at Southeasterners who were, by turns, voiding their liberal private manumission statutes, increasing their grip on the "peculiar institution," and driving forward from the Missouri Debate the rapid development of the slavocracy as the arena of conflict over the value of slavery and the Black race.

Between this period and the organization of the Methodist Episcopal Church (1784), Methodists set the standard of conscience for Evangelical Protestant denominations by making nonslaveholding the litmus test of good standing for clergy and lay ministers, missionaries, and members of Methodism.

Close behind the Methodists were the Presbyterians, but both the Arminians and the Calvinists slipped at this pinnacle of grace and goodness and commenced their slide down the slippery slope of moral and spiritual excellence.

Hence effectively until 1816 in North America, non-Quaker churches were a consummate presence conspicuous by the absence in their ecclesiastical and civil power bodies of color caste/captive cancellation principles, policies, processes, and programs. Synchronically, between the Revolution and the 1830s-upspringing New Abolitionists--who initially opposed both systemic anti-Black race interest and systematic slavery overtly and covertly--what also transpired was equally consequential.

Northern members of the (emerging New England-bound Trinitarian and Unitarian Congregationalist) one and united national Episcopal, Methodist, and Presbyterian denominations left Southern-slaveowning pastor and parishioner members of their churches to set the Christian standard of love and justice; national sacred and secular criterion of cultural values; ethical principle measures of ecclesiastical and civil lawmakers and laws and the Moral Law; and the political (but not the economic) pace.

ORTHODOXY'S POST-THEOCRACY RESPONSE

TO BLACK NORTHEASTERNERS

The critical analytical factor is that Churches of Christ in New England did not abolish slavery but it involuntary servitude was proscribed by the state. When the reality of anti-Black race preference in Massachusetts is compared with the commanding presence of the Congregationalist establishment, and the interjection of its will by the clergy in every other cultural sphere, Orthodoxy demonstrates an impoverished ethical leadership in the era of her New England preeminence.

A further equally plausible supposition follows: The Commonwealth of Massachusetts and her public taxes-funded Orthodoxy or Puritan Congregationalist churches were discriminately viewed as not synonymous but synergetic ecclesiastical and civil powers by residents and nonresidents alike throughout the colonial period. The pre-Independence Colony of Massachusetts boasted the largest population of White and Black (enslaved and free) New Englanders, and hegemony over the Calvinist Puritan theocracy.

Neither the positive poles of antiblack white-ethnic virtue and pro-Black race virtue that when engaged produce pro-White race virtue and pro-Black virtue possibilities, nor the negative polar extreme power points of antiblack white-ethnic virtue and anti-Black Race virtue that when connected form the dynamic twin values of the Calvinist Puritan spirit passed with the colonial era.

Just as certainly they did not vanish in the Standing Order churches the original Calvinist Puritans bequeathed their Yankee descendants who managed a pre-Revolution and post-Independence severely modified church and state connection instead of an absolute disestablishment disconnection; to survive the greater shock to the ecclesiastical nervous system than surprise to headship caused by gradual transfer from Boston and Harvard to New Haven and Yale of the titular leadership of Orthodoxy; and to construct a positive correlation between the church and state which silent supposition argued that abolition by the Massachusetts made her the first abolitionist member of the Union, the state free and clear of slavery, and the church absolved of all color caste/captive responsibility.

In the early national period, Massachusetts reported "zero" for the number of slave inhabitants--and rested on these laurels. Her failure to take the lead in ameliorating the enduring-Puritan and increas-ingly-Yankee problem of Black race insouciance--especially within the varieties of religious communions which were influential communities--boiled down to the litigious litigators and litigants who formed her secular and religious power elite (A) refusing to accept the burden of erasing the lasting effects of the inherited color caste/captive existence, on the grounds they did not either cause or perpetuate the caste system but ended the bondage condition; and (B) claiming "states' rights" preempted moral responsibility no less than legal accountability for the continuation of slavery in the Union.

Creative opposition to anti-Black race interest failed to emerge for these reasons and others that were not due to the absence of a fundamental intellectual, theological, and operative instrument.

The State of Massachusetts retained a minority presence of and majority respect for the historic Puritan antiblack white-ethnic virtue (of opposing sin and evil), whose rational private faith and public ethics means to the common good ends the observant faithful proclaimed the way, the truth, and the light. The sharp break in the public interest moral action continuum, following the slave-free Constitutions of Vermont and Massachusetts and the slave-permissive United States Constitution, was scarcely due to the absence of Black Massachuset people or unawareness of the color caste/captive condition. Black New Englanders were neither an invisible nor a burgeoning body of residents. They constituted a real minority the Yankee sons of Puritan saints and sinners could manage handily, minister to efficaciously, and develop successfully as American exemplariness if the able preceptors were willing.

Given the virtuous Yankee-Puritan antiblack white-ethnic values-related ability to measure anti-Black race vitality--and its certain benefit for White and Black Congregationalists--the following illustrative Massachusetts population census data are useful if they assist in setting in perspective the missing motive of the people of uncommonly resourceful ways and means, and their realistic opportunity to advance toward competitiveness their deethnicized and deculturalized Black-race cultural kin-group. The data refer to Black and White Massachuset people respectively: 1790 (5,463, 373,324); 1800 (6,452, 416, 393); 1810 (6,737, 465,303); 1820 (6,740, 516,419); and, in addition to the single slave reported in 1830 (6,048, 603,359).[2]

Compared to this sparse Black race population and setting the standard for curtailing anti-Black race demands, when contrasted with Vermont State that was conspicuous as the absolute presence of liberty and relative absence of Black Vermonters, slave-free Massachusetts enjoyed more than a statistical advantage over the Middle Colonies if resources are matched with population variables; and the less authoritative and powerful ecclesiastical compared to the civil power but formidable force of the churches is bracketed as a constant.

The statistics for slave, free Black, and White residents respectively of New York (1790: 21,324, 4,654, 314,142; 1800: 20,343, 10,374, 556,039; 1810: 15,017, 25,333, 918,699; 1820: 10,088, 29,279, 1,332,744; 1830: 75, 44,870, 1,873,663); New Jersey (1790: 11,423, 2,762, 169,954; 1800: 12,422, 4,402, 195,125; 1810: 10,851, 7,843, 226,861; 1820: 7,557, 12,460, 257,409; 1830: 2,254, 18,303, 300,266); and Pennsylvania (1790: 3,737, 6,537, 424,099; 1800: 1,706, 14,564, 589,095; 1810: 795, 22,492, 796,804; 1820: 211, 30,202, 1,017,094; 1830: 402, 37,930, 1,309,900) demonstrate, in the aggregate, that enterprising White Massachuset churchmen were not numerically overwhelmed by Black Massachuset neighbor.

Black Americans in sparse (rather than dense) numbers hardly prevented the

American vanguard from developing drawing blueprints of offensive strategies and tactics designed to compute the chances of neutralizing anti-Black race interests at first, and finally transmuting anti-Black race values in the Northeast from negative to positive possibilities.

Arguable legal doubt regarding the number of pro-slavery fine points of law and nice nuances in the Constitution of the State of Massachusetts remained a moot point for theoreticians, because with their 1780-ratified slave-free state constitution the Massachuset citizenry had communicated the will of the Bay State people so forcefully few if any Commonwealth constit-uents believed they could hold a Black inhabitant in bondage with impunity.

Coinciding with the Massachusetts constitutional jurists who declared it an act of justice when they struck slavery with their judicial pens, the Puritan legacy of anti-Black race values was enacted into synchronic statutes by legislative lawmakers, it is beyond dispute, and remained enforceable as anti-Black race virtue survived in the hearts of the Yankee faithful.

The pro-White race Puritan mind and anti-Black race spirit apparently could be changed but only by the establishment defenders and opponents of the saints and their successors--that is, the Yankee liberal religious humanitarians and secular humanists. They were anything but puzzled concerning the distinction between slavery and anti-Black race virtue.

Yankee Calvinist traditionalists, religious liberals, and secular humanists both affirmed the Hopkinsian dictum that nothing is settled until it is settled correctly--and elected not to initiate the process of eradicating anti-Black race laws and social values as squarely and fairly as adjudicators abolished human bondage.

No less certain and clear is the truth that the Congregationalist clergy class could claim no credit for the abolition of slavery. As a matter of fact, while Bay State establishment ministers did not pretend to cherish the challenge but publicly revealed their reasons for being chary of the risk, Bostonian parsons lost the opportunity to counteract effectually anti-Black race virtue in the congregations at the same time the capital of Orthodoxy was being translocated from Boston to New Haven.

Maine, New Hampshire, Vermont were the three New England states most deficient of the prerequisite resources required to provide general interest-securing faith and ethics leadership for traditional Congregationalists. The historic condition continued after Boston Orthodoxy (Trinitarian Congregationalists) lost her historic ecclesiastical and educational hegemonic role to the Unitarian Congregationalists: the theological liberal and social conservative Yankees who retained selective Puritan values and jettisoned the Calvinist heritage.

Similar inadequacy also appeared the condition enveloping Rhode Island, the old New England slave mart capital, whose slave, free Black, and White population bore a rough relation to her peripheral Puritan power role: 1790 (952, 3,469, 64,689); 1800: (381, 3,304, 65,437): 1810: (10, 3,609, 73,314); 1820: (48, 3,-554, 79,413); and 1830 (1?, 3,561, 93,621).

BOSTON'S DECLINE AS THE CAPITAL OF CALVINISM

New Haven and Yale replaced Boston and Harvard as the center of aggressive Orthodoxy shortly after the Second Great Awakening commenced. Connecticut theocracy succumbed in a much slower death than Massachusetts theocracy even though Bay State tax-supported church and clergy appendages were not removed until 1833. Moreover, with the demise of theocracy in Connec-ticut the political ministers (Timothy Dwight) and professional politicians (Theodore Dwight) continued to communicate long after the great Boston Puritan divines died and their worthy successor William Ellery Channing opted out of Calvinism, competition for civil control, and politics. The partisan Federalist Party power politics parsons passed prior to but were buried with the internment of Dwight in New Haven, preceding whose death at Yale Channing emerged as Regent of Harvard to lead the Boston anti-political Moral Reformers in a reversion of politics-intensive Puritan values.

Prior to the death of President Ezra Stiles of Yale (in 1799), the New Haven of Northeast patricians and Southeast aristocrats was fast becoming an attractive educational, recreational, and economic magnetic pole for Southern upper-class planters, middle-class merchants, and clerical members of the leisure classes. In the same time and space, Yale advanced the Edwardsean-Hopkinsian rational defense of Evangelicalism and Timothy Dwight (Edwards' grandson and Stiles' successor) was introducing his radical post-Edwardsean revision.

These Northeast-centered public political ingress and egress progressions, coupled with private corporation and parochial academic connections, were Calvinist clerical innovations and constructive engagements with the national sweep of Evangelical Protestant revivalism and revitalism, institutionalism and denominationalism, and millennialism and moralism.

All the cultural changes the establishmentarian evangelists and professionals precipitated supported social conservative views of church and state civil responsibility, and were commonly grounded mainly on the individual: the singular key to and critical common connector of the Enlightenment rationalism-grounded secular humanism and humanitarian Protestantism; and the principal principle of Calvinist capitalism, democracy, and Evangelism.

Dwight was admired by disciples for being as effective a Puritan and Anglican past and present conflict and conciliation continuum, and Calvinist channel of Congregationalist and Presbyterian direct communication and indirect correspondence, as he was an excellent cultural and political conduit of current and future "old school ties" in the "old boy network" that intertied "Connecticut Yankees" and Virginian with South Carolinian Cavaliers and other slavemasters who formed the English race-specific patrician and aristocratic class.

In the age of self-determination for the individual White ethnic male, states, and sovereign state, the growth and development of liberation from human bondage was undermined by the White Christian Gentlemen's proslavery parochial, private, and public pact. This alliance of the White Protestant power elite was not a conspiracy but a cultural compact sealed and signed in the manner of a blood brother oath, whose members ecclesiastical and civil connective tissues and sinews consisted of legalisms hidden beneath layers of moralisms.

Dwightesque Connecticut civil values that energized Orthodoxy confused preferred style, taste, and manners with genuine morals; cultivated a gentility whose debasement of civility equated gentlemanly and Christian virtues; and ignored the rancorous anti-Black race laws of Connecticut with a callousness that rendered the Southern "Black codes" imitated models of fairness and equity. Christian "Connecticut Yankees" confirmed as establishmentarians that distinctive Northeastern and Southeastern anti-Black race interests were in fact a distinction without a difference rational intentions and consequences.

What divided these fervently religious patriots was a subtlety so fine it seemed to escape their attention--and to function successfully albeit mysteriously as a uniting perception—until aggressive antebellum reality set in: "Connecticut Yankee" establishment Orthodoxy overestimated the cost of competitive Black males and underestimated their worth; and their Virginian and South Carolinian Cavalier compeers treated Black body as a not depreciating but appreciating national treasure of profit and pleasure, but an estimable and even expendable one if the entity failed cost/benefit analysis of productivity.

In short, Connecticuters and Cavaliers each knew the price of every Black body and the value of none partly because Connecticut also possessed slave, free Black, and White populations that statistically nearly matched those of Massachusetts: 1790 (2,759, 2,801, 232,581); 1800 (951, 5,330, 244,721); 1810 (310, 6,4533, 255,279); 1820 (97, 7,844, 267,161); and 1830 (25, 8,047, 289,603).

BRITISH-ETHNIC PRESBYTERIANS AND

ENGLISH-RACE CONGREGATIONALISTS

As the first quarter of the nineteenth century progressed, during which Dwight passed, New Haven increased her hold as the dominant center of Calvinist Puritan Orthodoxy. Cohort Bay State pro-Calvinist Congregationalists, who did not hide their Puritan Orthodoxy or "Massachusetts Yankee" pride and prejudice, argued from silence and bureaucratic offices the case justifying their failure to lead the interference interrupting anti-Black race repression.

Their excuse, disclosed in public ethical omissions more often than commissions at first, finally turned on nicely nuanced rationalizations that turned out special pleading. For example, a convenient excuse was the fact that they shouldered a double reversal of power and authority, to wit, Massachusetts Trinitarian Congregationalists suffered the loss of cultural hegemony to the Unitarians and the leadership of Orthodoxy to the New Haven Evangelical revisionists.

The latter was undeniably a friendly takeover by aggressive Connecticut warriors for "New Divinity/New School" Evangelical Calvinism. Connecticuters deserved the credit demanded for saving and revitalizing Orthodoxy in an ecclesiastical crisis, received but denied they earned and therefore disdained for choosing to develop a reracialization rather than a deracialization cutting edge role for determinative reasons besides those briefly mentioned above.

Another reason involved the denominational yoking of Presbyterians and Congregationalists. Their division of responsibility included Scotch-Irish Presbyterians taking the nation-wide proselytization lead for Orthodoxy/Reformed Calvinism, on the rising curve of revivalism and demonstrating on the Southern and Western Frontiers a strong determination to be a power in the regions beyond New England where Congregationalists were established in power and authority.

Free and clear of an identity crisis because they knew themselves to be the pure and simple English-race representatives and Puritan people descendants, Congregationalist Yankees were apparently a product of nature and nature like all other tribal groups, and, unlike other American tribes, as much a culture- as conditioned as a congenitally-constituted class who as a whole (and a rule exceptions proved conclusively) were born, bred, and bound in New England.

They had inherited the *"Promised Land,"* evinced awareness of no reason to leave their splendid insolation and isolation, and believed they had every reason to give the Orthodoxy-Congregationalist/Reformed-Presbyterian Calvinist mission to convert the nation to the enterprising British (Scotch-Irish) ethnic immigrants, for whom ecclesiastical expansion and extension enveloped opportunity, need, and vocation. Futhermore, if not more highly organized than Congregationalists the Presbyterians were differently structured and better prepared by the Reformed system of ecclesiology to meet the Evangelical competition; had formed a denominational establishment while the Congregationalists continued to revolve around New England-restricted independent but cooperating state Consociations; and developed a competitive edge sharply honed by the Presbyterian central church government, after whose rational arrangement the architects of the Union modeled the Three Branches of Government.

Entirely comfortable and satisfied with their regional existence, New Englanders welcomed in the churches of Orthodoxy Calvinists especially and other White Christian gentlemen from the South. Southerners were not only embraced by Congregationalists on the streets of New Haven and in the halls of Yale, but they were also proselytized in the South by swelling numbers of Presbyterians who envisioned a revivalistic presence equal at least to the once hegemonic Anglican establishment power.

Prior to the opening of the West and the subsequent post-Independence rapid extension and expansion of Northwest Territory, the colonial Southland was the growing edge and stronghold of the Presbyterians. Complementarily, the Old South was also both the identical opportunity region for and the field in which rival Methodist (Arminian) and Baptist (Calvinist) respectively beat their proselytism competition--and harvested and reaped souls at the expense of establishment Anglicans.

Anglicans (Latitudinarians) renamed Episcopalians--not unlike the establishment Yankee Congregationalists in New England whose Puritan fathers were also English rooted and nurtured former Anglicans--were creatures of historic hierocrats in command of ecclesiology and control of ecclesiastical and civil governance.

But unlike the Yankee sons of Patriot Puritans, the pro-Tory/pro-Loyalist legacy of a steel band of Anglicans left disestablishment era Episcopalian successors in a decidedly more defensive than offensive posture apropos sustaining power and authority, maintaining civil credibility, and making converts of the new and increasing ethnic immigrant populous.

Arminian Virginians, and the several varieties of Calvinist along with nonchurchmen Cavaliers, were competitive transmigrants on the Frontier of the West and the slavocracy. Combined with the loss of clout owing to being suspect British agents during the Revolution, and the resulting post-Independence church and state separation which entailed religious freedom that redounded to benefit the Evangelical sectarians, the West and the slavocracy were two attractive regions for migrating masses. These factors contributed to Anglicans being less successful than Puritans in limiting the numerical proliferation of immigrant inhabitants and the number upon whom status was conferred.

Puritan-English history, in spite of its different motive and mission, matched the Anglican-English record for repelling immigrants and presumed aliens in their presumed private territory. But Yankee Congregationalists differed from Cavalier Episcopalians by reason of sending other immigrants to complete the Puritan *Errand into the Wilderness* of North America.

Their Scotch-Irish Reformed surrogates enjoyed greater success among the class-conscious professionals and organizational men than as proselytizers of the untutored. Presbyterian central church government and educational requirements for clergymen set presbyters at advantage in the competition for attracting the middle class. These two standard operating procedures also developed a more rigid than flexible polity compared to the relatively less firm Methodist method and less inflexible Baptist organizational pattern.

As a consequence of their exquisitely logical and discipline-demanding hierarchy-which required presby-ters to be able to follow rational arguments and to be excited only by the cerebral exercise in discipline--Presbyterians remained at a comparative disadvantage in the competition for converting the masses, and attracting the regenerated into newly constituted churches.

Methodists and Baptists created hundreds of new congregations virtually on the spot and at every crossroad in their Evangelical trek throughout the South and West. They were formed by the initiatives of normally more inspired than educated evangelists who chose the route of experience over learning to rise from the non-professionals into the professionals.

Normally they comprised the non-ordained and self-determined "many called" competitors of the ordained "chosen few," whose direct action on the supposition that "many are cold but few are frozen" spiritual beings who cannot be revived if "born-again" guaranteed the Arminian Methodist and Calvinist Baptist numerical denominational superiority in the nineteenth century. Presbyterians met the competition but could not match or beat the competitive English race and British ethnic rivals in their Evangelical race to establish their tradition as the national church. The Reformed revivalists were determined to establish throughout the new nation's states and territories the Puritan ethic, and struggled to succeed as predominantly Scotch-Irish ethnics in the new opportunity era.

Presbyterian immigrants and emigrants initially penetrated the Deep South where the Puritan-Yankee Congregationalists elected not to send their missionaries; and extended their denomination in the West where the mission of Orthodoxy failed rather less precisely: because Congregationalists concentrated their domestic missionary ministers on the Frontier and not among the White immigrant settlers but the Indian ethnic emigrants they drove from the East.

These contributing factors to the relative proselytization weakness of Presbyterian agencies also constituted their comparative strength. The revivalist rivals of Presbyterian evangelists on the Frontiers were neither establishment connected churchmen nor experienced in civil power relations. Sectarian institutional command and control was not only the great ambition of the Methodist and Baptist Englishmen and Britishmen (Welsh and Scotch ethnic transmigrants predominantly) but the limited range and the limits of the parochial realm proved the absolute end of their real power and authority. Their solid sacred presence and secular absence occurred as a result of neither design nor desire but were occurrences caused by their cultural conditioning; were not as they claimed a classic instance of the virtue of necessity or when necessity is virtue; and materialized as a conscious partisan party power politics counterpoint in the color caste/captive cultural crisis or demonstrable moment when virtue is a necessity. Methodists and Baptists were devoid of positive relations with the five estates, as well as of church and state responsibility and connections with the power elite in England and America, that Presbyterians in the British Isles and North America enjoyed, engaged with their organizational skills in civil affairs, and employed to impact the decision-making power and conscience centers of the nation.

Methodist and Baptist immigrants preponderantly were English-race rather less than British-ethnic representatives, fighting for respectability, and distinguished from the Presbyterians who possessed status that was achieved and not inherited but either conferred or ascribed by Yankee-Puritan brethren for whom they served as emissaries in their Presbyterian/Congregational Denomination.

Fellow British-ethnic Baptists and Methodists were rival immigrants, and e-qually committed to achieving the grand Evangelical Protestant design--that is, establishing their sectarian body as the national church. They did not believe Baptists and Methodists were not prepared to face the facts and accept reality in this matter of their single purpose and ultimate purpose.

They dictated to objective-minded contemporaries that their chances of success were limited by being a people whose Arminian and Calvinist Independent church traditions in England and America did not bequeath centuries-long civil governance experience. But in initially alternately spurning and selectively limiting power politics plays to securing religious freedom and liberty of conscience, class-conscious Methodists and Baptists disclosed their awareness of the meaning of not being privileged with immediate and routine access to scores of successful Northeastern men, who possessed or controlled seemingly limitless wealth and boundless institutional power.

Whether or not they were satisfied to manage reality by declaring the defeat a victory, or the ecclesiastical power and civil powerlessness a virtue, Arminian-Methodist and Calvinist-Baptist Independent churches further lacked the credibility of the Reformed tradition: the special relation and continuum of historical and transcontinental connections in foreign and domestic missions of both American and English Puritan Independents and Church of Scotland and New England Churches of Christ; and the sacred and secular Puritan mission Congregationalist and Presbyterian Yankees advanced as a manifest destiny subsisting of the millennial mandate to be the presence through which the Kingdom of God would be established in America.

By the commencement of the 1800s Yankee Congregationalists and Presbyterians united as the new commissioners of the old Puritan commission originally directed by the international millennium mission missionaries John Eliot (in the 1640s) and Jonathan Edwards (in the 1740s).

Highly representative of the saints' first and third generation, and unrepresentative of the "Elect" as the select Evangelical evangelists and educators of the Native Americans, the giant Puritan parsons giants were in direct correspondence and intimately involved with English Puritans and British Presbyterians who sent funds from England and Scotland to finance their missions to Massachusetts Indians.

Linkages between American and Anglo-British Puritans as well as Congregationalist and Presbyterian Yankees were further secured in intellectual centers from Yale to Princeton: where the Calvinist theology of individual rebirth, regeneration, and growth in grace accelerated its elective affinity with venture capitalism and partisan politics.

Early Presbyterian White-ethnic immigrants in the Old South, and progenitors of Black-race Calvinists, immediately locked horns with the English-race representatives of the ancient enemies of British-ethnic folk at the helm of the Anglican theocracy.

The Scotch-Irish commenced a long and intense combative struggle to wrest from the Church of England vestrymen and burgesses the free exercise of Evangelical proselytism, joined in this quest Quaker Puritan foes and British ethnic friends, and differed decisively from these equally early-transmigrating and late-arriving immigrants among the original settlers as a result of decreasing conflict and increasing conciliation with English-race Puritans.

The positive Orthodoxy (Puritan race) and Reformed (British ethnic) connection occurred partly because the un-English Scotch-Irish were (A) a counterculture group Congregationalists considered a complementary Evangelical Calvinist tradition rather than a competing theological and ecclesiology alternative like Anglican and Arminian opponents; (B) a minority who as Presbyterians elected not to vie with the Congregationalist majority in New England but whose plurality concentra-ted happily on the frontier and on the boundaries of the region; (C) a peer church and state norm instituting-people in power and authority Scotland and whose governance experience and model were admired, respected, imitated, and even adopted as the system for the United States by the Founding Fathers; (D) an equally competent and competitive intellectual, military, political, and economic body of courageous secular and sacred civil sector leaders, partly as a result of centuries-long English/British hostilities; and (E) a proven resource of Protestant philanthropy from the outset of the experiment in North America, whose fiscal contributions from Edinburgh to Boston were symbols and signs of the continuous five estates' interlocking directorates and their inclining significance as Presbyterians expanded from the Northeast throughout the Middle Atlantic and Southeastern Colonies to the Northwest Territory.

In brief, British-specific plus English-specific Presbyterian Puritanism and/or Anglo-American Orthodoxy/Reformed Calvinist Puritanism, were energized especially by aggressive Scotch-Irish churchmen's advancement in their adopted or native nascent nation of the historic and current dynamic connection with John Calvin's Geneva: where in his ecclesiastical and civil hierocracy the founding father interconnected Calvinist capitalism-evolving mercantilism and power politics with church and state united faith and ethics as the governance model of Calvinism.

Along with first-hand experience as command and control ecclesiastical and civil authorities in a church and state related political economy, the Calvinist immigrants from Scotland brought with them a history of Presbyterian leadership of conciliation, cooperation, and conflict in Parliament; struggle between Englishmen and Scotsmen; and creative knowledge and experience that allowed the Scots-Irish to shape and to be shaped fundamentally by the new politics of the fledgling republic democracy.

Classic Calvinist and Scotch-Irish power culture leadership gifts and graces were combined with political skills and opportunity, and sharpened in the South as a result of clashes with the Anglican establishment.

Dissimilar from the Calvinist Puritans who were able and willing to channel Scotsmen creatively, and to be directed by Scotch-Irish Reformed Church leaders, their English brethren and sons of Anglican Puritans in the South sought to confine the un-English Presbyterians, to eliminate the British-ethnic Calvinist competition, and to counterbalance their ancient antagonist's indominantableness.

Over time and through time the truculent, combative, and strong willed Scotch-Irish proved in time they were the equals if not their betters in the contest of wills of the Puritan patricians and the Anglican aristocrats.

SAMUEL DAVIES AND JOHN WITHERSPOON

The Reverend Samuel Davies (1723-61) loomed large as the first of the great native American, Presbyterian, and clergymen-champions of the Scotch- Irish in the Old South.

A militant military minister who came by his bellicose propensity naturally, Davies struck the ScotchIrish patriotic theme when he preached to the Virginia soldiers, who fought under Colonel George Washington in the French and Indian War, the original religious version of a call to arms. (It effectively issued forth from the South as a notorious secular revision two hundred years later: When Senator Barry Goldwater asserted in his acceptance speech as the Republican Presidential Nominee his famous dictum that extremity in defense of liberty is virtue without vice.)

A master benevolent paternalist, and prototype of the slavemaster "redeemer governor" of human bondage, Davies solicited and received financial support for the instruction of his dearly loved personal slaves and the bondmen owned by his White-ethnic immigrant parishioners from the Church of Scotland Society for the Propagation of Christian Knowledge.

One hundred years before the Davies factor, Anglicans in London and Parliament established the Society for the Propagation of the Gospel in New England (1649) to underwrite the mission in Massachusetts of the Reverend John Eliot (1604-90) mission to the Algonquian Indian ethnics.

One hundred years later, the Scottish Society supported the Massachusetts ministry to the Stockbridge Indian ethnics of Jonathan Edwards until the Congregationalist was selected to lead the Presbyterian academy. President (1757-58) Edwards of the College of New Jersey (Princeton) died a few months after his election, and as the immediate predecessor of President (1759-61) Davies who was succeeded as President (1768-94) by the Reverend John Witherspoon (1723-94)--a native of Scotland who emigrated to accept the post.

Witherspoon promoted the Scottish Common Sense (realism) philosophy that the Reverend Timothy Dwight (1752-1817) quickly adopted and adapted as President of Yale. Dwight appropriated Scottish empiricism for his revisionist/deconstructionist method, means, and medium; reconstructed the constructive Evangelical theology of his grandfather, Jonathan Edwards; and established for Yankee-Puritan Calvinism the new "New School" which downgraded high idealism and upgraded low puritanicalism.

In addition to integrating into his systematic Orthodoxy theology Witherspoon's psychology-replete and sociology-deficient social conservative philosophy/theology transplanted by the peerless director of the Reformed tradition, Dwight led the recognition and acceptance by Orthodoxy of Witherspoon's exceptional organizational skills.

Due in no small to this blessing, Congregationalists, who preferred the local church autonomy and regional consocation system of Congregationalism and elected to retain Calvinist hegemony in New England, evidenced a growing appreciation for the Presbyterian central church government structure.

The Reformed polity was engaged as compatible with and not as superior to Orthodoxy's system, and embraced as an earlier established and effective national organization. This collective judgment of the pro-Federalist Congregationalist clergy was confirmed by the Federal Government's adoption of Presbyterianism's sacred rational governance arrangement as the civil model for representative republican democracy. For these and other well-known reasons, Congregationalists delighted in acquiescing to the leadership of Scotch-Irish immigrants and emigrants whose denomination was better prepared for the Orthodoxy/Reformed Evangelical mission to the nation.

Timothy Dwight turned up in the Independence era a fierce Federalist Party partisan to lead his clerical brethren and follow his layman and lawyer younger brother, Theodore Dwight, who emerged in the vanguard of New England Federalist Party leaders. The pro-political "Connecticut Yankee" Dwight brothers emerged Jonathan Edwards' curious "Consistent Calvinist" couple of grandsons, who deviated sharply from the anti-political style and substance their grandfather established as the Evangelical-Calvinist Puritan norm. Just like the theocracy experience which turned Edwards from a terrestrial into an extraterrestrial political professional, they were eyewitnesses to the slow death of their Federalist Party. After Timothy Dwight entered the stages of irreversible his disciples appeared defeatist as they endeavored to the Democratic Party's defeat of their Federalist Party into a spiritual and moral power triumph. Wherefrom surviving Yankee-Puritan parsons, parishioners, and parishes retreated posthaste from power politics as politics-intensive Scotch-Irish ethnics advanced as Jeffersonians in the Democratic Party with the plurality of the proletariat electorate.

The Presbyterian polity neither chastened nor checked so much as the parochial process (revolving around rules of reason ruled rational and right by ruling elders) disciplined Scotch-Irish denizens' birthright political instincts, sharpened their political skills in ecclesiastical and civil politics, and accelerated rapid development into church and state professional politicians. Church politicians and bureaucrats directed the principles, process, and programs of the measurable ecclesiastical and civil law-venerating Reformed tradition's comparatively superior faith and order and inferior faith and ethics promise and performance in race and religion relations.

The leadership majored in advanced logics and higher rationalism and concentrated the mind as they produced through these refinements an efficient rational, legalistic, and legislative national system of local churches, overseered by regional presbyteries that governed according to the laws enacted and enforced by the sovereign legislative and judicatory Presbyterian General Assembly. This supreme power and authority of the central church governance polity, composed of annually elected presbyter ruling elders, chief architect Witherspoon served initially and frequently as the chief ruler (moderator).

Pure politics arranged and passed laws, rules, and regulations of the General Assembly enabled the Reformed body to compete in the era of rapid church and state expansion.

Wherefore, Presbyterian political prowess proved the perfect complement of a-political Congregationalism's economic competitive edge, the Scotch-Irish materialized the nice counterweight of Puritan Calvinist capitalists, and Orthodoxy's clergy were satisfied with limiting their Congregationalist local churches and state consociations to the New England region and electing not to enter the national race for denominational hegemony or to meet the stiff competition established by the ecclesiastical and civil powers.

In a word, the compelling force of Scotch-Irish churchmen's aggressiveness, British-ethnic exploratory drive, and Reformed Calvinist direction encouraged the Congregationalists to defer to Presbyterian ecclesiastical kith who took charge in the leadership circles of the Evangelical national mission and extension of Calvinist churches, ecclesiastical and civil politics, and social ethics in secular and sacred race relations and antislavery/proslavery questions.

Parenthetically, Samuel Hopkins and Ezra Stiles, successively, failed in their role as the elder Puritan pastors of the youthful Puritan William Ellery Channing less precisely than in their bid to solicit Congregationalist Harvard and Yale to facilitate their Christianized-Civilized-Colonized color cast/bondage mission as the respective parsons of the First and Second Church of Christ in Newport, Rhode Island, and succeeded as deterrence-benevolence ethicists in enlisting President Witherspoon: who consented to educate at the Presbyterian College of New Jersey Samuel Hopkins' two Black parishioners to become the pioneers in his indigenous North American Black-race deculturalization, denationalization, and deportation to Africa scheme.

In a domestic complement of his efforts to educate Black Calvinist leadership for foreign service, Witherspoon, who also played a significant political role in the formation of his adopted nation as a New Jersey delegate to the Continental Congresses (1776-82), most probably tutored privately the Reverend John Chavis (c.1763-1838): the Black Patriot and the Presbyterian General Assembly's first Black missionary to Black free and slave Virginians.

As an educator learned in the classics and Presbyterian clergyman, Chavis founded and developed a private academy by arranging the schedule of his school to facilitate his function as the successful preceptor of sons powerful White and powerless Black North Carolinians.[3]

SOUTHERN MIGRATION OF BRITISH ETHNIC IMMIGRANTS

In the 1740s, the Scotch-Irish ethnics emigrated by the thousands to Pennsylvania; and by the 1770s additional thousands had settled in New Jersey, New York, Virginia, and North Carolina. These Presbyterian Calvinists were as often as not similar and dissimilar to other frontiersmen, both as rugged individualists and competitive challengers who extended in the Old South their British Isles-conditioned disrespect of England-underpinned establishment rules and every thing Anglican (though not everything or everyone English).

Straightaway, Scotch-Irish churchmen taking charge of Independent Presbyterian churches expanded their constituency in the three most populous slaveholding states.

In the pre-antebellum South they demonstrated quickly their boldness in their proselytization of the statistically significant and comparable respective populations of slave, free Black, and White inhabitants in Virginia (1790: 293,-427, 12,766, 442,115; 1800: 345,796, 20,124, 514,280; 1810: 292,518, 30,570, 551,-534; 1820: 425,153, 36,889, 603,074; 1830: 469,757, 47,348, 694,300); in North Carolina (1790: 100,572, 4,975, 288,204; 1800: 133,296, 7,043, 337,764; 1810: 168,824 10,266 376,410; 1820: 205,017, 219,629, 638,829; 1830: 245,601, 19,543, 472,843); and in South Carolina (1790: 107,094, 1,801, 108,895, 1800: 146,151, 3,185, 196,-255; 1810: 196,365, 4,554, 214,196; 1820: 258,475, 6,826, 237,440; 1830: 315,401, 7,921, 257,863).

Self-determination was the real and pervasive if not predominant affirmative action and equal opportunity principle in the pre-Independence and early national era, prior to the arrival of the tidal waves of European ethnics in the post-Independence, and even the declaration of universal liberty would have surprised far fewer citizens than the number of inhabitants who anticipated and expected to hear the peal of freedom. Certainly for many Northerners--and comparatively relatively few Southerners--unconditional liberty from human bondage was a reasonable and realizable hope.

Freedom in liberty was a real possibility for all free-born and slave-born Black Americans, and White denizens and citizens howbeit at once turned into a legal impossibility upon ratification the Constitution which competed for reverence with Bible. This presumed God-ordained Moral Law and man-instituted law or Calvinist compromise and *White Gentlemen's Agreement* equivalence British-ethnic immigrant Witherspoon joined representatives of the English-race (Congregationalist and Anglican and other) types in visiting with his official stamp of approval as a previous Signer of the Declaration of Independence.

Yet the optimistic hope of self-determination was kept alive by incidents and accidents of history upspringing without prediction from the Northwest Ordinance, synchronously negotiated in the settlement between proabolitionist and antiabolitionist White Anglo-Saxon Protestant representatives who dominated the critical Continental Congress.

Synchronical unrepresentative secular and sacred Southerners, not the least of the Christians among whom were Presbyterian clergymen and laymen, affirmed the ideal of universal, unconditional immediate abolition. In time and that space withstanding their antislavery stance and progressive Protestant press, they felt the Black race liberty-denying and White race freedom-diminishing push of the powerhouse Protestant proslaveholding class dominating the South--and the pull of the free and open West. Some Presbyterian manumissionists, who heard and answered the call to manumit their slaves, forthwith journeyed to the West, and to freedom of conscience no less than to religious liberty, where, driven by love and grace, they struggled as public servants to align law and reason with justice, good public policy, and the general interest.

DAVID RICE'S ANTISLAVERY ACTS IN PROSLAVERY KENTUCKY

The Reverend David Rice (1733-1816), a Virginian and Presbyterian who established a record of success after nearly three decades as a presbyter in his native state, relocated on the Western Frontier in 1783. Rice emerged a political ecclesiastical and civil lawmaker as an organizer of the Presbytery of Transylvania and a delegate to the Kentucky Constitutional Convention. Endeavoring as legislative lawmaker to eradicate slavery in the Kentucky Territory, Rice delivered (in 1792) a speech before the legislative assembly wherein he argued boldly but unsuccessfully for a constitution that would surpass the liberal Virginia private manumission statute and imitate the abolition model of the sovereign British Isles, colony of Vermont, or state of Massachusetts.

Rice's remonstrance illuminated the salient situation wherein "*states' rights*" catapulted slavery into a lively system which not only each state but apparently every territory praying admission as one was authorized by the Constitution (or her current Federal interpreters and consensus of the Three Branches of Government in power) to legalize.

In a period of flagging Northeastern Evangelical Christian antislavery leadership, the failure of Rice's plea and similar appeals for a slave-free State of Kentucky revealed the proslavery rule of law in the Union and South to be slowly but surely rising from a minority view in the abolition-committed states of the Northeast; the undivided reason and will of the solid Old South proslaveholding mind could not be changed by a White Southern Christian gentleman who issued the most rational moral call to change from universal slavery to universal freedom North Americans were capable of delivering to Southern civility and Christianity; to set a higher value on true interests than real interests; and to give the highest priority to human liberation than to human bondage.

SOUTHERN PRESBYTERIAN ABOLITIONIST ETHNICS IN THE WEST

Although he was not only early antislavery Southerner and Presbyterian clergyman, Rice distinguished himself as a professional church and state politician, ecclesiastical and civil lawmaker, and private and public parochial moralist who combined antislavery and Southern Christianity.

The Reverend Elihu Embree (d.1821), Jonesboro, Tennessee Quaker, and publisher of the first strictly American Abolitionist paper: the *Manumission Intelligencer* (1819). The Reverend David Barrow (1753-1819), Virginia-born Baptist minister, and universal manumissionist migrated to Kentucky with his antislavery views in 1798 where the Kentucky Bracken Baptist Association dismissed him (in 1805) for preaching the antislavery principles he previously practiced.

Barrow was caught unawares and taken entirely by surprise when the Bracken Baptist clergy enacted and enforced a law that violently violated the only Baptist rule: Baptists are by definition independent power and autonomous authority, whereby a Baptist rule is a contradiction in terms of the Baptist rule that there be no rule!

This period was the end of the beginning of abolitionism and the beginning of the end, for the exact opposite reasons, of the gradual state manumission statutes in the Northeast and liberal private manumission laws in the Southeast.

The Reverend John Finley Crowe (1787-1860) advanced in the ranks of the Presbyterian leadership cadre of the antislavery movement when he acceded to the post and served as the first editor of the magazine published by the Kentucky Abolition Society: the *Abolition Intelligencer and Missionary* (1822).

In the course of the migration West, Crowe joined the significant minority of public ethics-creative, Southern-born, and Presbyterian-bred presbyters who moved to Ohio. First among the equals were the Reverend James Henry Dickey (1780-1856) and the Reverend James Gilliland (1769-1845).

Gilliland was one native South Carolinian who had his priorities so straight until his South Carolina Presbytery ordained him (in 1796) only after he pledged to cease and decease from future public promotion of liberation from human bondage for Calvinists. He violated the spirit (if not the letter) of the ecclesiastical and civil law, and migrated to Ohio (c.1804) where for fifty years the Scots-Irish clergyman proclaimed self-determination the rule of righteous, the principle of right to be obeyed, and the higher law of conscience than the lower law of "states' rights" slavery that the church and state promulgate as the highest law of the land.

Fellow Southerners were especially active as antislavery advocates in the Ohio Chillicothe Presbytery, where they inaugurated Old Abolitionism as the official principle and policy of the body in the late 1820s. These transplanted Southern Presbyterians were antislavery voices whom no Northern brother clergyman or layman member of the General Assembly could avoid learning of in that august body.

A plurality of the Presbyterian clergymen in the West, who led the post-Independence/Old Abolitionist early national era antislavery discussion in the relatively few proabolitionist churches, were also involved in various and diverse Old Abolitionist Societies which formed a consensus on the principle of pro-manumissionism rather than proabolitionism.

Most of these private and nonsectarian organizations, that churchmen led as nonecclesiastical or non-church related societies, were effectively brain-dead (if they were ever alive) in New England upon the arrival of the day when state-mandated gradual manumission laws finally proscribed slavery in all the states of the region; composed of a growing Evangelical minority and decreasing Quaker majority in the leadership ranks until the Old Abolitionist Societies were effectively supplanted by the American Colonization Society; located predominantly in the border slaveholding states (before 1830, wherefrom they dissolved with the formation of New Abolitionism); and orchestrated primarily by Friends.

Between 1784 and 1830, the only mainstream Protestant churches-sponsored (non-Quaker or Evangelical sectarian) Old Abolitionist societies were located outside the Northeast. Even as the 1830 approached, the year in which A-bolitionism burst forth from the antiabolitionist American Colonization Society to defeat American Colonizationism and buried expiring Old Abolitionism, it was perfectly understandable why even antislavery societies in the Western Baptist Associations such as the Kentucky Friends of Humanity (1807) were manumissionist bodies at the core; antiabolitionist in the spirit and letter of their antislavery law; and moderates in the majority among whom even the minority who shared the universal eradication of caste and bondage common coin of dying Old Abolitionism and borning New Abolitionism still shared the praying for time and time is the great healer major dynamic of the former and difference between these two schools of proabolitionism.

Nearly all church-related antislavery consociations in the antebellum West, functioning as under the auspices of a competitive Evangelical sectarian ecclesiastical body, remained predominantly gradualists and increasingly approached the rule of instant dual abolition comprising the distinguishing factor of universal and unconditional immediatism that set New Abolitionism from all previous antislavery movements--as they crossed the counter-cultural line from liberal thought to direct action.

The earliest private (but neither parochial nor sectarian) Old Abolitionist societies were produced by Quaker catalysts in the Northeast and activated as extra-ecclesiastical bodies of Protestant Christians on the Frontiers of the South and the West.

The Western and Eastern societies were essentially committed to stabilizing rather than to expanding or to contracting their associations, between the finalization of the Northwest Ordinance (in 1787) and the mainstream Protestant denominations' 1817-organization of the antiabolitionist American Colonization Society as their para-denominational antislavery institution. Whereupon the rapidly declining (in significance) and vanishing (in history) Old Abolitionist Societies collapsed from internal paralysis of analysis and appeared to out live their usefulness.

This perception of failure was precipitated by the New Abolitionists' success in revealing the reality of slavery to be self-serving special interest, and thereby stripping the human bondage advocates of their general interest pretense as often they laid bare the dehumanization nature of anti-Black race values. The difficulty of Old Abolitionists entailed an ethical complexity and perplexity whose lesson initially was lost on all the New Abolitionists. It revolved around possessing indisputable facts and figures, producing incontrovertible evidence, drawing correct the conclusions as well as developing undeniable interpretations and then believing they did not require political force but were capable of generating sufficient spiritual and moral power to challenge conventional wisdom and to make the status quo change.

Representative of the varieties of Old Abolitionist Societies inclusive of the Manumissionist Societies, whose aggregate seemed to think they could solve the problem of slavery by avoiding or managing the conflict of dynamic moral values and static real interests, were the Manumission Society of Tennessee (1814);

the Kentucky Abolition Society (1815); and the Manumission Society of North Carolina (1816).

Over seventy years after Cotton Mather formed a school for Black Bostonians, and Elias Neau (c.1661-1722)--the Puritan Calvinist's Huguenot (French Calvinist) contemporary whom he applauded for his religious humanitarianism as vigorously as he condemned for converting to Anglicanism--founding for the Church of England's Society for the Propagation of the Gospel (1701) a school (in 1705) for Black Manhattanites, the New York Abolition Society (1785) organized the New York African Free School (1785).

On the one hand, the New York Society was chiefly organized to secure gradual manumission statutes, that did not end legitimate human bondage in New York State until 1826. On the other hand, Massachusetts effectively outlawed slavery in 1780: but the purification act in the Commonwealth of the Puritan saints structured in reality what was previously only a spiritual climate of virtue, and established the State of innocence and ignorance in which a non-student Old Abolitionist Society could not be established.

On yet another hand, the New York Abolition Society's educational performance in Manhattan was complemented by the White Bay State citizen who formed for Black Massachuset youth a Boston school (1798) in the home of Black Bostonian Primus Hall.

Last but not least in supporting elementary educa-tion for Black Americans abided the members in good standing of the first abolitionist Protestant church. The Reverend Anthony Benezet (1713-84), a Huguenot like Neau but unlike him a convert to Quakerism and second only to the Reverend John Woolman (1720-72) as the Old Abolitionist standardbearer in the birthplace of Old Abolitionism, obtained the support of the Religious Society of Friends and constructed a school (1774) in the City of Brotherly Love for Black Philadelphians he also served as the principal preceptor.

Later, but prior to the reversal of values with the birth of slavocracy in 1822, religious humanitarians who were everywhere far more active agents of positive good than secular humanists developed separate schools for Black sectarians--from New Jersey and Delaware through Virginia to Ohio. Quaker women in Cincinnati, whose southern boundary was the northern border of slaveholding Kentucky, formed the Female Association for the Benefit of Africans and established a Black school (1821). Unlike Calvinist Puritans who established a record of fits and starts after the initiatives of Cotton Mather, and Anglican Puritans who vanished before the missionary Society for the Propagation of the Gospel in the English New World Colonies was established in London by the Church of England, Quaker Puritans sustained antislavery and schools for Black pupils in the Middle Atlantic, Southern, and Western states.

PROSLAVERY ANGLICAN RIVALS

Compared to the Quaker Protestant church model of a slave-free Religious Society of Friends Denomination, principle of gradual abolition in the civil sectors, and approved standard of instruction for the slaves Friends manumitted--and the varieties of variations from this criterion of Christianity and civility produced by the isolated minority elite corps within the major Evangelical denominations--a precious few anti-slavery Anglicans were discernible who elected not to be faithful to the proslavery Anglican norm, but these standard deviants emerged the clearly conspicuous few by virtue of being both outstanding and very unrepresentative Protestant Episcopal churchmen.

It followed logically from the Southeast being the stronghold of the Protestant Episcopal Church that the Southern establishment's cautious proslavery/antiabolitionist approach and cost-conscious amelioration automatically resulted in the General Episcopal Convention's-decreed and episcopacy-enforced official silence on the slavery question: in all ecclesiastical legislative bodies as well as every high and low church in the denomination. This national promulgation guaranteed the antislavery or abolitionist Episcopalian could only speak for himself/herself--and express his/her sentiments outside of Parochial officialdom--in private and/or public spheres.

Inevitably, therefore, deviant behavior was the rare effective Episcopalian abolitionist. Indeed, s/he stood out dramatically as an exception who proved the rule of limited antislavery influence within Episcopal Conventions.

Even in the Philadelphia and New York dioceses, which were the most flexible and fluid of all the mercurial ecclesiastical districts parallelling the Southern Way of Life, the proslavery-antiabolitionist Anglican preponderancy had a lasting effect in anti-slavery/antiabolitionist dioceses. The official pro-slavocrat position ruled out nearly everywhere and forever (until the 1970s) the very idea of initiating antebellum or postbellum opposition to anti-Black race church and state premises, principles, procedures, and process--to say little of laws, rules, and regulations. Concernment with Black Anglicans reached the seldom breached consensus that they constituted an immutable class united by color and divided by caste and bondage: notwithstanding the bishops, priests, and vestrymen who were brilliant exceptions to Episcopalian nineteenth-century race law and order.

Forming a distinct complement as distinguished from a contrast with the real intentions and consequences of "Consistent Calvinists," relative to their near unanimity rather than uniformity in cherishing "separate and unequal" religious and secular values, White Angliican lay and clerical canonical authorities could not be fairly indicted for hypocrisy.

This aristocratic and Episcopalian character trait exhibited candor rather than failure, since success was the near universally asserted Anglican equation of true justice and legal justice and specified as upholding proslavery "states' rights." This Latitudinarian dogma and pragma translated literally and figuratively the virtue rather than vice of disinterest in Black race interests. The anti-Black race interest preferred prerogative of privilege Anglican/Episcopalian powerhouses demanded as not British-ethnic but English-race representatives, and promoted proudly as the productive standard of Christian values.

Anti-Black race virtue initiative was evidenced in high and low Episcopal churchmen's willingness to accept responsibility for marketing in the parochial, private, and the public sectors their overriding pro-White race priorities and ethnic group real interests. The Anglo-American continuum of the historic English race of Anglo-Saxon superiority includes color-conscious and class-conscience Church of England adherents' promulgation of anti-Black race values. They demonstrate that the Anglican triumph of consistency contrasted sharply with establishment Puritans' consistent exceptionalism in this matter of color caste/bondage class carelessness. According to this standard of civility,

Victorian Age Episcopalianism was indistinguishable from the establishment Anglican religion of the onetime British royal and proprietary colonies; iden-tified with the constituted Anglican authorities totally; and, distinguished from Britain's antislavery Independent churches, embraced the Church of England's proslavery spirit and policy absolutely.

Arguably, at the zenith of English imperialism during which the sun never set upon the British Empire, the American Anglican-Episcopal Church advanced as an anti-Black race and proslavery ethical clone of Canterbury.

As such, the unbroken continuum of the denomination was striking due to the fact the plantation owners formed a presence that passed for a law unto itself and into a class by itself; a body competing with Puritan theocracy patricians and theocrats of Anglican monocracy aristocrats and monocrats; and a ruling group of the proprietary and royal colonies who selectively de-termined with impunity to make law and to obey, bend, or break the laws of the crown, the bar, and the Church of England.

Specifically, pre-national Southern planters were not only economic powerhouses but the host in themselves of the secular/civil-political and ecclesiastical powers who as burgesses and vestrymen controlled the local church.

Their total command of the parishes, which was surpassed only by their absolute rule of their plantations, involved usurping the power and authority of the Bishop of London to dispose by requiring their priests to pastor under the arrangement of a one-year contract that laymen renewed or not at their option.

This measure of ensuring the quality of professional ministry was appropriated during the English Civil War--howbeit the office of the Bishop London retained the right to propose, since prior to and following the Protectorate the London diocesan's ecclesiastical jurisdiction included the American colonies and British West Indies.

Their model ministerial management masterfully mixed municipal and munificence motives to advance state-of-the-art damage control techniques; an innovation born of the necessity of forcing poor performing priests from England to operate under constraints; a typical instance when necessity is a virtue; and, as a vestryman-burgess lay rule of the clergy, a *de jure* and *de facto* anti-juridical interdiction.

Southern Anglican laymen (and clergymen willy nilly whose limited or long tenure and termination were life terms and livelihood conditions dictated by the good or bad but finally absolute will of vestrymen-burgesses) were in charge of the church, congress, and corporation no less than of the color caste/captive class, and thus their Black race interest disinterest was demonstrable power rather than powerlessness.

Due in no miniscule degree to the laity being the parochial-private-public power people who protected their demanding real interests through the exercise of leadership, neither the Church of England (before the British Abolition Act of 1833) nor her New World Anglican extension nor her transformation as the Protestant Episcopal Church (prior to the close of the Civil War) ever challenged as ecclesiastical power the civil power in the matter of legalized human bondage. Doubtless the Church of England and the American Episcopal Church discovered antislavery and abolitionist clergymen and vestrymen who were engaged in direct opposition to the official ecclesiastical policy of proslavocrat/-proslavocracy.

Just as certainly, Episcopalian antebellum denominational tolerance of concerted efforts to destabilize anti-Black race priorities were necessarily nonexistent in the Cotton Kingdom.

And even Episcopal priest and parishioner antislavery initiatives in the Northeast were predictable and measurable consistently ambivalent, because the dramatic better promises than performances of the denomination were designed and had normally realized their desired effect of reducing to an impotent aberration the rare high or low churchman and churchwoman committed to advance the interests of Black Episcopalians.

The self-revealing relevance of Anglican-Episcopalian managed reality leaps from the facts and figures, especially when they are interpreted in the context and light generated by the anti-Anglican (even more than anti-English) diligence of the un-English Presbyterians.

Pursuant to these intensive ethnic minorities, the perception is reality perspective gains validity when the Scotch-Irishmen's historic British identity and experience with the English in the British Isles and colonies are reviewed against the background of positive Presbyterian and Congregationalist clerical relations as English and British Calvinist cousins in New England.

English Orthodoxy and British Reformed traditions were interlaced in North America with ties originating in the British Isles and on the Continent. The correspondence commenced with the original French and Scottish connection established in Geneva by the respective Frenchman (founder of Calvinism) and Scotsman (apogee of Reformed Presbyterianism) and fellow former Roman Catholics, the John Calvin and the Reverend John Knox (1514?-1572).

The Scotsman convert from Catholicism to Protestantism joined clansmen British émigrés who evolved a collective conscience and moved to Geneva, materialized a conscious body scarcely motivated by fear and driven by reaction to either real or threatened physical persecution, and were determined to exercise initiative in a Protestant middle-class class action suit to place all the power of pressure at their command in a protest of the return of the Crown to Catholicism by Queen (1553-58) of England Mary I (1516-58).

Best known to history as the Marian Exiles, Knox emerged among these pro-Protestant and anti-Catholic churchmen distinguished by their invincible refusal to compromise principle as the pastor in Geneva of constituent congregation primarily composed of English Puritans, prior to their countrymen engineering the decapitation of "Bloody Mary" and their returning to the British Isles only to be ruled (as British ethnics in Scotland) by Mary Queen of Scots (1542-87): whom Elizabeth I, the Queen (1558-1603) of England and Church of England of head whom traditionalist Anglican contemporaries celebrated as the pluperfect Protestant hater of Puritans, finally ordered beheaded.

Transplanted English-American Puritans (Congregationalists) and British-American Puritans (Presbyterians) expanded their millennial mission in North America on the strength of their powerful ecclesiastical and civil interests and matching theological and missionary minds, from the naturalized Englishman John Eliot through native-born American Jonathan Edwards to British-ethnic immigrant John Witherspoon and beyond the 1801 Presbyterian-Congregational institutional linkage.

During the ensuing four and one-half decades following the alliance of the English-race Congregationalists and British-ethnic Presbyterians in their Orthodoxy/Reformed Denomination, the predominantly Scotch-Irish Presbyterian Church functioned nationally as both an independent denomination and an instrument of interdependent or interchangeable local Congregationalist/Presbyterian churches and foreign and domestic bureaucracies.

But bold faith innovations were not matched by creative ethics as presbyters strove to shape the sacred and secular society. "Old School" and "New School" theological liberal and conservative Reformed establishmentarians remained social conservatives, before and after their 1837 schism of their single national denomination. Preceding and succeeding this division into separate denominations, Presbyterian denominationalists faced and moved flat in the teeth of the opportunity to lead the Calvinist denominational establishments in an institutional assault upon anti-Black race hyperexclusivity.

Whether or not to complement the finally slavery-freeReligious Society of Friends, and the Quakers' civil sector directed antislavery structural change agency, was a free choice. This presence of means and rejection out of hand of possibility was not the result of lack of awareness but the absence of motive. British Obviously Presbyterians and their English Christian brethren, including the Quakers, were not the only Protestants who inconsistently marched right up to the color-conscious caste walls ecclesiastical and civil societies constructed, and consistently marched around the race bulwarks.

They were matched by each and every communion in this church and state dual antislavery and pro-caste style of faith and ethics deliverance from double damnation in history and eternity rather than salvation in society. Due to its paucity of substance, liberation from bondage and freedom of association or the right to hyperexclusion was popular ethics among the populous proselytized by British Christian cousins but competing establishment and nonestablishment churchmen.

Among the selective engagement sectarians meeting the competition, the "New Light" Baptists advanced ahead of the "Old Light" or Standing Order British Baptists, who persisted through the eighteenth century as separate evangelical and traditional Baptist types comprised of predominantly Calvinist but also Arminian constituents. Last but not least in this line of march moved the preponderantly Arminian English Methodists (or Evangelicals in the Church of England prior to 1784), who were organized to beat the devil and beat the competition for communicants.

The momentous French Revolution and American Revolution evolved mysteriously from magical and mystical oriental mysteries less directly than from the rational manipulation of material matter occasioning the Occidental Enlightenment, whose power of reason empirically verified the power of choice and validated the possibility of making the right choice.

These dynamics of empirical rationalism concentrated the mind of inspired Westerners on the European and North American Continents, who generated in their class clashes the idea that self-determination is the indispensable essence of existence; the way of possessing and exercising appropriate rights and responsibilities; and the end justifying the means of optimal fairness and equity.

Self-determination emerged from an abstract into the concrete ideal that these agents of enlightened self-interest termed the means justifying the ends of existence; translated natural individual responsibility and right to the "pursuit of happiness;" and determined it would be guaranteed by the justice principle of the rule law for each independent, interdependent, and dependent individual White-ethnic male, community, and state. Apparently due to the conflict of pro-White race and pro-Black race interests, universal liberation from human bondage surfaced instantly and was quickly submerged.

Just as positively, from the turn of the seventeenth- into the eighteenth-century, the synchronous conviction that it was imperative to defuse the explosive device of anti-Black race vice. Certainly this value judgment was as national as it was notional among Christians whose prominence flowed from their perceived discernment: when partisan power politics parsons and parishioners--who possessed influence in the churches that shared values as well as the power and authority redounding from their support of the Federalist Party--could have taken the initiative in the relatively slave-free Northeast where free Black Americans concentrated.

Pro-White race mainstream churchmen remained persuaded of their anti-Black race persuasions during the first three decades of the nineteenth century, because instead of positive negation and correction in the power denominations and establishment churches they met strong persuaders of opposite principles far less often than they were persuasive.

The leadership of every nationally united Evangelical denomination simultaneously managed to challenge their sectarian competition, to manifest their capacity to sustain intertribal war over dogmatic faith issues and peace based on uniform social conservative ethics and solid class opposition to the color caste/captive group, and to deny White advocates of Black respect access to the power organizations'institutional resources.

The minority were endeavoring to induce Christian changes in secular and religious values that would lead to attitudinal and behavioral modifications of profane and sacred anti-Black race thoughts and actions, and the refusal of the powerful clerical and lay majority to lead the mainstream toward praiseworthy public principles and to support therein the countermarching leadership cadre may have been as inevitable for Evangelical denominations as it was consistent for the Anglican communion.

Nonetheless, their bare minimum social redeeming values were of limited value and neither necessary nor sufficient: when viewed in light of the direct actionist minority's valiant endeavor but inability to form a consensus behind their leadership, and the Scotch-Irish British ethnics' direct opposite history and experience among and with the English/race-specific Puritan and Anglican establishments.

PERIPHERAL NEW ENGLAND INVOLVEMENT IN OLD ABOLITIONISM

The bad faith and worse ethics of the color bondage caste condition nonchalant Evangelical Protestant denominations provided the sharpest contrast imaginable, after New England abolished slavery (specifically between 1794 and 1830), to the Old Abolition Societies that were steadily sprouting (between the 1790s and the 1820s prior to the germination of the ACS) from seeds sowed primarily by the Quakers basically in local communities external to New England.

They were scattered, with varying density, across the landscape of the new nation within the boundaries of Connecticut, Delaware, Kentucky, Maryland, Massachusetts, New Jersey, New York, North Carolina, Ohio, Pennsylvania, Rhode Island, Tennessee, Virginia, and Western Pennsylvania.

These overwhelming gradual but general Old Abolition Societies were distinguished from and effectively extinguished by the New Abolitionist Societies erupting as immediatists from the ACS in 1830, whose distinctive criteria were immediate, unconditional, and universal abolition of color caste and bondage.

Diversity in unity and nonsectarian Old Abolitionist Societies located strategically throughout the nation, whose formations Quakers fundamentally originated and exercised hegemonic powers over between the Revolution and the War of 1812, the Old Abolitionists comprised a cross-section composite of religious and secular Protestants; ranged across the spectrum of social moderates to liberals; and forged a solid consensus.

Essentially the members proposed to liberate Black slaves from the human bondage civil constraints legitimated by states in the North and the South, and to educate and incorporate in the civil order and political economy (without integrating in the churches and the social status system as well as the private associations) free-born, freed, and fugitive Black Americans.

Changes in motive, means, and opportunity occurred with the rise of the first Evangelical clergy-dominated and churches-centered consocation engaged with the secular and sacred civil Convention of Abolitionist Societies. It was conceived by 1776 when two standard deviations from the Calvinist Puritan norm of apathy emerged as antislavery mavericks and the first Old Abolitionist Congregationalist clergymen. They were the uncommon "New Light" Samuel Hopkins and "Old Light" Ezra Stiles, who respectively served synchronously as the ministers of the First and Second Church of Christ in Newport, Rhode Island.

Their handbook was composed of pages from the new Christian social ethics guidebook that the American Abolitionists developed from the mid-sixteenth emerging and mid-seventeen century crystallizing Quaker anti-slavery ethic, and a leaf from the early 1170s-upspringing British Abolition manual.

The latter rational race and religion relations moral theory and practice subsisted of a living text, entailed an Old and New Testament authorized revised standard version of high Christianity and civility private and parochial public ethics, and included the section detailing the precedent setting British Abolition plan that inspired English Abolitionists created.

Being the ultimate insider-as-outsider and outsider-as-insider Members of Parliament and the Church of England, English Abolitionists could not be missed as one of "our kind" by the English race-conscious royalty and nobility, could not be dismissed for being far more respectable than respected standard deviations from the English "class will tell" norm of the realm, could not be displaced from their perfect position to place potent pressure (not only over and through as well as in but before its time) on Parliament to enact into law and enforce through the British Empire their desired, designed, and directed British Abolition Act.

The Act authorized the official transportation of the British-African bondmen and bondwomen English slavemasters manumitted in the British West Indies to Sierra Leone--the territory in Africa that Parliament purchased, renamed, and transformed into a colony for the settlement of Black British-African Americans.

This pacesetting sovereign state record of rational rethinking and repairing (rather more than either repentance and reconciliation or reparation) excited Hopkins' imitation and innovation, whose inspiration for White Calvinists and aberration or divine apparition for Black Calvinists turned out to be establishment Protestantism's antislavery standard and the American five estates' final solution to Black bondage and caste.

Apparently this Anglo-American imitation of the English Anglo-Saxon Protestants' perfectly *amazing grace* and ethics was in essence and manifestation the Stiles-embraced Hopkinsian Evangelical revivalizing, evangelizing, and missionizing progressive Protestant program and process. Demonstrable deterrence-benevolence, its rational means and end consisted of (first) Christianizing-Civilizing-Colonizing the color caste/bondage class; (second) the deculturalization and denationalization of native Black Americans in order to transmute the African ethnic-deethnicized Black race-only body into re-ethnicized naturalized Africans; and (third) the inability to admit the error of their truth claim, or refusal to accept responsibility for the cultural consequences of their rational intentions and thought as well actions, but no less real for being denied brute force of brutal benevolence deployed by benevolent paternalists to deport the Black American race to Africa.

Hopkins and Stiles were (A) into their Halfway Piety power as the high principled principal Protestant public ethicists created and promoted in the marketplace of ideas their demanding *tabula rasa* principle; (B) more embarrassed than either surprised or shocked into reversing the direction of their social change ethic upon meeting neither acceptance nor rejection but invincible blazé resistance from Yankee-Puritan Congregationalists, or no demand in Orthodoxy for their patented and marketed immediate Black presence erasing instrument that they guaranteed to be the pure and simple as well as easy solution to the problem of Black-race and White-race/ethnic coexistence in North America; and (C) denounced Evangelical establishment Protestantism's response of complete unconcernment with the plight of Black folk and their Black parishioners whom the parsons took seriously and to heart.

Clergy and lay Calvinists' heartlessness, White Old Abolitionists' lackadasicalness, and instant rejection out of hand of the Hopkins/Stiles plan of salvation from double damnation in infernal and supernal time and space as wrongheaded thought and action by rightheaded Black Old Abolitionists argued the case for its being nothing more or less than demonstrable nonsense.

Nevertheless, Hopkins and Stiles defined prototypal White Nationalism in the process of creating this positive deprogramming principle and progressive transformationist policy of constructive engagement, and emerged paradigmatic White Nationalists whose transparent deterrence-benevolence intentions and consequences produced enduring results that may be telescoped instructively.

(1) Puritan Hopkins was unable to gain sufficient support from the Congregationalist Consociations to launch successfully his Evangelical Abolitionist deportation program; (2) Congregationalist clergymen-abolitionists deceased as a class soon after Hopkins was buried; (3) compeer John Witherspoon was engaged as the peerless triple (public-private-parochial) professional parson politician in the power politics of the new state (representing New Jersey in the Continental Congress), church (directing the Presbyterian General Assembly into a formidable denomination), and corporation (building the College New Jersey at Princeton); (4) the Baptist, Episcopal, Congregationalist-Presbyterian and Methodist denominations were both forming and concentrating on Foreign Missions; (5) the dearth of Evangelical establishmentarian denominationalists in Quaker-led Old Abolitionist Societies was replaced by the plurality of parsons fast becoming antislavery agents and replacing the proabolitionist nonchurch-centered old agencies with their new church-centered and antiabolitionist ACS; (6) promptly upon organizing the ACS, the preponderancy of powerhouse Evangelical denominationalists effectively abandoned the sacred/secular civil Old Abolitionist Societies and directed the bulk of their antislavery denominational resources to support their para-church and antiabolitionist ACS (whose two-tracked single organizing principle and primary purpose as well as first priority was to liberate slaves if possible but in any case to ship all newly freed and free-born Black Americans to Africa by any means possible and necessary); (7) the concurrent inclining significance of the ACS and decline of the Quaker-underpinned Old Abolitionist societies was as swift as the rapid rise of the ACS to the hegemony of the American antislavery movement; and (8) the pro-Colonizationist Evangelical de-nominations' ASC and the Quaker-led Old Abolitionist Societies increasingly cooperated, and from divergence virtually converged when

the former effectively vanished into the latter.

Evangelical Protestant initiative embodying a power-hunger drive and driving need was evidenced by Colonizationists proclaiming proudly to the public their social conservative shared values, and rational organizing principle.

Among these celebrated certainties and realities their consecrated motives, concerted means, and com-mitted ends were one set of things, entailing the e-limination of White race/ethnic folk's Black-race and competition or conflict of conscience as if it were a noble act of removing a negotiable conflict of interest; their self-determination delaying gradualism and bondage in perpetuity extending antiabolitionism were another set of things; and their co-equally imperialistic foreign and domestic mission were altogether different set of things, subsisting of the perfect contradiction in terms of Christianity and civility perforce the "charity begins at home and spreads abroad" Evangelical adage--that is, they equated secular fairness and equity with their sacred exchange of Protestant philanthropy for ecclesiastical and civil citizenship.

Hyperexclusion of the color caste/captive class from the American church and state was the distinctive design distinguishing the ACS and preventing its merger with all competing antislavery societies. All three major ACS measures made entirely necessary if not inevitable the revolt of the New Abolitionists who bolted the ACS. As a direct result of this incredible turn of events precipitated by the American Colonizationists transfigurated New Abolitionists the Old Abolitionists disappeared, as the pro-Colonizationists strove bent on demonstrating the superiority of gradualism and inferiority of immediatism repeatedly performed their antislavery-proslavery dance on the national stage.

At this point in the overview, a sharp turn in focus will be less disconcerting if it proves useful in furthering its purposes of comparing Protestant possibilities by contrasting the Calvinist Puritan with the Quaker Puritan actualities.

Slavemaster William Penn (1644-1718) served West Jersey as a trustee, purchased East Jersey (in 1681) with fellow Englishmen, accepted that year additional lands in payment for the debt the crown owed his rich and famous father: Admiral Sir William Penn (1621-70). King Charles II (1630-85) issued a charter bestowing upon Penn sole ownership of Pennsylvania (1681), which Province the upper class Anglican convert to Quakerism named for his father, developed as the near Quaker hierocracy, and cultivated as the "holy experiment" in religious freedom and liberty of conscience.

In the same year that Penn purchased East Jersey and planted the Pennsylvania Province Quakers shook the foundations of fellow countrymen who held each other in mutual contempt, namely, their challenged pre-English Civil War and post-Protectorate settlers from Britain, competitive mercantilists, and champions of rival Protestant traditions.

Adversarsies described these aggressive Friends as violence-provoking Quakers, and/or violent violaters of the physical space (albeit not the corpus) of the body of Christ as forcefully as they disturbed the domestic tranquility.

These assertive early religious freedom-demanding and liberty of conscious-exercising Friends resided outside the proprietary colony; switched from a defensive to an offensive Protestant posture to demand their civil liberties and civil rights as a result of which domestic tranquility disturbing direct action became the first Quakers to incite and become victims of Puritan wrath and retaliatory violence of riots; and were charged by Calvinist theocrats and Anglican monocrats with contempt of their established ecclesiastical and civil law.

They survived the struggle for self-determination in ecclesiastical matters, whereas their descendants earned respect finally for their peace faith and pacifism ethics.

Equally like and different from fellow English race-representatives and colonial governors of the theocracy just north and the monocracy just south of the Friends hierocracy, Quaker Puritans exercising hegemonic powers in the Pennsylvania Province Legislature were themselves exercised by British-ethnic immigrants who protested they were vulnerable to the arbitrary aggres-sors in the French and Indian War (1744-63); demanded that the Friends in power and authority authorize a Province militia and the appropriation of sufficient funds for the military force; and direct the volunteers or conscripted servicemen to protect their lives and interests in Western Pennsylvania threatened by the French solders and Indian warriors.

Forced to choose between waging war and peace and whether or not to compromise pacifist principles, in the midst of this accident of history and incident of the French and Indian War the Religious Society of Friends ordered Quakers to abandon abruptly power politics forever.

Relieved of the burdens of governance, and electing the force of parochial influence and personal persuasion rather than coercion of political power and military might to reform civil structures, Friends were free from the re-sources-absorbing responsibilities inherent in military defense of the civil order; able to contemplate the appropriate means and ends of selective engagement in the moral equivalence of war; and willing to concentrate their peace and prosperity public interest-ethics initiatives perforce adopting and adapting the liberalism of Quaker-style social change principles and practices to Old Abolitionism.

Friends mastered spirituality no less than mercantilism and capitalism; engaged economics along with morality rather than politics and managed reality as they determined it to be; arranged in this ethical order their ecclesiastical house and affairs according; and delivered in the profane sector less than they promised despite their great performance.

It is neither new news nor surprising nor irrelevant but noteworthy that Quakers most certainly did not manage secular private sector and civil sector social change, lack sufficient capacity to effect their will, and prove deficient of power when they exercised their radical potential and new standard of Christian public ethics which reversed the traditional Calvinist interpretation of *The Social Teaching of the Christian Churches*.

Doubtless the Friends made a singular contribution to Protestant principles and practices perforce, by turns, turning on the faulty premised beginning and end foundational point that law (enforceable rule) or commandment is the true nature of morality or virtue, turning up being perfect as the standard of being moral and employing the principle of perfection to secure the maximization of negative good, turning around the Quaker Church-based experience of resolving contraries through imposing consensus community-conscience on individual-conscience apropos the presumption there exists no multiplex but only single polar opposites, turning out the strictly limited and restrictively ecclesiastical effective church method of resolving simple contraries, and turning down or away from the opportunity to develop a relevant Christian social ethics approach to secular reality whose permanent human nature and condition subsists of absolutely complex civil sector conflicts of interests.

Paralleling the Friends' spectacular disjointure of Protestant political and moral power in the age of the Protestant Protectorate, and development of the single moral and spiritual force from undeveloped and underdeveloped into developing potential, what the Quakers unwittingly but no less realistically advanced was the historic and current classic Christian continuum of comparatively effective parochial and private ethics and ineffective public ethics.

In short, the charity and amelioration cause and effect of abolitionist Quakers entailed the maximization of negative good and minimization of positive good. Their moral power lost force partly because instead of politics-restrictive benevolence being a minor constituent element of Quaker morality it was the major dynamic of their demonstrable harm-limiting or negative good benevolence-ethic.

Quakers evolved from the best slavemasters into quintessential specialists in freeing and educating Black North Americans, and in this special interest and single issue Friends gained peer respect for their permanent significance. But what was no less true and transparent in spite of its being the direct opposite of their reasoned and reasonable intentions is equally relevant: A mechanism of limited instrumental value as a positive social structural vice-changing-to-virtue device was the end result of their updating and applying in the civil sector and secular state the church method of politics-free pure moral and spiritual, howbeit the preemptive strike of human bondage in the Religious Society of Friends proved to their minds that pluperfect Quaker liberalism was equally efficient and sufficient productivity.

Nevertheless, however perfectly or poorly Quakers practiced their principles relative to their pertinent and impertinent positive possibilities and power prospects, Friends were fearless yet not peerless but the equal of rival Protestant power people as an ecclesiastical elite from whom they differed distinctively as rational spiritualists and materialists in matching Jews in harboring among their perceptible pretensions no driving desires to attain universe-wide religious dominance.

What Friends strove unsuccessfully to be the world-class model of Occidental and Oriental spirituality, but they succeeded along with Christian compeers in raising the standards and value of world-wide principles--including the unique universal self-determination Western principle--and facilitating the liberation of human bondage Domestic Mission. Quakers and the Quaker Church mangaged distinction as moral perfection peers of parallel sectarian and secular Protestants who ap-peared professional proponents of this persuasion proponents.

Ethical excellence eluded their efforts as moral agents in their moral agencies partly due to being absolutist rather than relativists regarding embracing perfectionism as the ultimate means and ends. Nonetheless, in this concrete certitude as well as measurable other principles they approached with absolute certainty that they knew and possessed *the truth* (rather than some truths and many truth claims), Quakers were disparate decision-makers determinatively different from the mainstream denominations and who stood out from moral means ministers by being indiscriminately opposed to the Evangelical Protestant worldwide ambition and imperialism inherent in their Foreign Mission top priority.

Yet forward from 1817, from which principal principle-perversion pivotal point Evangelical denominations escalated in intensity and extensity their antislavery activity, the number of Evangelical Protestants (the electorate plurality and body politic majority) experiencing a heightened antislavery consciousness continuously increased, joined the ACS, and decreased proportionately both the influence and importance of the Friends' antislavery leadership class and the local Quaker-style Old Abolitionist Societies that they dominated).

Mainstream proselytizing Protestants advancing as late-bloomers from unconcerment through concernment to make a difference in the antislavery movement were naturally disproportionately engaged in and attracted to the ASC, since they designed this powerful deculturalization, denationalization, and deportation corporation.

What followed in logic and life was neither necessary nor inevitable nor predictable but consequential. The strictly expatriation-minded antiabolitionist leadership of the major Churches, the demonstrable Protestant power presence and conspicuous absence of a rational antislavery component comparable to the Quaker contingent, created the ACS as the original and (for a quarter of a century) the only internal sectarian-specific or external ecumenical-explicit antislavery organization the proselytizing Protestant Denominations officially sanctioned and sponsored. Congregationalist and Presbyterian clergymen enjoyed an advantage over competitive Protestant churchmen through their established interlinkage, whereby these power elites acceded automatically to command and con-trol positions of the church-centered and antiabolitionist-specific antislavery movement as the interlocking directorates of the Congregational/Presbyterian Denomination's ecclesiastical bureaucracies and ASC board of trustees.

Calvinist capitalists concentrated in the command positions of this potent power organization of Protestantism primarily because these charioteers uniquely possessed control of the chariots of charity, direct connections both with and as parson and parishioner Protestant philanthropists, and access to the Congressional leadership in charge of disposing the national treasury. Clergy and lay Protestant leaders in the parochial, private, and public sectors emerged the well-known pilots of power who were respected for their capacity to secure unification of the potential and actualized peerless political, economic, and social resources.

The pluperfect parochial/private/public partnership in philanthropy constituted the Protestant power elite. Their dearly loved ACS was cherished for its African Colonization program, and advanced rapidly as an extraordinary reactionary organization as a result of being underpinned by these solid ecclesiastical and civil power realities.

Howbeit far from securing perfect realization its chief objective, contemporary critics certified the ACS was far too successful in its (A) endeavor to render the North American Black race obsolete, indivisible, and invisible in their native land; and (B) refusal to expend resources on the education of society generally and Black folk particularly, to advance Black Americans' equal access to opportunity, to republican democracy means to attaining their legitimate interests, and to the prerequisites required to acquire the skills necessary to compete fairly.

Over and above being imperialistic, the ACS passed for the mind of the American elite parochial, private, and public powers it served. The ACS's deterrence-benevolence principle this consensus conventional wisdom professionally reflected, perfected in the course of developing its policy and process, and programmed as a protectionist philanthropic principles and practice power tool. Hence the ACS rational race and religion revenue-riveted national means-ends proved to be the most effective deceptive strategy ever devised by the power elite to divert the quest of Black Americans for equal individual responsibility, respect, rights shared ways and means to contribute their fair share.

(Furthermore, African Colonization of indigenous Americans was the divisive and disruptive Protestant tactic that assured seriously combatted anti-Black race virtue would be delayed until the twentieth century--and then promptly undermined by the descedants of these brutal benevolence paternalists and abandoned by rational powerhouses who denied random recurring deterrence-benevolence is a uniquely harmful American value).

However, in spite of their gradualism unanimity and consensus anti-Colonizationism, the original Quaker Old Abolitionists were not evenhanded in their efforts to protect and nurture free Black Americans, and the early Evangelical Old Abolitionists were more reliable and effective in securing the protection of Black Calvinists than in managing the education of free Black con-gregants. In this matter, proabolitionist Calvinist Puritans formed a better contrast than comparison to Quaker Puritans who managed to protect, to educate, and to exclude Black folk from their Religious Society of Friends and Old Abolitionist Societies.

Quakers instructed their slaves and free Black neighbors whom they converted to Christianity, who were then directed by the Quakers' silent but compelling force of positive negation and race/ethnic rejection to find a religious home in segregated White Evangelical churches and denominations--and/or to create parallel autonomous bodies.

These dynamics were generated by the same collective Quaker mind that synchronically produced the positive feedback Old Abolitionist Societies--a limited power national alliance of local auxiliaries that frequently associated with a state-wide coordinating committee. Whether or not local affiliated units chose to co-ordinate their efforts with state and regional exten-sions of the nation-wide organization, they were eligible to send local community delegates to the national meetings of the confederation.

Thus delegates from local and/or state subsidary societies formed the umbrella organization officially they entitled *The American Convention for Promoting the Abolition of Slavery, and Improving the Condition of the African Race.* The national meetings of the societies convened in varied sequences that persistently were not consistently adhered to--that is, the Convention generally assembled annually (1794-1804), triennially (1806-1815), and biennially (1816-1829).

The private local groups were neither parochial nor secret societies but open to the public; and their national conventions were scarely convened as covert operations. At the very least, their nationally disseminated promulgations to the American people occasioned their being the object of curiosity.[4]

During the life span of the Old Aboltionist Socieites, there were seventy-one distinct organizations directly involved in the Convention. Official member groups of the Convention included thirty-nine societies from the Northern states, which were most consistently represented at the annual meetings by Pennsylvania and New York; twenty from Maryland and Delaware; and twelve from the other Southern states--although the combined total never gathered at one time.

Strange as it may seem, New England was not represented in a any one of these sessions by a single society, delegation, or delegate. This absence was due only in part to the fact that the New England mind-set was either that she had settled the issues of slavery and anti-Black race virility or that she possessed neither slaves nor a critical mass of free Black inhabitants and therefore no color caste/captive class cancellation responsibility. The error of perception turned from a false into a self-fulfilling prophesy that proceeded apace the positive Puritan race and religion Yankees' projection of their New England presence as the total absence of either accountability or liability in democracy's

slavocracy. In this "Hub of the Universe," and the Commonwealth of Massachusetts that claimed to set the national standard of managed reality, state-tax supported clergymen and churches were authorized and paid to raise the ethical
standards, to heighten the social consciousness, and to excite the moral conscience of the Commonwealth.

Parsons as a class were explicitly bound by the oath of office implicitly administered by state authorities; took equally seriously their Orthodoxy and
sacred/secular-civil duty; and increasingly avoided color caste/bondage class-re-
lated general interest ethics, as well as elected to attend private morals as frequently as they asserted the equivalence of parochial moralisms and public ethics (wealth, welfare, and well-being of the whole and each member part of the
Commonwealth including the color caste/captive class constituents). The clerical
professionals argued logically and demonstrated conclusively in their rational
thoughts and actions that they were faithful ministers of the gospel according
to Saint Paul and his messengers, especially the Latin and French model-Cath-
olic predestinarians Saint Augustine and John Calvin; delivered as ministers
their apostles' natural law and reason message; and determined as emissaries of
the classical conservative Calvinist ethicists that their critical imposition and
interpretation of the "Rule of Scripture" is the "Rule of Truth" and standard of
Christian faith and ethics.

These Calvinist Puritan preservationists not only accepted the philosophical
and theological social conservative bases of their inherited predestination dogma but continuously revised the double election sacred cause--in the face of its
double damnation effect and perception is reality unanswerable charge of un-
fairness leveled by secular authorities at the helm of their civil order. Precisely
because of these factors, not all the arguments were on the side of secular humanists who declared the religious humanitarians anything but model modern
moralists.

Evangelical Calvinist parsons and parishioners in ecclesiastical power and authority appropriated for themselves Jonathan Edwards' "self-determining power"
philosophical/theological foundational premise. No less naturally and certainly,
they faithfully translated it literally and figuratively "self-determination"; took
their liberty and freedom for granted; and argued with impunity their interests
from this advantage as intentionalist ethicists.

Ethicists noted for not being consequentalists but intentionalists, they were
more careless than careful concerning the relatively equally well-known and universally nonaccepted fact that the consequences of demanding security at the
expense of the disadvantaged set in the more dynamic than static concrete culture-created captive condition, compromising the double damnation destiny-bound
Black New Englander free-born losers and the birthright double election Black
Calvinists.

Modern Calvinists' classical-predeterministic faith and ethics were informed
by Catholic and Protestant theologies, that were in turn based on Enlighten-
ment-engendered and empirical rationalism-energized Western philosophies.

Evidently, their classic conservative Christian faith and social ethics translated the equivalence of (1) order as the first principle and foremost priority of
human beings the grace of God created to exist in bondage, and the primary
one to be obeyed, honored, cherished above liberty and freedom; (2) rational
rule--that is, each and every legitimate positive law and constitution to be
treated in civil affairs as a higher authority than conscience for all White
Protestant masters and indentured servants as well as Black free born and in-

voluntary slave Christians; (3) nature's God-predetermined inferiors' respect for Providence-ordained superiors--namely, White indentured or do-mestic servants and Black slaves total obedience to English-race and British-ethnic race, reason, and revelation masters; and (4) reverence for either underived and/or both nature-derived and God-established static natural law-ordered higher authority.

Exactly due to these presuppositions, and therefore because New England parsons' official license as quasi-officers of the state was a given, the ecclesiastical and civil authorities emerged in their contemporaries' appearances as decision-makers who acted on the apparent belief they were not at liberty to countenance rational and radical rapid constructive social structural challenges or change.

Thus for "Consistent Calvinists," for whom routine employment of their selective secular/sacred-civil rule and principle of interpretation was so far from a pure and simple contradiction and as near to an unmixed and full completion of consistency as rational election can guarantee, the sacred Scripture "Rule of Faith" and "Rule of Truth" for sacrosanct secular order required the observant to positively engage neither the White male-dominated American Convention of Old Abolitionists nor the Black bondage nor the Black free-born whose un-form caste chances caught their attention and captured imagination.

This church ruling class' rule was scarcely either illogical or nonsensical but made perfect sense if the premise of their logic was accepted, to wit, given the White Gentlemen's Agreement, the ecclesiastical and civil powers-established and honoring power parsons were reasonably suspect of abolitionism, since the spirit and therefore the substance of the principle was at least a technical violation of the Constitutional legitimacy granted slavery by the negotiated "states' rights" law and order of the land.

No less understandably, this perspective promoted by the ruling elders of Protestant power denominations was not examined as fully as it was embraced as a sacred law of God and man. It reinforced Orthodoxy's basic insensibility to the perpetuation of dehumanization inherent in the power elite's tolerance of delaying and thereby denying justice to their color caste and cap-tive congregants.

Prior to the determination by the parsons to press for antislavery on their own sectarian turf and terms, they sustained the system either through innocence or ignorance by overriding higher priorities such as church bureaucrats' abhorrence of secular/civil social change Christian ethics; proclivity for sacred faith-specific theological controversies; and propensities for Evangelical denominational-controlled humanitarian institutions.

Thus nothing so great as distance separated the ethical means and ends of establishmentarian Colonizationist proselytizers from those of the Quaker Old Abolitionists. This reality was made perfectly clear in the books, pamphlets, broadsides, and addresses published by the American Convention.

They stressed with increasing sharpness their power points: (A) "Although liberty be a blessing, when we obtain the freedom of the slave our work is not completed," because "religious, moral and intellectual improvement" is essential and "how much depends on the careful instruction of all who are free" (beginning in 1809); (B) "retribute justice" (from 1821 forward); (C) that the colonization message, method, and mission is absolutely "incompatible with the principles of our government and with the temporal and spiritual interests of the blacks" (after 1817); and, forward from 1825

(D) **Whereas** the abolition of slavery in the United States must emphatically be the act of the people: and *Whereas* there is good cause to believe that this practice is now mainly upheld by mistaken self-interest, prejudice, and an incorrect estimate of its nature and tendency, and that much good would result from convincing the public mind in the slave-holding states of the impolicy and injustice of slavery, therefore, *Resolved*, That the acting committee be instructed to collect, digest and circulate throughout the slave-holding States, such facts and other information as is cal-culated to prove the impolicy of slavery and the practicability, safety and advantage of emancipation.

These printed principles were relevant and remarkable as well as both unmistakable and unavoidable Old Abolitionism counterpoints to the American Colonizationism's scores orchestrated by the Evangelical Calvinists and Arminians.

Concurrently, Presbyterian, Trinitarian Congregationalist, and Unitarian Congregationalist denominations were emerging as the peerless power and prestige communions, whose congregations included as communicants leading American intellectuals, aristocrats, and industrial capitalists. But being custom-laden social conservatives, moderates, and liberals, these Protestant philanthropists were preoccupied with faith and order conflicts, and serious disputes over which Yankee sons were the authentic inheritors and conservators of the genuine Puritan tradition bequeathed by the wayward worldly saints.

Hence Yankee Puritans left the distinct impression they were institutionally deaf, dumb, and blind to the relevant American Convention declaration of 1825: "By the law of Nature all men are entitled to equal privileges." Subsequently, into their power and posture of irreversible reflectiveness, they argued successfully that their saving grace was the lonely Yankee-Puritan parson, here and there, who, now and then, spoke out against the "indelible disgrace" and "glaring inconsistency."[5]

NEW ENGLAND'S COLONIZATIONISM PREFERENCE

Without doubt, every educated non-specialist interested in this examined subject understands the critical point: Neither the absence of Black New Englanders nor the presence of Yankee-Puritan ignorance determined that the New England Yankee-establishment (Trinitarian and Unitarian) Congregationalists would perpetuate Orthodoxy's tradition of great inattention to their Black Calvinist cultural kith and kin.

When establishment Trinitarian Congregationalists finally seriously considered slave and free Black Calvinists in their churches, and their national Foreign and Domestic Mission bureaucracies, their reaction took the form of perverting the positive negation (of evil and error) dynamic ethical principle of the authentic Puritan antiblack white-ethnic virtue they inherited.

This conscious activity occurred most dramatically during the mid-antebellum in a singular one among the routine instances when their sacred churches served their civil community as the town hall, for the public discussion of any secular issues the citizenry deemed a matter of general interest. Pro-Colonizationist Congregationalist parsons turned the New Abolitionist good-seeking truth squads into forces of evil and error, and overriding the long and honorable public freedom of speech and assembly tradition commenced driving them from their meetinghouses.

New Abolitionists were disaffected Yankee-Puritan American Colonizationists (rather than Old Abolitionists) who had grown accustomed to enjoying the time-honored free speech prerogatives and privileges, to exercising their rights and responsibilities in legitimate assemblies, and to engaging Christian citizens in the secular/civil sector as religious agencies committed to dispelling slavery and dispersing anti-Black race preferences from the Congregationalist towns and churches.

New (unlike the rival and replaced Old) Abolitionists were feared by Congregationalist clergy because they constituted a real threat to the classic Catholic and Calvinist social conservative Christian faith and ethics that traditionalists established as the standard of truth and justice.

The parson protectors of Orthodoxy united with the presbyters of the Reformed tradition as the original architects and financial underwriters of the ACS and its Black race removal plan. Their reaction to New Abolitionism followed in logic and life from the fact that Congregationalism's first ACS champion was the influential minister of the First Church of Christ in New Haven and the citadel of Orthodoxy--the Reverend Leonard Bacon (1802-81).

The perceived outrageous approach of New Abolitionism, by those who envisaged New Abolitionist centurions as competitive challengers rather than champions of conventional wisdom's consensus, contributed to the fact that the Congregationalist clergy neither heard nor heeded but finally ran rough shod over the Old Abolitionist agents they formally cooperated with and damned by feint praise far less than deadly disinterest.

The up-to-date Yankee Calvinists and liberal Puritans who had turned on each other were turned on by New Abolitionism, turned up social conservative Trinitarian and Unitarian Congregationalists, turned away from being divided over theological tactics, and turned to each other--whereupon they turned out united in cultural commitment to securing the status quo strategy of progressive transformationism.

Initiative was evidenced in the compelling certainty with which Presbyterian, Congregationalist, and Unitarian establishmentarianism ignored Old Abolitionism and opposed New Abolitionism, because, irrespective of the failure of New Abolitionists to practice their principles, antiabolitionist Congregationalists understood they were committed to render anathema both slavery and anti-Black race values.

This great reality was transparent in the dress rehearsal which the New Abolitionists' rejection of Old Abolitionism and American Colonizationism constituted. The New Abolitionists' case for rejecting Old Abolitionists and American Colonizationists was argued by a Southern pro-Colonizationist who unwittingly made their point stick in a letter to the Reverend Benjamin Lundy, the foremost Quaker agent for the Old Abolitionist Societies and antislavery editor, which he published under caption "A Friend to Colonization" in *The Genius of Universal Emancipation* (1821):

> These societies, proclaiming principles injurious to the slaves themselves, and dangerous to Whites, are yet the bitterest enemy of a society whose aim is simple, safe, and *really humane*, and whose prosperity is the only rational ground of hope of getting rid of the evils and sins of slavery consistently with the true interest of the Blacks. The real friends of the Colonization Society think that the

success of their scheme will have an inevitable tendency to effect
a gradual emancipation, as the convenience, the interest, and the
safety of our country shall permit.

Synchronical antislavery Southern Christians who shared the experience of
being forced out of their slavocracy by slavocrats--at least a decade before the
New Abolitionists existed who were driven out of the New England churches by
proslavocrats--persisted as exiles in the West. Among these émigrés, who were
exiled in their native land no less unmistakably than they demonstrated initative
in seeking either to secure to find their fortune on the Frontier, emerged Old
Abolitionist Presbyterians.

Progressive Presbyters sustained their counter-Colonizationism on the Western periphery of the Eastern establishment's dominance of their denomination,
where they sounded the alarm and rang all the changes on the false hope in
the note penned by this "*Friend*" of pro-Colonizationism.

Synchronously, the Reverend William Ellery Channing (1780-1842) emerged
the social conservative ethics and liberal philosophical faith founder of the Unitarian Denomination; appeared the power elitist who possessed among other
great gifts and graces peerless Protestant private ethics and perfect moral
pitch; and evolved a powerhouse who believed all the "Friend" proclaimed concerning the virtue of gradualism and vice of immediatism.

As Unitarian Congregationalism's standardbearer, Channing shared values with
his New England Trinitarian Congregationalist opponents--and none more solidly
than reverence for pro-gradualism. Channing, the advocate of anti-Calvinism,
and his pro-Calvinist adversaries united similar social conservative ethics and
dissimilar theological principles to affirm the truth claim of the pro-Colonizationist for the same antiabolitionist reasons. Rigid moral consistency was advanced as these English/Puritan-race representatives who once diverged from
their common Congregationalist tradition as a result of counterdemanding faith-
specific conflicts of interest currently converged in conformist social ethics.

Concurrently these English Easterners' British-ethnic cousins, the Presbyterian Scotch-Irish immigrant descendants and Southern exiles, formed a creative moral minority who challenged the rival moral majority and immoral majority who battled for hegemony of the lawless Frontier. Extending from the
South their expanding ethics in the West, the Southern Calvinist ethicists exercised antislavery leadership in the local Presbytery and national Presbyterian
Conventions. In this pro-manumission posture, the predominantly British ethnic
manumissionists shook the English ecclesiastical establishment dominated in the
South by the proslavocracy Anglicans, and in the North by the Yankee sons of
the Calvinist Puritans who divided Congreationalism and united as proslavocrat
Trinitarian and Unitarian Congregationalists.

On the Western Frontier, "New School" Southern deviants from the Northern
and Southern traditionalists and the "Old School" norm of their Reformed
Church protested the retention and extension of the "peculiar institution," advanced against the recalcitrant slavocrats at the helm of the massive Old South
resistance gradual but complete manumission in the forseeable future, and promoted Christianity and civility which they equated with granting native North
American Black folk the same civil guarantees bestowed upon White ethnic immigrants.

These maverick moralists' principle of respect for their color caste/captive
cultural kith and kin, whose irreducible minimum they declared encompassed ac-

cepting the Black body as not an African but an American people entitled to all the rights and privileges appertaining there to, the pre-proabolitionist Calvinist clergy from the South in the West were not always able to practice with equal rigor and vigor.

No comparable ecclesiastical and civil legal contraints or coercive conditions existed in the East to check the conscience of the Protestant power elite, which they followed as conscious proslavocrats and foes of their dearly loved and dutifully defended slavocrats' antislavocrat brethern in the West.

In the East and this same time frame, Channing reached maturity and grew in stature as the developing standard of anti-Calvinist Puritan/Yankee culture. He accomplished this feat by forging secular humanism and Puritan humanitarianism into a private-elitist lance for the cultivated religious-moralist Yankees.

Channing was certain he had developed the cutting edge of Unitarian Congregationalism, the affirmed new religion and denied new Denomination, and a-vowed that the relatively faith-free and ethics-energerized Unitarian principle subsisted of a point sharp enough to bear the weight of its truth claims, which, for Chan-ningesque "true believers," entailed the optimism-intensive belief in pure reason as the inerrant means ensuring the irreversible advancement of moral man, and ethical society, and vice-declining and virtue-inclining linear progress.

Channing's finely honed rational lance's logical point was sharp enough to pierce the New England whole way of life; to divide into Puritan Piety and Halfway Piety the New England Congregationalist religion or faith and ethics tradition; and to sever publicly, finally, and forever the sacred Calvinist soul (theology-faith) from the sacred/secular-civil Puritan body (politics-ethics).

Given the inextricably interlinked Calvinist Puritan faith and ethics constituent elements and coordinates, that is, disciplined daily affirmation of the pure goodness and rightness of God and practice via implementation of the positive evil-driving and positive good-attracting antiblack white-ethnic virtue principle, the enigma of Yankees promoting Puritan anti-Black race values as the device of not vice but virtue is disclosed in the person and presentation of Channing, the leader of the American cultural center. Instead of ramming the anti-Black race interests hard realities, that formed the race reason and revel-ation substance of the Calvinistical theological ramparts, young parson Channing initially primed Puritanism's personal-private cultural pump and then directed the powerful Puritan civilization currents to energize creative human ventures.

As he neared mid-career and the increasing tremors of anti-Black race demands that jarred his sensibilities, the professional preceptor of principles continued to tarry, to pray for time to change the culture-created crisis in Christianity and civility, to wait for the propitious time to direct the divergent antislavery left and proslavery right of center protagonists to converge in his proslavocrat middle-of-the-road (half slave and half free) moderate principle until the antislavocracy/proslavocracy undercurrents built up pressure that forced him to act.

And finally near the end of his career, when the torrents of Yankee and Cavalier conflicts of real interest srushed forth, Channing attempted (but was too late) to cap the geyser.

The reversal in fortune of Orthodoxy and pro-Cal-vinist Congregationalists proceeded apace the apperceptive anti-Calvinist Congregationalists' fully developing appreciation of the color caste/captive class con-dition, who, in their "irreversible reflectiveness" upon the transcendent terrestrial pursuit of the spiritual and material happiness (securing eternal rewards/salvation and escape from eternal punishments/damnation) of the people in history and eternity common cause and uncommon effect of the original New England Plantation, understood the cause and effect of the sacred and secular purpose in light of the failed Puritan peculiar mission (*Errand into the Wilderness* of North America).

The discerning comparative culture critics of the Puritan and Yankee cultures determined the descendancy from ascendancy of the Puritan Commonwealth to be at once arguable; relative or absolute depending upon the casuistical perspective of the reality interpreter; and the result of neither design nor accident but the plethora of choice and consequences of power (seeking and possessing) people in a powerful culture.

Antislavery analysts related their rational analysis and conclusion drawn from the evidence; published their finding; and asserted that the empirical facts and figures argued unavoidable *Original Sin* (pride and prejudice power of choice preferences elected by proverbial Adam and Eve in the Garden of Eden, imitated by the Puritan fathers and Indian natives in the Promised Land and their sons as Founding Fathers of the color caste-precluded Constitution whose *White Gentlemen's Agreement* crystallized the *American Dilemma* as certainly as they created the American Dream and United States in North America) is evidenced in the intertwined inevitable rapid rise of the special interests (mercantilism/capitalism profit-making means as ends) and necessary sharp decline of the general interests (Christianism/communism profit-sharing ends as means) or good of the whole (common weal) faith of the fathers and ethics of the sons of the wayward worldly saints.

Informed analytical antislavery agents conjectured that like the laws of nature and parallel natural laws of human nature the natural fall of the society for the good of all men, and/or of good men (undivided mind and will to the good) from grace and graciousness, necessarily followed in life from the irreversible human being reason faculty, capacity to select the right or wrong choice, and civilization-produced enigmatic networks of historic and current culture consesquence-laden values.

They were convinced by their ratiocination that among the contributing catalysts precipitating the cultural crisis not the least significant were the overpowering reality-transforming dynamics generated by seventeenth-century Western Enlightenment theory and eighteenth-century American Independence experience. But as Orthodoxy advanced in the final stages of death and dying, Evangelical Calvinists increasingly turned from theological controversies to focusing their energies in ecclesiastical and civil cultural conflicts and claiming they possessed the solution to the problems.

The relevant relation between antebellum Black folk and the status quo guaranteeing Protestant determiners is the color caste/captive class-stabilizing function of the power elite, and the connective linkage of their reverence for the individual or the constituent element of republican democracy and the Christian denominations. The individual-in-the-community and community-in-the-individual New England Commonwealth ethic was evolving into an individual v. community morality in the civil order dominated by profane public servants, as a result of empirical rationalism priorities crit-ically imposed upon sacred church values and ecclesiastical power by the secular humanists and state authorities in power.

Congregationalism simultaneously united descendants of the Calvinist Puritans, suffered schism from the separated the sons and daughters of the wayward worldly saints and sinners, and divided Bostonian and other New Englanders into Trinitarian (faith first) and Unitarian (ethics foremost) Congregationalists.

Channing contributed cerebral and structural form and function to the Puritan private moral-specific Unitarian Congregationalists he led in initiating the formal and final severance from the Puritan personal faith Trinitarian Congregationalists.

Essentially Channing broke forth as the crystallization of the Boston "Old Light" anti-Calvinism. Interlaced with the Channingesque act of synthesis advanced a liberal profane and sacred synergy involving secular and religious individual-only responsibility and rights constituent elements. Channing intertied these com-ponents with pure rational and pure moral coordinates to produce an unprecedented Protestant religion of humanism. Unitarianism burst forth from his word and deed as a social consciousness-lowering rather than public consciousness-raising new church, a morality of higher mathematical (or quantitative rather than qualitative) ethical principles distinguished from higher conscience, and a faith-limiting elitist Protestant religion of personal morals and private ethics.

This *tour de force* turned the Evangelical Calvinist justification by faith priority inside out and stood it on its head. What was no less real for being neither the primary nor the secondary objective of Channing's near single-handed turn of events contemporaries considered a matter of record and considerable consequence.

Specifically, in his powerful Puritan promise and performance, Channing divided authentic Puritan Piety ethics into private and personal v. parochial and public ethics, and appropriated the former while discharging the latter; merged his ethics and anti-Calvinism and subtracted ethics from pro-Calvinist Puritan Piety faith; and manipulated an addition from his division and substraction whose bottom line was syncretistic moral monism and the monocracy of Unitarian liberalism.

Monocrat Channing illuminated the elusive unity of the Puritan bifurcation of reality and Yankee ethical dualism and disclosed the binary contraries to be (A) an undivided mind and will to unite mutually exclusive polar opposite principles; (B) the perversion of positive and conversion of negative antiblack white-ethnic virtue into pro-White race interests and anti-Black race interests; and (C) the asserted equivalence of diametrically opposed pro-White race values and pro-Black race values.

The Channingesque single-minded idealism-replete and realism-deplete critical interpretation of the national standard of values, and critical imposition of value judgments and descriptive facts as high Christianity and civility upon a half-free and half-slave culture in crisis, raised the standard of religious and secular Moral Reformers: who employed intentional premises, principles, and priorities to achieve consequences produced by logically coordinated and presumed relevant facts and values.

These factors model modern moralist Channing believed to be equally correct and accurate, right and good. Inarguably, the superimposition of Channingesque experience-deficient rational theory as reality shaped Black life and thought because it gave foundational structure and shape to American culture.

His situation social ethic was celebrated by the initiated as the antithesis of ignorance and innocence empowered by a dialectical sacred and profane order-stabilizing principle. They understood the complexity of the Channingesque dichotomy and admired the dysfunctional morality-contracting and functional ethics-expanding fashionable form, enhancing in his capacious capacity to se-lectively unite and disunite truth and error depending on the priority real values and interests. Few challenging compeers discovered any reason to doubt that the plethora of preferences constituted at once the great possibility and perplexity factors facilitating the propensity of rational Puritanism to fashion superior sacred/religious-faith and inferior secular/civil-ethics thought and action.

Antiabolitionist Channing attempted unsuccessfully to sever the sacred and secular dynamics of Puritanism. In point of fact, Calvinist Puritanism, as an E-vangelical movement driven by a universal mission and ambition from the inception of Orthodoxy, was as irreversible as its direction and misdirection of virtue and vice--despite their being determined by the intentionalist ethicists' complete sincerity and seriousness.

An objective consequence of this random sequence is the predictable actuality that these dynamics often alternately and simultaneously protect either/or both pro-White race interests and anti-Black race interests. On a no less rational plane, and one of far more na-tional consequences-conducing compelling power and authority, the double standard of values and two track ethical principle and practice rules (one for powerful and one for powerless people) were rationalized in a structural system by the antiabolitionist ACS.

The dual rules regulating ruling elders formed the ACS as the first (initially one and only) antislavery agency of all the Evangelical churches one decade after Unitarianism was organized, and fifteen years before Channing felt called and chosen to compete in the class over caste competition, experienced a rush of heightened consciousness caused by the conflict of interests confrontation between the Northern proslavocrats and antislavocrats whose aggressive defense of and offense against the slavocrats challenged him to compete for the hegemony of moral gradualism, and entered the race to set the pace of rational race and religion relations.

In the aftermath of the previously dead or dying post-First Great Awakening Old Abolitionist Congregationalists, whose demise occurred nearly a decade before the end of the Second Great Awakening, and as an aftereffect of this A-merican culture changing Protestant conversion movement, the Calvinist churchmen-led ACS first re-awakened old Puritan and awakened new Yankee antislavery rational organizational concerns among Congregationalists and Presbyterians, competing Calvinist Baptist cousins and Arminian Methodist Evangelicals, and even establishmentarian Episcopalians.

But in spite of the fact a singular initial effect of the constellation of mainstream denominations' ACS was to reduce the Old Abolitionist Societies to diminished capacities, and nearly render them obsolete, within fifteen years of the birth of the Old Abolition-counterdemanding ACS this moving contradiction in terms self-produced internal conflict of interests and values, and propelled a minority of its faithful Evangelical Protestant establishmentarian members into iconoclastic liberationists.

At this stage of these immediatists' emergency, and election of a radical alternative to gradualism, the former American Colonizationists and new-born radicals in the cause of human liberty and freedom distinguished themselves from ASC and Old Abolitionist gradualists, self-generated the New Abolitionists, and included in their ranks an influential minority Protestant disestablishmentarians.

These antisectarian pro-immediatists found Protestant denominations and denominationalists to be neither Old Abolitionist nor New Abolitionist but either antislavery/proslavery and/or both antislavery/proslavocrat and antiabolitionist/-proslavocracy churchmen and churches. The Protestant proabolitionists considered the antiabolitionists the Colonizationists unrepentant witting foil and bulwarks for the human bondage experimentation, and as dehumanization rationalization specialists so repulsive that the Evangelical professors of the Protestant self-determination principle turned anti-establishment denominations crusaders for Christ and civility.

These rational and rapid radical social structural realists/idealists understood power is never given up gratuitously but must always be forced by pressure to choose at least the lesser of two constraints on their priority privileges to relinquish the intolerable grip of the powerful on the powerless. Thuswise, they comprehended why in his *Divine Comedy* Dante Alighieri (1265-1321) reserved a place within the lowest of his seven circles at the deepest pit in Hell for citizens who chose to be neutral in a national crisis.

Analogous to Dante's condemnation appeared an element in their anathematization subsisting of the high priority private and personal morality principle and practice of establishment Protestantism that the Trinitarian Congregationalists shared with Unitarians like Channing.

Their social conservative moral rule focused on the individual's radical or gradual conversion from low to high morality on one side, and on the other side coinstantaneously discounted community transformation and condemned massive eradication of the democracy-contradicting slavocray cause and effect of the enlarging caste-cancer on the body politic (both out of fear of mastectomy or radical removal and favor of limiting lethal lymphs to local areas), pervading the American superstructure and infrastructure.

Before and after the New Abolitionist Calvinists, the pro-Colonizationist Calvinists declared themselves the voice of the establishment Evangelical denominations, and the American social conscience. This presumption of being the principal practitioners of principles was an assumption supported by an arguable affirmation. It followed in logic and law particularly in Massachusetts where until 1836, the mid-antebellum date prior to and after the mid-1820s withdrawal of parsons from partisan Federalist Party power politics and favors, churches were tax-supported and clergymen were paid by the state to function as guardians of the Commonwealth's morals.

The spin-off claim by the ACS to being the instrument of national values was based upon facts and figures promoted by its agents, that were as indisputable as the agents' interpretations were refutable by critics who did not accept the premises of their arguments. This truth claim turned on a self-evident matter of importance. The ACS existed as the unprecedented trans-denominational, trans-regional, and trans-sectors (ecclesiastical and civil powers) Federal Treasuryfunded organization, and therefore as the model of parochial-private--public partnership.

Equally positively, but not as direct and exact as its connections to Samuel Hopkins' Christianizing-Civilizing-Colonizing scheme, the ACS presented itself as a Society of men engaged in a purely benevolent Christian enterprise: as if the Colonizationists were an altruistic general interest agency completely devoid of all public, private, and parochial political as well as other special interests.

What ACS agents believed in absolutely but totally erroneously was that their ends justified their means. Both the objective process and subjective objective revolved around the cancelliation of the caste/captive class' cultural contract primary nature and prime purpose of the ACS. This capacious chief

subject and object contenious charitoteers wheeling their chariots of charity c-
ommended to the citizens as neither a controversial nor a caparicious but a
world-class motive, measure, and mission.

Colonizationists proclaimed proudly to the public that the incontrovertible
proof of their non-partisan, non-sectarian, non-ideological, and/or absolutely
neutral antislavery/proslavery approach was their dedication to the removal from
North America of neither the chattel slave nor the fugitive property legally
possessed by their denominational brothers and sisters whom they considered
their vital real interests and coveted so highly but both the free-born and the
freed indigenous Black Americans.

ACS humanitarianism was further advertised nationally as unimpeachable
charity: a conclusion all reasonable investigators would reach after careful a-
nalysis, they averred, since the free Black Native Americans the Society transported to Africa were volunteers.

Beyond these stipulations, the ACS understood itself to be in league with the
unitary English-Evangelical/British-Abolitionist Protestants and their British Abolitionism model modern moral message, method, and measure of not only antislavery means-ends but also civilization, Christianization, and colonization ef-
fects-results. ACS agencies considered their claim to expanding a vice-free and
virtue-embedded device empirically verified and validated universally because the
Society provided slaveowners a way to solve their conscience; absolved the body
politic of liability; and essayed to fulfil the essential benevolence mission of the
Church.

Any lingering serious question about whether the ACS simultaneously complemented and clashed with the cerebral/moral-only social change condoning Unitarian Association, or whether Colonizationism evinced better faith and worse
ethics than Unitarianism and the Unitarian Society promulgated better ethics
and worse faith than the Colonization Society, suggests the absence of adequate
assessment of one salient factor. It is that on Colonizationism's primary theological (distinguished from Unitarianism's primary philosophical) plane, the Colonizationists coordinated efficiently mainstream Protestantism's evangelism
method, millenarianism message, conversion mission, voluntarism medium, and
crusade mentality.

ACS member parishes, parishioners, and parsons presumed that good Christians are Evangelicals whose primary task is to spread the Gospel to every person in every nation. They understood the indispensable element for efficacious
evangelization to be the exercise of free choice by each and every individual.
Complementarily for these proselytizers, predetermined principles of the principal Protestant process of personal conversion and/or regeneration, parochial
nurture and growth, and private development and expansion in Christian maturity required the "born again" to be indoctrinated in elementary civil moralism; instructed in the three R's; and self-instructed in the self-revelatory Word
of God.

Contradistinctively, the ACS agencies did not lack acute awareness of underestimated constraints undermining the latter-day wayward worldly saints' up-to-
date revision and completion of the Calvinist Puritan "*Errand into the Wilderness*" of North America. But somehow they managed the revelation realities as
cultural certainties, whose double-edged (equally provoking and provocative) dimensions they frequently addressed and understated.

Their ruminations included rationalizations leading to aver that (A) the illegal international slavetrade and slavetraders prevented the evangelization of

Black Africa and Black West (not White South) African ethnic groups; and that (B) domestic slave-breeding and slavesellers limited the Christianization of Black-race Americans. These formidable foes pretending to be fast friends of the Black African-ethnic major and the American Black-race minority were coldly calculating color caste and captive class conditions as natural frustrations of life, whereby the dehumanization of whole people did not deter the absolute certainty of the pro-Colonizationist antislavery gradualists.

Their absence of doubt was firmly reinforced as a result of being reformist advocates and revolution adversaries able and willing to agree tacitly with moderate to radical Northern enemies of their conservative status quo-stabilizing antislavery means-ends on two key points: slavery is detrimental to the virtuous quality of a free society, and slave labor is less productive than free labor. And they were just as able and willing to believe that they had dominated the middle ground, which these proslavocrats priding themselves in being centrists were convinced all reasonable men were forced to turn upon--including the slavocrats for whom the end of slavery was the unconscionable and unthinkable.

THE NEW ABOLITIONISTS

Orthodoxy/Reformed defenders of the revisionist Calvinist conservative faith and ethics against the New Abolitionist advocates of re-revisionist liberal Evangelical Calvinism were champions of gradualism who appeared to their pro-immediatism adversaries better prepossessors than professors of the Protestant principles.

Yale-schooled and Princeton-trained professionals evinced absolute certainty that their *bona fides* guaranteed they possessed the "Rule of Truth" and were not possessed by the "Rule of Scriptures." Opponents never doubted they were impeccably credentialed Presbyterian/Congregationalist pastors of Puritan captains of industry, they proved Calvinist capitalists and capitalism-certified public accountants, and they believed themselves automatically right and righteous rule of law rulers.

Wherefore it obviously surprised no initiated contemporary that Yankee natural rights and natural law theologians were completely confident they knew the whole truth, they delivered nothing but the truth, and they were the truth--or engaged in being and doing the truth. They seemed to the critical social observer total "Rule of Scripture" and absolute "Rule of Truth" rulers of the "Reprobate" who were altogether sure they constituted "the Elect," entirely satisfied in the knowledge they were the "select," and wholly safe and secure "chosen few people of God." The revisionist ratiocinators of traditionalist Calvinism formed a presence to be reckoned with by New England pro-Cal-vinist and anti-Calvinist opponents.

Congregationalist clergy's classic crusader consciousness--plus "the friend of my enemy must be my enemy and not my friend" mind-set--made an entirely negative significant difference. They predetermined the permanent refusal of these ACS loyalists to countenance the consequences resulting from one plain and plump fact: No less solid Christians existed who were not Evangelical missionary-minded and millennium-centered churchmen.

In truth, it was their fellow observant Protestant brethren but proabolitionist adversaries who informed them of the facts in no uncertain terms, and hurled them flat in their teeth, when they asserted that whether or not self-determination leads to a being "born again" individual liberty is (A) one of the four (life and reason plus freedom of choice) absolute preconditions for human existence (whose essence is ever-expanding native endowments toward excellence), at the minimum no less than maximum range of human being-ness; (B) the first and last principle that (howbeit negotiable) any ultimate choice between liberty of conscience and either the legitimate constitution and/or both ecclesiastical and civil law is always the higher priority; and (C) the primary means-ends that in a conflict with select principles such as religious freedom and freedom of association to exclude takes precedence everywhere at once.

In this correctly prioritized order of human principles, values, and interests, the religious humanitarian proabolitionists demonstrated they had far less public interest-expanding ethics in common with the pro-Colonizationists than they shared with either the abolitionist or antiabolitionist secular humanists. These secular civil comrades included the preponderancy of sacred and profane citizens who remained impassive to the caste and captive conflict of the dynamic conscience and Constitution after Evangelical tradition-alists became conscious antislavery churchmen.

New Abolitionists published the data documenting their implications and inferences from which they drew their consensus criticism. Its double bottom line asserted antiabolitionists were congenital security-conscious social conservatives, whose chief objective is to secure a risk-free environment in the middle of a cultural crisis--and as the means to achieve this end direct their considerable rational thoughts and actions toward limiting liabilities rather than expanding possibilities.

Hence, they informed contemporaries, their former friends and current firm foes in the ACS major in minor matters; consistently marshal the facts and analyze them accurately from a questionable premise; and invariably draw exactly the wrong conclusion, repose in the wrong interpretation, and argue the wrong arguments. They castigated their opponents as the proponents of rescuing their real interests at the expense of the true interests of the beneficiaries of their beneficence, which conformance they manage to justify with rational expedience and rationalizable convenience reasons.

Compliance with instituted laws of God and man was the rule of law and life which cautious conservatives accepted naturally as the positive confirmation of their Halfway Piety convictions, which proved the direct opposite of the social values affirmed by the Puritan Piety exponents and opponents of their ethics: the proabolitionist churchmen who were in complete agreement with the antiabolitionist churchmen in matters of faith, and not infrequently on a given critical interpretive point in the proslavery/antislavery controversy.

New Abolitionist and antiabolitionist Protestant majority dominating the Christian Church in North America, like and unlike their Dutch Afrikaner Calvinist cousins who constituted the minority in South Africa, revealed their poor perception and poorer perspective resulting from culture transmitted congenital Puritan bifurication of reality and Yankee myopia when they avouched, that, whether or not Black West (like White South) Africa should be evangelized, the Black African multi-ethnics would not be proselytized by Protestants as long as the domestic (to say little of the foreign) slavetrade existed.

This was the case--they argued patently falsely and plainly curiously in light of the perfectly clear one hundred and fifty years of Dutch Afrikaner proselyization in South Africa, and the even older mercantilism-originating (East Africa Oriental competitors-circumventing) West Africa-specific Occidental slavetraders' income being the outcome of the spirit of Calvinist capitalism--because the enormously productive if not entirely peerless profit-making and wealth-producing slavetrading principle and enlightened Christian virtue are not only diametrically opposed but also mutually exclusive values. Of course, like most cost-conscious conservatives, the "Consistent Calvinists" were right in what they affirmed and wrong in what they denied.

Contrariwise, in opposition to most Evangelical Southeastern slavocrats, Northeastern American Colonizationists shared the persuasion that Black Americans could not be Christianized satisfactorily while in bondage. This consensus was reached and preached at the same time these Northern proslavocrats were in profound disagreement with Northern proabolitionists.

Pro-Colonizationists thought their ACS process was superior to the alternative because at least it was a simple solution to a compounded complexity, whereas the antislavocrats had no risk-relieved and violence-free or security-guaranted plan to realize their conviction, were convinced that after slavery Black folk would be fully integrated into the American society, and opined that biracial equal access to opportunity would occasion equal results automatically.

As a consequence of the proslavocrat and antislavocrat Northern churchmen's nonnegotiable discord over whether a future in America or Africa served the best interest of their Black Protestant cultural kith and kin, and the belief of abolitionists who disaffiliated from the ACS because they came to understand the antiabolitionists at the helm who confirmed their suspicions and conspiratorial theory that they unwittingly but willy nilly turned the ACS into a proslavocrat plot to shore up the slavocracy, the New Abolitionists were transformed from independent into interdependent individuals.

They forged on the diversity in unity anvil crusading unity in diversity societies that were unalterably opposed to colonization. They self-transfigured into bands of fierce freedom fighters committed for the duration of the declared moral war on captors and capitivity to liberate their captives--and determined both to vanquish error or perception-bound proslavocrat warriors and to defeat the error of deception-fixated Christian vanguard at the helm of the ACS.

The liberators were met by either bogus or bankrupt moral and therefore offensive as well as defensive Southern slavocrat and Northern proslavocrat specialists in antiabolitionist-resistance, and combative professionals counterattacking their declared ethics equivalence of war upon slavocracy and the protectionists of the structural dehumanization system.

By the 1830s, the proabolitionist and antiabolitionist advocates' adversarial exchanges of truth claims and recriminations turned their agencies into mutual contempt societies. Their countermarching truth squads revealed the hardened immediatist versus gradualist positions as clearly as they betrayed their livid disdain of each other's motives and measures.

No less rigorous and vigorous than the Calvinist and anti-Calvinist theological wars waged between pre-antebellum Trinitarian and Unitarian Congregationalists, the exhaustive and exasperating war of words consuming proslavocrat and antislavocrat Evangelical Calvinists was intensified by an ever-expanding difference in interpretation of the correct ethical principle and practice, engendered by a conflict of principles and interests whose cause and effect was the unbridgeable gulf between their approaches to private versus public rights and responsibilities.

One nation-wide consequential outcome was the critical comparative cultural values analysis of the universal virtue of self-determination and vice of involuntary servitude published by New Abolitionist moral analysts. In its multiform versions, it made evident and unavoidable the color caste/captive chattel property self-serving, real interests-specific cause and effect of the slavocrats, on the hand, and, on the other hand, the truth and consequences stemming from the fact that Northern proslavocrats' commitment to democracy's slavocracy was deepening, widening, and intensifying.

The meaning of the expansive slavocracy, and the nature of the effectively different aim of the liberal and conservative antislavery Northern responses, advanced the division between the reactionaries and radicals, and forced the moderates to appraise the Northern versus Southern conflict of real interests, desires, values, and demands.

The unity of reactionaries contrasted sharply with the schism in the ranks of the radicals. This division in the house of immediatism occurred as a result of the contest between the rigid anti-political power and moral compulsion-only Old Moral Majority and their New Abolitionist Moral Reform compeers competing for hegemony of the abolitionist movement, as the flexible new political party power partisan minority.

Pro-political New Abolitionists moved to add to moral pressure the coercive force of pragmatism engendered from political involvement of a number of antislavery men and societies. Quite like anti-political Calvinists forming the leadership cadre of both the American Colonization and New Abolitionist Societies, these pro-political Calvinists had been laboring under the Halfway Piety faith and ethics promulgated by Jonathan Edwards but reverted to the authentic Puritan Piety faith and ethics of public interest-advancing direct action Cotton Mather crystallized for Evangelical Calvinists.

These Puritan Piety New Abolitionists, who entered the political arena as Christian ministers and laymen, knew that all across the North churches were the centers of abolitionist rallies. There Black and White Protestants met to hear the "Good News" and the "Bad News" of the latest administration of victimization or legal injustice, success or failure of the agencies organized to beat the devil, and fugitive caught by or who escaped from being eclipsed entirely if not scot free of the system.

They also knew the Evangelical Protestant denominations were overwhelmingly antiabolitionist institutions, that like the pro-immediatism congregations, the sectarian churches hosting antislavery rallies were not even close to a representative minority number of any denomination--let alone represented the majority or even a consensus.

The churches in the West, not unlike those in the East, were frequented as civil auditoriums for every civic affair and therefore for antislavery public assemblies because few town meeting halls were erected. Antislavery gatherings in parochial parishes were preludes to principled-proabolitionist and proletarian-Protestant partisan participatory democracy, occasions for preaching to the converted and converting the preachers, arenas of pure politics and no less real for being more often denied than affirmed status political meetings of religious and secular abolitionist direct actionists, and not simply forums for the informed to discuss the issue dispassionately and to inform the uninformed objectively.

The citizen sponsors of abolitionist town meetings in each local community were not engaged in Evangelical spirituality exercises, to say little of what William Ellery Channing concurrently denounced to the public scandalous "enthusiasm" or "fanaticism" excesses.

They were exploring, through investigative first-hand experiences and innovative experiential experiments, creative ways of challenging the oppressive slavocracy regime. Moral Reformers embarked originally as moral-only social and civil change course engineers, and subsequently a minority turned pioneer pilots of moral plus political power-specific professionals who expected the two parties to converge in a confluence that would transmogrify the bondage-bound body politic into a corpse.

Late emerging political proabolitionist societies, compared to the initially and continuous earlier pro-political British Abolition Society, offended the anti-political sensibilities of the Northern liberal and conservative traditionalists who censured before the citizens for Christianity and civility as pure political public Protestants and therefore diminished moral agencies.

Pre-1840 political proabolitionists were the bane of strange bedfellows, namely, the religious anti-political abolitionists and antiabolitionists, and the pro-political and anti-political proabolitionist and antiabolitionist secular humanists, who criticized them for engaging in single-issue politics. But they were wiser than their critics, even if they were not as clever as their challengers in devising logic and rhetoric to further their defense and offense.

What power politics proabolitionists understood comprehensively, and religious humanitarian and secular humanist antagonists underestimated thoroughly, was that the slavocracy passed the test of a total culture; to take the whole Southern Way of Life on was to immerse oneself in every facet of complex and competing American parochial, private, and public conflicts of interests; and necessary and permanent differences cannot be arranged perfectly but can be settled relatively reasonably, and finally only through the exercise of rational power.

What is noteworthy because of its particular bearing upon this exploration entails the partisan party power politics initiatives of the New Abolitionists. By means of which participatory democracy form and function, these Evangelical Calvinist sons of the wayward world saints returned to the original Puritan tradition in both England and America.

Departure from this true type constituted the distinct anti-Calvinist and unique anti-Puritan turn from authentic Puritan Piety into Halfway Piety pioneered by strict constructionist and moralist Jonathan Edwards. This Edwardsean reversal of values proved a continuum Yankee rival Congregationalists alternately advanced and honored in the breach in recurring random cycles. Power politics convergence and divergence were selective engagement and disengagement decisions Yankees managed to protect their real interests. Anti-political moral power was a common error or more accurately a consensus reached in New England by odd bedfellows.

Power elite Protestants denied that moral power only against a pure power aggressor could be meaningful self-defense finally and only to Christian citizens enjoying such ample amounts of liberty and capital in history they could afford the luxury of grounding their hope in the millennium, moral man, and linear progress from legal injustice to justice in law.

New Abolitionists earned and deserved more credit than they received for arguing that the predestinarian, Western, and White race/class-conscious proslavery secular doctrines and pro-millennium sacred dogmas are Bible-based political profane and sacred ideological doctrines that may be (singly or in combination) attended by advocates and adversaries yet conductors of either the positive and/or the negative spirit of antiblack white-ethnic virtue transmitted through the historic and current proslavery (1) ecclesiastical and civil law; (2) Old Testament (Mosaic-Dueternomic) juridical statutes and New Testament (Paul-

ine/Greek-Roman-Judaica) codes; and (3) positive law of republican democracy.
In truth, attested the radical abolitionists equally imaginatively, class over
caste and bondage cultural custom consciences may be appropriated by *bona fide*
self-serving powerhouses who equate the rule of law with guaranteeing anti-
Black race interests and pro-White race/ethnic interests, and who are prolific
progenitors bent on abandoning their human experiments in dehumanization to
their fate.

Among such forehanded and apperceptive emerging proabolitionists evolved a
minority who refused the proslavocrat, pro-millenniarian, and anti-democratic
politics-devoid antislavery movements. Their preferred alternative involved being
engaged in a democratic political struggle against the all-encompassing legalistic
forms of suppression.

One public consequence of the biblical and political offense unleashed by
politics-intensive New Abolitionists was the predictable North and South interconnected counterattack by reactionary and conservative, liberal and moderate
antiabolitionists, who, understandably, naturally loved states' rights and/or the
Union more than they respected the Black race, community and individual responsibility, and Christianity and civility whose commonalities entailed the single demand that they grant precluded Black kinsfolk inclusion in the Constitution.

IRISH PROTESTANT EDMUND BURKE

English-race and British-ethnic proslavocrat Northern conservatives, who defended the slavocrat reactionaries by attacking their radical abolitionist
Northern brothers and sisters, could argue their status quo reasons theological-
ly, partly because of the Scottish Common Sense Philosophy they caught from
Reformed tradition leader John Witherspoon; and philosophically, partly due to
fact that their conservative political thought was informed by Edmund Burke
(1729-97).

An Irish Protestant (born in Dublin to a Protestant father and Roman Catholic mother), and critic of English politics in Ireland, Burke was born six years
before and died three years after Witherspoon, Timothy Dwight's preceptor.
Burke evinced unshakable confidence in political, social, and religious institutions for the same reasons traditional conservatives naturally are protectionist
and preservationist custodians of traditions and institutions, and join establishmentarians who cherish them as repositories of the wisdom of the ages.

Co-equally instinctively and fundamentally, Burke counted as all but inviolable the habits and prejudices of an race/ethnic people. From a perspective
paralleling the outlook of elder contemporary Georg Wilhelm Fredrich Hegel
(1770-1831), the Protestant Anglo-Saxon superior race philosopher who treated
"*the spirit*" as the distinguishing each folk group, Burke viewed race and ethnic
values as the creative folkways and mores forming the substance of meaningful
distinctiveness and continuity in the political experience. Burke was ded-icated
to the preservation of "*the spirit*" of the folk group at all costs.

Due to his respect for folk wisdom and values, oddly enough, the British-
ethnic political philosopher and professional politician opposed sheer rationalism
in civil and political human affairs--and considered unbridled logical empiricism
positively dangerous.

Yet in America, at least, the conservatives who defended "states' rights"
over the human rights of slaves were evenly divided in their preferences bet-

ween their love of habits and prejudices and belief in unrestricted rationalism. The problem they were for Black folk sprang from the consequences of conservatives who acted on their intentions, struggled to be both hyperexclusive ethnocentrists and rationalists, and ended in compromise which Burke declared a contradictory ethical posture.

If the abolitionists did not forget forever their Anglo-American Puritan general interest-advancing heritage, which included engaging their parochial faith and personal ethics in private and public politics as civil servants, the conservatives in America appreciated Burke as a British Protestant political theorist the more he vilified clergymen such as the Evangelical British Abolitionists, for their active role in combining political power and legislative justice to end the English state of injustice and liberate the slaves:

> Politics and the pulpit are terms that have little agreement. No sound ought to be heard in the Church but the voice of healing charity. The cause of civil liberty and civil government gains as little as that of religion, by this confusion of duties. Those who quit their proper character, to assume what does not belong to them, are for the greater part, ignorant both of the character they leave, and of the character they assume. Wholly unacquainted with the world, in which they are so fond of meddling, and inexperienced in all its affairs, on which they pronounce with so much confidence, they know nothing of politics but the passions they excite. Surely the church is a place where one day's truce ought to be allowed to the dissensions and animosities of mankind.[6]

In the antebellum era, British-ethnic Southerners either led or followed the solid proslavocrats who made a religion of their politics. As the slavocracy progressed, political theology became the high art of the Southern pulpit. Although comparatively late, relative to proslavocrat and Scotch-Irish birthright politicians' early and consistent political participation in the system, amid the antebellum era of undeclared war pro-political proabolitionists were realistic enough to endeavor to unseat the slavocrats and place a proabolitionist in control of the "bully-pulpit."

One among many contributing causes of the precipitous move by a minority of New Abolitionists to add political force to their moral crusade was the cruel imposition of pure and simple politics by White Southern clergymen-slave-masters who indoctrinated Black Southerners with a religion of dehumanization.

These English-race and British-ethnic American Christians declared Black folk were a group in human bondage because God willed the race descended from the Providence-cursed Canaan (eponymous personage) to be enslaved to the descendants of eponymous personages Japeth (White Gentiles) and Shem (White Semites). Since Black people were instituted a captive race by the law of God and man, averred the proslavocracy Protestants, they should be obedient and faithful; good slaves; and preserve the social order by not disturbing the peace.

If White and Black New Abolitionists shared a common cause, they also shared the common experience throughout their lecture circuit travels of discovering that the minority of White churches (in the majority of Northern communities) were the only sanctuaries--not the Federal courthouses and other law and order buildings--where they could find relief from their problems, and the resources to withstand the powers embattleling them.

Not the least of these embattled counterforces were the ACS-persuaded Evangelicals, whose arguments made it apparent they believed the overt slave system was a covert Providential mission. They pontificated in parochial and private as well as public circles that from the human point of view the enslaved Black race constitutes the "*White Man's Burden*," but from the view of Providence human bondage is divine motive plus opportunity.

Synchronic Colonizationists discovered new ways they proclaimed better ways of glorifying God that involved civilized transformation of African barbarism, Christian conversion of Black Americans through the process of evangelization-regeneration, and humanitarian colonization of the Black race. These rational means were justified by the millennium end.

Both sets of rational antiabolitionist Calvinists, the Northern "Rule of Scripture" and Southern inerrancy of the Word authorities, recorded on the record their interpretation of God-derived, Bible-ordained, and state-legitimated slavery. The Southern retention and Northern removal of Black folk clearly was not the relative but the absolute difference they made.

In spite of Colonizationists' internal different intentions and purposes, and the imperceptible difference in the consequences of their conclusion that begins and ends with the common belief in a subjective-free objective motive, means, opportunity, and end of Black race bondage, slavery translates literally and figuratively an instrumental cultural vehicle for the advancement of Christianity and civility from excellence to distinction; an institution for the structural expansion of the political economy and development co-equally of social and moral perfection; and an inviolable divine principle and process whose operation is in line with the Kingdom of God.

Northeastern proslavocrats and Southeastern slavocrats testified tirelessly that the law and order premise of their faith and ethics, and justification by faith in reason, commanded them to respect, protect, defend, and secure the slavocracy. Their reasons were equally logical and predictable.

Providence designed (or most certainly permitted) the slavetrade to carry the African to America for potent English-race and British-ethnic superiors to penetrate African multi-ethnic inferiors; predetermined the progenitorship to produce an African ethnicity de-culturalized and deethnicized race-specific Black cultural and genetic kinsfolk; inspired the progenitors to attract individual kith and kin to repel their American Black race kin-group coinstantaneously; directed the procreators to invent Black-race deportation/denationalization and other dimensions of deterrence-benevolence as the ultimate measure of objective love and justice and fairness, equity and charity, goodness and grace or as means to the end of saving the Black soul and re-creating the Black body a missionary force; and foreordained the final solution and purpose which unfolded in the right and will of the righteous to propel their Black-race flesh and blood to Africa--in order to make room for their White-ethnic relatives they bid welcome to the *Promised Land*.

In fine, the task-responsibility of the ACS and what passed for the mind of the White Anglo-Saxon Protestant Christian was defined in the Colonizationists' implementation of this Hobson's Choice ("that or none") fairness doctrine for their Black-race kinsfolk.

The Evangelical doctrine of Colonizationism, and the Colonization dogma of deculturalization and pragma of deportation, proved no less doctrinaire than the double indemnity-twice blessed select "Elect of God's" denationalization double damnation (that they preferred to call double election). It was in fact the critical anti-Black race vice the establishment moderates declared virtue and never decried seriously.

Pro-politics New Abolitionists correctly understood the pragmatic dogma and dogmatic pragma of Colonizationism to be in truth the error of terror; the affirmative action positively produced by deep-seated White ethnocentricity; a holy color caste/captive class cause and effect of such compelling force no rational argument or moral value could counterbalance the national value; and, therefore, drew from the universally empirically verifiable evidence the accurate conclusion they acted upon, to wit, only real power can command and control both bondage in the South and caste in the North.

ORTHODOXY'S ANTI-BLACK RACE SIGNALS

The dehumanization suffered by the Black race in American democracy and slavocracy no less than theocracy, according to the conservative view, was neither a disvalue or a value nor to be compared with virtue. Social conservatives equated virtue with both the private rights of individual White ethnics to enslave Black folk, and the rights of states to self-preservation at the expense of self-determination for Black Americans. This perfectly legal and logical position was exquisitely extended from spurious premises by rationalists and rhetoricians, whose posited enlightened self-interest was legitimatized by the Constitution and positive laws; sanctioned by the Moral Law and statutes of the Bible; and advanced by religious principles and principals.

Given this conservative persuasion, it was understandable that the William Lloyd Garrison-types of Christian New Abolitionists who included the Black race in their unyielding demand for human freedom in liberty, would counterreply. Garrisonians argued incorrectly that Christian deception was the only religion accessible to Black folk, and that they lacked the capacity to distinguish good from bad faith.

They argued accurately, and naturally to no avail, that the black, evil, and self-serving White race/ethnic religion of the Christian masters and the state should not be preached to Black Southerners. The Garrisonians comprised Evangelical Calvinist and anti-Calvinist, theological traditional and liberal, and moral moderate and radical Protestants transfigured anti-denominationalists and anti-Colonizationists. These male and female fully developed rationalists and logicians, who followed moral power-only leader Garrison, projected their antiestablishmentarianism verbal barrages in anticipation they would demolish the mainstream denominations.

Garrisonians thought the major Evangelical churches were bound by sectarianism, tied by antiabolitionism so tightly they were able neither to loosen or untie nor cut the immoral institutional knot, and therefore should cease to exist in order to free the moral individual members whom the national congregations were accused of binding in ethical neutrality.

The radical moralists stated for the record their absolute aim which they coupled with attestations of their intentions to be fair, and avowed that just as their word was their bond and as certain as the integrity of their testaments the consequences of their thoughts and actions were automatically right and good.

Truth to tell, the politics-free, morality-full, reason and spiritual force-restrictive abolitionists scarcely shunned intense controversy, circumvented conflict, or did not have physical punishment inflicted upon by White foes who did not like their Black friends. In their encounters with the White race power and White ethnic powerless they concentrated on the negative good--or on the a- voiding violence and preventing harm principle--and thus the anti-political paci- fists and moralists not only escaped the risk of power within the circles of re- alism but also missed the opportunity to expand positive good possibilites.

Pro-Garrisonians argued with force that the Bible and Evangelical religion are political instruments, and as such subject to the manipulations of Machi- avellian-types who simultaneously execute terror and the error of deception. They were accurate as far as their analysis went but it did not go far enough, whereby they drew the incorrect conclusion when they maintained that Black folk should have neither the Bible nor Evangelical religion because these instru- ments of power politics were currently fashioned to inflict harm upon them, nor access to their freedom and liberty potency. Unquestionably, the Evangelical nonviolence and pure moralists radicals among the pro-Garrisonians intended to place nothing so great distance between themselves and the deterrence-benevo- lence Evangelicals.

Still, in spite of the divergence of these proabolitionists from the antiaboli- tionists in matters relating to private faith and public ethics, Colonizationist Lyman Beecher and former Colonizationist William Garrison remained Protestant idealist rather than realist Moral Reformers who converged in personal moral- isms as traditionalists. White Calvinist antiabolitionist and proabolitionist arche- types Beecher and Garrison were identical twin moralists as Temperance advo- cates and benevolent paternalists.

Arguably, they extended their paternalism unnecessarily, mindlessly, and went too far in predeliberately exercising their powers to preempt choice. Specifical- ly, they needlessly underestimated the capacity of Black religious folk to elect-- if given the opportunity to select--their best known good interest. Complemen- tarily, they overreached yet failed to stretch or to extend themselves in this matter of caste or did not reach very far toward providing even in an experi- mental, localized way, a sound basis for Black and White Northeasterners to en- gage in egalitarianism.

Measured by their public principles and affirmations, that were given a higher priority than their preferences, Garrisonians should not have expended less but could have more energized antiblack white-ethnic virtue to expose fel- low New Englander proslavocrats' perversion of the principle into anti-Black race virtue. Garrisonian New Abolitionists' capacity for even-handedness was demonstrated in more random than reliable feats such as holding the feet of anti-Black race-intensive White ethnics to the fire, as well as by their aware- ness of the no less positive for being relative rather than absolute power of their social criticism (which was not lost on Black Garrisonians).

Correlatively, it was not beyond the range of their capabilities to add a searching self-critical feature to their fully developed appreciation of the nega- tive effect of their intended constructive criticism of antiabolitionist establish- ment denominations and denominationalists. Such a rational self-appraisal mech- anism would have not contracted but expanded discernment of their propensity to go beyond pointing out the spurious issue of organized religion to castigating institutional Protestantism as if were only the problem and not also part of solution.

A plurality of the Garrisonians were strident anti-Calvinist Unitarian Con- gregationalists. They followed theological liberal and caste-conscious Bostonians in the direct social conservative color class line from the Reverend Charles

Chauncy (1705-87) to William Ellery Channing. Their determination to override the great faiths of mankind because they did not like organized religion was explainable but no less surprising, and even shocking, precisely because their remonstrances flew in the face of Northeastern experimental theory and experience in reality.

The convincement of these rational Protestants that, paralleling their reversal of ethics, they could succeed in reversing the course of faith in human history and cultures approached demonstrable power of arrogance; arrogance of power; and the height of contempt for God and man. What was certainly odd and even peculiar concerning this commitment to eradicate religious systems creating and created by civilizations, and to replace community values and institutional world religions with individual morality or rights and responsibilities, involved its implicit compromise of the explicit humankind improvement principal principle and purpose of Unitarianism humanism, philosophical and theological humanitarianism, and moral liberalism.

Unitarian Congregationalist Channing and Calvinist Baptist Garrison, and similar and dissimilar social ethics leaders of bold brahmin Bostonians, enveloped Unitarian Garrisonians who as the religious power elite embraced the popular secular elitists' belief in subjective-free or pure objective reason; promoted Protestant private and personal linear ethical progress; and advanced the individual as the source and the standard of moral truth and ultimate reality.

Necessity seemed clearly defined in their asserted equivalence of individual existence and moral essence, and will to jettison White race/ethnic Protestant denominations. Perforce this pursued cause and effect inevitably occurred a sense of the greatest unimportance and desertion of the Black race body politic, body corporate, and body of Christ.

The anti-Calvinist and pro-Calvinist ethicists, for whom the exclusively individual moral actor was the only true moralist, did not believe they were fairly accused of being arbitrary. Synchronously, however, they revealed their remarkable Yankee disrespect for the Evangelical Calvinist authentic Puritan Piety faith and ethics concern for their Black bond and free Congregationalist body-- the Black parishioners whom before after but like their model Puritan pastor and preceptor Cotton Mather the "real" and "presumptive" saints sep-arated from the "Reprobate" and selected the "Elect" and educated--and no more dramatically than when these sons of the wayward worldly saints demeaned the intelligence of Black descendants of slave and free Congregationalists whom Mather taught to be Gospel exegetes and eisegetes.

This occurred most strikingly as the Yankee descendants called into question sons of slavemaster Mather's bondmen's Calvinistical Gospel-specific ability to extract the kernel of the antislavery message from husk delivered by the proslavery messenger.

If no more or anywhere else than just here and to this extent, the moral excellence of the Garrisonians failed to support imaginatively the one power base Black race non-citizens possessed; and the instrumental means for escalating Black American cohesion and progress towards participatory democracy.

This critical error committed by the rational johnny-one-note moralists, moral-only or one-dimensional power brokers, both illuminated and complemented the failure of the inflexible anti-political and restrictive moralism-bound radical abolitionists to provide a mechanism for free Black New Englanders to participate in the democratic process as earlier as New Yorkers.

Their stunning power stunting operation was not astonishing but demonstrable conventional wisdom. Disproportionately due to this dynamic linkage, the power preclusion policy was fully expected from the preponderantly Christian abolitionist-Yankees who were either/or both anti-Calvinists and pro-Calvinists during the course of their active life; self-identified Puritan descendants accepting unquestioningly an inherited cultural tradition that did not think the Black race important enough to warrant securing their inclusion and real interests; expanded the real interests of the advantaged at the expense of the disadvantaged; and chose not to risk the new conflict and competition they anticipated the entrance of the Black body into the system would guarantee.

What followed automatically from the rational design of American culture determiners, rather than from an accident of history or law of nature, was the profit and pleasure Protestants declared the prerogative of privilege and advised Black folk in no uncertain terms to consider their joy and to suffer gladly. Logical rationalization and non-denial denial to the contrary notwithstanding, prognostication- and prophecy-respect-ing liberals and traditionalists fastened Black race kith and kin in a fixed place between their fashioned private and parochial public device: whose coordinated polar opposite ends of Puritan individual virtue and community vice turned deliberately to meet in the middle the Black body, as the Golden Mean and the moral man, and to squeeze the life out of the Black presence and immoral society.

These Yankee descendants of the Puritans had better reason to hope than to think their truth claim reversed rather than both tolerated and managed reality. As evidently they had no reason to doubt that the Puritan race inheritance came to rest on their shoulders: the color-conscious pro-White race/ethnic values or anti-Black race values advanced as the dual secular and religious cultural legacy of positive negation of Black race's true and real interests, and calculated callousness regarding the consequences for their Black-race free and bond kin-group of their White Christian Gentlemen's Agreement to perpetuate systematic and systemic slavery.

The "perfect is the enemy of the best possible" classic collective conscious, whom contemporary critics averred constituted a picture perfect instance when perception is reality, the veritable force managed to escape the consequences but could not be innocent or ignorant of the bequeathed negative caste-specific attitudinal and behavioral intentions.

A singular reason why this moralist host advanced with impunity was the precipitous break out of the Calvinist pack of English-race and British-ethnic New Abolitionists, who publicly admitted the inherited caste/captive liability; professed intergenerational individual accountability and collective culpability; and demonstrated initiative in exercising leadership to form a consensus behind their assumption of the task-responsibility to remove the demanding free second class and first class slave outcaste race condition, which in traditional and non-traditional English/British-American ecclesiastical power circles their fore-fathers neither admitted or accepted nor performed.

The controversial pro-political Christian ethicists, who revealed the onetime concealed and currently congealed anti-Black race desire, were subject to citizen's arrest for indecent public exposure of pro-caste and proslavery priority principles and practices; quickly complied with the order to cease and desist from promoting the abolition of caste issued by the citizenry's antislavery/proslavery consensus; surrendered in defeat to the forces in opposition to their two track abolition plan of action; and opted essentially and finally howbeit reluctantly to abandon the double eradication goal for the single targeted-objective of abolishing slavery.

Abolition was difficult enough, but while the demanding crusade concentrated the mind of New Abolitionists it was not an all-consuming one. Ecclesiastical expansion and theological controversies were among the central concerns competing successfully for the boundless energy and resources of the optimistic antislavery churchmen.

And Evangelical Garrison, who in being equally anti-political and pro-pacifist proabolitionist was more precisely a strange breed of Evangelical Baptist than a standard deviation from the pro-political and pro-military Calvinist (Baptist) norm, never lost his life-long pro-Temperance verve.

Upspringing from these higher real interests and values higher priorities than anti-Black race drives were civil and ecclesiastical power conflicts of interests and compromises of principle, namely, logi-cally irrefutable reasons to trim the great ambition to abolish caste and bondage in the Union.

The color caste/captive statusless class condition constituted a church and state issue, whose outcome could be influenced through the skillful use of pragmatism by professional churchmen but which political opportunity was promptly ignored by idealists transformed selective realists.

In 1819 when the latter incident reflecting the abandonment by parsons of partisan Federalist Party power politics occurred, exactly two years after the birth of the American Colonization Society and eleven years before sometime ACS member Garrison bolted the ACS to become the first New Abolitionist, the General Assembly of the Presbyterian Church (and supreme judicatory of the undivided national denomination) demonstrated ecclesiastical power possibilities. Reformed Calvinism also disclosed the case for the critical perspective of this interpretive essay in a memorial submitted on the convention floor, that defined the prospects and made the point sharp enough to bear the weight of the analysis.

The point is made by accepting rather than arguing with two facts fixed by realists and idealists that no more lie than their figure. First, the American power elite and proletarian parties to the conflict of upper and lower classes divide in the middle classes during their random recurring class wars and unite as a whole White race in their persistent casting of the caste in culture. These factions form a factor who drive down and hold the Black race beneath the bottom of the lowest White ethnic group, and deprecate the depreciated for failing to pull up the Black body by its bootstraps.

Second, the point subsists of the difference made by the sectarian sources transformed by rational organization into an institutional power that proved to be both like and unlike yet distinctively different from the secular press or any other public organ. Several major Evangelical denominations--whose leadership appeared poised to begin their approach to the standard set by the Religious Society of Friends--comprised the only national institutions where Americans addressed seriously the issue of anti-Black race values, if only to vote their conscience and to register their despair:

> The situation of the people of color of this country, has frequently attracted the attention of this Assembly. In the distinctive and indelible marks of their color and the prejudices of the people, an insuperable obstacle has been placed to the execution of any plan for elevating their character, and placing them on a footing with their brethren of the same common family.[7]

This ringing resignation and hand wringing reflected the organized denominations' sharp decline into alternating regret for the caste and bondage bind of their color-bound class of Christian constituents, and reduced opposition to anti-Black race perversity, from color-conscious caste and bondage conscience-stricken Old Abolitionists' conception and nativity of the Methodist Episcopal Church and the Presbyterian Church several years before the birth of the nation at the moment of ratification of the Constitution.

Churchmen switched from the divine right of kings to the divine right of the republican representative Executive-Congress-Court or Three Branches of the Federal Government, to holding the Bible and the Constitution equally sacrosanct and inviolable documents, and to declaring them to be the presumed Providence-ordained and Creator-instituted in power and authority government heads' sacred testaments of or law of God and man.

Hence once the Constitution instituted slavery as one of the "states' rights" the churches changed from confronting race bondage and caste as a matter of ecclesiastical and civil rights and church and state responsibility, to considering preempted self-determination and citizenship natural rights of native Black Americans not only justice because it was legal rule of legitimate powers but also the proper domain of only civil law and not an ecclesiastical law as well, to promulgating total obedience to the Constitution rather than to conscience as the commandment of God and therefore the duty of Christians, and to parochial reflection upon and enforcement of private bondage and caste questions while considering the secular and sacred system the province of public authorities.

Forward from far fewer Arminian than Calvinist clergy's growing awareness of the ever-increasing domestic slavetrade after the 1808-outlawed foreign slavetrade, these new leaders of the budding Evangelical denominations experienced a heightened antislavery consciousness of caste and bondage that expanded and peaked with their 1817-formed ASC.

Hand in hand with Yankee Calvinist clerical origin, growth, and development of gradualism from Old Abolitionism and immediatism to antiabolitionism and Colonizationism went a universal refusal of establishment denominations to enable their Black-race class (or at least constituency) to ascend the ladder of competence and competition as a people in America, whereby the individual exception they permitted as a rule, and routine matter of management or convenience and expedience as often as expression of tolerance, confirmed the Black race exclusion rule of law. Establishment parsons and parishioners were Calvinist capitalists and Protestant philanthropists, and as the nonesuch Colonizationists were able but not willing to create and maintain a constructive benevolent alternative to the destructive deportation development of their ACS: because they developed this organized deterrence-benevolence ethic as their interdenominational, nonsectarian, and para-church antislavery surrogate.

These conscious church omissions and commissions positively correlated with the higher priority of the highly developed Protestant "*Foreign Missions*" relative to the gradually developing "*Domestic Missions*" the denominational bureaucracies were organizing. Their different stages of institutional development corresponded with the deliberate speed with which churchmen and churches advanced New Abolitionism after it sprang from American Colonizationism in parachurch private societies and denominational-instituted antislavery bodies. Compared to the contrasting leadership style and commitment exercised by Quakers at the helm of the Old Abolitionist Societies, at the commencement of the 1830s and civil sector change-directed New Abolitionism White Protestant New Abolitionist clergy and lay people in the Northeast were in descending numerical concentrations Presbyterians, Unitarians, and a statistically insignificant number of Congregationalists and Episcopalians.

The real presence of the Methodist and Baptist overwhelming Evangelical Protestant majority and conspicuous proportional absence from the initial New Abolition initiative was consistent with the fact that their ecclesiastical-supported antislavery activities and associations were more strictly church coordinated and connected. The poignant point of the self-called people of God is predictable but a no less pregnant one: The churches and churchmen comprising the overwhelming numerical majority of New Abolitionists were members of the denominations with the greatest scarcity of Black congregants.

In the contiguous Independence and Second Great Awakening eras, a statistically significant number of Black Northeasterners had opted for their own independent communions exactly because White church ecclesiarchs and bureaucrats would not consider their requests for fairness and equity. Undoubtedly the universal flat rejection by Protestant authorities of their equalitarianism-demanding Black constituents indicates they knew (1) that the plethora of Protestant free choices including the real alternative to the exercised preference of the American Colonization church and churchmen to follow rather than to lead the state in controversial public interest-ethics, such as the moral ecclesiastical and civil issues of conscience and the Constitution; and (2) that in addition to the enormous effort required merely to initiate the task of establishing solidly the Black race in American democracy, success requires parochial plus private and public resources interlinked with those of the Federal, state, and municipal governments.

The egalitarian objective involved including exclu-ded Black folk voluntarily as effectively as they were precluded from republican democracy. No one seriously doubted achieving this aim commenced with creating an unprecedented institution on the scale of a national Church-Congress-Corporation organization, that was even more sufficient and efficient than the picture perfect parochial-private-public partnership model the ACS proved to be.

But the establishment denominations' budgeted antislavery allocations had been earmarked for deterrence-benevolence, funds solicited to facilitate the denationalization and deportation program, and personnel committed to the ACS.

BENJAMIN FRANKLIN: FORMER SLAVEMASTER AND CALVINIST

TURNED ANGLICAN'S APPEAL FOR FREE BLACK PHILADELPHIANS

Old and New Abolitionists continued the Puritan tradition of not setting wrong right, and failing merely to strike on paper a comprehensive plan to connect Black Americans with the new demands of individual responsibility and rights, currently expanding with the evolving republican democracy representative government and free market-oriented mercantilism free enterprise system fast becoming a political economy driven by industrial capitalism.

They did not renege on their antislavery commitment in the face of the quantum leaping bondage crisis of conscience and culture, and the growing social problem free Black Northeasterners presented in urban communities. White abolitionists were scarely without influence or access to the resources to insure that slavery (human bondage) and the symptom of the deeper dehumanization problem of anti-Black race values--that these color-conscious Christians understood to be the un-touchable issue of caste--was set high on the national agenda of the Three Branches of Government, and acted upon up by representatives who were responsible to this electorate and other accountable governmental authorities.

But in Massachusetts, for example, cautious congenital conditions were the operating constraints of Congregationalist clergymen reinforced by the clerical professionals being state-authorized and tax-paid guardians of the Commonwealth's morals, committed to the agenda of the national denomination and its rational bureaucracies, and enamored with the spirit of the Evangelical-Calvinist deterrence-benevolence ethic. These priorities prefabricated and fostered more rigid than flexible restraints on the social structural change potential of the Calvinist clergy, who were the conscience of the community.

They did little or nothing to deter their negative good strong suit, and ever-developing positive Calvinistical contribution of dialectical parochial-private-public charity. Their dynamic individual morality and personal altruism principle induced an elite corps to act discriminately to include in their amelioration efforts for White ethnic immigrants the (post-1808 outlawed international slave-trade) increasing number of Black fugitives from the slavocracy bound for the *Promised Land,*" arriving in Boston, convicted of crimes, and ministered to less by ministers than by lay missionaries of the Boston Prison Discipline Society (1825) and the Boston Society for the Religious and Moral Instruction of the Poor (1815).

After their primary interest in the Evangelical conversion and benevolence-deterrence salvation of the incarcerated, slowly but surely after 1800 the Moral Reformers added to their religious humanitarianism a secondary commitment to distributive, retributive, and corrective justice.

A century earlier, charity for Anglo-American Calvinist Cotton Mather in Boston, French Calvinist convert to Anglicanism Elias Neau in New York, and French Protestant convert to Quaker minister Anthony Benezet took the form of founding schools for Black slaves and domestic servants of slaveowning Congregationalists, Episcopalians, and Friends. Their legacy of exercising initiative to create the new and relevant means of meeting the current urgent need of the double damnation victims did not survive their death.

Instead of Protestant professors and preceptors building upon this foundation a developing structure of education, on balance Black folk met in the next generation of parsons more opposition than opportunity. Singular among the many measurable factors contributing to this change from Puritan Piety to Halfway Piety proponents--turn in events and reversal in fortune at once--were the capacity of these formidable foes of Black folk to generate interminable frustrations within their towering infernos and to erect these legal ecclesiastical and civil barriers in the *Promised Land.*"

These secular and sacred moralisms and legalisms permitted the sectarians to interject confusion and thereby protect their personal priorities; to take advantage of their private plethora of choice; and to add compound complexity to public conflicts of interest, and to the difficulty of color caste/captive class disadvantage in order for the privileged classes to secure their own pursuit of happiness.

Perchance the permanent Christianity and civility faith and ethics competition and conflict pertinent connection is less obvious than it appears, and may be usefully illuminated when set in the beside the relevance of the relative presence of the color caste/captive condition and the comparative absence of the

Black race from the dedication of "Consistent Calvinists" to extending education and building academic institutions in the antebellum decades.

The cultural connection can be constructively clarified in a brief recollection of the importance of race and reason in the designs of three Calvinist-nurtured ex-slavemasters.

Black race education and salvation means and ends were anticipated and illustrated by the contrasting purposes of the Samuel Hopkins-created and Ezra Stiles-sponsored Christian Colonization Appeal (1776)--the original American dream and source of the American nightmare ACS, or demonstrable White Nationalism existence in essence and the effective cause of the counteractant Black Nationalism effect--and the *Appeal* (1789) endorsed late in life and in his career-ending role as president of the Pennsylvania Abolition Society for Public Aid by Benjamin Franklin (1706-90): the New England-born, Pennsylvania-translocated, and Presbyterian-nurtured convert to Episcopalianism. Following the model established for the Quakers by contemporary Philadelphian Benezet, Franklin solicited funds to enable his society to orchestrate a plan to promote the industry, morality, and education of free Black Pennsylvanians.

What Franklin's class valuable values challenging to change or correct caste valued disvalues disclose are American culture-long appearing and disappearing civil and uncivil race and religion relations, and that history neither repeats nor is repeated but like his story (or history of progress in higher conscience moving in the train of ever-improving ethical excellence, paralleling his ethics mentor Cotton Mather in being a slavemaster and becoming a Protestant philanthropist soliciting fellow philanthropists to underwrite a philanthropic education fund for their Black-race brethren of the cloth and laymen in Christ Church Philadelphia or Boston) the class over caste patterns are repeated as frequently as these lessons of history are learned and unlearned repeatedly.

The Mather (Calvinist Congregationalist) to Franklin (Calvinist Presbyterian turned Anglican/Episcopalian) found and lost both lofty and real possibilities and opportunities expose the Protestant powerhouses' relatively interesting intentions rather less than either the absolute consequences of their rational action and inaction or their enduring significance.

Mather's pacesetting Evangelical Calvinist Puritan-Piety model as not only the pastor but specially as the principal preceptor of his North Church color caste/captive congregants for whom he founded a school set a late seventeenth- and early eighteenth-century precedent for the education of Black youth and elders.

It was not heeded by Jonathan Edwards or the post-Edwardseans, who institutionalized as solidly as they perverted his Halfway Piety faith and deterrence-benevolence ethics systematic theology. It was heeded by Ezra Stiles, who evolved a stronger Matherean than Edwardsean Calvinist, less formidably than by Samuel Hopkins, his brother of the cloth in Newport, Rhode Island and the protégé of Edwards whom contemporary admirers and critics considered the faithful Edwardsean.

And it was heeded by the successors of the post-Edwardseans who became the headmen at the helm of the Evangelical Calvinist establishment after the New Englanders (ex-slavemaster converted Old-Abolitionist advocates of education for Black men as the elemental mechanism for their elevation from exclusion to inclusion in the competitive political and economic system of the acquisitive society) Hopkins and Franklin died, massive waves of White ethnic immigrants arrived on the Eastern Shore, and run-a-ways were locating with

freed and free-born Black Philadelphians and Bostonians in growing numbers.
For their own dramatic reasons, the Protestant power elite preferred their different deterence-benevolence priorities and purposes, whose charitably principles these charitots of charity charitoteers wielded principally as princes of the church. Instead of taking the Black race seriously by way of promoting secular and civil schools, economic opportunity, political participation, and social responsibility, Calvinist clergy majored in minor ameliorations: when they did not in engage in benevolence-deterrence human exper-imentations, and approach the Black body, mind, and soul as sacred objects and subjects.

Lyman Beecher evolved with other younger ancillary agencies of the elder and venerable Hopkinsian and Franklinesque corollaries, who emerged at the end of the eighteen-century, submerged Old Abolitionism early in the nineteenth century, surfaced as antiabolitionist civility standardbearers spurred by a heightened con-sciousness of the caste/captive crisis in Christian conscience, and extended the sacralization of the sec-ular/civil order objective of the religious humanitarians in their role as public interest-promoting public servants.

"Massachusetts Yankees" established The Boston So-ciety for the Religious and Moral Instruction of the Poor established two years after Beecher founded the Connecticut Society for the Reformation of Morals (1813) four years before the formation of the ACS.

They formed the Boston Prison Discipline Society a decade after Northeastern Calvinists joined Southeastern Calvinists in creating the ACS, among whose members when the Prison Discipline Society issued its first annual report in 1826 were Yankee-Congregationalist interlocking directorates of the ACS.

Members of normally competitive Calvinist groups managed their faith division and ethics union, to maximize the power of antiblack white-ethnic virtue, their common sin-driving and evil-repelling moral principle, including the Reverend Edward Beecher (1803-95), a Congregationalist clergyman son of Presbyterian presbyter Lyman Beecher; Arthur Tappan (1786-1865), the prominent Massachusetts Congrega-tionalist and merchant, relocated in Manhattan and currently a Presbyterian layman; and the Reverend Francis Wayland (1796-1865), the Baptist Boston pastor and future President of Brown.

In this first generation of post-Puritan Calvinists and new Yankee Congregationalists, and period after the death of Orthodoxy's Old Abolitionists marked by the parallel rise of the antiabolitionist American Colonization Society and demise of the Quaker Old Abolitionist Societies, the Boston Prison Society was composed of Evangelical Calvinist William Lloyd Garrison's fellow pro-Temperance members of the ACS.

The critical point and caste/captive connection in this constricted tracking of the color-conscious social ethics of Calvinists is noteworthy. Just five years after the Prison Discipline Society published its initial report, Garrison pressed the Protestant establishment's ACS on a public petard; renounced his mem-bership in the ACS as the transfigurated original New Abolitionist, to form the New England (Massachusetts) Anti-Slavery Society; and discovered he was followed in this defection by nearly only Arthur and his brother Lewis Tappan (1788-1873), who formed the New York Anti-Slavery Society.

The pre-1830 Boston Prison Discipline Society's Annual Reports were factual publications that detailed the rise in crime among the White ethnic and Black race populace. The cause of this effect Garrisonians and Tappanites subsequently attributed to the abject statusless and degraded station in which Black Americans were bound beneath the White-ethnic underclass.

This bind which profane and sacred culture determiners preferred, the Tappans averred, in turn deterred the development and implementation of even one effective education project. No secular or sacred Protestant power or powerless architect deemed it important to design a blueprint designed to guarantee the Black male equal inclusion in participatory democracy, access to opportunity, and chances to manage conflict by meeting the competition.

Civil no less than Christian ducation, Tappanites were persuaded, is not only everything but the only thing; anything but revolutionary; and nothing more than a reform measure in which most liberal and conservative advocates of Christianity and civility certainly should be able and willing to cooperate.

Thus the two bottom lines of the Tappanites' progressive color-conscious/caste-limiting process were to their minds inarguable, to wit, the education of Black folk is as a clear choice and a manageable possibility one of the primary priorities and best solutions to the cultural crisis. But the idealists were realists who seriously doubted that the anti-Black race forces could be mitigated, who everywhere faced down Black friends they were aiding in freedom.

Prior to this analysis of experience and reality, which led them to draw a radical conclusion and become New Abolitionists, Garrison and Tappan were committed American Colonizationists whose Society was dedicated to the proposition prescribed fifty years earlier by Hopkins, namely, that colonization in Africa of the Black race is the last and best hope of White-race/ethnic and Black-race Americans.

OLD ABOLITIONISTS' PROGRAM

Half a century after Hopkins and Franklin, the Calvinist-born and New England-bred representative religious humanitarian and profane humanist extremes of the sacred/secular-civil Puritan heritage, what advanced in the establishmentarian ecclesiastical and civil power sectors was stabilization of the norm of little progress in either developing a creative caste/captive-limiting project and/or designing a process to correct in the present past absolute wrongs for a relatively right future.

They could contend the previous one hundred and fifty years of culture determined anti-Black race virtue to be the righteous spirit of dominance. British-ethnic and other ethnic folk, who understood themselves to exist at disadvantage relative to the English-race and Puritan-race descendants persisting in power and at advantage, were persuaded and very persuasive in attracting the unpersuaded to promote their persuasion that the Black race was not the only collective victim of the powerful culture.

From this spurious premise and specious principle of common human species suffering they argued with (instead of) the facts in order to hide in relative difference the absolute distinction which they understood comprehensively--that is, Black people were grossly neglected, and denied the prospects for real progress by British ethnic laborers as well as by English race capitalists.

Bethinking the Black-race an inferior group, the British-ethnic groups apprehended the fact that the White ethnic class was deficient in the status English-race and ethnic groups were ascribed. They managed poorly the contradiction inherent in the contention that relative to the deethnicized African ethnic people that the White race created a Black race-only body they were different by dint of being descendants of a superior White race.

A proclivity to live out the fanciful and the fancied fantasises in either the mind or reality notwithstanding, in actuality the Yankee descendants of the English/Puritan race were, like their British ethnic relatives, unequal to the task-responsibility that the best and brightest at last freely admitted to be their duty. It is, they preached and published for parsons and parishioners to practice in public as well as parochial and private affairs, to make, to keep, and to improve power Protestants' promises (and plans) to match the ambitions of free Black kith and kin to the competitive expectations of a free society.

However relatively powerless antebellum churches and churchmen were to create and implement an escalation mechanism, their bureaucrat and technocrat leaders, in their formation of the formidable denominational bureaucracies and the highly rational ACS corporation, demonstrated that they were more unwilling than unable and certainly no less capable than the Colonizationists to imagine, design, and build experimental models in the ecclesiastical sector on a par with their parochial schools, that could be instituted in the civil society later.

Antislavery bureaucrats at the helm of the Evangelical denominations, who were neither Old Abolitionists nor New Abolitionists but antiabolitionist procolonizationists/proslavocrats, disclosed their remarkable social engineering skills and rational organizational genius in forming successful domestic and foreign mission enterprises.

These major Protestant parochial formations of the rival sectarians remained impressive due to the obvious fact these multifaceted and multiform multinational benevolent institutions endured, and also because they were created and expanded in the midst of denominational theological conflicts and antislavery controversies. A singular and necessary consequence of these conflicts is that they increased competence and competition no less than rational and rationalization powers, whereby, necessarily, antislavery/proslavocrat logicians and rhetoricians were continuously becoming more and more sensitized to the critical neglect of proselytized Black Northerners and Southerners.

Still the rigid traditionalist or social conservative given to Evangelical religious humanitarianism, and the Halfway Piety faith and deterrence-benevolence ethics, generally succumbed to the anti-Puritan defeatist sentiment and anti--Black race interest principle which argued that Black folk could only be positively instructed, advised, and qualified for civil society in Africa, or least in an extraterritorial space entirely removed from White Americans.

Apparently the unnecessary and inevitable proceeded apace *vis-à-vis* this Yankee Trinitarian and Unitarian Congregationalist failure to establish a modern model moral public interest-institution of linear progress, one energized by a will to achieve patient, progressive, and steady social change, and directed toward near-term and long range Christian-inspired elevation of Black folk.

If the antebellum power elite had not been bent on restraining rights but on releasing resources to restore they Black Americans to the natural state of natural liberty, and to natural rights freedom in liberty in the New World and newer social order, it would have contributed significantly to reversing the accelerating progression of their crisis in confidence and credibility condition.

It is clear enough that power people's election of unconcernment instead of concernment with their Black male and female neighbors was no more an exclusive East Coast phenomenon than anti-Black race legitimate claims was limited either to the elite or to the popular churches. The American anti-Black race value was nationally and notionally not considered a vice but a high virtue. Instead of disinterested will to the good of Black folk, their positive negation pervaded the cultural consciousness, and was mitigated only by charitable or harm-limiting thoughts and actions.

Charitable goodwill also included aiding the Black race to achieve liberty, and excluding the Black body from inclusion in freedom. This to repel bondage and to attract caste law of alternation was exemplified by the Indiana Yearly Meeting of Friends in 1826:

> We having received a communication from the trustees of the North Carolina Yearly Meeting describing the difficult and perilous situation of a number of persons of color under the care of Friends, and informing, that some of them inclined to remove to the States north of the Ohio river, and requesting our attention to them. After solidly deliberating on the subject, and having our minds clothed with feelings which breathe "good will to men," we have come to the conclusion to inform Friends, that we are free to extend such assistance to those who may be found among us, as our means will permit: and, although it is desirable to avoid an accession of this class of population as neighbors, we are concerned to impress it on the minds of all, that our prejudices should yield when the interest and happiness of our fellow beings are at stake; and that we exert no influence that would deprive them of the rights of free agents, in removing to any part of the world congenial to them; and that Friends everywhere render them such assistance, in procuring them employment, and promoting a correct department among them, as occasion may require.

Black Protestants who had formed their first national denomination ten years earlier than this Quaker confession of faith, later extended their initiative to establishing autonomous academies, colleges, and seminaries. These academic plantations were spin-offs of their rising expectations of achieving through education the civil status precluded by power politics, and individual and community responsibilities and rights in liberty denied by self-serving capriousness.

Due to being severely handicapped by a dearth of resources, this initial step in the participatory democracy process necessarily began at the top and concentrated on generating self-reliance needs in the lower-class and supplying the demands for opportunity of the lower middle-class.

Thus the initiative of the select and fortuitous few self-determinationists who enjoyed relative advantage was hardly an alternative to the total program and massive resources required to elevate the masses.

When Black leaders and builders of independent community organizations solicited support from Calvinist capitalists they were not as successful as they might have anticipated, usually because their concern with achieving their best good interest did not fit the agenda and priorities of Protestant philanthropists.

Black folk were greater victims than beneficiaries of system designed to keep slaves in bondage and the Black free-born and freed competitors wards of charity. Black independent-minded men and women who experienced the presence of liberty and absence of freedom, were forced to become beggars and subject to the whims of the power elite.

They were as selectively generous a class as they were sometimes resentful, and always arbitrary.

What passes for the mind of the Evangelical establishment moderate,

Protestant philanthropist, or antislavery Calvinist capitalist issues forth in a statement of one no less suspect for being a self-styled abolitionist:

> We, abolitionists, are laboring for the destruction of slavery, and, at present, can do nothing for you. Until that evil is removed, the free colored people can not rise into respectability, or be relieved from the prejudice which now bears them down. Universal emancipation, therefore, is the first objective to be gained, as, after, prejudice will disappear, and the best schools and colleges in the land be thrown open to the colored men.[8]

This may have been only the analysis of a single Southerner and a Southern conclusion; but the implication and inference were drawn from pure Northern logic.

EQUATION OF SLAVERY WITH SIN

The class of the original Old Abolitionists distinguished themselves in their overwhelming opposition to all plans to dispose of Black Americans by removing the whole people from their fatherland; were inclined to disturb the peace and harmony of the United States for the sake of granting liberty and justice to Black folk; and affirmed what Hopkins (the onetime slavemaster but reborn Old Abolitionist clergyman), Thomas Jefferson (the Virginian who bequeathed two hundred slaves), and Abraham Lincoln (the "Reluctant Emancipator") denied: an equalitarian society inclusive of equal fairness and equity as well as mutual respect between Black-race and White-race/ethnic peoples is possible in both North America and the future.

Old Abolitionist secular and religious egalitarians did not accelerate the eventuality of equalitarianism because the idealists turned realists as architects of the Constitution, cut the facts of anti-Black race interests and figures of proslavery demands to fit their formula fashioned to form the Union, and argued their compromise of conscience was not a compromise ethical principles because they elected the lesser of two evils.

They were as convinced that this act was one of not self-serving interest but enlightened self-interest as they were confident slavery would collapse under its own weight, and they would right their wrong as certainly as right would triumph in the end. What was widespread common knowledge and generally accepted by a majority in the North and a minority in the South no serious and sincere Old Abolitionist at the birth of nation questioned, namely, that as a moral evil and a heinous sin slavery was the sum and substance of the positively dangerous and deadly harm nature of anti-Black race values.

There was more error than truth or a measure of realism in this not only odd and even peculiar but fascinating fastening upon slavery the whole of the Black and White conflict of interests, Old and New Abolitionist shared value, and bad faith and worse ethics. In their unalterable opinion, slavery is a clear and consistent wrong and the truth that could not be doubted by those whom they respected.

The unrequited optimism Yankee sons substituted for the pessimism of the Calvinist fathers' vision of status quo stability, as the permanent condition of slavery and anti-Black race desire in America, combined cynicism with faith in a redemptive future, and two separate and distinct issues they were too logical to confuse.

These Yankee coordinates may not have been one and same millennium coordinates employed by their Puritan fathers, but they were equally as rational.

Distinguished from the Old Abolitionists, the Evangelical New Abolitionists were rationalists, reformers, and revolutionists.

Regarding their initative in the human bondage question, they were the chief catalysts among other precipitating figures. Despite their deeper diversity than unity in common cause, the alternately followed and led initiators accelerated the escalation of the people from a nation of individual consciences toward a social conscience.

One key to their dynamism was their refusal to be satisfied with abolishing slavery in Northeastern churches.

Alternatively, Evangelical New Abolitionists de-manded that the entire nation undergo moral conversion from proslavocrats to born again antislavocrats, a process that evangelists considered the prior condition for social sanctification (Calvinism) or perfection (Wesleyanism).

UNREPRESENTATIVE SOUTHERNERS AND PRESBYTERIANS:

OLD ABOLITIONISTS IN THE WEST

New Abolitionists sprang from the tension produced by the not identical but dynamic twin Old Abolitionist and American Colonizationist Societies, united in the American Anti-Slavery Society whose means and ends were diametrically opposite from the different purposes of the preceding antislavery organizations, and divided New Abolitionism into anti-political and pro-political bodies.

One-dimensional moral pressure was the single issue and special interest of the antipolitical New Abolitionists, whose defining characteristic was the sharpest contrast imaginable to the two-dimensional moral plus political power distinguishing feature of the pro-political New Abolitionists.

Demonstrable secular and civil order understanding and wisdom as well as initiative was evidenced by the Evangelical/pro-political New Abolitionists for social structural change. They accepted the positive possibilities of moral and power politics, and concentrated their limited influence on the politics of slavery in the new antislavery party they created.

Their political action and formation of a sacred/civil party in 1840 was the outcome of a combined religious income and emerging consensus that broke with secular humanist mind at the helm of the government; the pure profane intellectual community; and the pure pious establishment churches.

Less than two years before New Abolitionism burst forth and formed a friction and fraction factor fragmenting the forceful faith and furtive social ethics formation in the Northeast, a developing church-centered, counter-Eastern establishment and anti-ACS antislavery movement crystallized in the West.

At least as early as the first issue of the Illinois *Christian Intelligencer* (1829), the periodical Presbyterian-Congregational clergy established as their antislavery paper, a new alignment of Old Abolitionist ministers committed to speaking for and to the church proclaimed slavery illegal, immoral, uncivil, unscriptural, unconscionable, and anti-Christian.

From this rational premise and upspringing logic and law evolved a principal Protestant principle and practice that emerged a universal categorical imperative: (A) Evangelical churches should dismiss all slaveholders unwilling to accept the new found interpretation of the veritable Word of God; (B) Evangelical denominations' supreme ecclesiastical legislatures and judicatories should enact and enforce laws requiring the local churches and churchmen to be free and clear of slavery in the East and the West, the North and the South; and (C) Evangelical Protestant pastors and parishioners throughout their national, state, and regional associations should publish antislavery journals of opinion which proscribe proslavery expressions.

This plan of action was promoted by the Reverend David McDill (1790-1870), and his co-editors of the *Intelligencer*, before Protestant private-conscience and parochial-centered principals experienced a heightened social concern induced by public-conscious antislavery/proslavery truth claims in the churches; prior to the proliferation of antislavocracy/pro-slavocracy divisions throughout all major Evangelical denominations (save the Protestant Episcopal Church), and the national churches voted slavery up and down and disunited; and previous to the antislavocrat/proslavocrat sacred and secular civil conflicts of interest which galvanized churchmen and nonchurchmen and radicalized the body politic, body corporate, and body of Christ:

> When we consider what has been done, and is still being done by the Quakers, Methodist, etc., if these bodies of professing Christians which have been mentioned as having the subject under consideration, would only disenthrall themselves from all human schemes of policy and prudence, and stand forth on scriptural grounds, the decided advocates of justice, humanity, and equal rights and privileges to all God's rational creatures, in that system of things with which we are connected, what happy results to the family of man might not be anticipated... If, instead of folding up their hands and saying, we cannot touch the subject of slavery--the evils admit of no remedy, at least the millennium--the laws lay an embargo on the cause of emancipation;--they would only consider that public opinion is superior to the laws, so that tyrannical and oppressive laws cannot stand it out against correct and enlightened public opinion--that, if any of our fellow Christians are withheld from doing their duty, by law which are an usurpation on the rights of men, and an enormity under the government of God, it is because public opinion has become corrupt through the apathy and supineness of those who ought to have been exerting themselves to keep it in a pure and healthy state: and if every man who possesses a participle of influence, either direct or indirect, on the common wealth, would rise, and come forward, and bring with him all the aid in his power, to correct the stream of human blessing in its fountain head;--we should soon find laws relaxing from their rigor, customs melting down into goodness, and the obstacles which obstruct the current of emancipation giving way, sooner than many who make goodly professions would be willing to see them.[9]

REACTIONARIES' PREEMPTIVE STRIKES OF RADICALS
AND ABOLITIONISM IN THE DENOMINATIONS

Prototypic McDill fairly represented and spoke for a new breed of antislavery churchmen. Their direct knowledge of the pernicious and obscene caste/captive system, ascertained from first-hand experience in democracy's slavocracy, slowly charged their consciences and compelled them to act to reverse the anti-Black race course of American history. But their will was infinitely greater than their power.

Given two hundred years of a rational superstructure and infrastructure, whose powerful systematic and systemic color-conscious cultural values the idealists thought they could escape, ignore, or deracinate, their best efforts and enormous energy were expended in moral movements. Their boundless capacity for absorbing negative good and harm-limiting values were revealed by the presence of matching damage control experts, damn-ing up the flow of anti-- Black race passion operations, and the absence of positive good and constructive change.

The long range failure of the representative social change agent's call for denominational action was one thing, and its near-term impact as an indicator signaling significant change in direct action was another thing. Indeed, the prototype was a church-specific pure moral exercise in the struggle to undermine and to overturn historic and current culture-intensive anti-Black race values. But the difficulty of the task-responsibility was complicated and made impossible by the doctrine of the millennium pervading protypical McDill's premises.

Inarguably doubted, nevertheless millennarianism progressed as the lasting social conservative tradition of classical Christianity and Calvinism as irreversibly as it neutralized the rational civil order reform potentialities of the enlightened secular humanist and/or religious humanitarian power elite.

In the matter of stabilizing or changing the condition of the caste/captive class, the high priority of securing the status quo united the upper-, middle-, and lower-class Protestants. It was dictated as much as anything by the equally compatible and complementary connection between the logical social conservatism, the rational conservative realism revered by the secular and religious powerhouses, and the popular millennarianism embraced by the Evangelical patricians, proletarians, and pedestrians.

Of course, the clear directives McDill and company issued were neither rare nor common but preponderantly promulgations of Old Abolitionist churchmen primarily in the West. The minority formed the Old Abolitionist grassroots constituency in the Presbyterian-Congregational denomination before William Lloyd Garrison (1805-79) turned up New Abolitionism, and turned the abolition business of religion into a moral science; turned out a new profession; and turned into a professional by creating an alternative moral weekly to the secular dailies.

Profane newspapers were by design of editorial policy normally anti-Black race values voices of public opinion, in which pages an apology for slavery frequently appeared under guise of neutrality. Black and White churchmen had prepared the way for Evangelical Garrison's *Liberator* (1831), and while Black Old Abolitionists who had turned into New Abolitionists were responsible for its survival, they neither made it notorious nor popular.

Concurrently, as antislavery churchmen, various Evangelical denominationalists were well behind their Quaker brethren. But the mainstream White Protestant congregants and churches reached their antislavery zenith under the command of their ministers, who had abandoned partisan party power politics as decisively as if the public had discharged them from civil politics and charged with keeping taut the private morals and conscience of the community. These parsons and parishioners evolved in the West the majority in the nation among the abolitionist publications' financial supporters and subscribers.

Contrariwise, in the Northeast, Black churchmen were the critical mass whose subscriptions enabled the *Liberator* (at least if not Garrison also) to survive during the first years when Garrison reported to the public he attracted few White paid subscribers. As a creative minority, New Abolitionist clergymen predictably normally neither represented nor led either the majority or the consensus of their congregations--since the numerical and moral majority in the ecclesiastical and civil sectors frequently were indistinguishably. Prior to the dramatic presence of Garrison, as the white knight of truth in the shining armor of moral uniformity, the *Christian Intelligencer* appeared to certify (in March 1829) that Old Abolitionists were in large agreement on a matter of importance:

> *The Emancipation of the Slaves Practicable--*
> *their Mental and Moral Culture Impracticable.*

Current conventional wisdom passed for understanding in high and low circles wherein, also was harbored the self-fulfilling prophecy that the Black race could not be qualified for equality with White race or ethnic groups by anyone anywhere, in or out of slavery.

Forthwith civility and common sense fostered this fashionable canard as a petard by which establishment petardiers maimed the Black body and sharply defined the caste/captive question and issue of crisis. And no less evidently than they created the climate in which the ACS's deportation program was acclaimed the judicious and righteous answer.

But there emerged even in the antiabolitionist Colonization Society different emphases.

Some of its members arose to question the antislavery Society's pro-gradualism process and to state their preference for the immediatism principle of abolitionism was based on the demonstrable greater good of its end justifying the lesser evil of its means. As in other issues of faith and ethics where there appeared as many points of view as believers, churchmen held a hundred opinions regarding the complex question of slavery.

Thus it was not surprising that the majority refused to surrender their differences in interpretation of the slavery problem and solution to the single answer Garrison demanded. He commanded each Christian individual, church, and denomination to acquit the body, mind, and soul itself like the Religious Society of Friends in one sustained denunciation of slavery, and commitment to abolition.

Any doubt about whether slavery was an absolute or relative value for the class of secular and religious White Anglo-Saxon Southerners was removed when slavocrats managed to crystallize and to govern the slavocracy, with a commanding mandate from the electorate and the broad and deep consent of the governed who left no reasonable doubt they expressed the general will of the people, forty-five years after the ratification of the Constitution.

Democracy's slavocracy crystallization occurred as an aftereffect of the exacerbated Yankee and Cavalier conflicts of interests during the acrimonious Congressional debate over the Missouri Bill, which ended with the second great Compromise and White Gentlemen's Agreement.

In the aftermath of the Missouri Compromise when the uncompromising slavocrats established the solid slavocracy, as the evident Anglo-American Southern English imitation of Victorian Age British Imperialism, it was a foregone conclusion that foreign and domestic mission-minded Northern Evangelical Christians--who were enjoying their double covert and overt operations and Protestant power connections as interlocking operatives of the national proselytizing denominations and the ACS--would be unable to agree either to include or to exclude fellow churchmen-slaveholders from their national church.

The Northern antislavocracy v. Southern proslavocracy conflict of real interests and values expanded and contracted until the developing irreconcilable political and economic differences resulted in the frac-tionalization of the Northern antislavocrat and pro-slavocrat churchmen, which added severe stress to the already intensely strained relations between them and their Southern slavocrat brethren.

Finally the division of the Presbyterian national denominational body precipitated the schism of the Methodist and Baptist denominations.

This severance of the most populous Evangelical Churches occurred when the controversial issue concerning the Christian consistency or contradiction of either the antislavery or the proslavery principle and practice was pulled out of caucus to be debated and voted upon on the floor of the nationally united denominations' ecclesiastical conventions.

Without offering a thousand objections, the Northern bisected and headquartered "Old School" majority and "New School" minority Presbyterian Denominations initially managed to secure slaveholding Southern churchmen.

The establishmentarians in the competing Reformed Denominations continued to share values, and none more centrally than their common contempt for the Garrisonian call for universal opposition to a strict constructionist/static interpretation and affirmation of a dynamic interpretation of the sacrosanct documents: whose premise and process projects an antislavery God, antislavocracy Bible, and abolitionist Constitution.

Garrison's compatible dual Evangelical and abolitionist religion turned out to be for the union of pure reason and pristine ethics, and against the mixing of morals and power politics. He understood his ethical conclusion ("the United States Constitution is a covenant with death and an agreement with hell") to be merely an application of his moral analysis and principle of justice.

But the descriptive fact and value judgment was too political for the Colonizationist and antiabolitionist establishmentarians, and pure political rhetoric rather than reality for the pro-political New Abolitionists.

Aggressive pro-gradualist and pro-immediatist antislavery men and women formed competitive and marginally influential pro-political minority groups, existed in the churches on the fringes of anti-political ecclesiastical power, and sought to grow and convert the whole community.

For this reason and obvious other ones such as the disestablishment experience, Northern churches as a whole, (unlike the Southern churches generally, and Presbyterian churches variably, which were respectively active in partisan politics), were given to accept the warnings "against meddling with political parties, or secular disputes."

Of course, in spite of their strained relations, their natural rather than strange selective confrontation on disparate matters of importance, and cooperation on common interests, resulted in the consistent-in-principle and inconsistent-in-practice anti-political/apolitical establishmentarians--or standard de-viations from the Evangelical Calvinist pro-political norm--and Garrison sharing the free of politics moral force only rule of thumb.

Absence from political engagement proved a principle that high principled

Calvinist principals selectively strictly applied religiously, practiced perfectly as objective or subjective participants in the slavery controversy, elected not to apply as warriors in their battles for religious freedom, and rigid moral absolutist Garrison invariably implemented as his litmus test.

Exceptions proved the rule although they occurred frequently in the battles fought and won in his war on proslavery and anti-Temperance forces, wherein, despite his intentions of inducing peaceful and constructive radical and rapid rational moral change rather than violent transformation of cultural structures and values, apolitical Garrison's politics of moralisms effectively delayed more precisely than it denied or prevented the inevitable clash between right makes might wrong (Garrisonians) on the one side, might makes right (Northeastern proslavocrats/Southeaster slavocrats) on the other side, and might makes wrong right (Tappanites) on yet another side generated a force for radical social change.

He failed to demonstrate conclusively to the mind of the slavocrats and Northern proslavocrats that its power was distinguishable in consequences from partisan party power politics. The majority of mainstream Protestant principals were major moralists, for the same reasons Evangelical Calvinists were also as well as model moralists, because they were natural or birthright social conservative Christians; neither accidentally nor incidentally dutifully resigned "to enforce, by precept and example, cheerful obedience to lawful authority"; and at once rather less ironically than paradoxically alternately one and at odds with Garrisonianism.[10]

At this juncture in the overview, a brief consideration of the ecclesiastical politics of slavery ensues. Church power politics dynamics were the precipitating cause of the early antislavery legislation enacted in the Presbyterian and Methodist denominations, a brief statement of whose development is set forth to elucidate the difference (or distinctions and the difference they made) between early national era church-centered antislavery activity, nonsectarian Old Abolitionism formed in the eighteenth century, and the 1830-commencing New Abolitionism.

Prior to 1845, New England was preponderantly the self-imposed boundary for both the original Puritan fathers' Calvinist Orthodoxy and their Yankee sons' Congregationalism.

Congregationalism was a comparatively late-emerging national denomination, and like the Baptist Denomination will not be included here partly for this reason--and partly for the reason that Congregationalists and Baptists are treated in my volume entitled *Puritan Race Virtue, Vice, and Values 1620-1820*.

The Baptists will also be excluded because of their peculiar history as Calvinist cousins of the Congregationalists, with whom they vied in selective religious rather than civil liberty-demanding power politics battles; general opposition to central church government; and their very firm but not inflexible rule of local autonomy or self-rule of each congregation and independent authority of each minister, whom few Baptist Associations (or coordinating regional bodies) could presume to speak for on any question save religious freedom and liberty of conscience.

While Methodist Evangelical Arminians and Anglican Latitudinarians were polar opposite wings of the Church of England before they were transformed denominations (respectively in 1784 and 1789) with American independence from England the Methodist Episcopal Church and the Protestant Episcopal Church, and both suffered a credibility gap in the minds of Patriots who suspected a statistically significant number of being Tories and Loyalists, only the Methodists will be included in this narrowly scoped construction.

This limited analysis of the Arminians reflects reality, in which Methodists moved as a missionary sectarian rather than civil culture governing body of believers from their inception.

The broad theocracy and comparatively sharply reduced post-Independence ecclesiastical power in civil affairs of the Episcopalians was analyzed in my book on *Anti-Blackness in English Religion 1500-1800*.

And the Religious Society of Friends is exempted from this deconstructionist probative interpretive critique due essentially to the fact that the Religious Society of Friends--as a result of Quakers forsaking power politics in the midst of the French and Indian War--distinguished herself as the only American ec-clesiastical power to have, to hold, and to give up civil power; a pacifist Denomination unlike and like other Protestant peace Churches; and a competitive capitalist class from Calvinist capitalists and Quakers' other fellow English race representatives, who were similar onetime theocracy hierocrats but dissimilar current partisan political crusaders for Christ and civility as well as Christian combatants in war and peace.

BRITISH-ETHNIC PRESBYTERIANS' EARLY BRIGHT

BUT BRIEF PRO-BLACK RACE MEMORIALS

The Synod Of New York and Philadelphia formed the hegemonic core of the Reformed churches who founded and organized the denomination they denominated the General Assembly of the Presbyterian Church in North America (1787). The denomination's developing social ethics in the relatively liberal environment of the post-Independence early national era was partially reflected in the recommendations on slavery promulgated by the 1793 General Assembly.

They were informed by the Enlightenment-engergized and Revolution-realized doctrines of Christian universal liberty, and secular self-determination of each individual human being, legitimate independent church, and sovereign state. The presumption that all the "Old School" and "New School" congregants of the Reformed Church were true members of the one human species and family of God formed the background, as certainly as the "pursuit of happiness" foundational principle underpinning the Preamble to the Constitution existed in the foreground, of the Assembly's call for Presbyterians to "promote each others' happiness."

From this mutually fertile sacred and profane moral standard, and ecclesiastical and civil sector obligation, there followed the duty of Presbyterians to "maintain the rights of humanity" and to "teach the obligations of Christianity." Presbyterians were directed by the supreme judicatory, and therefore these all legitimate power and authority obeying and law and order abiding churchmen pledged "to use such means as are in their power to extend the blessings of equal freedom to every part of the human race." Reformed (Presbyterian) "churches and families" were urged by the General Assembly--in the very "warmest terms"--to do "every thing in their power, consistent with the rights of civil society, to promote the abolition of slavery, and the instruction of negroes, whether bond or free."

The predominantly Scotch-Irish Assembly's authorities promulgated this 1787 British-ethnic Calvinist memorial in the year the Constitution was ratified, and before the erstwhile Presbyterian son, Benjamin Franklin, issued his *Appeal* in

1789. But this pre-antebellum criterion of cardinal Christianity would not approach the point of implementation by the establishment "Old School" and "New School" Northern (to say little of the separate Southern) denominations until the Civil War carried forth waves of benevolent instructors from the North to the freedmen in the South.

By this time, the color caste/captive die was cast for Black free-born native Americans in the Northeastern and Middle Atlantic states--where English-race capital and management united in urban manufactories and industrial capitalism with Scotch-Irish labor and other British-ethnic working-class to exclude Black-race competitors.

Inevitably the Reconstruction-era exemplary deeds of Presbyterians necessarily could not be social redeeming actions they intended. This was particularly the case since these remarkable ameliorative programs of parochial and private charity--although combined with equally trendy and transitory partial public or Federal aid--were too late and too little for the positive structural change of a society whose majority-comprising intensive minorities held fast to their anti--Black race religion.

The dehumanization power inherent in the anti-Black race interest these White ethnic aggressors demanded was demonstrable deterrence-benevolence. Its conver-sion to equalitarianism could be achieved only by cultural determiners committed to elevating the color caste to equal status with the race/ethnic class.

While the postbellum society was not about to undo its past, in order to redo its present, Presbyterians revealed that the leadership of the Christian community concentrated their resources belatedly but as early as any American institution in education--which they both correctly considered indispensable and mistakenly thought was the alternative to real power and wealth rather than also a part of the complex solution to the outcast condition.

Earlier the 1787 Assembly addressed the Presbyterians throughout the nation in a pastoral letter wherein presbyters concluded that African ethnic folk were transformed deethnicized American Black

> men introduced from a servile state to a participation of all the privileges of civil society, without a proper education and without previous habits of industry, may be in many respects dangerous to the community, therefore they earnestly recommend it to all the members belonging to this communion to give those persons, who are at present held in servitude, such good education as to prepare them for the better enjoyment of freedom.[11]

A generation later, the 1815 Presbyterian General Assembly was reminded of the "action of 1785 with respect to the buying and selling of slaves by way of traffic." Apparently these delegates further listened to other promulgations communicated to previous representatives such as that however unavoidable the "transfer of slaves" might be, "in some sections of our country," the Presbyterians' final legislative and adjudicatory Assembly considered both "the buying and selling of slaves by way of traffic" and the "undue severity in the management of them" as "inconsistent with the spirit of the gospel."

BOLD BRITISH-ETHNIC ANTISLAVERY ACTIONS

Three years after the delegalization of the international slavetrade, the rapid decline in slavery was as firmly and widely expected by the surviving Old Abolitionists as the expansion of the domestic slave-trade was unexpected.

One branch of the Assembly, the Scottish Associates Synod of North America's Presbytery in Kentucky, drafted antislavery legislation for Synodical action in 1811 that was promptly defeated decisively by Presbyteries in Virginia, North Carolina, and South Carolina. The Synod's Kentucky Presbytery was equally as far reaching and unsuccessful in its consideration of its duty to prepare Black Calvinists for civil life. These were neither fully anticipated nor unanticipated nondevelopments, due in part to the optimistic spirit of the antislavery hopeful and the Presbytery's own powerless status relative to the power Presbyteries and its location on the Western Frontier. But the Kentucky Presbytery was as clear as the Eastern establishment Presbyteries in its operating assumption: Black brothers and sisters in Christ would abide in their native land as free citizens.

They were manumissionists from the South who converted to se Old Abolitionists in the West. Upon arrival, they embarked upon the business of making the Presbyterian Church an abolitionist clone of the Religious Society of Friends and Old Abolitionist Societies. But within in a few short years the Presbyterian clergy-led and Presbyterian Assembly-adopted ACS emerged as the matchless antislavery organization of the major Protestant Denominations, quickly neutralized through massive nullification strategies and tactics the Old Abolitionist Societies.

On the Frontier of democracy and slavocracy, the Southern manumissionist and abolitionist Presbyterians advanced their triple bottom line, which they published in lucid prose whose eloquence of expression matched the ethicists' ethical excellence:

It is a moral evil to hold negroes or their children in perpetual slavery; or to claim the right of buying or selling them; or of bequeathing them as transferable property.

This model moral and religious principle for private and parochial or public personal practice, and civil community standard, was a political and economic statement fully as much as it was an ecclesiastical legal prescription. As abolition law it ruled conformance to immediatism in order, whereby all Black bondage-owning Presbyterians under the Presbytery's care were "directed to set them at liberty, unless prohibited by civil law."

And regarding the form and function of education for civil performance and Christian promise, this Presbytery certainly considered it indispensable and efficient if not also sufficient that Presbyterian slavemasters and slavehirers ensure their Black Calvinist slaves were "taught to read, and instructed in the principles of religion."

By 1831, the majority in the Scottish Synod seemed convinced they had debated the issue long enough, and given the recalcitrant more than ample time to change their ethical attitudes and behavior.

In that year the Synod voted to exclude all slaveholders from all "its subordinate judicatories" forthwith. However, being idealists and intentionalists as well as realists, the rule of exception was appropriated as an instrument of simple fairness and equity for slavemaster members residing in the slave states who proclaimed their commitment to "*moral emancipation*." Its meaning for intentionalists was straightforward.

Slavocrats had rescinded the pre-slavocracy's (early national period's) liberal manumission laws in the slave states, and replaced them with "*Black Codes*" proscribing private and parochial (to say little of public) liberation of human bondage. Hence those slavocracy residing slaveowning members of the Synod were exempted from ecclesiastical law (A) whose declaration of agreement officials accepted as being in compliance with their ruling that "slavery is clearly condemned by the law of God, and has been long since judicially declared to be a moral evil"; and (B) who promised to disengage from direct involvement in slavery when civil laws established by public opinion and politics no longer bound the private conscience by prohibiting the manumission of slaves.

The fundamental flaw in this process was its bad timing. Between the original pronouncement and its promulgation the slave states were transmogrified into one solid slavocracy. Slavocrats tolerated in the slavocracy neither proabolitionist nor antislavery public thoughts and actions. And, as partially disclosed or at least reflected by the Kentucky home of this antislavocracy Scottish Presbytery, the slavocrats forced Southerners of both persuasions to choose between remaining either in the slavocracy or true to their principles.

Convening at Chillicothe, Ohio in 1826 as the Scottish Synod's antislavery compeer in the Presbyterian General Assembly, the Associate Reformed Church of the West Synod managed to unite the antislavery position promoted by the Scottish Synod with a pro-Colonizationist commitment. The expansion of the Synod's concern with Black Presbyterians entailed recommending that the body inaugurate and sustain "annual collections to aid the funds of the American Society for colonizing the free people of color."

Led by effective synodical presbyters, and antislavery leaders of this regional organization of local Presbyteries, the Synod initiated action and generated instant illumination on two levels--that is, revealed by its positive possibilities for the color caste/captive class on the hand, and endorsement of the American Colonization Society's absolutely sincere intentions and relatively good and bad consequences on the other hand, the true nature and purpose of the national Presbyterian Church's antislavery policy.

British-ethnic "Old School" and "New School" Presbyterians managed to negotiate an ecclesiastical alliance with the English-race "New Light"/"New Divinity" Congregationalists, whose 1801 Presbyterian/Congregationalist denominational union occurred at the moment when the Federalist Party began its decisive decline that was precipitated by the sharp rise of the Democratic Party.

Their Plan of Union simultaneously functioned effectively as a mirror image of the expanding Evangelical Calvinist proselytizing opportunity, and not to impede but to accelerate the progress of the Federalist Party partisan parsons' defection of power politics in direct proportion to the rapid demise of their revered Federalist Party. Coinstantaneously, on behalf of the Orthodoxy and Reformed traditions, Second Great Awakening Scotsmen expanded proselytization of Black Americans on the Frontier of the South and the West.

The subsequent ACS and evolving colonizing interest of the establishment Presbyterian Church demonstrated the regression and progression propensities inherent in the Second Great Awakening, the opportunistic revivalists and the opportunity evangelists channeled to develop Protestant institutionalism, and the imperialistic missionary dynamic of the Mother Church of Scotland and Evangelical Independent Churches in Britain.

FORTHRIGHT EARLY ENGLISH-RACE AND BRITISH-ETHNIC
METHODISTS' AND METHODISM'S ANTISLAVERY RULES

Simultaneously counterdemanding change from moral reform to ethical revolution advanced in the Chillicothe Presbytery. This largely missed but no less momentous Old Abolition preparation for New Abolition materialized in the early 1830s, when the Old Abolitionist minority of Presbyterians but majority among the predominantly "New School" emigrants and sons of immigrants from Scotland and the South who dominated the Chillicothe Presbytery were converted by Calvinist proabolitionist agents from gradualism to immediatism.

The Old Abolitionist pace set by the early national Presbyterian Church was met and matched if not surpassed by The Methodist Episcopal Church, the Arminian chief competition of Calvinist faith ethics, who formally separated from the Church of England and formed a new denomination organized as Annual Conferences (or regional bodies) in December 1784.

At this organizing Methodist Christmas Conference in Baltimore, the initial class of the previously all non-ordained White Methodist preachers were ordained clergymen (elders). Forthwith Methodists were no longer required to celebrate Holy Communion in an Anglican Church, and this change provided Methodist ministers with additional authority and disciplinary power.

They were empowered to deny the Lord's Supper to those members not in good standing. Correlatively, during this initial Conference, the rule was put into effect requiring bondage property purchased and inherited Methodist ministers and members to liberate their slaves. But it was unenforceable and therefore effectively suspended within six months.

Representatives of the heretofore autonomous Annual Conferences first collectively convened in the original Methodist General Conference at Baltimore in 1796. The initial *Methodist Discipline* (comprising the laws of) the Methodist Episcopal Church condemned the "crying evil," the "great evil of the African slavery," and made allowances for the fact that Methodism's largest constituency resided in the slave states.

Unlike the Congregationalists and Presbyterians who were stymied in their numerical growth by the high standards of education established to qualify candidates for the ministerial profession, and dissimilar to the Baptists, who recognized the untutored man who believed himself called of God and whose congregants followed suit as the local minister, the Methodists were less rigid than the former and more demanding than the latter regarding the matter of clerical certification.

Methodism advanced Arminian theology but also differed from these rival Calvinist denominations in its ecclesiology and methodology, rational organization, and method for expansion and discipline.

The uniqueness of the Methodist ministry lay in Methodism's systematic and systemic itinerancy rational organizing principle of the central church governance ecclesiology. This bishop-presiding elder (district superintendent)-pastor directed system included traveling ministers in charge of a number of churches on a circuit, as well as elders normally appointed pastors in charge of a single church for a year or two and routinely reassigned on a regularized rotation basis.

However, since great distances prevented circuit riding elders of several Methodist churches from meeting once a week with each local congregation's classes or lay societies and leaders, lay leaders were the hands-on trustees in charge of the day-to-day Methodist people and programs, albeit responsible to the minister for the spiritual care and discipline of the society in his absence.

This highly organized and efficient bureaucratic command and rational control methodical Methodism system operated efficaciously as a mechanism; gave the Methodists (in relation to Baptists) a competitive edge at first; and succeeded as a productive process because the principle practiced primarily promoted prescribed and proscribed lay involvement.

Pursuant to developing clergy and lay power and authority, the 1796 General Conference ruled in this context and without pretext that a slaveholder could join and remain a member in good standing in a Methodist society on one condition--namely that the preacher whose appointment by the bishop entailed "oversight of the circuit" spoke with him directly about the Church's antislaveholding principle.

Just as the slavocracy evolved and the power of the lay proslavocrat expanded apace, it followed axiomatically in neither fact nor experience nor reality but in logic and theory that a clergyman-slavemaster and/or layman-slaveholder was excluded once he had received and rejected the instruction of his bishop or elder.

Concurrently the abolishment of slavery by Vermont and Massachusetts, successively and instantly upon establishing their state constitutions, outmatched the gradual abolition laws in the other Northeastern states and exhibited a difference in degree so great as to be a different kind of liberation from Virginia's enac-tment into law of a liberal private manumission statute.

The synchronic intention of the Methodist instrument of realism in the pre-slavocracy era loomed no less self-evidently than its inevitable consequence in the slavocracy was necessarily the compromise of principle, and the principal parochial practice of the art of politics. Civil law and order abiding Methodist delegates to the General Conference were elected clergy/lay legislators and judges for the ecclesias-tical body, made law, and published their enactments and interpretations in *The Discipline*.

They achieved ethical distinction and earned high marks for ruling in order immediate exclusion of any member "who sells a slave." The church law was accompanied by the civil proviso that prior to completing their human bondage transaction, taking their purchased personal property title deed, Methodist slavebuyers should "execute a legal instrument for the manumission of such slave."

Hereby Methodism contributed significant to the voluntary involuntary servitude Christian paradox and paradise prolific Protestantism proliferated. Par for the competitive Evangelical inherited and cherished color caste/captive course as well, the implicit standard for the explicit antislavery/proslavery Methodist model is the slaveholding moral law of the Deuteronomic Code and conscience cut to suit the current fashion.

According to this Calvinist and Arminian legalists' so highly honored and violently violated Old Testament legislation, the God-ordained Jewish slave-master of his poor Hebrew brother and sister was required to liberate the enslaved Jewish cultural kith or kin either within seven years or at the "*Jubilee*"--which ever came first. In the liberal interpretation of the otherwise equally fateful and faithful inerrant truth of the Bible and literal Word of God transmitting "Consistent Calvinists" and Arminians, a necessitous member of their Black-race cultural kin-group could be purchased morally correctly if the "Elect" right and righteous slavebuyer committed himself in advance of executing the legal entitlement to liberate his human bondage within a definite delimited period of a few years at most.

METHODISM'S RUSH FROM ABOLITION
TO ANTISLAVERY/PROSLAVERY VALUES

In short, a Methodist slavemaster ought (A) to purchase in order to liberate a slave; (B) to liberate each and every slave; and (C) not to sell a slave either as a matter of personal privilege or as a means to the end of securing liberty for the slave.

Rather more than mere expedience and convenience, the demanding priority of securing real interests was the primary reason why the rule prohibiting the slaveowning rights and restricting the slaveholding responsibilities of Methodist churchmen was abrogated in 1784, and the effort to reinstate it was defeated in the 1796, 1804, and 1808 General Conferences.

Each minister, by contrast, was ordered in the legislation enacted by the 1804 General Conference to manumit his slaves legally forthwith, "if it be practicable," or "forfeit his ministerial character to the laws of the State in which he lives."

Relative to the Calvinist Baptists and Presbyterians whose expansion centered in Virginia, which had enacted a liberal private manumission law, the preponderant proliferation of Arminian Methodists occurred in North carolina, South Carolina, and Georgia.

Their pre-slavocracy less permissive and more psychologically inhibitive if not legally proscriptive private manumission civil laws prompted the introduction and passage of an amendment to Methodist Church law, that exempted elders in these three states from the nonslaveholding ecclesiastical rule and ethical regulation.

Substantially for the same reasons why Methodists relished their extraordinary growth in the Old South slave states, the 1804 General Conference (1) initiated innovative constructive engagement of "Consistent Calvinist" and Arminian Christian social conservatism; (2) overturned the proabolitionist standard raised by founder John Wesley; and (3) directed ministers to "admonish and exhort all slaves to render due respect and obedience to the commands and interests of their respective masters."

Thus the success human bondage owning British-ethnic Methodist clergy and laymen enjoyed in saving thousands of Black slaves' souls--in combination with the walkout of the denomination of Black parishioners in comparable numbers in the late 1700s and early 1800s to form independent Black Methodist denominations--rendered null and void any serious Christian and civil education systematic thought or plan for the inclusion in the warp and woof of American society of even their own considerable Black constituency.

White Methodists engineering their Black Methodist folk's relative ascendancy with all deliberate speed, compared to ensuring their descendancy beneath contempt but not beneath notice, was always the possibility--if never the promise--of the English race-inspired British-ethnic people who prided themselves in being methodical.

The Methodist people's failure to perform in line with their greater possibilities than promises was not impeded, of course, by the full course press of Calvinist revivalists against Arminian evangelists that Methodists scarcely suffered gladly. Yankee Congregationalist sons of the Puritan Patriots appeared to extend a continuum initiated by Jonathan Edwards in their theological attack upon the Evangelical Arminian-Loyalists, which emerged in the appearances as a thrust in the inferiority reflex directed by a superiority complex.

In reality, "Consistent Calvinists'" persistent Arminian-bashing most certainly did not give Methodists much reason to hope they could sustain the suspicion of being inferior "people of God," or the charge leveled by the superior "chosen people of God," and take charge in the crisis of confidence and conscience by developing a design for the advancement of their color caste/captive class that would be well received by the power elite whom the pro-Calvinist and anti-Calvinist Yankee sons of the Puritans dominated.

The Methodist Annual Conferences regularly agonized over the issue of slavery at their regional meetings, and in their local churches from their inception throughout the antebellum and Civil War periods, primarily outside the South which boasted the largest Methodist contingent. The ecclesiastical wars-excited determination to escape scot-free from the agony of defeat and into the ecstasy of victory set a sharp edge on the slavery debates at each subsequent quadrennial, or General Conference of the Methodist Episcopal Church.

The delegates found the polemic controversies on the pre-1845 denominational dividing convention floor not only argued the facts and figures but for surrender to the interpretation that in "the South and West all civil authorities render emancipation impracticable."

Officially, Methodists (certainly some Methodist officials) were concurrently concerned to see that "our colored preachers and official members have all the privileges" which the "usages of the country in different sections will justify."

In actuality by 1824, Methodists were without peer in refusing to ordain elders and granting local preacher licenses to Black pastors of Black congregations but not White churches also--save for the conspicuous exceptions who as exhorters to parishes peopled predominantly by slavemasters and slavemistresses were mostly slaves under the thumb of White clergymen.

The absolute difference between the preponderancy of White-ethnic elders and Black-race preachers issued forth unmistakably in the law passed by the 1824 General Conference, which made it legitimate to command and control the Black pastor in a stabilized state of dynamic powerless and statusless by authorizing that "any of the annual conferences may employ colored preachers to travel."

Any reasonable doubt concerning the simultaneous liberal and conservative faith divergence and social ethics convergence of the competitive British-ethnic Calvinist and Arminian English-race representatives was removed when the 1828 Methodist General Conference voted to adopt a resolution approving the ACS.

This good housing keeping stamp of approval, and declaration to Black people that they were an ungrateful body who (A) protested without warrant their being delivered into the good hands of the race removal *raison d'être* and (B) possessed no right to be wrong, put Methodist authorities in league with nearly every other establishment Evangelical denomination.

In light of the Methodism's embrace of the anti-Black race interest-specific ACS denationalization process and deportation purpose at the end of Old Abolitionism and beginning of New Abolitionism, condemnation of radical abolitionism by the 1836 General Conference of the Methodist Episcopal Church was neither astonishing nor alarming but an illuminating reflection of the central church government, social conservative faith and ethics, and mainstream Protestant-centeredness direct connection between the Cal-vinist Presbyterian and Arminian

Methodist mind.

QUAKER JEREMIAH HUBBARD'S PROCOLONIZATIONISM

These New Abolitionism era's antislavery/proslavery church-specific ambivalences were fairly characterized as being neither for either Black folk or abolitionism nor against proslavery public principles, state politics, and ecclesiastical and civil laws: or the private practice of proslavocracy privileges by Christians in the slave states. And because revered "states' rights" legalized-slavery and their Constitution were set above conscience, benevolence-deterrence generally prevailed throughout the denominations during the first three decades of the nineteenth century. Professionals expertly developed state-of-the-art antislavery/proslavery vacillation into antislavocracy/proslavocracy alternations and alternatives, whose delicate balance was maintained by antislavocracy/proslavocrat theological and social liberal and conservative Protestants in the North.

Precisely these polar contradictions in the Evangelical denominational hierarchies and local churches provided the indisputable evidence of their inability to manage change, crisis, and ambiguity. They preferred to facing reality, therefore, to presume the perverse pride and prejudice presence was so far from being a complicated many splendored phenomenon scarcely more complex than the pure and simple truth and consequences they alone possessed, preached, and proliferated.

No less incontrovertibly, in the different consciences of churchmen within these same collective color-conscious churches, their Black race positive negation critical impositions also created the wish that fathered the thought of a single standard, to wit, religious and secular civil liberty in freedom and justice with respect enjoyed by each individual North American.

And, in the ensuing debate between the color-conscious antiabolitionists and proabolitionists, the quest for pro-Black race and pro-White race/ethnic egalitarianism crested in the formal call for "instant liberty" and the "with all deliberate speed" response. In due course, the ecclesiastical engineered pro-immediatism v. pro-gradualism shaking of the founda-tions resulted in a divided house and a home for the wedge Garrison drove between Christian Colonizationism and New Abolitionism.

The heart of the matter for antislavery Christians was revealed in the June, 1834 issue of the antislavery Illinois *Christian Intelligencer*. The editors printed in that edition a copy of a letter sent by the Reverend Jeremiah Hubbard (1837-1915)--Clerk of the Yearly Meeting of Friends in North Carolina--to a Friend in England in which he articulated in a lucid and concise statement his vision of the American dilemma.

Elder Hubbard was in a good position to know the evidence validating the truth he published without fear of contradiction, and to encourage belief in his empirical data-based value judgment:

> The Southern people have no more idea of the general emancipation
> of slaves, without colonizing them, than the Northern people have
> of admitting the few among them to equal rights and privileges.

Hubbard's realistic analysis of the slavocrat solid mind and undivided will overpowering fellow Southern Colonizationists led him to a calm and clear statement of a correlative fact, the implications of which were as unsettling as he knew them to be:

> Not even the Friends of humanity here think that a general eman-
> cipation, to remain here, would better their condition.

This Southern Religious Society of Friends standard or deviation from the American Quaker norm undoubtedly constituted an informed reaction molded to fit public opinion, to facilitate consensus, and to adjust to reality. Southern realism and managed reality included the *"Black Codes"* prohibiting slaveholders from liberating their color-specific chattel.

Hubbard understood slavocrats enacted into law this private property rights-restricting state-mandated and public-approved restricted covenant (A) to preserve the "peculiar institution"; (B) to secure the slavocracy whereby the designed firm but not fixed legal instrument opposed in principle the means and ends of Colonizationism, yet made its mission impossible more difficult rather than a Cotton Kingdom exercise in futility through sharply constricting the ACS from a broad-gauged to a narrow-scoped movement operating under the constraints of delimited special exemptions from the law permitting manumission of select slaves for whom colonization in Africa was guaranteed; and (C) to protect the permanent perpetuation of the Southern Way of Life established a singular exception to the rule the sacrosanct rule of the exception or made a sacred exception the rule, to wit, the continuous antebellum slavocracy positive law-transcending custom law effectively commanding private manumission or immediate "emancipation" of each Black man or woman who saved the life of a White man or woman .

Hubbard was certain that the dyed-in-the-wool slavocrats and the ultra-abolitionists held in common a total reprehension of the Colonizationists, albeit for completely opposite reasons. New Abolitionists were equally confident of their double bottom line: (1) extinction is the near-term destiny of American democracy's slavocracy, whose certain terminal end is not prevented but postponed by equally unethical and advanced technology-based life support system manned by Northern and Southern proslavocracy efficiency experts; and (2) the utilitarian value of the American Colonizationists inheres in facilitating the extension of the Southern Way of Life, and thus neither frustrate nor deny but delay the fate of the "peculiar institution."

Reactionary extremist defenders sensed so sharply the clear and certain dissolution of the slavocracy until its imminent demise became the "primary cause of their discontent," pro-Colonizationist Hubbard averred. And the poor ACS performance that to his antiabolitionist mind appeared the great tragedy seemed to the pro-abolitionist comparative culture analysts a sad but true civics lesson in classic conservatism.

He confirmed his worse fears in his specious reasoned arguments. They argued that are conspiratorial frame of reference constructed by the proabolitionists induced the slavocrats to liken the ACS to a trojan horse in the slavocracy.

Were he released from the intense pressure and dynamic tension occasioned by being a devout Quaker and devoted Southerner, Minister Hubbard may not have chosen the ACS "mild" and gradual but irreversible deportation of the entire Black race solution he clearly preferred to the real alternative.

But his private real estate interests and personal conventions gave birth to his own invention of the not decreasing but "gradually increasing influence of the Colonization Society." The White Southern Christian gentleman's idolization of overreaching counterchecks of the color cast/bondage class' true and real interests that Black leaders proclaimed to the public was a shared value and vision, and one bifurcation of reality that the Northern American religious establishment revered and promoted as Calvinist charity.

Yankee adversaries relentlessly anathematized the advocates is if they were certified Yankee and Cavalier brutal benevolence marketeers, driven to manipulate the market in order to generate a demand that would supply their need for the elusive deterrence-benevolence fan-tasy; clear and present dangerous delusion; and positive harm-intensive White Nationalism cause of reactive Black Nationalism.

The Garrisonian militant moralists were so aggressively nonviolent until antislavery/proslavocrat Hubbard felt called upon to publicly admire their courageous truth, condemn their judgment as being a perfect prescription for violence, and report that the *Liberator* is "counted incendiary" in the slave states and instantly confiscated by Federal postal officers.

Antiabolitionist Hubbard's Quaker-specific repugnance for military and political force--which Garrison shared and published with intense passion--was greater than his repulsion of the psycho-physical violence Black folk suffered. In the tension between his rigid and inflexible principle, and the equally firm con-straints of dehumanization experienced by fellow Black Southerners bound in mind and body by mental and corporeal cultural chains, no real relief or choice ex-isted for the color caste/captive class.

Hubbard left the distinct impression that he was congenitally programmed to accept the slavocracy as the great reality and certainty, as he roundly condemned the New Abolitionists on the grounds that the "general course of their efforts...appear to be hardening the slaveholders." His solid White state solution that he launched in the Cotton Kingdom did not fly but crashed flat in the teeth of the cotton gin.

The pre-antebellum presence in the Old South of the initial "cotton picking" machine, and the subsequent revisions of the original patent advancing it throughout the antebellum era into an increasingly efficient "cotton picking" separation mechanism, guaranteed two certainties in the Cotton Kingdom: The permanent absence in the antebellum slave states of (A) known resident abolitionists, and (B) a solid reason to think that the planter class would discontinue determining policy in the slavocracy according to democracy's majority rule which slavocrats translated fifty percent of the ballot casting voters plus one; release their slaves voluntarily *en masse* to the ACS; permit the minority to overturn the institution; and end slavery on their own terms in time or even history.

THE FORCE OF POLTICAL INFLUENCE AND PRESSURE

PREFERRED BY QUAKERS TO THE POWER OF POLITICS

The Religious Society of Friends' ecclesiastical abolition set a precedent that mainstream churches did not follow, yet the Quaker Church failed as flatly as other Protestant Denominations in the private and public power realms to produce a "revolution in sentiment"; a caste/captive-deliverance driving desire to supersede "
the spirit" of the American culture and character; and an inclination to make the Quaker religious humanitarian standard the secular humanist model for ec-

clesiastical and civil law.

The Quaker initiative within the Society of Friends neither died nor found complete satisfaction in denomination. Certainly compared to the development of the Religious Society of Friends from their American headquarters in Pennsylvania, parochial Quaker Puritan abolitionism contrasted sharply with the pure public Calvinist Puritan abolitionism.

Specifically, with regard to the slave-free states of Vermont and Massachusetts, fewer religious-specific than secular-specific but no less real Yankee sons of the wayward world saints proclaim Massachusetts the first slave-free Colony to join the Union.

Their English Quaker and Calvinist Puritan disconnected ecclesiastical and civil abolitionist ethics set the standard for the church and state; demonstrated --over time and through time as well as in time--to the sensible and sensitive general interest-directed public servants and social ethicists the best known possible right and good of Black and White Americans; and revealed the indispensable need to execute constructive rapid social structural change.

The color caste/captive issue vanished with slavery among the pro-Calvinist and anti-Calvinist Puritans who were united as late as 1800, as Federal Party partisans prior to the commencement of its decline and the rise of denominations, and divided as professional sacred moralists and profane politicians with parsons turning anti-political agents of the state but concentrating upon creating the indivisible Evangelical body of Christ. Concurrently, Quakers advanced abolitionism beyond the borders of New England from a church to a state question.

In their Old Abolitionist Societies, Quaker Puritans originated antislavery political petitions, and influenced Calvinist Puritan-Yankees who later followed suit in their New Abolitionist American Anti-Slavery Society. Even after the near-identical twin birth of the ACS and the slavocracy, but before they began to wax and the Quaker initiative commenced to wane, agencies and agents of the Old Abolitionist Societies throughout the nation consistently engaged in praying Congress to enact "national legislation to be brought to bear direc-tly upon the slaves."

Hubbard apparently perceived these continuing developments as harbingers of different conditions, that required direct opposite plans and procedures instead of creative extension of the traditional strategies and tactics. He appeared barely distinguishable from compeer social conservatives and pacifists who are absolutely certain violence is never the best course of action because it is always wrong; and nonviolence is always best and right or never wrong.

Hence Hubbard affirmed and justified the eighteenthcentury eradication of slavery in the Religious Society of Friends by arguing from the strict constructionist premise the narrow-scoped point that Quaker abolitionism was not a public-imposed state law but a parochial-mandated private nonslaveholding church law; a prerequisite for good standing in the Stated Meeting of Friends only; and a model citizens were free to adopt or reject with impunity.

Since this critical imposition of ecclesiastical and not civil law was strictly a matter between Friends, Hubbard asserted, Quaker authorities were correct to "compel them to emancipate their slaves." But New Abolitionists were declared engaged in neither correct nor corrective action but only in the dangerous error and evil business of superimposing their private and parochial virtue as a public value.

Even Old Abolitionist political action, which Quakers restricted to the American pragmatism process of directing petitions "against the evils of slavery" to Congress, Hubbard determined to be at best neither praiseworthy nor blameworthy but incendiary. As a principled proslavocrat and anti-political Moral Reformer, and purist who managed to argue partisan politics was both an immoral exercise and a pure rational and power-free field, the rigid moralist denigrated advocates of single issues and special interests who used the democratic instrument of peaceful political pressure because they engaged indirect partisan politics.

Complementarily, Hubbard directly condemned partisan party power politics proabolitionists, who played hardball politics with slavocrats to secure public abolition, as provocateurs pressing "a style and manner that savors more of the spirit of those would ask for fire to come down from heaven to consume their enemies." The representative of what passed for the proslavocrat Southern Quaker mind, and the reactionary through conservative to moderate Christian mind in general, Hubbard could not admit that the political petition approach of Old and New Abolitionists was purely moral and democratic nonpartisan politics.

However a much a threat proabolitionists were to antiabolitionists, their radicalism fell far short of the full needs required to sustain the Black race in an egalitarian society. Abolitionists majored in liberating slaves in the North and the South whom they struggled to protect in the North, and minored in initiating experimental ways and means to secure equal access to opportunity for free Blacks in the North.

Proslavocrats in the North and the South were supported by the Constitution in demanding stabilization of the status quo principle, and declaring the Black American was not an individual--or a constituent element of republican democracy and Evangelical Protestantism--but the exception who proves the rule of Black race exclusion.

Self-determination, every Enlightenment instructed and enlightened self-interest observant post-Independence era American affirmed, is both an absolute and the distinctive feature of the human being; the bare essence of whose liberty in freedom nature and destiny is individual-in-community and community-in-the-individual existence for the mutual enrichment of the independent, dependent, and interdependent individual and community, whose rights and responsibilities appropriately begin with the pursuit of happiness and end in the improvement of the human condition.

Nevertheless, radical and reactionary antagonists in full dress rehearsal for civil war, to revolutionize or stabilize culture values, were proponents of mutually exclusive social ethics principles because the aggressive adversaries advocated different purposes and ends which justified their means.

Productive proabolitionist direct actionists per-formed in public as if they believed in the in eradicable identical "*Alien Dignity*" of and presence of the Creator in each created mortal; liberty as the gift of Providence to each new born person--that God cannot rescind without canceling history but man can abrogate; and in liberty as the indispensable precondition for full human existence and complement of "*Alien Dignity*." Few were discovered who doubted self-determination is the necessary possession both for full development of human potential and prevention of dehumanization; the universal natural birthright whose security is foremost second only to securing life or the first among equal high priorities; and anything less than self-determination is self-defeating, community-restricting ethnic group-limiting, race-diminishing, and human species-undermining.

The counter-culture liberationists' powerful pro-Colonizationist, proslavocrat, and pro-gradualist opposition acted as if deterrence-benevolence was singularly and solely for Black folk an empirical rationalism universally verifiable, valid substitute for liberty: in theory, logic, and therefore in truth and life. Whence the firm foes of Black Magic (experiential experimentalism) and friends of White Magic (experimental empiricalism) appropriated rationalism; engaged specious premises which if accepted produced incontrovertible logic; and denied liberty and delayed freedom for the Black race.

These sincere intentionalist and serious consequentialist social ethicists were not only solid rationalists but Protestants who believed in the "Rule of Scripture," the "Rule of Truth," and therefore understood comprehensively the Christian *agape*-love ethic. They defined it in their voluminous publications as acting in the best known good interest of the enemy, in order to persistently activate and consistently expand the fairness and equity possibilities of the democratic--secular justice ethic--that is, aiding each individual and group to gain their legitimate claim.

But instead of these color-conscious and caste/captive-securing "*true believers*" energizing the *agape*-love/power/justice ethic, the advocates of expedience conveniently neutralized these universal and particular virtue-enhancing and vice-limiting instruments of Christian social ethicists. This exercise of reason and the will to power enabled Protestant powerhouses to rise above demanding *agape*-love and justice to secure their expanding existence at advantage, paralleling the existence of Black folk at risk and disadvantage.

Like the Puritan and Anglican fathers, their English-race and British-ethnic Yankee and Cavalier sons' advanced the color caste/captive class continuum. Their achievement was also accomplished through the skillful deployment of the power tool of reason, which resulted in a successful execution of the deethnicization first strike--or preemptive strike--of African ethnicity, and immediate creation of their Black race-only genetic and cultural kin-group.

The progenies of the progenitors completed their positive negation/attraction act of creation with a critical imposition of sympathy, empathy, and charity upon their Black race: whereby the color caste/captive class was permanently pressed beneath the real interests protected by the pragmatic dogmatists and dogmatic pragmatists.

Being one of these innate English superiority complex types, Hubbard could not allow that the New Abolitionists' positive error-repelling and truth-attracting, rational organizing, and driving positive-intensive antiblack white-ethnic virtue principle was checking--if not balancing--the anti-Black race spirit; that it was attuned to "the first shall be last, and the last shall be first" dictum of the slavemasters' Master; that it was directed to advance the true (rather than the real) or the best known possible right and good interests of the Black race above not the true interests and values of the White race but their real anti-Black race interests and values; and that it was as liberationist faith and ethics direct action the courage to be, to know, and to do the relative truth or best good possible "of those that would feed them if they were hungry, and if they were thirsty, give them drink."

Hubbard was a revisionist Quaker minister, a Friend unalterably opposed to Protestant parsons and parishioners who interpreted their public servant task-responsibility to mean private and parochial employment of the *agape*-love and justice social ethic in the secular/civil sector to expand the general interest and common good.

He had managed simultaneously either to ignore and to deplore or to implore and to adore the power and wealth of William Penn--the upper-class slavemaster-Quaker and Pennsylvania proprietor--rather less than the Quakers who constituted the hegemonic power of the Pennsylvania Province legislature prior to the French and Indian War. The hostilities saddled Quakers with Hobson's Choice, and they elected as a class to abandon abruptly and forever civil power leadership and partisan party power politics.

Evidently Hubbard had conveniently forgotten the highly competitive as well as productive and wealthy Quaker capitalists could afford the luxury of practicing their principles unlike Black folk, on the one hand, distinguish themselves from White folk as peer-less practitioners of their principles, on the other hand, and, on yet another hand, comprise the non-proselytizing Religious Society of Friends whose success nation-wide as the model White presence and Black absence bare essence in manifestation was not matched non-rival denominations.

Hubbard was entirely satisfied to avoid the selective sacred/church and secular/state moral principles of Friends, and to attend their pacesetting promise and performance of benevolence. They interpreted conformance with the Christian ethic to require the harmony of love and justice in mutually fertile acts of private faith, parochial community, and public society. Forward from opting out of Pennsylvania legislative leadership and power politics, Quakers elected to move the benevolence of Friends from public-coordinated action to private/parochial sector-concentrated charity, and to leave love to pure reason/"inner light"-guided moral motives and money measures--unsupported by power politics-determined law and justice.

Thus their praiseworthy abolitionist activity left liberated Black subjects and objects greater beneficiaries than victims of their beneficence yet dependent upon personal relations.

This positive and strong support system proved to be equally invaluable and temporary or transitional. Without exception, after delivering to the liberated generous gifts and grants-in-aid such as liberation resources and start-up funds to compete in the system, Quakers abandoned the Black powerless to enter participatory democracy's public power politics competition and civil affairs realms of ethical suspension: dominated by the powerful intensive ethnic minorities who comprised the American majority Quakers could selectively engage and disengage.

The culture-pervasive anti-Black race interest-specific spirit Black folk could not exist clear of and Friends failed as Quakers either to manage and neutralize or to escape scot free of, was evidenced in the power elite's greatest strength and weakness: (A) the absence of not only both the need and desire of power but either the imagination and/or the reason and the will to relate appropriately real resources to the whole rather than only a part of the need of the poor and "truly need" they appeared to save; (B) unnecessary excessive reverence for personal influence and the power of the purse or faith in parochial charity and private philanthropy; and (C) undue disregard of the relative virtue and value of the rational exercise of power in American pragmatism, or faulty equation of vice and power politics public justice.

Instead of uniting private charity and public justice with parochial power in the civil sector to serve the special interests of the Black race, Quakers, in a classic demonstration of why in the conflict of real interests negative good ethics is neither positive good ethics nor good enough, chose perfection rather than the best possible--that is, to avoid the reality of power and selected the device of saving Black individuals from the vice of bondage.

Quakers elected to maintain their apolitical principle, and to refuse to permit the Black race to become an exception to the rule: presumably because principled Friends were consistent moral perfectionists who were earnest and honest but no less certain believers in the erroneous idea that an exception does not either prove or confirm but challenges or overturns the rule.

Friends liberated hundreds of slaves. They fed, clothed, housed, and instructed thousands of these Black fugitives and freedmen. Once this humanitarian task was accomplished, Black beneficiaries were directed away from the Quaker Stated Meetings and societies, howbeit domestic servants were encouraged to live in a separate enclave nearby, and encouraged to locate a church and domicile elsewhere.

Without equally efficient endeavors to remove the color/caste condition, Friends discharged Black folk before Quakers completed their self-initiated obligation--that is, Black folk were liberated without the rights of the White race/ethnic individual-specific American, barred from equal access to economic opportunity, and political participation rights and responsibility.

Precluding Black members of the Quaker ménage (whom Friends educated) from the Religious Society Friends, and excluding them from membership in Quaker-led Old Abolitionist Societies was one thing; including Black neighbors in the abundant blessings of charity was another thing; and not enabling the Black-race cultural kin-group their fathers enslaved, deethnicized, profited from, and turned into a color caste/bondage class to achieve economic, political, and social rights was an omission resulting in consequences of a different dimension and magnitude.

There were natural and cultural irreversible reasons why Quaker Puritans made a perceptible difference in reversing the color caste and bondage values relative to the nearly imperceptible difference Anglican and Calvinist Puritans made. Anti-Black race virtue was a fundamental dynamic determining American social reality, a preferred religion, and ultimate concern of White citizens in the North and the South, East and the West.

These values were inflicted by White race kin-groups upon their Black kinsfolk with vengeance, and such force until there resulted the mutual affliction of internal conflict in and between White-ethnic and Black-race communities.

This reality slowly advanced through ever-intensive dynamic interrelations of abstract theory and concrete experience to a heightened social consciousness, and convincement of a higher conscience than Constitution.

It ended in the truth and guilt elective affinity, whose demanding radical and rapid rational social structural change effect was a contributing factor to the rise of the New Abolitionists.

Precisely because they perceived the power of demanding anti-Black race drives, and knew that in isolation they possessed insufficient power to neutralize anti-Black race desire--let alone ride it out of the new Union--New Abolitionists became a righteous force composed of the tenuous combination of Enlightenment reason; Christian persuasion; and individual moral power. Even before a minority added political partisanship, the combination ethics bewildered nominal members of the church and society.

The unvarnished condition of Black Americans left them entirely without a viable option, and surviving between more debasement and less despisement. It could be underestimated only with tortuous logic--and then with the greatest

COLOR-CONSCIOUS CONSTITUTION, CHURCHES AND CHURCHMEN 135

difficulty--once it was attested to by a virtuous White Christian lady, and native of Hubbard's Southland. This revelation appeared after the eruption of New Abolitionism. Ironically, it was a factor contributing to the marriage between the male descendant of Northern "Old Light" Puritan Calvinism and a female descendant of Southern Anglicanism: the two American establishment religions of the English race, that fostered anti-Black race virtue as a matter of course from the beginning of the Anglo- American plantation.

ANGELINA GRIMKÉ-WELD'S PUBLIC

ACKNOWLEDGMENT OF HER BLACK NEPHEW

The near-Reverend Thomas Dwight Weld (1803-95), an Evangelical-Calvinist Congregationalist convert to New Abolitionism, married (in 1838) the Charleston born and bred Anglican, aristocratic Southern belle, and daugh-ter of a planter---Angelina Emily Grimké (1803-79). Several years prior to their nuptials, she moved from Charleston and relocated in Philadelphia where she converted to Quakerism--under the direct influence of her sister who had become a Quaker convert earlier--Sarah Moore Grimké (1793-1873). Angelina Grimké, in turn, after becoming a convert to New Abolitionism (in 1835), both converted her sister Sarah to the movement and led her out of the Quaker community.

Angelina flouted Quaker discipline, which forbade women equal status in public roles, when she not only began to speak in public on controversial issues but quickly became a sensation on the lecture circuit in 1838. She flaunted her independence by marrying a non-Quaker that year, and the choice of defiance rather than compliance with Quaker law resulted in the ex-communication of the sisters by the Friends. Angelina Grimké-Weld practiced her preachments to the point of arranging for one half of her bridal attendants to be Black Philadelphians. This unconventional biracialism shocked the sensibilities of the Friends and induced them to expose their fine distinction between violence and force, and nice nuance between exercising power and discipline, when Quaker elders promptly dismissed her on solid grounds of infraction--specifically, the violent violation of Quaker rules governing the relations of both a Friend and a friend.

In more serious matters, she spoke with unimpeachable authority. The Grimké sisters persuaded their mother (in 1838) to give them the family slaves as their share of the estate--whom they promptly freed. Any question regarding her thorough, if less than complete knowledge of slavery--obtained not from armchair theory but through intimate experience so concrete as to be uncontrovertible--was laid to rest subsequently as a result of public revelations of the relations between her brother, Henry Grimké (d. 1852), and a slave woman, Nancy Weston.

The children Henry sired and for whom Nancy bore the stretch marks made Angelina the self-acknowledged aunt of Archibald Henry Grimké (1849-1930): the crusading Black author, who, with her help, graduated from Lin-coln University (B.A., 1870; M.A., 1872), and Harvard School of Law (LL.B., 1874).

Eighteen thirty-eight was a memorable twelve month period in Angelina's life, and an exceptional one with regard to her relations with Black Philadelphians. During the course of that year, the Pennsylvania Hall in Philadelphia was dedicated and, on the occasion of a Feminist convocation during the celebration in the facility, Grimké-Weld offered a controversial resolution.

It revealed, in its adoption, that at least some radical abolitionists understood the anti-Black race value to be a phenomenon whose power and presence they might not have the capacity to eradicate but should floodlight:

> Resolved, That the prejudice against color is the spirit of slavery, sinful in those who indulge it; and is the fire which is consuming the happiness and energies of the free people of color.

> That it is, therefore, the duty of the abolitionists to identify themselves with the oppressed Americans, by sitting with them in places of worship, by appearing with them in our streets, by giving them our countenance in steamboats and stages, by visiting them at their homes, and encouraging them to visit us, receiving them as we do our fellow White-citizens.

In this statement for the record, Grimké-Weld did not simply put forth her own highly personal improvisation of a sentimental theme. She also sounded the major chord which the early New Abolitionist minority en-deavored to march to but failed in their short-lived attempt.

Their unsuccessful and fleeting crusade against color/caste was due less to failure of nerve and more to their interracial counter-culture style and substance striking the societal race sensor and color censor, inciting a collective conscious' vicious and visceral mass public reaction and massive resistance, and exciting in the stunned provokers of pro-White race pride and pro-White ethnic prejudice a value judgment: Whereas liberation from bondage had proven possible ever since its long history of success, abolition of caste proved impossible and even an exercise in futility not because it had been tested and proven to fail but because it had never been tried.

IMMEDIATISM AND PRO-BLACK RACE PRINCIPLES

In lieu of a comprehensive and long range plan to secure equal access to opportunity for free Black Northerners, New Abolitionists initially called for social equality.

The short-cut to the mainstream social engineering strategy and tactic was agreed upon by consensus and implemented to demonstrate, by turns, that the pre-clusion of status was the cause of the exclusion of competitive functional station, and that positive Black race respect is the best means to end immediately and permanently the outcast color caste/captive class condition.

Black and White cultural symmetry cancelling asymmetry was not the extreme but the mainstream view of New Abolitionists, when the immediatists began their crusade in the 1830s.

Biracial equality quickly became a private vision and personal persuasion of the precious few with little public expression--and thus failed to become a serious criterion of authentic New Abolitionism--largely because anti-Black race forces admitted no challenge to their rule for respect-worthy classes and races.

Affirmation and disaffirmation of the Black race as well as the Black person were competing alternate New Abolitionist tendencies, because proabolitionism was largely--at first and in the main--the synthesis of the Christian thesis (*agape*-love) and humanistic antitheses (individual liberty and justice).

This Protestant philosophical and theological, sacred and secular, and personal rational and private moral union of common essences--at their frail and extreme ends--disallowed serious respect for and sustained support of the unique and distinct Black race-only (rather than also individual-specific and ethnic-intensive) people.

All the normal complex reasons why the color/caste class remained an intractable cultural pariah group existence predetermined the marginal difference the Moral Reformers made. For one, the initially the New Abolitionist leadership cadre was primarily analogous to a nonestablishment Calvinist Puritan raising of the social ethical locks--by the power of Enlightenment humanism--which the fathers created to dam up anti-Black race virtue. For another, the driving force of original New Abolitionism entailed a particular Puritan Yankee Evangelical-Calvinist faith-restrictive and ethics-intensive personal moral salvation.

Its reform spirit sprang from the same cultural changes creating the Arminian mass evangelism movement, the democratic control of churches, the Enlightenment and Revolutionary views of individual liberty, and the voluntary associations.

Further, the humanistic theme of the equality of all men in the political state, where personal freedom was guaranteed by law and reason and the legal system of justice, complemented and complicated--when it did not compromise--the Christian verities: the love of God, neighbor, self, and the enemy; the fatherhood of God and the brotherhood of man; and the inviolable worth of the individual.

The state granted and guaranteed these rights to each individual or White-ethnic male--to promote his happiness and the prosperity of the general welfare.

The traditional Evangelical commitment turned on extending the blessings of faith, or primary means of grace and salvation, to the members of the church alone. This parochial proclivity excited the revivalistic, proselytizing, and missionary zeal to win everyone (including Black men and women) to Christ. But this very particularity set rival sectarian Evangelical churches on a collision course with secular universality.

Secular humanistic universalism transcended the Evangelical criterion by including all White-ethnic men, and creating its own preclusion rule which excluded all Black men from the citizenry and commonality. Secular humanists acted as if the fairness doctrine and equity principle were generalizable at best and not universalizable, when Black Americans were theoretically viewed as an additive in the "no taxation without representation" equation.

One result of this profane and sacred bifurcation of the White race/ethnic class and the color caste/captive body was the division among Christians, and between Christians and secularists, over the question of in-cluding and excluding Black folk in church and state--as *bona fide* full-fledged members with all the rights and privileges as well as responsibilities appertaining there to.

Some liberal parochial Protestants struggled to apply the secular rule of universality for the White ethnic individual-only to Black brethren in the private and public realms. Counteractant compeer churchmen appropriated the American standard constituent element of individual worth and dignity and endeavored to use it as a fair measure and power leverage mechanism to include Black faithful in the church--who were currently confined and segregated especially in their all-Black autonomous sectarian fellowships--and to preclude Black brothers in the sacred sector from securing competitive legitimate claims in the secular realm.

Counterdemanding other Protestant decision-makers were determined to exclude Black kith and kin from the private clubs and civic voluntary associations as well as the church, on the hand, and, on the other hand, to include them in the civil arena. And still others sought to Christianize-Civilize-Colonize Black beneficiaries of deterrence-benevolence, and to enable them to achieve full sacred and secular as well as well civil rights exclusively in Black societies outside America.

Predictably the preponderance of Evangelical Calvinists and Arminians, who were antislavery/anti-abolitionists, attempted to fuse faith with ethics in a Christian program for Black brethren, whose distinguishing feature was the presence of pure moral law and "Rule of Scripture" and absence of power politics.

The power politics heart and soul of participatory democracy Arminian and Calvinist capitalists and moralists naturally preserved for the exclusive rights and privileges of White race/ethnic individuals. Certainly the representative model of this powerhouse class was their ACS--whose overarching millennium theme was also the Evangelical Arminian/Calvinist rational organizing idea and ideal.

Thus mainstream millennarians were antiabolitionists dedicated to extract a religious morality from genuine Puritan Piety faith and ethics and perfect it as a Halfway Piety faith and ethics modern moral model. Its manifest essence was deterrence-benevolence constructive engagement and progressive transformationism, that was not designed to be either flashy or what if became: a fabulously functional and fashionable secular/civil-free, total obedience-proof, and church-bound bad faith and worse ethic promoted as good enough for Black folk alone.

Establishment White churchmen applied this Halfway Piety to the secular society selectively--that is, were careful to prevent mixing of morality and politics, to avoid any public elevation of the color caste/captive class, and to restrict its application to parochial moralisms and private interests.

Black folk who had created their Black folk religion/ethic, from direct encounter and intimate involvement with Independence-era Evangelical Old Abolitionists, were saddled in the slavocracy with Evangelical reversion of their progression, when slavocrats wrote the "*Black Codes*" which ended autonomous Black leadership of independent Black churches in the slave states; and set White ethnic males in command and control of official Black religious life. Post-Old Abolition Evangelicals declared they possessed true morality that was born of born of true religion, whose nature and purpose was no politics as usual or political ethic at all.

This anti-political morality was anti-Calvinist, Halfway Piety, and a sharp deviation from the authentic Puritan Piety. This historic tradition involved the public servant parson and parishioner directing positive-specific antiblack white-ethnic virtue to drive evil and to attract good in the secular state and civil society as well as the church, and engaging in power politics to expand the general interest with love and power transforming justice.

This line of development was derailed by the Half Piety faith and ethics Jonathan Edwards standardized as a deterrence-benevolence ethic of churchocracy for christocracy. The Edwardsean reversal of traditional Calvinism was itself reversed Puritan parson patriots of the Revolution and the Independence era.

During which early national period New England Congregationalist Orthodoxy and Eastern establishment Presbyterian Reformed traditions united, prior to whose connection the clergy had become partisan Federalist Party power politics parsons. But, both like and unlike the abrupt departure of Quaker Puritans from power politics to moral influence, with the vanishing Federalist Party Evangelical establishment parsons turned from power politics to pure rationalism and pure moralism--that is, to pure pious protestants of poor profane performers.

The anti-political motive, message, and mind was possible and productive primarily because of the dynamics produced by the Second Great Awakening (1787-1816). Nonestablishment, British-ethnic, and Evangelical beneficiaries or democratization-intensive revivals (Methodists, Baptists, and Presbyterians), were distinguished both from the class of the English race representatives' descendants--fairly represented by the Puritan patrician/merchant-Congregationalists and Anglican aristocrat-planter/Episcopalians--and by their sparse representation among the elite Northern and Southern Protestants educated at Harvard and Yale.

Except for the Scotch-Irish in the Reformed tradition--growing in real numbers and power at Princeton and in the alliance with Orthodoxy--these British ethnics, new immigrants or older emigrants, had few genetic and class ties but many positive/negative theological associations with the Puritan-Anglican legacy of establishmentarianism.

Concomitantly, the ethnic newcomers shared no appropriate sense of either blame and guilt or responsibility and grace with regard to the color caste/captive-cursed class. But the White-ethnic immigrants and emigrants instantly adopted the Americanization of virtue and vice, and vigorously embraced immediately anti-Black race values. Their millennium thesis also freed the preponderancy to suspend any serious examination of their public ethic, which, in any case, fully supported the philosophical, theological, political, economic, legal, and social conservative doctrine and system of the American culture.

Stable variations and variables of these traditional varieties advanced without serious challenge through the first three decades of the nineteenth century. As a consequence of being born and bred in this cultural mode, the 1830-originating New Abolitionist Protestant Evangelical host separated private faith and public ethics.

Thus the majority of these moral radicals compartmentalized the millenniarian doctrine but did not reject it out of hand. One result of endorsing the selective utilization rather than engineering the suspension of millennarianism was that it added more intensity than tension to their direct actions and political directions. This effect was partly due to the formal and informal education of Calvinists.

The Presbyterians, who merely appeared to produce as many immediatists as gradualists, were schooled in the tradition of Scotland toward a humanitarian humanistic appreciation of society as a democratic body of liberty. The fulfillment of this religious and secular civil liberty in freedom they believed could be achieved through combining the Scotch Irish Reformed ethic with authentic Puritan Piety--private faith, parochial community, and public-interest ethics--and applying the duo-ethics to the secular/civil governance sphere. In their enlightenment view of a religious-civil society--comprised of an American Civil Religion--there was no public difference between the spirit of universality instituted in the Church and the Constitution.

The theological diversity and controversy, undermining church unity and

Christian community, was inundated by the optimism of three conflicting univer-
sals, which New Abolitionists believed to be one in consequence for the well
being of Black New Abolitionists and their countermarching contemporaries: (A)
the Christian estate, in which in the projected future-state of the millennium
there will be the universal rule of Christians; (B) the human estate, in which in
the present the Christian ideal of the fatherhood of God and brotherhood of
man applies to all--irrespective of national origin, race, creed, sex, age or
previous condition; and (C) the political estate, in which human rights and
privileges accrue universally to those approved (or approved by) White Christian
Englishmen.

Conservatives, liberals, and moderates selected portions of each universal to
support their antislavery and anti-Black race sentiments. The unity overrode the
diversity and bound them, tacitly at least, after the 1830s to the American Civil
Religion agreement--that gentlemen would not offend civil sensibilities, or the
White race, by openly advancing the newly consigned non-issue of White-race/
ethnic and Black-race equality. They averred that, after all, equality of the
Black race is a social question--properly relegated to private sphere of personal
taste.

The parochial construction--of Black race and White ethnic group equity, as
a private matter of freedom of choice--was a deconstruction and reconstruction
of reality. Its pragmatic dogmatism permitted antiabolitionist and proabolitionist
opponents to settle their differences regarding slavery in the public arena,
where political battles are appropriately waged. Defendants of either/or both
slavocrats and slavocracy were convinced this Northern pragma advanced as
dogma set them at advantage. And they believed that, as a consequence, even if
they could not extend the boundaries of slavery, the status quo could be main-
tained--since "*states' rights*" could not be abrogated without disunion.

Proslavocrats opined, correspondingly, that only the pro-Black race New
Abolitionists--who thereby proved themselves irresponsible--dared to engage in
such reckless, unpatriotic, and intemperate pro-equalitarianism rhetoric.

The English race's New World Puritan and Anglican feuding brothers--as well
as the later arriving and therefore normally reactive rather than formative determinants of American culture, their British ScotchIrish-Presbyterian kinfolk
other ethnic emigrants--did not lack the courage of their convictions. Clearly
they   were   not   reluctant   to   press   their   disputants   to   the   point   of
convincement--or on to the edge of despair.

The sheerly moral Puritan height reached its apex in Unitarian Congregationalist William Ellery Channing, the self-proclaimed Puritan descendant. He
emerged above and beyond the full-breasted Calvinistic puritanicalism, that
Evangelical Presbyterian Lyman Beecher roundly developed.

Protestant public ethicists contribute singular understanding to the meaning
and bearing of Black folk, and their prospects in this American religion of civil
defense and offense. What follows is an evaluation of these establishmentarians'
convictions of their courage, that begins with the color caste/captive class interests of Channing and Beecher.

2

WILLIAM ELLERY CHANNING: ANATOMY
OF A MODERATE ANTIABOLITIONIST

ORTHODOX PURITAN PIETY: PRIVATE

FAITH AND PUBLIC INTEREST ETHICS

Old and New England cultures were celebrated by Puritans as the origin and orientation of their original Evangelical-Calvinist (Congregationalist) philosophical theologians. Systematic Federalist Theology was the invention of their innovative minds.

This philosophical theology was developed to systematize Orthodoxy, the tradition of authentic Puritan Piety faith and ethics that comprises the traditionalists' hallmark positive negation of evil and error antiblack white-ethnic principle; criterion of virtue and vice; and posited objective and subjective truth means and ends to the ultimate Subject and Object, purpose and meaning of individual and community function and being, and relevance of absolute and relative rational values.

These pioneer Puritan divines also evolved either/or both the standard and the progenitors of emergent Yan-kee "Consistent Calvinists" who were, by definition, principally Halfway Piety revisionists of genuine Puritan Piety faith and ethics. They were conductors of the ever-expanding Catholic continuum from two highly revered predestinarians, who at least in the appearances emerged first among equals in the no less real for being invisible parthenon of the Puritan saints--Saint Augustine (354-430) and John Calvin.

Although the establishmentarians were consistent in being committed millennialists, and strangely inconsistent in not following Calvin who broke ranks with the tradition to become an antimillennarian, in this line of march the principal New England religious and moral minds were primarily classical Catholic and Calvinist Christian social conservatives; masterful logicians and rhetoricians; and masters of myth and reality, symbol and ritual, style and substance, and reason and revelation. Their propensity for mastery of rational and mystical reasons was evidenced in the apparently natural and congenital howbeit peculiar Puritan proclivity to concentrate their cerebral powers in comparatively major faith and minor ethics thoughts and actions.

It is not necessary to guild the lily since it is common knowledge the Puritan parsons and parishioners form a common sense collective conscience. Doubtless what becomes this Anglo-American legend most subsists of their individual and community mind-changing intentions and consequences, that are legion cultural certainties of considerable importance. Demonstrable macro justification by faith (in the righteousness of God or Jesus Christ and reason) and micro ethics theologians, Puritan and Yankee professors proved powerful preceptors. Their Puritan principles and practices contributed lasting values to the kaleidoscopic color-intensive culture's caste/captive crisis, of enduring significance for Black and White American folk. They left the issue unresolved yet not an academic question but a public interest social ethics matter of singular importance. This compelling legacy is best accessed and assessed by employing the faith and ethics constituent elements to analyze evaluate their rational reflection and direct action.

Given the legions of scholars and students keeping the legends in perspective, it is sufficient for this probative and deconstructionist Christian social ethics interpretation to on the moral meaning of the color caste/captive class condition for the powerhouse Yankee Puritan parson. Pursuant to this race and reason revelation, it is presumed that generalists in the American Academy of Religion and specialists in the American Christian Social Ethics Society have reached a long and honored broad consensus that establishes as the prototypes-from the beginning to the end of the diverse Puritan parson class--the Reverends John Cotton (1584-1652), Cotton Mather (1663-1728), Jonathan Edwards, Samuel Hopkins, and William Ellery Channing.

What distinguished these uncommon from the common varieties of synchronical Puritan moralists, in addition to their degrees of distinction that amounted for their admirers and critics alike to a difference in kind of Puritan social ethicist, was their particular form and function in their specific ways and means of being (to a remarkable degree) the Puritan host in themselves; their will to power; and their existence in essence coinstantaneously as the majority of one and representative of the Puritan establishment to and for whom they spoke.

Contemporary firm foes and friends encountering each *tour de force* as either/or both beneficiaries and victims bethought this perception is reality, the accessible contradictory specifications to the contrary not withstanding, and published their evincement in voluminous communications. Certainly these complex and perplexing productive professionals formed a formidable presence, on balance, even though their impact upon the Puritan Moral Majority scarcely occasioned equal effect and respect from power Puritans and powerless New Englanders; and they each escaped through double indemnity the double election and double damnation Black folk suffered but experienced measures of the good will and ill will the power elite usually reserved for heroes, heroines, and heretics.

The line essentially ended with Channing, after whom the Puritan parson was no longer *the* person and the Yankee professional was pressed in competition. Massachusetts State tax-supported (until 1836) Congregationalist-clergymen predecessors, contemporaries, and successors of Channing enjoyed the status redounding from their role as pure pious bureaucrat officials and technocrat professionals, conferred by pure profane civil authorities. This benefit accrued to the parsons, even though the public servants had long since lost the compelling force accruing from their real or presumed power over life and death--and respect born of the real threat and fear the powerful figures were in fact and fiction.

Traditional Puritan divines were masterful men who mastered many good and bad social ideas and ideals. Indeed, they were "capable of" perfectly immense "cerebration" in the process of administrating psycho-physical harm, and superimposing their predestined permanent color caste/captive class predilection throughout the "social situation made to their hands."[12]

Original, vintage, and authentic Puritan Piety entailed each individual and community being engaged--interacting private parishioner and parochial parish directorates--in directing their personal faith and ethics to secure simultaneously their special interests and the general interest, or the asserted equivalence of the public interest and the pursuit of happiness. This principal premise and principle produced a process consisting of employing the Puritan antiblack white-ethnic virtue: a rational and radical social structural change axiom professors skillfully utilized to promote positive personal and public good, and to arrest evil in the individual and community.

Jonathan Edwards was celebrated as the original Evangelical-Calvinist philosopher and theologian, empirical rationalist psychologist and protectionist, and peerless professor, prophet, and preceptor of the First Great Awakening. Following his death, an unfortunate loss of greatness that was tragic because the occurrence was not the result of natural causes but due to an unsuccessful battle with small pox complications, the Edwardsean "New Divinity" school was led by Samuel Hopkins.

Hopkins survived as Edwards' strongest student, friend, and disciple; first biographer; and champion successor as a millennarian logician, rhetorician, and metaphysician. Hopkins and his compeer Edwardseans included the Reverend Jonathan Edwards, Jr. (1745-1801)--his younger compatriot who also died too early and before him. They were "New Light" Old Abolitionist associates of "Old Light" Ezra Stiles, First Church pastor Hopkins' cohort as minister of the Second Church of Christ in Newport prior to becoming President of Yale.

These Edwardseans (the ethics friends and faith foes of anti-Edwardsean Stiles) were replaced as the legitimate heirs of revisionist Edwards by re-revisionist post-Edwardseans, who were led from idealism and in the formation of puritanicalism by Edwards' grandson and "New Light" successor of "Old Light" Stiles at Yale--President Timothy Dwight.

The virtue as well as the vice power dynamics of the antiblack white-ethnic virtue-device were instrumentalized by experts. But few of the Puritan professionals matched Hopkins, and fewer of his contemporaries surpassed the public promise and performance of the philosophical theologian. He deserved the credit he received and earned the title Orthodoxy's first and last (and very nearly only) establishmentarian theoretician and practitioner of Evangelical Calvinist Congregationalism to initiate and develop an innovative faith and ethics systematic theology that Old Abolitionism as the rational law and order of Calvinist dogma and pragma; rule of logic; "Rule of Scripture"; and "Rule of truth."

Secular and religious Puritans had accepted Old Abolitionism as a relative rather than an absolute civil power principle, and not also as an ecclesiastical power principle, primarily because it was given legitimacy by the "states' rights" clause in the Constitution; and upon admission to the Union the state of Massachusetts abrogated involuntary servitude. Basically due to these reasons, the post-Edwardseans emerged the American Civil Religion hegemonic powerhouses who argued that the case for the separation of church and state on the moral question of abolitionism was irrefutable; liberation from human bondage is a state and not a church issue; and whether or not birthright self-determination for White-ethnic folk complements the dehumanization existence of Black-race folk as subjects for human experimentation follows in natural law is the business of business and not the business of religion.

Several years after slavemaster Jonathan Edwards deceased and before the Revolution commenced slavemaster Hopkins sold his slave and resigned as pastor of the Great Barrington, Massachusetts Church of Christ, accepted his election as minister of the First Congregationalist Church in Newport, Rhode Island, and discovered Old Abolitionism in Newport and preached his new-found principles in this slavemart capital of Puritan New England.

In their proclivity for proclaiming universal liberty the natural right of their asserted individual and White-race/ethnic male equivalence, nature and nature's

God designed the Black male not to possess, Rhode Island slavemasters proved, by turns, a perceptible difference in intentions and imperceptible difference in consequences for the color caste/captive class from their representatives who negotiated the White Gentlemen's Agreement they denominated the Constitution of the United States of America, indistinguishable from fellow former slaveowning establishmentarians in the New England states whose legislatures were currently enacting into law gradual manumission statutes.

Distinguished from onetime Puritan slavemasters turned Puritan proabolitionist lawmakers, pre-War and post-War Rhode Island warriors in defense of their private profit and pleasure, and personal real interests in the Black body, were social conservatives who managed reality to oppose rapid and radical rational social structural change by defining it as revolution.

By the mid-antebellum, these Puritan decedents' Yankee descendants turned from revolutionists to reformers who made law and nonsense: by combing logic-laced nice nuances of parochial law and fine points of positive law to argue with the facts the case for the "*Spirit of '76*" being an American Independence movement and not a revolution. Social conservatives of Calvinist custom law, no less than the Puritan tradition of ecclesiastical and civil law, in their lexicon revolution appeared at once by definition and manifest bare essence the French Revolution. Alternatively stated, revolution in reality and theory generally but the French Revolution in particular the nobility-revering notables in nineteenth-century Orthodoxy despised more than they feared.

Reacting to the threat of secular humanism and skepticism, religious humanitarian spokesman for Orthodoxy manipulated the Puritan-patrician and Anglican-aristocrat Patriots' visions of violent and vicious Frenchmen actualizing a middle-class and proletarian "Liberty, Fraternity, and Equality" French Revolution to impugn the character and values of the equally dreaded New .Abolitionists. God-fearing antiabolitionists specifically utilized innuendo and character association to castigate Evangelical Calvinist proabolitionists, condemned immediatists through guilt by association with the caricatured Godless French Revolution, and denounced the French Revolution to the public as being the villainous source of abolitionist ideas and ideals.

Concurrently selective Yankee proslavocrats chose neither to recall nor to remind the public of other perfect parallel (if not equally momentous) turn of events. A significant one occurred prior to the American Revolution when the Evangelical English Abolitionist Granville Sharp, the self-instructed litigator, successfully litigated the case for liberty of the British slave James Sommerset that resulted in the abrogation of slavery in the British Isles.

Regarding the accelerating international movement for the universal abolition of slavery, following the signing the Treaty of Paris that officially ended the War between the English and the Americans, apparently it was also easy and convenient to forget that the French Revolution was first preceded and then drawled by British Abolitionism, the politics-intensive creature of English Evangelicalism.

Actually, in addition to the imperceptible negative effect in the United States of the social structural changes occurring in France, the direct influence upon the American mind of the French Revolution-galvanized secular humanist and democratic self-determination for each individual French connection did not undermine but complemented and confirmed the concentration of Evangelical Protestantism on each person being reborn.

Certainly Hopkins broke with the proslavery sacred Calvinist and secular

Puritan faith and ethics tradition before the French Revolution, in the era when pro-Calvinists had surrendered the Congregationalist conscience and church to the state: whose citizenry had compromised the abolition principles of the Massachusetts Commonwealth in order to secure preferred real interests.

Hopkins opened the Calvinist locks whereby the common good damned up faith-half and other-directed ethics-half of genuine Puritan Piety was enabled to flow into the antislavery movement. Coinstantaneously, and just as decisively, Hopkins' dialectical New Evangelicalism (thesis) and Old Abolitionism (antithesis) reproduced, revised, and sustained the historic anti-Black race Puritan ethic (synthesis).

Parallel negative consequences occurred in spite of his different motive, means, and message. The Hopkintonian Old Abolitionist innovative interpretation of the convention projected Black Calvinists buoyed on the high seas by a millennialism-evangelism-missionism mechanism, and transported to Africa on the high powered Christianization-Civilization-Colonization ship of religious humanitarianism.

Hopkins was one peer-prepared professional prophet and perception is reality prognosticator who most certainly knew he had a large problem on his hands and did not know the enormous extent of the condition encompassed what emerged as actuality in the appearances: The Black body would not float and Black people could not walk on water.

He focused on the facts and missed the meaning of this simple truth--that revealed the profound error of his truth claim--partly because, like and unlike the destiny determiner's predetermined past and present and ergo future fate of the charitoteer's color caste/captive class charity subject and object, the publicly projected people prediction and control forecasting powers of the forthteller were ironically efficient enough to analyze the physical nature and cultural nurture components of the perplexing civilization-created difficulty compounded by complexity and paradoxically deficient of sufficient capacity to discern the difference between the complementary and contradictory divine designed and human imposed nature and function of the Black race-only group.

Since Hopkins could not divine the irreversible essence precedes existence nature of the Black race, it is not surprising to discover that he lacked a fully developed appreciation of the legitimate claim of Black folk to being a North America-indigenous entity or whole body (rather than whole way of life) that is greater than the sum of her parts, and one undivided mind and will to attain the true and real interests and values of the Black people in their native land.

The Hopkinsian color caste/captive class double election and double damnation damage control system was designed to solve the problem Black race existence presented, whose functional utilitarian principle and efficient process entailed soliciting sufficient charity from White race cultural progenitors to generate great waves of deterrence-benevolence for their Black race kin-group to ride with great ease and no expense, that, once amassed Hopkins fully expected would sweep the Black body from the American upon the African shores, and leave both the Black race-only and the White race/ethnic groups--as well as their North American society--free and clear of each other.

A model rationalist, and Evangelical Congregationalist, the mind of Old Abolitionist Hopkins was so polarized by the intensive Calvinist faith and Puritan ethic bifurcation of reality until his will and reason were divided in the cultural crisis of consciences and constitutions.

Hopkins' good intentions and impeccable integrity survived his struggle with the Black caste and White class system, and surrender to pro-White race values. But so did the consequences of his rational thoughts and actions for the Black race he wished to save from the White race, in God and the church, and for their eternal escape from hell and salvation in heaven. Hopkins materialized as an uncompromising and relentless benevolent paternalist, who thought that by reason of innate superiority he knew the best interest of Black folk; did not need to inquire of Black heroes of the Revolution and other Black community leaders the nature of their true values and real interests; and proved equally sincere and serious, correct and accurate, and right and good.

THE PURITAN CONNECTIONS OF UNITARIAN

CONGREGATIONALIST WILLIAM CHANNING

In writing for the record that he possessed full knowledge of pure truth and error, and boldly engaging good while bravely driving evil, Samuel Hopkins proudly proclaimed himself the standard of Congregationalist Puritan faith and ethics; seemed the perfect symbol and sign of the Calvinist crusaders for Christ and civility--who as "Good News" and "Bad News" messengers managed their manipulative method and message through the medium of bearing gilded guilt and gifts; and appeared the self-fulling prophecy and prophet of the tradition or its manifest essence.

Puritan justice (perchance poetic justice) is the curious connective linkage and direct connection rather than close correspondence between Hopkins and Channing in the appearances upspringing from their common culture, induced by Channing who recalls their church association to relate their different time and space common cause and conscience conformance in the civil color caste/captive class.

The implied heightened consciousness (and/or sense of being called and chosen to clarify the proper Puritan race and religion relation) positive correlation, and posited positive feedback comparison but inferred non-denial denial of their being Puritan parsons engaged in contradiction and the sharpest conflict conceivable, are highly relevant in this context and critique of the Congregationalism converging and diverging Puritan and Yankee comparative culture(s)' conscious color-consciousness, color conscience, and change and constancy.

In this context, the absolute relevance for Channing of the cross-generation caste and captive crisis concern--that he conduced to control the condition--is relative to the more paradoxical or less ironic relation between Channing, the mind of English/race Congregationalism, and Hopkins--the deceased elder of the two Puritan parsons who passed for the last wayward worldly saint.

It involves specifically the millennialism-missionism-evangelism equally consecrated and concentrated Hopkins, who emerged in the Evangelical-Calvinist conservative faith and ethics culture a moderate faith and liberal ethics ethicist or radical religion man of Yale and Newport--for Evangelical Puritan Piety and Orthodoxy--and Channing the social conservative, moderate modern model moralist, philosophical liberal, and radical (private v. parochial or individual v. community) for Puritan pro-personal/private linear moral progress and anti-Calvinist Puritan hegemony in the American culture, church, and state. "Connecticut Yankee" Hopkins relocated in Newport--rather than any Boston divine in the "Massachusetts Yankee" city and center of competing Puritan liberals (liberalism) and Calvinists (traditionalism)--was the last of the pure pious Puritan saints, Evangelical Calvinist Edwardseans, and Old Abolitionist Congregationalist parsons.

Likewise metaphysician Hopkins was the first experiential experimentalist Calvinist theoretician-logician-rhetorician--in the New England Evangelical Puritan establishment line--to make abolition the universal categorical imperative dogma and pragma of the tradition.

The Newport-based master rationalist was also the last man in the world to give a quarter to secular humanist atheism and liberalism, and the first post-Edwards metaphysical millennarian to challenge the alternative to traditional Puritan Evangelical Calvinism that was currently rapidly rising in Boston Congregationalism. Preponderantly in Boston, after his death, Trinitarian Congregationalism proponents made their point stick by defining their opponents who subsequently officially adopted the designation Unitarian Congregationalism (c.1819) as the name of their new denomination.

At the height of his career and peak of his powers precipitously advanced the sharp decline in his personal prestige and of the Calvinist Puritan civil power, and the rapid rise of the new Evangelical Orthodoxy that post-Edwardsean "Connecticut Yankees" at Yale engineered. Into his power and orbit during this cultural moment, Hopkins launched a violent attack upon Boston liberals whom he called "infidels," but the return verbal blasts targeted by the liberal "Massachusetts Yankees" were no less vicious for being rationalized as right and righteous indignation.

Without objection from the establishmentarian traditionalists, with whom in matters of faith he shared values and in social ethics issues he had little or nothing in common as an Old Abolitionist, Hopkins intemperately anathematized the Boston theological liberals and social conservatives as the great "apostasy." Predictably, given the historic Calvinist Puritan intertribal theological warfare, the Hopkintonian inflammatory missive, and boomerang, they were anything but reluctant to return in kind.

Thus it was neither either strange or accidental nor incidental that from his Rhode Island community, and the slave mart capital of New England, arose a Newport-born young neighbor out of Hopkins' reckoning to become in his majority the Reverend William Ellery Channing (1780-1842). Subsequently, becoming in his maturity neither an Old Abolitionist nor a New Abolitionist but antiabolitionist Puritan, social conservative Channing evolved in Boston the rigid anti-political and moral reason-only antislavery standard of liberal secular humanism and religious humanitarianism.

Similar to Calvinist re-revisionist Jonathan Edwards who attained fame as a theologian for executing expertly a sharp turn from Puritan Piety public ethics to Halfway Piety faith, Channing, who managed disengagement from Old Abolitionism and resistance of New Abolitionism until the end of his long life and productive career and thereby to reverse the Puritan Piety proabolitionism values Hopkins advanced, was highly acclaimed far less for his social ethics initiative than for his leadership of the new American Puritan Association of Unitarian Congregationalists.

Unitarianism was an outgrowth of an offshoot of traditional Federal Theology roots and "Old Light" branches of theology. They produced "liberal theology" partly due to their positive integration of religious humanitarianism and secular humanism, and rejection of both Edwards' "New Light" and traditionalists' "Old Light" Calvinism. Unitarian Congregationalism was from its origin through its growth and development into a denomination a contrapletal Puritan formation. The Unitarian Society matched the Religious Society of Friends in incorporating Black congregants in statistically insignificant (if not imper-ceptible) numbers. But her substitution of philosophical morality for theological faith was exceeded in consequences for the color caste/captive class only by the anti-Calvinist body's power of elitism. This critical element may have been far less obvious than appears to contemporary adherents and antagonists, namely, an individual-specific and community-limiting private Protestant and personal Puritan moral academy, countermarching against the Puritan Piety social ethics "New Divinity" cadre Hopkins led.

The English Anglo-Saxon race reverence force progressed from an old and venerated Western Civilization continuation of reason and right. Commencing with Plato (427?-327 B.C.) perchance less precisely than with his student Aristotle (384-322 B.C.), the *Great Chain of Being* social conservative philosophy--of permanently superior v. inferior classes, ethnic groups, and races--proceeded perchance relatively unconsciously in the Orient and comparatively consciously during the succeeding centuries throughout the Occident. There it developed from rationalism into rationalization before it settled in the foundation underpinning the premises and principles from which the establishmentarian pro-Calvinist and anti-Calvinist Puritan ecclesiologies and theologies diverged, and in which their similar secular and religious social conservative civil ethics were fixed.

Channing evolved a young professional in "Old Light" and Boston/Harvard-centered Orthodoxy. Distinguished from "New Light" Congregationalist and "New School"/"Old School" Presbyterian Calvinism, "Old Light" New England Puritanism was English race commanded and controlled Congregationalism. As such in essence and manifestation, Unitarianism was virtually untouched by the Scotch-Irish Reformed (Presbyterian) tradition that British ethnics dominated. Essentially Unitarianism emerged from ceaseless rational modifications created by not only the successors but also by the surviving cohorts of the Reverend Charles Chauncy (1705-87)--the nemesis of Edwards and Hopkins--like "Old Light" Ezra Stiles, who was young Channing's first minister.

Unitarian Congregationalism slowly evolved as faith-liberated and ethics-enclosed liberal religion from conservative theological Trinitarian Congregationalism and finally erupted from traditional Puritan-Yankee Congregationalist Consociations. As the successor to Orthodoxy, Trinitarian Congregationalism in New England was the establishment Calvinist presence--compared to the relative absence in power of the Reform (Presbyterian) tradition. The Unitarian movement was a Congregationalist development essentially led by theological liberal and social conservative clergymen, who were in overwhelming numbers graduates of Harvard College--the center of Enlightenment in North America--and thus distinguished as a core of clergymen from not only the majority of Evangelical churches as well as Episcopal and Quaker minority but from all other Protestant denominations as well.

These theological liberal Harvard alumni, who managed to jettison the historic Calvinist faith and retain New England ethics, were also the clerical defenders of the conservative Puritan cultural virtues, vices, and values. This social tradition and its doctrines they reinterpreted with more profound logic than sound sense (relative to the tradition's political wisdom).

Having abandoned even "Old Light" Federal Theology, and rejected the Evangelical "New Divinity" theology--that Yale Congregationalists and Princeton Presbyterians were concurrently revising and correlating--the Boston Yankee theological liberals found Calvinism a sacred faith perplexity they were unable to relate to their religious and secular ethics complexity. They steeped themselves in British empiricism, and raised Enlightenment philosophy so far above theology they virtually severed the connection.

And in that separation both theology (the faith and ethics teaching of the Christian Churches) and Calvinism were nearly exchanged wholly for wholly the asserted equivalence of moral philosophy and ethical religion.

Hence harboring a philosophy of religion and deficient at best theological system of faith and ethics (the constituent elements of the great religions of humankind), and irreconcilably opposed to Evangelicalism and Calvinism, the Boston/Harvard Congregationalists were in contention more with the Evangelicals' application of logic in their systematic theology and revivalism that with the rationalism and social conservatism promulgated by the "New Divinity" school at Yale or the Andover Theological School it spawned beyond Boston. Both agencies of revisionist Orthodoxy were Trinitarian Congregationalist seminaries united with Presbyterians and Princeton to create and lead the Evangelical Protestant establishment.

PURITAN CLAIMS AND CALVINISTIC DISCLAIMERS

Unitarians equated Unitarianism with optimism, progress, the pursuit of happiness (maximum pleasure and minimum pain), and the lively future of civilization; and Calvinism with pessimism, retrogression, and the dead hand of the past that refused to bury its dead. Ignorance and/or innocence of the common culture were two things these fellow English/Puritan-race descendants could not be fairly accused of.

Whence Unitarian Congregationalists undoubtedly were imbued with certainty when they accused Calvinist Con-gregationalists of not seeking knowledge for knowledge's sake; and condemned Evangelical traditionalists on the charge they were millennialists who used reason to advance either their principal predestination point or preferred parochial process, private principles, and personal prerogatives.

Calvinists pleaded guilty as charged, on the theory that an unbeatable defense is the best offense, and aggressively argued the case for the superiority of their high priority faith and low priority ethics or theocentrism. Checking a defensive posture, liberals took an offensive stance to countercharge that their opponents facts and figures argued they advanced the glory of God and the "total depravity" of man, sacred and pure pious desires above secular and pure profane values, and existence in eternity over life in history. Unitarians denied they were effectively doctrinaire humanists crusading against Christocentric dogmatists at the same time the counterindoctrinationists affirmed they asserted in no uncertain terms that Trinitarians proved by their own arguments (for the greatness and goodness of God and the "total depravity" and misery nature and function of humankind) they were unworthy of serious consideration by serious men and women.

Yet they were no less absolute certain than the rival Puritan social conservatives that their straight-forward unconcernment with the color caste/captive class-condition central controversy in American culture exacerbated a crisis in neither conscience nor confidence nor credibility. Indeed, Unitarian and Trinitarian Congregationalists united as philosophical and theological liberals and accelerated their developing diametrically opposed premise and process; burst forth as a direct actionist polar opposition empowered by pure profane reason they engaged as a driving rational organizing principle; and committed consciously their equally proslavocrat counterintelligence to glorify the grandeur of man.

Forthwith in the face of universally verifiable contrary experience, nontraditionalists contended the evidence supporting their new Christian Humanism theory and practice was their contemners' reaction of stubbornness who thereby proved the rule and not simply standard deviations from the norm, whereby, instead of admitting perception is reality in the matter of exceptions, traditionalists asserted such an incredible turn of events lacks probability.

Straightaway, Religious Humanism advocates appeared adversaries of Christian Theism and turned the tradition inside out and on its head. In this dramatic performance they not only captured the attention but also concentrated the mind of the pro-Calvinist hegemony.

Coinstantaneously, the anti-Calvinist leadership created competing societies. Their basic premise assumed moral man and moral society is the new reality; primary motive, meaning, message, medium, measure, and method involves faith in the matchless force of sheer moral reason and distrust of political power; and the ultimate selective objective and subjective goal subsists of a centered commitment to improving the White race/ethnic individual, with whose elevation rises automatically the human race and condition. High principled Protestant parson and parishioner elitists who practiced their selective universal civility principles, and won high praise from the power elite, promoted as their chief priority the contraction of the sacred theism dynamics and expansion of the secular humanism dynamics of Christianity and Puritanism.

Such aggressive anti-Calvinist Congregationalists were so thoroughly persuaded that the Enlightenment and Revolutionary ethos of individual liberty constitutes the pure profane, one, and only universal standard of truth and justice until they managed, by turns, either/or both not to believe and to forget the individual functioned equally successfully as the constituent element of Evangelical Calvinism and republican democracy, to believe Unitarian Societies were nonsectarian because they consisted of positive egocentric (ethnocentric) rather than Christocentric and substituted the one-dimensional moral for the two-dimensional faith and ethics critical poles of the worldwide major religions, and to be convinced the complementary parochial-private-public individual/community-centeredness of the church and state was an obsolete rational organizational and institutionalization process in the irreversible stages of death and dying.

For these obvious and many other similarly familiar reasons, it is well-known that Unitarians deemphasized the individual and community criterion of human improvement and emphasized the values of the solo individual and secular humanism. This Cavalier aristocratic-class complementing Yankee patrician-class coupled with the human individualism and secularism perspectives a moral individual responsibility only (and not also community responsibility) viewpoint.

Its correlation as a continuum of the Puritan bifurcation of reality was evidenced in their demonstrated capacity to frown down upon the free caste and bondage underclass and incapacity to support the entity's ascendance from beneath the White ethnic lower-class. Their unprecedented individual responsibility and rights moral code also took hold in the new-emerging convergence from divergence of Yankee pro-Calvinists and anti-Calvinists whose Puritan ties, that Boston/Harvard-Congregationalist liberalism inevitably informed and was thereby informed, formed, and bound.

Hopkins' faith and ethics system had long since plummeted from the height of high academic respect and formal study at Yale Divinity School as a result

of the thrusts and twists of theological liberal Boston Unitarian Congregationalists, moderate Andover Trinitarian Congregationalists, and the progressive
New Haven Trinitarian Congregationalists and Presbyterians.

During this post-Revolution rehearsal for the reversal of idealism-intensive
faith and ethics of Edwards and the Edwardseans, the re-revisionist post-Edwardseans at Yale created a new theology (the new "New Divinity"), a new value (puritanicalism), and a new heightened deterrence-benevolence ethic consciousness. There occurred, over time, competing Congregationalists who produced a three-way division of the Puritan Piety tradition of parochial faith and
publics ethics, and its Halfway Piety faith and ethics replacement.

First, as the national headquarters of the "New Light" (Congregationalist)/"New School" (Presbyterian) and center of the certified and solidified
hegemonic Evangelical Congregationalists, the Yale/New Haven citadel continuously updated Calvinistical Halfway Piety faith and deterrence-benevolence
ethics, re-fashioned rational rules and regulations of the "Rule of Scripture" and
"Rule of Truth" principal principle and practice of parsons and parishioners, and
promulgated these systematic theologies as the authorized new revised standard
version of Orthodoxy.

Second, as the professional parochial school that Yale conservative Congregationalists (who preferred to be identified as the engaged traditionalists or
preservationists of the Evangelical tradition) spawned and sponsored following
the take over of Harvard Divinity School by the liberal Congregationalists, Andover Theological Seminary emerged as the major Evangelcal Congregationalist
theological school in Massachusetts.

Andover admitted as theologues graduates of Yale and Harvard (as well as
other higher education academic centers like Amherst) College. They were attracted theological professors trained at Yale Divinity School who challenged
and were challeged by Harvard Divinity School philosophical theologians. Their
Calvinist/Andover-"New Light" and anti-Calvinist/Harvard-"Old Light" Congregationalist defensive and offensive battles in the "Hub of the Universe" apparently resulted in different mutual influences, whereby measurably more than
their adversaries the Andover advocates selectively mixed the "New Light" and
"Old Light" empirical rationalism-rooted extremes of historic New England theology to emerge moderates who concentrated on middle-of-the-road alternatives.

However, the champions of Englightenment-responsive reason and revelation
religion struggled unsuccessfully with their up-to-date Calvinistical truth claims
to preserve the presumed ecclesiastical leadership role of the New England
Church of Christ Congregationalist Consociations in North America and Boston
as the center of this hegemonic Calvinist Puritan faith and ethics tradition.

The lost cause did not ensue from a failure to search and find a
constructive theoretical methodology and technical means to secure these ends,
since Andover warriors selectively followed Yale leaders who appropriated for
Orthodoxy the Scottish Common Sense philosophy British-ethnic immigrant
theologians at Princeton borrowed from the Presbyterian Church of Scotland
when they translocated to develop the American Presbyterian extension of the
Reformed Church.

Yale-educated Andover professors integrated this philosophy with other Enlightenment philosophies to form the basis of their systematic theology essays.
With these rational tools of analysis, the Halfway Piety faith and ethics
scholars attempted to generate a "New Light" pro-Calvinist positive corrective
action connection with the "Old Light" anti-Calvinist revisers of Puritan Piety

Federal Theology that was fast becoming Harvard Unitarian liberalism.

Located near Boston, with a few "Massachusetts Yankee" Harvard alumni on a faculty dominated by "Connecticut Yankee" Yale graduates, Andover was created and sustained by defenders of the faith once delivered to "the saints." Puritan Piety and Federal Theology were constituent elements of the Boston and Harvard Calvinistical continuum advanced by Cotton Mather, from which norm Charles Chauncy emerged a standard deviation critic of Jonathan Edwards whose Halfway Piety was a difference in degree so great from Puritan Piety to amount to difference in kind of Calvinist faith ethics. In spite of this difference universally appreciated by the scholars of sacred history, Andover academicians appeared convinced that the Yale pro-Calvinist Halfway Piety and Harvard anti-Calvinist Puritan Piety poles of the tradition were mutually fertile conservative ethics--if not reactionary right ("Rule of Scripture") and radical left ("Rule of reason") faith in God and faith in man systems--and therefore not mutually exclusive motives, means, and measures.

Andover crusader conservativess for classic Calvinism evinced maximum effort and minimum results in resisting the liberals' emerging in command and control of the power elite Congregationalist church, college (Harvard), and culture. In fact, Unitarian Congregationalist social conservatives and theological liberals drove Calvinism from the power center onto the peri-phery (if not entirely out) of the Unitarian Church power circles, on which boundaries they also abandoned the authentic Puritan Piety Unitarianism was formed to replace.

The Unitarian Associations substituted for theocentric faith and ethics faith in reason and moral man. And the unpersuaded power people pursued by the persuaded, who found Unitarians persuasive and were persuaded by Unitarianism, declared Unitarian Congregationalism a new suasion--and decidedly not a new persuasion--revolving around belief in rational man as the equivalent of linear moral progress and humanistic values, and the universal criterion of high Christianity and civility.

Puritan Piety was reconstituted by all three (Orthodoxy, Reformed, and Unitarian) competing claims to be the legitimate heirs of the Puritan tradition. In the process of dividing over dogma they united in pragma as each accepted as the standard of values middle-class morality and respectability; imposed a common criterion of good taste, style, and manners that was a class preference they confused with virtue; and disregarded the public interest ethics of Puritan Piety.

ANTISLAVERY TIES OF THE SONS OF PURITAN

CALVINISTS, UNITARIANS, AND QUAKERS

Hopkins lived to a ripe old age, and died driving defensive faith and offensive ethics arguments flat in the teeth of social conservative philosophical/theological Unitarian and Trinitarian Congregationalists on his left and right. These Yale post-Edwardseans and Harvard theological liberals were challenging social conservatives. They managed indiscriminate indifference to his radical color caste/captive class liberation social ethic, their pro-Calvinist and anti-Calvinist counterclaims, and to share values.

In short, instead of interring with Edwards burdensome bones of contention regarding whether Hopkins' or his challengers' body of works constructively connected the correct interpretive principle ("Rule of Scripture"/"Rule of Truth" rightly dividing the divine Word of God) and/or interpretation of the Calvinist

Puritan tradition preferring to wield their differences like sharp sword of truth and to bury them deep into the body of Hopkins and each other, the decisively divided and uncommon clergy class in New England discovered their common social conservative interests and united their different motives and objectives to discredit Hopkins' underpinning philosophy (metaphysical system), theology (systemic millennialism), and ethics (systematic abolitionism).

But quite like and unlike his advancement of Edwards' millennialism-centered Evangelicalism, that survived the Unitarian and Trinitarian English/Puritan-race representatives' disesteem and surfaced in Calvinist Baptist and other British-ethnic Fundamentalists and Charismatics, Hopkins' faith and ethics theology of abolitionism struggled to life after death in the deliberate development of Calvinist Puritan Piety Yankees.

Just as at the beginning of the eighteenth century, when Cotton Mather deliberately understated his Evangelical Calvinist-Puritan theological litmus test in the hopes of effecting a political alliance with the Religious Society of Friends, just so effectively at the end of the century, Calvinist Puritan Hopkins made a rare concession to the historic Quaker Puritan brethren. It subsisted of refashioning his one-dimensional sectarian theology into a two-dimensional sacred and secular civil interest-directed system of dogmatism and pragmatism.

The remodeled methodology resulted in stabilized firm faith and flexible ethics components that enabled him to praise (for the Calvinists to appraise) Quaker Puritan abolitionism, at the same time that he found nothing of comparable value in his fellow "Connecticut Yankee" and "Massachusetts Yankee" descendants of the wayward worldly saints who had turned from pro-Calvinist to anti-Calvinist Puritans.

Hopkins informed the sons of "the saints" in pluperfect public prose and published pieces that the Quaker Puritans were closer to the admittedly undeveloped and underdeveloped yet developing special interest-enhancing and general interest-expanding ethical standard established by their Puritan Piety fathers than were their liberal and conservative Yankee Congregationalist sons. He made his point stick in the process of recalling to mind their sacred and secular history he believed the brethern knew and forgot.

In the late eighteenth and early nineteenth centuries, Calvinist-reared Puritans engaged former nemesises and current Quaker Puritan friends in the Old Abolitionist Societies Friends inspired, financed, and influenced. Quaker Old Abolitionists were impressive ethicists who attracted Rhode Islanders Samuel Hopkins and Moses Brown, and Philadelphians Benjamin Franklin and Benjamin Rush. Compared to the majority, they also won to Old Abolitionism a few Presbyterians (Calvinists), Methodists (Arminians), and Baptists (Calvinists and Arminians); fewer Anglicans (Latitudinarians); and even fewer Trinitarian and Unitarian Congregationalists, and secular humanists.

In brief, the establishment White Anglo--Saxon sacred and profane Protestants evolved in their preponderancy not only pure pious and pure profane bitter rivals but also a statistically insignificant presence in the nonsectarian Old and New Abolitionist Societies.

These unrepresentative creative minority of Old Abolitionists differed in their receptivity to the relevant bearing upon the social reality and cultural crisis of the Enlightenment-derived principles of universal self-determination, liberation from bondage, and freedom from dehumanization and human experimentation.

Yet the nonestablishment majority and establishment minority of (Quaker,

Presbyterian, and Unitarian) churchmen and churches at the forefront of the anti-slavery movement all shared with secular humanists a highly developed sense of the priority of pro-White race/ethnic-interests--in any conflict with pro-Black race-interest--and a fully developed appreciation of liberty in freedom for each individual.

In addition to the Moral Law overriding legal unjust and therefore immoral ecclesiastical and civil law, the mainstream Evangelical Protestant New Abolitionists shared a rational "Rule of Love/Power/Justice" and "Rule of Reason" approach to the Bible and the Constitution that turned on consciences overpowering the "Rule of Scripture" and "Rule of Realism" as the "Rule of Truth."

These men and women of social status and Calvinist capitalist substance who enjoyed expanding power and wealth that was evidenced in their increasingly varied benevolence contributions to White citizens--and the charity Protestant philanthropists dis-pensed to their Black race--were endowed with greater material resources than other religious people.

The relevant matter is the cold fact that Quakers invariably, and even Baptists selectively, clearly demonstrated that securing anti-Black race values and interests was neither necessary nor inherent in the inevitable protection of pro-White race/ethnic real interests and values.

However, most establishmentarians were bound and determined to secure the status quo and their advantage at the expense of the disadvantaged. They were fully conscious of reality and thus that radical and rapid rational social structural change was the necessary renewal process for equitable access to equal opportunity and fair competition, and the indispensable prerequisite for the Black race to rise from outcaste statuslessness to equal status with the White race in North America.

Setting aside in this context the Anglicans who dominated the planter class in the slavocracy, and the British-ethnics who comprised the overwhelming majority of their overseers, protection of privileged status that the members of the English race's representative class inherited, achieved, were ascribed, or otherwise acquired in North America was a precipitating cause of an odd and even peculiar singular effect: The Quakers, Unitarian Congregationalists, and Trinitarian Congregationalists welcomed into their fellowships comparatively fewer Black members than all other transnational denominations.

Their English race competitors as theocracy powers were the Anglicans at the helm of the royal colonies, emitting fierce loyalty to the crown that was exceeded in intensity only by their love of their Black property whose body of profit and pleasure they incorporated in the body of Christ to protect their real interests.

Quaker, Anglican, and Calvinist English race-derived and/or power elite churches and churchmen were Puritan descendants as certainly as they differed with regard to the value of Calvinism. The net negative outcome of this Puritan (triple preclusion and exclusion faith and ethics) process was consequential: Free and slave Black Southerners (and Northerners effectively) were essentially abandoned to the care and feeding of capricious British-ethnic Evangelicals, who, possessing the least resources, were the most vigorous recruiters of Black souls.

The establishment communions and class congregations who had a perfect right to their own parochial acceptance and rejection standards, and private association entrance approval and prevention rules and regulations, clearly exercised the prerogatives of privilege with impunity. They included electing to preclude or to exclude Black folk from (they did not segregate within) their sacred religious and sacrosanct secular communities, and the free choice not to elevate on their own terms in the civil community and their native land their Black race cultural kin-group.

GREAT CHAIN OF BEING SOCIAL CONSERVATIVE
PHILOSOPHY UNDERPINNING PURITAN LIBERALS

Channing expressly verified and validated his cultural and genetic Eng-lish/ Puritan-race heritage amid affirming his self-identity in a letter he addressed (August 29, 1828)--fifteen years after the death of Hopkins--to his English correspondent, Lucy Akin (1781-1864):

> We here who have Puritan blood in our being are
> never tired of celebrating their virtues.[13]

Pride in Puritan race and virtue naturally were the inherited cultural values reinforced by the Yankee elitist's connective linkage with (1) the Boston Brahmin; (2) Harvard College, his alma mater and the American Enlightenment citadel from which towering cathedral of liberalism he emerged to become the "apostle of Unitarianism"; (3) the intellectual compatibility of Christianity and humanism through his influence upon Ralph Waldo Emerson, who after resigning as minister of Boston's Second Unitarian Church nurtured Transcendentalism; and (4) Henry David Thoreau (1817-62), who rationalized the Old Abolitionist English and American principle that New Abolitionists had long since practiced in his work on *Civil Disobedience* (1849).

(Thoreau's development, like John Locke's (1632-1704) *Two Treatises on Civil Government* (1690) that included a justification of the Glorious Revolution (1688) in England which was subsequently appropriated as the legitimization of the American Revolution, had a positive influence upon the British Labor Movement; Mohandas Karamchand (Mahatma) Gandhi's (1869-1948) passive resistance revolution in India; and the nonviolent Civil Rights Movement the Reverend Martin Luther King, Jr. (1929-68) led in America.)

The common Puritan mettle of Channing, Emerson, and Thoreau is the source of their very considerable "virtues." Their individual, hero, and great man moral theory and principle advanced unevenly and differently the unexamined premise of the social conservative *Great Chain of Being* philosophy, whose superior/inferior people presuppositions were those of their fathers along with other commonly shared values; and the empirical *Great Chain of Reason* logic, that links each independent individual in an association charged with optimistic faith in mankind and linear human progress.

Boston liberals' enthusiasm for rationalism, and passion for optimism, harnessed a dynamism permitting these anti-Calvinist sons of the Calvinist fathers to transmogrify the sacred millennialism of Calvinism into secular Transcendentalism.

For the Transcendentalists Transcendentalism took subjective shape and objective form as pure Protestant, Puritan, and private soul-enraptured mysticism, that corresponds with the elementary force of the solitary individual. Mysticism was articulated differently but equally by other English-informed American Puritan rationalists.

Clearly Jonathan Edwards' and the Quakers' differently composed and directed rationalism, individualism, and optimism were present with such power in Transcendentalists that these white truth-revering and black error-repelling Puritan descendants rejected--when they did not ignore--the powerful presence and phenomenal social evil the White Devil superimposed upon the Black vulnerable.

While engaged in penetrating reflection during their pre-antebellum and mid-antebellum residence on Southern plantations, the sharp moral reflexes of Channing and Emerson were never more striking than when they passed by on the other side of the color caste/captive class, and turned permissive regarding the perpetuity of anti-Black race values and interests.

Strange to say, like their fathers, this perversity the apperceptive were reluctant to admit. But unlike their forefathers who believed God and the Devil were real beings, whom humankind should respectively perpetually engage and drive in history, they tolerated the pervasive anti-Black race spirit; denied and delayed before they chose to contribute their moral real to correct the condition; and refused to accept responsibility for the consequences of their acts of commission and omission.

Certainly the elite liberal establishment consciously closed their minds to the empirical evidence of anti-Black race desire needlessly in their space, heed-less-ly in their time, and recklessly in their sphere of influence. But the surging submerged ant-Black race reality finally surfaced, soared, and was seriously engaged at last--in the liberals own medium of symbol and ritual, myth and reason--in Herman Melville's (1819-91) *Moby Dick* (1851).

Being a Yankee descendant of the English race like the moral intellectual giants Channing and Emerson, Melville makes the pertinent point by illuminating the power the secular and religious elite Yankee sons of the Puritans commanded and controlled in their management of the color caste/captive class reality.

Melville joined the Emersonians, best known to history as the Transcendentalists, in the search for the totally subjective-free and objective absolute with the mystical fire they supplied. While his first-hand experience of evil was neither unique nor distinct but comparable to the similar direct engagement of the phenomenon by other devotees of Transcendentalism, apparently unlike most of these cohorts Melville could not avoid pessimism by escaping permanently into the mystical stratosphere of optimism that the anti-Calvinist Yankee liberals substituted for the millennial realm of the traditional Calvinist Puritans.

CHANNING'S CHRISTIAN COMMITMENT AND RATIONAL MORALITY

Channing, of course, progressed on a parallel but different astral plane from the Transcendentalist Yankee brethren. First, he remained throughout his life a Congregationalist, and commenced and ended his professional career as the Puritan minister of a single Boston Unitarian Society. Second, Channing's pure passion for reason was accompanied by precious few mystical tendencies. This distinction made a relative rather than absolute difference between the Protestant professor and fellow academic moral powerhouses, since their reverence for rational mysticism postponed and prevented positive possibilities as certainly as they denied proabolitionism the critical confluence of social justice the devotees were when they retreated to their private inner circle of the initiated.

Demonstrable seduction of pure reason, and the ancillary moral man making individual linear progress the critical criterion for creating not only a less unfair and inequitable but more just and moral society, deterred a plurality of Transcendentalists from being distracted by serious antislavery endeavors; and from initiating a personal penetrating analysis of inherited anti-Black race values. The corollary commonplace and common sense for contemporary admiring critics of Channing was that his cherished rationalism without mysticism--which also served as an inadequate definition of Transcendental intuitionism--together with his embraced social conservative Puritan "virtues," constituted the rigid constraints of Channing's social-limiting ethical character and principles.

The self-revelation of his public moral monitor of the caste/captive contradiction of Christian Humanism, no less than of the Christian Church in the West, automatically appeared unmistakably in the antislavery moralist's definitive antiabolition declaration. This moral monism principle that he set forth, as an extension and expansion of the moral principality within his moral monocracy, permitted the moral monocrat to rationalize as not only reasonable but so far from vice and near to virtue his refusal to risk his life and career in the cause of abolitionism, and to light the fuse to what he knew to be the explosive power elite's dynamite keg of anti-Black race principle.

Compared and contrasted to Old Abolitionist Samuel Hopkins who was an uncompromising immediatist long before Channing publicly praised him and took his moderate antislavery stand, years after the 1808 statute outlawing the foreign slavetrade marked the beginning of the intensified domestic slavetrade, Channing elected not to be either an Old Abolitionist in the Old Abolitionism era or a New Abolitionist in age of New Abolitionism; preferred antiabolitionism to proabolitionism for his own more dramatic purposes than solid reasons; and averred that for the same precipitating factors contributing to the correlation between Hopkins' ever-increasing proabolitionism and declining reputation, which ended in an irreversible credibility gap, no known greater real risk to the prestige of even a peerless Protestant powerhouse existed in the antebellum era than for an establishmentarian clergyman to promote immediatism.

His own personal reputation as a rational mind would be ruined, Channing ingenuously wrote in a communication to Lucy Akin, if he became associated with "vulgar modes of thinking": since there exists "not a few persons" in Puritan New England who think "slavery a low topic." Channing was naturally wary, albeit he did not avoid so much as selectively engaged controversy. But this congenital cautious condition scarcely proved to be his problem.

Channing's altogether different difficulty involved his penetrating clarity, with which he characteristically laid bare ethical issues. It was the evident failure of the ratiocinator to apply his potent powers of perception effectively --even though the Anglo-American made the Puritan power point and made it stick in this "Old and New England" comparative culture critique--that is, to place in great perspective the self-disclosed grandiose gift of anti-Black race ideals that he inherited and accepted uncritically from his New England fathers.

These perfectly enormous endowments encompassed neither accidental nor incidental spin-offs of the historical human bondage-bound powerful Puritan culture: the forceful theocracy or ecclesiastical and civil political economy, and whose dynamics were engendered by entrepreneurs engaged in expanding material wealth and physical health, energized by the sacred faith and secular ethics components of their Calvinist religion, and determined to ensure for each individual and community spiritual security plus social salvation in history and eternity.

On the contrary, the class over caste and classy charitable chassis bequests bequeathed along with their culture constancy conducing chariots of charity by charioteers were the primary cause of the entirely unique and distinct African slavetrade that was itself a secondary effect.

This difficulty was exacerbated by Channing's overreaching belief in the primacy of moral duty as the vicar of reason. Complementarily, in his moral theory, solid logic-underpinned inenarrable reason inexorably results in inerrant subjective-free objective judgments. From this data right and good knowledge emerges as automatically as dusk precedes and succeeds dawn, whereby, for the wise and prudent, full compliance with the analysis and conclusions reached by impeccable rationalists follows the dictates of the cultural determiners reason for the identical natural reasons night follows day.

Channing succinctly stated his principal social ethics principle, the low priority of community responsibility and rights and high priority of individual responsibility and rights, when he declared that the rational being who begins with the "conviction of the paramount worth and importance of duty"--and that his "first concern" regarding "inquiries into human affairs" is to learn his responsibility--will both see the light and do "what is Right." The paradigmatic Puritan publicly proclaimed "this is the fundamental truth, the supreme law of reason." But the critical matter that Channing consciously denied was equally true and consequential, to wit, what the facts and figures of fellow Northern proslavocrats, and the statistics of the slavocrats, revealed were relatively interesting, but what they hid was absolute.

Anti-Calvinist Channing carefully analyzed the pro-Calvinist works of Jonathan Edwards and Samuel Hopkins, and understood comprehensively that they teach the source and power of the saints is the *Nature of True Virtue*--that is, to know, to be, and to do the truth, or, to actualize the will to love the will of God. This will to power, will power, and will to realize and to exercise real power--made efficacious by God's infusion of the Holy Spirit into the soul of each "real saint--presumably empowers the "Elect" with peerless possibilities, and transforms absolute justification and relative virtue.

Channing studied millennarian mystic and philosophical theologian Edwards, and concluded from his analysis that the rational faith and ethics Edwards developed by perverting Puritan Piety into Halfway Piety advanced the classic Christian and Calvinist social conservative principles and practices, on the one hand, and, on the other hand, the historic continuum which entailed placing disproportionately greater weight on faith than ethics.

It is most difficult to determine whether he admired or whether he simply took for granted the nature and function of Edwards' benevolence. Edwards established benevolence as the means and ends of his Evangelical Calvinist faith and ethics, that revolved around the central operating principle of Calvinists in the church and civil community dispensing personal Christian benevolence, that, predictably, Edwards equated with virtue.

Channing found no flaw in the connective linkage between Evangelical-Calvinist Edwards' parochial theology and private morality, and found little fault with its tendency to limit for all but the strongest Puritan parties to the conflict inherent in the Puritan bifurcation of reality the social structural change potentiality of the powerful Puritan culture. On the contrary, he accepted this deficiency as demonstrable efficiency and sufficiency as certainly as Edwardsean Halfway Piety abandoned the civil power dual conformance and challenge dynamic of authentic Puritan Piety public-interest ethics.

Ironically, in his sequential sharp disconnection with revisionist Edwards'

Halfway Piety faith and ethics, and poor reconnection with Boston public servant Cotton Mather's special interest-enhancing and general interest-expanding Puritan Piety, the consequence was that Channing's common good ethics more nearly matched the Edwardsean criterion than it approached the Matherean standard. Moreover, in preferring contracting to expanding social redeeming values, Channing repeated Edwards' strictly limited public promise and performance.

Unquestionably, Edwards and Channing were committed equally alike and unlike in rational thought and action to raising the Puritan standard: one by promoting Cal-vinism, and the other by demoting it. Instead of advancing traditionally underdeveloped but cyclically developing Puritan Piety--or the coordination of private faith and parochial community in public interest ethics-- Channing separated its individual and community inextricably interconnected coordinates; at once abandoned the sacred and secular social redeeming virtue and opted for the private and personal individual-intensive moral virtue; and called it the way, the truth, the light, and the will to love God.

The Unitarian apogee short-circuited or depleted rather than completed virtue, an accomplishment he achieved by asserting erroneously that the rational and political power are not positive factors in the fusion of faith and ethics. Part of reason for this confusion is that he deprecated what he thought was depreciating in value: the appreciating *agape*-love (virtue), justice (principle), and power (middle axiom ways to the justice-means and love-ends) dynamics of disinterested will to the equally different and mutually rewarding best good and right of all individuals, communities, and race and ethic groups.

Restated, Channing substituted simple truth for the profound truth and complexity of the Christian *agape*-love/power/justice ethic; and one-dimensional reason or rational morality for tri-dimensional reason-faith-ethics triad. This error in principle derived from the faulty premise that reason alone is the sure-fire source of positive moral will possibilities and their actualization.

Moral reason and will translates conscience for Channing, whose evident meaning is inherent in his convincement that reason produces knowledge; reason plus knowledge generate power; and the power of reason and knowledge, the reason of power and knowledge, and the knowledge of power and reason are never powerless either when they fail to be matched with power or they face real power.

Thus a Channingesque basic belief is that men of conscience will not "inquire first for our interests." Channing asserts this ground rule with confidence so towering that he is fundamentally unperturbed by either the experience of slavery or the knowledge of anti-Black race attitudes and behavior.

Pursuant to these proclivities, Channing attempts to override the essence of Puritan Piety with his preference for Yankee morality. This propensity is prominent when he sharpens the difference between theological and non-theological Puritan ethics, and never more striking than in his communication to Lucy Akin (August 2, 1829):

> To realize our connection with the Supreme Being seems to me the great secret and spring of moral energy, moral victory, and unlimited progress in whatever ennobles our nature. It is for these influences that I value religion. The joys which the fanatic boasts of finding in piety, which have little or no connection with moral improvement I hold cheap indeed.[14]

What he means by "moral improvement" for the Black race, and the nature of his contribution to the rise of Black folk as a competitive color/caste class are--on his terms--central questions to examine and reflect upon even though like the Black body they exist as marginal matters in the body of his life and work.

UNITARIAN AND TRINITARIAN CONGREGATIONALISTS' INDIVIDUALISM AND COMMUNALISM HIGH PRIORITIES

No reasonable and serious synchronic critic worthy of respect, among those who called into question his judgment in the color caste/captive cultural crisis, ever accused Channing of courting danger. Not one of the synchronous counterculture figures ever doubted the better part of his valor. This primary positive virtue denotes bold and brave strong character, constitutes the distinguishing nature of Puritan integrity and nobility, and envelopes what he declared the fortitude to "look beneath 'the flesh,' to 'the spirit'" and not to "overlook" "color." Color conditions "brotherly regard," Channing attests, because to affirm the color-blind value is to disaffirm Black-race existence in particular, and to "violate the great Christian law" and the "spiritual principle in man" in general.

Ancillary significance inheres in the no less real for being neither obvious nor intentional culture-consequences connection between Channing's public avouchment of his total identification with Puritan virtues (shorn of Calvinistic theology) and the nature of Puritan virtues. They include Black bondage and anti-Black race values, and slavery is not most lethal of all the Puritan virtues.

The Channing and Puritan virtue connection revolves around liberalism, which he approached as logic-laced and empirical rationalism-rooted ethics; understood as philosophy independent of theology; claimed advanced necessarily as free of ideology as it was the absence of theology and presence of pure reason; and, therefore, contended it was neither dogma nor doctrine. But his belief in reason was the cause and the effect no less than the objective of his Christian Humanism: a rival of Classical Christian religion whose essential dimensions subsist of faith in God (not man) plus individual and community ethics.

Channingesque Protestantism was deficient of Christian *agape*-love/power/justice ethic. In point of fact, this universal categorical imperative was overruled by Channing's overriding cardinal principle of simple rather than profound justice or the absence of political power and the presence of moral will power, which force alone, he averred, is sufficient, efficient, and "even more necessary than the intellectual to the security of the just rights of the many."

Doubtless the indisputable positive parochial and private and public value for White race/ethnic citizens of both religious and secular liberalism enhanced their anti-Black race values, and the prospects of the color caste/captive class, neither more efficaciously nor less salutarily than Unitarian Congregationalists' discredited Trinitarian Congregationalists' Halfway Piety: the justification by faith and deterrence-benevolence ethic of select grace and "Elect" virtue. These "Rule of Scripture" and "Rule of Truth" Trinitarian rationalists used reason no less adroitly than the Unitarians. This facility enabled the Evangelical Congregationalists to combine confidently total obedience co-equally to the laws of nature, man, and God; the Bible and the Constitution; and man-centered values and God-based virtue.

Demonstrable divergence in their vying for hegemony of New England's religious and civil culture with different instrumental means and motives, and convergence as the establishment Trinitarian pious and Unitarian profane Congregationalists by the common purpose to secure the salvation of the whole man and society: as if they were the divided mystical Yankee body, seeking and being driven by an unknown elemental Puritan force of the spiritual or third kind demanding reconnection, and mysteriously drawn irresistibly in union perforce the religious (ying) half and secular (yang) half of the sacred and profane "just rights" whole Puritan body.

By the age of twenty-three, when Channing was ordained and elected minister of the Federal Street Congregationalist Church in Boston, Puritan parsons had reached their apex as Federalist Party partisans; their high point as advocates of democratic ideas and idealism bent on being unbending in their commitment to a strong Federal Government; their aggressive posture that complemented Congregationalists' official connection with Presbyterians and their republican representative democracy-influencing central church government; and their zenith as social conservatives enamored with structured hierarchal class privileges, and a stable order they were prepared to defend from their high status positions.

Consequently, as clerical members of the Boston elite class, Massachusetts paid officials (albeit distinguished from authorities) of the state, and indistinguishable Trinitarian and Unitarian establishmentarian Congregationalists, Puritan parsons centered the weight of their primary individualism-intensive ethics so squarely on the White race/ethnic individual-specific basic element of the Puritan church and democratic state until they displaced community responsibility half of the tradition effectively, and moved it from a co-equal moral standard of the common wealth and welfare with the individual to an essentially secondary one.

Whether the cause or whether the effect of the predictable cultural consequences, salvation or wholeness for powerhouse Trinitarians and Unitarians flowed to the society automatically from the quality of the individual moral character and/or conscience. As the parsons disaffected from the partisan power circles of political republican democracy to place their faith in reason and capitalism, producing and acquiring wealth accelerated as the criterion of moral worth; and distributing social health and welfare spiraled as a controversial fiscal accountability question, rather than as a means-needs test and means-ends measure of individual and community mind-will ethical responsibility and possibility.

The social ethics of updated Evangelical Orthodoxy, and her up-to-date revisionists/preservationists, was based on the unchanging traditional premise of the Standard Order, to wit, if the will of each individual is changed to will the will of God, by that process of voluntary conversion s/he will be in harmony with God and, therefore, do the will of God for mankind. The social ethics of the new Unitarian "orthodoxy" was guided by the alternately complemental and counteractant premise, namely, if the mind of each rational human being is constructively changed and switches to be (in the fine tuning mode at that very least) on Divine Being's sound sense frequency and moral wavelength or channel in universe, s/he will know the mind of God to her/his certain knowledge, and inexorably the new and different mind therewith will as well will be and do what this clear knowledge of certainty demands.

Their mutually fertile rather than mutually exclusive public ethics downgraded community force as well as peer pressure and power; upgraded in the period of "rugged individualism" the idea of a truly autonomous individual, as if even an independent-minded man in an immoral society could engage a conscious color caste/captive cast v. captor class captivated culture without being tainted or had a choice between being moral or immoral; and focused so sharply on the solitary conscience in the age of the solid slavocracy they blurred the anti-Black race values-specific content of "*the spirit*" and character of the culture.

Having either lost or not found *agape*-love, the absolute and one and only true virtue--as well as the exact opposite of the individual acting alone and for himself always and everywhere at once, whose polar opposite is the individual and community or collective guilt and grace advancing the best known right and good possible of each necessary conflict of interest or individual person, ethnic group, and race body member of the commonwealth--Bostonian Congregationalists majored in absolutizing the relative and relativizing the absolute, whereby affirming the existence of the absolute rather than the relative moral individual and Christian society they denied their creation and preservation of the sacred and secular anti-Black race value.

Bay State Congregationalists managed reality for establishmentarians and/or passivity regarding the outcast condition of their color caste/captive class with power and poise by the mid-antebellum decades. And the pure pious and pure profane Protestant power elite were challenged by neither conventional wisdom nor common sense nor active conscience successfully, partly because liberal and conservative churchmen's Black race cultural kin-group existed at best on the far edge of the peripheral margins of their real interests and priority values; on the fringes and in the "colored corners" of their congregations; and on the slippery spiritual and material surfaces set in concrete both above these two primary Puritan substances and beneath concernment, as routinely as their anti-Black race interest-specific Southern slavocracy and Northern democracy cultures persisted with impunity--just beyond the range of the rational clarity and moral power influence produced by divided theocentric and egocentristic but united ethnocentristic Puritans.

And these secular and religious real power alternatives to the moral power Puritans consisted of as much truth and error in actuality as Congregationalists were shielded from by their New England insulation and Northeastern isolation, and resisted while the power elite social conservatives insisted they secured the one and only ultimate reality.

Above this Puritan bifurcation of reality and great divide of Trinitarian/Unitarian Congregationalists, the liberal and conservative clerical establishment slowly but surely joined forces to stabilize the social order. This sad and sorry subvention symbol and substance included a tacit and silent solemn White Anglo-Saxon Protestant Gentlemen's Agreement, that they concluded as effectively as the fathers of the Constitution who also firmly clasped their hands prayer as the preyers prayed for time to change the double damnation they inflicted upon their Black race.

Religious and secular establishmentarians were satisfied no mind and will of stature, or figure of consequence, would object to their taking the offensive to make the defense of the status quo a matter of national security, which they contended would perfect the Union they wished both to protect and extend.

Ensconced in their joy, and sublimity, the Eastern establishment remained oblivious to the truth, the error, and the terror of power proliferating in parochial, private, and public political circles--and social consequences--no where being either balanced or checked by the high priority principle of restricting moral influence to the force produced by individual character. Increasingly anti-civil and pro-ecclesiastical politics church bureaucrats and technocrats, who directed the revision of Orthodoxy, argued that no mind will change the will; and no will will change the mind; but "*the spirit*" of the culture, which mind and will will follow, can be transformed (without changing the cohesive social discrimination and segregation) through repentance and conversion into one sustaining a spiritual affirmation of Black race liberation from bondage and caste. This theology of hope and realized eschatology was born of the knowledge representatives of the Puritan race of saints were not only slavemasters but progenitors of Black folk, who as benevolent paternalists *par excellence* "Christianized, Civilized, and Circumscribed" Black bondage before they cut their ties with their progeny, in pre-Independence private acts of manumission and post-Constitution state statutes mandating abolition.

Antebellum Yankee Evangelical sons of the wayward worldly saints, currently in throes of engineering a White race/ethnic individual-geared depreciating predestinarianism and an appreciating puritanicalism, were Calvinists seeking to replace double election/double damnation Calvinism with double indemnity for White race and ethnic males. But in eliminating "Reprobate" punishment and offering "Elect" rewards for White folk, re-revisionist Calvinist remained in democracy and slavocracy too optimistic concerning the anti-Black race legacy bequeathed by the pessimists.

They proved the rule of race and reason reigning in their Calvinist pride and prejudice, when Yankees rendered Black folk excludable from North America out -Puritan Puritan fathers who merely precluded the Black male from the Constitution: The color caste/captive class is the symbol and substance of cultural values, and a hard reality that no mind or will can ever change by the use of moral and spiritual force as the surrogate for political power; approaching Black persons as if they were individuals neither tied nor bound inextricably by Black race identity; and circumventing full and equal respect for the whole race.

VANGUARD CALVINIST-PURITAN ANTISLAVERY PARSONS AS PASTORS OF YOUNG CHANNING

Channing received a religious education in his pre-college years from the original complete Old Abolitionist Calvinist clergy, It was a nurturing experience that seemed to set him apart from nearly all other synchronous Congregationalist ministers. First among his parson preceptors stood out a "Connecticut Yankee" urbane lawyer, theological liberal, and social moderate: the Reverend Ezra Stiles (1727-95).

After twenty-two years as minister of two parishes--the Congregationalist Church of Christ in Portsmouth, New Hampshire, and the Second Congregationalist Church of Newport, Rhode Island--Stiles acceded to the Presidency (1778-95) of Yale College. Following his move to New Haven from Rhode Island in the middle of the Revolution, the unsettling conditions created by the War and the early national era--including the decline in the number of Harvard students preparing for the clerical profession--ten years passed before a successor replaced Stiles as minister of Second Church Newport.

Towards the end of his professional career and exceptional life, "Rhode Island Yankee" Channing gave public expression to the high esteem in which he held "Connecticut Yankee" Stiles. The Harvard alumnus wrote concerning the Yale alumnus to state for the record that as a "consequence of Dr. Stile's

164   CONSTITUTION, CONSCIENCE, AND CALVINIST COMPROMISE

removal to New Haven, my father was accustomed to attend on the ministry of Dr. Hopkins." Hopkins, as Channing recollects in a (February 14, 1840) letter, was "the first minister I heard" and instructor in the Westminster catechism. Reflecting later on his teen-age years, during which period Channing stated that he "grew up," Channing recorded his recollection of Hopkins: "I was accustomed to attend worship in our church, where Dr. Parker was settled, so that for years I knew little of Dr. Hopkins."

It is most difficult to determine the inference to be drawn from what are arguably only apparent conflicting recollections of his experience with Hopkins, given the Newport years of his youth and Stiles' pastorate, that two years before Channing died he penned. The problematics concerning Channing's attested to early intimate and later nonexistent association with Hopkins do not merely arise because of their similar rational analyses of faith and ethics--from which they drew different conclusions, largely dictated by conflicting philosophical and theological premises. They inhere in specific facts. A singular one is that his father's home, where Channing resided during his first twenty years, was located a short distance from Hopkins' parsonage.

But it is not critical for this undertaking to construct a reconciliation between the letter in question and Channing's *Memoirs,* where the profound influence of Hopkins is acknowledged as beginning in his youth. In this document, Channing avows he "first gained his conviction of the iniquity of slavery" from Hopkins while listening to him share his Old Abolitionism persuasion at the Channing family table, that he attests the "apostle of abolition" frequented often.

Anti-Calvinist Channing published his assessment of pro-Calvinist Hopkins at the height of the New Abolitionism, whose immediatism the antiabolitionist had previously rejected as flatly as Old Abolitionism, in order to demonstrate the Channing and Hopkins direct connection in the antislavery continuum and to obscure their disconnection in abolitionism:

> It was not until I left college that I became acquainted with him, and a short intercourse dispelled all the fear and reserve which my early impressions and left in my mind. His conversation was free, rather abrupt, blunt, and often facetious. We saw, at once, that he lived in his study, and borrowed very little from the manners of the fashionable world. He took pleasure in talking with me of his past life, his controversies, etc., and I regret that I took no notes, and did not, by questions, acquaint myself with the progress of his mind.[15]

ANTI-CALVINIST CHANNING'S DEFENSE OF
PRO-CALVINIST HOPKINS' FAITH AND ETHICS

What can be stated with certainty--concerning the relevant relation between the two Newport apostles--is that Channing was educated at Harvard in the era Hopkinsianism was at the height of its influence at Yale. Equally unobscured and noncontroversial is this conspicuous actuality: the first fifty years of his life had passed and been lived as an antiabolitionist before Channing publicly set forth his antislavery thoughts. At the end of the initial decade of New Abolitionism, Channingesque antislavery principles differed from those of Old Abolitionist Hopkins less in sentiments than in process and purpose.

What is interesting and noticeable is also pertinent and to the point: Channing did not improve the antislavery conclusions he shared with Hopkins; and he failed to offer a real alternative to Hopkins' solution to the problem of the White race/ethic citizenry's determination to perpetuate in perpetuity their color caste/captive class, and to exclude the body from participatory democracy (a stricture that he rejected as illiberal).

Without pretext in this context, Channing recalled he "preached for him once" in 1803: the year of Hopkins' death and his own ordination and installation as minister of the Boston Federal Street Congregational Church, in which initial office he remained the rest of his life. Amid the controversy in which he was accused of being a traitor to his English class and Puritan race,and e-merged a crisis in confidence for the power elite who provided the resources for the style to which he had grown accustom, Channing outlined a fully developed appreciation of his Newport social ethics inspiration, and attributed to Hopkins his own most highly prized virtue: "He revered reason, the oracle of God within him."

Channing did not positively follow the Hopkins he reported "labored for the education of the colored people," or, regarding intimate involvement in the advancement of the color caste/captive class and improvement of their condition, share with him experiences such as "the happiness of seeing the fruits of his labors in the intelligence and exemplary piety of those who came under his influence." But Channing appeared a suspect revisionist who was subject to arrest and fairly charged with rewriting history.

Evidently he adopted a new perspective that was diametrically opposite to the point of view of the Boston and Harvard traditional Calvinist opponents of nontraditional Jonathan Edwards of New Haven and Yale. They were championed by Charles Chauncy--the uncompromising social conservative who argued that so far from a messenger of "Good News" Hopkins was nothing but "bad news"--whose "Old Light" liberal Puritanism Channing constructively channeled in the creation of Unitarianism. In short, what Boston theological liberals considered a flaw in Hopkins' character Channing apparently transubstantiated through a positive gloss of the Rhode Island patriarch: "He wanted toleration toward those who rejected his views."[16]

The value of Channing's critical re-evaluation of Hopkins lay not in the accuracy of his re-examination, since his assessment and that of Chauncy and other formidable foes whom Hopkins fought fiercely were irreconcilable. What is instructive is Channing's personal attestation to his affinity with the spirit of his fellow Congregationalist minister, whose affirmative action occurred in the New Abolitionist era when the inextricable proslavery Calvinist tradition and preferred color caste Puritan heritage Channing respectively despised and cherished--and the Trinitarian Congregationalist-establishment he bolted no less than the Unitarian Congregationalist-establishment he founded--were under attack for their certified antislavery/proslavery neutrality.

Fellow Unitarian and Trinitarian male and female New Abolitionists currently argued that while divided by faith the two establishments were united by a common social conservative ethic, and cited Congregationalism as historically and currently proslavery in nature, design, and function. Channing understood that the whole Evangelical Protestant Christian enterprise--and the establishment denominations in particular--were being indicted as one entity of uniform neutral parties in the middle of a cultural crisis.

At least in the appearances of his apperceptive compeers, Channing increasingly respected, the New Abolitionists' value judgments and descriptive facts were verified by solid antiabolitionist Congregationalism's proslavocrat/antislavocracy posture, that enhanced nothing so much as proslavocracy expansionism. Unitarian proabolitionists entered the antislavery race dominated by the Colonizationists for the Unitarian antiabolitionist soul of Channing and fellow establishmentarians, steadily gained over the long distance to close with Channing in a strong photo finish, and met and matched yet did not beat the competition but induced greater cooperation than conflict with the gradualist Congregationalists that exceeded in high anxiety the high intensity previously inciting Calvinists to foment theological riots.

Channing was born and bred in antislavery/proslavery Rhode Island a Puritan but not a antiabolitionist. He lived and died the antislavery antiabolitionist he was made in theory and experience by the Yankee Boston and Cavalier Virginia cultures that nurtured and cultivated the form and function of his antislavery nature and purpose. Trinitarian Massachusetts immediatists, and Unitarian Boston "bold brahmin" converts to proabolitionism, concluded Channing was a needlessly stubborn antiabolitionist. Thus as an antislavery adversary of immediatism the advocate of gradualism was a special target of the criticism leveled by New Abolitionist Unitarian and Trinitarian Congregationalists.

His pro-immediatist Boston admirers expected a higher standard of moral promise and performance from Protestantism's "Reluctant Emancipator" than cost-conscious and cautious-conscience pro-gradualism. More was expected of him because he demonstrated leadership in not seeking but forming the con-sensus behind his initiative in fashioning rational moral principles; championing secular humanism and religious humanitarianism; and guiding the liberal Congregationalist clergy out of the Boston Congregationalist Association into the Berry Street Conference of Ministers (1820), who formed the American Unitarian Association (1825).

CHANNING'S PURITAN PRINCIPLES

Caught in this cross fire between Boston proabolitionist and antiabolitionist Puritan parties to the Yankee conflict of true interests and values, Channing's several purposes were served at once by recalling in the New Abolitionist era the Old Abolitionist record and performance of Puritan Hopkins as a model for Yankees ignorant and innocent of his achievements. They had been lost for a generation as consummately as he had been buried beneath notice by Yale post-Edwardsean creators of the Hopkinsian "New Divinity" counteractant "New Haven Theology," and contempt by Boston theological liberals who visited an anti-Calvinist plague on both pro-Calvinist schools.

First, in the process of memorializing Hopkins positing no "new creed" as the principal principle of Unitarianism, Channing certified his highest priority primary principles subsisted of securing liberty of conscience, religious freedom, and ecclesiastical and civil together with secular and sacred tolerance.

Second, having fought fierce foes for decades and won the battle for the anti-Calvinists but not the war they waged, that left the optimist neither a pessimist nor a cynic but a sobered skeptic challenged by the reality that the liberal victory did not vanquish the defeated pro-Calvinists, the memorial permitted Channing to argue the case for Hopkins' reform theology and radical ethics being the sharpest contrast imaginable to Evangelical Calvinism rather than a standard deviation from the norm of Orthodoxy.

In this revised interpretation, Channing elevated the Hopkintonian innovation and effectively turned it into rational instrument of his own vindication. The implication and inference he left his readers to draw inhered in the paradox that in spite of his impeccable credentials as a Congregationalist establishmentarian and uncompromising defender of Orthodoxy, Hopkins was repudiated as flatly as his "New Light" millennarianism and Old Abolitionism were rejected out of hand by the Yale and Andover Seminary post-Edwardseans he battled for the hegemony of Boston on the one side, and, on the other sided, by his Boston anti-Calvinist theological liberal-forerunners.

This anti-Evangelical Calvinist line of Puritans expanding from Edwards' and Hopkins' archenemy Chauncy to Channing the original Unitarian advanced as the leader of the "Old Light" Calvinist to liberal anti-Calvinist continuum in Boston. Neither the Evangelical Calvinist protectorate, nor the progressive party of liberal Calvinists fast becoming the anti-Calvinist secular humanist alternative within the Congregationalist clerical establishment, called into question the Christian clerical credentials and competence of either Hopkins or Channing. But these courageous character and integrity profiles in conscience shared values and the uncommon experience of being as a conscious clerical class a classic crisis in conservative consciousness, confidence, and credibility.

Third, Channing presented Hopkins as the model independent-minded and objective rationalist because he formed his own "religious opinions." Hopkins, Channing averred, existed in creative independence, emerged "superior to human authority," and "broke away from human creeds." Doubtless this high gloss and convoluted communication of gross error as the truth occurred as a direct result of Channing's personal predicament. Nevertheless the difficulty compounded by complexity inherent in the accurate analysis and incorrect conclusion Channing drew is that he obscures the self-evident truth attested to by synchronic Black and White folk: Hopkins created new demanding, religious, and "human creeds."

Fourth, and finally, Channing asserted that Hopkins arrived at his Old Abolitionist position at least as early as (1) Benjamin Franklin--the admired Boston-born, Calvinist Puritan-inspired, Presbyterian-reared, and Quaker Pur-itan-influenced convert to Anglicanism in Philadelphia; (2) Benjamin Rush (17451813)--the native Philadelphian and Presbyterian-nurtured University of Pennsylvania physician; and (3) Anglican John Jay (1745-1829)--the native New Yorker and first Chief Justice of the Supreme Court (1789-95).

Thus in an era when Trinitarian Congregationalist clergymen closed ranks to resist the Unitarian philosophical radicals, and the Evangelical-Calvinist New Abolitionist ethical radicals, Puritan Channing reminded the expanding antiabolitionist establishment opposition to proabolitionism that there is no inherent conflict between being a Puritan (or a Calvinist not to mention a Christian) a New Abolitionist (or totally opposed in principle and practice both to slavery in general and the "peculiar institution" in particular).

Channing's veneration of Hopkins, and therefore of Puritan virtues, outlined a liberal's vision and revision of the theological reactionary, radical public interest ethicist, and social conservative. Channing managed to neglect Hopkins' advancement of Edwards' teaching of the doctrine of millennialism in his systematic theology, and which Hopkins singled out as his greatest achievement; to acknowledge that Hopkins developed a new interpretation and defense of rather than a commitment to retreat from the cardinal Calvinist dogma of predestination, that Channing considered its great offense; and to laud Hopkins with high praise for grounding his dogmatics in empirical logic and metaphysics.

Channing featured Hopkins as one who "imagined himself a disciple of reason as well as of revelation." Hopkins' "free spirit of inquiry" was in fact Channing's salient orientation. But having rediscovered and recovered for contemporaries the inquiring mind in Hopkins, Channing saddled Hopkins with the misrepresentation that Hopkins "wholly rejected" Original Sin, or at least the hermeneutical principle of interpretation which translates the dogma to mean "imputation of Adam's guilt to his posterity"; the doctrine of Christ's imputed "righteousness or merits to the believer"; and the tenet that "Christ died for the elect only." Channing's selective analysis resulted in the production of arguments based on erroneous premises from which confusion ensued a cacophony of right and wrong.

He managed this error and this paradoxical perplexity or part of the complex plain and plump both profound and simple truth: "Consistent Calvinist" Hopkins most certainly insisted that "Christ suffered equally for all mankind" as clearly as he persisted in adding the universality of the justification by faith in the righteousness of God (Jesus Christ) entailed profound consequences, such as those upspringing from Hopkins' central doctrine of millennialism that Channing intended to erase no less cleanly than Hopkins endeavored to eliminated the Black body from the White mind of North America.

Channing's varnished appraisal of Hopkins' real thought, rational intentions, and logical objectives reveals his understanding of the value of rescuing the jewel in the crown of social ethical reason Hopkins produced from its discredited state. The illumination produced by his rescue operation also discloses Channing's need for legitimation.

Of course the contrast in their form, function, and fashion is styled to highlight Channing's false notion, namely, that in-stead of Puritanism being in essence and manifestation Puritan Piety perforce the rational faith and secular and sacred ethics it appears--Puritanism is a pure and simple religion of rational ethics.

In addition to separating dynamic and neither static nor eradicable Calvinism and Puritanism, from specious reasoning of the spurious opinion they can exist as autonomous phenomena, ethical religion or the Puritan resolve to reason (above all) constitutes for Channing the heart, soul, mind, and will of authentic Puritanism:

> The system of Dr. Hopkins was, indeed, an effort of reason to reconcile Calvinism with its essential truths. Accordingly, his disciples were sometimes called, and willingly called, Rational Calvinists. The impression which he made was much greater than he supposed. The churches of New England received a decided impression from his views; and though his name--once given to his followers--is no longer borne, his influence is still felt. A conflict now going on in our country, for the purpose of mitigating the harsh features of Calvinism, is a stage of the revolutionary movement to which he, more than any man, gave impulse. I can certainly bear witness to the spirit of progress and free inquiry which possessed him. In my youth I preached in his house at the request of the venerable old man. As soon as the services were closed, he...said to me, that theology was imperfect, and that he hoped I should live to carry it towards perfection. Rare and most honorable liberality in the leader

of a sect: He wanted not to secure a follower, but to impel a young mind to a higher truth.[17]

Channing's mid-antebellum re-evaluation of Hopkins illumines especially when it is compared and contrasted with antebellum era antiabolitionist and pro-Colonizationist Harriet Beecher Stowe's postbellum *Old Town Folks* (1869), in which mid-Reconstruction piece the Puritan re-revisionist credits social conservative Jonathan Edwards for contributing the identical liberationist ideas Channing praises social liberal Hopkins for contributing to model New Abolitionist Yankee sons of Puritans like Theodore Parker.

CHANNING'S PURITAN SOCIAL CAUTIOUSNESS

The distinguishable style and substance of Hopkins and Channing, two Puritan-rooted and self-identified Congregationalist reformers, is evident in their demonstrably dissimilar interest in private faith and public ethics. The difference is dramatic where Black folk are the subject and object of their moral thoughts and actions. The fact that their respective ministries were actualized at different times, and in different places, were factors contributing to Hopkins' significantly greater direct involvement with Black Congregationalists, and personal commitment to Black folk's immediate liberty unconditionally and universally. In their rational sincerity and serious purpose--that contributed disparate components to the clarity of Calvinist charity or crystallized Yankee deterrence-benevolence--they were equals and perhaps unequaled.

What is debatable is the extent to which their Puritanism and rationalism interlaced philosophy and theology distorted their vision of reality, in which myopic civil and bifurcated secular and sacred narrowed-scope point of view appeared a distorted image of the Black body. In this Puritan perception is reality perspective the true and real interests of their Black race plummeted to the lowest concern beneath their high priorities, hopes, dreams, and desires.

What is inarguable is that they were given to speak to White Christians about their Black Congregationalist brethren in a way that belied the brotherhood they honestly preached practiced equally poorly. Their White class superiority and Black caste inferiority complex was not an underived presumption but inherent in the premises of their realized and presupposed transcended social conservative *Great Chain of Being* philosophy, that underpinned the culture and metaphysics they both inherited and thought they transmuted personally.

No one doubted they were educated above their race, in a class by themselves or a least a select circle, and acted ahead of their age and on ideas before their time had come. To the extent they were (or were not) ineffectuals in the power realms, and condescending in their relations with Black folk, the fault lay in either/or both the community design and the individual mind.

Neither they nor many other pro-White race/ethnic moralists may have been effectively pro-Black race ethicists. But Black contemporary Calvinist and Arminian clergy certainly were confounded by their dif-ferent premises. They left Black Americans with the precept they should learn to fend for themselves, in their systems and ideal constructs, while they appeared to labor to eliminate the Puritan-Yankee contradiction, that is, the perversion of positive good antiblack white ethnic virtue into positive negation anti-Black race virtue.

They attempted the impossible of feat of resolving the differences between permanent and contraries, that resulted in foolish failure to eradicate the necessary and basic conflict in individual and community inter-ests, rights, and responsibilities.

One reason why they made this error in judgment clearly is rudimentary: the raticionators' power instruments were philosophical-theological principles sub-sisting of deficient culture correcting capacity diminished by their limited and narrow social premises. Whence ritualistic revelation and reason rhetoricians were unequal to the task-responsibility they felt obligated to perform.

Each in his own way and different (Old Abolition and New Abolition) times succeeded in reaching the logic of some, and raising the consciousness of others. But at critical junctures, they both failed to connect relevantly and realistically the heightened conscience of the individual and the community--partly because their coordinates of accuracy and correctness were not harmon-ized with the best known right and good interest of their freely affirmed and denied Black-race cultural kin-group. In this connection, Channing's tribute to Hopkins serves equally well as a description of his own character:

> He had many qualities fitting him for a reformer--great singleness
> of purpose, invincible patience of research, sagacity to detect and
> courage to oppose errors, a thirst for consistency of views, and
> resolution to carry out his principles to their legitimate consequen-
> ces.

CHANNING'S EARLY AND PRIVATE VIEW OF SLAVERY

Channing's consistent conservative cautious creeping change approach to morality made him the voice of tolerance in religion, and moderation in the antislavery conflict. The basis for this Channingesque cost/benefit prudential insurance and assurance is the classical Christian continuum extended by the traditional establishment Calvinist and Puritan values that his reason approved. Channing's defense of this Western Civilization heritage was as inspired as his demonstration of humanitarianism was admired and won him just praise for be-ing neither a revolutionist nor a radical but a prudent prognosticator who con-jectured that "reform is sure."

This public exposed Channingesque distinct decency and instinct for Golden Mean morality and middle-of-the-road social ethics also demonstrates, in un-guarded moments, whom he identifies with as "our people." Channing's English Puritan race and religion self-identity was communicated in his view of "the elective franchise." It was set forth in a letter he wrote to Lucy Akin of Hampstead, England (August 29, 1831) eight months after the first issue of the *Liberator* was printed by founding editor and publisher William Lloyd Garrison, the apogee of New Abolition, all three of which proabolitionist voices antiabolitionist Channing denounced to the public:

> In this country the right of suffrage is next to universal. It may be
> said, everybody votes. But our situation differs from yours. Our
> people are *used* to the right. Then an immense majority have *prop-*
> *erty*, and are directly and strongly interested in the support of
> order and the laws....Then the vast majority of our citizens may be
> called educated; and this we owe partly to a very honourable cause,
> our public provisions for instruction of all classes and partly to

what is our great reproach, I mean *slavery*. In the slave states, the
only voters are the masters, and these from their condition enjoy
many advantages of education of which they generally avail
themselves.

Channing clearly caught himself immediately, and did not (for his own good
reasons) rewrite the section where he approves universal suffrage and, apparently also as a conventional wisdom matter of common sense, the fact that in
every state suffrage excludes free Black Americans (whom he seldom attends
seriously) as well as slaves:

I forgot that the slave was a part of the community having the
rights of a man--so easily do established abuses obscure our
perceptions. I now perceive that we have less cause than I
supposed of boasting of the extension of the elective franchise
here: for if our slaves are men, what a vast number do we exclude!

Later in this same letter Channing develops the private and personal or pure
individual essence of his antislavery position, whose quintessential pro-
gradualism the antiabolitionist was unwilling to publish because he was not yet
prepared to state in public his antislavery position. Just here, as well, he also
reveals his suspect knowledge of the number of Black British inhabitants in
Victorian England, and his surface comprehension of the pervasive power of the
Americanization of anti-Black race values. Although he argued the argument
rather than the facts at an earlier point in the letter, he restates it as he explicitly relates his idea that slavery is a problem of the moral will only and
implicitly denies it is one of power politics also:

On this subject of slavery, you are far in advance of us. I almost
envy your country the pure glory it has won by its sympathy with
the oppressed negro. In truth, when I think of the state of the
public mind here in regard to slavery, my national pride dies within
me. Never did a people deserve chains more than we, who are
vaunting of our freedom and holding one or two million in bondage.
This is truly our foulest blot, and I fear nothing will rouse us up
to wash away but the deep, stern, irresistible indignation of the
civilized world.

In their extended correspondence, Channing and Akin covered incisively and
brilliantly addressed every conceivable academic issue intellectuals were likely to
engage. Slavery was not a major but a minor topic on which they narrowly
focused their broad and ranging analytical minds--during the years English
Abolitionists were making British Abolition law and policy--although Akin and
Channing condemned human bondage with righteous indignation.

In an argument with respected peer intellectuals, Channing customarily drove
every point to its logical conclusion. He therefore did not hesitate to remind
Lucy Akin that the North American "slaveholders reconcile themselves to this
guilt," and to compare their treatment of Black-race slaves to the English
treatment of Irish-ethnic peasants.

Channing had in mind proslavocrat Northeasterners and slavocrat Southeasterners who resented the challenge pressed by adversarial British Abolitionists, assumed what they presumed to be the position of leverage, and reacted by stating that when Englishmen provide their peasantry "as comfortable a hut and as good food as we provide for our slaves," they may then "come to improve the state of things here."

This sophistry did not beguile Channing. But the combination of his awareness of the class problem as a foundational one in the English social experience, and the compulsion to defend the American culture that was under attack for its caste system excited Channing who felt "compelled" to advise the English and counsel Akin that--if for no other reason than fear of the "*formidableness* of the lower classes" and their capacity to seek retribution through eruption-- "the great and rich and educated should be roused to their duty."

Late in 1831, Channing finally declared in private his personal antislavery position--following Garrison's unsuccessful solicitation of his participation in New Abolitionism. Channing wrote: "I have no spirit of violent revolution"--and even

> dread civil convulsions on account of the crimes which follow in their train, and of their tendency to give ascendancy to force and reckless ambition, and to issue in re-morseless tyranny....I have hoped for gradual progress, and have thought, and still think that our present social condi-tion contains the elements and promise of a happier state. I may err, and Providence may see that subversion, not improvement, of existing establishments is the only hope of the human race. Such will be my inter-pretation of violent revolutions, if they come; and I shall see in them motives to the disinterested and generous, the more strenuous efforts and more sparing sacrifice for the regeneration of the world.

Channing's succinct statement articulates the sum and substance of establishmentarian anti-Black race policy and antiabolitionism.

RELUCTANT PIETY AND PROPHET

This articulation of his moral verve and vision was Channingesque pessimism-checking and realism-deterring vintage optimism. Optimism fortified Channing throughout his life, constituted the dynamic content of his character, energized his propensity to focus on the ripple of hope in a sea of despair, and supported his consistent complete confidence in a brighter tomorrow and better future throughout the slavery crisis: "My hopes greatly prevail over my fears as to the result of the present struggle."

Quite like John Calvin, the architect of rational Calvinist faith and reason for his fathers and his intellectual nemesis, Channing did not believe might makes right. But unlike Calvin Channing was certain right makes might. Thus dissimilar from Calvin who taught that the moral evil of the majority could not be defeated by the "Elect" minority, but that it could be counterchecked and kept from becoming the overbalancing presence only by civil military force and the political power exercised by the magistrate, the source of Channing's optimism was his convincement of the imminent "regeneration of the world by the peaceful influences of Christianity and increasing knowledge."

Neither in this arguably Channingesque secularized version of the sacred millenniarian enterprise--that Edwards and Hopkins expended enormous energy in exciting--nor in his unpublicized antislavery sentiment did he differ from the Rhode Island Old Abolitionist Puri-tan. But instead of witnessing the Hopkinsian "improvement" that Channing had doggedly insisted (since 1803) would evolve over time, through time, and certainly in time from the sets of rational principle, process, and program plans pioneered by the professionals, he was persuaded (finally in 1835) by the proliferating mass-ive evidence publicly disseminated universally that the problem of slavery was worsening.

Certainly Channing's optimism was not chastened upon "learning somewhat slowly how possible it is for intrigue and fanaticism" or "vehement impulse and selfish calculation" to meet in the same mind, which, he averred, is at once left with a disordered reason, as well as a disturbed conscience, and thereby "moral as well as intellectual perceptions" are disheveled.

As he grew "older," Channing discovered "morbid bigotry"; and that he had become less indulgent of both fanaticism and that "more cheerful form of insanity, enthusiasm." Concurrently, he experienced along with his expanding rational powers and reasoning capability a growing reverence for the power of reason; and especially a deeper assurance of his rational comprehension of "universal truths" and "great moral principles."

What Hopkins and the Puritans called Piety also developed in the host in himself of the Yankee secular variation on the sacred tradition: "I am kept more and more in peace by my deeper, more reverential conviction of the mysteriousness of Providence." Unexpectedly for a Religious Humanism protestant and professor, Channing went so far as to confess that whereas once he [I] had "presumed to be a prophet,...now I hope and submit."

Of course, he did not simply hope or entirely submit. His belief in the linear moral progress of the civilized world, advancing through "gradual, gentle, peaceful processes," continued uninterrupted with his observations that made him less certain that the "worn-out, corrupt state of things is to be transformed by a quiet transition into a fresh and healthy one." Pursuant to these stable change developments, Channing reveals unwittingly the basic worldview he shares with Hopkins:

> There are elements of good in all societies, but often so overpowered by evil growth of centuries, that convulsions are necessary to set them free. I do hope that destruction is not required for renovation: but if they to whom society has a right to look for beneficent renovation, concentrate all their powers to resist, the same awful Providence which has in past times shaken the social state, will again leave it from his foundations.

The social conservative/philosophical liberal anti-Calvinst Puritan disclosed to readers of his rigorous reasoning and racionative reaches why it would be difficult for Calvinist Puritans to put the matter in Evangelical Calvinist terms more clearly than their fellow Yankee set forth in his new testament, and self-revelation of the faith in reason gospel of goodness and rightness according to Channing.

Evidently, what distinguishes Channing from Hopkins is not their equally like and different adamant refusal to rest upon political foresight. The distinctive factor is the millennial doctrine constituting the ultimate hope of Hopkins. Yet, this critical component in the counter-culture critique of the pro-Calvinist so highly praised by the anti-Calvinist compares rather more nicely than it contrasts sharply with Channing's ultimate ground of optimism:

> My religious faith in human nature, in God's purposes towards his spiritual family, never fails me.

Black folk, whom Hopkins and Channing compared to White folk and contended they possessed adequate if not equal "human nature" gifts and graces, could not be so sanguine. The *de facto* and *de jure* undergirding rationalistic structures of both men were not *ipso facto* harmless to the Black Americans, even though Hopkins and Channing were one insofar as their course was fixed upon the stars. Quite like two ships in the dead of night passing over victims adrift in the sea, they generated great expectations. They saw the individual Black people, but did not see the whole Black race they were members of, and therefore failed to rescue their perishing Black body of free-born, freed, fugitive, and bondmen contemporaries.

CHANNING'S PUBLIC ANTISLAVERY AND
ROMANTIC VISION OF BLACK FOLK

The antislavery undercurrents in Channing's moral precepts were not produced spontaneously in the splendor of isolated contemplation. Prior to serious slavery ideas entering his irreversible reflectiveness, there emerged moral giants blessed with not only courage and conscience but sufficient common sense to know they could not single-handedly cause the desired social structural change effect; and who, therefore, organized as the British Abolition Society, the Old Abolitionist Societies, and the American Colonization Society. Fifteen years after the formation of the ACS, which was the last of these three rational antislavery bodies to be established, Channing was driven to discover and defend his pro-gradualist sensibilities by William Lloyd Garrison--the original Boston pro-immediatist who departed the ACS as decisively as Channing disaffected from the Congregational Association.

Forthwith Channing's pro-gradualism sympathies were deepened and broadened as his heightened reaction to the aggressive pro-immediatists increased, whom he preferred to refer to contemptuously as the "professed Abolitionists." Channing did not appreciate the fact that the New Abolitionists appeared suddenly to fill the Puritan Old Abolitionist vacuum. He seemed equally oblivious to the truth that the void was partially created by his absence--with the Congregationalist clerical host--from the Old Abolition Societies that had continued since their inception on the eve of the Revolution, whose contingent Samuel Hopkins was the first Calvinist Puritan clergyman to join.

Channing thought the New Abolitionists' bid for dominance of the antislavery movement would divert and delay his prophesied linear progress of moral minds in accelerating the declining significance of slavery. He had "received severe criticism" from New Abolitionists for his opposition to swift social change of the superstructure and infrastructure, that he neither took lightly nor suffered gladly. The protypical liberal appeared, in the perception of radicals, quite like the reactionary slavocrats and Northern proslavocrats. Contrapositively, he came to believe, New Abolitionists were so "unwise and intemperate" that they reduced to silence the "intelligent and intellectual people" or the voices of moderation. Yet, until the awakening as a result of the shaking of the foundations by the New Abolitionists, he chose not to make public his mature views on the subject.

Channing felt severely constrained on the one side by the New Abolitionists, who, in his estimation, had turned the antislavery movement into a professional enterprise and held it captive to their private strictures. His anger turned to scorn when he attacked the host of immediatism--and Evangelical Calvinist who proved his match as a model modern moralist--William Lloyd Garrison (1805-79). Editor Garrison printed his unconditional, universal, and immediate abolitionism position in the first edition of his Boston-published *Liberator* (1831).

Garrison's New Abolitionist paper originated in the year he was organizing the New England (renamed Massachusetts) Anti-Slavery Society that Channing refused to join. The Boston Society emerged one of the founding bodies of the 1833-organized American Anti-Slavery Society (AAS). The AAS understood itself as the original antebellum complement of the British Abolition Society, but surfaced as so strong a statement that it appeared un-American to liberals like Channing, conservatives, like Lyman Beecher, and other contemporaries identifying themselves as moderates but who could not be distinguished from the legalistic literalists. These positive bad and good law-ruled ruling elders, more precisely than high Chrisitianity and civility informed conscience-conforming law and order respecting respectable rulers, believed the proslavery Moral Law of the Bible and the positive law of the Constitution were instituted by God and therefore should be obeyed and not questioned.

While the *Liberator* was a radical paper because it countenanced neither untying nor loosening but condoned cutting the Gordian Knot, and thereby this medium of the print media incited a counterbalancing reactionary establishment, Garrison's most forceful work was his anti-Colonizationist *Thoughts on African Colonization* (1832).

On the other side, Channing was constrained by his distaste for controversy; and by his reluctance "to encounter the dissuasives, disapprobation and frowns" of the respectable people, who were his associates and parishioners:

> All my feelings, and, I may add, my interest, dictated
> silence to me. But I could not, I dared not, be still.

Channing's initial polished public antislavery testament, a slim volume entitled *Slavery* (1835), was written against this background: four years after the first issue of the *Liberator*, two years after the formation of the Massachusetts Anti-Slavery Society, and a year and a half after the organization of the AAS. His chief goal was to discuss human bondage in the light of basic principles: "What I esteem universal and eternal, truth"; the general "grounds of justice and humanity"; and liberty or self-determination. In this context, what the English Puritan race Channing represented thought of the Black race their progenitors created in North America is less grand than what the Puritan romanticist thought of slavery and freedom:

> Of all the races of men, the African is the mildest and most
> susceptible of attachment. He loves, where the European would
> hate. He watches the life of the master, whom the North American
> Indian, in like circumstances, would stab to the heart. The African
> is affectionate.[18]

The perversion of positive into negative antiblack white ethnic virtue and interconnected with Channingesque gradualism, proceeded apace mid-antebellum linear moral progress, and produced the solidification of antiabolitionism and anti-Black race interests. The development is unmistakable in the Yankee-Puritan "apostle of Unitarianism." It occurs in his humanistic romanticism of charity, exactly where it was located by "apostle of abolition" Hopkins in his Half-way Piety deterrence-benevolence ethic.

Prior to the death of Edwards and his own relocation in Newport, Hopkins' Evangelical love and affection was expressed in his earnest engagement of the Algonquian Indians, who were located near his parish in Stockbridge, Massachusetts. These sentiments intensified with his outreach to them--in their compounds on the Massachusetts reservations--early in his ministry. Hopkins' real concern with Black-race slaves--among whom he ministered usefully after the middle of his career--was equally solid, and demonstrated in direct action.

Hopkins was too fully informed by his millennial-evangelical mission, and Evangelical British Abolition relations, for him to have been inspired to engage either the Indian ethnics, or the Black race, merely in the humanistic spirit of his world-influential contemporary, Jean Jacques Rousseau (1712-78): the Swiss-French philosopher who escalated and elevated romanticism to a virtue, and doubtless was the original mind in which appeared the cult of "*the noble savage.*" Rousseau lived briefly in England, but had a significant affect upon the English Romantics. Without ques-tion, his impact upon the French Enlightenment-informed and British Enlightenment-influenced Thomas Jefferson, American individualism, and the French Revolution was no less consequential.

Paralleling these English descendants' national union on the basis of shared values such as a common belief in the superiority of their English race heritage, and regional political division due to different economic interests, howbeit patrician Channing was no more a natural or native Boston brahmin because he represented the older New England families than aristocrat Jefferson was a pure democrat because the slavemaster founded the Democratic Party, there is a high probability that Rousseau had a more indirect negative than direct positive effect upon Channing.

Channing was developing from Rhode Island childhood through adolescence in the late 1700s to manhood in the 1800s, and/or a "Rhode Island Yankee" divergence advancing as a "Massachusetts Yankee" in Boston toward American convergence. This constancy and change condition was contributed to substantially by his unexamined embrace of the American White Gentlemen's Agreement (Constitution), the "more perfect Union" of opposite real interests, and the English commonality without due regard for the Northeastern patrician and Southeastern aristocrat different real interests and values made explicit by the Massachusetts and Virginian competitors forward from the early national period.

Yet the naturalized and certified neither born nor baptized Bostonian, like the Yankee preponderance of Channing's Anglo-American class and profession, passed for a certified pro-Federalist Puritan parson; abhorred the French Revolution; and loved order even more than he adored the British.

As a rational idealist and romantic optimist, Chan-ning was like and different from Rousseau and the Ro-mantics to the degree he was a Puritan elitist--that is, effectively one of the power elite who found the "simple peasant" somewhat unappealing, and the American Indian no "noble savage" at all.

Nonetheless, there existed no missing link and primarily dynamic connective

linkage between the European and American Enlightenment confluence. Chan
ning's Romantic inclination-and natural cultural instinct nurtured if not inspired
by the Continent-influenced Romanticists in North America--was too strong and
poignantly related to the Black race for him to have been unaware of the
French Romanticists. Relative to each Western power and political economy engaged in the European, New World, and African Triangular Slavetrade, French
intellectuals emerged the pioneer theoretical developers of Romanticism, and
experts in experiential experimentalism, who, combining theory and experience
in reality, initiated the new school of thought which concentrated on viewing
through the Romantic perspective their Black-race African ethnics and New
World folk they deethnicized.

Correlatively, there existed within the range of Channing's worldwide intellectual inquiry and perception the Abbé Henri Grégoire (1750-1831): a French
Jansenist priest, revolutionist, and writer whose lib-eral literary publications
emphasized racial equality. Grégoire published--in the year the Constitution
man-dated the termination of the international slavetrade--the widely read De
La Litterature Des Negres (1808), in which work he celebrates the eighteenth-
century Black American writers who were widely admired in Europe and ignored
in America: Benjamin Banneker (1731-1806); Gustavas Vassa (1745-1801); and
Phillis Wheatley (1754?-84).[19] Either compared and contrasted to or within this
sphere of influence upon Channingesque liberal secular/sacred Christianity and
civility, the reflective romantic rationalism of Yankee-Puritan and major moralist Channing illuminates the virtue and vice of the standard conservative social
values and liberal individual principles device:

> The African is so affectionate, imitative, and docile, that in favorable
> circumstances he catches much good; and accordingly the influence of a
> wise and kind master will be seen in the very countenance and bearing
> of his slaves. Among this degraded people, there are, occasionally, exam-
> ples of superior intelligence and virtue.... We also witness in this class,
> and very often, a superior physical development, a grade of form and
> motion, which almost exhorts a feeling approaching respect.[20]

The Reverend Ralph Waldo Emerson (1803-82) shared this perception, that
most certainly was a step behind Grégoire if not a step ahead of the model
Puritan public parson, person, and servant--the Reverend Cotton Mather
(1663-1728), whose management manual entitled A Good Master Well Served
(1696) remained the standard color class/bondage class command and control
handbook for Christian slavemasters. Compared to the Channingesque and
Emersonian rational romantic racialism, Grégoire approached Black folk with
greater appreciation and attention to their achievements which the Bostonians
may have read in the English translation (1810) of his book entitled An Inquiry
Concerning the Intellectual and Moral Faculties, and Literature of Negroes.

Neither Channing nor a statistically significant number of the Puritan clerical elite managed to mention positively the creative works of Black Americans
in their published prose--to say little of either treating seriously the writing
projects of Black folk or eval-uating critically their significance. Channing
avowed that in experience (and theory howbeit seldom if ever in reality) he
approached the point of being able to "respect" the body singly and not also
the mind of Black folk.

Therewith Rhode Islander Channing evinced the difference in value of the color caste/class values for the Puritan and Anglican slavemaster, whereby, unlike the former (Yankee) and the latter (Cavalier) slaveholder, the native of the former slave capital of the North determined the profit and pleasure he found in the Black body to be a difference without a distinction.

Channing has to be taken at his word, that he was motivated by his peculiar attraction to motor phenomena to "respect" the physical prowess of the Black race, whether or not his equally compulsive class and caste consciousness reflected his social conservative Puritan nature he inherited as honestly as his being a birth-right cautious parson person, radical rational romantic racialist, and liberal moralist.

But his remarkable gifts of grace and grit notwithstanding, he could determine the real possibility inherent in the opportunity he was presented by Garrison to contribute "respect" to the Black race was an offer he could afford refuse. Albeit his free election and selection of an alternative choice was a viable option without any cost to pure profane principle, nevertheless he missed an accessible connection with social redeeming power. Although Channing may not have been imbued with the anti-Black race spirit, the value judgment that he was no less a potent and primed pro-Black race interest-specific agency than he was a powerful promoter of pro-White race values lacks compelling force only where ideas are without meaning, and values are innocent of social consequences.[21]

Praiseworthy for not advocating the social conservative color-bind rule of ignorance, and blameworthy for being as color-conscious as his admired predecessors Mather and Hopkins, Channing received more credit from the class of conventional wisdom and centrist common sense than he earned and deserved for either looking straight through or overlooking contemporary Black Patriots who were not only Revolutionary War heroes but synchronous Black community leaders and brethren of the cloth.

Among the productive and published New World Black Americans who were sufficiently famous to attract the attention and receive the serious critical praise and criticism of Old World race relations specialists such as Grégoire, Channing's liberal elder contemporary, who focused sharply on their productive life and work in his books as early as 1790, stood out the one representative power person whom naturally White Americans studiously ignored for the same reasons that the Black self-liberator not only provoked fears but evolved into a phenomenon presence who posed a real threat and struck terror in hearts of some Frenchmen, to wit, Francois Dominique Touissant L'Ouverture (c.1744-1803): whose military-patriotic achievements including defeating the British (in 1793) and winning Haitian Independence from France (in 1801).

Currently Channing, who never doubted the value of the American Sons of Liberty in whose front ranks Black Patriots were active, wrote off Black hero contemporaries and the descendants of these Freedom Fighters who made the supreme sacrifice.

So far from demonstrating great graciousness, real grace, or appropriate gratitude, Channing did not threatened but promised Black free-born and slave men of proven promise and performance they could be certain of one thing: whenever and wherever a North American Touissant L'Ouverture type of self-liberationist emerges, to imitate the Black Baptist insurrection (1800) bent Gabriel Prosser or preacher/self-determinationist Nat Turner (whose 1831 insurrection impacted the senses of all discerning Americans), "our physical power is pledged against him in case of revolt."

The Unitarian father proudly proclaims himself to the public an unqualified anti-Black race interest agent and dedicated promoter of pro-White race interests; one "with a deep feeling" of total opposition to any action that could "put in jeopardy the peace of the Slaveholding States"; and a modulating moderate moralist who identifies with the Protestant powerhouses in legitimate control of legal injustice and the repub-lican democracy's slavocracy, whom he pronounces honorable White "men," "Christians," and "citizens." The exciting reality and glowing attractiveness to Channing of White Anglo-Saxon Protestant is natural and evident in his antiabolitionist appeal to slavocrats to switch to his antislavery principle, poignant as he pontificates that the proslavocracy principle the class of the slavocrats promote "wants the vision of a Christian," and a sharp contrast to his idea of the ideal Black-race "fellow-creatures who in outward circumstances are repulsive," naturally, simply because they are "burned by a fiercer sun."

If not a throwback to the English continuum of chiaroscurists that Anglo-American John Cotton initiated in North America, and Cotton Mather and Jonathan Edwards extended imaginatively, the traditional Calvinist moral tone and Puritan function of chiaroscuro is sustained in Channing's admonition to White folk that their Black bondman is "yet a brother, a child of God, a man possessing all the rights of humanity, under a skin darker than your own."

Channing employs the hue, lightness, and saturation dimensions of color to adorn the tale; to point "the moral importance of the question of slavery"; and to elicit "moral goodness, virtue, religion," or to incite "sympathy" and empathy, from Protestants prone to seduce and engage in the pursuit of illicit pleasure and profit without pain or happiness. But despite the good intentions of Channing, transmitted in his encounter with minds resolved to protect their real interests and to expand different purposes, he failed to heed his own advice and accept the truth that his fine "distinctions cannot add to the dignity" of the Black race.

In his high-wrought opposition to human bondage--in principle--he elucidated elaborately all "attributes of our common humanity which reduce to insignificance all outward distinctions," and reasoned so carefully the responsible rationalist never came close to recommending the abolition of the domestic slave-trade, slavery, and anti-Black race values. Electing to approve for the White male and disapprove for the Black male immediate and unconditional universal self-determination, for rationalizable prudential reasons of expedience and convenience that settled on excuse, Channing ended his disquisition on *Slavery* by arguing the merits and demerits of the deterrence-benevolence policy promoted by the American Colonization Society, whose serious criticism had the effect of legitimatizing the recognized *bona fides* of the ACS.

PRO-GRADUALIST CHANNING'S ADMIRATION

FOR PRO-IMMEDIATIST HOPKINS' CHARITY

Challenged in the cultural crisis to connect Christianity and civility and effect change in the social system, Channing responded with this small but comprehensive book on *Slavery*. In his slim volume, he develops Hopkins' Calvinist revisionist social ethics indictment of human bondage into an electrokinetic moral power primer; and a guidebook for ethicists whose electrogalvanized ethics were so powerful its discharged varying decibels of resounding condemnation of slavery was heard by alert Americans throughout the land. His exquisite juxtaposition of moral judgment, clear commitment to an absolute end, and expedient "means of removing slavery" added lustre to his fame as an evenhanded model modern moderate moralist.

Channing wrote to establish the middle ground, he was certain he could dominate if not control, upon which tough turf he hoped the proslavery and antislavery forces might compromise their principles (like the Founding Fathers who negotiated the Constitution) and reach a civil solution. His moral negation and positive resolution principles were steeped in goodwill to Black and White folk--rather than in disinterested will to the good and right best interest of both the Black-race minority and the intensive White race/ethnic minorities comprising the American majority.

Due to many more reasons than his emergence as a rationalist, such as being an intentionalist rather than a consequentialist moralist, Channing confused good intentions with positive consequences; and fused the best known good interest possible of the Black race with the real estate interests of the White race. His critical imposition of the real values of White folk upon the true values of Black folk was in thought and action as sincere and serious as its premise (what is good for White folk is good for Black folk) and consequences were harmful.

The peril of this fine point differs as a harm-intensive nice nuance in degree but not in kind from Hopkins' deterrence-benevolence. Channing abolishes the dual individual and community coordinates of ethical duty, and advances the individual as the sole change force. Thus he promotes the instrument of private charity as the single public means of social responsibility; and the instrument of public justice as the private means of social accountability. As a result of his lost and misplaced Puritan Piety public interest functions--such as the individual and community engaging power in the civil order to promote love and to expand justice--his recommendation of political power-devoid pure moral reason meets with confusion, rather than the hoped for agreement.

Channing published his dogmatic pragmatic and pragmatic dogmatic morality less than eight years after the gradual manumission acts of New York finally outlawed slavery in the Empire State. But onetime passionate Federalist Party parson Channing overlooked this recent experience: as absolutely as he had abandoned politics for morality with the demise of the Federalist Party, and wrote to defend the proslavery Constitution.

He argued the arguments whose premises asserted that intellectuals and Northerners in the free states could offer "general vicar and principles"; the slavemaster "alone has an intimate knowledge of the character and habits of the slaves" and thus only the slaveowner knows the effective "means of emancipation"; and, therefore, that to the "slaveholder belongs the duty of settling and employing the best methods of liberation, and to no other."

As an up-to-date power elite protectionist's reinterpretation of the law and order the White Gentlemen's Agreement (to strike conscience and compromise principles to construct a Constitution and Union) legitimatized, Channing's Protestant dictum of "no right of interference" demonstrates conclusively his defense of "states' rights": as well as the progressive transformationist's interpretation of the Constitution as a static rather than a dynamic sacred document. His rigid rather than flexible approach concentrates the mind because it is the direct opposite of his treatment of the Bible, the other sacred of the republic.

His literal dictation and strict constructionist interpretation of the civil/secular sacred document upsprings from Channing's doctrine of fairness. Channing-esque "noninterference" turns on the liberal's positive thinking, and guarantee that a rational "friendly relation between master and slave" can be produced by appealing to the enlightened self-interest of slavocrats whose realism dictated that self-serving interests were far more productive. Channing was con-vinced he needed only to remind each slavemaster who presumably could follow the logic of an argument of the prudential value inherent in developing harmonious master/slave relations.

He certified that common sense dictates to the prudent slaveholder that stubborn refusal to institute a humane human bondage system will precipitate intervention by the Federal Government. Moreover, he averred, slaves should be set free as an "an expression of benevolence." In a word, slaves ought not to be liberated by force because there is no known good reason to doubt and every reason to fear the inevitable outcome of any Touissantesque or Turner-esque liberation, namely, un-mixed "jealousy, vindictiveness, and hatred."

The slavemaster who initiates Channingesque deterrence-benevolence with high "regard for his rights," and for those of the slave as well, becomes the "benefactor and deliverer" who retains his role as the superior to whom the inferior will look "cheerfully and gratefully for counsel and aid." Channing, in effect, counseled suspension of reality. He argued with the facts the case that Northerners lacked experience with slaves and, therefore, were devoid of com-petence to offer efficient solutions to the problem of bondage. The argument he put forth was deficient of efficient force essentially because it failed to counterbalance two facts: a majority of slave-free states had rela-tively recent-ly become nonslaveholding commonwealths; and the flow of Southerners to the West--both with their slaves and to expand slavocracy by admitting territories to the Union as new slaveholding states--was as continuous as their interaction with Northerners in the South and the North.

Channing's pontificated moral command to observe his universal and irrevo-cable essential human qualities was candidly and publicly delivered. Partly be-cause of this overt rather than covert operative mode, once the closet conser-vative moderate discovered the moderate conservative ingress and egress and exited from the ethics closet a middle-of-the-road ethicist, Channing blind-sided few if any public morals professionals yet shocked and surprised many of his slaveowning Christian auditors. His arguable case for liberty being the natural condition and right of the involuntary servitude dehumanized Black American as well as his White American dehumanizer was advanced without fear of contra-diction, on the presumption that slavocrats were either ignorant or innocent of his pure reason and moral truth, and with the certainty that once conscious and convicted rational men of heightened conscience would undergo a moral conver-sion from whence "the whole intellect and benevolence of the South" would create a plan that would carry out his principle of gradual emancipation.

His philosophical cultural premises and therefore his logic determined the Black race to be without virtue, and presumption of perpetrated by the premier Protestant rationalist reinforced the analysis and conclusion similarly high-mind White Northerners and Southerners readily accepted. However, while White Nor-theasterners agreed with his corollary that in sum and substance the Black race is without significant value, slaveholders reacted violently as if a fragrant limitation of their fundamental fiscal stakes and economic shares in the system had been committed whenever anyone dared to intimate that their great profit and pleasure producing chattel property was worthless. Channing completely missed or dismissed the real interests heart and soul of the matter: partly because he was neither able nor willing to believe the facts and arguments slavocrats and proslavocrats relentlessly published; and partly because Yankee-Puritan tribalism overwhelmed his secular humanism, and surfaced as an anti-Black race estimate even slavemasters found totally unacceptable.

Beyond his own need to make a public confession of his private identification with the superior class and inferior caste social convention, the concession served to validate his credentials as a lover of the White Puritan race. It followed in logic--but not in faith and ethics as automatically--that Channing possessed the right and the responsibility to improve the value of the White race in order to protect its interest. His devaluation of the Black race, and non-judgmental appeal to the self-interest of the White race and ethnic groups to initiate moderate cultural attitudinal and behavioral modifications rather than fundamental change, was on its face bad ethics but great psychology: when compared to Hopkins' flawed and Edwards' flawless Empirical Rational psychology.

Correlatively, the application of ethics by Edwards and Channing to their understanding of the White American Religion (anti-Black race interest) was less praiseworthy or more blameworthy than Hopkins' deterrence-benevolence. Old Abolitionist Hopkins was too wise in his certainty to believe, for a moment, that White race and ethnic groups possessed the capacity to apply to their color caste/captive class and cultural kin-group the principles promoted by Jonathan Edwards in his slim and slender but fibrous book on ethics, *The Nature of True Virtue* (1765)--not to mention the Hopkinsian ethic of benevolence and extension of the Edwards' manifest essence of Evangelical Calvinism or true religion.

Contrariwise, Hopkins was absolutely certain White race/ethnic folk would not actualize charity and fully embrace their Black-race cultural kinspeople in America. Whence his rational mind, Evangelical heart, millennial soul, and Calvinist will overrode the *agape*-love-power-justice ethic with mercy and charity whose transformation process resulted in deterrence-benevolence, whereby Hopkins proposed to dispose of the Black race in Africa.

Hopkins believed his audacious and arrogant parochial and private Black-race removal criminal syndicate served the public and the best interest of Black Americans. He managed this error as the truth effectively because he and Stiles and their Congregationalist clergy cohorts, in this so insensitive Black-race excludable defensive and offensive as to be nothing short of a crime against humanity, elected to insult and demean the intelligence of the free Black community by choosing not to consult the Black leadership of the independent Black denominations.

As if to leave no one mistaken about his motivation who accepted the convention that imitation is the sincerest form of flattery, and neither accidentally nor incidentally but predeliberately like "Consistent Calvinist" Hopkins, blue-chip Channing rushed to press his blue ribbon emancipation blueprint for the Boston as well as Virginia and Kentucky blue blood. He raced right passed not only the co-equally prominent and hegemonic Manhattan and Philadelphia but also the Boston-based brilliant and *bona fide* Black leadership class, as if the visible color caste class dematerialized into an indivisible invisible Black body. But unlike Hopkins, his moral mentor, Channing at least ensured the blue-blooded citizenry his emancipation plan was designed to liberate the Black race in America, to be a "benevolent enterprise," and to guarantee "a happy result" for each and every White and Black American.

Channing's blameable pro-gradualism process neither made law nor policy but won the praise of honorable men and women because it was good in theory; and even though the imperceptibility of its experience base was exceeded only by the absence of its correspondence with the color caste/captive condition-securing Northern democracy and Southern slavocracy reality. This pro-White race interest-intensive and anti-Black race values-specific American cultural soul Samuel Hopkins accurately analyzed but leaped to the incorrect conclusion fifty years earlier: because the facts and figures he drew on skillfully argued the direct opposite arguments of those he advanced to make his point.

Briefly stated, Hopkins was correct in what he affirmed and incorrect in what he denied. Hopkins was satisfied White male theory and Black male experience validated his truth claim: pro-White race real interests and values directed to nullify pro-Black race real interests and values are latent and manifest vice, but cannot be corrected by any device including eternal vigilance or sustained virtue.

Channing drew the logical conclusion that voluntary private emancipation by principled planters, and other slaveholders of less massive numbers of chattel prop-erty, was the best alternative in a condition where the state normally enforced the law proscribing personal liberation by any individual slavemaster. He was accurate in abstract reason and inaccurate in concrete application because (A) Northern White and Black New Abolitionists obstructed the justice meted out by the lawless White ethnic mobocracy, and befriended the lawbreaking fugitive from legal injustice who elected self-liberation or help to attain self-determination; and (B) proslavocrats in the ambiguous North and slavocrats in the solid South were united (1) in their general opposition to any violations or violators of the civil law, including infractions by slavemasters who take the law into their own hands and execute acts of manumission, and (2) in total resistance to sacrificing their private property, profit, and pleasure on principle such as either the pure pious or the pure profane antislavery altar.

Necessarily evolving from total lack of neither either judgment or courage nor competence but into nonappearing credibility apparently occurring as a direct result of the Yankee proclivity to be pragmatic--that followed in logic and life the Puritan propensity for avoiding terror and falling into error--Channing emerged a self-fulfilling prophecy, as his wish for cautious and careful civil conformance became fulfilled as the truth and consequences of the establishment Trinitarian and Unitarian Congregationalists.

Taking the counsel and advice of Channing seriously, or at least his prestige as the confirmation of their convincement and proof they were not avenging vindictiveness but the right and righteous committed to vindicate truth and justice, Protestant establishmentarians expanded their endorsement of the expedience or prudence value; denied it was a blameworthy principle and process or policy; and affirmed it to be a praiseworthy ethic which the peter principle prototypes consummated by accelerating their application of their prudential morality to a moribund solution.

The Puritan Piety overriding Halfway Piety deterrence-benevolence ethic's idea of private virtue as the parochial answer to any public problem--including legal slavery and anti-Black race desire--had long since been discredited. What seemed less astonishing than illuminating to proabolitionist Garrison, the nemesis of antiabolitionist Channing, was that partisan power Federalist Party politics parsons knew the idea was dead upon the arrival of the Constitution for ratification by the colonies--whether or not he believed that the lesson was lost on establishmentarian parsons because they had abandoned competition in the civil sector.

Channing further moved against Garrisonianism to make it nearly impossible for any reasonable citizen to harbor any doubt concerning his posture, when he qualified and clarified his pro-gradualism premise upon stating "I intend" "immediate emancipation" "by no means." Hopkins' original formula for removing the Black-race body, which through error of not deception but perception he conceived as the answer to eradicating slavery immediately and efficiently, was up-dated by Channing's counterdemanding contemporaries and implemented as the driving rational organizing principle of their American Colonizationist Society. Channing precluded the pro-Colonizationists' "colonizing" scheme from his itemized catalog of macro and micro ways and means he recommended the public adopt and adapt to end slavery gradually, and thereby placed distance between himself and other advocates of gradualism as a result of fashioning two fundamental factors among other apparent reasons.

First, as distinguished Evangelical Protestants who were not only fellow advocates of antiabolitionism but his adversaries as rival sectarian evangelists and revivalists, Channing believed himself to be a model nonsectarian: a liberal Protestant for whom proselytization is a meteoric rise of "enthusiasts" to stratospheric spiritual heights, that frequently ends not in the climatic "born again" experience but a crash landing and thus is too crass a course for champions of civility.

Second, on this major matter of moral reason and relevance, he agreed with Garrison--his sharpest social ethics critic--and argued to make the Evangelical New Abolitionist's compelling point stick: Colonization of the Black race in Africa is a bewitching "compact with hell" or barefaced White Christian Gentlemen's Agreement, averred Garrison, the consequences of whose rational thoughts and actions is the perpetuation of "the evil without end."

ANTIABOLITIONIST EMANCIPATIONIST

Old Abolitionist Hopkins believed slavery must end by any means necessary. Contrapositively, in 1835, emancipationist Channing believed slavery should end by all honorable means possible. Currently the faithful Unitarian host in himself was declared an infidel in principle by Hopkins' dogmatics, and in practice by contemporary doctrinaire pro-Calvinists.

Yet the Evangelical Calvinist New Abolitionists who initiated correspondence with Channing, and were not a failure to communicate their desire for conciliation and cooperation rather than confrontation, discovered themselves charged by Channing with contempt of civil-ity and for being in error.

Materializing in the appearances as a classic Christian contradiction in terms, Channing anathematized the New Abolitionists as a sad and sorry presence. This damnation issued forth from the anti-Calvinist host in himself despite the fact nothing was more perfectly clear than their existence as the authentic Puritan Piety public interest ethics-expanding heirs of Old Abolitionist Hopkins, whose spiritual kinship was their demonstrable union with him in demanding immediate, universal, and unconditional abolition.

Strange to say, Channing acclaimed the illustrious rational powers of Old Abolitionist Hopkins at the same time he denied the Puritan's New Abolitionist Yankee heir apparent (Garrison) was his match as moral rationalist, and denigrated New Abolitionist Evangelical Calvinists upon he pinned the deprecative label "enthusiasts." Compared and contrasted with his broad perspective, antiabolitionist Channing adjudged the proabolitionists held "too narrow views"--for example, their insistence upon interassociating slavery with slavocracy, and upon denouncing this slave system and functional unit of democracy an intrinsic "evil."

Counteragent Channing turned livid in the face of this vivid character judgment, that he censured as uncivil character assassination. In reacting to the deconstructionist analysis and conclusion swiftly, Channing countered with an early reconstruction slavocracy history. He strove to confute proabolitionists he accused of perpetrating a proliferating sweeping generalization, and an unfair characterization of proslavocrats.

Proslavocrat Channing charged the anti-slavocrats were not only pure "pomp and circumstance" but also a clear and present dangerous crusade against the slavocrats: who plainly assigned blame; induced in slavocrats unmerited "guilt"; and adduced groundless aspersions of the White Christian fidelity of his Southern firm friends of the slavocracy, and permanent enemies of his antislavocrat formidable foes.

New Abolitionists were agitators, Channing countercharged, claiming this was a fitting characterization because what he committed his professional career to eradicating they created: a "system of affiliated societies" modeled after the denominations he and Garrison similarly found objectionable for different reasons. New Abolitionist societies were correspondent with the new rational organizing systems being developed by church and state bureaucrats and technocrats, to promote special religious and secular interests--in either/or both ecclesiastical and civil affairs.

But, in the judgment of Channing, the denomination (unification of local churches into a superchurch) constituted a collective or community organizations united to secure their common interests; the opposite of his cherished individual angels of mercy only, as Protestant organized religion composed of national churches and institutions; and the unmistakable ubiquitous presence of demonic political power and absence of pure moral power and, therefore, to be regretted, renounced, and repelled.

Contrapositively, countervailing Channing argued, an equal fault is that community organizations, public partisan parties or private associations, and class action collectives--formed for competitive pursuit of conflicting or common interests and shared values--are not alliances for progress. Improvement of the human condition, counteractant Channing pontificated, can be achieved only by "individual action."

In this one fell stroke Channing mixed the social conservative secular humanist individual-only responsibility and rights principle (unnecessarily selectively promoted and frequently without appropriate connection to community rights and responsibilities), underpinning the republican democracy, and the Evangelical Protestant principle perforce personal individual rebirth in and for the parochial society. In the process of driving the private principle to sever the public political force-dynamized and *agape*-love/power/justice-responsive community of law and order, Channing set a prece-dent for Protestants and Other Americans United for Separation of Church and State (1947) and calcified American Civil Religion.

Channing elevated the collective community wisdom and foolishness neither correcting nor corrected by individual conscience so high that at the climax of his escalation process the solitary individual soul was perched above risking the advantage and disadvantage of community consensus. Channing presumed he had eclipsed neither military nor cultural but only political power, or transcended majority rule apropos the masses voting with their feet to defeat the elite.

From this olympian height of contempt and conceit, the liberal escaped both political pragmatism and theological dogmatism. But a singular result was that he became an unwitting catalyst precipitating the merger of the divergent secular pragmatists and sacred dogmatists who emerged pure pious and pure profane partisan party power politics moral convergents, and organized to beat the devil behind an alternative pragmatic and dogmatic moralism.

His denunciation of the New Abolitionists, whom declared the anathema and instigators of the Black race, was scarcely delivered either to impugn their motives or to dismiss them as the enemy. It was squarely intended to pinpoint their passion, the instinct that Channing identified as the flaw causing them to embrace proabolitionism; exposed publicly in the expectation they would cease and desist upon reflection; and associated with neither warriors or revolutionists nor crusaders but with "enthusiasts," whom he thought common knowledge attested both were too easily excited and could not be rational or reliable.

White Abolitionists him as incredulous as Black Abolitionists found him incredible, specifically when he took it upon himself to lecture these recent fugitives from injustice: "To instigate the slave to insurrection is a crime, for which no rebuke and no punishment can be too severe" precisely because such "rashness and passion" automatically guarantees the opposite of the intention, or ends not in equality of liberty and justice engaged in unrestricted personal pursuit of happiness but with the "slave and master in common ruin."[22]

DISCREDITING ENTIRE BLACK RACE

Channing stood out as the prototypal powerhouse parson and parishioner who was neither willing nor able to credit productive Black clergy and lay contemporaries with independent minds. This was understandable, howbeit inexcusable for the host of wisdom and wit, since by definition of their existence outside the Constitution with no rights or interests the White male was obligated by law and justice to respect Black males were not individuals like White ethnic males for whom life is good; liberty is precious on a par with if not better than gold; and freedom in liberty is life.

Indeed Channing, the representative moral mind of the Northeastern region, could not locate in his perceptive imagination the responsible Black slave and free persons currently concentrated in the South, among whom existed a minority capable of reading. Apparently the unthinkable for young Channing was the current Colored captives commanding the cerebral capacity they were created with to resist counterchecking culture determiners, to evaluate rationally the proliferating readable reports of the revolutionary events taking place in France and Haiti, to hold liberty more dear than absolute obedience to the proslavery laws of their otherwise sacrosanct Bible and Constitution; to distinguish between the message and the meaning of the civil rules-abiding and moral law-abrogating Northern democracy and Southern slavocracy; and to prove the premise faulty and therefore the principles flawed underpinning the human bondage system Channing preferred for them to honor, cherish, and bless.

Channing may have been innocent of the consequences of his priorities, yet he was neither fatuous nor ignorant of the facts that he chose either to ignore or to override in order to manage reality--that is, a more safe and sane than sound and solid society secured from swift serious social correction. Specifically, Channing's stated implication left no one able to follow simultaneously the logic and the argument with no alternative to drawing a single infer-ence from his distinct impression: It argued that Black slaves were functional entities but not human beings since they show little evidence of possessing a fully developed appreciation of reason or being in possession of rational faculties.

It is noteworthy that in logic, principle, and prose Channing chose to discredit the color caste/captive class--along with the Black and White New Abolitionists--and to credit White proabolitionists only. The enduring effect of his careful thought and careless action, that survived his existence, was no less real for being an unwitting consequence. Channing charged the culture with the compelling force that misdirected contemporaries and history when he essentially asserted as fact the fiction that Black New Abolitionists did not exist as early, and unconditionally, as any pro-immediatist leadership class. The pertinence of this poignant point is as explicit as the reasons are implicit why he failed to credit the Black Stationmasters in Boston or the Black Conductors on the Underground Railroad.

Pursuant to his capacity to assign blame and incapacity to extend praise to Black folk, initiative was evidenced in the willingness of Black insurrectionists Denmark Vesey and Nat Turner to accept responsibility for their actions. But instead of attributing to Black self-determinationists the credit they deserved for being self-liberationists, Channing states that the White male invaded and exercised mind control of the Black body Channing came so near to "respect" as a fantastic physical machine:

> They preached their doctrine to the colored people, and collected these into their societies. To this mixed and excitable multitude, appeals were made in the piercing tones of passion; and slaveholders were held up as monsters of cruelty and crime. Now to this procedure I must object, as unwise, as unfriendly to the spirit of Christianity, and as increasing, in degree, the perils of the Slaveholding States. Among the unenlightened, whom they so powerfully addressed, was there no reason to fear that some might feel themselves called to subvert this system of wrong, by whatever means? From the free colored people this danger was particularly to be apprehended. It is easy for us to place ourselves in their situation... And it would be wonderful, if, in a moment of passionate excitement, some enthusiast should think it his duty to use his communication with his injured brethren for stirring them up to revolt?[23]

You could drive the Puritan out of Calvinist Congregationalism and into the Unitarian Association: but you could not drive out of Channing the historic social conservative Catholic and Calvinist and therefore Puritan principal priority of authority, principle of hierarchal order, and propensity to demand obedience to all the moral laws of God and civil laws of man. The admonition encompassed conformance with all the self-serving laws written and legitimatized by human beings in power and authority, such as the Moral Law and the positive law of the sacred and profane proslavery Bible and Constitution ecclesiastical and civil powers established as sacrosanct documents to serve their religious and secular real interests.

It is Channing the apostle of fear who proves the permanent potential of the power elite to constrain the positive and accentuate the negative dynamics of Puritan Piety's antiblack white ethnic virtue, and to pervert it into anti-Black race virtue. He demonstrates this will to positive negation or reaction rather than attraction in his dogmatic moral restatement of Hopkins' theological doctrine. Hopkins asserted that each human (lower being) ought to be willing to sacrifice life, if necessary, to effect the greater good of higher being; whereas Channing contends there is need for "zeal" such "as will sacrifice life to truth and freedom."

New Abolitionists did not accept the premise yet understood the antislavery moderate's message. It translated antislavery radicals should not curb their zeal but "the believers" ought to transfer their immediatism to gradualism, or to submit their commitment to direction by the "Moral Law and by Christian Love" as interpreted in the gospel according to Channing. In this moral principle and practice practicum for the power elite, the ways and means employed to end slavery is more important than achieving the ultimate objective.

Strangely, Channing's antiabolitionism argued the means justifies the ends. Contrariwise Garrison, who engaged in this altercation with an alternative alternation method, effectively averred that if the ends do not justify the means it is most difficult to determine what in fact does.

Channing offered himself as an additive alterative of the presumed proabolitionist vice squad, functioned as the antiabolitionists' truth squad's squadron commander, and admonished the New Abolitionists to seek "virtue more than success." Channing guaranteed that if what is right is pursued first prosperity will follow. In a word, he called immediatists to relax the positive good and right expanding antiblack white-ethnic virtue, to intensify the negative good dynamic of antiblack white ethnic virtue, or to assume the presumed mode of the Puritan saints and to "keep ourselves unspotted from every evil thought, word, and deed."

This limits-intensive law and justice was the nature and function of the "wisdom and universal charity" litmus test of high Christianity (morality) and civility (civil conformance) Channing insisted Yankee-Puritan and other White race/ethnic antislavery advocates adopt who place the best interest of the Black race first:

> If by one wrong deed we could accomplish the liberation of millions, bad in no other way, we ought to feel that this good, for which, perhaps, we had prayed with an agony of desire, was denied us by God, was reserved for other times and other hands.

Black Old Abolitionist leaders who emerged as members of and models for the original preponderantly White Evangelical cadre of pro-immediatists, and the Black New Abolitionist sons of these fathers forming the Black proabolitionist leadership corps, experienced being the direct object and indirect effect without being the engaged subject of Channing and discovered they had better reason to hope than to think they were not "in the hands of an angry God."

Of course this sense was not due to mere suspicion or fear of the unknown but occurred as a result of Channing and his elitist cohorts never seriously considering or addressing them, neither as independent-minded ecclesiarchs at the helm of independent Black ecclesiastical antislavery bodies nor as dependent and interdependent agents and agencies nor as initiative-intensive biracial proabolitionists.

Black idealists were realists in the pursuit of betterment and for whom reality was survival in the determined will of Channing: one Puritan saved by Yankee reason from Calvinism, though not with grace sufficient for the efficient improvement of the Black race. Being realistic in the face of the Channing's publicly preached and practiced faith in man and version of Hobson's Choice ("that or none"), Black folk put their trust in God rather than in either Channing or man: and their lives in the hands of the Black and White Evangelical New Abolitionists.

Coinciding with the rise of Transcendentalism, the intuition of Black folk (whom Channing accused of lacking common sense) seemed to suggest to his apperceptive critics and admirers that Channing could be trusted to be fair, if the Yankee-Puritan could determine the rules of life, just like and unlike his Puritan fathers who wrote the Black race-preclusive Constitution.

Channing appeared analogous as the Puritan host in himself to the post-French and Indian War anti-political successors of the pro-political original Quaker Puritans, or demonstrable Pennsylvania hegemonic power and English race representative Religious Society of Friends, who no less than their Calvinist Puritan rivals were preponderantly distinguished from British-ethnic immigrants and emigrants. He certainly shared their illusion and lived out their fantasy: a pure pious and moral solution to any complicated power-intensive civil conflict of real and true interests is not infeasible but the impossible possible, since the model of utilitarian sufficiency and efficiency that functions successfully in the conflict-free sacred community of the Friends need not be dysfunctional but can be transferred and made to work in a competition-centered secular society.

In short, albeit unwittingly, Yankee Puritan Channing imitated the Quaker Puritan visionaries. He attempted to superimpose upon reality the dream and absolute certainty that a rational/economic-individual influence style of pure moral leadership, composed of private and parochial civil culture-pervading but public partisan party politics-avoiding components, was a real alternative to power politics (the mother's milk of the American pragmatism system), could change the real interests and values of slavocrats, and entice proslavocrats--driven by Evangelical fervor to convert the world to their opinion--to inaugurate a systemic attitudinal and behavioral modification system.

Channing struggled to raise the moral stakes and standards, and to elevate the Northeastern power elite to the position of undisputed command and control cultural determiners. In truth, their moral leadership of at least the establishment center of the nation was neither in question nor in doubt nor the issue. The heart of the matter, during the era of the Virginia Presidents when three successive slavemasters filled the office of Chief Executive, was the hegemony of the political economy; the arrangement of power; and the problem inherent in the actuality that the Southeastern rather than the Northeastern set of powerhouses existed in power and authority and dominated the Three Branches of Government.

Correlatively the Southeastern fanatics generally and particularly--whom he both knew South Carolinians especially to be and yet did not call "enthusiasts"--and evangelists were far more aggressive than the progressive. Cavaliers challenging Yankees were clearly miscomprehended by Channing, aggressors, and possessed by not only keenly different purposes but also sharply competing legitimate claims, great ambitions, and real interests.

The meaning of this profound misunderstanding is plain: Channing did not believe perception is reality and therefore could not conceive either the truth or the consequences proceeding apace his non-acts of omission and acts of commission, because he was incapable of both perceiving and admitting that the ecclesiastical and civil powers coalesced in demanding obedience to any and every moral or immoral legitimate government; conformance with the instituted legal injustice promulgated by the rulers of the Bible and the Constitution, or the Deuteronomic ("eye for an eye") and Draconian (Black-race preclusion from participatory democracy and total control in the slavocracy) codes; performance to secure the Union as the philosophical Secular/Religious Humanism and Christian Church establishmentarians for (not the separation) but the union of church and state; and compliance with the priority principle of permanent stabilized order, whereby it abides as not only the first and foremost one but above liberty and conscience for each and every civilian.

Since Channing was rigid in his arrangement of the individual and the moral deeds of the private person, as not simply everything but the only thing of importance, it is understandable why there appears nothing he cared less about than the fortune of the Black race. Yet in the matter of national leadership, relative to their achieving liberty in freedom, there was little choice for Black folk between master Puritan and Mr. Unitarian Channing, the Calvinist masters of establishmentarian Evangelical Presbyterianism/Congregationalism, and the Southern slavemasters.

This apparent difficulty made it quite beside the point that Channing was an antislavery moderate, challenged in his antiabolitionism by establishmentarian Unitarian proabolitionists, and unwilling to condemn totally the abolitionist movement "as only evil." The complexity of this perplexity, relative to Channing being to Black folk nearly as overbearing and unbearable as he appeared overreaching to proslavocrats in the South, inheres in the fact that Channing presented himself as the real alternative master of the color caste/captive class--and the champion of the Black race--whose "chief strength" as "a Reformer lies in speaking truth."

DEFENSE OF A FREE PRESS AND FREE SPEECH FOR RADICALS

And from this rarified position of no less questionable for being self-elected moral authority and power, Channing declared that the New Abolitionist societies "must not supercede or be compared with Individual action" because "the enthusiasm of the Individual in a good cause is a mighty power"--that is, implicitly latent and explicitly manifest capacity, capable of cultural triumph and civil victory even against the solid and undifferentiated critical mass of proslavocrats and slavocrats.

One among the salient reasons why the conservative clout-concentrated and controlling central cast of the contemporary Boston brahmin caste honored Channing by bestowing upon him the title "virtuous influence," and lauded him as the constellation of the best in Christian and humanist cultural values, is the fact that he could be trusted to act only after knowing "the Right"--and to place thereafter his "entire confidence in well-doing"--according to the "first principles of freedom, morals, and religion." Channing spoke to and for the power elite who had no reason to doubt, and every reason to believe, him when he avowed that he would not sacrifice "honor, freedom, and principle." His word as his bond and was as good as his defense of the New Abolitionists' civil liberties, and criticism of what he adjudged their uncivil tongues.

One singularly illuminating demonstration of his promise and performance for White folk occurred following a turning event in the life and commitment of radical liberationists. In 1833 Beecher left Channing and Boston to relocate in Cincinnati, where the pro-Colonizationist antislavery clergyman was installed as President of Lane Seminary.

But the antiabolitionist promptly found himself in conflict with fellow "Connecticut Yankee" Congregationalist Thomas Dwight Weld who took charge of the pro-abolitionist seminarians, as their student body lea-der, following their long and controversial antislavery debate early in 1834 that attracted national attention. James Gillespie Birney (1792-1857), a Kentucky lawyer and sometime slavemaster, was a singular adult among the Southern Presbyterians that the Lane Student Antislavery debate attracted, and the over two weeks-long rational and constructive controversial argumentation inspired. Weld was instrumental in twice converting Birney--first from a proslavery to a antislavery churchman, and, after he joined the American Colonization Society, from gradualism and Colonizationism to immediatism and New Abolitionism.

Birney developed as a "New School" Evangelical Presbyterian, and into the founding publisher and editor of a moderate abolitionist periodical he established in Cincinnati and called the *Philanthropist* (1836).

Subsequently Birney was victimized by White-ethnic Cincinnati rioters, in 1836, who broke up his establishment--and eventually drove him from the city in a ruthless attack upon the editor, New Abolitionism, and the freedom of the press. The mobocracy's act of suppression so exasperated Channing that he was moved to write Birney a long letter (November 1, 1836) for publication in the *Philanthropist*, that was separately reprinted as a pamphlet and distributed by the New Abolitionists' American Anti-Slavery Society.

Channing wrote to rebuke the criminal cowards and to renounce in public the outlaws and their perpetrated crime. He condemned it as a disastrous precedent, and one so uniquely despicable in the annals of the Union that there exists nothing "more disgraceful to us as freemen" than this macabre Cincinnati malformation.

In this antiterrorism mass march and rally of the power people, the antiterrorist stated that these terrorists were not minor minions in the West but major menaces in the body politic who placed the Union in eminent danger by perpetrating the "first systematic effort to strip the citizen of freedom of speech." Channing challenged the champions of liberty to eradicate instantly the crusaders cruising the culture to cancel the White race citizens-dominated vigilance committee, to rule out of order immediately the pro-terrrorists, and to reverse the perversion of principle pernicious effected by the White-ethnic mobocrats.

Nothing provoked to be provocative like the vigilantes' violent and vicious violation of a representative White-race New Abolitionist's space in the name of preserving domestic tranquility; in the spirit of patriot defenders of the Southern Way of Life in the West determined to protect the status quo social order; and in order to arrest and punish a White Christian Southern gentlemen on charge of committing the "great crime" of carrying "the doctrine of human equality to its full extent."

Juxtaposed with his repudiation of the forcible rapists, of the virgin and virile voice of virtue, Channing managed to mix and match with his admiration

for the ex-slaveholder convert to immediatism chastisement of the New Abolitionists, who had his entire gratitude for their resolution in the face of deadly
assault, as he challenged them to "maintain the liberty of speech and the press"
while forthwith ceasing and desisting from writing in a "spirit of intolerance,
sweeping censure, and rash, injurious judgment." From his perspective, New A-
bolitionists remained simply too "intolerant towards the slave-holders," and their
Northern opponents and proponents:

> I do not, cannot believe, that the majority of slaveholders are of
> the character now described. I believe that the majority, could they
> be persuaded of the consistency of emancipation with the well-be-
> ing of the colored race and with social order, would relinquish
> their hold on the slave, and sacrifice the imagined property in him
> to the chains of justice and humanity.[24]

Birney and his New Abolitionist associates--who formed an elite corps of
preponderantly Ohio and New York secular democratic and religious "New
School" Presbyterians--were instructed along with Garrison by Channing to
stand fast in free speech but to "exercise it as Christians, and friends of your
race."

One hundred years of religious controversy and Black race disinterest produced Channing, the voice of Protestant civility, who, in his most "deliberate
moments," looked upon "reproach, poverty, persecution, and death, as light evils
compared with unfaithfulness to pure and generous principles, to the spirit of
Christ, and to the will of God."

These principles for the White pious and profane elite were developed for
powerhouse Protestants in power and authority as parochial, private, and public
decision-makers. Compared to his daily correspondence with these "Church, Corporation, and Congress" interlocking directorates, Black folk, with whom Channing was uninvolved, shared values with their Black and White New Abolitionist
leaders whom Channing, and other leaders of establishment denominations they
knew, considered unprincipled activists.

Evangelical Birney's reaction to Channingesque antiabolitionism, over time
and through time, varied in its forms from civil radicalism to reactionaryism
relative to his basic moderate conservatism and liberalism character and content. These culturally active varieties and variations of power postures were
struck in the several roles he played within and without the politics of church
and state as the New Abolitionists' paradigmatic partisan party power politics
politician.

SECULAR EMANCIPATIONISM AS THE RATIONAL

TRANSPOSITION OF SACRED MILLENNIALISM

The struggle of the pro-immediatists was revealed in the descriptive facts
and value judgments Birney drew on successfully. The professional civil and
church lawyer proved instantly credible in the ACS and AAS because his logic
and reason was based on rational theory, he had direct experience in the South
as a former slaveowner, and he argued the case against the antiabolitionist
establishment denominations in his anonymously published book on *The American
Churches: The Bulwarks of American Slavery* (1840).[25]

Also during this critical year for New Abolitionists and their American Anti-

Slavery Society, Channing wrote a sequel to his disquisition on *Slavery* in a monograph entitled *Emancipation* (1840). Once his attention was drawn to slavery his mind, functioning like a steel trap, grasped and treated the subject of human bondage dehumanization and liberation every way but right. Somehow he managed in brief and bright moments to overcome his natural reluctance to engage in controversy; to publish his findings and formulas in several occasional writing projects; and to become fascinated by the complexity of the color caste/captive class no less than by the enormity of involuntary servitude's cultural impact.

The particular attraction apparently occurred as evocative Channing was provoked by the provocative Garrison, whose challenge he answered by offering his "final solution" to the dual caste and bondage color class condition. The process of formulating a liberal moderate antislavery Protestant principle and practice was activated by his instinct for the juggler vein of a cultural problem, which he thought he had precisely located and pressed in his work on *Slavery*, upon discovering to his chagrin the power he applied to the private manumission pressure point had been thwarted by the vigorous resistance of the slavocrats and Northern proabolitionists to his theoretical and technical personal manumission process.

Dispassionate Channing shared with "Consistent Calvinists" a passion for rational consistency, which as a cardinal counterpole of emotive power politics facilitated a flexible aesthetic and fashioned an inflexible principle of limits under whose rigid constraints his moral sense operated. Consistence in Channing's operative pure rational and moral method and measure required the subjection of each problem to objective analysis; the careful checking and balancing of the engendered quantitative and qualificative data in the mode of irreversible reflectiveness; and, after working through to the answer, the pronouncement of the problem solved only if the logical conclusion is also demonstrable right.

Channing's predicament inhered in the simple truth: He did not have the issue of color caste and bondage perpetuation right. This difficulty compounded by complexity expanded rather than contracted because of his failure to apply his own theory and methodology. He appeared the most surprised benevolent dictator in the world upon discovering that, in spite of his aesthetically beautiful and logically impeccable Golden Mean and inspired middle-of-the-road progradualism solution, the antislavocracy and proslavocracy counterforces were rapidly escalating rather than deescalating conflicts of values.

The wonder is how he could reason so logically, write so elegantly to elucidate universal values, and be so sincerely wrong. Even more wondrously surprising is Channing's remarkable facility for fashioning a more intellectual than ineluctable transposition of sacred Calvinist virtues into secular Puritan values. This is especially interesting ratiocination exercise, given the consensus view of Channing as the measure of liberal Boston religious humanitarianism and secular humanism, the quintessence of antislavery advocates of anti-Black race interest, and the model of felicitous pro-White race virtue--meticulously inoculated against contagious pro-Black race values.

It was Channing's recollection that in the previous generation of "Consistent Calvinists" the disciples of Samuel Hopkins were known as "Rational Calvinists." Curiously enough in this single dimension and special relation, if one applies to Channing his own strict constructionist definition of a Hopkintonian, "the apostle of Unitarianism" proves to be an odd and even peculiar "Rational

Calvinist." In actuality and spite of his strenuous efforts to be entirely free and clear of them, Channing's Calvinistic proclivities were exposed in relation to the doctrine of the millennium. This indirect connection deepened in reality and direct opposite secular moral nature and function the further the millennarian doctrine progressed as a critical divide between select Calvinists and Arminians on the one side, and religious and secular humanists on the other. Channing saturates the dogma with Enlightenment logic in a process of desacralization and re-religionization.

As a result, the doctrine is so highly secularized as to be all but unrecognizable and yet on his own terms acceptable. Arguably the distinction between the traditional sacred millennialism and his nontraditional secular millennarianism remains more real than apparent.

Samuel Hopkins, like Jonathan Edwards, was much more than a mere systematic philosophical-theologian. His systemic rational faith and ethics began, centered, and ended in the millennium. Thus he was both a rational Puritan and an Evangelical Congregationalist. Yet the Puritan Pietist was primarily a "consistent Calvinist" and Channing an inconsistent one.

But as a persistent moralist-rationalist, Channing was not a consistent secular humanist or religious humanitarian. It is "wondrously strange" that relative to the millennialism and humanitarianism counterpoles of authentic Puritan Piety, the Newport innovators counterbalanced their Black race life-enhancing and death-enhancing contributions to Black Americans.

Certainly these opposite yet not mutually exclusive but dynamic sacred and secular components of the Puritan ecclesiastical and civil power were, in nature and function, analogous to the equally different and indispensable conflict and conciliation male and female parts of the human species.

In a word, millennialism and humanitarianism were calculated by the select "Elect" to be among the mutually fertile positive and negative ideals in history that "pleased the Providence of God," as Channing was given to say, in the traditional Puritan way. After affirming Providence in *Emancipation*, in the very next passage the Unitarian pleaded piety in a form that, relative to the mystical myths and rituals revered in Trinitarian Congregations, evinced a difference without a distinction:

> We know indeed, that good is to triumph over evil in this world:
> that "Christ must reign, till he shall put all enemies beneath his
> feet," or until his Spirit shall triumph over the spirit, oppressions,
> corruptions of the world. Let us then work against all wrong, but
> with a calm, solemn earnestness, not with vehemence and tumult.
> Let us work with deep reverence and filial trust toward God, and
> not in the proud impetuosity of our own wills. Happy the day, when
> such laborers shall be gathered by an inward attraction into one
> church or brotherhood, whose badge, creed, spirit, shall be Univer-
> sal Love. This will be the true Kingdom of God on earth, and its
> might will infinitely transcend political power.[26]

MUTUAL GROWTH OF THE COTTON KINGDOM
AND CHANNING'S PROSLAVOCRAT INTERESTS

What is useful to recall for context at this juncture--despite the risk of being charged with redundancy--revolves reiteration of the critical point: The ever-developing original New England theology formed the norm relative to which Channing arrives at the end of his career a standard deviation. He had nearly completed a one hundred and eighty degree turn from flatly opposing the Calvinist conservative faith and ethics tradition--that he found determinative perpetual positive error (evil and damnation) rather than positive truth (good and salvation)--to finally affirming its negative good as the best good possible ethic.

Puritan-Calvinist evolving into Yankee-Calvinist Halfway Piety (rational spirituality and morality) reached its climatic explication height expressly in the Enlightenment-grounded philosophical/psychological/theological mind of Jonathan Edwards. Between the death of the New England theocracy and the birth of the North American democracy, Halfway Piety erupted as pure profane people-converting and pure pious Protestants-attracting Evangelicalism and millennialism out of the Halfway Covenant. And the enduring unbroken continuum and permanent connection of Halfway Piety faith and deterrence-benevolence ethics commences and ends as it continues in opposition to the spirit and letter of John Calvin, John Cotton, and/or Cotton Mather--that is, as a selectively anti-political/pro-political presence with its efficient capacity for secular/civil social redeeming values diminished.

Contrapositive authentic Puritan Piety is private-individual and parochial-community public interest-enriching rational faith and ethics direct action: an undeveloped and underdeveloped sacred and secular responsibility dogma and pragma developing amid alternating expansion and contraction cyclical recurrences, instrumentalized by the ecclesiastical and civil power correcting positive and negative antiblack white-ethnic virtue. Prior to the New Abolitionists, Channing argues with compelling force, special interests-attaining and the general interest-advancing Puritan Piety reached its highest stage of development in the Evangelical faith and ethics of Old Abolitionist Samuel Hopkins, where the cyclically recurring common good realizing responsibleness ended its current extension in frustration (as Channing reported accurately on the record) and turbulent deterrence-benevolence (whose terrible and terrifying cause and effect the benevolent paternalist fails to record correctly for explainable reasons).

Edwards and Hopkins were "New Light" pro-Calvinist metaphysicians who engaged, grasped, and sometimes absorbed the best ideas of their "Old Light" anti-Calvinist contemners--whom they gave an argument as good as they got in their stiff competition for the hegemony of the New England Calvinist-Puritan tradition, and challenged fundamentally but not always fairly and fully the opposing Congregationalist party to the conflict of Puritan interests and values.

Master Edwards and Hopkins (his disciple) had a similar counterirritant affect upon the Evangelical Arminians. They also made major contributions to Congregationalism: as their learned treatises structured and set the framework for the debate on their merits of pro-Calvinism and anti-Calvinism Orthodoxy, ensuing after the First Great Awakening (1720-45) that entailed the Evangelical evangelism and revivalism of the great unwashed and unchurched populous.

A singularly significant consequence of this movement for the proselytization of the masses, especially in the West where the new nation and her foreign-born immigrants and native-born emigrants were expanding, was the attraction of a critical mass who became churchmen/women; did not simply join the established local parishes but organized new congregations and built new churches; and extended the expanse of the churches through organizing them as national denominations.

An American Civil Religion ecclesiastical component in the democratization of the White Protestant people, Evangelicalism survived the dying intensity of the First Great Awakening and kept burning as an American cultural eternal flame, although temporarily reduced to candle power by the all-consuming Revolution. The combination of the undead Evangelical presence and intense spiritual need, that the unsettled political economy of the post-War era fed, fanned the religious incandescence until it ignited the Second Great Awakening (1797-1810) flame that sparked a post-Independence renewal movement, during which period the popular Evangelical churches swelled their ranks with the common man.

The Second Great Awakening exhorters--whose over-whelming majority in the East and the West were Northern and Southern White-ethnic males (rather than females)--effectively expanded, rationalized, organized, and institutionalized not only the proliferating churches, developing denominations, and the predominantly English race-led First Great Awakening pattern of involving slave and free Black Northerners and Southerners. They updated and intensified this pattern, whereby White-ethnic evangelists and revivalists dominating the Second Great Awakening issued forth as the first White-race Americans to seriously engage Black folk *en masse*.

Certainly this was the first time a massive crusade for Christ and the color caste/captive class occurred in the South: where Black-race folk were concentrated as slaves, and White-ethnic new immigrants and old emigrants amassed (especially nonestablishment Evan-gelical Calvinist-Baptists and Arminian-Methodists in statistically significant numbers. This demographic change was due to accidents of history such as greater opportunity, and to design prior to the industrial revolution when the Congregationalist (Orthodoxy) dominating New England made the immigrants unwelcome in the region.

Something new and of significance for the future of the secular and civil society occurred in this sacred movement. And it paralleled the rise of the Quaker-initiated Old Abolitionist Societies in the Independence era, when universal liberty was a principle preached and practiced by a Northern majority and Southern minority of cultural determiners. Evangelical evangelism in the local churches for congregants and contiguous inhabitants of the community, mass revivals in the fields open to the public, and direct personal encounters between Black and White participants were occasioned by the experimental conversion method and "born again" experience. These cultural changes and change agents generated conditions in which rapidly increased positive possibility thinking and acting evangelists and revivalists consciously and unconsciously drew upon Enlightenment-derived and Independence-inspired humanistic themes and techniques of liberation to appeal to Black folk.

Whence a goodly number of messengers in the North and the South, as solid rationalists and spiritual mediums, developed into a method the deliverance of the message to Black folk that they should possess self-determination of their body (on a par with White folk); freedom of their mind; salvation of their soul. Bethinking the "no taxation without representation" rallying cry of the War for Independence, in which Black Patriots made the supreme sacrifice, White evangelists in the post-Constitution ratification years coupled conversion with the with the declaration to Black converts that should gain equal access to opportunity both to compete in the political economy and to engage in participatory republican democracy.

The further they were removed in time from the era of Independence, however, the more White-ethnic Evangelicals imitated the English race-specific hegemony of the Puritan and Anglican theocracies, calcified the color caste/captive system by rationalizing the pro-tection of pro-White race interests and stressing pro-Black race interests entailed the division rather than the union of spiritual and civil rights and liberties, and argued fairness and justice meant less is more and good enough for Black brothers and sisters in Christ.

This sharp and swift reversal in secular and civil values was reinforced by the public virtue-distracting sacrosanct concern with the millennium. This was an enduring rather than new effect, that advanced from a sacred counterbalance of the secular to the central concern of eternity in history for Christians. The anti-Calvinist overreaching interest in ecclesiastical rights and disinterest in civil righteousness was not a tradition for establishmentarian Puritans but an incredible turn of events. It was initiated at the emerging end of theocracy and beginning of democracy by Jonathan Edwards, when the master of millennialism preached preparation through the Churchocracy and Christocracy for reception of the imminent Kingdom of Christ on earth.

The lasting effect of unconcernment with the presumed transitory and unimportant civil order pervaded the Southeast during the post-Second Great Awakening era: when liberal private manumission laws were replaced by "Black Codes" proscribing liberation; slave states outlawed independent Black leadership and autonomous churches; and slavocrats mandated White-ethnic command and control of all Black community endeavors. Millenarianism concentrated the mind when the slavocracy crystallized partly as a result of and during the year Congress' Missouri Compromise and Denmark Vesey's insurrection electrified the citizenry, before ten years had elapsed after the effective dissolution of the Second Great Awakening, and millennialism took the form and shape of religious determination to unite the slavocracy and the Kingdom of God, and to establish it as the Cotton Kingdom.

Enjoying power and authority over the life and destiny of the Black race, and being unpaid officers of the state both like and unlike Massachusetts parsons who remained state tax-supported until 1836, self-serving White-ethnic evangelists and revivalists attempted to please each local English race plantation master--whom they confused with the Master--as the ministers of the Gospel increasingly became slaveowners. Between preaching the gospel of liberation to Black folk at the commencement of the Second of Great Awakening, and substituting the gospel of Black-race slavery in perpetuity and perfect obedience of slaves to masters forward from its demise to the end of the antebellum era-- along with the promotion of White race/ethnic basic self-interest--the spiritual need and demand White minister/masters both generated and supplied had the analogous effect of nearly cornering the market and eliminating competition.

In this double damnation pernicious and obscene state conditioned by predestinarian Southern Calvin-ists' version of predestination, far more hearts of the Black masses were eagerly sought than steadily won by the proslavery ministers and missionaries. While the Black majority was not captivated but too large a minority swallowed both hard and the whole slavocrat hook, line, and sinker--which was not only understandable and predictable but inevitable given the relative resources of the powerful arbitrary and powerless vulnerable White and Black folk cultural kin-groups--each Black body, mind, and soul was compromised in the system no less than each White counterpart.

Thuswise the Black masses were disproportionately caught unawares and captured entirely by surprise. They became the captive body within the major E-vangelical denominations, that sought praise as "Consistent Calvinists" because they prevented Black folk from enjoying rights in the ecclesiastical sector as solidly as the Constitution precluded them from civil order. Black free-born, freed, and slave congregants in the churches of the slavocracy were as significant decision-makers in the ecclesiastical society as they were in the civil community.

Bondmen were important in the denominations only because they were highly valued in the private sector--where as chattel property or real interests their bodies provided pleasure and profit--and in the public realm due primarily to the republican democracy system of pragmatism. It revolves around the basic process wherein population determines the number of Congressmen every sovereign state is eligible to elect, whereupon each Black existence in involuntary servitude counted three-fifths of a person for the slaveholding states and thus the body politic. Thus while, like all save the rare few and far between and hard to find free Black Northerners and Southerners, slaves were permitted neither to vote nor to be represented, but, unlike free and freed Black males in the North and the South, they were scrupulously counted by White race/ethnic Southerners since their numerical preponderance of slaves provided the South with an edge in the House of Representatives.

Nonestablishment Evangelicals, in official control of the Black masses, were not normally the advisors of American establishment leaders--outside the South --who determined the intellectual, political, and economic directions of the society. Within the South, White-ethnic British Evangelical immigrants, and emigrants, were frequently and increasingly filling the void in the civil arena. The vacuum was created by the diminished power the English race-representative Anglican establishment incurred as a result of being suspect pro-Loyalist/pro-Tory Americans during the Revolution. Evangelical White ethnic Southerners were influential reactors, who, decidedly in the spheres of religion, carried out the social dictates of the community. Their chief concern with Black folk--whom they knew were struggling for human dignity and liberty--was to keep them profitable servants by mechanisms which guaranteed conformance with the commandment of slaves to be obedient to their masters.

Christian and non-Christian Black body owners demanding their self-serving Black bondage property in-terest, and system based on the error of deception, were slavocrats whom Northeastern proslavocrats appraised as being perfectly natural and justified systems managers and well within their rights as enterprising entrepreneurs in generating the need and supplying the demand for maximal disincentives and minimal incentives to guarantee their Black race cultural kinsfolk fairness and equity in the slavocracy.

In the appearances and imagination, lived out fantasy, and therefore managed reality of the Evangelical Southerners emerged a no less real for being far less obvious powerful myth. English-race and British-ethnic slavemasters and overseers, as a rule in their role as lower-class as well as upper-class and middle-class rulers, managed no more or less justice than prudence dictated was necessary to prevent distraction from preparation by the White Anglo-Saxon Protestant faithful for the ultimate (if not imminent) Kingdom of Christ, that their Cotton Kingdom they were establishing would welcome once its firm structures were in place.

Correlatively Edwards, Hopkins, and the host of Orthodoxy or the predestination and predetermination White Man's Burden of Calvinism concentrated in the Northeast, and in managing equally great pretentions and tensions with Enlightenment values and claims. These Evangelical Congregationalists appeared in their isolation and insulation to extend the Calvinistic variables to engage the aggressive Methodist proselytizers of slaves and their Arminian theological axes on which Black folk turned--as the New England-bound establishment progenitors stood dead center--upon the firm Puritan ground of tradition.

Inner-directed   rather   than   outer-directed   and   region-oriented Congregationalist ethnocentrism demonstrated real advantage and disadvantage, just as it predetermined that neither the Black race nor authentic Puritan Piety (private faith, parochial ethics, and public interest politics) could advance in the culture crisis (in either the interior or exterior environment and world New Englanders made) beyond the standard of religious and secular civil service Cotton Mather set for Calvinist Puritans.

Channing's Protestant *Emancipation* proclamation constitutes his particular significance in this race and religion connection. The Puritan culture's class over class continnum advanced with the anti-Calvinist *master of the situation* in this context, as he touched the theological ground of Calvinism conveniently, expediently, and ever so lightly in order to promote his protectionist Puritan principle without advancing the perfectionist Calvinist point. Synchronously the premier Protestant moralist refined and extended as the determinants of American society the Puritan cultural tastes. He achieved this accomplishment by combining secular humanist and patrician Puritan values generally, and in his Unitarian Congregationalist Church humanitarian instrument of personal morality particularly.

Channing exercised leadership as neither a public servant nor a professional politician but a prominent parson, and fashioned his not in the general or public interest private and parochial ethics as a social status quo-stabilizing civil service. Channingesque social conservation turned into a protectionist principle that burst forth with his essay to circumvent public power in not only the parochial but primarily the private sector as the right of right and righteous rationalists. Being a disengaged Archimedean leveling lever and an engaged elitist social engineering instrument, the Channingesque middle-class pure moral power point efficiently accelerated the advancement of White folk to even greater advantage over the disadvantaged, from which real leverage edge rich White race and poor White ethnic males placed all the pressure on the backs of the Black body.

Leaving aside the irrefutable personal integrity and exemplary character of Edwards, Hopkins, and Channing--who were outstanding spokesmen in their works and times for the diverse range of Protestant establishmentarianism, and personified in their life the highest ideals of contemporary Puritans--these masterful Congregationalists' ideational plantings produced full, new, and overripe fruit in the thoughts and actions of descendant Yankee-Puritan men and schools who developed their original plantations and sometimes revised them in their imagination beyond recognition.

Among the enduring virtues and lasting values transmitted consciously and unconsciously as a direct and indirect result of the Puritan fathers' *Institutes of the Christian Religion*-based color caste/captive interpretations and teachings were antebellum Congregationalist institutions. At their earliest--or latest--and best these Yankee denominational organizations gave their Black race constituency perfunctory consideration. Just as in other endeavors they were peerless pioneers, just so efficaciously in this sphere of class and caste cultural crisis these Yankee-Puritans were "peculiar" exemplars of the establishment views of leading Christians, who thought as little of the Black race as Yankee-Puritans thought about the Black body.

Channing enjoyed the advantage of preaching the equivalence of tolerance and rational Christianity to the affluent and influential Bostonians, in the post-Puritan and post-slavery Yankee center of commerce and culture. There, as the "observed of all observers," he did not so much set, or raise, as unfurl the Puritan-Yankee standard of rational and reasonable rationalizable anti-Black race interests.

In the brilliance of his rhetoric, Channing white-washed establishment Puritan wrong right; and ruled, almost without objection, its anti-Black race interests past dead and buried--with extreme unction--beneath the formal interment of slavery. From thence arrived jus-tification by faith in facts, and the righteousness of the New England "chosen people" of God. He argued basically from silence the truth and error inherent in his prime unexamined premise--perforce which the wayward worldly saints sons of the "Elect" fathers blessed the Puritans and their Yankee-Congregationalist descendants whom they set free from past, present, and future responsibility in the new Republic for their color caste/captive class and cultural kin-group upon establishing Puritan Massachusetts as the first slave-free state to ratify the Constitution and enter in the Union.

This official Black bondage liberation policy and act of law Yankees translated a public apology for Puritan slavery, and condemnation of involuntary servitude as the cultural root evil transplanted by Anglican, Quaker, and Calvinist Puritans; declared the incontrovertible evidence and vindication of Puritan values that were fragrantly flouted at their peril by peer Protestant ecclesiastical and civil powers; and flaunted as the *mea culpa* exonerating New England Congregationalists from caste and class cultural change obligation.

The premise of Channing's indistinct rationalization of the culture-cultivated color caste condition alleged there was no need for Yankee ecclesiastical and civil acts of repentance, forgiveness, and correction. Purification rites inclusive of hallowed observance of past deeds that resulted in the eradication of human bondage in the Bay State, and rituals of cleansing in the New Abolition era revolving around praise and thanksgiving for Old Abolitionists who abolished slavery in Massachusetts and ratified the sacred Constitution, revolved around declaring "states' rights" not only sacrosanct and inviolable; involved asserting the equivalence of the legal and the right their legitimatization of slavery in the sovereign states; and emitted by means of self-revelation the New England right and way.

This Channingesque transference of 1780s Old Abolitionist virtue to the New Abolition decade of the 1840s post-Channing Congregationalist establishmentarians would declare superiority; and shift from Channing's Puritan defense to Yankee offense in order for Evangelical Orthodoxy to prove its truth claim.

Channing articulated this Puritan virtue with such freshness and finesse until the myth that the Puritan antiblack white-ethnic virtue (black personal sin and moral public evil opposing parochial ethic) is automatically everywhere at once the formidable foe of anti-Black race interest was accepted by New Englanders as an article of faith; universally empirically verifiable evidence of Calvinistical justification by faith and its utilitarian value in history and eternity; and a transferable utility ethic utilizable as a high Christianity and civility securing virtue in the civil sector and social circles by the saint and sinner cultural determiners alike.

Congregationalists propelled this Halfway Piety deterrence-benevolence ethic throughout the cultural crisis to the point of near unassailableness. To a significant degree, this grand Puritan cultural reification was the accomplishment of William Ellery Channing: the dogma and pragma transcending Unitarian Congregationalist whose track record conventional wisdom appraised and praised for being totally opposed on principle to doctrinaire theology and secular ideology doctrine.

This comparative culture vacuum and void of critical analysis of the difference between coexisting positive truth and positive error, apropos the permissiveness of color caste Puritan connection of the Old Abolitionists and New Abolitionists, was filled with such expansive appreciation of Puritan culture until the depth of evil, good White Christian establishmentarians wrought, was lost in enlightened self-interest.

COLONIZATION AND THE WEST INDIES' SOLUTION

Produced by the representative Protestant mind, singularly signifying that neither the Protestant mystic nor the Protestant myth but the Protestant is the attribute that most becomes a legend in his own time, this mysterious and magical immaculate conception of Puritan vice-free virtue was the moral marrow of the message Channing published in his *Emancipation* epistle. He begins the monograph by indicating his objective means with lengthy excerpts (that do not telegraph his subjective end) from an English Friend's *Familiar Letters to Henry Clay, of Kentucky Describing a Winter in the West Indies* (1839).

A highly prized investigative piece, *Familar Letters* was written a respected friend--of his esteemed Quaker friends Jeremiah Hubbard and Benjamin Lundy-- the Reverend Joseph John Gurney (1788-1847). These *Letters* from a leader in the London world headquarters of the Religious Society of Friends were originally addressed to Presbyterian layman Henry Clay, the lawmaker who would emerge one of the chief proslavery United States but currently served in the House of Representatives and as first Vice President of the American Colonization Society, focus on Gurney's investigation of the British West Indies one year after the archipelago's emancipation (1838).

Gurney was transmitting London to Clay in Washington, D.C., the near peerless Christian slavocrat political powerhouse and House Majority leader, Parliament's political and civil adoption and adaptation of the radical surgery and slavery removal technique that American Quakers pioneered in the ecclesiastical sector. Gurney reported progress with regard to the expanded post-liberation support contributed to their freed Black Britishmen by the English state.

Channing captivated cultural determiners who called him the conventional wisdom because he shared with these fellow centrists a conscious consensus-seeking cautious conscience committed to secure a civility-controlled civil order--and/or status quo society--consisting of risk-free social constancy and change.

Thus Channing was in character when he openly admired the Church/Congress/Corporation-funded American Colonizaton Society's gradual approach to eradicating the American slave system, applauded the ACS's economic ways and means employed to achieve the approved end, and dismissed the Society as a neither functional nor dysfunctional nor morally bankrupt organization but one whose fiscal principle-based Black-race excludable process and program he determined to be not unethical but unworkable because his analysis of the problems and prospects led him to conclude that the ACS was unable to secure the resources required to achieve this great ambition.

In addition to damning the powerful ACS with faint praise and full disclosure of its inability to fund its forceful fancy, that was not fanciful but as foolish as the endeavor by ACS' agents to live out their fantasy in reality, Channing reflected on the utilitarian principle Parliament practiced by enacting laws abrogating bondage in the British Empire and paying partial compensation to English planters for losses suffered when the state confiscated their chattel property.

But he rejected on grounds of economic efficiency and ethical expediency the British political model for state abolition, whose universal yet neither immediate nor unconditional change of the captor and captive classes to a single citizen class entailed a ten year plan of preparation whose progress Gurney detailed and excited Channing to examine for himself in the British West Indies.

Straightaway, arguably a decidedly less stubborn and stupid or more sane and safe than sound sense champion of an American alternative way to end slavery, Channing produced his personal Protestant *Emancipation* Proclamation, (private) Manumission Plan for White Southern Christian gentlemen, and simple solution synergy subsisting of a synchretistic synchronization of British (public) Abolitionism and American (parochial) Colonizationism.

While he did not join the ACS whose financial plan he doubted was feasible, a singular one of the many more obvious reasons why he appreciated the fiscal form and final solution was the influence upon him of the Reverend Ralph Randolph Gurley (1797-1872): the impressive "Connecticut Yankee," and Yale graduate (1818) who served as Executive Secretary (1822-72) of the ACS, Presbyterian powerhouse, and the ACS's most effective solicitor of funds from Calvinist capitalists and Protestant philanthropists in the Northeast.

Channing clearly knew, as well as any man, that the South opposed general emancipation as firmly as the slavocracy rejected abolitionism. This left Colonizationists the class of superhypocrisy, impossible dreams and loyalties, dedicated to a lost cause. These proslavocrats' embracement of the slavocrats, structural fiscal underpinning of the "peculiar institution" and moral fiber support of the slavocracy, presumably was delivered at a high cost to principle matching the high price of transporting the Black race from America to Africa that the Colonizationists were ethically and economically prepared but not fiscally able to pay; and without cost to holiness because they believed their answer to the anti-Black race reality was the only adequate one: all things being equal Colonizationists added, but failed to include in their equation the fact that they never are.

The data in Gurney's book, a copy of which the English Quaker reformer personally handed to Channing during his visit (1837-40) in the United States, added serious purpose to Channing's contemplated sojourn in the British (and of course not the French) West Indies for personal reasons. The West Indies experience, Channing related, gave him such "satisfaction" that "I [he] could not confine myself" and commenced to write, "with little labor," the "Protestant *Emancipation* Proclamation" he called an "exciting one"--and produced the handbook "with perfect calmness."

The Antilles experiments with large concentrations of recently freed slaves, and especially the Black populations in the British and French West Indies, were in the direct experience and mind of Channing. He commended them as useful models for the American slavocracy but made Haiti the excludable exception: Unquestionably because its independence (unlike the precedent setting colonization form of dependence Parliament enacted and enforced British Emancipation entailed) was won by Black freedom fighters from the French Colonial Power through military might, political power, and violent revolution.

Channing's boundless free speech and freedom of conscience liberalism had its definite limits, and stopped decisively at the hint of imminent clear and present danger to domestic tranquility. Channing denigrated Black liberationists and self-determinationists, would not permit toleration of even the positive portrayal of Black insurrectionists, and defamed as totally reprehensible the hint of an overturn in the presumed self-delivered American nation. He had misgivings in the extreme regarding the value of power "politics"--and professional politics whose decision-making chambers he considered as vile a den of iniquity as the drinking establishments Evangelicals condemned.

Hence in his approach to resolving the color caste/captive class' condition, and the cultural crisis one critical constituent element of which appeared the appeal of the bondmen to the rule of right (*apape*-ethic) precipating the conflict and competition between the rule of law (Union's republican democracy) and the rule of might (democracy's slavocracy), Channing was impelled to plan for and bank solely upon "our means of education, and on moral and religious influence." His chief aim was to secure the Puritan-sacred (moral/spiritual) and profane-secular (material/cultural) American "happiness." This ultimate objective required, for its beginning, the emancipation of slaves: whose gradual liberation he thought and wrote to initiate through "a new wisdom, a new temperance, and a new spirit of brotherly love."

Although he had occasion to change his mind later, and took advantage of the opportunity, Channing's gem of a little book on *Emancipation*--he informed his large reading public--served as his "fitly ending" or last and final word on the subject of slavery. He prayed it would "communicate." Certainly it reverberated in the high registers of the resonant voice of resident nemesis William Lloyd Garrison. The radical immediatist had penned his maxim, "Anything but slavery! Poverty sooner than slavery!" And Channing wrote in his Protestant *Emancipation* Proclamation critically of Garrison, whom he caricatured the Pied Piper of "this good City of Boston."

Channing naturally respected solid social conservative White race and White ethnic citizens at large, including the Trinitarian Congregationalists by and large: even though at least as late as 1842, the year in which he died, their institutional interest in the Black race was directed through the ACS; which tra-dition continued until 1845, when liberal Trinitarian Congregationalists organized against the conservatives and traditionalists and formed in the Congregationalist Churches of Christ Denomination Congregationalism's antislavery American Missionary Association (AMA).

The ACS's unmatched, and unmatchable, parochial-private-public treasury was a repelling force, one surpassed only by its excludable Black race deterrence-benevolence compelling power. Precisely because the ASC was the official antislavery organization of the White race/ethnic Evangelical Protestant denominations for thirty years, the good will chariot of charity was taken for granted and misconstrued to be disinterested will to the good for the Black race.

To tell the truth, were it not for this pre-ante-bellum to postbellum bad luck the Black race may have had no luck at all in the mid-antebellum major denominations had not the real presence of Garrison proved a conspicuous absence in the national conventions of the body of Christ.

HUMANISTIC FAITH IN MANKIND OR
JESUSOCRACY FOR CHURCHOCRACY

Pre-slavocracy Unitarian and Trinitarian theological controversies often approached a state of hostilities that frequently turned their "New Light" and "Old Light" Congregationalist traditionalists out of Evangelical Calvinism and New England churches or upon each other. The conflict produced anti-Calvinist and pro-Calvinist warfare that turned Channing away from Orthodoxy, toward transcending the fractionist theological tendencies he believed to be a painful cry for deliverance from dogma, and to reunion of select Congregationalists on a theology-free and philosophy-exclusive Enlightenment ethic of reason, moral values, and humanitarianism.

He directed this synergy of universal moral truth, Unitarian Church of Western profane rationalism and sacred Christian charity, and secular humanism and sacred humanitarianism toward his dream of a Religious Humanism synthesis devoid of sectarian divisiveness.

Contradistinguishingly, Channing's patented poor perspective externally of reality and internally in reality producing his poorer perception is reality stemmed from studiously avoiding taking social psychology seriously; escaping entirely engaging his exactitude in emerging sociology that was currently evolving with the New Abolitionists' analysis of the social (individual and community) being nature and function of human existence; and attending cerebrally selective (greater either metaphysic or aesthetic and lesser ethic) elements of philosophy.

Being an elitist divine who not only defined ultimate worth by positing his deep devotion to the individual and disdain for the social (community) being equation but one for whom excellence and the elite were one and nearly the same thing, and entailed excellent ethics ethicists, it was perfectly understandable why this narrow-focused and sharply delimited philosophy turned out deficient in social philosophy; turned up a diminished capacity social conservative philosophy undergirding faulty premises whose shaky structures formed the fundamental form in which his fraught with flounce yet flaunted individual-exclusive principles and surrogates for social principles both floundered and were grounded; and turned out the solid base of his more rigid than flexible principal means-ends principles.

In addition to the *Slavery* and *Emancipation* texts' self-revelation of the method in the madness and the madness in the method perforce the Protestant powerhouse's proclamation of peace and prosperity attained through being true to pluperfect profane principles of perfection, this process of public persuasion and profession disclosed he was persuaded that his personal intentions dictated the outcome or outflowing social consequences; this persuasion of the persuasive perceptor to be the prime point of the high principled protest ethics; and why Channing was convinced that the consequences of his intentions are not only the legitimate but also the high standard measure of moral thought and action.

This perspective--if his premise and logic are accepted--appears neither a specious mental manipulation nor a spurious piece of reasoning. But inextricably bound in his presupposition is the pretentious presumption that because his less religious or more ethical (faith in God counterbalanced or cancelled by faith in man) society was the demonstrable absence of theology--therefore presumably of dogma as well--and the presence of philosophy, Channingesque Unitarian

Congregationalism could be neither either ideological or doctrinaire nor a new creed.

He designed Unitarianism to be the relative absence of faith (in the trinity and centermost characteristic of his bequeathed Puritan tradition) and the absolute presence of ethics (espoused equivalence of faith in reason and rational man or linear moral progress). This dual highly abstract and concrete set of secular humanistic beliefs functioned effectually to facilitate the core private ethical idea that he posited as the transcendant moral plane. From this astral turf he projected the positive values and disvalues of dogmas and doctrines no less pontifically than he propounded the principle that the measurably greater worth of the ideas and ideals of pure reason can be easily evaluated, disaffirmed, and/or enveloped for affirmative action.

Channing failed to take his own advice and counsel, and missed the meaning of his own revolution, which turned on the argument that interpretation is everything and therefore the centrality of dogmas for theology and doctrines for philosophy that need not be either doctrinaire or ideological.

Yet his misinterpretation of theology as the dogma and pragma of faith and ethics, whose constructive meaning and possibilities he both comprehended and knew their destructive propensities obscured, was one thing. And another thing altogether was his underestimating the equal applicability of logic and imagination to scholarly secular and sacred investigations and explications of profane and religious texts and experiments, experimentalists in empirical and experiential experiences, in personal and social history in cultures and civilizations.

Undoubtedly it was due as much as anything to his belief that endlessly repeatable universally empirically verifiable experiments prove conclusively both the existence of subjective-free objective reason in reality, and that securing and expanding this state of perfection in history is ratiocinators' great promise and greater performance. He was entirely comfortable with the notion that what can be proved cannot be disproved by the same scientific method and suchlike processes of empirical rationalism that successfully produce successive hypotheses, theses, and theories.

The death of God may have been (A) wished for no more than he reflected upon the continuous creation of lesser gods like pleasure, profit, and reason by secular hedonists, Calvinist capitalists, and Puritan rationalists; and (B) desired so strongly that he became a "*true believer*" like millennarian Jonathan Edwards, who wrote for the record eighty years earlier that he could see clearly and nearly "taste" the imminent millennium. Synchronously, Edwards stated that he was completely convinced of one thing: Either he or contemporaries who survived him would soon see his hoped for vanishment of the great religions of the world, with all similar community-centered organizations as well as institutions and systems, and their replacement by individual reason and wisdom knowing the truth and thereby being free.

What is no less real but far more apparent is the high probability that Channing knew the difference between faith in God and faith in science (and empirical rationalism or man and human wisdom) often depends upon the appropriation of their mutually fertile like and unlike different set of beliefs and assumptions--and doubted it amounts to a difference without a distinction.

Arguably, indistinguishable from other Western rationalists in Boston, his vision was distorted by not only the Puritan bifurcation of reality but also by a myopic Occidental mind: one that was rather less dead to universal perspective than to the presence in the universe of the Oriental worldview.

Consequently, Channing either did not apprehend or stubbornly refused to accept the fact that faith is by definition each human being's ultimate concern or concern with his/her ultimate interest, as well as the source of either and/or both religious and secular beliefs; that faith is by nature the cause and effect of sacred theology/dogma and profane ideology/doctrine, or, rational constructs quite like faith as well as theocentric and humanistic religions, are inextricable reason-spawned realities and certainties of the human condition and as permanent as man or God and the Devil in history; and that faith is the subject and object of subjective and objective worldwide faiths of mankind.

But while he located consciously at the margin of his intellectual concern the academic subjects of faith at the heart of Christianity, and all the great religions of the world, Channing combined wittingly and unwittingly the ethics of theology and philosophy in his quest for moral dominance based on a purely rational universal categorical imperative. And the syncretistical synaeresis enabled him to release the brakes on his dream of a class-divided if not also either caste-permeated or color-conscious church for all people--based upon the brotherhood of man. Coincidentally, although he rejected consciously the terms church and denomination as inappropriate descriptions of Unitarian Societies, Unitarians created organizations no less real or viable than those of rival Trinitarians for being denominated Associations.

Subsequently, Channing failed to perceive that equal fairness and equity proved historically and currently no more the strong suit of his cherished Puritan-Calvinist people than public ethics or civil justice. In bare essence, justice is securing the legitimate claim of each individual and race or ethnic group. A civilized society coinstantaneously based on human bondage and caste systems, and challenged to eradicate these not identical twin forms of dehumanization by champions of civility, requires (compared to Channing's contrasting relative deficiency) an ample amount of *agape*-love in order make demanding distributive and corrective justice efficacious. The *agape*-love/power/justice ethic persisted in principle as clearly as it was obscured in practice as the vital meaning and purpose of his universal church.

Limited to this single issue and special interest of general interest-expanding social ethics, and what Channing claimed was the central business of religion--howbeit he could not admit the empirical evidence he validated--Channing's ultimate concern and commitment to create a new earth through a new church or fellowship of individualists/moralists was effective for White folk. But it was effectively also in its positive negation of power politics and social redeeming values public consequences, for the civil life-enhancing versus death-enhancing chances of the oppressed color caste/captive class, as political or mystical and visionary as the "Apocalyptic Vision" of Edwards and Hopkins.

What does not require elucidation is the obvious difference between the pro-Calvinist faith and ethics of Trinitarian Congregationalists and the anti-Calvinist pure reason and moral marrow of Unitarian Congregationalists on the one side, and the Edwards/Hopkins Evangelical millenniarian vision of ultimate reality and that of religious humanist Channing on the other side.

But the distinction that is important in itself for the American majority takes on added significance because it makes a difference to the Black minority. The unity of the Trinitarian and Unitarian establishmentarians demonstrates that the instrumental value produced by their power elite coordinating religious and secular anti-political counterpoles redounds as a great benefit for the White ethnic/race, and greater liability for the Black race.

The millennialists require an ethic of deterrence-benevolence: the dynamic form, fashion, and function enabling Christians to advance the Churchocracy as Christocracy. Marching in lock-step to this millennium-centered rhythm of deliverance through the ritual of escaping from history into eternity, Evangelicals are in league with the unbroken line evolving from the seventeenth-century British and Continental Evangelical millenniarianists. In this mode and mood they increase the efficient Puritan cultural ethic.

The powerful and powerless pure pious neither misstep nor are distinguishable when they break their sacred ranks and join the pure profane in the secular sector. They develop in the civil order the English-race and British-ethnic folk-rooted American Puritan ethic, whose hierarchal order entails a highly struc-tured arrangement of natural Anglo-Saxon race status and superior/inferior class stations beneath which exists the outcast color caste.

The ethic expanded by virtue of its vice, or White race/ethnic-folk's natural real interests-realizing driving need to plunder their Black race; to equate the Black body with negotiable property; and to hold Black folk in disrespect. This Western Christian religious and secular culture-derived device guaranteed the expanding relative advantage and disadvantage of the arbitrary and the vulnerable, and increase in the resources of White folk and decrease in the value of Black folk.

Expansion and extension rather than contraction of the Western Civilization-pervasive caste class condition was alternately accelerated and deaccelerated by rational and radical rapid social structural change: principally in principle and practice by violently vi-olating the African space and body; and through what principled-secular/religious cultural determiners called either a peace process or a process of peaceful changes, whose rationalization appeared reasonable because the change process resulted in neither a revolution nor a reversal but the stabilization of European and Anglo-American real values and interests.

The security and defense of this national treasury was aided immeasurably by the vice expanding and contracting Puritan virtue, whose work ethic and other utilitarian moral values were proliferating parallel to the profit motive and wealth-accumulating purpose or spirit of the Calvinist-capitalist ethic. The elective affinity between the Puritan ecclesiastical and civil powers, and their hegemonic intellectuals who shared responsibilities and implemented the domestic and foreign policies of their powerful sacred parochial and profane private as well as competitive political and economic culture, enhanced the secular and religious viability of the Puritan ethic; its broad and deep culture-pervasive both irreclaimable and irreproachable national influence; and viability as an independent phenomenon that survived in democracy and the demise of theocracy, Orthodoxy, and slavocracy.

These enduring realities have been documented so thoroughly by specialists and generalists in the multiform Puritan culture field that it comes as no surprise to the educated non-specialist to discover, or to recall upon reflection, that in its preponderance, the universal brotherhood approved by Channing subsists of a Western rationalist Christian-rooted and humanist-informed ethic of benevolence and justice for White Protestant males primarily; Anglo-Saxon females secondarily; and other ethnic moral men and women of goodwill generally. However, his heroic moral individual ethic is promoted by Channing as not only the perfect private and parochial model but also as the only public standard of moral excellence.

What transpires is transparent relative rather than absolute certainty,

Trinitarian and Unitarian Congregationalists' corresponding intentions and consequences to the contrary notwithstanding: The rational morality Channing fashions as faith in mankind, and denominates the universal brotherhood ethic and endeavors to activate in the North and the South, differs from Evangelical-Calvinist Congregationalists' millennial-centered Churchocracy for Christocracy.

This millennarian instrumental means Evangelical sectarians created to achieve the ends of Halfway Piety faith and ethics, whose self-revelatory nature and purpose is the deterrence-benevolence message, method, and mission; in essence and manifestation exemplified by White Protestants uniting church and state for the separation of the Black body from the White body politic and shipping the Black race from America to Africa; and related to but different from the Puritan theocracy.

Nonetheless flexibly for being more paradoxically than ironically connected, Channing's theocentric-humanistic ideal interlinks with Puritan Edwards' revisionist Churchocracy and the Puritan theocracy, from which real norm Edwards' standard deviates sharply.

The not rigid but flexible connective linkage is no less real and revealing than--as the moral arm of his Calvinistical variation of Christocracy--Edwards' revision of the peculiar Puritan *Errand into the Wilderness*: The human species-redeeming in history for eternity faith and ethics task-responsibility accepted by the called and chosen select "Elect" saints, or their proudly proclaimed and publicly published dual mission, to provide a faith for personal salvation from damnation and for eternity; and a universally applicable ethic as a moral means whereby the faith works in civilization for the Kingdom of God.

In the process of developing a method whereby he does not totally reject and jettison but positively rationalizes the premises and doctrines of Calvinist-Puritan social ethics, Channing creates a philosophy-grounded humanistic religion and ethic whose arrangement is in tension with the Calvinist-Puritan theology and may be fairly described best as a Jesusocracy.

Jesusocracy is the rea-son overriding as well as underbuilding more anemic than barren Channingesque faith, and virile humanistic ethic instrument for worldwide person-specific attitudinal and behavioral moral character modification and culture-specific reform. Exactly for this ultimate purpose the man of intellectual gifts and graces to match his great ambition structured this functional form of rational morality to be the facilitating mechanism to improve the utilitarian value and implementation of his boldly reasoned Christian faith-free ethic.

Succinctly restated, as an alternative ways and means, the ethical individual prime Channingesque ethics principle was developed for the religion and church of the moral man: to be applied in an era when Massachusetts state tax-supported Congregationalist churches and clergymen (until 1833) understood existence as the instrument for the realization of the Kingdom of God on earth to be the primary purpose of the Church.

New England Congregationalism had developed into a regional church or denomination, composed of churches at once resisting dependence and retaining independence while developing interdependence in state consociations, that was not without influence. Precisely due to the evolvement of the New England church as a rational organization of Congregationalist Consociations it was widely perceived by Unitarians as a collective (whole apart from autonomous churches and greater than the sum of these functional members of the body); in nature and purpose as well as form and function indistinguishable from either secular or civil institutions albeit an ecclesiastical arrangement; and an end in itself.

Nevertheless, existence in essence as Congregationalist establishment clergymen is the dynamic link connecting the Unitarian's Jesusocracy and the Trinitarians' Christocracy. The Anglo-American Puritan race and Congregationalist Church of Christ common heritage was downgraded in their concentration on the polar opposite binary and not diametrically opposed faith and ethics differentials of Puritan culture.

Unitarians fastened upon uniting the secular in the sacred, and Trinitarians upon separating the pure pious from the pure profane Puritan mind, proved theological (faith) and philosophical (ethics) proved respectively undeveloped and developed different constituent elements of the bipolar legacy, and the central cause and effect of the tenuous continuity between the three representative types of conflict and competition prone Puritan Yankees in Boston, to wit, Channing, who evinced reverence for the two if not equal profane and sacred halves of the tradition; the "Consistent Calvinists" ever-revising Orthodoxy; and the secular humanists.

This theistic, Christocentric, and humanistic establishment confluence developed as combative competitors as successfully as Calvinist Congregationalists and Presbyterians organized to beat the devil and the competition (provided by the very competitive Evangelical Arminian Methodist evangelists and revivalists) for the souls of Black folk.

Moreover, the Yankee tripartite in Boston advanced in the stiff competition for and on the strength of Calvinist capitalists and Protestant philanthropists, while virtually avoiding or escaping and certainly without encountering the Black experience. This class and caste gulf Channing occasionally endeavored to bridge with his purely theoretical humanistic ethic.

In point of fact, Channing entered the antislavery/proslavery field of conflict and competition between antislavocrats and proslavocrats to exercise leadership and form the consensus behind his antiabolitionist initiative; to take charge by challenging White New Abolitionists--united with Black New Abolitionists and divided as Protestants variously engaged with the Christocracy and disengaged from Churchocracy--to join him in the new one-dimensional moral monistic and anti-political johnny-one-note Jesusocracy.

He had organized the Jesusocracy to be the American Puritan Religious Humanism alternative to the European Christian Humanism transplanted as the New Church, or Church of the New Jerusalem in North America, in which alone, Channing averred, their zeal could be directed rationally and efficiently effective.

Howbeit a day late and a penny short, the color caste/captive cultural crisis finally had the attention of Channing: if not as fully as he felt the intense heat of the one hundred year old pro-Calvinist/anti-Calvinist embroilment, that left the combatants more exasperated than exhausted. Evangelical Congregationalists were excited about their developing humanitarian mission. It was calculated to be of incalculable value for White America, and therefore proved of questionable social redeeming value for Black America.

Heretofore emerging with an undivided will and mind to resolve through pure reason the theological (faith) v. philosophical (ethics) battles, which had escalated into full scale Puritan intertribal warfare, Channing conditioned himself to avoid--at all cost--active participation in issues that were certain to erupt in civil and secular controversies.

CORRELATIVE DOCTRINAIRE MORAL
IDEOLOGY AND ANTI-POLITICS DOGMA

Channing was convinced controversial parochial and profane affairs inevitably turn on political questions, power plays, and personality clashes, which he thought were questions of style rather than matters of substance. Due directly to his reflection upon the Puritan experiment and experience from a patrician's vision of high idealism distorted by a demonstrably poor perception of realism and worse pragmatism posture limiting the possibility of placing in perspective the aristocrats' power-wielding dominance of the Three Branches of Government, Channing, unlike the Yale and Harvard Federalist Party power politics partisan parsons who were his Newport pastors and Cambridge preceptors, refused to take seriously either power politics and economics or conflict and competition as the ineradicable and indispensable condition of a complex culture composed of different legitimate claims and interests, yet not necessarily either an inevitable or permanent state of confrontation in any particular instance of demanding disparate desires or determinations of man as demonstrated conclusively by American pragmatism.

In spite of counterpoised empirical evidence and experience in reality, as well as because of the high priority he placed on stability and order, Channing acted on the patently false premise that constant absolute conciliation (like linear moral progress and ever-spiraling economic prosperity) rather than alternately expanding and contracting or relative domestic and foreign harmony is possible: and not like heaven a co-equally necessary and elusive ideal that functions effectively in history to improve the human being, race and ethnic groups, and cultures.

What followed in logic and life, from this Channingesque elitist ethical analysis and conclusion, was predictable given the fact that he believed the human being is in essence and essentially a moral and rational but not a political animal: Channing reached the final judgment that church and state power politics are neither the necessary result of inevitable conflicts of real interests and values nor rational means for managing conflict and competition nor moral engagements but irrational immoral exercises.

He reached this decision by arguing with the facts the argument that because nonnegotiable differences are settled between international enemies by war; between national rivals by pure power; and between neither foreign nor domestic hostile parties by pure reason; and, therefore, being counter-productive and non-rational measures that serve no useful purpose, parochial or public partisan parson and parishioner power professional politicians and politics are both unnecessary and dispensable.

Thus his logic outran theory and experience in reality, as he argued the case for power politics being a more dysfunctional than functional process of raising the emotions to a fever pitch level, whereby the mind is clouded with suspicion and a clear perspective is obscured.

On this elitist conservative corner, Channing thought to escape power politics and to avoid controversy which he determined were harmful in the extreme.

In addition to demonstrating his characteristic dispassionate rather than impassable nature, this value judgment disclosed a new peak in his low-level concern with public matters of importance had been reached. It reflected Channing's escalating reasons to act and will to direct quiet, deliberate, and peaceful social change. To attend appropriately this uncharacteristic role and attain the challenging goal, Channing quite naturally adopted and adapted the leadership style of a moral "prophet" rather than that of a policy maker: a posture that was consistent with the fact that his reverence for most politicians was on a par with his disdain for politics.

In his efforts to escape from the Congregationalists' fiery theological furnace, that his Calvinist brethren stoked with seemingly unrelieved passion, Channing was determined not to jump into the ethical fires the pro-Calvinist and anti-Calvinist New Abo-litionists were lighting. In his estimation, immediatists could only engulf the nation in a conflagration. He could share the New Abolitionists' antislavery premise while finding their principal principle and practice repugnant to his sensitive sensibilities; agree to disagree as a pro-gradualism proponent with their pro-immediatism as amicably as possible; and vigorously and rigorously denounce proabolitionist strategies and tactics to public as inflammatory and therefore despicable.

For a non-controversialist, so-called by academic admirers, Channing was very definite in his opinion of the New Abolitionists. He did not hesitate to express it in the strongest negative language he was capable of producing for public consumption. The obvious pertinent correlation that is relevant to recall in the context of Channing's pretext entails the point that Black Americans, if not Whites citizens, might have been his beneficiaries had Channing elected the viable option of choosing not to depreciate and to appreciate as well as to support Old or New Abolitionist policies and politics early.

The impossibility is not more apparent than the possibilities inherent in the fact that liberal Yankees (if not Puritan Trinitarian or Unitarian Congregationalist traditionalists) dominated the politics of Boston in the era of his ministry.

Channing knew these politicians personally; and well enough to exercise his influence with them. They provided him with the first-hand information and raw data that he transformed into knowledge. And he used the facts, he harmonized with his values, as ammunition to deprecate politics as a necessary evil and profession, and one producing a preponderance of professionals existing without art or science and just so little rhyme and reason to make this lowest form of human communication barely tolerable.

Channing juxtaposed his affirmation of the office of statesman, he identified with and as the classical role of the ruling patricians, and disaffirmation of the validity of the professional politician: most of whose class he decried as experts in seeking the lowest common denominator, while securing rank bargain basement self-interests, and downgraded as professionals fixed in a profession beneath the profiteering merchants.

This public posture suggested a probable cause why and how Channing's attention was drawn away from de-manding anti-Black race interest, currently enlivening the uncompromising spirit of Northern and Southern proslavocrats. As a result of more narrow-minded than broad-minded primary concern with the real interests and values of White folk, and their peace and prosperity in the Union, the prospects of Black Americans all but escaped Channing's positive resources entirely.

Channing who was the nonpareil advocate of private emancipation by only but any personal moral suasion means possible, and the adversary of pro-politics proabolitionists who assumed ethical awareness requires for its effect the acquirement of the amount moral plus political power necessary to shake the slave structure loose from its foundation, were commonly inspired by the "spirit of Christianity"--and the "Great Emancipator." He was at work in the host English Abolitionist Evangelicals from Granville Sharp (1735-1813) through William Wilberforce (1759-1833) to the Reverend Thomas Clarkson (1760-1846).

Channing's "Great Emancipator" empowered these observant British Abolitionists and churchmen with suf-ficient Enlightenment reason and political power to initiate the liberation of Victorian England from a state of human bondage. But his discriminating judgment fastened on the narrow social conservative point, whereby, along with the American Independence, Channing preferred to overlook the power politics of this English Christian radical structural change movement and to distinguish the British from the French and Haitian Revolutions: whose social change systems Channing described as "the low motives" inherent in other revolutions that involve "policy, interest, state-craft, church-craft."

Yet at the same time the apperceptive was appraising soulcraft and statecraft, forehanded Channing was oblivious to the critical factors and their meaning, to wit, the British Abolitionists were Evangelical Anglicans and Independents predonerantly as well as descendants of English Puritans (the Marian Exiles fathers of his beloved John Milton and John Winthrop); largely a partisan party power politics force of parsons and parishioners, whose civil law and order correcting rational power connection Channing disconnected in the process of cutting himself off from its comparable American Puritan source; and led by Protestants who had no difficulty matching their moral powers and promise with their performance as direct actionist Members of Parliament.

Channing also failed to observe the meaning of the difference between ending slavery in the British Empire without driving Black British free-born and freedmen residents out of the British Isles--where they never existed in substantial numbers--and the general emancipation of Black North Americans. The difference between the small and large Black minority and Anglo-Saxon majority in England and America entailed a distinct difference in real (rather than true) interests and values, subsisted of a distinction that required a different solution from the one Channing demanded, and was a difference in degree so great as to make all the difference in the world.

The power point was missed or dismissed entirely by Channing when he publicly promulgated his preference for voluntary emancipation of "the most despised and injured race on earth" by slavocrats whom he called (or appealed to as fellow) Protestant philanthropists but who were primarily concerned to secure their expanding chattel propery real interests, that they equated with enlightened self-interest and believed were best served by securing an ever-expanding slave-labor rather than free-labor political economy.

As late as 1840, the year when Channing published his *Emancipation* proclamation, divided antiabolitionists and proabolitionists were united progradualist and pro-immediatist opposites as absolutists who tolerated moral-only antislavery methods and dominated the movement in the United States. These principled moralists were formidable friends and foes of their pro-politics proabolitionist and slavocrat opposition, as well as a study in contrast when compared to the moral plus political power leaders at the helm of British Abolitionists in England.

In keeping with their inflexible moral law and order, whose rigid rules and regulations they thought were the standard of morality because the "true believers" in moral monism were consistent monocrats, this Northern antislavery class understood all residents in the slavocracy were forbidden by Southern positive law to obey or honor their Northern moral law: still, they preached to

Christian Southerners to practice the principles of Protestant Northerners as if the antislavery Northeasterners were not also proslavocrats but only antislavocrats.

Congregationalist Channing and the central cast of the countercharging New Abolitionists--who were predominantly Calvinist varieties led by a Presbyterian preponderancy--fostered the distinct impression they believed Southern Christians in general and Protestants in particular were perfectionists, philanthropists, and protectionists (if neither angels of mercy nor avenging angels of true interests and values) but not like themselves: New England pure pious and pure profane citizens; indistinguishable sacred and secular defenders in the civil sector of their real interests and values; and--analogous to war as the ultimate moral breaker of an unconscionable bind such as when the consciences of ethicists are bound by either/or both conflicting principles and unresolvable national security or unsecurity choices between two equal superpowers--powerhouses possessing counterbalancing resources and frequently caught in a conflict of interests, whose tie neither consummate reason nor sheer moral power but only superior real power can break.

For example, moral monocracy professors of monism like moralist Channing approached the solid slavocracy but singled out for special reproach the proslavery Methodist and Baptist "prevalent sects at the South." Channing condemned their clergy for being "content with silence" and thereby supporting slavery. They were chastised as a class that "preached known falsehood"; indulged their own "self-interest" and "private affection" in company with the "tyranny of opinion and the passions of the multitude"; and promoted the advancement of the slavocracy system as if human bondage in perpetuity was "consistent with justice, equity, and disinterested love."

It is far more curious than either surprising or shocking that Channing never grasped so firmly the relationship between the ethnocentrism of Englishmen and their no less potent for being rather more latent than manifest anti-Black race values or pro-White race virtue. The pristine principled Protestant knew with absolute certainty the Evangelicals in England originated the British Abolition movement, and that their equally strong and sustained half century-long antislavery protest eventuated in Parliament's abolition of the slavetrade and slavery.

Whether or not he was willing and able to understand the moral power cause and real power effect of Christian British Abolitionism, well within the range of Channing's powers of discrimination was the capacity to appreciate how and why as much as when and where Evangelical British Abolitionists accomplished what American White and Black New Abolitionists observed as an incredible reversal of real values and interests and called the miracle of England.

He knew in theory and/or in fact the abrogation of the English human bondage system was at once a pure political triumph--over a difficulty compounded by com-plexities subsisting of competing positive law and social order values as well as legitimate economic claims--and not a defeat for either the British Empire or its world-class enterprise system.

Undoubtedly Channing knew that and thereby why the British were able to achieve this remarkable Victorian Age turn in events partly because there were few Black British residents in the British Isles, and, as he may not have believed, in spite of the fact England--both unlike and like the Yankee Independence era descendants of the English Puritan settlers of New England--a minority of Englishmen found the African slavetrade as morally indefensible as it was currently profitable and economically dispensable and therefore politically intolerable.

The penetrating mind of the moralist was preconditioned by the constraints of concentrated moral power to preclude the possibility of factoring into his analysis these real power-specific complex certainties. His fixed critical focus on the British intellectuals among the upper-class and middle-class English was a predetermined corollary, whose predictable ancillary appeared an equally automatic failure to connect the Evangelical and political realities of British Abolitionists with the potentialities of their New Abolitionist American counterparts.

These were among the contributing factors of a mind that was pre-set and satisfied to berate Evangelicals in the American South, where slaves were numerous and cherished as highly profitable and pleasurable chattel property. Channing advanced arguments supporting the reasons why he believed Black race real interests-protecting Evangelical Southern slavemasters existed, and could recognize and accept their obligation to perform "the most common duty of morality"--or know and do if not be the truth--like their Northern Evangelical adversaries. He was of this entire convincement, even though Northeastern antislavery warriors distinguished themselves distinctly by not possessing slave property; and thus were engaged with different real interests and values, and motivations and opportunities.

Whether considered an irrelevant incidental accident of history, or whether a tragic story but one barren of instructive possibilities, Channing paid no attention to the decisive fact that mainstream Protestant manu-missionists had long since been forced out of the sla-vocracy with the Southern abolitionists--and to prac-tice their antislavery principles in the West where they were vigorously contested--by slavocrats at the helm of an equally intolerant of criticism and mono-lithic slavocracy.

In this context, the social consequences-conducing double standard that Channing automatically places in the operational mode--consciously or unconsciously--is in itself the evincement of his personal ambiguity. While he writes in one sentence to prove Northern and Southern Evangelicals are "enthusiastists" in manifest esesence and existence, and associates them with zealots rather than with crusaders for Christ and civility, in the next sentence he asserts enthusiasm is the Achilles heel of Evangelicals in the South, whom, in the third sentence, he challenges to take up the antislavery cause by reminding them they are "expected to be less tainted by a worthy spirit." For his own co-equally silent and transparent reasons, he does not identify the Anglicans and Presbyterians of the South by name but includes them among those unspecified "other denominations in which luxury and fashion bear great sway."

Channing and the New Abolitionists personally knew, in the North and West, a respectable number of Evangelical ministers who opposed slavery; signed petitions; and, as a permanent minority, voted antislavery resolutions in various ministeriums and other denominational "associations, conventions, presbyteries or conferences." They knew few more New England Congregationalist clergymen than they could count on one hand, compared to the number of rival Protestant pastors, who successfully opened their meeting-houses for abolitionist rallies. But they also knew that while many independent-minded clergymen and laymen were staunch antislavery Christians--in the North, West, and South antislavery was neither authorized by major churches or on the official agenda of any establishment denominational movement. Most churches, and every national denomination throughout Channing's life, "in the main looked coldly on the subject."

Thus there were one hundred antislavery-proslavery ambivalents for every Evangelical like the near-Rev-erend Theodore Dwight Weld, and his financial supporters Arthur (1786-1865) and Lewis (1788-1873) Tappan--in whom Evangelical Christianity and opposition to the color caste/captive were united in perfect harmony. And for all the official denominations, including the Unitarian Association--and their establishment ecclesiastical bureaucracies and other institutional extensions--Channing's general rule held: "The Christianity of this day falls fearfully short." Consistent in ignoring power politics on the grounds the profession was both impotent and corrupt, Channing declared the "pulpit and the press," having deferred to "public opinion," were--"in no small degree" --virtually "reduced to silence as to slavery."

The Evangelical New Abolitionist radicals stood foursquare with Channing in subjecting Protestant churchmen, churches, and denominations to their withering criticism. Being observant Christians but not rigid institutionalists, they understood the denomination to be distinguished from the Church; but, in their critical assessments, they often failed to discriminate between antislavery and proslavery local churches as well as between the national denominations and the Church universal.

As a consequence of sweeping generalizations that were interesting but lacked compelling force because their emphases revolved around misplaced priorities and frequented the haunts of misarranged principles, the pure profane nonchurchmen critics as much as the pure pious churchmen treated a generalizable as a universalizable criticism. Forthwith scholarly specialists and generalists transmitted as a fact the fiction that not even a creative minority of antislavery churches existed in either the Northeast or the West.

Of course, a precipitant factor in this misconstruction and misdirection being sustained instead of the mistaken impression being corrected was the salient fact that the majority of churches ratified the enactments of their leadership and national representatives, promulgated by the supreme judicatories annually, whose policies and programs were as overwhelmingly anti-Black race and anti-abolitionist processes as their principles.

These underpinnings illuminated the complete eradi-cation of slavery by moral power force only--first and last and always--the principle shared by proabolitionist Garrison and antiabolitionist Channing, the repre-sentative spokesmen for radical and moderate Protestant moralists, as well as their nearly career-long irrecon-cilable pro-immediatist and pro-gradualist differences.

Evangelical Garrison, for example, in spite of his reputation for torrid rhetoric, parted company with Channing on one sharp point the Unitarian never doubted --"Christianity lives and acts among us"--as he man-aged to make contradictions of his moral absolutism appear consistent or to superimpose, "salutary re-straints" and to inspire "good deeds."

They also held similar anti-Black race values which they communicated in dissimilar expressions, although it was not unexpected that Channing disclosed the substance of their premises in more revealing poetry and prose since he was in the sphere of literate writing an artist--and model for other men of letters.

AN ENLIGHTENMENT RATIONALIST'S ROMANTIC BLACK IMAGES

In line with his elitist values and elegant style, Channing exercises his power and authority in defining by describing Black folk as Christ-like in their na-ture--"meek, long-suffering, loving virtue." By this figment of an imaginative mind of the age of Christian romanticism, he intends nothing less than to set forth--against the general denigration of the Black race--"the noble elements of the negro character."

Compared to Protestant traditionalists extending the collective high culture suspicion but selective en-gagement and disengagement continuum Puritans expressly expanded, who were less receptive to the secular cul-tural determinants than to the empirical logic as well as philosophical and psychological developments of the Enlightenment than the liberal elite, such positively race/color-intensive discriminations were the distinguishing marks of secular humanists.

Color-conscious intellectuals both followed the Abbé Henri Gregoiré and jumped the track he laid to respect race-specific descendants of Black African ethnic groups--through connecting their literature and first published creative artists with Western European, American, and other men and women of letters. But the sharp distinct between these Occident varieties is the unmistakable fact that Channing, and the American literati, simply did not read seriously the poetry and prose works of Black Americans.

This is one reason why Channing, who is unable to empathize with either the whole Black race--that is greater than the sum of its individual and community parts--or free Black men, sym-pathizes with slaves. But he would not, like Samuel Hopkins, defend Indian ethnics--each brave among whom, he believed, would send a knife deep into the heart of the White man if he were a member of any White race/ethnic ménage. But Black human bondage are to the mind of the romantic liberal rationalist "the mildest, gentlest of men."

It was no mean accomplishment for Channing to keep current with the illuminati who praised the Indian as the primitive original and "noble savage"--and the African as the "Ignoble savage"--and, in counterpoint to the intelligentsia, to transubstantiate the Black man into the "noble savage" possessed of a rare "gracefulness and dignity of form and motion." His aesthetic judgment here is one thing--and not called into question. But, the demur he offers notwithstanding--"I have aimed only to express my sympathy with the wronged"--the logic of his position leaves little to choose between the romanticism of the Boston moralist and the "enthusiasm" of the Southern Evangelical Pietists he decried.

Channing's nicely nuanced romantic descriptions of the Black race are intended to reinforce his central point, to wit, the "religious tendencies" of Black folk are "the noblest in human nature." Northern White Christian gentlemen engaged in protecting their anti-Black race interest, like compeer Southern slavemasters they supported, were pleased to have these common sentiments rehearsed by the voice of American rational moralism. Doubtless the initiated religious no less than the secular Protestants--who knew they were transpositions of major Continental secular themes in a minor American religious key-- were even more overjoyed to have their convictions confirmed on an international scale.

Universally accessible scholarly investigations provide ample evidence documenting the conventional wisdom that the full orchestration of the clashing crass class and color and conscience symphony Channing first heard played or read in the East from the score published in the West by the near-Reverend Alexander Kinmont (17491839): the Scotland-native, American emigrant, and Swedenborgian whom Channing credited in his Puritan *Emancipation* testament. Kinmont had won the respect of the establishment Evangelicals whom the re-located large family of the Reverend Lyman Beecher (1775-1863) embraced in the West; while chiaroscurist Channing, in the East, wrote his own script.

DECEPTIVE BLACK-RACE EMOTIONAL RELIGION
AND WHITE-ETHNIC RATIONAL RELIGION

The relevance of the connection is implicit in Channing's explicit superior White race moral principle and affirmation of faith: "The European races have manifested more courage, enterprise, invention." This pro-White race declaration was set forth to illustrate the difference between the compared and contrasted superiority of the White race and the superiority of the Black race: White race and ethnic groups demonstrate peerless cerebral power, "but in the dispositions which Christianity particularly honors, how inferior are they to the African."

What he has specifically in mind concerning the strengths of the Black man is piercing weakness: "His nature is affectionate, easily touched; and hence he is more open to religious impressions than the white man."

This "Good News" and "Bad News" both religious and secular social gospel according to Channing, Western rationalism, and romanticism is not the essential Christian person/people/public redeeming promise but the secular humanist sentiment in essence and manifestation. Channing both confuses and fuses the two: partly because his Enlightenment Philosophy is diminished rather than increased by a counterbalancing Enlightenment Theology; the Christian ethic of love, power, and justice is divorced from the public interest politics of the Puritan tradition; and charity is reduced by romanticism to a slender reed--and one deficient of the tough moral fiber Channing requires.

Without doubt, a stereotype quite like a generalization is, on the one hand, inaccurate and unconscionable when it implicitly or explicitly functions either/or both to override each unique and distinct individual and as a universally applicable categorization of a race-entity, ethnic-group, or other human community; and, on the other hand, intrinsically neither unfair and unjust or demeaning and degrading nor evil and error but may be extrinsically a context-specific instructive construct in the abstract or concrete, especially when skillfully designed and applied fittingly in a restricted academic field as the subject and object of disciplined analysis and reflection; and, on yet another hand, risk-prone since its inherently harm-intensive potential may be readily appropriated for human abuse by the harm-intensive mind and will.

Precisely because Channing is a man of integrity and competence, whose intellectual character and content renders him incapable of enmity and malice a-forethought, his impeccable character automatically lends powerful credibility to the stereotype he transmits and translates gratuitously or not for contemporaries and posterity. Irrespective of his intentions, there follows from his conscious rational romantic racialism negative good/positive harm public consequences for White and Black Americans. Exactly in this moral construct Channing reveals the anti-Black race virtue he advanced as conventional wisdom in the circles which set the standards of American culture, civility, and character.

Unquestionably for an individual-only rights and responsibilities absolutist it is odd and even peculiar that he should attend the idea of race as an ideal devoutly to be wished--to say little of engaging and disengaging his Black-race essence (precedes and succeeds individual existence) presence so selectively that he confirms his high-minded disregard of the life-enhancing and death-enhancing chances of the whole Black body.

Black race wholeness is the ultimate concern of this American Christian social ethics probative, deconstructionist, interpretive essay. It is the ultimate subject and object because the condition of the Black community is not a matter of relative but of absolute importance: since the individual member of the color caste class can be neither whole without the whole becoming whole nor become whole apart from the whole, nor exist wholly apart from the Black American race.

Contrapositively, there is no reason to doubt that on the conscious level Channing wishes to credit the Black race with a single solid natural virtue, nature-conditioned and nature's God-derived gift to humanity; and the one good trait which he believes everyone at once should acknowledge, appreciate, and accept with thanksgiving. Doubtless in punctuating this gratitude note--without the counterpoint grace note it demands--he does not make music. He makes exactly the wrong point--at the wrong time--in his influential environment.

Instead of elevating the Black race in the estimation of his readers, his albatross-intensive neither objective nor descriptive facts but culture-specific caste/class scores of value judgments are hung around the necks of Black people.

Indeed, his demonstrated capacity to explore the truth and falsity in the race and religion myth was diametrically oppositely directed to exploit fantasy rather than reality for his own moral power purposes. The creative achievements of Black individuals and communities he knew as well as he knew the Black race to be capable of manly arts. But Channing intentionally excluded these assertive and aggressive realities from his disquisition, because the self-serving absence of this presence in his *Emancipation* proclamation promoted his primary point and purpose which was to keep the Black race docile. And, in line with his final wish he recorded in the manuscript and intended to execute, Channing published *Emancipation* as his last testament to Black folk. No less certainly than the income from this interest earned him no fortune, fame was the outcome as White folk praised him for his living will posthumously.

Alternately stated, by rephrasing the relevance of the bottom line and the difference Channing made in race and religion religions during his professional career that ended in 1842, what the works of the informed moralist make unmistakably clear is this: the chiaroscurist knew the difference in private intentions and public consequences between notions and deeds of commission and omission, and therefore understood comprehensively in theory the harm in fostering a tortured color caste/class caricature subsists of being misleading at best; proliferating misconceptions and misperceptions at least; and--at worst--promulgating a dangerous error.

For at least a century in New England, White race and ethnic residents had been intoxicated by emotional religion and their wild enthusiasms. While denied by "New Light" Jonathan Edwards, his challenging contemporary critics like "Old Light" Charles Chauncy adjudged Evangelical "enthusiasts" to be less in than out of control during the First Great Awakening.

The "reborn" appeared progressively less violent until the spiritual phenomena broke forth again with sufficient force to be known to history as the Second Great Awakening. In both national spiritual revivals, varieties of silent and serene or clamorous and physical high intensity and high anxiety religious experience were as real as they were the obvious bane of his heritage and ministry.

Certainly, Channing was privy to the facts. There existed no more "gentle, meek, and mild" people--who were coinstantaneously open to immediate "religious impressions" and politics of pressure placed upon power to persuade authority--than the strong, rich, and famous Quakers. Correlatively, corresponding pro-abolitionist English Evangelicals, whom he understood to be the catalytic agents of British Abolitionism, were "subdued" by the moral individual and civil community redeeming "religion of Jesus." Indeed, Channing wrote to affirm it "struck root among them"--and to deny the English Evangelical and Quaker "born again" spiritual and/or moral experience was encountered by the American Evangelical and Quaker New Abolitionist minority.

Pro-immediatists' amazing grace he wished to silence, while Black New Abolitionists were enthusiastically cheering and singing in harmony the lyrics of the Negro Spirituals the Black slave community were spontaneously creating, namely, if liberation be the theme of Christian faith and ethics--preach on in the parochial and profane pulpit and press, public political party and presidential "bully pulpit," and Congress and the Court. What Channing extended was far less equal access to equitable law and justice or competitive political and economic opportunity, for Black advocates of biracial fairness and equity, than a helping hand to White race/ethnic-adversaries seeking to turn the strength of Black performers against the Black race.

His rational thoughts and actions had the effect of paralyzing intentions and consequences, as he planted, picked, produced, packaged, and promoted--in the public market he cornered--the profitable and pleasurable value which guaranteed Black folk were weak, complacent, servile, and docile. The motive of the method and medium was the message Boston brahmin liked and there-fore did not stone the messenger--which he delivered in order to sacrifice Black race to his grand scheme of emancipation.

Channing proved he had the courage of his convictions when he admonished Black human bondage not to grow weary in submissive and subservient well-doing, but to suffer gladly or to be cheerfully obedient and hardworking; a credit to their slave race and worthy of their slavery in perpetuity natural selection and divine election; earnest and honest to God; and to be passive and wait for deliverance (one by one) by the proslavery moral law and civil positive law and order abiding White slavemasters--no matter how long it might take for the property owners of their Black body, whom the Bible and the Constitution set in absolute command and control of the destiny of the Black race, to experience a new birth of conscience (individually seriatim).

BLACK RACE ESSENCE AND PRESENCE IS THE
ABSENCE OF A BLACK INDIVIDUAL IN EXISTENCE

A mind undivided in either reason or moral will power and will to power, energized by the *noblesse oblige* content of his character, Channing combines rationality with romanticism and spirituality to strain credulity. Demonstrable ignorance and innocence rather less than expedience and convenience is Channing carrying coals to Newcastle, as he preaches to proud owners and progenitors of their Black property who take great pleasure and profit from their human chattel with whom they engage in intimate licit and illicit intercourse.

The self-determination preempted and dehumanized Black man, Channing pleads with the slavemaster class to acknowledge, is "my brother" in "Christ and culture." He is to be showered with Puritan-specific antiblack white-ethnic virtues, Channing pontificated, apparently because the Unitarian truly believed either their mutually exclusive and equally intrinsic positive and negative dynamics were not counterbalancing potent realities, or that the former over-powered their negative power energies: whereby they "bear a small proportion" to the double damnation vices of the Evangelical Calvinist sons and distant cousins of his Puritan brothers and fathers.

Positive moral power and reason and a classic nondenial denial is Channing affirming that "undoubtedly the negroes are debased," or, what by way of admitting he proves conclusively he believes, yet, as certainly, actually admits only in order both to deny the belief and to disapprove what he disbelieved as definitely it was widely alleged: expressly that Black people possess a "peculiar incapacity of moral elevation." Without exception, Channing would accept the point that in accord with his intentions these were mutually exclusive proposi-tions, and categorically deny what is nevertheless true beyond a shadow of a doubt: they were manifestly mutually fertile principles evolving in his color caste/class life and work from his typology of classes and races.

As Channing integrated these types as universal categories, the relatively powerless and statusless lower classes within the ranks of each race and the inferior beneath the superior races, are, in relation to the nature-derived high born and therefore high status and powerful classes, to be submissive and obedient to every hierarchal ecclesiastical and civil power and legitimate authority instituted by God and man; and in compliance with every positive law enacted and civil order issued by powerhouses in their paro-chial/private/public offices that is moral.

The pertinent Channingesque critical point in this American Christian social ethicist's interpretive essay is that, Channing, the moderate modern moralist model, represents the White upper-, middle-, and lower-class religious and sec-ular Protestants: who are against slavery, for liberation, and can afford to delay and thereby deny self-determination to their Black cultural kith and kin because they possess liberty and enjoy freedom. Prerogatives of privilege include self-de-termination and are exercised by Channing as he sets forth for public imita-tion his protypical social classification. In this hierarchal arrangement for capi-tal, management, and labor--and their slaves, serfs, and servants--order and stability is a higher priority the liberty.

Without doubt, his gradualism in principle and practice is in consequence a stabilizing moral power--whereby Channing aggravates rather than eases the predicament of slaves in the slavocracy. In the pursuit of happiness for Black and White folk, his categorization of racial "types" serves his principal purpose --which is to point up and out the "typical" member of a race group. As a re-sult of consciously lumping together all members of a "race," Channing uncon-sciously dramatizes the differences between "races"; totally ignores individual distinctions making each human being unique; and thus leaves Black folk he rose to grant the advantage of liberation at a greater disadvantage than he found them.

Doubtless as incontrovertibly as the ethics exemplar emerges a managerial master of morality and masterful moral man of stronger *Emancipation*/liberation words than deeds. Yet as the diametric opposite of a value-free intellectual, the converse of Channing's intentions is the consequence of his middle-of-the-road direct action-devoid and rhetoric-restricted ideals. Channing advances in this moral mood and mode even as he protests strongly that Black folk are "selected to be trodden down and confounded with brutes." In line with his high princi-pled *Emancipation* process and program, evidently it was outside liberal limits of his conservative mind and will but not beyond the range of his cerebral capacity for Channing to think it useful to extend verbal endorsement (if not more substantial support) from his boundless resources to Northern and Southern Black and White men and women, whom he personally knew and observed placing their bodies on the line to increase the number of meritorious Black individuals.

But an antithetical congenital moral verve--reflected in his reflex reaction including the use of words like bullets as his choice of weapons--controlled Channing's iron will, nerve of steel, and Puritan-Yankee brains and brawn when challenged to be provocative and even provoking rather than simply evocative; pressed to defend the national security and wealth by uninvited foes of regional values and interests, and unwelcome aggressive enemies threatening the Union's peace and prosperity as well as the national social health and welfare; and/or forced to break his normal chain of command and channel of discretion, and to forage in unchartered deep and dangerous waters in order to protect American life and liberty.

These submerged but surging certainties surface and soar paralleling the deliberate speed with which Channing switches from being disengaged to becoming engaged in the cultural crisis. Wherein, unmistakably, the perfectly plain and inherently self-revelatory logic of his applied *Emancipation* philosophy and psychology requires no interpretation of the message that translates figuratively and literally that the Black individual is fated to rise and fall with his "race."

After building a national reputation partly on the peculiar premise for a Puritan parson that religion (spirituality) like theology is weak and limited and philosophy is strong and boundless, especially for the progressive development of high moral principle and practice which he proclaimed the subjective and objective means and ends as well as measure of man, Channing avers that religion (weakness) is the God-given strong suit and strength or nature of the strong Black "race" complemental inferior of the superior White "race."

Contrariwise, for the White "race," religion is a human culture-created derivative of civilization; a reason-replete configuration of "*the spirit*" making the North American society distinctive; a public parochial matter of personal preference and private choice which the White-ethnic individual can elect to accept or reject; and a subject and object for both subjective and objective irreversible reflection.

The Channingesque natural spiritual bare essence and pure power unique and distinct constituent element of Black folk religion complements and contrasts with the natural reason substance and force of White folk religion. Upspringing from this comparative difference is the distinctive capacity of White folk to use rational religion either to spur Black folk and their spiritual religion or to spare Black folk White folk religion--neither of which, naturally, Black Americans can spurn. Whether the result of accident or design, it turns out that by means of rational religion or morality White powerhouses can predict, determine, and control the Black powerless as effectively as Western man imposes his will on any other element of nature.

In brief, Channing constructs a color caste/class spire on top of a moral crystal cathedral which is founded on faulty premises, specious logic, and spurious principles. His straightforward natural religion of the Black race--whose quintessential nature and function Channing he characterizes as equally spontaneous and infectious physical "touching," "tender thankfulness," and "beautiful emotion"--works together with the natural rhythm of Black folk which, presumably, God provides them as the complement of the grace (good and goodness) Divine Being bestows freely and uniquely upon the Puritan race.

Precisely on this rational romantic racial and religious social structure change point, he thought was sharp enough to bear the weight of his moral counter-culture critical imposition, Channing is right in what he affirms and wrong in what he denies: Puritan grace functions to stifle the life chances of the Black race in direct proportion to progenitor Channing's promotion of the presumption each Black American, who is culture-preempted of nature-derived individual existence and identity, can be recreated a third time through either reversing or overriding cultural values from an unnatural into a presumed if not a real individual--or the uninterrupted nature-endowed and God-created natural condition of each member of the White race and other ethnic groups--and assisted to rise one by one each to his/her highest values by virtue of demonstrating individual ambition, talent, and achievement.

The romantic idealist moralist managed to be a "true believer" in the absolute superiority of the individual, the relative inferiority and subordination of the community, and his pure pride and prejudice in the supremacy of the Puritan race and individual. Consistent with this will to believe he could unite opposites, like his belief in Puritan tribalism and Yankee individualism, excite civil sector-specific religious and secular forgiveness followed by rational moral growth and development from recognition and repentance through reconciliation of differences. Coinstantaneously both activate conciliation and cooperation and avoid contradiction as well as conflict and competition. Thus Channing's mutually exclusive individualism and race "typology" was transformed by his skillful manipulation of the utilitarian Puritan/Yankee bifurcation of reality into a mutually fertile one for the White-race/ethnic Americans.

A conscious culture determiner, Channing designed this scenario to be implemented by not secular but sacred social/moral engineers he attempted to lead in the management of reality. His underpinning premise is the transparent axiom that unlike Black human beings, who are condemned to hang together as a de-ethnicized race, White individuals are free to affirm or disaffirm their race or ethnic group. Channing did not stress, as would subsequent and unconditional proslavery warriors, the *White Man's Burden*. Yet, howbeit unwittingly, he demonstrated conclusively the *Black Man's Burden's* to be the irrevocable externally induced task-responsibility of (not the White race creators of the Black race or the White-ethnic individual but) each Black person to carry the whole race--in every positive and negative act (or failure to act).

Channing's Southern English aristocrat and planter "brethren" who formed the upper class, and a distinctive enity that through personal employment in the Old South and experience in the slavocracy the Boston patrician discovered grew accustomed to and even "fond of calling itself Anglo-Saxon." But instead of Anglo-Saxon types, in his judgment, they were solely--and as solidly as they certified Black folk were born of a different gene pool--"Normans": The "terror" spreading, preying, pirating, and conquering un-English "chivalrous race" descending as a standard deviation from the "nobler families of England."

But unlike the Black race, that he attends incorrectly as if the race-specific people form an unmixed ethnic-specific group, the character of the Southern master class "is still a mixed one, impulsive, passionate, vindictive, sensual; but frank, courageous, self-relying, enthusiastic, and capable of great sacrifices for a friend." These traits of the Cavalier were identified by the Yankee because, in his estimation, they proved inclusively his "Southern brethren" are not equal to the "steady, persevering, unconquerable energy" of the Northern Puritan "Anglo-

Saxon."

Whatever the measure of rational religion overbalancing self-inflicted emotional religion, pervading Puritans and Yankees as a result of the Evangelical Calvinist preferences of fellow New Englanders distinguishing themselves as "enthusiasts," Channing was persuaded their persuasion is both an unnatural or nonauthentic and reversible Puritan mutation. But the presumed absence of rationality, and presence of natural emotional or spiritual religion in the Black race, results in an opposite effect within Black people--that is, Channing certifies, Evangelical religion renders "them harmless" ineffectuals. This was the color class/caste "effects test" of his sharp moral principle and practice which, as a self-fulfilling prophecy, neutralized his intent. Channing knew Black people well enough to assert on the public record and in the media that their "powers are undeveloped"; to leave them in that poor condition, where he attended them briefly at last with characteristic hope for their "generous nature"; and to profess his certainty that the "day of improvement" for Black folk "is to come":

> I should expect from the African race, if civilized, less energy, less courage, less intellectual originality than in our race, but more amiableness, tranquility, gentleness, and content. They might not rise to an equality in outward condition, but would probably be a much happier race.--There is no reason for holding such a race in chains: they need no chains to make them harmless.

ABOLITIONISTS' RESPONSE TO REAL

BLACK FOLK AND SOCIAL REALITY

All the crusading New Abolitionist radicals may not have doubted that the Black man's "nature is affectionate." But they were too engrossed in expending themselves in Channing's leisure-time antislavery activity to develop--for the management of slaves--a psychological theory of constraints matching Channing's manual for scientific command and control of human bondage. This primer bid fair to update and complement as well to compete with Cotton Mather's 1696 moral manual of discipline. Channing's theory had the effect of curbing the Black race's rising expectations, and limiting the people's horizons: a consequence caused without incurring culpability while currying favor from White folk, whose convictions he confirmed by creating in the Black people's mind the suspicion of diminished capacities.

Countermarching proabolitionists formed the checks and balances of Channing who frequented the haunt of invectives to hurl them in the teeth of the slavocracy, which they believed to be monstrous on its face and "one of the provinces of Hell." The immediatists' truth was denied free discussion and open debate in the Cotton Kingdom proslavocrats honored and adored as the edge of eternity or Kingdom of God in history: namely, that slavery is evil, sin, in-humane, immoral, and unconscionable. The immediatists discerned the character of slavery and the contentious slaveholder to be the necessary extension of each other: which formed a total system, institution, and Southern Way of Life.

Channing thought, that in this instance of condemnation, the New Abolitionists were working at cross-purposes with antislavery interests. And he harbored "no doubt" their antislavocracy anathema were uniformly "false and pernicious." The absence of overriding antislavery sentiment in the North, complimenting his own response that was a far cry from action, and the wide-spread Northern sympathy and empathy with "Southern brethren," Channing declared to be the direct result of the "coarse" spirited proabolitionist Northerners: whose taste and manners were in striking contrast to the genteel ambiance accorded Northerners who engaged Southerners in social and business intercourse.

Thus while Channing is uninterested in differentiating between Black persons and their "race," he adamantly opposes the New Abolitionists who pass the same judgment upon his own Puritan "race" and the slave-holding "class of men indiscriminately as the chief of sinners." He replied that "among its upholders may be found good and pious people." The immediatists clearly understood and accepted this fact they believed to be entirely beside the point, as definitely as Channing apprehended the "horrible nature" of Black bondage he declared an "atrocious wrong"--which "works fearful evil to bond and free."

But pro-immediatists were concerned with slavery's systemic and systematic vices, whose institutionalization of human bondage in perpetuity when compared and contrasted with the personal virtues of slavemasters insisted upon by Channing demonstrated the proslavocracy-stabilizing or abolitionism-counter-balancing individual acts of civility were deficient of social redeeming power. Antislavocrats knew there was good in every evil--and evil in every good produced by man. Abolitionists in fact did not disagree with Channing's analysis of slavery, but they simply were confounded by the contradiction between his profound conclusion and election of the simple solution, which, being the choice of cautious moderation and toleration, was a no more cost-free than value-free conscious acceptance of continuous Black involuntary servitude victims and White dehumanizationists as an intractable yet manageable condition:

> The worst institutions may be sustained, the worst deeds performed, the most merciless cruelties inflicted by the conscientious and the good.

In the considered judgment of many immediatists, Channing was engaged in not merely an antiabolition/proabolition contradiction but one that had social consequences. And most could not see how, or why, "Slavery is not then absolved of guilt by the virtue of its supporters." Channing determined that bondman "persecution is a cruel outrage, no matter by whom carried," because, as he also stated, it "breathes a moral taint, contaminates the young and old, prostrates the dearest rights, and strengthens the cupidity, love of power, and selfish sloth on which it is founded."

Then, according to his own discernment, immediatists inquired, why make a virtue out of necessity--by arguing either "that men acting from conscience and religion may do nefarious deeds," or that "in good company we may do the work of friends"--unless the point is "to speak plainly of wrongs" as independent and autonomous phenomena "which good men perpetrate," but who are separate and distinct from their creations. Channing could not but perish the thought that a man may be simultaneously good in some spheres of his life, and evil in others. His preference was to leave the inference to be drawn (or not) that the personal "virtues of slave-holders" make them wholly virtuous:

> I readily grant, that among slaveholders are to be found upright, religious men, and especially pious, gentle, disinterested, noble-minded women...under whose kind control much comfort may be enjoyed.

FAIRNESS TO WHITE AND UNFAIRNESS TO BLACK FOLK

Proabolitionists bethought there is something to Channing's calculating attempt at fairness--but not much more than its being so very much beside the point of the immediatists. His bottom line is that slavery is an evil institution, dominated by good men and women ("slavery rests mainly on the virtues of its upholders")--without whose sanction institutions "would soon die." Therefore, Channing contends, slaveholders cannot enjoy this monopoly and be in their role as Christian slavemasters "the selfish, cruel, unprincipled" slaveowners.

He avows, contradistinguishingly, capitulation to such obscene and pernicious caprice--upspringing from culture-specific solid South values whose rank infamy and domestic slavetrade system he determines to be both of a piece and unworthy of White Protestant Anglo-Saxon Christian gentlemen and civility--is the "peculiar" singular characteristic of the relatively powerless White ethnic classes, and not tolerated for a moment by the class of good Christian aristocrats dominating the master planter class and the slavocracy.

As an additive insight to his accord/discord descriptive analysis and prescriptive solution, Channing bethinks the saving grace of the slavocracy is that "good and great names" in command and control of the system manage "the evils of the institution" so professionally they are kept within the tolerable limits of Christianity and civility. Channing certifies that these standardbearers can be appealed to successfully as ladies and gentlemen of serious intentions and sincere goodwill--and/or Channing's asserted equivalence of good manners and morals and true virtues and conscience--by their peers who hold them in high esteem, rather than beneath contempt.

Channing understood himself to be one of the many called and few chosen and finally accepted this "solemn duty"--fully aware of the fact that in being for a bold brahman so uncharacteristically unconventional as to call the public to engage in moral reformation of the slave system he left himself vulnerable to arbitrary Puritan peers, who possessed no qualms about confronting even the Pride of the Yankees and preferring the charge of being a traitor to his English-American Puritan race, ethnic group, and class:

> What is especially demanded of the Christian is, faithful, honest, generous testimony against enormities which are sanctioned by numbers, and fashion, and wealth, and especially by great and honored names, and which, their sustained, lift up their heads to Heaven, and repay rebuke with malice and indignation.

Thus without fear or favor, Channing proclaims "truth is truth, and must always be spoken and trusted." Thereupon he leaves the strong impression that, in relation to the abolitionists, his gradualist-emancipation truth and *the* truth are one and the same. Immediatist-Unitarian firm friends and formidable foes of his Trinitarian Congregationalist enemies countercharged that the Channingesque truth claim is as far from truth and near to expediency as he appears the man with the *"Golden Mean,"* caught in an antiabolition/proabolition exigency he understood comprehensively but refused to respect.

They were joined by productive nonestablishment Black and White New Abolitionists who found Channing's truth claim difficult to reconcile with his proud public profession, to wit, "our fathers brought the African here to make him a Christian" (slave, he would not add partly because, to the mind of the model modern moderate moralist, being a Christian and a slave is a contradiction in terms; nor would he acknowledge his Puritan progenitors and those of Black folk admitted no intention to affirm their Black race cultural kith and kin--a past error he was in a position to help correct.

Instead of immediate and unconditional universal self-determination and self-respect for his Black-race cultural kin-group, Channing instantly alternately responded in the affirmative to the Old Testament question ("Am I my brother's keeper?). Channing shared with the sons and daughters of English-African bondman counterfeit Christianity, civility, and the "simplicity and godly sincerity" surrogate for *agape-love*--or *agape*-love/power-deficient rational and relative justice, truth, and humanism. This clear charity was so cold it left his publicly admitted but admittedly rejected rather than accepted Black cultural kin-folk comfortless, if not frozen in place, as the Protestant professor passed by on the other side.

His mind was fixed on arguing that his virtues overbalanced his vices so overwhelmingly until they emitted nothing less than relevant values, on the one hand, and, on the other hand, that the difference between his rational thoughts and actions as well as intentions and consequences and those of the Good Samaritan were imperceptible:

> To be just is a greater work than to free the slaves or propagate religion, or save souls....To free the slave, let us not wrong his master. Let us rather find comfort in the thought, that there is no unmixed evil...

Pursuant to his pursuit of happiness and identity of this managed reality with the truth, Channing affirms the Roman Catholic philosophical/theological rule of double effect--perforce the equation of the moral right and good with the election in each concrete choice of either the greater of two goods or the lesser of two evils--and disaffirms the Calvinist doctrine of double election/damnation as flatly as he rejects the Christian doctrine of Original Sin.

Perforce his experiment with the fusion of philosophy and theology or experimental confusion of philosophy with theology, in the process of nearly dispensing with theology and replacing theology (the faith and reason teachings of the Christian Churches and traditions) with philosophy (faith in sheer logic)--as if the great religions of the world were not distinguished from the major philosophies of humankind by pure reasons of the heart (conscience) that the head can check and balance or frustrate and override but neither eliminate nor render null and void--Channing retains the *Great Chain of Being* social con-servative philosophy which forms the presumed common sense underpinning premises of his private-intensive macro and micro culture-engineering ethical principles, that are too public-limiting to bear the freight of his theoretical and applied superstructure and infrastructure psychology.

For example, he believes in individual and not also collective ignorance and innocence, rights and responsibilities, consciousness and conscience, and guilt and grace. Thus he denies collective slavocracy complements of what he affirms --that is, Christian slavemasters as individuals-only are neither entirely either ignorant or innocent nor guilty but fully responsible and partially accountability.

Counterdemanding Original Sin holds that generic Adam-man/Eve-woman, as human species eponymous personages and representative gender types, form the primary human community; each male and female is endowed by the Creator with His ineradicable "Alien Dignity" presence as well as both reason and freedom of choice, and born of human beings who rear the individual in their family-community and nurture him/her in the culture parents form and are formed by parents; every competent person who enjoys consciousness and exercises choice is relatively responsible and guilty or not absolutely ignorant or innocent; and, being the true and real values and interests source of the human being, each competent cultural body--inclusive of the interdependent nuclear family, ethnic group, national church and state community, and human race--is a complemental agency of collective responsibility, guilt, and grace.

Channing observed the asserted equivalence of innocence and ignorance Puritan philosophy of good and evil perspective inherent in Calvinist theology--or secular and sacred culture-correcting dogma (faith) and pragma (ethics)--when the consequences of calculating Christian captors of captives claiming innocence (ignorance) and to be the criteria of Christianity and civility are computed. In the interpretation of observant churchmen/churchwomen true believers in Black bondage being their best good and real interest, the meaning of their innocence or ignorance truth claim translated literally and figuratively that if guilty, not responsible; if responsible, not innocent; and if innocent not guilty.

He did not, however, see the problem of conferred status intrinsic to his liberal psychology--upspringing from its underlying classical social conservative philosophy--and therefore missed the point that was nothing was lost in the alternative free translation, to wit, if innocent, not responsible; if responsible, not guilty; and if guilty, not innocent (or ignorant). The slavemasters who professed to be innocent of guilt were by their logic guilty of innocence--which no man can be.

Straightforwardly living according to and by expanding and extending this rule of making sense out of nonsense, pure profane as well as pure pious parson and parishioner Southern slaveowners decreed their flat refusal of Channing's challenge to engage in personal acts of manumission. They elected not to become the private and parochial catalytic agents precipitating public emancipation demonstrable civil law and order breaking leadership and moral initiative--and evincement of being completely absolved of legal and ethical responsibility and accountability, no less than lia-bility and culpability. The rejection of the Channing challenge was evidenced by their appreciating human bondage values and interests, being not only legitimatized but also mandated by "States' Rights" statutes.

Restated, proslavocrats found their proslavery benevolent paternalism fully defensible and therefore quite satisfactory moderation--as would Channing's experimental philosophy and applied psychology in theory and experience--and he would not in principle and practice.

Appearing to turn a deaf ear and his back to the cavalcade of Christian-crusader proslavocrats' all is fair in love and war rallying cry, and driving rational organization spirit, Channing concentrates on psychology and advances his theoretical uniform conscience hypothesis ("the most hardened, conscience never turns wholly to stone") in principle--but demonstrates in reality a conscience limited by more lower than higher heightened consciousness-raising experiences.

His negative good philosophical ethics complementing positive psychology begins in process of desacralization and re-religionization which ends in a secularized version of Arminian psychology--if not a secularization of the revisionist Calvinist Evangelical competitive alternative--apropos which any one willing is able to become whole at once or a new "being born again."

The tension between his rigid philosophical-ethical principle and flexible applied psychology generates greater stability than constructive change possibilities, whereby Channing is neither able nor willing to entertain the truth and consequences of the fact that good, informed, alert, and conscientious men may also love to do evil for the sheer pleasure and profit it brings.

Clearly Channing believes the "most prevailing voice on earth is that of truth." The belief requires him to attribute high moral standards to the Southern White "multitude of upright compassionate, devout minds." They only need to be "awakened" to the "insensibility of habit to the evils of slavery," in the view of Channing. Correspondingly, "if awakened," the moral conscience will necessarily activate virtue and not vice--and "soon overpower the influence of the merely selfish slave-holder."

There most certainly can, ought, and will arise everywhere throughout the South a new moral rather than spiritual born-again slavemaster, directed by brand new correctly prioritized principles of right and good--without but like the regeneration of the soul which Edwards and Hopkins made the prior condition of the new moral being--accompanying whose transfor-mation automatically is the "principle and kindness he should set him free."

Channing is also a "true believer" in the self-realization of the truth and the real existence of the truth in a pure state: precisely where true and real values, interests, and principles do not exist either permanently or ever in conflict but persist in harmony necessarily and always. Thus the anti-Black race principle--he and Northern White antiabolitionist/antislavery Protestants shared with Southern White proslavery Protestants--is demonstrable truth and reality as a priority preference, and not simply a rationalizable and reasonable value but an inevitable and natural fact of nature and history. As such, anti-Black race values constitute so great a difference in degree from the issue of slavery as to be a different kind of problem.

However, as the proabolitionists insist as vigorously as the proslavocrats, Channing fails to relate accurately such relevant facts and figures as their unalterably opposing bottom line, either/or both ultimate or preferred real interests and priority values, and therefore to interpret correctly the meaning and consequences of their different motives and purposes.

The permanent conflict of principles, inability to recognize the relative merits of the counterdemanding truth claim and false claim as well as struggle to improve through accepting the superior and rejecting the inferior idea, and failure to distinguish between the reconcilable and irreconcilable differences and proved equally predictable and significant occurrences argue forcefully the point: Channing's moderate means and ends main point is not sharp enough to induce the sufficient amount of efficient power necessary to force antiabolitionists/proabolitionists to disengage from destructive deadlock and engage in constructive change.

Undeniably, the end in the stable forces of counterpoint mutual recrimination societies arguably was as inevitable as its beginning with the Western Civilization translocated by the New World settlers from the European Continent and British Isles. Between divergence in the English transplantation and convergence in the Americanization process, the color caste/class Puritan-Anglican worldview--or basic philosophical/theological culture-specific principle guiding the English Christian religion of race--evolved into neither a value-neutral nor a value-free but a very judgmental and secular/religious-charged system of principles and interests in conflict with each other and real values.

ANATOMY OF A MODERATE ANTIABOLITIONIST 229

COMPROMISE AND PROMISE OF CHANNING AND
FELLOW EASTERN ESTABLISHMENTARIANS

This natural consequence and continuum of the English tradition expanded as the cultural substance and style of Southern Englishmen: who directed the Royal and Proprietary Colonies forward from turning even when the Pilgrim Fathers landed, several years before the Puritan Fathers disembarked in New England.

It is noteworthy because it is instructive to recall in the context that Northern Englishman Channing wishes not to accept these Southeastern establishment men either on their own terms or for what they are--the conscience or "moral power of public opinion" of their region fully as much as he emerges the voice of the Boston elite.

For equally like and different reasons, revealed in the sign and symbol of his height of condescension, Channing could not respect either the Black race or the Southern will to power. Whether the minority or majority of slavocrat gentlemen once upon a time regretted their slave culture inheritance, and believed their human bondage constituted a problematic political economy, Channing labored under no illusion there existed fewer than a great plurality of Southern slave-masters who considered the slave system a manageable rational culture, a "peculiar institution" that beat any probable alternative, and defensible against all foreign and domestic critics as a result of being a known entity and pleasurable estate.

Channing's profound misjudgment of his own and pride and passion, as well as that of proslavocrat Southerners and antislavocrat Northerners, figured significantly in his self-knowledge that he had been called--in his time and place --by God to end the caste and class crisis in Christianity and civility by providing the hardball politics players at the helm of the Union with his peculiar moral power panacea. Channing challenged the ideological slavocrats and masters of the art of power politics, plus idealism and realism or *realpolitik* pragmatism, with sheer rationalism. This Channingesque liberalism subsisted of being free and clear of the posited demonstrable essence of irrelevance or real interests needs and demands forming the heart of the patrician and aristocrat increasing conflict and confrontation and decreasing cooperation and concilation.

His complete confidence and comfort in solitary and unilateral morality, faith in man and rational prog-ress, were matched by his possession of pure reason that he termed the irresistible elixir of life. He asserted that pure reason produces pure truth with which no reasonable men will differ, and not different logics and reasons whereby alternative right and truth claims compel reasonable men to differ and agree to disagree whether they choose to accept their differences as unresolvable conflicts or whether they determine to resolve them either by reason of compromise or coercion. It was, then, hardly a coincidence that his *Emancipation* proclamation was quickly written and published a few months after the New Abolitionists' American Anti-slavery Society suffered a schism: a result of the dispute between the Garrison/Boston-led and Tappan/ Manhattan-led rival societies, following which fractionalization the factions never reunited.

Channing interpreted this decisive cleavage of the New Abolitionist body as the unmistakable sign that New Abolitionists were mortally wounded: despite the instant new nonsectarian and sectarian variations that erupted to compete as different immediatist constellations--attracting the advocates of exclusive moral persuasion to one and the adherents of moral power plus political force to another proabolitionist body. Straightway the excited opponent of "enthusiasts" announced the death of the New Abolitionists prematurely to the public when he exclaimed, with delight, pro-immediatists are "broken by internal divisions."

Forthwith his ideal of unity (or uniformity) approached the status of a categorical imperative, and distorted his perception of social reality. This myopic vision expands and extends even as he experiences first-hand the Evangelical rule of amoeba church growth through constant division, that crowded the landscape with new churches almost daily. Yet he could not com-prehend this process of concentrated power that showed no signs of being ephemeral.

And therewith Channing failed to appreciate ecclesiastical and civil power concentrations adequately enough to develop a plausible interpretation of the implications of the empirical data he had to accept.

Paralleling the sharp rise in heightened consciousness of the color caste/ captive and class cultural crisis, this inherited and coveted Puritan private moral monism and public myopia bifurcation of culture reached its apex of power and powerlessness in the life and work of Channing. The effect of this calcification upon the cultural determiners and determinants included his evident uncommon success in relating individual personal and community responsibility that was exceeded only by the failure of his social ethics middle-axioms, utilitarian means, and ultimate ends. Channing's redoubtable will-driven and need-blind moral rule, ra-ther more than blind ambition, both limited his social redeeming vision and led him to mistake the New Abolitionists' build-up/proliferation process for loss of "true strength, that is, moral influence." Whereas, in reality, their splintering form functioned much like the church/sect/cult-type reproductive multiplication, that entailed conflict and competition between mini-leaders in mini-societies (as opposed to the great man theory Channing shared to some degree with anti-clerical Evangelical Garrison).

This assessment, that the antislavery "associations are waning," was followed by an appraisal that came as close to being the will of God for him as anything: "It is time for the individual to be heard." He could imagine the future shock consequences of the currently rapidly expanding rather than contracting New Abolitionist movement (as distinguished from the reverse experience of the new American Anti-Slavery Society divisions): whose inexorable dynamic included a slowly developing change in the locus of its national leadership from private and parochial societies to hege-monic professionals at the helm of public politics in the Capitol of the nation. Self-claimed prophet Channing could not prognosticate reliably in this sphere of his prediction (determination and control) because he could believe proabolitionism was a phenomenon whose time had come.

New Abolitionism was a moving force whose growth violently violated values he staked his credibility on promoting. It was so sharply in conflict with his principles he devoutly wished and prayed for deliverance from the threat, and strove to dismiss it as an aberration. Consequently, he both missed the true virtue and real value of New Abolitionism and misled the liberal establishment.

Once the onetime united New Abolitionists divided their American Anti-Slavery Society, Protestant professor Channing immediately changed from preceptor of private ethics; slipped on his prophet mantle; switched into his public moral leadership role model; and moved to fill the perceived proabolitionism-created antislavery vacuum. Channing entered the presumed antislavery void as a neither dependent nor interdependent but totally independent social consciousness-raising voice, appealing to the conscience of the "enlightened virtuous" individual. It is each identically awakened individual acting autonomously whom Channing considers to be the principal social redeeming power.

Thus absolutely certain his principle and program is the only workable process possible, Channing propounds his point: if every antiabolitionist White race/ethnic individual (female and male) who professes abhorrence "of what they have called the violence of the Abolitionists" will think, feel, and speak like pro-gradualism advocates, and as forthrightly as their pro-immediatism adversaries against all the (A) "unjust monopolies, and prejudices, barbarious punishments, oppressive institutions," (B) "conspiracies against humanity," and (C) insults to truth and rectitude, these combined "moral efforts" will demonstrate conclusively two relevant facts and values: First, that men and women need not be "starved into justice and humanity"; and second, that the individual possessor of moral truth, religion, and conscience when acting alone or in concert is power sufficient and efficient enough to eliminate the evil human bondage system.

He guarantees the large audience he commands his analysis and conclusion are as valid as his prescription is verifiable by universally repeatable empirical experiments: All that is necessary to achieve the gradual elimination of the "peculiar institution" is for "each of us to bear our conscientious testimony against slavery." Further, Channing preaches persuasively his persuasion to the persuaded, only the personal protest against slavery and for private emancipation by each profane and parochial individual can so "swell that tide of public opinion" that alone has the capacity to "sweep it away."

What may be tracked instructively is the interesting but scarcely curious course of moral power development, and specific evolvement into a standard deviation from the Puritan public ethics and public servant norm, of Channing: the erudite "Boston Yankee" who was born a "Rhode Island Yankee" and educated a "Massachusetts Yankee." Compared and contrasted with his conflict and competition with the Boston contingent of the New England-wide "Connecticut Yankee" hegemony of Evangelical Calvinist Congregationalism on one side, and the direct correlation between Connecticut as the Northern leisure time location of Southern upper class powerhouses at play and Rhode Island as the center of the Northern slavetrading complement of the Southern slaveowning system, on the other side, the remarkable fact is how near Channing came in close encounters of the third kind to breaking for his own person the historic and current upper class color caste/captive connection between the English Northeastern patricians and Southeastern aristocrats.

Channing may not have been the first American of more faint or less feint Calvinistic dissociation, and Congregationalist connections, to direct establishment Puritan culture into the antislavery fray. But the moderate went further, faster, and more fully than any managed equally rational and modest change minded Boston clergyman predecessor: during this brief but intense moment in which he resisted revolutionary and radical change procedures, and endeavored without significant success to replace them with reform measures based on the union of religion and morality.

Nevertheless, however neatly Channing's ethics of individualism fit-hand-glove with Puritanism, Calvinism, Evangelicalism, democracy, and secular humanism, as he flails the fibrous connection the social ethicist bids fair to sever the moral/immoral individual from his immoral/moral community--the individual's greatest power-failure source and power resource--and then saddles him with the responsibility of securing complex social change by the single and simple

means of moral suasion. He projects as positively primary the hero/heroine-her-
etic as the lone and lonely individual against the whole society, rather than the
individual with community resources working upon the society flat-footedly in a
"country of licensed, legalized wrongs," where arbitrary and historical rights of
the privileged White race/ethnic classes are maintained at the expense of the
elementary human rights of the color caste/captive class.

The contrast between Channingesque principles and practice in theory and
experience are most striking in reality, when he coinstantaneously affirms pro-
White race values and promulgates his analysis of the dual nature of moral man:
there is nothing "more common among ourselves, than a courteous, apologetic
disapprobation of slavery which differs little from taking its part," yet "there is
a strong tendency to indifference, and to something worse." In his own humanistic version of Calvinism, Channing goes as far as Edwards and Hopkins in demanding that Christians be born again--not spiritually of course but--to ethical
benevolence:

> Home is to be a nursery of Christians; and what is the end of
> Christianity but to awaken in all souls the principles of universal
> justice and universal charity. At home we learn to love our neigh-
> bor, our enemy, the poor, the oppressed. If home do not train us
> to this, then it is woefully perverted. If home counteract and
> quench the spirit of Christianity, then we must remember the
> Divine Teacher, who commands us to forsake father and mother,
> brother and sister, wife and child, for His sake, and for the sake
> of his truth.

MORALS OF FEDERAL ERA OLD CONFEDERACY

VERSUS NEW CONFEDERACY POLITICS

The animus of this radical individualism appeared to Black New Abolitionists
so far from universal and unconditional either instant elimination of dehumanization and immediate institution of self-determination, or a principle of fairness
and equity, and very near to total opposition to their White New Abolitionist
friends who were organizing politically. Channing emerges in the appearances of
White and Black pro-politics proponents an exponent of a static rather than
dynamic Constitution, and a strict constructionist interpretation of the "states'
rights" White Gentlemen's Agreement architects of the Union and old Federalism
negotiated.

He clearly defends the proposition that the Federal Government is without
constitutional power to interfere in any sovereign state, and argues that the
national government should relate to the Southern states in matters of slavery
as "foreign communities." These suggested "limits of the Federal Constitution"
made political organization among New Abolitionists appear to his mind exercises in futility; and he took comfort in the fact that his view was widely
shared by onetime Northern Federalists and current proslavocrats. But this was
not the only reason why he regrets so deeply "the willingness of the abolitionists to rely on and pursue political power."

Channing is also convinced that individual moral power is pure, perfect, and
reliable force--which he holds to be incorruptible once the ethical agent evolves
from self-serving into enlightened self-interest. Contrariwise, he asserts that
political power is inherently "pernicious" because the pragmatism sys-tem of

republican democracy intrinsically and extrinsically revolves around the compromise of real values and interests which he confuses with true interests and values; and, while neither equally necessarily nor frequently, even compromises principles in crises analogous to the one occurring during the process of transforming the "Disunited States" into the United States.

Moreover, Channing harbors no doubt, by "assuming a political character" the New Abolitionists "lose the reputation of honest enthusiasts"--and are at once written off as "hypocritical seekers after place and power." He was engaged in total opposition to the newly formed "third party," that the Evangelical New Abolitionists organized as the Liberty Party several weeks before the publication of his manual on moral-specific *Emancipation.*

Channing opposes the Liberty Party by arguing the argument of conventional wisdom, to wit, there exists without the Liberty Party for the liberation of human bondage sufficient "intelligence and virtue in the community," and "good and true men enough to turn the balance on all great questions": if they will commit themselves to active regard of "the moral, Christian law."

This aggregate of moral individuals will totally reform society as well as end slavery, Channing averred, without being organized into a pressure group: which he bethinks is co-equally deficient in reason and fairness because organized political pressure begets more of the same politics as usual, and generates a collective individual free will-counterdemanding element. Channing berates the liberationist "third party" as a pro-Black race-values single-issue and special interest Liberty Party. Synchronically he is not eager for Evangelical conversion but anxious for "political regeneration," even to the point of recommending "revolution of the press." Channingesque "revolution" upsprings from the presumption that the fourth estate can be influenced to change into the kind of establishment organs that will communicate the moral perspective he identifies with truth:

> It is by such a broad, sensuous improvement of society, that our present political organizations are to be put down, and not by a third party on a narrow basis, and which, instead of embracing all the interests of the country, confines itself to a single point.

It is difficult to discern whether the Unitarian's circumscribed respect for the pragmatism or the American version of utilitarianism--with its inherent special interests and single-issue politics that compete with the general interest--is grounded solidly in his reflection upon the particular politics that characterized the institutions he knew, or whether it is rooted rigidly in his general disaffection from politics principally on the grounds of ethical principles: the essential one being his belief that partisan party power politics is an unfit arena for a pure moralist. Certainly antebellum politics left him less than sanguine regarding the democratic process. Concomitantly, the post-Federalist Party experience bears some relation to his entrance into the clerical profession at the point when the Puritan parson was consigned, by church and state, the apparent moral and non-partisan political role of policing moralisms, howbeit an official duty he did not prefer.

Wherever the truth lies, Channing feels secure in this judgment: "The Federal Government has been and is the friend of the slave-holder, and the enemy of the slave." His high anxiety and high intensity presence but absence of despair is stimulated by the Federal Government's (1) Fugitive Slave Act (1793), the effect of which enactment into law rendered slaves the personal property of slaveowners and mandated that fugitives from legal injustice be returned upon demand to the slavemaster; (2) perpetuation of slavery in the nation's capitol; (3) formal opposition to emancipation of slaves in Cuba; and (4) Congress' refusal to consider "petitions against these abuses of power."

These perceived political failures suggest to his mind that the nonslaveholding states ought "to resolve that they will free themselves from every obligation to uphold an institution which they know to be unjust"--a most important Channingesque task-responsibility that involves withdrawal from commerce with the South.

Contrapositively, while individuals should raise their voices in moral indignation, liberation from human bondage must be the "gift of the masters" for same reason private emancipation or personal manumission must be "their own act and deed." This remains the case even though these acts of liberation emerge from ulterior motives devoid of any real "sense of justice," since even if they arise from a "sense of interest"--that is good enough.

Perchance perception is reality wherein Channing's passionate appeal to dispassionate self-interest and the prudential ethic is his ultimate solution to avoiding his deepest "dread." Evidently it is his paranoia rather real fear that for Northerners to "touch slavery in its own region" would be tantamount to inciting "insurrection and tumults."

Channing looks into the future and is convinced that "emancipation, universal freedom, must come"; that liberation will advance primarily through Christianity working on "human affairs," with an "all-comprehending" philanthropy; and that that "is at length to be understood at the South." The good, pious, wise, and "self-respecting" slavocrats will stand against the "selfish men," given to "cupidity and love of power," who constitute the majority in the slavocracy; think tyranny can be voted right, because they are "brave enough to defy all personal danger"; and are wise enough not "to defy the moral sentiment of mankind." In these "wise and good" Southern masters there "is power enough to put down the selfish and unprincipled."

The classical Christian social conservative values Channing upgrades to progressive transformationism indicts slavery as an irredeemable evil. Precisely for this reason, albeit from different interpretations of reality and motives as well as purposes, his moral remonstrances reinforce the anti-Garrisonian and pro-Tappan New Abolitionists in their convictions, to wit, that political power is an essential element in the destruction of the slavocracy. Basically, Channing does not believe the Southern gentlemen he appeals to are prepared to defend their real interests and values as true ones and at all costs--exactly in the modes and by the means he describes--largely because he cannot accept the reality of co-existing, equally logical, and defensible diametrically opposite values and determinations of the right and the good.

Since he knows that what women and men value is not thereby valuable, he is positive that by proving conclusively (with evidence utilizable in empirical and experimental tests by each individual) why specific desires are not intrinsically desirable--that is, inherently either universalizable right or generalizable good--the seemingly intractable practitioner advocates of human bondage experimentation will be moved (through initial conviction followed by convincement) to leap from error into truth. Because he knows virtue when he sees it--as well as knows that men are bound to disengage their ties with self-defeating or blameworthy thoughts and actions, and engage the self-fulfilling or praiseworthy attitudinal and behavioral possibilities--Channing has no doubt but that he can define the essence of this manifestation; and establish the principles, rules, and regulations certifying authentic virtue.

Despite the nonpolitical abolitionism espoused by rigid pro-Temperance and radical-antiestablishment (as well as anti-denominational) moralist Garrison, and by his Boston neighbor and nemesis the liberal-establishmentarian moralist Channing, two Evangelical Presbyterian moralists and maverick establishmentarians initiated political abolition: The New York philanthropist Gerrit Smith (1797-1874); and James Gillespie Birney, the corresponding secretary (1837-40) of the American Anti-Slavery Society until its schism that final year of its united existence, following which Garrison served as president of the old American Anti-Slavery Society during the ensuing two decades and Arthur Tappan organized the new American and Foreign Anti-Slavery Society.

Smith and Birney were founding fathers of the antislavery Liberty Party (1840) that, in 1840 and 1844, nominated Birney as its Presidential candidate. The non-clerical headed but Evangelical lay-directed Liberty Party emerged strongest in New York. There it was initially energized by the support of Black and White New York New Abolitionists aligned with the American and Foreign Anti-Slavery Society: the in-strument through which Yankee and Calvinist sons of the Federalist Party Puritans reentered partisan party power politics as a social conscious Protestant block.

The Evangelical Federalist Party power politics parsons and parishioners formed a moral force, even though as they played a spoilers hand in the 1844 Presidential election. The Federalist Party survived Channing, retained power at the local level in the State of New York for sixteen years, and evolved as a critical merger unit in the formation the Free Soil Party (1847-54) that was itself absorbed into the Republican Party (1854).

Evangelical Liberty Party partisan power brokers and players did not require the theoretical defense Yankee Lysander Spooner (1808-87) outlined in his book entitled *The Unconstitutionality of Slavery* (1845). But attorney Spooner's reasoned legal arguments were especially useful for New Abolitionists who had not previously arrived at this persuasion advanced by the Liberty Party Calvinists.

For one thing, litigator Spooner courts the liberal and counters the conservative political theory variously advanced by English, Scottish, and Irish philosophers and the observant Protestant churchmen John Locke (1632-1704), David Hume (1711-76), and Edmund Burke (1729-97). For another thing, he develops for the proabolitionists the arguable case that the laws of a government are not arbitrary, or established by might, but intelligible rational principles of right derived from human rights and/or natural rights that are compatible with empirical reason and natural law or the "rule of natural justice."

Approaching the Constitution as a legal scholar, he instructs the pro-immediatists in broad and ranging deconstructionist interpretations. Thus for a third thing, liberalist Spooner recalls for litigation-minded Calvinists the general knowledge that as a means of civil order men institute governments, that are compacts based on natural justice that do not abrogate natural rights. For a fourth thing, Spooner states his double bottom line: if a constitution is in point of fact determined by the majority, but also binding in injustice upon an individual or a minority it is illegal and immoral; and the duties of the victims of such legal immoral laws and authorities in power "are disobedience, resistance, destruction."

Spooner's study counterpointed traditional ethics-limiting law and logic, challenged the unexamined precious few ethical legal principles underpinning civil litigation and legislation, confronted the preponderantly less dynamic than static strict constructionist interpreters of the Constitution, approached positive law to set justice rules and regulations in not rigid but flexible concrete moral foundations, and managed through adding to the rule of law and right or ethics real but neglected continuum a more firm footing in the rule of right as the right rule and the only right to rule. His work contributed to the formal foundation of right over might law and order, to the future of this legal ethics feature (albeit better logic than law) of the Constitution, and to Henry David Thoreau's (1817-62) futuristic *Civil Disobedience*, which work Thoreau published during the year that the second Fugitive Slave Act (1850) was enacted. This combination Deuteronomic and Draconian *anti-Black Race Code, that lawmakers in Congress established as the law of the land eight years after Channing died,* radicalized Boston New Abolitionists and occasioned Spooner to write *A Defence for Fugitive Slaves.*[27]

Forward from their mature years and before their mid-careers, Yankee-Puritan Baptist Calvinist Garrison and Unitarian Congregationalist Channing were the chief Boston professors of principled moralism. They united in solid opposition to violence, to moralists participating in partisan party politics, and to sectarian religion. These rule of law moralists were also of the equally fixed opinion that the United States Constitution had to be changed but only should be changed through referendum from a proslavery to an antislavery document.

Contrapositively, lawyer James Birney and lawmaker Gerrit Smith were controversial ironic and even paradoxical counter-traditionalist strict constructionists: They believed the Constitution did not legalize slavery in fact but was only so interpreted, and thus could be reinterpreted if their Liberty Party candidates were elected.

These different antislavery interpreters of the Constitution as a dynamic rather than static instrument were each right in their analysis and equally disappointed by their dissimilar motivated and consequence-laden political rebuffs. Yet the anti-political and pro-political antislavery competitors kept their alternative pressure forces on the multifaceted system of slavery.

Between the Garrisonians and the "Barnburners," Black and White Christians illuminated brilli-antly the reality of the dual class and caste/captive cultural system. What had a very peculiar effect upon Black folk was the very deep interest in ending slav-ery evidenced by these intelligent White Protestants: who were engaged in con-flict and stiff competition rather than in conciliation and cooperation among themselves over methods fully as much as they were at odds with the establish-ment and the Three Branches of Government.

The faith (of absolute assurance) and ethics (of absolute certainty) equation, or constituent elements as well as keys to the success of Evangelical religion, alternately converged and diverged as the instrumental dynamic of sacred and secular values and interests in the civil sector.

Because they both defined and determined the point of being moral in the special and general interest at the public power point, it was not surprising that Calvinist Baptist Garrison engaged and disengaged this complex source of Evangelical Protestant convergence and divergence as selectively as he appropriated successfully its preferred resources; and proceeded unsuccessfully to disorganize and dissolve organized mainstream Protestant denominations and Evangelical religion, that functioned effectively as the strongest Old and New Abolitionist center of the Black community.

Demonstrating a preference for different variables and variations of the pro-political and anti-political varieties encompassed by Calvinist Puritanism, representatives of both liberal and traditional establishment denominations withheld their resources from free Black brothers and sisters: whom they encountered either directly or indirectly as local residents in adjacent neighborhoods. White Protestants in the Northeast offered native-born and other free Black neighbors, they located in permanent residence, moral preachments rather than strategy for greater success. Black leaders were intelligible (and understood if not forgiven as easily) as they appeared puzzled by the liberal and conservative confluence of Yankee moralists engaged in disconnecting the Puritan moral monism and pluralism connection; embracing as well as transmitting as the whole legacy one-dimensional moral monism; and baptizing, by the power and authority of the Puritan race of wayward worldly saints, moral suasion as Black Americans' only hope for effective change.

Thus it most certainly was not only or primarily but also because they were not interested in the rough and tumble of politics that opposing anti-Calvinist, pro-Calvinist, and pro-Garrisonian Boston monocrats--who united for a monism monocracy infrastructure and re-publican democracy superstructure and against slavocracy--did little or nothing of sacred and secular civil consequence to prepare Black folk for a future outside their spheres of direct influence.

Simultaneously, Black Northeasterners knew a mi-nority of nonestablishment or Evangelical White race/ethnic mavericks and a majority of Black-race mainstream and nontraditionalist denominationalists were, virtually alone, providing slaves with a counter-religion to the slavocracy's dominant faith of justification by obedience, ethics of capricious repression and oppression, and erroneous universalizable or at least generalizable realized eschatology or false prophecy of hope in this world--that hope in history being realizable only in another country like Africa--if not hope only out of this world or in eternity. Northern and Southern either benevolent paternalists and/or both denomination-specific protectionists and preservationists were mutually fertile experimentalists of this Word.

Black folk appeared confused as the objective subjects and objects of revisionist "New Light"/"New School" Evangelical Calvinists' human experimentation, and their entirely updated and up-to-date if not new experimental experiential method of psychology they designed as the new authorized standard version of the old Calvinist-Puritan predestination doctrine. They were especially frustrated by the interpreters of the dogma and pragma that translated into a experience of being damned if they do--and if they do not--obey the voices of the opposing White masters in the North and in the South: Who posed as their friends, vied for their loyalty, and judged their faithfulness according to conflicting standards.

This potent mix of pro-White race values and the positive perversion of not the positive but only the negative dynamics of antiblack white-ethnic virtue into anti-Black race virtue kept Black victims of the capacious caprice off balance: as inevitably as the powerhouses were necessarily forceful intentionalist moralists and also consequentalist ethicists, neither incidentally or accidentally whether or not by design.

Black-race Americans were at once powerless people and the possessors of direct knowledge of White race/ethnic powerhouses, who shared values in the antebellum era. Black Northerners and Southerners were greater victims than beneficiaries of the liabilities and assets expended in the experiment.

Perchance it is far less obvious than axiomatic that Black people's experience encompasses the power elite perforce rational men promoting moral evil; moral men proving to be equally rational and different in their purposes apropos approving the greater rather than the lesser possible evil, and the lesser rather than the greater possible good; evil men excelling in performing minimal rather that maximal good deeds (relative to the real alternative), and good men promoting comparatively evil means to achieve unconscionable ends; and immoral men refusing to do the immediate good at once possible and required by the "truly needy," in order to insure the anti-Black race interests-specific ultimate design is honored at least in the observance.

These certainties were no more the whole of life for Black folk than they constituted their whole way of life, but these great realities were the constantly expanding experience of the Black race.

In the North, free Black inhabitants were denied access to civil opportunities rigorously. Vigorous li-beral Unitarians like Channing--who not unlike their Puritan fathers were social conservatives in touch with the leadership of the political economy--added lofty indifference to the dehumanization experience Black free and freed males were told, throughout the North and the South in no uncertain terms, they were to suffer gladly. Yankee Evangelicals committed to extreme moralisms like the radical Garrison who was beaten black and blue but scarcely suffered the insufferable, certainly enjoyed the "all in all of the affections of the anti-slavery host,"[28] and expended major time and talent in the New Abolitionist and Temperance movements--compared to the either imperceptible or relatively inconsequence resources they contributed to assisting free Black Northerners to become greater community resources.

At the same time, Garrison vigorously opposed pro-viding slaves with the Evangelical religion in which he was nurtured and evolved a radical, on the grounds the Bible had been translated into a greater debit than credit book by the translators of the proslavery Old Testament and New Testament: and even by the interpreters in the slavocracy of the gospel according to the slavocrats who perverted the "Good News" of the Gospel into "Bad News" by defending the oppression and claiming to be offended by the accompanying brutal repression.

The logic of the adverse decision was the perverse presumption Black folk lacked his powers of discrimination and were deficient of the capacity to pick and choose and select the truth from the error of conception, perception, and deception.

Thus the no less real consequences for being the perfectly obvious reverse results of the color caste/captive class' rational thoughts and actions--stemming from those promoted in public by the Garrisonian and Channingesque types of moral monism monocrats, who proved to be as exemplary leaders of goodwill far better intentionalist moralists than consequentialist ethicists--were the predictable absence of both respect for the Black race and disinterested will to the Black body's real good and best interest.

Black Americans were whipsawed between the varieties of benevolent White Southern and Northern masters, among the latter of whom Garrison materialized in the jaundiced view of the Reverend Daniel Wise Garrison a distinct and fixed sensation: where he unwittingly left indelible impression he considered himself the "whip-master-general and supreme judge of all abolitionists."[29] North and South, Black free and slave women and men were privy to the debates between White Prot-estants regarding the comparative worth of the real interests and values of White Northeasterners and Southeasterners.

They heard them no less clearly argue on the merits the case for the absolute absence and relative presence of Black folk, the justice of demanding Black individual responsibility and preempting Black rights, and the virtue of rendering null and void Black-race real interests and values. Black Americans could no more be permitted to develop from dependence, through interdependence, to independence than they could be prevented from listening to White Protestants argue the arguments for the best good means and ends of the Black race: as if their management of reality was neither deficient in facts and figures nor based on interpretations rooted in deception nor devoid of truth and fairness.

And precluded from securing sufficient time and space, isolation and insulation, to consolidate a total culture and response over time, through time, and in time, Black folk were naturally relatively powerless compared to the absolutely powerful White folk and frequently a preponderancy of human bondage subject to the suggestions of the slaveowner of their body, mind, and soul. Irresistible and irreversible superior White power was reality and as necessarily reflected in the Black drivers who challenged White ethnic overseers and were their White-race master's voice: and in the statistically insignificant number of Black slavemasters who owned their "poor brother and sister" for the best of reasons, which proved conclusively absolute power corrupts absolutely in the process of demonstrating White supremacy's absolute corrosive vice and relative salutary virtue.

Forced to choose between greater evil and lesser good, common sense dictated to Black folk that the perfect is the enemy of the best. But they did not receive the credit they deserved for appreciating this commonplace that escaped entirely the understanding of White Evangelical formidable friends and foes. Black folk in this perspective of irreversible reflectiveness opted, as often as not, to take the Gospel seriously after electing to follow the advise and counsel of their selected masterful free and slave Black Northern and Southern interpreters of the Bible transmitted by White proselytizers.

These White evangelists, as the antebellum era pro-ceeded apace, sharply declined from high and good translators into low and poor propagandists of the "Big Lie." In the North, former slaves created on their own initiative entirely autonomous congregations--whose separate and distinct churches evolved into the first Black American denominations. In the South during the synchronical early National era, ex-slave and free Black exhorters formed the first Black churches in North America from the congregations permissive White Southerners authorized to secure autonomous organizations: before they revoked their legitimate independent ecclesiastical bodies at the outset of the slavocracy.

The initial one was the Baptist Church (c.1775) in Silver Bluff, South Carolina (located across the Savannah River from Savannah, Georgia). The Evangelical Calvinist Black Southern bondmen and free churchmen who established it were released on their own recognizance and by exceptional "born again" slavemasters who manumitted some men to be ministers: before Old South slavocrats in the throes of giving birth to slavocracy retracted the official stamp of approval granted by Independence era-inspired Southern manumissionists, and what often in lieu of freedom papers passed the litmus test of a license for the select elect Black free or slave preacher to be at liberty in the Cotton Kingdom.

Black folk's memories of their experience in this experiment with a license for liberty, as an alternative to self-determination, could not be erased when it was cancelled. Paralleling the rise of the slavocracy and demise therein of the independent Black church--or pastor and parishioners as well as parish and parsonage--free and slave Black Southerners developed clandestinely what is known to history as the "invisible institution": beneath the visible official churches for Black folk currently instituted, led, and controlled by White Southerners, as illegal surrogate congregations for the once legitimate and autonomous Black church.

They proliferated after the insurrections organized by African Methodist Episcopal Church layman Denmark Vesey (1767-1822)--and the (Baptist) near-Reverend Nat Turner (1800-31). These model Black self-determinationists and liberationists demonstrated leadership--to the entire satisfaction of the livid proslavocrats and slavocrats who made them pay with their lives for having the courage of their convictions--when they formed the consensus behind their direct actions and initiation respectively of the 1822 and 1831 insurrections. Rulers of the slavocracy instantly reacted to these direct actionists by enacting "*Black Codes*," that included continuously updated laws proscribing the Black-led independent churches that had been promoted by unrepresentative eighteenth-century Northern Evangelical White-ethnic evangelists, and authorized by the Southern slavemasters they converted during their sojourn in the South (c.1773-1822).

Concurrently, free-born and ex-slave Black Philadelphians united as Methodist and Episcopal churchmen to create the nonsectarian and mutual aid Philadelphia Free African Society (1787): the precursor of the 1794-organized Mother Bethel African Methodist Episcopal Church and St. Thomas Episcopal Church of Philadelphia. These Black independent churches were led in the City of Brotherly Love by former leaders of Black members of all-White led St. George's Methodist Episcopal Church and Christ's Episcopal Church who were in their all-Black Free African Society: the Reverend Richard Allen (1760-1831), and the Reverend Absalom Jones (1746-1818). Classic instances of when necessity is a virtue, Black folk demanding respect and no taxation without representation formed these historic churches to exercise liberty in freedom. But these creative cradles of liberation were ill-considered by the hegemony of mainstream denominations.

These facts and figures argue that the consequences of the color caste/ class-specific rational values of Channing and Garrison--which gave short shrift to Black leadership of Black institutions in the North and the South--were more harmful than helpful to the slavery-free life of Black folk and the Black race, to the extent their serious thoughts and actions supported all the leverage of White folk who placed all the pressure on Black folk.

Channing advanced as no ordinary but an especially illuminating luminary. In this role as rule, moral excellence as the antiblack white-ethnic virtue/eth- ic triumphed--or the positive negation of ignorance, poverty, disease, cruelty, and crime--only to be compromised in close encounters with publicly displayed obscene and audacious anti-Black race values at the apex of his power. Such positive negation acts transpired exactly when and where anti-Black race interest burst forth beyond his power and authority, although not necessarily forever beyond the control of compeers. The cultural crisis over the relevance of anti-abolitionism and proabolitionism produced forces precipitating the severance of his great head from his good spirit. The separation occurred after he had sustained the challenge of his chief rival in Boston--evangelist Lyman Beecher.

Ten years before Beecher's mid-1820s arrival in Boston--where he relocated to challenge Channing's liberalism, secular humanism, and man-centered values with counteractant God-centered values--European powers were in a transitional phase of their relationship with Black-ethnic Africans. Essentially, they had completed their human bondage forages and trade in indigenous Africans--and were some seventy-five years away from commencing their thorough penetration and colonization of the African Continent. This late Victorian Age Colonial Powers' conquest would expand into the sharp division of the African ethnic communities into client states of Western nations: as a result of a colonization process the imperialists completed successfully between 1890 and 1914.

These Occidental forces in opposition to the idea of Africa for the Black-ethnic Africans--or even for the Afro-Americans--were the dynamics of realism demonstrating the irrelevance of the denationalizationism-cen-tered American Colonization Society Beecher favored: the British-founded Sierra Leone and American-established Liberia Colonies (that emerge the only two African territories to escape European colonizationism) to the contrary notwithstanding. The simultaneously submerged Black independent churches in the South, and surfacing and soaring American Colonization Society were indicators of the depth of cruelty inherent in the Colonizationists living, moving, and finding their meaning and being in Black-race deculturalization, denationalization, and deportation.

The growth of the ACS and decay of indigenous Black African ethnic and Black-race American life and culture was an uncoordinated European-American principle of imperialism, and a White church and state program of millennialism. These secular-religious demonstrations of opportunism gave realism and pragmatism the bad name of dogmatism, and included middle-class respectability covering pernicious real interest and values with a very thin veneer of virtue.

3

LYMAN BEECHER: CHAMPION OF RADICAL RACE REMOVAL REACTIONARIES

Throughout its eighteenth-century emergence, colonial Connecticut was dominated by New Haven and Yale College--whose Evangelical Calvinist social conservative centeredness reached its intellectual climax in Jonathan Edwards. Concurrently in the 1740s, the Reverend John Woolman (1720-72), Edwards' contemporary, was a direct actionist engaged in his productive life's work and successful struggle to free Black human bondage from the bonds of Friends. Synchronously, Edwards was primarily freeing White ethnics who were bound by "*the spirit*" of pro-White race values and to determined to keep Black folk in the constraints of the color caste/captive system.

CONNECTICUT PURITANS AND TRADITION

New Haven evolved from a nascent seventeenth-century mercantilistic market center into an important eighteenth-century small city, emerged the competitive commercial and cultural cosmopolitan capital of the commonwealth, and challenged Boston successfully for post-1730 New England hegemony of Evangelical Puritan Calvinism. Like their seafaring English forefathers who formed the powerful London and Boston mercantilist middle-class, post-theocracy and pre-democracy Calvinist mercantilists emerging capitalist entrepreneurs in New Haven dominated the political economy of Connecticut. New Havenite businessmen centered and revolved around their developing productive enterprise and wealth-generating selling and buying system, whose traffic in trade of raw materials for market generated and distributed goods and services turned on slave-trading and manufacturing axes.

From "Old New England Families" spawned mercantilistic commerce, or masterful merchants and masters of mercantilism, evolved expansionist industrial capitalism and Calvinist capitalists who created the five estates best known to history as the Protestant patricians (inherited land personages, parsons, pecuniary principal producers, press preceptors, and profane professionals such as lawyers and politicians as well as professors).

The conciliation and confrontation prone parsons and parishioners, and the Protestants they produced who not only protested but pressed the professors out and replaced them in power and authority, appeared in their preponderancy secular and religious political economy and culture determiners who organized a leadership elite corps of ecclesiastical and civil power interlocking directorates of the New Haven Church, Corporation, Congress, and College.

Of course a measurable significant difference in degree of commitment to advancing the traditional Calvinist continuum, initiated by English Puritan settlers and wayward worldly saints, eventually developed as the distinguishing factor of clergy sons (or clergymen) of White Anglo-Saxon "Old New England Families" who acceded in the eighteenth century to command and control of the commonwealth church in New Haven and Boston.

The contrast was sharpest in First and Second Great Awakening developments wherein, unlike "Massachusetts Yankee" scholars in Boston and Harvard, hegemonic Congregationalist "Connecticut Yankees" in New Haven and Yale distinguished themselves by the greater amount of academic sacred and secular resources professors in their academy expended as "Consistent Calvinists" in constant rational re-revisions of Calvinism (A) first to defend and protect Evangelical Puritan-Yankee Orthodoxy; (B) finally to ensure growth and to secure the fulfillment of the peculiar Puritan *"Errand into the Wilderness"* of North America; and (C) foremost to expedite the rapid expansion and extension of the New England Church of Christ as the ecclesiastical establishment power in the nation legitimated by professional litigators in their role as lawyers and lawmakers in the parochial, private, and public sectors, and actualized by the confluence of affluence and influence, power and authority, and moral plus positive law and pure reason concentrated in the "Moral Majority" triumvirate (clergy-church, capitalists-corporation, and congressmen-congress).

Preponderantly in the period following the death of theocracy, between the birth and early growth of democracy and her slavocracy, New Haven materialized in the appearances as the bare essence of a Yankee Puritan/Calvinist-Congregationalist company town: whose apparent difference from Boston included the empirically verifiable distinctive cultural characteristics created through its evolvement as a city wherein the interchangeable spirit of the Northern patricians and Southern aristocrats, relaxed as the power people and leisure class at work and play, merged with their constructive engagement as nearly identical twin interlocking directorates of the color-conscious caste/captive American social system.[30]

The "Connecticut Yankee" positive-limiting and negative-intensive social conservative ethic, and variable compared to the "Massachusetts Yankee" varieties and variations on the traditional Puritan perversion of praiseworthy antiblack white-ethnic virtue into blameworthy pro-White race (anti-Black race) values, appeared to perception is reality pro-abolitionist advocates (most sharply in their role as adversaries of antiabolitionist combatants) a difference whose distinction was not so subtle and elusive that could be missed as easily or regularly as it was dismissed by their apperceptive proslavocrat critics. New Abolitionist "Connecticut Yankees" and "Massachusetts Yankees" understood that because the perception of rather more distinct than unique Connecticut anti-Black race values prevailed in the appearances, the peculiar nature of the phenomenon in reality is equally arguable and disputable and therefore readily dismissed as an infinitely impotent and grand illusion by litigious witnesses for the defense and prosecution of offensive English/Puritan race virtue.

Proabolitionists took seriously "Connecticut Yankees" who disavowed they were agents of anti-Black race values and pretended they were affirmation action and equal opportunity American Colonization Society angels of mercy. The process of deconstruction and denial, counterclaimed radical reason and revelation revolutionists, begins and ends with antiabolitionists establishing an objective and subjective-free fairness doctrine as the criterion for testing ethical standards. From this principle they impose the rule that moral thoughts and actions can be accurately assessed as to their relative praiseworthy and blameworthy merits only by an evaluation that excludes consequences and includes intentions.

Since the reality of motives can no more be measured than the existence of God can be proved or disproved conclusively, averred the proabolitionist minority who apprehended their disadvantage as critics of the anti-abolitionist majority, and intentionalist rather than consequenialist modern model moralists were the cultural determiners of right and wrong social ethics standards the predictable inevitably occurs: The re-ligious and secular values-empowering "Connecticut Yankee" White class/status superiority and Black caste/captive inferiority consciousness is rendered either/or both nonexistent and irrelevant.

What New Abolitionists revealed to heightened consciences was that this managed reality misdirection perpetrated by the American Colonizationists clarified the truth the error was calculated to obscure. It illuminated the power and permanency of the mutually fertile rather than mutually exclusive positive and negative dynamics of antiblack white-ethnic virtue, by making unmistakable the self-evident moral conflict and competition between two great sacred-secular American Civil Religions: The Evangelical Puritan Piety positive antiblack white-ethnic virtue, or eternal vigilance engaged in repelling negative values produced by ignorance, immoral, and sin; and English-American pro-White race virtue translated anti-Black race virtue, or God-created and nature-derived, culture-cultivated and history-demonstrated Black race inferiority.

New Abolitionists were declared radicals partly because the revolutionists propounded the precise point their peers wished not to hear: These sacred and profane cultural coordinates are so purposive and perpetual they cannot be denied reality by arguing as fact the fiction that they are mere myths devoid of reason and power in society, as if symbols are the signs of the powerless and barren of substance for the powerful, and the authoritative pronouncement that pro-White race and anti-Black race values are mere sound and fury indefeasibly deracinates their potency.

The positive symbolic and substantive power of the phenomenon of blackness master rationalists can attempt to confine, as experts in obscuring their truth claims and value judgments *vis-à-vis* arguing descriptive facts as if they are actual facts: either by defining rather less precisely than identifying it as "*black magic*" and the *ersatz* of Western empirical reason and logic ("*white magic*"), and/or both by denying the phenomenon reality through associating it with the equation of religion and ultimate unreality apropos asserting the equivalence of black magic and spiritual force in history and the universe. But whether Orient generalists or whether Occident specialists, Black New Abolitionist professionals universally attested to their daily and empirically verifiable race-specific first-hand knowledge of and experience with Black race positive negation: the Black body whom White race/ethnic powerhouses create and proliferate, equate with national virtue, and apprehend comprehensively, but by definition of their essence and reason of their existence cannot experience.

This dissimilarity in knowledge of the truth and consequences of the color caste/captive system, between White-ethnic theory and Black-race experience in reality, is the demonstrable difference between absolute power and relative powerlessness. White and Black New Abolitionists were decidedly decisive in deprecating the New England race and religion mythical phenomenon, and declaring determinative the diabolical dimensions, that, being peristent antebellum "Consistent Calvinists," "Connecticut Yankees" erratically reveal both naturally and sponataneously as well as consciously and unconsciously.

Dissimilar pro-Calvinist and anti-Calvinist critics similarly stated the racism-rife Connecticuter clone of the Carolinian and Virginian racists disclosed the reality of the American positive antiblack white-ethnic virtue-intensive values. The full disclosure included the positive principal principle of the antiblack white-ethnic ethic, to wit, the Puritan-derived opposition to the black and evil effects of the Devil. And its positive negation and perversion counter or com-plemental anti-Black race values, subsisting of the total exclusion of the deethnicized race-only group and on the one side, and, on the other side, pro-cedural prevention by corruptive and collusive capital and management imitating (or alternately following and leading) labor of the Black body from attaining equivalent status with the equally culture-created race/ethnic groups on prin-ciple (which is primarily based on the premise that the inherent and inextrica-ble character of the Black race is the manifest essence of the Devil).

White combatants of the contenders for the title world champions of the caste compartmentalization class reported on the record that Connecticut posi-tive antiblack white-ethnic virtue was converted consistently, and persistently perverted into negative devices or anti-Black race vices. Critics claimed that the commonwealth's systematic and systemic driving of caste beneath class groups impacted all Connecticuters. The veracity and validity of their charge they certified with documented data, whose evidence was not disputed but deconstructed by interpreters determined to make their opposite point stick. Its corrosive culture cerebration extended from White to Black Connecticuters ex-isting within and beyond the state boundaries simulataneously but at once alike, and differently.

The Connecticut culture *malaise* evolved over time--and through time--and the coagulation transpired after the disestablishment of the Connecticut theocracy, whose progress was not impeded by the connective linkages of the established Connecticut Church of Christ (if unofficial religion) and the parson and parishioner patricians in the democracy with the establishmentarian aristo-crats whose "peculiar institution" they solidified in the slavocracy.

Eli Whitney, a "Connecticut Yankee"-educated "Massachusetts Yankee"-bred as well as born and reared son of the saints, guaranteed the correlative growth, development, and expansion of the Northeastern capitalists and Southeastern planters into a patrician and aristocrat convention with his design in the South of the cotton gin to accomodate the wishes of his slavemaster hosts. Whitney invented his cotton picking machine in 1793, one year after graduating from Yale.

Lyman Beecher, who matriculated in the College that year, subsequently became a lightning rod for Northern and Southern White and Black political and religious interests: after the old Puritan theocratic turned Yankee Federalist Party partisan parsons once again abandoned power politics as their Federalist Party entered the stages of death and dying, and the clergy accepted the new Connecticut Constitution (1818) as the civil law and order instituted by *God and Man at Yale* in the year that Ralph Randolph Gurley graduated.

As a result of the demise of the Federalist Party precipitated by the Democratic Party that also was a catalyst in the formation of the Whig Party, the two relatively recently formed political parties and their dominance of the new two party system, a dramatic change occurred whereby the once united Federalist Party clerical body divided between old Republican (new Democratic) new-emerging Republican (Whig) Party preferences; the old lay and clerical coalition lost credibility; and the command and control power of the parson/parishioner sacred and secular force in the civil sector diminished precipitously.

But if Beecher can be trusted to write accurately for the record, he turned the apparent ecclesiastical adversity into opportunity. Forward from this turn of events that occurred at the close of the Second Great Awakening, Beecher certified in writing his public record and defense that he led Connecticut Calvinist Puritans turned Yankees toward the forty-year old Quaker way of exercising political influence in lieu of wielding political power, to the new Calvinist parsons' way of political indirection. The process resulted in large and not infrequently undue influence; and the turning of parsons from partisan party power politics players back to Jonathan Edwards' apolitical and anti-political reversal of the politics-intensive Puritan tradition public servant Cotton Mather epitomized.

Among the precipitating factors contributing to renouncement of partisan politics fast becoming the new law and order of the clerical class, as well as to New England parsons quickly discovering themselves in near total conformance with the reversal of values and rules and regulations, a singular one is noteworthy. Beecher acceded to the office of "field marshal general" of Evangelical Calvinism previously held by his Yale preceptor and mentor Timothy Dwight: who had superceded his grandfather Edwards by returning to the pro-political Puritan tradition; followed his layman and Congressman brother Theodore as a dyed-in-the-wool Federalist Party partisan parson; and died the year before the 1818-ratified Connecticut Constitution.

A brilliant strategist and tactician, Beecher's audacious manifesto effectively proclaimed the political vanquishment of the Federalist Party (whose dissolution precipitated the vanishing partisan parsons) a victory; and set a precedent his Southern brethren appeared to imitate two years after he died and the Civil War ended. Beecher preferred fighting for his fixed hierarchal arrangement of his principles to switching the order of their priority, even after it was demonstrated conclusively his rigid ranking lacked utilitarian value: because they ran counter to the flexible compromise system of American pragmatism, and resulted in his functional principles being effectively dysfunctional in the civil sector. He put the best face possible on the worse defeat imaginable, counseled resignation, advised cutting losses by cutting power ties and running from political conflict and competition.

Whereas predecessors and compeers of Theodore Dwight and the political leadership of the Connecticut Federalist Party formerly sought out the clergy for advice and consent, post-Federalist Party clergy had to seek out the many more Whig than Democratic establishmentarian Connecticut politicians: and either pray for their consideration or apply pressure in the hope they would respond as desired. This power loss distinction proved the difference between being certain ministerial wishes would become translated into law, and being surprised when they were. The development of the rule of law and reason into a government of laws rather than men, and therefore the diminishing preponderancy of the systemic White Gentlemen's Agreements forum as well as form and function of governance, proceeded apace the change from a political system dominated by a ruling class representing the interests of the five estates to a power game in which intensive White-ethnic immigrant minorities played hardball politics.

These new political measures and players were in large measure occasioned by Thomas Jefferson's break with the Federalist Party and formation of the Democratic Party in 1800. The success and expansion of Jeffersonian participatory democracy and the failure and contraction of the Federalist Party were interlinked concurrent opposite developments. Due in a significant degree to the initiative of three successive Presidents from Virginia, the rise of the Dem-o-cratic Party and fall of the Federalist Party con-tinued until the latter died.

The internment effectively occurred when Federalist Party leader John Quincy Adams, seeking a coalition to defeat the Presidential Candidacy of Andrew Jackson, gave life to the fledgling Whig Party in 1824.

The relevance of this slavocracy matter inheres in this better known than understood fact: The rapid reversal in fortunes of the Federalist Party, that the erstwhile political and establishmentarian parsons dearly loved, was scarcely impeded by their synchronic desertion of the Party and disaffection from power politics. In the words later used to describe another unsettling unbridgeable gap between promise and performance, penned by the quintessential English Protestant Poet Matthew Arnold (1822-88), prior to publishing these lectures that he delivered in the United States a quarter of century after the death of Beecher as *Discourses in America* (1885): For the conscious clerical class and Federalist Party devotees, their idolized Federalist Party devolved into the home of lost causes, misplaced loyalties, and impossible dreams.

The voluminous accessible studies by Puritan specialists obviates the necessity of developing in this probative and deconstructionist interpretive essay a broad and deep comparative analysis of the politics the clergy class played within the sectors of the ecclesiastical and civil powers, the relative competence of the pure profane and pure pious professional politicians as public servants in the civil order, and the value of the clerics' demonstrable courage of their convictions in relation to their political commitments in the sacred and secular sectors. Sufficient context, providing an efficient background for perspective on the development of Beecher as a superior parochial and inferior public power politics politician in New Haven and the Connecticut environs, is attained by juxtaposing this representative individual and the clergy class in the shifting political sands of their hegemony of Protestants united alternately for the union and separation of church and state.

What is obvious is the net loss to the public or general interest--and the net gain to the parochial or special interests to the contrary notwithstanding-- of the clerical class' recurring and random but far less arbitrary than selective alternation between engaging and disengaging the secular order to secure the improvement of the moral health and welfare of the ecclesiastical and civil realms, and their leadership of church and state divergence from convergence and convergence from divergence. It appeared as unnecessary and certain as the consequences of the non-acts--or acts of omission rather than commission--of the clergymen resulted in their being as much the cause and the effect as the beneficiaries and victims of the color caste/captive class system.

Compared and contrasted to the lack of serious commitment to his civil politics avocation, Beecher succeeded as a peerless parochial power politics professional in Connecticut during the era of Jacksonian Democracy--only to fail when he attempted a repeat performance in Boston. His developmental stages from a local and regional to a national ecclesiastical political presence commenced after the end of theocracy and the beginning of democracy, and were completed prior to the eruption of the irruptive slavocracy.

He participated in beginning of the end of the old order of exclusive and elite politics. They previously entailed the sacred and secular civil duty of the select elect to vote, as well as an obligation that could be fulfilled or not as a matter of personal choice or privilege. The business of casting a ballot in church and state elections was the right of the freemen: who was preponderantly an English/Puritan race male, and less frequently a British (or other White) ethnic inhabitant.

This right as the power of choice was a culture determinant created by culture determiners of the problematics of human experience and a powerful culture--that is, it was a conferred rather than a natural right and underived principle inherent in either nature or the human condition. Limiting the franchise to the property owning profane and sacred privileged classes was tantamount to securing special interests and equa-ting them with the general interests.

Certainly prior to the full emergence from the Age of Reason and the Age of Enlightenment of the enlightened self-interest principle, the Puritan premise that each individual would surrender his real interests to the presumed higher real interests of the community in any conflict of interests underestimated the natural human propensity for blameworthy self-serving interests; praiseworthy self-interest; and creating conflict and competition with the good of the whole commonwealth rational organizing ethic via underpinning the priority of English/puritan race and class interests and values. Alternatively put, it generated rather more than it degenerated the tendency of the power elite to selectively engage and disengage in church and state politics according to whether or not the process served their real interests.

Moreover, theocracy's equation of inherited race and class, church and state power, with status, privilege, and power were prerogatives that proved perfect prescriptions for disaster in the republican democracy. There power was extended from the White-race male to the White-ethnic male, established the rule of law and the individual, and based on the one man one vote principle that set the English race minority at relative disadvantage and the British ethnic majority of minorities at comparative advantage.

Forthwith the tendency to be lax in civic duty and propensity for non-involvement in civil politics advanced from manifest to latent proclivities: except in cultural crises when the real interests and values of the power elite were threatened and they were forced to fight either/or both in the political arena and on the battlefield. Naturally, of course, during the pre-National era and continuing into the early National period, New Haven governance corresponded with the policy of the privileged few, who were diligent and realized their will disproportionately.

Framers of post-theocracy governance determined to secure the permanent change from oligarchic and theocratic rule, and end to hierocratic polity. They managed to institute a republican democracy based on regular elections as the permanent method for guaranteeing representation and orderly change, and subsisting of the electorate-specific citizenry between elections identifying with (or submitting to) the community will that normally is identified with that expressed by the voting majority.

The architects of the new politics of democracy, who, instead of inflexible impartiality adopted and adapted for the system of American pragmatism the sensible utilitarian (greatest good of the greatest number) flexible principle and process. The end of utilitarianism justified means of pragmatism as the American way of adjusting for the ever-expanding peculiar needs and abilities of all White race/ethnic males and legitimate associations in the Union. Their plan was devised to assure every White race/ethnic citizen and community equal access to the competitive system, to enable them to compete fairly and equitably.

Hence they designed and implemented American pragmatism as the rational mechanism for each individual (White race/ethnic male by definition of the "pursuit of happiness" premise and principle as well as practice), class, and secular and sacred no less than each ethnic group to acquire relatively balanced and proportional partial measures: rather than the disproportional or absolute whole aggregate of their competing and conflicting real interests.

Presbyterian central church governance was adopted as the representative form of the Union and helped to shape the wisdom and knowledge of presbyter Beecher. He understood instantly and completely what in theory and experience turned out to be in principle and practice the rule of fifty per cent plus one.

What made him singular was his immediate grasp of the mechanics, and instruments, of effective democratic politics. Instead of the solo and solitary moral individual, as Channing was wont to believe, Beecher apprehended the fact that republican democratic politics begin and end with power exercised and realized through the vigilant press of permanent interests through different varieties of many more temporary than fixed coalitions--of special interests united on one and divided on another single-issue--rather than through the self-defeating process of arraying permanent friends and enemies in adversarial postures.

The utilitarian value of uniting in power politics formations with formidable foes as friends to secure a single common interest Beecher accepted and defined as the genius of American pragmatism--the art of persuasion or the ability to know when to bargain and what to trade. He apprehended the critical point as well: compromise is both the key to success and effective only if the parties to the conflict and competition possess a combination of (a) attractive or desired and negotiable values and interests, and (b) counterbalancing real power or force.

This business of professional politicians--that political scientists term "logrolling"--Beecher effectively disengaged from in the civil power order and engaged in the church and corporate sectors, where he developed his rational power politics experimental method systematically and selectively. Between private experiences and innovative parochial experimentations Beecher managed to merge substance and style with fashionable form and function so effectively until, in the course of trial and error, he became a masterful ecclesiastical politician, if the master of church politics did not set the American pace for the civil politics ebb and flow of nineteenth-century partisan and nonpartisan Protestant parsons.

It is not inconsequential that the final consequence of the consent given in 1818 by the "Connecticut Yankees" to their new state constitution--that enfranchised every White male citizen--was not the end of church power in Connecticut. The new civil law functioned effectively as the catalyst stimulating the beginning of art of parochial politics, directed the reorientation and revitalization of ecclesiastical power and its exercise in the private and public sectors.

Undeniably a critical factor of the fallout from that happenstance entailed the loss of state tax support the "instituted" Connecticut Congregationalist Churches of Christ previously enjoyed, and a privilege status their Massachusetts cousins retained as late as 1833. But while Connecticut Congregationalist clergymen lost public funding they did not lose their resourcefulness. In fact, Beecher avows, they actually managed to gain greater private sector resources from the Calvinist capitalists who were fast becoming rich and famous Protestant philanthropists--and the only real economic sources of state revenue.

Instead of wringing their hands in the anxiety of defeat, the once state-supported Congregationalist clergy and churches rapidly developed the voluntary rational organizing principle; and developed innovative techniques by means of which they expanded into a wealthy and competitive voluntary society of congregations united in a state Consociation.

In short, the relative loss of support from the increasingly greater number of secular than religious professional politicians was more than compensated by the clergy brethren's fellow Puritan sons of the wayward worldly saints. They constituted a preponderancy of the Yankee merchant princes; underwrote the political economy and the state treasury; and were solicited to finance the local churches and national as well as international enterprises of Congregationalism.

Calvinist capitalists obliged the clergy's plea for voluntary contributions through increased pledges, that regularly took the form of purchasing pews especially in the metropolitan churches of the establishment (Congregational, Presbyterian, and Anglican) denominations. Deaccelerating public contributions and accelerating private fiscal support of parochial institutions in the old Puritan mercantilist and new Yankee capitalist centers of commerce--rather than the power of righteousness that was the presumed authority of the saints in previous generations--automatically redounded to increasing the parish lay leaders' final decision-making powers, universally in theory and fact howbeit irregularly exercised in reality.

Parishioners gained increased if not unprecedented ultimate command and control of the seating arrangement in the church; the physical plant; and the clergy. At the very least, parishioner power over the parson was based on the measure of lay benevolence, that was frequently presumed to be a partial reflection of their true faith and ethics.

This pro-Calvinist development anti-Calvinist Yankee-Puritans adjudged near deterrence-benevolence and ironclad lay control, through the power of the purse rather than the state, establishmentarians promoted as the standard of Evangelical Northern voluntarism. The New England way differed in style and substance from the model of lay dominance pioneered in the Church of England, during the Anglican theocracy, by the class of aristocrats and slavemasters. Lay leadership in Cotton Kingdom Anglicanism took the shape of an interdiction. Master planters were not infrequently at once both vestrymen (lay officers in the parish) and burgesses (selectmen), and thus in total control of the established Church of England and the legislature in the royal and proprietary Old South Colonies.

Concurrently and correlatively but contrapositively, the parson as the person in the Puritan community of the Calvinist theocracy evolved as a continuum predominantly in the Yankee evolution of voluntary churches. In New England, traditionally and predominantly, ultimate lay power and authority was not asserted but bestowed upon the minister who exercised it as the authorized final word--except in crises of confidence.

The pre-National Anglican establishment--in the Southern colonies--suffered from a nondeveloped intellectual body of professional priests as well as from one other denomination-wide problem that the Orthodoxy and Reformed traditions never experienced: a clerical class crisis in competence, credibility, and courage. And, usually, the Anglican clergy in the Old South were subject to a renewable (or non-renewable) annual contract.

Contrariwise, preponderant conciliation and cooperation rather than conflict and competition normally characterized the nominal counterbalancing economic power of leading laymen and the respect conferred upon the Congregationalist (and the Presbyterian) minister with ordination--who was as a rule a graduate of Harvard, Yale, or Princeton--and effectively meant for the Puritan as well as the Yankee parson and parishioner that neither was in (nor could be out of or beyond) the control of the other.

A predictable but not insignificant consequence emerging from the difference between the respective general rather than universal Anglican priest/parish discord and Puritan parson/parishioner accord was the pre-Revolution and post-Independence confluence of the latter in the intersecting spheres of mutual interests and influence. This New England harmony enabled clergy and laity to share values and to work together in parochial and public politics on political common concerns of the ecclesiastical and civil powers.

For these among many other commonly appreciated factors, the impactful and sometimes impacted hegemonic qualities of Lyman Beecher were parlayed and deployed affectively in the politics of church and state. His relatively small civil sector persuasive presence and large religious political effect was the direct result of the evangelist's skillful translation and translocation of power politics techniques to the field of evangelism, where revivalist Beecher developed into the leading institutional orchestrator of the resources generated by the revivals. And revivals, due in large measure to continuously developing professional psychological proficiency from the Second Great Awakening throughout antebellum era, became the life blood of the emerging voluntary churches.

Their centrality within the local establishment churches of Orthodoxy and the Reformed Church, as well as within the congregations of the plain folk, was the outcome of the revivalism's production of vitality and utility.

Revivals functioned effectually to keep alive the spiritual tenor and moral tone of the private person and parochial parish; and equally productively as the instrumental means assuring growth in membership and contributions. A non-state supported church was an American Evangelical Protestant invention and experiment--and a new model ecclesiastical form and function distinguished by being totally dependent for success upon the voluntary tithes and offerings of the people.

Particularly in the rural areas and small towns, where the handsome gifts of princely merchants were rarer than in the cities--or even in the urban-suburban corridors where there were few generous rich merchants and the local church contributions were limited to personal appeals--a full and lively house was indispensable to the maintenance of the denominational ecclesiastical superstructure and infrastructure; the sustenance of the national and the local church's program; and the furtherance of foreign and domestic missions.

Revivals also allowed one who had large ability and larger opportunity, like Beecher, to engage in more than regenerating the saved--and saving the domestic infidel and foreign heathen. A church full of folk, in cooperation with other churches, could engage in limited political change--and unlimited moral reform and religious humanitarian endeavors.

Just as certainly as Beecher was born (in 1775) and bred in New Haven his emergence as the calcification of the "Connecticut Yankee" cannot be explained away as an accident of history, and may be explained only in part by attributing this forged glaciation result of a fortuitous correlation of a race-genetic and ethnic-cultural as well as birthright-religion inheritance to his wise cultivation of natural intelligence and the advantage afforded him of joining the ménage of powerhouse Timothy (or choice of mentor). Just as unquestionably as mere circumstance alone hardly made New Haven the pivotal center of the Colony it was scarely the result of sheer coincidence that Connecticut, out of all proportion to its size and reputation, graduated into a critical crossbreeding region of Northern and Southern color caste/captive values.

The cross-fertilization of English Puritan and Anglican superior race and religion values expressly occurred in New Haven partly because it was a significant Atlantic seaport city for industrial capitalist investors. Venture capitalists earned interest on their investments in free labor and slave labor, or the profits they produced in Northeastern manufacturing plants and Southeastern cotton plantations, associated in business and leisure time activities with the owners of Northern industrial and Southern agrarian profit-making and wealth-generating industries.

These ordinary and enduring interconnections between extraordinary English-American gentlemen of the North and the South were solidified as they journeyed to New Haven bearing different real interests and purposes together with disparate gifts and graces. They were each fiscally dependent upon the other, both to do well economically and socially and to do good politically and morally, and shared Cavalier etiquette preferences and Anglican aristocratic priorities, and converse Yankee capitalist virtues and Puritan Calvinist values.

Concomitantly due to the convergence of Calvinist capitalism and Cavalier culture in New Haven, the city evolved into the cross-cultural rather than counter-cultural heart of the American soul.

She was energized by the pres-ence of diverse and divergent determiners of the political economy transacting ship building and rum distillery commerce, whose national and international commercial enterprises initially revolved around trade in slaves no less profitably than in raw materials and other negotiable property and goods produced in the West Indies and Caribbean colonies; Black-race involuntary servitude and free men encountering Scotch-Irish immigrant beneficiaries and victims of indentured servitude, who, as the un-English British-ethnic representatives, appeared in conflict and competition with Black folk they precluded from the competition for jobs in the free labor market and with bondmen whose slave labor household employment they eliminated as White-ethnic domestic servants of the Northeastern English-race aristocrat class; and entrepreneurs and ministers whose clerical-mercantile "patrician" ties insured autocratic rule of the allied capitalists and Calvinist Congregationalist.

What may be easily either missed or dismissed yet neither explained nor explained away is the opportunity-limiting consequence for free and slave people of color of the dynamic Evangelical Calvinist growth and development in New Haven of the "Connecticut Yankee": whose social redeeming nature and function contrasted sharply with the parallel evolvement from the English and Puritan race people of the "Massachusetts Yankee" in Boston. In the "Hub of the universe," a larger minority of old Puritans and new Yankees were translated into liberals; evolved into an influence within the ruling class as well as within the class of religious humanitarian and secular humanist intellectuals; and dictated cultural tastes and moral standards.

PARALLEL RISE IN ANTI-BLACK RACE

STATUTES AND BRITISH ETHNIC STATUS

In 1638, the original New Haven Puritans--who were preponderantly English-race as distinguished from British-ethnic representatives and dissimilar from the Puritans who journeyed from the Continent to North America--arrived directly from England not unlike the earlier arriving Massachusetts Bay Company who dis-embarked from the *Arbella* with leader John Winthrop at Salem in 1630.

In June 1639, these original Connecticut colonists adopted their first constitution of government which they based squarely upon the Bible, whose ordinances were had the authority and force of positive law.

The relation of this ecclesiastical and civil law and order of colony to the connection between antiblack white-ethnic virtue and anti-Black race values is apparent in the correspondence between the Connecticut statutes of 1715--that mandated strict observance of the Sabbath Day together with suppression of immorality--and statute passed by the lawmakers in 1750 regarding the Connecticut enforcement thereof the "Hebrew *lex talionis* was applied under this enactment, in the case of a negro slave for the mutilation of his master's son."

In 1650, exactly one hundred years earlier, the General Court of Connecticut sitting in Hartford adopted the conclusion reached by the United Colonies of New England (September 5, 1646) and created the statute and precedent known as the Black race-specific "code of 1650." This "*Black Code*," enacted and enforced by the New England Confederacy, solidified in statutes and social structures private and parochial slavery with the public force of positive law. Under the Charter of 1662, the several Connecticut colonies were joined in one colony a century before the commonwealth formulated the constitution of the sovereign State of Connecticut (1776).[31]

Connecticut led the New England mind in developing a secular and sacred intellectual rationalization of slavery, within the time frame that the Chief Jurist in England responded to the British Abolition litigation of a self-taught litigator by proscribing slavery throughout the British Isles (in 1772). His singularly significant decision for the English, British natives of Wales, Scotland, and Ireland, and the Black British and American slaves, he issued thirty odd years before Parliament outlawed the British slavetrade (in 1807) and three score years before Parliament abolished slavery throughout the Empire (in 1833).

Briefly recalled for context, Indian and British ethnics formed the original labor force for the Anglo Connecticuters. But apparently these working classes were insufficient masses for mercantilists or unable to supply the demand produced by abundant commercial possibilities and land. Equally apparently, they were simply sufficient or proficient enough to engender the motive, means, and opportunity for the Connecticut ruling class to introduce Black African ethnic bondage in perpetuity as the slave-labor (involuntary servitude) competitors of free-labor and servants temporarily bound by their voluntary indentured servitude contract. Slaves were the plentiful and cheap neither necessary nor necessarily inexpensive abundant, affordable, and accessible labor force who became increasingly available in the New England slavetrading capitol of North America.

Indentured servitude like race and religion, reason and revelation, class and caste or even color-conscious Western Civilization, was transmitted and translocated altered and alternating states of color-intensive unconsciousness and preconsciousness as well as consciousness from the Continent and the British Isles with the English transmigrants. Once bondage surfaced in the virgin body politic of Connecticut, as elsewhere in the "*Old and New England*" New World settlements within and beyond the boundaries of North America, far less an immaculate conception than a magnificent obsession the extraordinary exception met a remarkable reception because it was marvelously marketable.

Human bondage commenced in English settlers with opportunity, the functional surrogate for necessity as the mother of invention in this instance of classic Calvinist conservative conscience and consciousness, and as instantly progenitors produced a greater demand than need they generated and supplied as New England slavetraders.

The market-created color bondage class need produced its own color caste class demand whereby the artificial need and demand turned into a real interest and value necessity, turned up a legitimate claim and virtue, turned on a virtue of necessity or a specific case when necessity is a virtue and the virtue of necessity, and turned out the necessity of virtue at the same time that it revealed unmistakably the necessity of virtue (*agape*-love) it denied.

Upon opportunistic Puritan merchants taking advantage of the market opportunity to generate the need and supply the demand ministers were in the black market, and certainly no less in the market for Black bondage than profane Puritans and sacred peer parsons and parishioners. The Black body was found equally attractive and irresistible by Connecticut farmers, and an inexpensive luxury that the growing urban upper-class and middle-class thought they could well afford.

Without ever forming a statistically significant population, the number of Black Connecticut inhabitants multiplied quickly. Black Connecticuters totaled 5,500 in the 1790 census, one half of whom were slaves, comprising as slave and free Black women and men a color caste/captive class that barely added up to a fraction over two per cent of the state's population; and approached three per cent (7,976) in 1820, at the outset of the rapid growth of the capitalist formation into exploding industrial capitalism that paralleled the explosive expansionist Southeastern slavocracy.[32]

Several years after Vermont abolished slavery (but delayed ratification of the Constitution) Massachusetts not only followed suit but trumped and triumphed when the Bay state entered the Union as the first abolitionist colonial commonwealth member of the United States. Concurrently Connecticut imitated other New England states in enacting a gradual manumission statute into law, expressly with the legislature's 1784 revision of the laws of the Connecticut Colony.

These revised statutes resulted in a state constitution that did not specifically mandate continuation of the tradition, whereby each Black male resident was excluded from becoming a citizen or freeman of the commonwealth.

But whether enslaved or not--the colonial laws disallowing any legitimate legal contracts for Black Connecticut males were preserved in the state constitution.

In point of fact, several provisions emitting conflicting color caste/captive class signals were added by the legislature, dominated by lawmakers who represented the interests of the patricians. One of these laws (rescinded in 1797) required free Black Connecticuters to travel only with a "certificate or pass"; and another outlawed any further importation of African ethnic slaves.

The latter law passed by antiabolitionist "Consistent Calvinists" was neither a proabolition-ist nor a antislavery code. It was a statute enacted into law in response to the protest of the new wave of Scotch-Irish ethnics.

With the help of pro-Calvinist and anti-Calvinist Free Labor leaders in Scotland, the female and male churchmen and non-churchmen who used their leverage to place pressure on their sacred and secular friends in the North and the South, Northern and Southern British immigrant brethren (who formed mutual help coordinating coalitions and political pressure groups to protect their interests as industrial and agricultural workers) protested successfully that slave labor unfairly robbed free labor of the opportunity to gain employment and advance their wages in Northeastern manufacturing companies, and fair market value and prices for their crops and cattle grown on small farms in the South and the North.

Yankee capital and management both reluctantly and assiduously joined labor and farmer associations in welcoming White ethnic immigrants. British (and other European) ethnic skilled free labor Yankee mercantilists and Calvinist capitalists valued because it served their real interests, supplied the productive workforce required to turn their growth industries into expansive enterprises, and maximized efficiency and minimized costs whose essential profit-making factors and capacities rendered free labor preferred to the slave labor Connecticut Puritans owned.

What Yankee capitalist sons of Puritan mercantilists owed White-ethnic folk was as obvious as the no less real and consequence-laden (if perchance less transparent) fact that they were bequeathed by their "Elect" progenitors equally powerful color caste/captive class benefits and liabilities, between which they could no more pick and choose effectually than they could reject summarily either successfully. Co-equally perfectly clear and bound to be denied truth was no less consequential: Yankee Calvinist historic and current slaveowning and slavetrading descendants of the Puritan saints owed an incalculable debt to their Black folk.

It was incurred as a direct result of Puritan foreign slavetraders, as well as domestic slavebuyers and slavesellers and slaveowners, foreshortening the cultural roots of the Black African multi-ethnic people so drastically they translocated with their Puritan race transplantation until the potent procreators recreated their own deethnicized and deculturalized Black race-specific genetic and cultural kin-group. The Black race-only consequences of English Puritan/Anglican race-specific truth were neither merely parochial redemption nor simply private exemption but primarily public preemption of virtue; a transmogrification that transpired in the transparent process of remaking the Black body pure property, and leaving the asserted equivalence of vulnerability and obsolescence in dramatic disadvantage.

There were myriad unmistakable reasons why new-arriving White ethnic Roman Catholic groups were preferred to their North America-indigenous Black race cultural kin-group. But the preference most certainly was not due to any discernible either parochial or private not to mention public pro-Black race concernment upspringing from the Connecticut Yankee power elite, in the establishment Congregational-Presbyterian denomination. Positively prior to the 1837 division of the united "New School" and "Old School" Presbyterian Church into two Northern-directed North and South united denominations, neither Orthodoxy nor the Reformed tradition of Calvinism determined the state of human bondage to be a condition of intolerable dehumanization and unconscionable injustice.

These underlying realities were the abiding certainties along with the misleading opposite impression that churchmen evidenced precious little interest in discrediting. The misperception was sustained by the new economics of capitalism emerging from mercantilism--and the new politics resulting from the Democratic Party and Whig Party evolving a two-party system from the one Federalist Party--both advancing parallel with the Connecticut gradual manumission statutes (that compared to the immediacy of abolition in Massachusetts slowly but finally proscribed slavery in the state) and proceeding apace the necessary end of the international slavetrade and inevitable beginning of the expanding domestic slavetrade.

Contradistinguishingly, color-consciousness materialized as a singular reason why European immigrants were embraced--despite being less real religious cultural kinsfolk than their Black-race kith and kin who were rejected--by White race representatives. Undeniably because in the appearances even the Catholics whom Protestants dreaded and loved to hate among the ethnic folk from Britain and the Continent were conceived and perceived by Calvinist Puritans to be more of their genetic race or ethnic type than their Black race genetic kinsfolk who were nearer their cultural kith and kin than the ethnic kinspeople.

For no more or less solid reason than pure English Puritan race protection religion and revelation, dictators of Yankee manners, morals, taste, and style predetermined the increase in the numerical growth and genetic quality of White ethnic folk would be limited if free and open--licit and honest instead of illicit --intercourse with Black folk were either sanctioned or permitted and not prohibited. Yankee patricians demonstrated conclusively that their success in ignoring the counteractant experience of revered Anglican aristocrats--that matched or surpassed the relationship between Thomas Jefferson and his dearly loved slave woman Sally Hemings--was exceeded only by their failure to take seriously the progenies the powerful and prolific English-race/British-Ethnic procreators produced with their Black-race property.

Connecticut cultural determiners managed to make the assertion stick that the universally empirically ver-ified natural and not completely preventable issue produced by the White female and Black male is unna-tural; repulsive; and, therefore, nature or both natural law and natural rights must be overridden by custom laws reinforced by positive laws of church and state enacted to proscribe honest and to prescribe dishonest biracial relations.

As the eighteenth advanced into the nineteenth century, even the domestic servant descendants of the White-ethnic indentured servant class were given pre-ference over the traditional involuntary servitude and the new free-Black class of household servants. One no less real if perchance less obvious singular factor contributing to this changing color preference, and unchanging color consciousness in Connecticut, turns on the fact that a preponderancy of the White ethnic domestic servant class was related to Protestant (Pres-byterian rather than Catholic) Scotch-Irish labor.

In the new era of industrialization, British-ethnic labor represented a pool of not only free and skilled but productive artisans that was equally indispensable, highly prized, and politically potent. Thus while simultaneously experiencing the dual sense of being attracted to America and pushed from the British Isles toward the land of opportunity, by the press of the British economy and the English--who concurrently were shipping from the West Indies to England secondarily and to Sierra Leone primarily the Black British they passed in the transatlantic crossing--the combination of being White-ethnic British subjects and experienced skillfully trained workers in industrial England set the Scotch-Irish ethnic immigrants at advantage over the North America indigenous Black-race people in their native land.

Contradistinctively, one year after American Independence and during the period when the economy of the new nation was suffering from havoc wreaked by the Revolution, and Old Abolitionists throughout New England and the "Disunited States" were pressing their states to follow Vermont in abolishing slavery or at least enacting liberal gradual manumission statutes three years before Connecticut Continental Congress representatives signed the slavery-permissive Constitution, it was more ironic than paradoxical that the 1784 Connecticut law proclaimed it to be "injurious to the poor, and inconvenient" to increase slave labor.

Implicit in this act was the emerging explicit pull of the Scotch-Irish who would press from strength and force the English-American five estates into a negotiating position. Power elite Yankees were so enamored with the Federalist Party their perception lost perspective, and as result of their deformed vision they did not anticipate the foreseeable consequences of the intensive ethnic minorities' political agitation: until they were coerced into sharing the vote and competing with the real interests and values of the immigrants, who disaffected from the Federalist Party joined the Democratic Party.

High culture and the apex of existence were conscious and unconscious aspirations, and as decisively affirmed and denied as they were implicit in the explicit presence of the "Old New England Families." The first families, or the notable rather than the noble people yet the nearest American culture came to developing the classical continuum, possessed the val-uable land upon which they built a permanent mystique of natural superiority that survived not only real power and wealth but also the enormous capital amassed by the "Robber Barons." Traditionally, nobility was equated with inherited virtue and "old families" and nobility were assumed equivalences.

It followed in reason and reality that instant credibility and influence and near full faith and credit were the automatic inheritances the old families and what passed for nobility bequeathed Northern patricians and Southern aristocrats, who formed the foundations of the American hierarchal social status system that was as fixed as the upper-, middle-, lower-, and under-class stratification was fluid for the White race/ethnic individual (leastwise male if not also female citizens).

While the well-born inherited and therefore neither earned nor lost status, and status could be achieved, ascribed, or otherwise acquired by other fortunate White folk, by reason of these cultural realities and most importantly the a-massing of economic wealth and political power--either singly or in tandem--the individual member of the White-ethnic labor class, no less than White-race capital and management class, could ascend the social ladder rapidly and descend precipitously depending upon the circumstances.

Beneath the equally firm and flexible class structure persisted the permanent and absolutely different culture-determined nature of Black folk and White folk, apropos the division between human bondage and indentured servitude or the Black slave and White servant conditions: that in function was also not rigid since the Black bondwoman/bondmen could become domestic servants.

Yet free Black females and males were not equal to their White working-class and middle-class counterparts. The positive negation imposed upon the superstructure and infrastructure by the culture determiners precluded Black competitors from equal access both to the "pursuit of happiness" they guaranteed each White-ethnic individual.

The act of preemption compared to the competitive opportunity they conferred automatically upon White ethnic immigrants as a group or class upon disembarkation at the port of entry. Preclusion and exclusion was the predeliberate presence of the absence of fairness and equity, and reflected the reality the power elite managed to proscribe the Black race permanently.

The rational repression, in lieu of irrational oppression, was so effective it preempted the Black-race bound Black "individual" from attaining status and limited him to functional success.

This was true for the productive Black male whose gifts and graces matched his great ambition and achievements in the American enterprise system, and whom the system of flexible command and control permitted to be the exception who neither tested nor undermined but proved and improved the rule: Black body members may be accepted as performing peer personages while their Black race is denied equal respect attributed to the White race, and therefore he is left at last subject to the arbitrary whims of each White-race or White-ethnic individual formed by informing the anti-Black race interest "*Spirit of '76*."

Of course, little or nothing mitigated the American culture-specific anti-Black race values driving the "*Spirit of '76*": including regular individual and community acts of amelioration that were as natural for secular humanist advocates and their religious humanitarian adversaries as they were necessarily initiated to advance pro-White race interests, or the asserted equivalence of Christianity and civility.

This perverse phenomenon of antiblackness pervaded the unconscious and preconscious mind of English settlers.

And, induced by the conducive circumstance of 1630s, anti-Black race values erupted in their conscious mind (capacious cerebral capacity) and therefore ceaselessly as the powerful rational mind and will of their descendants and British brethren, including the three English-American classes, the two un-English Scotch-Irish classes, and the indentured servitude under class.

The anti-Black race "Spirit of '76" advanced as self-revealing phenomenons (A) in those states electing to reject the immediate and unconditional abolition route Vermont and Massachusetts ruled the law and order of the Green Mountain Colony and the Bay State, and to inaugurate step-by-step abrogation in order to permit mercantilist slavetraders and private slaveowners to recover their capital investment if not earned interest on their Black property by selling their human bondage down the river to highest bidder in the slave-intensive states; and (B) expressly in the 1784 Connecticut gradual manumission statute whose law mandated that Black Connecticuters born to slave parents after March, 1784 could be kept in bondage no longer than their twenty-fifth birthday; and its 1797 revision (during the year Lyman Beecher entered Yale) wherein the age limit was changed to twenty-one.

The progress of gradual manumission with all deliberate speed was evident four years later in the act of 1788--whose revision ruled it illegal for a Connecticut resident to engage in either foreign or domestic slavetrading, slavebuying, and slaveselling--and eight years later, in 1792 (the year before Beecher graduated from Yale), when the Connecticut Legislature decreed the manumission of all slaves between the ages of twenty-five and forty.[33]

The new State Constitution the Connecticut Legislature enacted into law in 1818 evenhandedly granted civil rights and civil liberties to every legitimate Connecticut individual--denoted throughout the document as "*citizen*--who was by definition one of the "white male citizens of the United States" and members of the class to whom the elective franchise was limited.

Color caste/captive-conscious Calvinist conscience continued to be enacted into law as late as the eleventh year of Presbyterian clergyman Lyman Beecher's pastorate of the Litchfield Congregationalist Church of Christ.

It was evidenced in the 1821 Connecticut penal code that revised the statute outlawing aiding and abetting a slave to take flight as a fugitive from legal injustice, and detailed the crime and punishment of self-kidnapping:

Provided, that nothing in this section shall operate to prevent persons coming into this State, for the purpose of temporary residence or passing through the same, from carrying with them their servants, nor to prevent persons moving out of the State, for the purpose of residence, from carrying or transporting with them such servants as belong to them, or to prevent persons living within this State from directing their servants out of the State, about their ordinary and necessary business.[34]

Human bondage ownership and existence remained legitimate Connecticut dehumanization conditions authorized by positive law and enforced as the moral law by officers of the state, whom Beecher revered as the church and state governors instituted in authority and power by God and therefore to obeyed by the bondman and freeman, until the last revision of the gradual manumission statutes ran its course and Connecticut law finally abolished slavery in 1848-- four years before he returned from his long and productive career-closing post in Cincinnati to write his memoirs in Brooklyn.

Complemental conservation of the Connecticut color caste conception was evinced in the case of *Prudence Crandell v. The State* (1833), whose notorious trial reached the docket one year before Beecher moved from Boston to Cincinnati. Following his deliberation on the arguments by the prosecution and defense lawyers, Judge Charles J. Daggett of the Connecticut Supreme Court of Errors delivered an opinion which upheld the constitutionality of the "Connecticut Black Act."

Lawmakers shaped this piece of legislation in response to the demands of the solid Christian citizenry, and passed it to insure that New Abolitionists would cease and desist from engaging in interstate interreligious, interracial, and integrated private schools. In the aftermath of the ruling by the justice, and the enactment of the legislators, New Abolitionists apparently found it difficult to determine if the adjudicator was an authentic strict constructionist, and impossible not to believe the law and his interpretation violated the spirit if not the letter of the State Constitution with absolute impunity.

The virility of "*the spirit*" of anti-Black race virtue, that the proabolitionist Connecticuters reported, on the record was systematic and systemic exercised itself continuously years thereafter. Perchance the fact that it was taken for granted to be the norm was illuminated most strikingly when the New York and New Haven allied Black and White New Abolitionists were admired by their advocates and admonished by their adversaries for committing their considerable resources to a pilot project they developed to establish a private school for Black Americans.

During this controversy apparently no one pointed out that the Connecticut Constitution did not mandate that its guarantees of civil liberties and civil rights (with the exception of voting responsibilities) were explicitly inapplicable to free Black Connecticuters, whom the document denied the franchise and therefore were not citizens, or leave unprotected non-residents who might venture there for education. This point is instructive because the defenders of discrimination presumed that the state authorized wholesale segregation, whereby its relevance is its revelation that these anti-Black race attitudes and behavior patterns were the positive law, equated with moral law, and constituted custom law which the establishment Christians respected and sanctioned by their silent observance and/or active promotion.

Traditional Connecticut anti-Black race values were advanced by more substance and symbol than the force of law. They were propelled by the pure profane and pure pious power of morality. Pro-White race powerful and powerless Connecticuters embraced them as their inalienable right--which the Lyman Beecher power initiatives never questioned. Daggett's ruling was based on his reading of the United States Constitution, and the strict constructionist reached the incontrovertible conclusion that the sacred document precluded Black slave and free native Americans from becoming citizens:

> They (free negroes) are not so styled (citizens) so far as I am aware, in the laws of Congress, or of any of the states.

The jurist did not make law but adjudicated the law in rendering his judicial opinion--whose interpretation of the Constitution and published judgment proved that the Black-race male was not like the White-ethnic male the asserted equivalence of an individual and a citizen--and argued the law and the arguments in his with such compelling force that his judicial decision withstood judiciary review; remained an authoritative juristic ruling in the matter of legalized color caste/class; and legitimated the "truth claim" of litigious pro-White race/ethnic litigators that asserted their anti-Black race values were virtue-pure and vice-free demands.

In truth, Daggett's juridical judgment was solidly confirmed by the Justices of the Union's highest court in *Dred Scott v. Sanford* (1857): who therein reaffirmed the Original Sin the first Americans committed when the Puritan Old Abolitionist Founding Fathers compromised principles to negotiate their *White Gentlemen's Agreement* with antiabolitionist Anglican-reared Framers of the Constitution. Put another way, after hearing the litigation Scott pressed in suing his slavemaster for self-determination, the overwhelming majority of the United States Supreme Court ruled this Black American male (and therewith every other one) was not a citizen.

Led by major Maryland slavemaster and Chief Justice (1836-64) Roger Brooke Taney (1777-1864), during the Democratic Administration of presbyter Beecher's bachelor and lay Presbyterian colleague President (1857-61) James Buchanan (1791-1868), the proslavery Taney Court promulgated the pro-caste/pro-bondage doctrine from the pinnacle of justice, as the national principle and value to be practiced throughout the parochial and private as well as public sectors.

In addition to other meanings, in the interpretations of New Abolitionists, the Daggett and Taney law ruling the Black male out of the body politic translated literally that by force of either/or both power and persuasion the presumed so sacred and sacrosanct as to be inviolable Constitution had to be amended if Black men were to be conferred citizenship like White men, and if human bondage were to be eradicated.

Forthwith, rational reform if not revolution or civil change of the Constitution's premises, principles, and laws (if not the national values) was certified to be the co-equally irreversible and realizable way to universal liberty in freedom with justice for the proponents of fairness and equity.[35]

EARLY AMERICAN CRUSADES FOR HUMAN ADVANCEMENT

During the last year of the eighteenth century, Presbyterian Lyman Beecher departed his alma mater Congregationalist Yale, to which he had returned for post-graduate professional study and where he was pri-vately tutored in theology for nine months by President Timothy Dwight: (A) to accept his first pastoral call as presbyter in charge of the Presbyterian Church in East Hampton, New York; and (B) to marry Rosana Foote.

By the 1790s, and certainly before the close of the decade, the White-ethnic individual as the constituent element of the secular republican democracy and sacred Evangelical Protestantism had united church and state in the Federalist Party; begun to divide Federalist industrialists and agriculturalists and to lay the ground for the formation of the Democratic Party; and determined the fundamental rules of the new nation and developing republic.

The ill-liberal repute of double jeopardy Calvinist faith and ethics of Evangelical Puritan Congregationalists withstood its public morality dimensions of double election/damnation that Dwight transformed from tributary moralisms to mainstream puritanicalism, exercised in the through the initiative he exercised in the process of alternating between anti-political idealism and pro-political realism and then ending in pure pious moralism. Re-revised "New Light" Orthodoxy and "New School" Reformed Calvinism notwithstanding, the legacy of sacred predestination and profane predetermination induced the anti-Calvinist secular and religious new American people to look elsewhere for their cultural values, when they were concerned to enrich them; and inspired the disaffected pro-Calvinists to vouchsafe their politics to other Christocentric and humanistic spirits inclusive of the deists, theists, and antitheists.

Evangelical Calvinists evinced a disquieting and unsettling sense of being deserted and politically discredited by the culture elite, whose defection they perceived to be the result of neither the errors nor the sins of either the Puritan fathers or the Yankee sons so much as their contemporary critics' corrupt interpretations upspringing from misconceptions of rational Calvinism.

This experience of greater frustration than embarrassment was a precipitant reason why these descendants of the wayward worldly saints were bound and determined to retreat to Halfway Piety faith and deterrence-benevolence morality; from brethren committing their genuine Puritan Piety public interest-enhancing direct actionist ethics to competitive review in civil conflict and competition; and to give their best minds to upgrading a defensive and offensive Calvinist faith and downgrading Calvinist ethics to the point of neglecting its defensiveness and offensiveness.

The consequences of these factors were increased by another factor, to wit, the Evangelical Calvinists' relocation of their intellectual from Boston-Harvard to New Haven-Yale in the aftermath of the Trinitarian and Unitarian Congregationalist division. There occurred, as a result of these realities, abandonment by establishmentarian Evangelical Calvinists of the original Puritan Piety public ethics and politics tradition Cotton Mather left underdeveloped for the pursuit of the deterrence-benevolence and anti-political Halfway Piety developed faith and underdeveloped ethics re-revisionist Jonathan Edwards bequeathed traditionalists.

Evangelical Calvinist rationalists' expenditure of enormous intellectual energy produced counterbalancing learned ecclesiastical debates and acid civil rivalries. In the process of achieving an apparent net loss rather than gain from propagating popular piety among the populous, and reporting progress in the proselization of private faith and ethics during the mid-antebellum cultural caste crisis, the radiant religion and race defenders dissipated in parochial politics vast quantities of the substantial Puritan reserves of public politics and political abilities. What they generated as surrogates for social redeeming values were new priorities, inclusive of greater concern with protecting parochial rites and private rituals than with expanding public rights and contracting public wrongs.

Orthodoxy's rational Yankee Congregationalists, and descendants of the Calvinist Puritan elite cultural leadership class, could not conceive that between Black and White peoples' different needs and interests--born of mistrust of and neglect by as well as stemming from disgust with deterrence-benevolence millennarians--their historic political resources were at once necessarily lost to the old cause of predestined human bondage and unnecessarily lost to the new opportunity of universal liberty in freedom with justice.

At the synchronous birth of the nation and the Second Great Awakening, when the proselitizing Protestant preachers attracted to the parish the populous in nearly the same proportion the people rejected the pure pious for the pure profane power politics professionals, what was remarkable and seldom noted by the crusaders for Christianization-Civilization-Colonization but concentrated the mind because it was neither surprising nor shocking to the enterprising ethical engineers subsisted of this succinctly stated situation: "Consistent Calvinist" political parsons' demonstrated diminished capacity to learn the lesson of success in failure, or to discover the key to victory in defeat, resulted in the defeated disclosing they were befeft of sufficient grace and guilt no less than healthy doubt as they turned defeatists, tail and retreated, and from common sense to not recouping but curtailing their losses by cutting and running.

Upon reflection during the antebellum political aftermath of this apolitical aftereffect of the emergence of slavocracy in democracy, ratiocinators who reverted to the partisan parishioner and parson power politics principal Puritan pattern found it no more accidental than it was an incidental matter to the clerical class who lost clout that the proselitized proletarians predeliberately permitted the treasured Presidential prize to pass, at once, from the Northeastern clergymen's cherished Federalist Party, out of the hands of their dearly loved New England Federalists (John Adams and John Quincy Adams), and into the hands of the Virginians--George Washington, Thomas Jefferson, James Madison, and James Monroe--who were born, bred, and died dyed-in-the-wool owners of massive numbers of the masses, good slavemasters, and great aristocrats (whether or not greater republicans and democrats).

The Federalist Party's serious loss to the Democratic Party was neither an irreversible political power drain nor the consequence of Calvinist Puritans being inherently less learned men and less skilled either ecclesiastical or civil politicians, whose competitive capacity could not be doubted by fair-minded comparative culture critics who contrasted the church and state clergy and lay churchmen litigators to anti-Calvinist and non-clerical Yankee Puritan public servants and their Anglican Cavalier compeers. The dissolution rather than redirection of their Federalist Party was both indirectly rather than directly and only partly due to the partisan party politics parsons' discontinuation of participatory democracy; withdrawal of demonstrated Federalist Party corrective ethical and developing political skills; and surrender of the advancement of their ecclesiastical interests and moral values in the secular civil sphere to their lawyer and professional politician parishioners, and/or to their rejection by the more profane than pious new liberal class of Federalists.

Partisan party power politics parsons emerged in the new nation with a profound understanding and underestimation of the republican democracy and the centermost pragmatism rational instrumental mechanism of the American political system. The extraction from the civil power sector and insertion in the ec-clesiastical power circle of their theoretical and experiential knowledge and wisdom contributed to the rigid Federalism structure of the Federalist Party and the challenging Anti-Federalist politics of change--that produced Republicans-Democrats.

Diminished political presence was not the only real alternative but the priority option that was selected by establishmentarian clerical leadership cadre partially because they were seduced by and preferred the alternating apolitical and anti-political role of state-supported custodians of the Commonwealth's morals. While being Federalist Party partisan parsons meant their Puritan fathers were in essence and mani-festation for the union rather than the separation of church and state, the post-Dwight Yankee sons chose protection of the theological and ecclesiastical traditions over perfection of secular and civil order.

The majority of clergy from the political right and left of the New England centrists, and across the broad post-Dwight theological conservative to post-Chauncy and pre-Channing ethical liberal Congregationalist spectrum, were united in social conservative Halfway Piety civil ethics and secular politics as consistently as the solid preponderance of the best and brightest Puritan men were locked in interminable debates for a century. They were mistaken in the conclusion drawn from their analysis as evidently as they were resolved to manipulate the ends of this debating device to squeeze the life out of vice by virtue of necessity or the virtue of necessity; committed to proving conclusively the necessity of virtue and its irresistibleness; and determined to realize the ultimate objective of securing and managing in reality the objective truth.

Equally inevitably, of course, because their irreversible reflectiveness operated under these self-inflicted embracive constraints, they were self-pre-empted of the time and interest necessary to prepare adequately to participate appropriately in the new nation and political system. But any reasonable doubt about their capacity to master law and logic, and to implement these rational powers in politics, is removed when the pro-Calvinist and anti-Calvinist cler-gymen-graduates--respectively of comparatively traditionalist Yale and nontradi-tionalist Harvard--are recalled to mind as engaged formidable friends and enemies who took pains to hone their faith and ethics reasons to an edge as fine as they placed on their hatchets, and preferred burying them in each other's body of Christ to burying their differences.

Simultaneously competitive champions of establishing Calvinistical theology in the nation (not the Church of Christ as the state or establishment Church) appropriated the identical arguments from the laws of "nature" and "reason" that their secular humanist and religious humanitarian (deist, agnostic, atheist, and latitudinarian) rivals were employing with power and authority to command and control civil politics--and drove their razor-sharp ratiocinations deep into the sacred body of their fierce foes either to change the Methodist mind and method (the free will and freedom of choice moral medium and media is the message messengers) or to mortally wound the Arminians whom Jonathan Edwards stoned to defend the Calvinists because he did not like their universal human being absolute freedom to make the relative right choice (for God and greater good) or wrong choice (for the Devil and energized evil) message.

Beginning with the commencement of the nineteenth century, warring theological conservative and liberal Congregationalist-clergymen parties engaged in eccles-iastical power politics, disengaged from civil power politics, and counseled and advised the Federalist politicians they supported. But while they distinguished themselves from professional politicians and statesmen, they understood themselves to be as commonwealth tax-funded managers of the ethics of both the pure profane and pure pious community members.

In their role as moral guardians, agents of Orthodoxy essentially endeavored to prove the relevance of their Evangelical Calvinistic tradition. Pursuant to this sacred objective in the secular sector, they directed their efforts primarily in improving parochial values, personal manners, private benevolence, and public morals.

Prior to the arrival of Beecher in the historic Calvinist capital of Boston, Channing advanced the liberal theological continuum. It entailed endeavoring to disconnect Puritan Congregationalism from Evangelical Calvinist faith and ethics. His progress proceeded to the point of turning the faith above ethics dialectical order on its head, and ended with the reduction of authentic Puritan Piety's faith and ethics dual coordinates to one--that is, ethics without faith, religious humanitarianism without theology, and benevolence based on rational morality. Driven by humanistic logic, Channing anticipated the ethic or Religion of Humanism would enable the well-educated select and well-bred elect to progressively improve the human condition--and therewith reform the public mind in its own Puritan image.

Unitarian and Trinitarian Congregationalists were engaged in rational revisions of the opposite ethics and faith poles of the common Evangelical Calvinist Puritan Piety tradition.

Yet along with direct conflict and competition, convergence from divergence persisted in their equally like and different emphases on the centrality of the individual, the authority of Puritanism, and the power of pure morality. But the disparate revisionists' wisdom did not extend to the understanding that they elevated nearly so high above the other as to diminish the efficiency of the religious faith and secular ethics coordinates of their sacred-profane civil order-improving tradition.

Neither party to the Puritan intertribal warfare believed they violated violently the historic ecclesiastical and civil Puritan culture they were promoting. Nonetheless, Yankee antebellum clergymen were courting cultural cross-purposes and division by demanding uniformity in the name of preserving the Union; limiting their real interests and influence in the social and political economy; and surrendering hegemonic power in civility and civil politics to the challengers of their leadership of the culture.

Relative to the relationship between moral power and real power they were right in what they claimed (it is never non-adversarial), and wrong in what they disclaimed (it always involves the compromise of principles). Establishment clergymen, as public servants, attended morality with little deference to power politics for several further instructive (among many other) reasons.

Specifically, underpinned by the premises of time-honored classical social conservative Catholic and Calvinistical ethics, Protestant moralists understood (A) moral power and the moral laws of God to be unattended, unlike political power and the civil laws of man, by other professionals; (B) making, keeping, and improving individual and community good conduct to be the explicit role clergymen were consigned by the elected state representatives, and tacitly agreed to by their constituency; (C) the force of moral power to be equal or superior rather than inferior to the force of political power; and (D) moral power in relation to political power to be autonomously derived from nature, moral power to be an independent natural agency and as such the co-equal of political power, and moral power to be not only more substantial than political power but also the force that will ultimately triumph. This premise asserted the principle that the Moral Law is the power of the moral law and truth and God, revealed in religion and the Bible, whose eternal purpose alone the Church serves.

Both because and in spite of better analyses of the facts and figures than interpretations and conclusions drawn from the data--and logical arguments stemming from spurious principles based on specious premises--rational Calvinists lost more than opportunity in their revisionist Puritanism, that centered on the presence of private morality and absence of political power. They also practiced a Puritanism of reason so nearly exclusive of authentic Puritan Piety that Congregationalists in principle lost the great unwashed. These thousands of converts whom the aggressive Evangelical Calvinists and Arminians gained were the indispensable empowerment force Congregationalism required to achieve its great ambition of national ecclesiastical hegemony, and to complete the inherited millennial "*Errand into the Wilderness.*"

The defense of diametrically opposite pro-Calvinist and anti-Calvinist Puritan liberalization schemes riveting Trinitarian and Unitarian Congregationalist denominations in parochial gridlock, on the one hand, and the elitist individual-specific and moral-only social structural change process these establishmentarian and social conservative theological moderates and liberals proffered for public reform, on the other hand, placed nothing so great as distance between power elite Yankees and the White masses--and the Black free and slave Protestants who were conspicuous by their absence in both Yankee-Puritan denominations.

It was this propensity of Congregationalists to equate moral excellence with negative (rather than with positive) good, and their limited regard for the real interests of the common folk, that their Reformed Calvinist cousins appeared determined to counterbalance with the power of revivalism. Pursuant to this task-responsibility, aggressive Evangelical Presbyterians migrated to Channing's Boston prior to the War of 1812--whose commencement was the effective end of the Second Great Awakening.

By 1810 (and certainly prior to 1820), Unitarians had secured the Boston brahmin (if not ecclesiastical dominance in either Massachusetts or Boston) and hegemony of Harvard; and the Trinitarian Congregationalists were out of power but not, of course, without influence. Unitarian Congregationalists (some of whom remained liberal Trinitarians)--without pretensions of being custodians of either the old or newly revised Calvinistic dogma and doctrines--were in control of public affairs.

The change of real interests was reflected in the declining and inclining political parties, and the shift of the balance of power from Northeastern to Southeastern masterful power politics players. Simultaneously, New England's clear educational and economic dominance was limited to private and parochial priorities. In this poor public direction of the Puritan resources, Congregationalists were permissive of the Original Sin architects of the Constitution committed; and tolerant of its spread with the proliferation of democracy's color/caste democratic sin and undemocratic slavery.

Compared to Philadelphia, the City of Brotherly Love and birthplace of Old Abolitionism as well as the cra-dle of democracy and the initial capitol of the United States, and contrasted with the emergence of New York City as the capital of capital no less than of both emigrant Yankee capital from mercantilist

Massachusetts and immigrant labor from Europe along with Black migrants from the South, Boston emerged not only from a colonial citadel of human bondage also but successively as the Puritan acropolis; arsenal of liberty prior to becoming the first slave-free state in the Union; original hub of New Abolitionism; and theatre of the absurd where in stiff competition for the popular mind diverse companies of morality players staged their dramatically different public ethical culture, Evangelical moralism, and antislavery tragedies and comedies.

These varieties of Protestant public performers created innovative dramas and dramatic performances that were exciting Yankee-American New England versions of the old English Puritan morality plays, whose up-dated revisions revolved around the sacred far less than the secular experience of evil in freedom, knowledge of the freedom of evil, and theme of salvation or freedom from evil.

Among these dissimilar moral artists in residence, the New Abolitionist professionals formed two companies and established their alternately mutually fertile and exclusive headquarters in New York and Boston. Congregationalism allied with the Reformed tradition of Calvinism the Presbyterian-Congregationalist Union and therefore did not form a congregation in Manhattan until the mid-1840s.

Subsequently, the Massachusetts Puritan mercantilists turned Yankee capitalists and transformed proabo-litionists who relocated in New York attended Presbyterian churches--and these two Evangelical Calvinist types of pro-immediatists overwhelmingly comprised biracial Manhattan New Abolitionism.

In Boston, the Evangelical Calvinist leader Garrison was supported by Unitarian Congregationalists and the rare exceptional Trinitarian Congregationalist. Each company of method actors and actresses were moral mediums who appealed to the commonwealth for the common good, attracted disparate segments of the public, and played to entirely different audiences. These disparate Christian congregants clashed consistently, never engaged seriously or casually, yet seldom even met face to face in matters of faith and ethics or in close encounters of the third kind (spiritual and moral dimension)--and then normally unknowingly specifically during the course of passing on the way to and from their separate dramatic productions.

These Manhattan-transplanted and Boston-ensconced Yankee sons of Puritan fathers were a bewildering variety of traditional and nontraditional White Angl-Saxon Protestants, a majority of Evangelical and minority of anti-Evangelical churchmen, and an observant preponderance who by the same proportion frequented Presbyterian and Unitarian establishment churches. But they were distinguished by their different beliefs in the freedom of salvation--and the saalvation of freedom.

Congregationalists of all varieties either denied or down played the value of immediate and universal unconditional or conditional liberation from human bondage, and mechanically delayed liberty in freedom for Black folk. The ancillary of this corollary advanced equally automatically. In fine, from the ruling class--imitating (and/or both following and leading) ruling elders' implicit premise and explicit presumption which expressly assumed self-determination to be the natural wrong and demasculinization the natural right of Black-race males--and liberty to be the natural right and dehumanization the natural wrong of White race/ethnic males--power Protestants perforce preservationists of pro-White race prerogatives values who were lovers of freedom of choice assigned to the individual and the society exactly the wrong responsibility.

Channingesque liberal Congregationalists were antiabolitionists who believed slavery to be neither either a complex matter or a question of raw political power and rigidly-held prerogatives of privilege nor an issue of real interests and values but a pure and simple moral power problem of correctly prioritizing ethical will and reason, that the moral individual could solve. Competing Evangelical Congregationalist reformers were antiabolitionists/procolonizationists who believed slavery is not the business of religion or the church, exists as the sole business of the state or secular order, and persists strictly speaking as not a moral power problem but only as a policy question and civil political affair.

However, whenever and wherever whomever considers human bondage a problem for either/or both Christianity and the culture and the Christian and civility, the only ethical correction principle, process, and program entails singularly the initiative of each persuaded individual slavemaster directed by perfect obedience to the proslavery Moral Law of the sacred Bible and the positive law of the sacrosanct Constitution.

This group of humanitarian-minded Evangelical moralists, projecting themselves as the class of Orthodoxy's moderates and conservatives, further believed that the Constitution and the American pragmatism dynamics of the republican democracy and political economy are based on the freedom of the individual (White race/ethnic male); *a priori* his freedom to engage in private evil (immorality) and/or public evil (slavery); and therefore could not effect the change of either fairly and equitably.

Given their point of view, the White Gentlemen's Agreement could not be abrogated without either breaking faith with the parties to the compact or placing the Union at risk. But they were not prepared either to admit or to accept responsibility for the consequences following from the logic of their argument: their manipulatable error of not only both con-ception and perception but primarily deception proved the apparent cause and effect of the paralysis of the political system, the efficient magnificent Machiavellian instrumental value of the national crisis, and the widespread indifference to the color caste/captive class which constituted its universally pervasive pernicious and obscene law and principle.

Evangelical Calvinist traditionalists were by definition social conservatives, and by necessity of their nature and function litigious litigators who argued the arguments supporting their "truth claim": Social health can be realized through the Christian Church solely, because the Church alone is the means (and the clergy the medium) of grace who guarantees the freedom of salvation.

Forthwith they superimposed interpretations and conclusions, and pressed the judgment that once the chosen or "Elect" elects to accept his selection, the saved (regenerate) individual would redeem and purify the nation as a redeemer redeeming and being redeemed by a redeeming community (local congregation).

The Evangelical reformers did not always act in concert with the fundamental primary antiabolitionist and secondary procolonizationist fundamentals of their antislavery belief about slavery: Human bondage is (1) a matter of personal and/or public discretion; (2) an ethical value, and if not pure good most certainly a lesser evil than immorality or impiety; (3) nearly an intractable opportunity or even problem; and (4) resistant to change, and cannot be assaulted without ex-pressly inexpediently and inconveniently undermining the national order, peace, and security of the high powered many for the sake of the unfortunate few. Mainly through being nothing more intolerable than standard deviations from this norm and self-styled high ground, and electing not to break new ground, Congregationalist "Consistent Calvinists" treated slavery with great circumspect--quite like most Evangelical churches and all mainstream denominations--and left the distinct impression they fully expected that once the immoral majority was saved and converted into the moral majority emancipation would follow apace.

Concurrently the crusading New Abolitionists erupted during 1830--not in either New Haven or Yale which by that year arguably was the biggest and best American college but--in New York and Boston, beyond the dictates of the establishment churches and denominations. These predominantly nontraditional Evangelicals believed that slavery, fully as much as less socially volatile immorality, was an eradicable evil--whose removal as the absolute contradiction of freedom would contribute saving grace to the republic. Pro-immediatists did not--and William Lloyd Garrison being at once the original New Abolitionist and a rigid pro-Temperance moralist could not--entirely dismiss the traditional Evangelical conservative doctrine, to wit, all individual and community moral problems are due to sin and solved by being born again, therefore, the twice born slavemaster will end slavery.

Experience was the reason these radical proabolitionists and reactionary pre-Prohibitionists did not completely reject this individualistic and simplistic doctrine of puritanical Evangelicalism. New Abolitionists possessed first-hand knowledge of the dual spiritual and moral conversion of one or more rich and famous individuals, to whom the warriors for moral-only social structural change pointed as proof of their assertion, and who apparently knew better than most Americans what real exceptions they were.

Indubitably, Northern Protestants' Southern churchmen brethren who converted from proslavocracy slavemasters to antislavocracy New Abolitionists were the dramatic living evidence that the exception neither tests nor overturns but confirms the rule, namely, that a born again churchman may be dead to Christian-conscience concerns and consciousness-raising demands.

Normally, the Christian New Abolitionists both were and had been nurtured on the logical argumentation for the virtue of pure pious moral power and the vice of pure profane political power,recurring during random cycles in the course of the post-First Great Awakening history of Evangelicalism. But moral monism especially concentrated the mind of Evangelical Protestants between the defection of the partisan Federalist Party power politics parsons from the *realpolitik* sphere and resignation of Garrison from the American Colonization Society.

Typically, monocrats developed and exercised their penchant for *ex cathedra* moral monocracy measures in this adversarial atmosphere, that was highly compatible with the authoritarian spirit energizing the Independence movement.

They were also equally smitten with freedom as a socially applicable universal imperative and well informed rationalists. These Freedom Fighters approached the South as a complex slave-based economic, religious, political, and social culture; considered the slavocracy demonstrable tyranny of the majority established by and for a minority of tyrants harboring delusions of grandeur, and forming a paper tiger rather an impregnable power; and concluded that unlike the military might required to secure American Independence from England, as well as dissimilar from the political pressure British Abolitionists combined with moral vigor to coerce Parliament into abolishing human bondage prior to the Victorian Age (1837-1901), the organized solid South and Southern real interests and values formed in actuality a difference in degree so great as to be a different kind of "peculiar institution," namely, one requiring only moral force to induce rational and radical rapid both constructive and peaceful social structural change.

Ironically ignoring and overriding the well-known British Abolitionists' near half century-long employment of moral force plus political power prior to achieving their objective, Christian New Abolitionists proceeded as if their mission was substantiated by the success in abolishing slavery throughout the Northeastern states--that resulted from enacted gradual manumission statutes and civil politics managed without perceptible support from the churches. They were convinced pro-immediatists could hit slavery directly with sufficient efficient moral compulsion that would cause the slave system--following saturated pinpoint ethical detonations--to collapse like a house of cards and with social consequences in the culture similar to falling dominoes in the physical universe.

Slavery for the mostly Protestant New Abolitionists was not the private affair of the slavocracy but the business of the nation. In their judgment the enduring state-permissive human bondage system was primarily due to the moral relapse of the individual, and the related failure of the collective will, that once shocked into maturity would implement the eradication of involuntary servitude.

The Boston Evangelical Calvinist union of moral monism managers, specifically as the principal principled advocates and adversaries quickly united on the antislavery principle and divided over its practice, proved the remarkably relevant and instructive as well as the perfectly clear representation of the historic and current Yankee-Puritan bifurcation of reality norm. Complementarily, a real distinction is discernible that makes a difference between the White proabolitionist and the White antiabolitionist reformers. It subsists of the absolute immediatism of the former and absolute gradualism of the latter, whose demonstrable propensity for repercussion upspringing from irregularly exerted capacities to alternately attract and repel each other are based on common and uncommon premises, principles, and priorities.

Alternatively stated, it is noteworthy that Bostonian proabolitionist and antiabolitionist antislavery men and women shared distinct and conflicting interests, demands, and desires, because each antislavery body was equally steeped in reason and led by brilliant logicians and rhetoricians of comparable ability.

For example, as determined Protestant rationalist experts in empirical rationalism, who were persuaded by the also Enlightenment-produced political and social secular humanism, immediatists and gradualists differed in their preferred tastes in evangelism and revivalism, the form and function of fashionable Evangelicalism as well as the nature and purpose of Evangelical Calvinistical revisions, and precious little in the style and substance of their positive rejection of double damnation/jeopardy Calvinism and acceptance of double indemnity Calvinism: or salvation of each regenerated individual inherent in which process is not only ultimate security obtained through justification by faith in the righteousness of God (Jesus Christ) and reason but also the ultimate authority of efficacious co-equally sufficient and efficient spiritual power and moral power.

Christian moral reformers wrote for the record and certified as public accountants that both power components were essential, and rendered civil secular political power nonessential for rational social structural change. Deconstructionists at once distinguished themselves as New York-Tappanites, and their two-dimensional (spiritual and moral) power conversion-grounded religious humanitarianism, from the one-dimensional moral power conversion means and end of Channingesque Christian Humanism and enlightened secular humanism.

No less inarguably, Boston Christian and non-Christian moral reformers, in all their varieties, re-vered self-determination and salvation from dehumanization as the universal constituent elements of the one human nature and race. This imperative constituted the source of their common optimism, the evidences corroborating the validity of this common principle were equally omnipresent and unmistakable. Its manifest perception is reality essence turned out to be equally applicable in the sacred and secular sectors: If properly cued, every comparatively rational and relatively immoral Christian and non-Christian individual and necessarily influenced community also, save the statistically insignificant recalcitrant, can procure a basic change to a more moral heart and mind--that is, one creating a sharper consciousness of the only virtue (agape-love) and highest principle (justice); generating a new appetite for the right and the good; and producing a properly reoriented, coordinated, and directed reason and will, or united rather than divided moral body, mind, and soul.

The predilection of Evangelical immediatists and gradualists to engage in affirmative action, identically inspired by this cherished optimistic premise, vied for frequency of public expression with the different secular moral motives and measures of not only the preponderance of the two groups but also the divided and competitive majority and minority wings of the pro-immediatist party. The latter proabolitionist varieties of Congregationalist/Orthodoxy and Presbyterian/Reformed Calvinist traditions were no less real Yankee-Puritans in spirit for being an obvious diverse mixture of English-race and British-ethnic representatives, who, albeit separated as Boston moral monists and New York moral pluralists, united to form the critical mass of the American Anti-Slavery Society. Their sharp conflict and competition was as natural as spontaneous combustion, and the nature of Evangelical Calvinist anti-political and pro-political moralists to promote conflicting world views and priorities.

Yet proabolitionist Manhattan churchmen and pluralist moralists, like the countermarching Boston es-tablishment churchmen/gradualist and anti-establishment non-churchmen/immediatist mono moralists, were an interesting study in comparative public ethic. This is the case because as unity in diversity they managed coexistence and the sharpest contrast imaginable to the existence of Channing, anti-Calvinist moral monocrat. It is also due to the fact that as diversity in unity they were Calvinists, who, theoretically if neither experimentally nor experientially nor principally, affirmed the singular American Evangelical Calvinist teaching whether or not they preached and practiced the principal principle or doctrine of the millennium.

Millennialistic social ethics in its broadest expanse and admittance of the positive value of history, compared to its normal narrow restrictive limits and concentration on eternity, essentially consisted of a single point of moral monism. It is that each regenerated individual is saved in and for the Universal Church Militant and Triumphant, and the plane on which the Kingdom of God is to surface in history, whose individual-in-community and community-in-the-individual inextricably dual mission is to secure the improvement of all the current local and world societies for the superior sacred society imminently arriving to supplant its inferior secular surrogate/sacrosanct or civil order.

Without question, the crusading Protestant New Abo-litionists could reject readily the Calvinist reward and punishment psychological thesis/antithesis as well as philosophical principle and theological practice, because their rational analysis and conclusion argued it followed as inerrantly in reality as in theory and experience that the perverse and even pernicious immoral moral man and society--and obverse of the projected progressive moral individual and community--was the equally necessary and actual primary effect or synthesis of the Calvinist thesis and antithesis.

As a theological predestination/rational predetermination-based both psychological and social attitudinal and behavioral modification instrumental means-ends, for the public and private as well as parochial individual and community, averred the Evangelical Calvinist social liberals, classical Calvinism advanced in the antebellum regions of democracy and slavocracy as a perfect proslavery system: irreverently and irrevocably expanding unfairness and inequity; driving the greater good and evil and the retained lesser evil to crowd out even the lesser good; demanding the suspension of the love/power/justice universal categorical imperative or subordination of the general interest to the special interests; promoting the preferred value relative to the alternative of an expansive human bondage-secured moral debt and contracting ethical credit system; and rationalizing dehumanization effectively through desacralizing the justification by faith in the righteousness of God and reason principle of ethics, and translating it as the demonstrable proof of the virtue of the pragmatism and realism coordinates of democracy or the asserted equivalence of the utilitarian greatest good of the greatest number and republican democracy rule of the majority secular ethic.

Just as certainly, radical pro-immediatist Calvinists could accept the minor assets, howbeit more unreliable than rare spin-offs from the major debits of tradition-conscious and conscience-bound Evangelical humanitarianism. Proabolitionists preferred flaunting to flouting the exceptional public performance of the extraordinary Calvinist promise, to wit, the regenerated individual secures with his/her eternal salvation from damnation in history and eternity personal self-esteem and social redeeming values--that automatically translate into the only public benefits that can pro-duce the good society.

Inevitably, both the positive and negative powers of Puritan antiblack white-ethnic virtue at once pervaded and united the Yankee gradualists and immediatists: who divided in their preponderancy as exclusively church-enhancement and inclusively church/society-enrichment sacred agents in the secular civil society; impacted Black Calvinist brothers and sisters inordinately; and stroked anti-Black race virtue disproportionately. Relative to these complicated alternating conciliation and conflict and competition dynamics, when compared to Boston as the citadel of Unitarian Congregationalism and Princeton as the national headquarters of Orthodoxy's "Old Light" and the Reformed tradition's "Old School" theological conservatives, what emerges the relevant matter of importance occurs with the advancement of New Haven and Yale as the hegemonic center in the nation of Congregationalist "New Light" and Presbyterian "New School" theological liberals, in whose establishment Evangelical alliance developed puritanicalism along with rational anti-Black race morals, moralities, and moralisms.

Yalies and New Havenites in the establishment Evangelical Edwardsean-Hopkins line preached with consummate conviction in academic circles and complete con-vincement in Congregationalist Churches of Christ both the doctrine and for the religious salvation of each private person--but the class did not emerge a witness for the prosecution of anti-Black race values, because their rational thoughts and actions combined positive faith and negative ethics which not only limited their spiritual and moral power but prevented them from converting individual and community pro-White race/ethnic interests-protecting advocates to public servants, or parochial parsons and parishioners demanding in the parish respect for the Black race.

Their faith over ethics priorities and values empowered a leap over high regard for Black Calvinist brethren of the cloth, and the Black clergy's highest priority of equal human worth that they proclaimed publicly proudly and loudly to be their true and real interest and value, to embrace with high praise White Calvinist powerhouse's deterrence-benevolence: the counterfeit charity surrogate for love and justice they audaciously claimed, without a trace of White "Christian shame," a pro-White race/ethnic good and good enough benefit for Black folk.

These deterrence-benevolence charitable contributions were abundant, completely voluntary, and not the sole means of grace they were capable of distributing. They were simply the only ones the power churches and establishment denominations were willing and prepared to administer as gifts and grants to Black Christians.

It goes without saying that as experts in indiscriminate indifference and disrespect for their Black Calvinist fellow professionals, Evangelical Congregationalist traditionalists were not superior theoreticians and technicians to their more liberal religious and secular humanist Yankee-Puritan confederates.

Contrariwise, on balance, the conservative, moderate, liberal antislavery religious and secular establishmentarians differed radically from the stellar few nonestablishmentarian Evangelical abolitionists--both within and towering above the grateful mainstream majority cowering before the great tradition--who resisted their opponents' strong arm tactics, and extended their own right hand of fellowship to Black folk. They taught, and at first sought to practice, re-spect for the Black race.

The two great pro-Calvinist/anti-Calvinist Manhattan and Boston minorities within the White New Abolitionist minority challenging the antislavery majority --whose radical *bona fides* entailed demonstrable advocacy of abolishing slavery and anti-Black race values--appeared at the outbreak of New Abolitionism for the equality of the Black race and English Puritan-race/British-ethnic groups to be biracial respect engaged in concrete experience, whether or not they believed racial equality to be true in the abstract. The most consistent direct actionist among these proponents of equalitarianism were three-dimensional immediatists--that is, pro-spiritual, pro-moral, and pro-political power proabolitionists.

Black New Abolitionists were left to discern for themselves the White men and women who were superior in principle to the principles of the two-dimensional gradualists, and better performers of their three-dimensional promise than the practitioners of one-dimensional immediatism. Black Old Abolitionists exercised the limited choice allowed them at the begin-ning of the nation, when the Black race was Constitutionally determined relatively unimportant; and normally ill-considered when Black folk emerged in the peripheral vision on the boundary line of perception in what passed for the American mind and will at the heart of the three concurrent watershed crusades.

The *first* crusade was the humanist for democratic rights and individual liberty, the religious liberal Deist Virginians and liberal religious Massachusetts Puritans led together with compeer Federalist secularists. It directly benefited Northern and Southern White males fundamentally. The indirect benefit of the White Gentlemen's Agreement to Black exceptionals--that enhanced the Black race imperceptibly--was the class of Old Abolitionists who formed Old Abolitionist Societies to force the reversal of the compromise of principles.

Northern Old Abolitionist signatories of the Con-stitution were primarily Christian humanitarians, who, in spite of competitive beliefs resulting in a conflict of values with Deists, Latitudinarians, agnostics, and atheists, differed undetectably as a divided Northeastern antislavery bloc from the solid Southeastern proslavery confederation when it came to negotiating their conflict of interests except that Southerners did not compromise their principles and Northerners did when Old Abolitionists elected the Union and the exclusion of their Black-race Patriots and cultural kin-group from citizenship rights and responsibilities as well as privileges appertaining to American liberty, fraternity, and equality.

Evangelical Christians, paralleling the Quaker hegemony of the Old Abolitionism as the original dynamism of the New Abolitionism movement and *second crusade*, were united in Calvinist capitalism and against human bondage yet divided over personal and social theology and psychology far more sharply than over issues of philosophy and morality, church and state, slavery and union, salvation and humanism, liberalism and conservatism, Federalism and states' rights, missionizing and Christianizing, humanitarian manumission and colonizationism.

The rise of the humanist and antislavery crusades corresponded with the e-mergence of democracy and Evan-gelical reform of the republic, a public initiated individual and community moral change arrangement and outcome of the parochial community-directed income from private corporation-funded. A far less secular and civil than parochial and private sectors-concentrated religious humanitarianism, this Protestant Second Great Awakening aftereffect or the *third crusade*--along with the Channing-led Unitarian thrust-out of its orthodox Trinitarian Congregationalist circle--effectively marked the end of the beginning of Evangelical Calvinist Presbyterians and Baptists, and the beginning of the end of Orthodoxy's Yankee-Puritan Congregationalist prominence as a national instrument--even before Con-gregationalism emerged as the last major establishment tradition to form a denomination.

Yankee secularist sons of anti-Calvinist Puritans had long since left Congregationalist ecclesiastical bureaucrats and technocrats--or moral monocrats managing the theological disputes and improvements of their hierocracy--to become lawyers and the political presence. Yet the professional politicians in Massachusetts continued to appreciate parsons and parishes as guardians of the Commonwealth's morals and to fund their mission with state taxes, at the precise time Evangelicals were on the verge of their Northern and Southern ascendancy as the protectionists of society's mores and moralisms.

Between the death of theocracy and birth of democracy survived the remnant of the clerical hegemony, the once bold and commanding Calvinist Puritan force known to history as the Old New England Confederacy, and the Boston Congregationalist procession from John Cotton through Increase and Cotton Mather to Charles Chauncy.

Finally, at the top of Boston's liberal Calvinist bent, and unification of private and public Puritan Piety ethics, Unitarianism broke free of Trinitarianism's bonds and binds; jettisoned the public ethics component of the tradition and combined the sacred Calvinist and secular democracy dynamics of their common individual constituent element but uncommon ecclesiastical and civil "pursuit of happiness" guarantee and objective.

FROM STATE INSTITUTED PURITANISM TO
CHURCH ESTABLISHED PURITANICALISM

Unitarian Congregationalism functioned as a catalyst who transformed universal personal regeneration into the interchangeable pure pious and pure profane individual or private and personal rational moral power. It was adopted in the cultural crisis by Trinitarian Congregationalism, whose clergy accelerated the passing of authentic Puritan Piety public interest-specific ethics from English race Congregationalism into the leadership hands of socially and politically aggressive British ethnic Presbyterians: who developed it singularly until Congregationalists returned to politics on the eve of the eruptive new Confederacy.

The century long transatlantic cooperation between English Orthodoxy and British Reformed churches was intensified by the First Great Awakening, in spite of its being the precipitating cause of Congregationalists dividing as "New Lights" and "Old Lights" and Presbyterians into "New School" and "Old School" camps. The connection was revealed in the life of Congregationalist Jonathan Edwards, who emerged the solidification of the Orthodoxy and Reformed merger movement in the moment of his inopportune death, that occurred weeks after being appointed President of the Presbyterian College of New Jersey at Princeton. Four decades after his death, the Congregational/Presbyterian Plan of Union became effective in 1801: whose formal alliance of two Calvinist traditions and emerging denominations due in no small measure to the contributions of the Reverend Jonathan Edwards, Jr. (1745-1801).

He died in his prime, during the year the Calvinist denomination was established, as had his father. These birth and death events occurred two years before their good friend Samuel Hopkins died. He was the Edwardsean master and major disciple of Edwards with whom Edwards the Younger shared a commitment to Old Abolitionism, and something less than optimism and more like total pessimism regarding its future prospects in the New England Churches at the hands of the post-Edwardseans engineering the new Evangelical realignment.

Edwards the Younger graduated (1765) from the Col-lege of New Jersey: and remained there as a tutor until President John Witherspoon replaced Edwardsean philosophical theology and psychology with Scottish philosophy and theology. Jonathan Edwards, Jr. respond-ed to the new order by accepting a call (1769-95) to the New Haven White Haven Church of Christ: whose "New Light" congregation dismissed him for his opposition to the very Half-Way Covenant the prior generation of founding churchmen bolted (in 1742) from the New Haven First Church of Christ to protest, only to reinstitute the ecclesiology (in 1760).

Limited in his opportunities by this reversal in fortune, Edwards the Younger who was both unlike Edwards the Elder and like his father pressed by Calvinistical exigencies to earn a living on the fringes of power. He also relocated on the urbane margin and edge of a small town in (not the Massachusetts but) the Connecticut frontier (1795-99), as pastor of the North Colebrook Church of Christ. Similar to his father additionally, near the end of his existence that was also cut short of natural termination, on this far periphery of the center of Orthodoxy he was elected President (1799-1801) of Union College, Schenectady, New York.

At these crossroads the early national church and state commenced united separate and distinct subordinate-ecclesiastical and predominant-civil powers of the new Union, as the New Haven/Yale proabolitionist Edwardseans descended and antiabolitionist post-Edwardseans ascended respectively through the dying and borning stages. Between the celebrated death and birth of these celebrities the Old Abolition body of the Churches of Christ in New England teetered and tottered on the edge of neutrality and verge of unconcernment prior to its final collapse in Orthodoxy.

In the appearances, Old Abolitionist Congregationalist parsons and parishioners (who dominated the permanent parishes) were neither agile nor hostile nor mobile but very few, far between, and hard to find anti-slavery agents. There the collective (*E pluribus Unum* body of sacred and secular civil servants) persisted analogous to the representative Western Civilization-wide *Mr. Hyde* half of the *Dr. Jekyll* split (subject/object) personality--especially as the conscious "Consistent-Calvinist"/classic-conservative clerical class--and expressly so when perceived in perspective perforce the synchronous partisan Federalist Party power politics partnership of the New England parsons and parsishioners. They were in the front ranks of the Northern and Southern Calvinists allied in secular state and sacred sectarian affairs to secure a more perfect ecclesiastical and civil Union.

In reality, whose time frame is the passing of the first decade of the United States and the nineteenth century and the last decade of Hopkins and Edwards the Younger, abolitionism in Congregationalism could not withstand the death of the elder "Connecticut Yankee" and the younger "Massachusetts Yankee" conscientious objectors to slavery in the Union, who were Orthodoxy's last living major two--complete clerical--Old Abolitionists.

Whether or not intended and expected by Calvinist Puritans--whose powers of predictive reason and perception cannot be easily overestimated or underestimated without courting risk--what was no less consequential for Black Calvinists followed from these turning terminal events inexorably in logic and life.

The Old Abolitionist Congregationalist-clergymen remnant could not compete with rise of the Second Great Awakening or survive the new device of virtue and vice the cultural change movement produced, to wit, the ecclesiastical compact and imitation of the civil contract or Constitution: the binding Congregational-Presbyterian *White Gentlemen's Agreement* that the Northern and Southern "Consistent Calvinist" brethren felt duty bound to honor, whose firm faith bonding proved an equal ethics constraint consisting of kith and kin ties that tied their consciences in a *Gordian Knot* they could neither loosen nor untie but had to cut.

In the aftermath of the Calvinist color-conscious compromise of conscience and principle, the flickering flame of spiritual and moral power Yankee-Puritan Con-gregational/Presbyterian-Calvinism retained to counter anti-Black race values was snuffed out by the expert hand of the "Connecticut Yankee" grandsons of "Massachusett Yankee" Jonathan Edwards: the Reverend Timothy Dwight (1758-1817), and Congressman (1806-07) Theodore Dwight (1764-1846), two powerful brothers in their dual church and state united roles as ecclesiastical and civil lawmakers.

Reverting to the pre-Edwards Puritan tradition of engaging in civil politics, and defending declaration of war to secure peace and security by means of associating it with the asserted equivalence of just war and ethical right and good, Timothy Dwight emerged to energize in the early national or Independence era the pro-Patriot connective linkage initiated by his elder brothers in the Revolution between New Haven and Bos-ton Yankee sons of Puritans--the ancillary of whose pro-American corollary being their equally automatic and predeliberate will to suspend their anti-Calvinist/pro-Calvinist parochial hostilities for the duration.

Thus as a proponent of the use of military might and political force to secure Independence, and in his dual role as President (1795-1817) of Yale and titular head of Evangelical Orthodoxy, Timothy followed the lead of his brother (Theodore) in the *realpolitik* arena and evolved the chief Federalist Party partisan parson. As a pro-politics Evangelical Calvinist, Timothy Dwight launched the sharp reversal of his grandfather's anti-political faith and ethics.

Dwight not only shared values as a Federalist Party enthusiast with New Englanders who boast of the Anglo Saxon roots of their English ancestry, along with the erstwhile old Anglican and new Episcopalian Virginia aristocrats as well as the Boston and New Haven Yankee-Puritan patricians, but the English/ Puritan race representative united the Northeast Evangelical Calvinist consensus behind his leadership. It included a productive positive connection with President Witherspoon of the College of New Jersey--the immigrant from Scotland and national voice of the North American British-ethnic Calvinists--and the adoption and adapation for Orthodoxy of the Presbyterian powerhouse's Scottish Common Sense Philosophical/Psychological/Theological school of thought.

Single-minded moralist Dwight redacted the Princeton Reformed theology and singlehandedly instituted his single-hearted re-revision of Calvinism at Yale, and deserved the credit he received for the results of his perfectly predictable progressive transformationist public ethics principle and process. Straightaway, Dwight successively introduced his new curriculum successfully; turned out the remaining light of Edwardsean proabolitionism and social ethical idealism effectively; and turned Yale, the academic head and ecclesiastical heart of Evangelical Congregationalist Orthodoxy, into the an antislavery-antiabolitionist bastion of social conservatism.

Dwight superimposed his revision with impunity, howbeit the critical imposition appeared a presage of deconstructionism to his contemporary critics who could be excused for confusing it also with a convoluted analysis. In actuality, the process subsisted of deconstructing and reconstructing the sacred roots of authentic Puritan Piety faith ethics, together with the secular and civil roots of Puritanism, and producing from the cross-fertilization process the breed of puritanicalism--the re-rooted new transplants whose shoots flourished after he vanished.

Since this misconstruction was the work of the representative Evangelical Congregationalist, it could not be fairly judged a mismanagement of reality. Albeit equally unwittingly and inevitably, Dwight's puritanicalism proved both the bare essence of Halfway Piety faith and deterrence-benevolence ethics and to be confused with authentic Puritan Piety faith and ethics. Normally recognized in the ends justifies the means arguments of social conservative intentionalist ethicists, as challengers of social liberal consequentialist ethicists, and advocates of private intentions and parochial conventions overriding public consequences--the nature and function of Halfway Piety faith and ethics is in essence and manifestation the demonstrable purpose of its deterrence-benevolence ethics half, whose maximum value is positive negation and reverence for risk-free limits or negative good.

By concentrating on these constraints of idealism and principles of realism Dwight held a mirror before the public which provided a picture perfect of the general interest-limiting Halfway Piety he advanced as the negative power canceling the positive power coordinate of antiblack white-ethnic virtue and thereby restricted severely the positive enrichment potential inherent in the original Puritan Piety tradition. Contrapositively, in the identical looking glass the risk-intensive positive help and advancement or positive good true substance of genuine Puritan Piety appeared as clearly.

What is of moment centers on the fact that prior to their death, Dwight and Witherspoon presided over the formal unification of Congregationalists and Presbyterians--whose consummation formed the major power denomination(s). An instant model of ecclesiastical bureaucracy and functional efficiency, and the utilitarian standard of rational organization, the real power the potent denomination directed in ecclesiastical institutions was the singular effect of an ingenious conjunction of "*the spirit*" and peculiar genius of two cultures--namely, the historic and current English-Puritan Calvinist capital formation and Brit-ish-ethnic Calvinist political power experience.

In addition to these basic underpinnings, the Union authorized mutual full accreditation and acceptance of Presbyterian and Congregationalist ordination, whereby clergymen ordained in one (either Puritan Orthodoxy or the Reformed Calvinist) tradition could be called and installed as the pastor of a church in the other. And an ordained Presbyterian presbyter functioning as the pastor a Congregationalist congregation or vice versa was accorded full privileges in both legislative bodies--since Congregationalists and Presbyterians continued to convene separate juridical assemblies. The more venturesome Presbyterian Presbyteries, composed predominantly of native Scotland-immigrant and American born -emigrant British ethnic laymen and clergymen, extended themselves both in the South and on the Western Frontier.

British-ethnic Scotsmen/Irish-men brought to this institutional linkage, with the equally disproportionately English-American/Puritan-Yankee Congregationalists, the Scotch-Irish ideas, ideals, and ideologies nurtured in the British Isles. These birthright values included vigorous involvement in partisan politics as Independent Protestant church or members of the Presbyterian Church of Scotland and combatants of the Church of England protestants; self-identity and undaunted self-esteem, strengthened through ties with the controlling religious communion of Scotland; and, relative to avoidance and acceptance of opposition, the preference for aggression which was not impeded by the experience of being British in conflict and competition with the English.

Determination and drive complemented the cooperation and conciliation capacities of Scotch-Irish ethnicity, and were given public expression alternately when appropriate as regularly as the aggressive spirit of the individual and collective occurred when challenged by or challenging the dominant English in "Old and New England," and the Anglican colonies of Virginia and the Carolinas.

English race and British ethnic tensions to the contrary not withstanding, the century and a half of common involvement tied the ecclesiastical knot between the two Calvinist churches and folk. Moreover, unlike the English Puritan Presbyterians the Scotch-Irish Presbyterians enjoy a distinct advantage over North American Congregationalists in not only statecraft and soulcraft but also churchcraft when it comes to organizing and developing a nation-wide denomination. The Congregational system revolves the autonomy of each local congregation, and its boundless potential within the urban/suburban or small town/rural community reaches its maximum influence and affluence in direct proportion to the powers of persuasion of a persuaded and persuasive parson; a commanding if not charismatic leader; and one whose natural pastoral talent or skillfully developed parson and parishioners synergy results in extraordinary decision-making freedom in all parish affairs.

Essentially a system based on parishioner and presbyter confidence in elders selected and elected essentially due to demonstrated centrist common sense courage of their convictions, competence, and credibility--its relatively high success and low failure rate over time and through time is partially attributable to the positive effect of the frequently negative force of Puritan tribalism. Congregationalists always understood aberrational instances of parsons pitted against the people were not only as inevitable as they were rare but necessarily dimmed their potential for meeting new challenges, and therefore instituted in their regional consociations clergy crisis management teams which overrode local autonomy in emergency situations to advise and counsel the parties to the conflict on expeditious ways and means to solve the problem.

Antithetical Reformed ecclesiology is the direct opposite of local autonomy structure, and the power point of Presbyterian polity functions to prevent ministers, laymen, and churches from being a law unto themselves. They are subject to the Presbyteries--or constituted regional governing bodies acting under laws established by the General Assembly or supreme judica-tory of all Presbyteries.

In brief, central church government form and function fairly describes best Presbyterian ecclesiology: it turns the rule of the majority of General Assembly representatives into the majority rule of the General Assembly and/or the collective will of Presbyterians.

Ever since the Founding Fathers rejected the coal-ition formed during the Continental Congresses and prior to the Constitutional Convention by James Madison and like-minded aristocrats to making Frederick II or the Great (1712-86), King of Prussia (1740-86), king of the "Disunited States" and adopted the Presbyterian central church government system as the Union's republican democracy governance mechanism, serious minds questioned the durability of the not absolutely rigid but very firm and relatively flexible church and state order of the ecclesiastical and civil powers.

The first stiff faith and ethics as well as ecclesiology test of the General Assembly of the United Presbyterian Church in the United States of America occurred in 1837, when the "Old School" majority ejected the "New School" minority and produced incon-trovertible proof that the driving ambition of demanding Scotch-Irish immigrants, and the freedom and order disciplinary nature of Presbyterianism, formed efficient as well as powerful ying and yang middle-class coordinates of the Reformed arrangement of rational command and control power and authority.

With systematic and systemic Presbyterianism in the operative mode, the social conservative Presbyterians divided the United Presbyterian Church into two Northern (free states) and Southern (slave states) competing national Churches each headquartered in the North: the overwhelming majority of theological conservative Presbyterians forming the Princeton-centered "Old School" Assembly, and the minority of theological liberals directed by the New Haven-centered "New School" Assembly.

Previously, directly due to the 1801 Congregational/Presbyterian Plan of Union, "Old School"/"New School" Presbyterians revolving around Princeton and "New Light"/"New Divinity" Congregationalists revolving around Yale united in the two common foreign and domestic agencies Congregationalists established and directed as interdenominational bureaucracies--the American Board of Commissioners for Foreign Missions, (1810) and the American Home Missionary Society, (1826).

Until the 1837 Presbyterian schism, following which Congregationalists moved with all deliberate speed from New England-bound Churches of Christ to form an inde-pendent national denomination, the preponderantly social conservative yet disproportionately theological conservative and liberal establishment Congregationalists and Presbyterians coordinated their Calvinist antiblack white-ethnic virtue as method and message of their international and national mission to eradicate moral evil and infidelity.

Following the death of "Old Light" Calvinists--who were reborn Boston Unitarian Congregationalists--"New Light"/"New Divinity" Evangelical Calvinists were the overwhelming numerical body and nearly if not the only type of traditional Puritan or Trinitarian Congregationalists; predominantly amassed in New England as the plurality of establishment clergy and congregants or churches; and effectively led in ecclesiastical and civil affairs of church and state by the Yale-hegemonic Congregationalist philosophical and biblical theologians. Further illumination of the relevant point in question follows upon recalling that when Unitarians secured hegemony over traditionally Puritan Congregationalist Boston and Harvard, and, to the mind of the Evangelical-Calvinist/Trinitarian Congregationalists, added insult to injury upon establishing Harvard Divinity School as a Unitarian seminary, Yale challenged the usurpers of the historic tradition and turf by spawning and founding near Boston--in Andover, Massachusetts--the Andover Theological School (1808).

Thus empowered by a millennium-intensive expansionist missionary and proselytization dynamic, generated by the Second Great Awakening, Yale-centered "New School" Presbyterians and "New Light" Congregationalists combined with the Yale-created "New Divinity" Congregationalists in Andover to form a tripartite formidable force formal friends and foes appraised differently. The forged Evangelical Calvinist phalanx initially foraged Boston to overturn their social conservative Puritan brethren--the Harvard theological liberals; directed Protestant resources and organizations to establish parochial colleges and sectarian seminaries, private institutions and enterprises, and religious humanitarian public works.

Calvinist capital's real interests and values no less than fiscal contributions especially enabled the theological liberal alliance within the Presbyterian/Congregationalist Union to lead the American churches in creating civil charities, and/or in establishing--out of all proportion to its relatively small numerical constituency compared with the massive membership sta-tistics Methodist and Baptist evangelists boasted--a disproportionately greater number of Protestant philanthropic societies. The New Haven and Yale Congregationalist generals and field marshals, and "led captain" Princeton Presbyterians, first and primarily directed spiritual and moral power and possibilities produced by the revivals in Foreign Mission corporations--and veered last and least the secondary excess in Domestic Mission agencies, beginning with the non-sectarian or interdenominational Evangelical American Colonization Society and counterpart Moral Reform associations.

Developing rapidly between 1800 and 1830, throughout the continental states and contiguous territories of the Union, the umbrella Protestant Moral Reform confederation formed regional, state, and local affiliated groups which uniformly placed Temperance at the top of their individual and community moral reform agenda--as well as varied in nearly all other private and public moral problems selectively targeted and prioritized as the primary and secondary ethical issues for their social reform mission.

Upspringing from the Second Great Awakening, Evangelical Anglicans (Episcopalians), Arminians (Methodists), and Calvinists (Baptists as well as Congregationalists and Presbyterians), were driven politics-free and moral power means and ends only; expended massive amounts of time, talent, and tender to secure the ethical man as the standard of culture and ways and means to convert the unethical society to conform to this moral individual norm; and reached their apex at the point they formed the ACS as their para-denominational antislavery organ.

Paradoxically, for a pure moral and politics free and clear social ethics and cultural change ecclesiastical establishment coalition, precisely in explicitly affirming the intrinsic and extrinsic politics-intensive ACS and implicitly denying its sacred and secular political nature and function they proved to be (A) better at preaching than practicing their principles; (B) either innocent and ignorant or capricious and stubborn; and (C) the classic individual and collective demonstrable error of conception, perception, and deception.

It is nothing if not ironic that in era when Federalist Party partisan parsons were abandoning power politics for moral power, and the major churches and clergymen were anti-political rational moralists, the Evangelical Protestant denominations created and supported the ASC which, by turns, found power politics and policy essential instrumental mechanisms for successfully achieving its Black-race denationalization and deculturalization as well as deportation *modus vivendi* and *modus operandi*, evolved and devolved into an antiabolitionist body from the proabolitionist as well as both the First and Second Great Awakening-inspired mind of Samuel Hopkins--the Newport pastor and moral hero/heretic of the model modern moralist and Newport-native William Channing, and provided the first (albeit neither the foremost nor final) paradigm for William Lloyd Garrison--the onetime dedicated member of the Society, subsequent first New Abolitionist, and major Evangelical Calvinist social ethicist.

Since Channing was completely cognizant that this efficient moral power delivery system added extensity to humanitarian intensity and density, and revealed the new power and effectiveness of rationally organized national institutions and special interests, what appears just amazing is that Channing elected not to update and integrate individual and unified individuals or allied moral power but opted to overrule collective moral power and to superimpose upon reality his ideal moral man hero construct as the sole social change agency.

But despite Channing's moral wisdom and wit, and more subjective or less objective criticism of anti-slavery associations that he called formations as obsolete as the appendages of Neanderthal Man than he was prepared to admit, the denominational force revealed by its existence his power point to be an irrelevant value judgment and demonstrable nonsense.

Synchronous with Channing's development of his Unitarian moral monism, interdenominationally inter-linked Evangelical Foreign and Domestic ecclesiastical bureaucracies led by clerical bureaucrats and technocrats were as important as eleemosynary corporations as they were significantly financed by the philanthropy received from solicited Yankee merchants. And their distribution of Calvinist capital to fund their anti-Black race interest-specific Half Piety "bad faith" and deterrence-benevolence "worse ethics," to wit, Black folk transatlantic transplantation, awakened in a minority authentic Puritan Piety: or fusion of individual and community specialist interests and the general interest with personal spiritual-power/moral-power empowered social ethics.

Pure Puritan Piety's private faith and public ethics nature--religious and secular pursuit of primary sacred and secondary profane happiness function and common good securing objective mission--evolved from the Puritan fathers and saints who associated the moral means-ends with the ethical heart of the *Westminster Confession* (1643-45): the purpose of man is to glorify God and enjoy Him forever.

This affirmation seemed to the Trinitarian Congregationalist brethren to be reversed by the Unitarian Yankee sons of wayward worldly saints to mean the purpose of man is to glorify man and enjoy him forever. Yet it appeared to remain sheer potential after expanding and contracting for two centuries, or in a permanent state of underdevelopment, as a result of Yankee-Puritans' higher sacred and secular personal priorities; more pressing ecclesiastical and civil values; and diversionary church and state interests and demands.

Concurrently Victorian Age emerging power-acquiring and wealth-accumulating world-foraging exploits of the British Empire, and spiraling profits from the rapidly expanding industrial revolution and capitalism, were contributing causes of the Continent-induced and consequential color-specific caste/captive class crises; driving new formations of universe-wide underdeveloped cultures-corrupting Protestant international Evangelical and missionary imperialism; and precipitating forces pulling and pushing the equally arrogant and aggressive American Foreign and Domestic Mission agencies and agents.

They advanced on the frontiers of Occidental and Oriental cultures bearing the largess gained from the new industrial investment income and outcome of the old African slavetrade of independently wealthy productive Protestants generally, and particularly Calvinist capitalists whom clergy counseled and moved from conviction through convincement to commitment. These great realities also brought authentic Puritan Piety from the unconscious and preconscious to heightened consciousness, human bondage to mind, and a creative minority of counter-culture Yankees to conscience and conscious New Abolitionism.

Prior to the advent of the New Abolitionists and their break out of the moderate madding crowd packed in the middle-of-the-road, and jockeying for post and pillar position, and forward from the Independence era-commencement of Old Abolitionism, initiative was evidenced in the national antislavery leadership capacity and responsibility Quakers accepted: and far more West-relocated Southern Calvinists (mainly Presbyterians and a modest number of Baptists) than Arminians and Anglicans or Northerners shared.

They shouldered the antislavery task-responsibility between the death of Jonathan Edwards, Jr. and Samuel Hopkins until relieved by the ACS that establishment Protestant denominations formed as their quasi-official antislavery Society: whose incorporation conference commenced late in 1816, the year Roxana Foote Beecher died; and was completed early in 1817, the year Lyman Beecher married Harriet Porter.

Evangelical initiatives in Foreign Mission enterprises supplied the Moral Reform motive, means, measures, and opportunity Moral Reformers declared the Evangelical Domestic Mission, and demonstrated their heightened Protestant social consciousness in creating the anti-slavery ASC their antiabolitionist agency. The ASC emerged an establishment overt and covert operation, extrinsically cooperative but intrinsically in conflict and competition with the Old Abolitionist Societies, and matured into alternative whose effect was to override the Quaker-led Old Abolitionist thrust and movement.

A Calvinist ideational ideal that Congregationalist Samuel Hopkins created,

282   CONSTITUTION, CONSCIENCE, AND CALVINIST COMPROMISE

Congregationalist Samuel Joseph Mills, Jr. rediscovered and shared with his Reformed Church neighboring minister in New Jersey, Presbyterian Robert Finley transformed into a precedent-setting organization and model perfect parochial-private-public partnership, and Presbyterian Ralph Randolph Gurley developed into a multi-denominational and multinational corporation--the American Colonization Society (December 1816-January 1817)--succeeded in no small measure as a result of the ecumenical antislavery agency's able agents' productive professional solicitation of Yankee-Puritan magnificent munificence minds over money and matter, including market margins making-merchants and monitoring-managers willing and able to fund with their discretionary income its vaunted Black race excludable motive, means, and opportunity. But despite their shared affordable interest after profit on their principle, they invested in color chattel propery and real estate as well as other wealth-generating market-valued real interests, the Protestant philanthropists financed neither sufficiently nor efficiently this, nonetheless, far too effective deculturalization, denationalization, and deportation organization for Black New Abolitionists.

The ACS agency and agents--or demonstrable contradiction in terms, and compromise of principle--suffered gladly and survived their self-inflicted critical wound. Its expert executer (who was neither an executionist nor a chief executive action officer) cut to the bone but by-passed the heart less than fifteen years after its inception, when Garrison led out of the antiabolitionist ACS and into the proabolitionist AAS independent-minded Evangelical Calvinist churchmen and churchwomen. This counter-consensus Protestant minority the establishmentarian pro-gradualist majority could no more control than they could concur with their pro-immediatism principle.

The arrangement of power and range of authority of the formidable ACS was maneuvered skillfully by professional people and systems managers. These moralists directed management teams consisting of efficiency experts and rational organization men and women, who guided with their ethical engineering expertise crusaders for an antiabolitionist Christ, Christianity, and civility. The ratiocination-replete "true believers" in the right they distinguished from wrong--and in their truth claim subsisting of the complete certainty that they were right and so right and righteous in their harm-limiting acts unitl they translated help-extending gifts and grants--were good men and women engaged relatively more than absolutely in maximizing the greater evil and minimizing the greater good in the name of being right and doing good through actualizing the lesser of two evils rather than geater of two goods. They manipulated local, state, and national governments to secure resources to bring challengers of their ACS gospel to heel, and to heed its cost-conscious conscience.

In other words, the Evangelical Orthodoxy and Reformed Calvinist traditions initiated change and constancy in the color caste/captive crisis. The benevolent paternalists insisted their persistent critical imposition of the ACS' Halfway Piety deterrence-benevolence faith and ethics was neither spurious Moral Law nor specious positive law but the instituted law of God and man, the Bible and the Constitution, and, therefore, the right and righteous race reason and revelation.

Thus in the parochial effort to engineer the predominantly negative good Halfway Piety, to replace the positive good potential of Puritan Piety as the mainstream public-interest ethics, Protestant Colonizationists restricted the possibilities of the latter. ACS agents of virile Reformed-Orthodoxy managed to promote sacred and secular social ethics divisiveness in ecclesiastical and civil affairs, the sharp division between traditionally united faith and ethics of public-interest directed Puritan Piety, and to invite church and state ethical controversy in a spirit of rancor and dissension historically reserved for Calvinist faith issues.

By the time the Evangelical Moral Reform movement was crystallized in the ACS, it discovered itself to be at cross purposes with the secular motive and purpose of Unitarian Congregationalists' elevated ethical civility Christian idea and ideal--and one which Reformed-Orthodoxy Calvinists sought to contain in their own escalated sense of civil moralisms. The highest priorities of Evangelical Moral Reformers included purifying White and Black souls, and saving the approved social structures from rapid and fundamental change. These social conservative middle axioms and ultimate goals enabled the mid-antebellum denominational power institutions to be positively helpful to White folk and positively harmful to Black folk.

The liberalism of conservative Christian churches churchmen constituted catholic consecrated charity, and translated the religious humanitarianism complement of secular humanism, was evidenced in prolific Protestants' proliferation of sectarian higher learning institutions no less unmistakably than the conservatism of Protestant philanthropy was evident in establishment Protestantism's reduction of the color caste/captive system to a more curious than serious "peculiar institutionalization" of greater benign benefits than malign liabilities.

Antebellum establishmentarian proslavocrats' public defense of the slavocrats reached the height of paradox with those Protestants who asserted that the effectively adopted and adapted binary American Calvinist double damnation and Roman Catholic "Rule of Double Effect" Christian social ethics argued their case for social order over individual self-determination--or White folk stability over Black folk independence; there existed neither a real alternative nor a choice between universal and uncon-ditional immediate liberation of the Black masses and perpetuation of the civil peace and national security guaranteeing Black bondage system; and the systematic and systemic involuntary servitude is the lesser of two evils in the conflict between White freedom and order and Black liberty and justice.

High powered churchmen promulgated this social conservative premise as the promise and performance of the Catholic and Protestant higher law of obedience to civil and Christian authority than to civil and Christian conscience, which turned on concentrating the mind on consecrated charity as the medium of grace and salvation for the parishioner that permitted the parson to superimpose with impunity surrogate justice (principle) for *agape*-love (virtue).

Conservative Christian charity cultural determiners were as candid as they were confident they were a civics lesson. They communicated their constructive engagement in published promotions for public education where they stated the purpose behind absorbing the positive evil for Black folk and exposing the positive good for White folk inherent in the slavocracy was to produce a policy of containment that would keep the dehumanization acts of slave system within the range of tolerance.

Exactly in this posture the establishment churchmen revealed their two sets of rules, disclosed their as-sumption that the Protestant power elite possessed a right not only to their own opinion but also to their own set of facts, and inserted in the record that their impeccable credentials certified they were a body of public servants worthy of public trust.

In brief, the Moral Reformers asserted that their Moral Reform movement and agents were free of anti-Black race interest and proabolitionist contamination; quite without risk to faith and ethics but at once proslavocrat and antislavocracy churchmen both at liberty and under obligation to slavocrat Protestant brethren and their sister slavocracy Christian institution; and bound by duty as much as loyalty and honor to challenge on New Abolitionists on behalf of White Christian gentlemen slavemasters, because proabolitionists held antiabolitionist Northern proslavocrats' and Southern slavocrats' defense of each other equally offensive.

The Moral Reform collective body was the diadem of the Church-commissioned Protestant public works. As the jewel in their crown, the ACS appeared the brilliant symbol and substance representing effectually the joint Northern and Southern Presbyterian/Congregationalist will to promote the negative-intensive antiblack white-ethnic virtue of Colonizationist deterrence-benevolence, and the anti-Black race virtue of antiabolitionism.

Moreover as their highly negotiable pure pink pearl of great price, the ACS guaranteed the diabolical Halfway Piety White Gentlemen's Agreement. When this ACS Christian compact was signed, sealed, and delivered--and substituted Halfway Piety for previously restricted authentic Puritan Piety faith and ethics at the critical choice moment in church history for American Civil Religion agencies--all hope disappeared for the development and implementation of a sound plan that would initiate the acceptance of the Black race. In truth, the Protestant establishment was the only national resource with the capacity to spearhead this drive.

NEW LEADER OF YANKEE-PURITAN
HYPERORTHODOXY AND MORALISM

It would be difficult to discover a more representative powerhouse of the Congregationalist-Presbyterian/Moral Reform syndicate than the Reverend Lyman Beecher (1775-1863). This is the case because the New Haven-born, "Connecticut Yankee"-bred Presbyterian, and Yale-educated Evangelical Calvinist founder of the Connecticut Society for the Reformation of Morals, (1813) was an importunate organizer earlier--and consistent longer--than compeer members of his Moral Majority.

Following his graduation from Yale College (in 1797), and after undergoing a "born again" experience, Beecher was tutored in theology for nine months by influential Yale prexy Timothy Dwight: the successor in that post to President Ezra Stiles, who earlier shared with fellow Newport pastor Samuel Hopkins the Congregationalist nurture and development of Old Abolitionism among the clergy and lay members of Congregationalism; the scheme to ship the Black race to Africa as an Evangelical missionary people to the Black African ethnic groups; and William Ellery Channing.

Beecher dearly loved Dwight and defended his mentor: who was dubbed an old curmudgeon by antagonists who did not appreciate his uncompromising defense of the dead theocracy, aggressive leadership of the clerical offense for Federalism in the new democracy, and "intense moralism in theology."[36] Some of Dwight's critics took serious exception to his rejection of the philosophy and psychology developed by John Locke: the liberal Church of England lay philosophical theologian, whose empirical rationalism informed the theoretical and experiential principles of the philosophical-theology and psychology Dwight's grandfather Jonathan Edwards developed into an Evangelical Calvinist system.

Dwight preferred to the Edwardsean idealism the realism of Scottish Common Sense philosophy, appreciation of which he gained through communication with President John Witherspoon of the College of New Jersey at Princeton, and inculcated in the new "New Divinity" or "New Haven Theology" he founded.

Dwight changed the pace, pioneered a new direction, chartered a different course for Orthodoxy. Instead of advancing Edwardsean liberal idealism and countermarching genuine Puritan Piety toward greater realization he scotched both the Federal and Edwardsean Calvinist faith and ethics systems, and substituted his own revised Halfway Piety theology. He emphasized the weak and narrow limits negative good dimension of antiblack white ethnic virtue rather than its strong and broad social ethics suit, and replaced the tradition of positive possibilities enhancing Purity Piety when he established the negative legalisms and minor moralisms major verities of positive thinking Halfway Piety as the authorized revised standard version of the tradition.

Jonathan Edwards and Samuel Hopkins had directed their driving English (or Anglo-American) philosophical and theological idealism to challenge secular idealism, which Dwight rejected for the counterdemanding British premises and principles preached and practiced by the Scotch Irish. He exposed the Reformed and Orthodoxy traditions' common civil conservative Calvinism constitutions, whose social systems stabilizing values he accepted and sought through his own thought to further.

His national legacy is arguably so negligible a presence in the Evangelical Calvinist premise and principle promulgated by the European-American White Protestant middle-class as to be nearly imperceptible; and absolute presence as negative antiblack white-ethnic virtue cancelling the positive antiblack white-ethnic virtue inherent in authentic Puritan Piety faith and ethics and therewith its pure potency and potential (at the very least) for securing mutually fertile pro-Black race interests and pro-White race interests.

Admittedly far more latent than manifest, nevertheless this equalitarian idea and ideal surfaced rather than soared in the public servant Puritans Cotton Mather of Boston and Harvard and Samuel Hopkins of Yale and Newport. In their direct action as the public ethicists of Evangelical Orthodoxy, "Old Light" theological liberal Mather and "New Light" social ethics liberal Hopkins demonstrated the positive possibilities of Calvinist egalitarianism as clearly as they developed and bequeathed them to Yankee sons of the wayward worldly saints in a more underdeveloped or less undeveloped dynamic state.

When set in this context and perspective, "Connecticut Yankee" Dwight succeeded in undermining pro-Black race values with anti-Black race values--rationalized as disinterested will to the good of the color caste/captive class. He elected not to update and to upgrade his White and Black race cultural kingroup ties, and choose to ignore the color-intensive strings attached inherited Calvinism tying Black and White Calvinist kith and kin in a knot that Hopkins and Jonathan Edwards the Younger neither cut nor untied but loosened.

Doubtless these factors are far less important and apparent than Dwight's distinct legacy of antebellum era-enduring and lasting values, to with, the indelible impression and mark he left upon his most prized student--and Beecher's good friend and advisor--the Reverend Nathaniel William Taylor (1768- 1858).

Following Dwight's replacement with his post-Edwardseanism upon displacing in the Yale curriculum of Edwards' "New Light" and Edwardsean Hopkins' "New Divinity" (Hopkintonian theology, the Yale re-revisionist Evangelical Calvinist selected Taylor to be his successor as the official philosophical theologian of

286   CONSTITUTION, CONSCIENCE, AND CALVINIST COMPROMISE

Congregationalist "New Divinity"/"New Haven Theology." Taylor successively revised and advanced his mentor's narrow and negative sectarian, rather than broad and positive cosmopolitan, public moral ideas and ideals in what he defined as a "system of duties" authored by the "moral governor." The Dwight-Taylor or New Haven philosophical theology altered the Edwardsean Calvinist conception of God and faith far less than the school changed the meaning of Calvinist ethics as transformed and transmitted by Hopkins and Edwards the Younger.

Church-bound Dwight-Taylor ethics reversed the instrumental nature and purpose, as well as sacred/secular civil function of the Christian *agape*-love (virtue), power (parochial/private/ public politics), and justice (principle) social ethic that Jonathan Edwards left undeveloped as an approach in the small but powerful and beautiful ethics book he wrote in 1755, that was posthumously published in 1765 and entitled *The Nature of True Virtue*. Therein Edwards determines virtue is the distinguishing distinction of Christian faith and ethics--that is, TRUE VIRTUE is BENEVOLENCE or God BEING RIGHT and GOOD.

Edwards propounds the Protestant principle as his principal point: Benevolence (ethical right-justice and good-virtue) is the ethical nature of God, standard of human nature, and criterion of conscience. He argues the prerequisites of self-determination and moral value were essential for the development of the true nature of the human species, whose essence in existence he asserts in this descriptive fact-filled and value judgment-intensive volume is the demonstrable equivalence of manifest human being benevolence to BEING, to each human being, and to oneself. Alternatively stated, Edwards proclaimed rational and relevant thought and action is the true human being or demonstrable existence in essence.

But if Edwards and Dwight were not one in their substantive social ethics theory and practice--to say little of their ethical nature and its meaning in reality--they appeared to converge from their divergence in the matter of their major dysfunctional and minor functional value for the color caste/captive class: Effectively Edwards' parochial/private ethics revolved around nice nuances and the Dwight-Taylor public morality turned on fine points of law but their real differences were devoid of a distinction in repeating the history of perpetuating rather than propelling the White Man's Burden born by the Black man, upon whom English Orthodoxy and British Reformed faithful superimposed the destiny in history of double damnation as the double effects test and ethic their Calvinism.[37]

Beecher caught these subtle anti-Black race values as Dwight taught him the proper critical methodology, interpretive "Rule of Scripture," and "Rule of Truth" perspective in his study of the yet current Yale theological curricula-pervaded Evangelical faith and ethics works of three Yale alumni and sometime slavemasters, career-long Congregationalist pastors and theologians, and best professional friends: Edwards, Hopkins, and the Reverend Joseph Bellamy (1719-90).

The emerging evangelist was also schooled by these revivalists in the value of revivals springing forth in New England and reverberating throughout the region, as a result of the interplaying Western to Southern revivalistic Second Great Awakening outbreaks: whose commencement in the 1790s corresponded with the beginning of Beecher's career as solidly as the breaking forth of the First Great Awakening and Hopkins' conversion at Yale and Evangelical ministry positively correlated. Revivals were to be developed as both a rational principle and principal rational organizing method for Protestant sectarians, as well as a systematic and systemic formal and functional dual power generating medium. Revivals were not only routinely arranged annual local (Congregational or Presbyterian) church revival or renewal rituals for several generations, but also the spiritual power and moral power producing services from which Moral Reform associations sprang to life.

At the outset of the Second Great Awakening, Presbyterian Beecher moved from New Haven and relocated in Long Island, New York to accept his initial professional post as presbyter (1799-1810) of the "East Hampton and Freetown" Presbyterian Church. His national reputation as a revivalist and a Moral Reformer commenced in these communities, and skyrocketed after his crusade and published sermon against dueling--the Beecher solution widely disseminated and read throughout Calvinist circles as *The Remedy for Duelling* (1806).

Beecher attested in his *Autobiography* (1863), and last will and testament originally published in London during middle of the Civil War and the year he died, that during his New York ministry the "sight of a black audience" excited him and inspired the evangelist to preach continuously "to just such folks from 1800-1810." After he requested dismission from his office in 1809, on the grounds the pastoral support of the congregation was inadequate to meet the needs of the Beecher ménage, the "Connecticut Yankee" revivalist was attracted to Litchfield, Connecticut where the presbyter served as minister (1810-26) of the Congregationalist Church of Christ, and his direct involvement with Black congregants was less significant or at least noteworthy. Yet, even in the Connecticut Valley--albeit a region far less subject to cosmopolitan influences than his two previous habitations--Black folk remained out of his mind but never his sight as always. Litchfield-native Harriet Beecher Stowe, reflecting on her first sixteen years which were spent in her hometown, certified that her father encountered regularly at least one Black Connecticuter: "our portly old black washerwoman, Candace, who came once a week to help off the great family wash."[38]

Beecher's return to his native state put him in constant touch with "Connecticut Yankee" clergymen's distinctive unconcernment with the color caste/ captive class condition, and the investment of Calvinist capitalists in the Southern slave-based political economy. This disinterest was not due to their being either ignorant or innocent of the fact that the slave-labor generated profits of capital and revenues of the State of Connecticut had been growing, since the Revolutionary War, along with the proslavocracy real interests and values of New Haven proslavocrats. Their Connecticut parishioners and peers among the New Haven manufacturers, merchants, and farmers were selling to Southern urban slaveowners and slavetraders as well as plantation slavemasters their horsedrawn carriages, carpets, shoes, ships, beef, oats, and corn. Definitely by the time Presbyterian Beecher had switched to Congregationalism and secured his Connecticut Congregational Church of Christ connection and leadership, New Haven had become a favorite place for Southerners to summer--and Yale attracted aristocrats from across the nation.

Furthermore, the sons of plantation owners--a statistically number of whose class preponderantly were educated in England and France before 1776--experienced no quota and comprised nearly ten percent of the undergraduates at Yale in 1831, when thirty-one sons of Southern gentlemen were enrolled in a student population of three hundred forty-seven.[39]

Rich and famous as well as powerful slavocrat Yalies no doubt ascribed as first among equals the Reformed Calvinist John Caldwell Calhoun (1782-1850) of South Carolina, who graduated from Yale in 1804. Indeed Beecher, who received his undergraduate degree seven years earlier, later charged Calhoun incited Southern Presbyterians who with the Northern "Old School" formed a majority that ousted the "New School" from the once united Presbyterian General Assembly. Certainly for antislavocrat contemporaries, slavocrat Calhoun existed as the "Consistent Calvinist" descriptive fact and figure as clearly as he and proslavocrat Beecher persisted in the appearances as *God and Man at Yale* prototypes, and classic instances when perception is reality.

Several years prior to Beecher arrived to take up his duties as the Congregationalist parson in the small city, Calhoun studied law in Litchfield under Tapping Reeve (1744-1823)--who founded (in 1784) one of the first law schools in the United States--before the antebellum era and the representative British ethnic powerhouse became a model master planter: in the normal manner and typical traditional pattern included purchasing a large number of slaves and holding a greater number of united slave families than he divided and either traded or sold down the river. Calhoun ably represented the human bondage interests of the class of the Southern planter aristocracy in Congress; served as Secretary of War (1817-25) in the Administration of President James Monroe; and acceded to the office of Vice President (1825-29) under Chief Executive John Quincy Adams.

Beecher did not study positive law as formally as he studied and practiced church law and the Moral Law during his residence in Litchfield. Advancing in theory and experience, the ecclesiastical litigious litigator finely honed there an uncanny but not uncommon Calvinist capacity to present a brief; and to argue the case for causes he chose to advance with rational skill that matched for national influence the best work of many professional prosecutors and defense lawyers. Fairly described as the hierarch if not the bishop of Evangelical Yankee Orthodoxy-Reform moralism, Beecher stood between "old Pope Dwight" and his cardinalitial grandson, the Reverend Timothy Dwight (1828-1916): the silver tongue of "Yankee" negative antiblack white-ethnic virtue perverted into anti-Black race values, and pro-English/Puritan race-ethnic interests, who also served as President (1886-98) of Yale.

The Dwight/Beecher/Dwight ecclesiastical trinity passed for an informed and aggressive intergenerational moral power triune, and/or charitoteers who launched a color caste/capitive class (defensive rather less accurately than) offensive. Each charity charitoteer in his time--as well as turn at the helm of the church, state, and academy concentric circles of influence--drove the anti-Black race values-specific Protestant chariot through the nineteenth century. They were near equal hardliner hucksters of superior English/Puritan race worth, and the lively legalistic Calvinistical and moralistic puritanical coals they snatched from the dying fires of the powerful Calvinist Puritan culture. Arguably the third person in the trinity was the most bold and brash public promoter of pro-White/anti-Black raving rational romantic racialism, yet the archetypal triumvirate were near identical triplets in their color caste class condition-indifferent private and parochial intentions if not public consequences.

This perfunctory cultural and/or both rational and natural cause and effect appeared as necessary as it was instinctive for "Connecticut Yankee" "Consistent Calvinists" to equate English/Puritan-race values with noble virtues and *True Virtue*. Consequently, the high powered predeterminationists and high priests of the predestinarians, who proclaimed they knew evil and error when they saw it and that the truth is one, were inevitably unable and unwilling to admit evil/-error and therefore this truth claim: they had better reason to hope than to think consummate Calvinist capitalists translated into peerless Puritan philan-thropists do well and good always and everywhere at once as automatically as they acquire power and accumulate wealth.

Multiform varieties of similar disputable (not charges leveled at the saints but Calvinist claims and publicly pontificated) pretensions of Puritan pride and prejudice were based on indisputable Yankee capital, culture creating and deter-mining Ivy League colleges, and Federalist/Whig Party power. These and well-known complementary certainties that powerful Yankees published proudly were to their minds the only great realities, and utilizable resources for illumination remaining, which, of course, they used to generate as much moral heat as ethi-cal light. The trinity and their fellow Trinitarian Congregationalist crusaders for a stable color caste class were certain they had extracted the pure Puritan cultural values. Perchance with less humility than was warranted, they never doubted the perfect applicability of superior Yankee values even apart from the sacred/secular Puritan whole way of life--or the superiority of the Puritan Way of Life Yankees promulgated to the alternative Cavalier Southern Way of Life preferred by slavocrats.

These straightforward church/college/corporation/congress interlocking direc-torates pressed the status quo in lieu of appropriately downgrading the negative and upgrading the positive dynamics of the Devil/evil-driving and God/-good-expanding antiblack white-ethnic virtue heritage--relative to the new technology as well as political economy and thereby ecclesiastical and civil culture--or fitt-ingly translating and transforming in the process of transmitting and transferr-ing authentic Puritan Piety public faith and ethics in a post-Puritan Yankee world: of White race/ethnic and Black race cultural kin-groups requiring a con-text of grace nurtured in love to realize their kith and kin potential.

Positive good Puritan Piety power included in its arsenal of public ethics cast iron will power, that impacted subjects and pierced targeted foes like bul-lets. But in their fiery furnace firing hands it was melted like lead and poured drop by drop into two Half-way Piety casts: where it solidified in one mold as negative good lead shot ethics, and in the other as deterrence-benevolence flesh and blood burning prods. While the heat these ethical instruments produced left a superficial and transitory mark analogous to a sun tan on the skin surface of White folk, these branding irons were pressed and held at length upon the wh-ole anatomy of the human bondage class. It necessarily seared a deep and per-manent impression upon the Black body, mind, and soul: which Evangelical spir-itual and moral human experimentation experience as often as not was followed by chilling comfort.

Doubt concerning whether these Yankee Calvinistical and puritanical estab-lishmentarians positively associated their Puritan values with strictures vanished when, in a perfect translation of John Cotton's *Moses His Judicals: An Abstract of the Lawes of New England as they are Now established* (1641), Beecher not only described but defined the culture-long positive negation thrust in the title of his paradigmatic sermon on *The Bible A Code of Laws*. He managed, unwit-tingly of course, in the cool and crisp clarification of the teaching of his Half-way Piety tradition to demonstrate conclusively that therein the negative good and positive limits ethics were not the minimum but the maximum virtue or as far from the maximum vice of values as conceiveable; and that Halfway Piety moralists' accentuation of the negative to the point of eliminating the positive public good of the outcast human bondage and the color caste class were the result of a rather more constrictive than constructive interpretation of the Bible and the Constitution.

His negative good parochial or private intentions and public consequences most of the eleven children he fathered, and many other contemporaries, made plain and explained in Lyman Beecher Stowe's *Saints, Sinners, and Beechers*. But Lyman Beecher and his cohorts effectively pioneered the analysis of deconstructionism, advanced their strict construction conclusions in a Yankee conversion of Puritan Piety into Halfway Piety faith and ethics, and interlinked manners and morals as differences without a distinction. There resulted a revision of Dwight's revised authorized equation of ethics and moralisms, and one their critics called the new standard version of puritanicalism.

Thuswise Protestantism-pervasive Evangelical Calvinism-specific old and new hyperintensive anti-Black race values, quantum leaping throughout the antebellum era in tandem with surging Puritan hyperexclusivity, surfaced, soared, and survived slavery, the Civil War, and Reconstruction. This American Protestant peculiar phenomenon, and version of the universal Western Church perversion of *the spirit* of Jesus (the Christ and/or the meaning and measure in history of the Christian faith and ethics for Christians), is one singular infectious and contagious cause and effect of the color caste cultural *malaise*.

The enduring race/religion reason and revelation related presence, constituting the culture-created ca-pacity of the capacious Christian charity and caprice confusion, in reality relative to the Yankee Calvinist continuum of the Calvinist Puritan norm at once re-vealed the *Scarlet Letter* sign and symbol to be by contrast a matter of comparative pale significance.

In this direct connection, Beecher expressed with unchecked verbal profluence a singular infallibilism when he proclaimed his Yankee negative moral monism was equally like and the improvement of the positive/negative two-dimensional antiblack white-ethnic virtue-coordinated Puritan New England values; the one ray of truth; and the only way to social reform and refinement. Beecher was the host in himself of the masterful Evangelical Yankees who were convinced these truth claims made the difference that turned the Puritan "Bible Commonwealth" into "the most perfect society," and dedicated their active professional life to the rebirth of the values.

Lyman and Roxana parented three sons and two daughters during their East Hampton ministry, and were expecting Harriet when they decided to act in line with their calculated conclusion that the pastor's salary budgeted by the Presbyterian Church did not increase commensurate with the growing inflation, rising cost of living, and expanding Beecher household. Concurrent with his struggle to earn a decent living, the East Hampton community was not conducive to his growing ambition and actually restricted his opportunity to launch there a forceful assault upon what the combination Puritan culture reactionaries and Evangelical Calvinists agreed were barriers to the reinstallation of the tried and true moralisms in America's nascent national social order.

Forward from the commencement of his Litchfield ministry, especially Trinitarian and Unitarian Congregationalist clergy and laity in the community and throughout Connecticut characteristically respectively emitted a fully developed appreciation and depreciation of the Evangelical Calvinist warriors' aggressive crusade for Christ and civility. Anti-Calvinist varieties of religious humanitarian churchmen and secular humanists perceived as un-American the pro-Calvinist's conceived pro-American values equivalence of his pro-establishmentarianism and antidisestablishmentarianism, positive attraction of good (verity/virtue or morality), and positive negation of evil and error (vice and immorality).

These moral principles were not abstract but concrete affirmative action ideas and ideals of the social conservative establishment agenda, enveloped without being exhausted by controversial sacred and secular vectors intersecting in the civil sector, and revolved around color caste-bondage-preclusive White race/ethnic class-specific conflicts of interest: such as unrepentant rigid commitment to puritanical morality; state instituted churches; and Federalism. Beecherite values--produced between the virtue and vice ends of his inflexible Moral Reform device--reflected and reinforced the autocratic respective Presbyterian and Federal central church and state government power and authority, no less than the sacred and secular Federalism coordinates of the ecclesiastical and civil powers.

The parochial and public moral monism united and moral power divided monocrats for a moral monocracy and aristocrats for aristocracy demonstrated the strength and weakness of Federalism advocates. Their stiff competition and sharp conflict of interest as adversaries guaranteed the permanent demise of the Puritan patrician theocracy no less than the Anglican aristocrat theocracy, expedited the eruption of the Democratic Party out of the Federalist Party and accelerated the corollary rise of democrats from the divided Republicans/Federalists, and precipitated the growth of the residual binary bonds of Northern and Southern proslavocrat proponents of static aristocratic and patrician order: from whose expansive extension of mutually fertile ecclesiastical and church law and reason developed systematic and systemic republican democracy and slavocracy.

Pro-Calvinist powerhouses and the anti-Calvinist power elite managed to mask their conflict of real interests and values with finely honed and skillfully shaped differences they drove like wedges deep enough to split the outcaste subject and object, to sever the captive/caste mind and soul, and to bury the Black body and spirit beneath conscious concernment instead of each other (the White race and ethnic classes). This continued until gnawing greed and great grit girdled their just *amazing grace*, and galvanized a counter-culture creative minority who emerged a countermarching heightened consciousness: demanding a new cultural consensus composed of individual and community common sense, conscience, and courage of convictions.

First and foremost at Litchfield, in keeping with what appeared to his survivors in the Reconstruction era a post-theocracy unshifting fidelity to the theocracy that set a precedent for the unshrinking Confederacy allegiance of post-Civil War Southern Confederates, Beecher stepped out of the front ranks to lead the opposition to the increased Connecticut presence of Episcopalians.

Beecher was unprepared to accept the fact that he could no more prevent the nineteenth century out-growth of Episcopalianism--from the old Manhattan Northeastern center of Anglicanism along the expanding New York/New Haven axis and urban/suburban corridor--than fellow Yale alumnus Samuel Hopkins could curb the eighteenth-century extension of the Church of England in Great Barrington, Massachusetts fifty years earlier. This was the case as certainly as Beecher considered himself no less falsely accused than Hopkins believed that, like his mentor, Edwards, he was unfairly charged with the ecclesiastical crime of preaching "New Divinity" Calvinism by the Reverend Charles Chauncy (1705-87).

Edwards and the Edwardsean essayed to be responsible reason and revelation ratiocinators, but were held liable for inciting the populous to religious riot and outrageous spiritual exhibitions in public by the Harvard "Old Divinity" apogee in Boston. Whether Yale or Harvard Congregational Clergy were the true "Consistent Calvinists" in the post-Edwards years of their conflict and competition for the soul and body of the Church of Christ, Chauncy determined that the denominated "New Divinity" or Hopkintonian theology that Hopkins developed and proclaimed pure Edwardseanism was sheer error corrupting truth.

And as positive prove of the accuracy of his accusation ajduging Hopkins culpable, Chauncy, who matched his adversary as a litigious litigator, asserted that Hopkinsianism was so revolting to birth-right Congregationalists and enemies of Anglicanism that they fled in droves from the Great Barrington Church of Christ and--if not to the Church of England in that Congregationalist place--created the vacuum filled and opportunity taken advantage of by priests from whom the fathers of the parsons transmigrated from England to escape. In this time and space, Chauncy argued, Hopkins was the culprit cause and effect of the Anglican extension and expansion in the New York-bordering small town near the western edge of the Commonwealth.

Beecher's formal education took place in the momentous period of English and American Independence, when the disinclination toward Puritanism of the master merchants and plain people concerned with their commercial interests converged with the agnostics' attack upon Calvinism to shake the foundations of the new Yankee-Puritan Federalist Party establishment; and to drive the Calvinist clergy out of Federalist Party partisan power politics and historic confines of the "instituted churches." The Calvinist ministers did not fall prostrate. They grew imaginative in their use of revivalism. Evangelical evangelism's secular dynamic and civil order-impacting power potential secularists ignored at their peril, in the long range if not the near term, as certainly they misperceived and underestimated the necessary public connection of the church and state in the republican democracy.

While Dwight-led partisan party power parsons survived him in a poor posture, and with their backs against the wall, in that period of beleaguered Federalism and state of seige for the Federalist Party they redirected their will to power in concentrated church sectarianism and aggressive Evangelicalism.

Ecclesiastical power politics were the positive possibilities and viable alternatives to civil policies provided by the Second Great Awakening, whose Congregationalist Halfway Piety rational determinants Timothy Dwight broadly sketched for his strategic and tactical disci-ples. Consequently, although out of power and authority in the civil sector, the Connecticut Calvinists were not degenerating in theological disputes--or simply generating their own power for their own exclusive use. Ministers advanced as parochial servants rather than public servants of the people with the nineteenth century. They directed with increasing bureaucratic expertise and technocratic competence the resources created by the revivals in parochial-monitored private and public works.

But as a source of towering optimism and vanishing pessimism, post-Dwight Calvinist Evangelicalism ignored his pro-political re-revision of the anti-political Edwards revision of the Calvinist Puritan vision; turned their back on the challenge inherent in accepting the responsibility to engage creatively in the new politics inherent in the tradition they pro-claimed they preserved; and flatly rejected Puritan Piety public interest ethics and embraced rigidly the Halfway Piety Jonathan Edwards superimposed when he suspended the sacred and secular civil order tradition public servant Cotton Mather advanced.

While it is clear that Federalist Party era partisan parsons were not encouraged to change from the old politics (in which forward from Governor John Winthrop's pastor and "chief theocrat," John Cotton, the power and authority of civil advice and counsel inhered in the office of the parson) to the new process of being elected representatives of the people. It is no less certain that they were neither forbidden nor prohibited by law from becoming professional politicians.

Since rejection seldom if ever deterred a Puritan Yankee who possessed the courage of his convictions, it was scarcely due to being discouraged by secular humanists and religious liberals that partisan parsons chose to avoid campaigning for public office; to call American pragmatism a diabolical innovation of the ancient politics power game and politics an immoral profession; to retreat under pressure less precisely than to cut and run rather than to risk defeat; and to put the best face possible on this worse decision imaginable by denouncing power politics to the public a curse without a cure, while simultaneously pronouncing their unwelcome in the business of bargaining values a blessing in disguise.

In other words, the problems of their Federalist Party were turned into excuses to abandon the conflict and competition, and not into power politics opportunities, essentially because they fastened upon the viable alternative of Evangelicalism which the Second Great Awakening presented them: whose abundant possibilities included instant gratification.

They deserved to be credited for discerning immediately that liberty and politics were not the only new frontiers challenging the bold and brave rugged individual because they were there to explore, expand, and/or exploit. Along with the unknown dimensions of the social sphere, the free market, capital enterprise, and the physical universe, the unexamined parameters of the spiritual world emerged as an exciting field to forage. The inconstancy of spontaneous religious combustion and recurring mass evangelism meetings among the masses was one constant experience of the eighteenth century. Orthodox Calvinists continued to believe the revivals were the mysterious movements and acts of God in history--and therefore the authentic people's movement. In their version of power to the people, the religious were the true majority--with and through whom the Church militant would inevitably become the Church triumphant in the world.

In short, pure profane civil political and economic power and pure pious ecclesiastical political and moral force diverged from the identical Puritan source and converged as optimistic belief in linear moral progress, whose leadership was provided by the same Puritan sons of Puritans in their different modes of being secular and religious Yankees. These church and state citizenry connective linkages were not dysfunctional surviving appendages of the theocracy. They were functional coordinates in democracy and slavocracy of American Civil Religion and the body politic.

Precisely in these spheres White Christian citizens cooperated in cultural and social affairs. Secular and sacred heroines/heroes and heretics intersected with their moral and immoral individual and community rights and responsibilities in the common civil society, where stabilizing the status quo structural order and domestic tranquility was elevated as their highest priority value--just beneath life and above liberty. Hence the Christian *agape*-love ethic, and the secular humanist ethic of justice, were diminished in their capacity to enrich their separate and distinct but mutually com-patible social ethical natures, capacities, and obligations.

CLASSICAL BLACKNESS PURIFICATION POLITICS AND RELIGION

An uncanny intuitive understanding of the direct opposite rather than diametrically opposed Protestant Puritan work ethic and puritanical ethic empowered Beecher. His logical direction of their productive connection and counterproductive disconnection patterns, and efficient use of their natural and artificial attraction and rejection configurations, enabled the masterful moralist, opportunist and master of possibilities, to generate the spiritual and moral power need, create the desire, and supply the demand.

A no less real if equally obvious key to success proficiently manipulated by the highly skilled intentionalist ethicist, and expert manager of parochial people and problems as well as priorities and systems, entailed comprehensive command and control that the rational moral power produced from his precis-ionist contraction of the positive element and expansion of the negative component of antiblack white-ethnic virtue.

This evidenced strict constructionist social conservative morality apparently took fundamental shape during the progressive transformationist's undergraduate years (1793-98) and subsequent professional studies with President Dwight at Yale, and evolved toward a crystallized perversion of positive antiblack white-ethnic virtue into hardened negative antiblack white-ethnic vice. The positive negation power device shaped scalpel sharp spiritual tools and blunt moral instruments to be used by more rationally trained than organized highly efficient evangelists and skilled professional revivalists operating upon thousands of American hearts--entirely confident they performed successful spiritual and moral soul transplant operations as promised. The operative critical factor in the Beecher faith and ethics method was the hardcore moralism (crowding out ethics) handed down from Dwight. Beecher moralistic rules and regulations turned into laws that integrated the Edwardsean philosophical-theological-psychological unifying theme of millennialism successfully, and altered its logistics drastically.

The lofty "*Apocalyptic Vision*" Evangelical Congregationalism inherited from Jonathan Edwards and Samuel Hopkins was not transmitted but transmogrified and foreshortened. This accomplishment the post-Edwardseans achieved by advancing the critical time for churchmen to storm the kingdom of this world for the Kingdom of Christ is at hand rational organizing principle of the Edwardseans on the one hand, and, on the other hand, by introducing a counteractant to the Edwardsean anti-political central dynamism perforce mixing religion and morality with politics in both the ecclesiastical and civil power sectors during the early national era; primarily only in the ecclesiastical power sphere preponderantly throughout the antebellum decades; and finally moving the two from divergence to convergence on the eve of the Civil War, prior to returning to the one-dimensional church politics essentially but not entirely forward from the Reconstruction era.

Beecher demoted the positive and promoted the negative force of antiblack white-ethnic virtue that, as he understood and promulgated it, subsisted of the imperative moral conversion of each "born again" and non-reborn person to sobriety, propriety, decorum, order, and temperance. This equation of moral truth with moralistic truth claims featured moralisms as the standard of virtue as frequently as the moralists insisted upon legislating morality and demanded a "*Blue Law*" against Sabbath-breaking, theatre-going, card-playing, and intemperance. Beecher's early analysis of the immoral public dictated the corrective action conclusion he acted upon to make a moral difference throughout his long and puissant career:

> Our institutions, civil and religious, have outlived domestic discipline and official vigilance in magistrates which rendered obedience easy and habitual.[40]

The Presbyterian Congregationalist clergyman was primed for Moral Reform leadership and encouraged to initiate rational and rapid radical moral structural change of the individual, after concluding that "the laws are now beginning to operate extensively upon the necks unaccustomed to the yoke." Beecher stated that he acted to "preserve our institutions and reform the public morals" in line with the major civil order mandate of the clergy, and chief objective of the ecclesiastical moral "Yoke" he pressed upon the public and argued required reinforcement by the civil authorities if not civil law enforcement to raise the standards effectively.

General knowledge of the issue that Beecher resolved to answer reduces the range of recollection required to recall appropriately the commonplace for context to pinpointing why critical contemporaries claimed Beecherites appeared part of the problem fully as much as part of the solution.

(A) Alcohol was the boon of labor and bane of capital in the industrial revolution centers of "Old and New England"; (B) management contended that alcoholism was the real rather merely the alleged single source and its cure the simple solution of the workforce's poor productivity; (C) in actuality, monotonous assembly line tasks plus bad pay and worse working conditions were not the precipitating causes of the working-class use of the drug as not merely a-pleasure maximizing but also a pain minimizing narcotic imbibed to relieve the drudgery and survive the miserable employment and existence; (D) just as persistent antislavery moderates and proponents of gradualism, just so con-sistent Beecherites demonstrated their solid social conservative credentials in failing to concentrate on the cause and choosing to focus on the effect; and (E) thereby, as antiblack white-ethnic virtue advocates of Temperance (abstinence as the solution to sin), Moral Reformers blamed the victim alcoholic and intoxicated lower-class for lowering the community standards of moral purity and monetary productivity (a day's work for a day's pay) or the virtue of work (slave-labor and wage slaves as well as slave wages for free-labor), and diminishing the profit-making capacity of capital by indulging their habit that was counterproductive to the maximizing efficiency and minimizing costs *sine qua non* of the wealth-producing means and end of capitalism.

By the natural moralist's similar simple private moral approaches to complex public ethical issues, congenital reverence for the Puritanism and Calvinism expressly filtered through Dwight into puritanicalism (convoluted antiblack white-ethnic virtue). It was dictated by private priorities and his confusion of public interest ethics with preferred parochial morals and manners, individual style and fashion, and personal taste and values.

They were developed in the presence of a plethora of choice for the fortunate few, but when Beecher came face to face to live options he did not believe were real alternative to his Puritan-specific Yankee lifestyle he challenged deviant behavior everywhere he discovered "profane swearing," "traveling on sabbath," and "drunkards" who "with entire impunity" daily "reel through the streets."

To his mind these private acts appeared perilously close to barbarism, feeding and fed order-destablization, and culture-corroding attitudinal and behavioral modifications. They were not simply symptomatic but paradigmatic parallels of indecent public exposure prompting insidious civil disobedience, ceaseless conspicuous consumption and sensational sin, and disorderly conduct. These personal pleasures and for him poor tastespecific preferences so offended his decency and decorum sensibilities that he felt impelled to eradicate what he determined to be positive evil and error, caused by neither cultural nor societal conditions but their provided right choice being overridden by the individual consciously making the wrong choice.

In this strangely strained moderation mode and mood for a professional moderate, the leader of the Evangelical Protestant power elite trained his undivided mind and will to sustain the charges of the secular power elite social drinkers. They countercharged that, unlike the color caste/captive culture *malaise* Beecher managed to tolerate by refusing to recognize its serious conflict and competition with the Constitution he declared the height of high Christianity and civility, social drinking and the social disease of alcholism created in the industrial revolution age by the wealth-producing and wealth-acquiring Protestant or Puritan Work Ethic rather less precisely than the Calvinist capitalistic and manufacturing system (as clearly as the distilleries produced alcoholic beverages and the industry made them not only easily affordable and accessible for labor and management but plentiful and profitable for capital) so affronted the Puritan-specific cultivated taste of the Yankee Calvinist revivalist that Temperance took hold of his patrician senses.

Preoccupation with the social symptoms of and personal solutions to the triple White ethnic problems of poverty, ignorance, and disease, that he treated as the greatest human harm because alcoholic beverages were equated with the diabolical, provoked Beecher to organize to beat the Devil whose spirit materialized as demonstrable fragrant violation of cultural stability and social order.

From this identification of the worse kind of dehumanization the predictable followed in Beecher's reason and race relations, and finally meant that free and open serious consideration of the true and real values of his Black-race cultural kin-group was automatically ruled out of his hierarchal arrangement of Christianity, civility, and civil order priorities--along with other possibilities for the healthy reorganization of society.

He essentially directed his moral energy and the energies of Orthodoxy's officialdom neither to secure either liberation for Black bondage or freedom in liberty and equal access to opportunity for free Black folk nor for direct action in line with the best known right and good interest possible of the Black race. The social consequences of his intentions such as his alternating benign and malign neglect desires and designs resulted from the fact that his negative good and strict limits-revering morality functioned to render positive good neuter; and to delay the available and required resources for fashioning precision instru-ments that could correct the societal causes of the immoral individual effects he found so despairing.

But he was less concerned with approaching the harm-intensive social conditioning nature of human bondage, and the culture-induced White and Black derelicts from the experience of the victims than with (A) eliminating the physical predicament by throwing the baby out with the bath water; (B) spiritual salvation of infidels, pagans, prisoners, drunkards, and all other members of this "Reprobate" class; and (C) regeneration of the "Elect" backslider.

These basic conceptions and perceptions of the protypical Moral Reformer were set in concrete perspectives at least as early as the first decade of the nineteenth century. Beecher's Presbyterian social ethical ideals were translated into Congregational-working public moral ideas during the Presbyter's Congregational ministry and participation in the 1812 annual consociation of the Congregational General Association of Connecticut. Beecher was particularly interested in the clergy group the ministers assigned to assess the state of domestic morality the parsons were charged by the civil community to secure.

Upon hearing the chairman report progressive regression, and that his committee concluded nothing could be done to reverse reality howbeit regrettable "that intemperance had been for some time increasing in a most alarming manner," Beecher "rose instanter" and called for a three man committee he volunteered to head "to report at this meeting the ways and means of arresting the tide of intemperance." The next day, Beecher recalled a half century later, he read on the floor of the supreme judicatory body the report that evangelist called "the most important paper that I [he] ever wrote":

> Immense evils, we are persuaded, afflict communities, not because they are incurable, but because they are tolerated: and great good remains often unaccomplished merely because it is not attempted.

> If the evil, however, were trivial, or the means of its prevention arduous and uncertain, despondency would be less criminal... Let the attention of the public, then, be called up to this subject. Let ministers, and churches, and parents, and magistrates, and physicians, and all the friends of ci-vil and religious order, unite their counsels and their efforts, and make a faithful experiment, and the word and the providence of God afford the most consoling prospect of success.

> Our case is indeed an evil one, but it is not hopeless. Unbelief and cloth may ruin us; but the God of heaven, if we distrust not His mercy, and tempt Him not by ne-glecting our duty, will help us, we doubt not, to retrieve our condition, and to transmit to our children the previous inheritance received from our fathers.

> The spirit of missions which is pervading the state, and the effusions of the Holy Spirit in revivals of religion, are blessed indications that God has not forgotten to be gracious.

> With these encouragements to exertion, shall we stand idle? Shall we bear the enormous tax of our vices--more than suf-ficient to support the Gospel, the civil government of the state, and every school and literary institution? Shall we witness around us the fall of individuals--the misery of families--the war upon health and intellect, upon our religious institutions and civil order?

> To conclude, if we make a united exertion and fail of the good intended, nothing will be lost by the exertion; we can but die, and it will be glorious to perish in such an effort. But if, as we confidently expect, it shall please the God of our fathers to give us the victory, we may secure to millions the blessings of the life that now is, and the ceaseless blessings of the life to come.[41]

Beecher commanded complete knowledge of New England religious history, including apprehension of the inescapable detail that forward from the first English settlement in the Northeast benevolent societies in the Northeastern region had originated nearly invariably in England with English and British Protestants. He also knew the exception proving the rule, to wit, the Newport scheme cultural Calvinist values social ethics engineers Samuel Hopkins and Ezra Stiles concocted: pursuant to which his elder fellow "Connecticut Yankee" clerical brethren interlaced in a parochial and private public consequence-laden Evangelical matrix antislavery, foreign missions, and colonization sentiments.

At his finger tips abided further accessible information concerning the conceded fact that contemporary Evangelical Anglican and Independent churchmen's moral reform initiatives involved dual dedication to British Abolition and Temperance. But Beecher opted to retreat from the proabolitionism forefront; to engage in rear-guard antiabolitionism; and to fight on the "intemperance" front lines to raise the Temperance standard, and to force "total abstinence" from a matter of personal freedom of choice into not only an absolute parochial dogma and pragma rule of law but also a pre-Prohibition public policy or even positive law and order of the land.

Beecher's selective civil engagement and disengagement and segregation and integration of pure power politics, religion, and morality was not entirely based upon either nostalgia or an exalted view of an earlier symbiotic relationship between church and state in Connecticut. This is evidently the case albeit arguable or even demonstrable that in his testament of the correspondence between the ecclesiastical and civil powers Beecher inadequately assessed the legislative votes cast against clerical interests in the 1790s:[42]

On election day they had a festival. All the clergy used to go, walk in procession, smoke pipes, and drink. And, fact is, when they got together, they could talk over who should be governor, and who lieutenant governor, and who in the Upper House, and their counsels would prevail.[43]

At least as early as the commence of his professional career the time had passed when "ministers were all politicians," and "always managed things themselves," Beecher averred with little regret. In reality, the transition of the secular state and sacred church politicians from the old theocracy to the new democracy in Connecticut was relatively smooth and on track. Connecticuters ratified the Constitution on the advice and counsel of establishmentarian Federalist Party partisan clergy and layman, who initially engaged in *realpolitik* policy making "on the same level" as Connecticut entered the Union.

The deliberate development of the English-race rep-resentative parson and parishioner Federalists' new alliance for power and authority, that his mentors such as the Dwight brothers symbolized as the vanguard of the secular humanist and religious humanitarian professional politicians, was aborted by the sharp political rise of the British-ethnic immigrant "civilians." Beecher recollected in his memoirs that new White ethnic electorate embraced Jeffersonian Democracy, changed their loyalty *en masse* and pledged allegi-ance to the Democratic Party, and grew in influence as Democrats who opposed not only "the Federalist Party" but specifically the "influence of the clergy" and their like-minded "deacon justices" who enforced the "Sabbath Laws."

In truth, as a "Consistent Calvinist" who revered the church and state united model John Calvin established in Geneva and the *Institutes of the Christian*

Religion, Beecher preferred power politics but ecclesiastical and civil conflicts of interest inspired him to make his secondary choice (professional parochial politician) the primary political field of endeavor. And it was only after the clerical Federalists were challenged by anti-clerical Democrats, and refused to meet the stiff power politics competition, that Beecher discovered in retreat or defeat the virtue of necessity: whereupon he declared his new-found power of persuasion demonstrable necessity of virtue.

Beecher rationalized calling a solid retreat and defeat victory or vice virtue by the skillful employment of descriptive facts and figures--whose statistics were relatively interesting while the value judgment they masked was absolute: and no where with greater misdirection force than when he certified that almost instantly after the Connecticut disestablishment the "ministers and churches, by the voluntary system, recovered, and stood better than before."

Beecher switched from the dual ecclesiastical and civil power politics course Dwight correlated with spiritual and moral power to church politics and Moral Reform measures easily: partly because he chose not to compete with the secular who were replacing the sacred lawmakers at the helm of the Connecticut State Legislature and thereby contributed to the defeat of the Federalists by the Democrats, whose triumph he at once anticipated and did everything in his power "to avert." Once resigned to accepting his own self-fulfilling prophecy and philosophy, he began to prepare for a secular and civil power politics-free but sacred and sectarian politics-intensive morality through the "association of the leading minds of the laity with us in counsel":

> They say ministers have lost their influences; the fact is, they have gained. By voluntary efforts, societies, missions, and revivals, they exert a deeper influence than ever they could by queues, and shoe-buckles, and cocked hats, and gold-headed canes.[44]

INSTITUTIONALIZATION OF VOLUNTARISM AND

VOLUNTARY ANTI-BLACKNESS IN THE CHURCHES

Proabolitionist crusaders were engaged in direct conflict and open competition for the hegemony of rational and relevant social and personal moral truth with antiabolitionist warriors, and therefore academic impartiality was no more their central business than mathematical fairness was the primary mission of their opponents. Pursuant to validating their value judgment, New Abolitionists compiled massive quantities of descriptive facts which they were satisfied argued their final value judgment and made their critical point stick--namely, that New England regional and national Yankee Halfway Piety faith (puritanical moralism) and social ethics (deterrence-benevolence) proponents advocates majored in rational and radical rapid individual revolution (conversion) and minored in community transformation.

Whatever questions remain from this assessment of antiabolitionists by their combative proabolitionist challengers, one that does not is the incontrovertible fact that their pro-gradualist adversaries were formi-dable advocates and professional implementors of Evangelical-Calvinistic "New School" theology, revivalistic techniques, and organizational skills. Calvinist establishmentarians demonstrated conclusively their prowess as they attracted parishioners--possessing the power and authority of peerless economic wealth if not comparable political influence--and united them with parsons in voluntary associations to em-

power missionary, reformatory, millennial, and benevolent societies.
Beecher fully developed these Evangelical Calvinist unifying principles and practices during his Litchfield ministry. Forthwith the *tour de force* was either a director of or indirectly involved in nearly every one of the parochial-private-public partnerships and associations for Moral Reform the major Protestant establishment denominations authorized and supported. Being by definition and convincement antiabolitionist bodies, they excluded pro-immediatist societies and included their enthusiastically promoted pro-gradualism ACS on principle.

For example, the varieties of Moral Reform associations and board of directors Beecher either served on or enjoyed direct access to and influence within included cultural change and correction church corporations such as the American Board of Commissioners for Foreign Missions (1810); the New England Tract Society (1814), from which evolved the American Tract Society (1823); the American Education Society (1815); the American Bible Society (1816); the American Sunday School Union (1824); the American Society for the Promotion of Temperance (1826); and the Boston Prison Discipline Society.[45]

According to the consensus conclusion confirmed by a preponderance of professional church history scholars, Beecher's status among the Protestant culture determiners and interlocking directorates spiraled from the earned reputation and credibility he gained following the publication of his *Six Sermons on Intemperance* (1826).

In this brilliant Protestant problem and solution publication, Beecher advanced rational strategies and tactics that became prototypes for the Temperance movement, and won him wide acclaim as the stellar Evangelical Moral Reformer.

Beecher was a "New School" Presbyterian complement of the Congregationalist "New Divinity" Calvinists in the constantly revised and updated but always discernible Yale Divinity School Evangelical Calvinism. His Reformed tradition-specific social moral power chassis may have been out of alignment, but its suspension was no less well-connected to the School's ethic of deterrence-benevolence.

He began--and nearly ended--his useful life as a national figure committed to as committed to the dual Foreign Mission and Domestic Mission ASC project, that had serious social consequences for the color class/caste class. Beecher was no where more earnest and honest than his dedication to ASC's deportation of the Black North American race to Africa major goal, end of the beginning of the regeneration, missionization, and colonization antislavery mission and chief objective generated by and at the beginning of the end of the foremost Puritan-Congregationalist Old Abolitionist theologians: Samuel Hopkins, Ezra Stiles, and Jonathan Edwards, Jr.

Beecher developed into an uncommon rationalist as well as rhetorician and logician in the Evangelical Calvinist-specific theological liberal and social conservative revivalistic mold, whose pattern of evermore and greater successes--through immediate transformation of the individual with its rewards of instant gratification. He doubted his stellar strings of victories would be broken in the systematic and systemic process of engaging and disengaging Black folk selectively in the church sector and attempting in the civil order to exclude and include the Black race.

Enslaved and free Black Calvinists presented a fundamental challenge to reorganize the basic structures of society that Beecher cherished because they were stable and secure. Beecher appeared less completely confident realization of the rising expectations of Black folk was entirely remote and rather more threatened by the prospect of liberation; resisted their anticipated achievement of color caste/captive abolition because he discerned the ways and means to this end to be in direct conflict and competition with his preferred real interests and values; and bethought the motive and purpose of radical social *status quo* change reprehensible.

In this inflexible public ethics judgment and rigid posture, Beecher epitomized the unconcernment of the American profane and sacred establishment with sharing values such as fairness and equity with the Black race--before and after their temporary acceleration of reverse values on the way into and out of the Civil War and Reconstruction eras--and the determination of the Yankee power elite to work their normative desire and demand as well as individual and collective will of the people in or out of ecclesiastical and civil political office.

The not so crystal clear color caste/captive condition disinterest interconnection between the majority of White Northerners and Southerners, Easterners and Westerners--whose vital links the non-deviant attitudes and behavior of Beecher tightened--were as strong as the complementary magnetic forces of denominational evangelism and sectarian revivalism; moral reform church societies; and personal benevolence contributions to the commonwealth. These parochial-orchestrated, public-limiting, private-directed potent charitable acts--and often as not generous expressions--of positive antiblack white-ethnic virtue were implicit bad faith and explicit good faith efforts.

Their reason/revelation-replete race religion and rhythm of deliverance from evil was alternately beyond belief, above reproach, and beneath respect as demonstrable positive human bondage in perpetuity principles rather than social redeeming values. Precisely their intrinsic anti-Black race interest-specific intent, content, and portent values were defended as nonexistent interests they appeared extrinsic realities.

Beecher and the Evangelical Protestant Moral Reformers were intelligent and educated men of expanding capacities--and extensive inducements--who felt called and accepted the challenge to secure and stabilize the millenniarian and evangelical resurgence, as the demonstrable superior ecclesiastical relative to the inferior civil power in the universe. These Evangelical power dynamics, and derivatives of the ultimate millennium faith and ethics, made Protestant performers more than facile rhetoricians flying by their instincts, and in the face of Black-race folk disproportionately suffering when compared to White-ethnic folk. Divided English-race and British-ethnic sectarian groups united in Evangelical Calvinism.

As classical conservative Calvinist ethicists, their confidence and arrogance sprang from the undebatable and unexamined premise of the Constitution, and into the power principle Protestant principals argued with the truth and logic to superimpose as the civil rule of reason and law: North America is the White ethnic individual's inheritance, a White man's country, and one to be directed by and for the English-American race and British ethnics, their descendants, the other immigrants they chose to grant citizenship.

This pro-White race/ethnic interpretation of history and management of reality Protestant powerhouses issued in the new age of industrial technology and industrial capitalism, that attracted the rising tidal waves of immigrants, who made once affordable Black folk too expensive for White Connecticuters and other Calvinist capitalists to treat fairly and squarely.

And this Pro-White race sense of destiny transmitted to the new White-ethnic transmigrants made their proliferating Northern Christian-humanitarian societies, and the aggressive slavocracy expansionism advocated by their Southern White brethren in church and state and business and social affairs, harmonize and conflict.

Of course this ying and yang cultural effect was only partially caused by the reaction of Northern and Southern churchmen to their Black cultural kith and kin. They appeared expendable obsolescence for Puritan patricians and indispensable to Anglican aristocrats, and their regional brethren of the cloth and class, in which different Yankee and Cavalier reaction to Black bondage they illuminated the difference in degree so great that it was nearly a difference kind of Black race interest indifference. But in mutual and splendid insouciance, beguilingly arrayed as magnanimity, their execution of human bondage experimentation rites and exercise of spiritual and moral power exploitation rights to plunder Black Christians--for entirely different near term short-sighted goals and long range ultimate objectives--were in fact and in total effect variously civil and uncivil dehumanization means and ends.

Powerhouse denominationalist activists preached and practiced conformity but were anything but an unenlightened and simple-minded body of uniformity. Protestant humanitarians offered the handicapped, hungry, and homeless something more than soap, soup, and sleep. At once promoters of special interests and multi-issue rather than single-issue reformers, they most certainly were for benevolence and not simply against sin, chaos, and ignorance. On the contrary, Evangelical humanitarians vigorously supported what they determined to be the good of the social order. In pursuing rigidly their inflexible premises, priorities, and principles they were as serious in their purpose and sincere in their intentions as they were generous to a fault with their deterrence-benevolence.

However, this characteristic negative good temper, tone, and tenor made their major default monumental--that is, the primary expenditure of their extraordinary wisdom and resources was limited to promoting parochial principles, policies, and programs that were directed toward solving nearly every social problem save the pressing issue of liberating their Black cultural kin-group from caste and bondage. Contrariwise, synchronously, both English-race and British-ethnic Northern Christians denied they inherited their Black race-specific and deethnicized body, whose American dilemma they did not admit e-ven as they made every attempt to resolve the contradiction by organizing to finance arbitrary acts of Black body banishment or vanishment.

In place of mystery and the mystical elements of benevolence, pervading Jonathan Edwards' White Christian-race/ethnic *Nature of True Virtue*, Halfway Piety post-Edwardseans substituted white magic or Western reason in the concentrated form of rational deterrence-benevolence. The Occidental empirical rationalism logic and method of manipulating signs and symbols as well as substances appeared indistinguishable from black magic to Black folk caught between a rock (democracy) and a hard place (slavocracy).

If anything, the all-White leadership cadre of Colonization Society turned professionals and specialists in executing Black race disappearing acts. To the minds of White and Black New Abolitionist Manhattanites they were as credible as current Broadway magicians' sleight of hand and eye coordination performances.

What Halfway Pietists orchestrated poorly was the positive and negative components of their antiblack white-ethnic virtue. It entailed avoiding error and opposing evil, knowing and doing good, and being benevolence (the bare essence manifest *Nature of True Virtue*). They issued forth instead pro-White race values joined with anti-Black race values, whose virtue of double damnation subsisted of first deethnicizing and deculturalizing Black folk, and then deporting the entire body from their homeland.

Their union of ethical opposites to create dynamic neutrality can be explained as unques-tioning acceptance by the electorate of the establishment Puritan-Anglican heritage. This is not to say that the minority of male and female citizens who elected to form a counter-culture movement challenging the validity of the Americanization of shared anti-Black race values, which majority rule made the law and order of the land, were either imperceptible or a lonely and powerless voice crying the wilderness. It is rather to indicate that White and Black New Abolitionists were also necessarily smitten rather than possessed by establishment anti-Black race virtue, as they struggled against this private affliction to reverse its being evaluated as praiseworthy and further extended as the real values and interests.

Black Calvinists had never been a Puritan race priority. Yet the Evangelical Yankees preferred to their advancement to ensure the declining rather than inclining significance of the positive possibilities potential inherent in the authentic Puritan Piety politics-intensive tradition. Jonathan Edwards was the standardbearer of Halfway Piety post-Edwardseans reversed and then followed and revised. His unconcern with politics for politics' sake was exceeded only by his lack of concern for the Black race for Heaven's sake.

It is useful to recall that Cotton Mather, in his role as Evangelical Calvinist Puritan public servant and messenger, never received the credit he deserved for having the courage of his convictions and to risk failure, but was stoned because the Boston citizenry did not like his message and their descendants declared his endeavor wrong-headed.

Hence unlike Puritan Piety model Mather, neither the "Old Light" Congregationalists who succeeded him and followed Charles Chauncy in Boston, nor "New Light" leader Edwards and his grandson Timothy Dwight who led the Yale post-Edwardsean movement away from the Edward-seans, sought true moral reform of the secular order with church resources. Beecher was in the mainstream of his establishment tradition, and reached maturity as an antiabolitionist during the last days of the venerable Old Abolitionist "Connecticut Yankee" Congregationalist-clergymen.

One clear meaning emerges from the variable vectors of the tradition the Moral Reformer engaged as a disciple of the Yankee sons of the Puritan progenitors. Beecher was not incapable of advocating the best interest of the Black race. He simply preferred his priorities and forthwith elected selective parts of the Puritan heritage, and to equate them with the whole, whereby he chose to affirm the tradition's millennial dogma and pragma and to deny its double predestination doctrines.

While he proved the undeveloped and abandoned authentic Puritan Piety potential to be dead in the establishment traditionalists, Beecher was equally instructive in the perception where he materialized, by turns, the reformer White knight in shining moral armor, the sharp seller and bargainer of antiabolitionism in the market place of social values, and a striking figure who not only added perspective to the contrasting image presented by competing proabolitionists but also illuminated the integrity of these both conscience-heightened and unconventional "born again new beings" in whom Puritan Piety was being reborn.

Finally and foremost, the absence of disinterested will to the good of the

Black race in the American presence--or the national treasure as his admirers preferred to call Beecher--was a revelation of an essential part rather than the manifest essence of pure Puritan culture. Yet even in exposing the dual dynamics of Puritan Piety unevenly, as a result of making its negative good propensities perfectly clear and remarkably obscuring its positive good potentialities, Beecher disclosed that the Puritan spirit is autonomous sacred and secular cultural phenomena; either/or both can overpower and exist independent of the original Calvinist theology and ideology constituent element; and can be the common religious and secular moral power transformer competing Halfway Piety and Puritan Piety custodians of the multiform tradition can access to empower their countermovements.

Given these juxtaposed parameters at this turning point in the interpretive American Christian Social Ethics essay, it may be serviceable to recall that Beecher possessed sufficient means and opportunity but not motive to take serious note of what the Black Calvinist clergymen brethren and leadership corps of Black Connecticuters determined to be the best known possible right and good interests of the Black race, the social conservative eminence of New Haven and his Moral Reform constraints to the contrary notwithstanding.

LEONARD BACON: "NEW SCHOOL" ORTHODOXY'S

MAJOR MORAL REFORM BENEVOLENT BUREAUCRAT

Synchronous with Beecher's departure from Litchfield for Boston, the Reverend Leonard Bacon (1802-81)--a recent graduate (1826) of Andover Theological School and disciple of Moses Stuart (its major professor)--arrived in Connecticut to succeed Nathaniel William Taylor (upon his appointment to the new Yale Divinity School that was established for him) as minister (1826-81) of the First Congregational Church of Christ in New Haven.

Bacon--for whom Stuart functioned effectively as not only mentor but the model predecessor of Taylor as pastor of First Church Bacon--would himself become Presbyterian Beecher's Congregationalist ally director of the currently ten years-old ACS that fellow Calvinist Ralph Gurley ably served as chief executive officer, and other Eastern denominational boards when Beecher migrated from Boston to the Mid-West.

Prior to acceding to the New Haven post, and during his years as an idealist theologue, Bacon was employed as a researcher (1822-23) by the Boston Society of Inquiry for Missions, for which agency he developed and published his analysis and conclusions "On the Black Population in the United States." Three years later, and six years before Beecher wrote his famous Plea for the West, Bacon preached as one of his first homilies in New Haven the sermon entitled a *Plea for Africa (July 4, 1826)*--which he delivered previously as an address in Boston.

Later that month, in Bacon's office at First Church, four young White male Congregationalists joined with him to create two societies: an Antislavery Association, and the African Improvement Association. Existing in defiance of the New Haven custom if not positive law proscribing mixing Black and White inhabitants in public affairs, the African Association initially comprised an "expedient" White majority who were to assist the Black minority leadership in the development of an United African Congregationalist Congregation.

The separate Black Congregationalist congregation was inaugurated by Nathaniel Joceylyn's brother, a New Haven native and Yale graduate who earned a modest fortune as a commercial engraver in their enterprising partnership, the Reverend Simeon Smith Jocelyn (1799-1879). Neophyte evangelist S. S. Jocelyn met frequently with Black New Havenites to promote spiritual regeneration and moral welfare in their segregated community. Learning of their dream (which began as early as 1820) of an independent congregation, he remained after graduation to assist them in its materialization.

A quarter of a century earlier, the Congregationalist General Association of Connecticut created the Connecticut Missionary Society (1798) "to christianize the Heathen in North America." After the Congregational-Presbyterian Union (1801) and the Massachusetts Missionary Society sent (during the year 1812-13) the Reverend Samuel John Mills, Jr. (1783-1818), and the Reverend John Schermerhorn (1786-1851)--following their joint authorship of *Communication Relative to the Progress of Bible Societies* (1813)--to estimate in the West the ways and means for the Associations to "support and promote knowledge in the new settlements," the Massachusetts and Connecticut Societies joined to form the consolidated and Presbyterian-connected Congregationalist American Home Missionary Society (1826).

At the final stages of preparation for official confederation, in 1825, the New York-based A.H.M.S. selected Simeon Jocelyn to be one its first urban missioners and commissioned him its missionary to Black Congregationalists in New Haven. Previously he was one of the four White male architects of the Antislavery and African Associations for Black Calvinists originating in pastor Bacon's study, and later served as the founding minister of the Black congregation whom he helped to organize as the New Haven Temple (remamed Dexter Avenue) Street Congregational Church.

Along with the intensity of his Domestic Mission commitment, Jocelyn's respect for the Black race increased as he evolved into an authentic New Abolitionist. Correspondingly, Foreign Mission-minded Leonard Bacon devolved from a liberal antislavery moderate into Gurley's pro-Colonizationist cohort and an inflexible antiabolitionist. While Bacon was moving rapidly toward the center of the social conservative Evangelical establishment, proabolitionist Jocelyn was as swiftly and firmly repelled to its periphery. In 1828, after two years under the heel of Connecticut anti-Black race militancy, Detroit-Born Bacon concluded that the New Haven "People of Color" were "branded with ignominy" by "Connecticut Yankees"--and the victims of seemingly instinctive discrimination and segregation in all walks of life, from the cradle to the grave.[46]

This first-hand knowledge and experience of the discrimination inflicted upon the Calvinist color caste/captive class--whose excruciating pain he did not believe they should suffer gladly in North America--was a contributing factor to his rapid development from a convicted to a convinced pro-Colonizationist. Bacon brought his mind to his heart and fastened his will to eliminate neither the cause nor the effect but both the object and subject of anti-Black race vice. In this mood he sought from and was sought after by Gurley, in his post as executive secretary of the Washington, D. C.-headquartered ACS, and accepted (in 1828) a commission from the directors to be the New Haven ACS agent. Forthwith the young New Haven leader advanced with the Protestant power elite, who were marching lock-step as a deterrence-benevolence offensive unit.

Also in 1828, the ACS initiated plans for a school to train Black North Americans to become missionaries and teachers in Liberia. But, as in the case of the presage and precedent setting 1776 plan originated by Samuel Hopkins, this parochial and sectarian education project failed to attract a requisite number of students. The Society floated this quasi-education trial and error as an experimental educational model for the nation. Its instructional plan pivoted around educating young Black exslaves, from their earliest years, who were manumitted to the Society on the condition American Colonizationists would transport them to another country. Deportation of the Black race comprised the single purpose of the Society, and thus the sole intention and objective of providing Black free (or freed) Americans with a modicum of instruction was to further this mission of the Foreign and Domestic antislavery agency.

Simeon Jocelyn sponsored a different plan--initiated by a Black colleague--for the higher education of free-born and freed Black residents in the North. He envisioned a Black American college near Yale that would provide equal access to opportunity automatically the Black males whom it prepared to compete in a system based on fairness and equity. Naturally, being a proponent of the excludable Black race parochial principle and policy, Bacon rejected out of hand this higher education plan Black folk initiated and White folk chose to fund.

He defended his anti-Black race interest advocacy by arguing the identical facts and personal knowledge that inspired the Reverend Ebenezer Baldwin (1790-1837), Beecher's fellow Yale graduate and "Connecticut Yankee" as well as colleague Congregationalist pastor, to attest in a published text that the class of New Haven was too "prejudiced against the mixture of the two classes of population" to insist that the Black race was an indigenous North American group; assist Black folk in gaining equal access to competitive opportunity; and tolerate the liberation Black human bondage without demanding simultaneously their colonization elsewhere.[47]

COLONIZATIONIST AGENCY DIRECTING THE INTERESTS
AND PROGRAMMATIC FUNDS OF WHITE PROTESTANTS

"Immediatism!" was the national battle cry of New Abolitionism that Garrison sounded. It rang in Bacon's ear like a call to arms. And the pro-immediatism alarm deepened his reverence for gradualism and loyalty to colonizationism, along with his dedication to developing a disciplined cost-conscious social conscience that he continued throughout the balance of his long life and ministry in New Haven.

This cautious social ethics stance was the moral public posture mutually endorsed by his good friends Nathaniel Taylor and Lyman Beecher--but not for long by Simeon Jocelyn and Arthur Tappan. Presbyterian layman Gerrit Smith, the philanthropic millionaire from Western New York, who, successively, severed his ties both with the American Colonization Society in 1834 and the Presbyterian Church with its schism in 1837, and spent a substantial measure of his fortune on reform causes like John Brown's radical solution at Harper's Ferry in 1859, appeared to Bacon simply too great a financial loss to the ACS not to challenge to reverse his decision. Consequently, communicating his Moral Reform theology and ideology in letters published in the *Religious Intelligencer* (1834)--that Garrison remarked revealed to his mind the "jesuitism of his reason"--Bacon wrote in the identical Yankee-Congregationalist moral meter that on this Puritan score found Beecher and Channing phrasing differently the same gradualist melody.

Advocates Beecher and Channing of establishment old Puritanism and new Congregationalism might be prominent theological adversaries differ imperceptibly (if at all) on the ethical public principles and processes, springing from their mutually embraced and unexamined social conservative *Great Chain of Being* philosophy--and ethics of permanently predominant and subordinate races, ethnic groups, and classes. This common foundation of their social conservative ethical premises and practices undergirded the anti-Black race ideology and idolatry Puritan patricians overtly denied and covertly affirmed.

Bacon's significance as a establishment Moral Reformer is revealed in his adversarial advocacy of antiabolitionism. In this role the religious lawmaker in ecclesiastical legislative and juridical bodies demonstrated--in making and ruling in order moral laws proscribing instant universal liberty from human bondage--that he was a prisoner of his own rhetoric who made more news than sense.

The Congregationalist ra-tionalist and legalist was too solid a litigator and too sound an oral Moral Reformer not to learn from the testimony of a cloud of unimpeachable witnesses for the defense of proabolitionism. But the logic of pure reason, positive sacred and secular conservatism, was turned into a sharper rationalistic mechanism for deception than for critical analysis of the solidity of the premises in which--like Channing and Beecher--Bacon grounded his unchanging antislavery principles, rules, and regulations.

He managed selected statistics well enough "to prove that our southern slavery is wrong, if only the reader is gifted with a moral sense." But not having learned the relevant facts--or to relate them to his values--he was persuaded by the irrelevant data to draw the wrong conclusions and value judgments, and to forego any thought of attempting real risk-intensive such as endeavoring to root out of New Haven its systemic and systematic institutional anti-Black race values. As a consequence of better common sense than ethical principles and priorities, he settled for joining compeers committed to rout out Black folk whom they would provide a prepaid all expense-free ticket and route one way to Africa.

In the light of his assessment of the good and right, he was a goodwill rather than ill-will benevolent paternalist advocate of brutal benevolence. Like his fellow Northern proslavocrat and Southern slavocrat deterrence-benevolence moralists, Bacon did not consider the ideas of the color caste/captive leadership class seriously, and/or think of these brethren of the cloth much beyond what he thought he knew to be best for them. Contradistinctively, the established fact that White-ethnic immigrants were his primary positive and Black-race natives his secondary concern is understandable. Bacon argued the antislavery analysis and antiabolitionist conclusion regarding the slavocracy, it adjudged that the "wrongfulness of that entire body of laws, opinions and practices" is one regrettable thing, and the proabolitionist way to "rectify that wrong" another reprehensible thing. Without objection from establishmentarians, Bacon summarized the heart of the matter by asserting that the slavocracy error cannot be corrected, as New Abolitionists insisted, by stressing "the criminality of the individual master."

Taking pen in hand to make the point in the Congregationalist *Quarterly Christian Spectator* (1833), Bacon addressed his article on "Slavery" to the Presbyterian-Congregational Plan of Union members, to fellow Calvinist brothers and sisters in the united denomination identified as the peculiar "hereditary masters of bondmen, or who live in the midst of a slaveholding community," and to Northern churchmen.

The latter he anticipated would relocate in the Cotton Kingdom--since he recorded as informed speculation the observation that "thousands of the natives of the north" are "continually becoming citizens of the south." Bacon's New

Haven experience accelerated his fully developed appreciation of this intersectional intercourse, and left little serious reason to question his credibility or his accuracy in interpreting his first-hand knowledge:

> We at the north, are fellow-citizens with slaveholders; and between us and them, as fellow-citizens, there is, and must be, a constant intercourse. We and they not only meet by our representatives in the national legislature, but meet personally, both in our part of the country and in theirs. Many slave-masters are associated with us, in our various benevolent and Christian enterprises. Often individuals from among them, brought either by business, or in pursuit of health, come in and worship with us in our temples, or as members of sister churches, sit down with us at the table of the Lord. Not less often, one and another from among us, finds himself carried by his business, or is driven by disease, into those parts of the country where slavery prevails; and these slaveholders not only offer him the civilities of ordinary hospitality, but, if he is a professor of religion, invite him to worship with them in their families and in their temples, and to commune with them in all religious ordinances.[48]

As an exemplary colonizationist, gradualist, and outspoken opponent of human bondage in principle, an-tiabolitionist Bacon was a model throwback to the Old Abolitionist Congregation-alist-clergymen who differed from the New Abolitionists basically in terms of the different means that justified their disparate ultimate ends. Bacon brings to bear "the great principles of Christian morality"--and "a scriptural inquiry respect-ing the morality of slavery"--upon the slavery question as though it were an academic religious and secular matter, and an intellectual and moral issue of consequence only to White folk.

He holds in abeyance the anti-Black race interests-specific burden he was so acutely aware Black New Ha-venites had to grin and bear. As a direct re-sult of this counsel of patience and perfection he advises Black folk to heed, Bacon minimizes the systemic color caste evil preceding and succeeding as well as pervading slavery in the North and the South. He could not believe that even if it were possible to eliminate the intractable phenomenon, it could not be terminated by the full achievement of the impossible ultimate objective of either the simple moral abolition of bondage or the unmixed colonization solution. Color caste and class enduring values were considered a White problem of the will and spirit, well-known, and left alone by Baconesque types: in contrast to the system of slavery that mid-antebellum Evangelical denominations finally addressed as a matter of institutional concernment.

NEW AND OLD PURITANS: RESPONSES TO

BIBLICAL AND CONSTITUTIONAL SLAVERY

After setting forth a compressed exegesis of Old Testament legislation and polity as the center piece of his compact essay on "Slavery," and advancing his updated Calvinistic "Rule of Scripture" and "Rule of Truth" in an applied eisegetical interpretation of the Deuteronomic statutes, Bacon reaches his climatical point underpinned by a modern version of the traditional Protestant twin premises, to wit, the Bible is the literal and inerrant Word of God or divine truth, and the juridical law and order Moses composed was established "for Israel by Divine authority."

It followed in his logic and life from this hermeneutical principle and interpretation of the evidence in the sacred Old and New Testaments, predictably, that the right of human bondage and righteousness of slavery constitute the special prerogative and privilege as well as governance rule and regulation for the "chosen people of God." Hence it neither provides a warrant for either an involuntary servitude culture and a slave-based political economy or institutional slavery nor sanctions individual indulgences in the American domestic slavetrade system.

At the high point of his article, Bacon bids his "southern readers to compare their *code noir* with the slave laws of Moses," and challenges Northern "extra-zealous abolitionists" with the absolute certainty they will neither defy his logic nor deny his truth claim nor fail to conclude with him that Moses did not "peremptorily forbid and abolish" slavery "on the plan of immediate abolition." In the persuaded Moses-established sacred and secular as well as ecclesiastical and civil powers-functional both Moral Law and Dueteronomic Code ethical perspective of the proslavocrat and anti-slavocracy churchman, who wrote to promote procolonizationism and to convert his antislavery and proslavery extremist adversaries to this moderate position and solution Bacon guaranteed would enable them to escape through the middle by riding both horns of the color caste/captive dilemma, slaveholders were admittedly an offense yet not "to public sentiment, but to the law."

In keeping with his crusade for Christianity and civility and against brutal physical cruelty, Bacon admonished Southern Christian slavocrats to imitate his Moral Reform principle and practice; to cease and desist from continually lobbying for statutes and other legal means "to fortify the system"--and strengthen the "exercise of a power so absolute, so odious, that nature stands horrorstruck at the bare description," to say nothing of its "limitation against righteousness, against compassion, against religion"; and to enact positive legislation after the design of Moses.

The precedent Mosaic and Dueteronomic statutes he proposed for slavocrat lawmakers to model their positive legislation after would translate the Moral Law were slavocrats to enact laws that would (A) grant Black human bondage "their freedom" gradually; (B) authorize instruction of slaves entailing strictly supervised and limited to enabling them "to read the Word of God," and (C) "relieve the helpless and protect the defenseless."

A "New Side Congregationalist" pro-gradualist leading a counteroffensive against the pro-immediatism warriors, Bacon was sanguine that his pro-Colonizationist prescription was not value-free, value-neutral, irrelevant in the New Abolition era, or, as affirmative action antiabolitionism, the missing link with Revolu-tionary era Puritan Old Abolitionism. On the contrary, he claimed his proposal was a perfect translation of the Independence era Old Abolitionism that both Northern and Southern Old Abolitionist creative minorities advocated. This error he propounded as the truth Bacon presumed conferred instant credibility to his remonstration against the New Abolitionists.

According to Bacon's averment, the injudiciousness of proabolitionists was universally empirically verifiable and evidenced in Garrison's declarations--and no where more accessibly than when he asserted that in condoning slavery the American Constitution was beneath contempt. Bacon reminded the informed majority, and informed the uninformed minority of his readers, of the profound difference between antiabolitionists and proabolitionists by quoting accurately Garrison's notorious deduction: the Founding Fathers negotiated a White Christian Gentlemen's "agreement to act in opposition to the principles of justice."

But Bacon ignored the interpretation of the Constitution that was generally accepted by the South and specifically ruled the law of the land by his Connecticut neighbor, Justice Charles Daggett of the Supreme Court of Errors, that allowed Black residents to be slaves and free or freed inhabitants in Connecticut but not citizens.

A careful consideration of the accepted prerogatives and privileges of liberty automatically granted to new arriving White-ethnic immigrants and withheld from free-born Black Connecticuters, along with other rights and responsibilities of freedom and equity, might have induced him to re-think the adequacy of his activism in the Black community. Such an evaluation could have heightened his consciousness of the depth of dehumanization suffered by the color caste/captive class, the unfair social system, and the only high principle for a moralist publicist to preach, teach, and practice: the primary and immediate ethical need to amend the Constitution first and foremost in order to eliminate the White race/ethnic-only citizen and Black-race non-citizen laws, rules, and regulations. But he preferred living out his fantasy to being rudely awakened to the absence of real alternative to this prodigious undertaking.

An intentionalist moralist turned temporarily a utilitarian consequentalist ethicist to secure his real interests and values, and because demanding self-serving pro-White race priorities overriding serious consideration of the true and real interests of the Black race made it expedient and convenient to suspend the "Consistent Calvinist" rule, Bacon was less complacent than content to denounce the "agitators" who cursed the Constitution--and "the memory of all the framers of that august compact"--whom he proceeded to lecture on the facts in an interpretation in which nothing is lost in translation: (1) the Union was founded by striking a co-equally "undesirable" and necessary proslavery Constitution, that entailed a compromise of principles by the proabolitionist Puritan only and not also the antiabolitionist Anglican Founding Fathers; (2) the benefits of the White Protestant male's "cause of liberty and human happiness" to humankind "over all the earth" outweigh the price of perpetual human bondage and preclusion from citizenship paid by descendants of the Black Patriots in the Revolution; and (3) the deepest comprehension of this justification by faith in the righteousness of the Union New Abolitionists can gain by reading the Bible's "concessions to a hard-hearted and stiff-necked people, which are interwoven with the law given to the Hebrews by the inspiration of the God of love."[49]

Bacon not only addressed himself to New Abolitionists--whom he knew to be Christian men and women almost without exception--but he did so in the garb of a superior biblical and constitutional scholar. While he focused on the right to rule, what concentrated the mind of his real and imagined opponents was their engagement in instituting the rule of right as the right rule that counterbalanced the Baconesque critical imposition of the right rule as the rule of right and righteousness. Proabolitionists' commitment to libera-tion rather than to stabilization of the ecclesiastical and civil law and order redounded to their being too knowledgeable of history and current reality to be stymied by Bacon's prior interest in establishing the higher law of order than self-determination or liberation from dehumanization. They were too well informed to be fooled for a moment by his clever logic, which he fastened upon the proslavery laws of the

Bible and the Constitution to attribute to the sacred covenants the reasons of his heart.

Doubtless a model unprogressive moderate, yet, ironically, Bacon approached the Bible and the Constitution equally reverently and differently as respectively dynamic and static docu-ments, and argued for a liberal interpretation of biblical laws and a strict constructionist interpretation of civil laws. This selective progressive and regressive social ethic matched the social conservative moral theory and practice of the ACS as unequivocally as Bacon confidently maintains that Article IV, Section II of the 1788-ratified Federal Constitution--that he understood provides for the retrieval of fugitive slaves from free states--"is necessary to reclaim a runaway apprentice," and "will be indispensable after slavery shall have been abolished":

> No person held to service or labor in one State, under the laws thereof, escaping into another, shall, in con-sequence of any law or regulation therein, be discharged from such service or labor, but shall be delivered up on claim to the party to whom such service or labor may be due.

Bacon is equally impeccably logical and certain that the constitutional provision creating the Black man (or precisely every slave) "three-fifths" of a person--in an act of compromise designed to achieve proportionate or disproportionate representation in Congress by giving the slave states the advantage that accrued from thuswise counting each slave--was in point of "fact a motive to the abolition of slavery" that will "one day have a powerful operation": because, his irrefutable logic and questionable presumption led him to believe slavocrats would see and secure their real interests once they appreciated the point that the elimination of slavery will change each Black male from three-fifths to a whole person, and by this two-fifths additive the "now slaveholding states" will gain "immediately fifteen or twenty additional representatives."

Clearly Bacon assumed that the slavocracy was un-appreciative of this enlightened self-interest nice nuance, but discerned and determined there was no advantage in the universal emancipation he considered an advantage and certainly no disadvantage compared with slaveholding. The antiabolitionist found hope in the knowledge that Christian and non-Christian slave-holders were civil persons, and too gracious to release their slaves upon the society everywhere at once. New Abolitionist adversaries were not persuaded by his pro-gradualist arguments in lieu of any evidence that slavemasters were keeping Black folk their chattel property as the most efficient means to prepare them for freedom.

Still no less persuaded by the power of reason than the gradualists, the immediatists were united in the belief that oral suasion was the best and most effective moral means to achieve their abolitionist objective; although a division in the house of abolition led pro-politics proabolitionists to add direct political action to their arsenal of equalitarian de-mocracy. And these political abolitionists' moral turn to the political arena was committed with a mind to change the United States Constitution rather than to honor the slavery compromise.

They had become convinced that a period for training slaves for freedom may have been a live option in the past--and an effective one behind closed household doors--when the Puritan interest was distracted more by theology than by policy. But, New Abolitionists averred, it was no longer possible, necessary, or acceptable.

Correspondingly, immediatists were satisfied that the beauty of the Constitution flows from its self-contained provision for revision. They understood the republican genius of the democratic process to be plain and simple realism: nothing is settled until it is settled justly. Above all, for the "New Abolitionists," given the fact that the compromise of Black race existence in essence by means of which the Constitution was fashioned and ratified expressed the near-unanimous will of the establishment South (and at least the consensus of the establishmentarians in the North), the certitude solidified that slavery was a fundamental motivation of the Union. This meant that "a motive to the abolition of slavery" did not exist in the slavocracy and therefore they had to create one. In sum, it was exactly this determination which the Bacon doctrine of expediency and error of deception confirmed.

The New Abolitionists set about reconstructing the events surrounding the compromise that proved fatal for so many living and dead North American outcastes. The radical reversal of the rules essay of these rational revolutionists, was designed to sharpen their offense by turning their ideas into bullets that would penetrate the defenses of the uncommitted; lay waste the powers of proslavery advocates; and drive slavocrats with the force of reason-empowered moral power intoo rational retreat and defeat. In the early antebellum development of their strategies and tactics, the New Abolitionists recalled the nature and function of the Old Abolitionist vanguard.

One among them was Timothy Pickering (1745-1829), the Salem, Massachusetts native, lawyer, and member of the Massachusetts Correspondence Committee (1774-75), that, along with compeer organizations in her sister colonies, called the First Continental Congress at Philadelphia (1774) for united action against the British. Commissioned a colonel in the Massachusetts militia, Pickering rose to the rank of quartermaster general (1780-85) in George Washington's army.

In this post Pickering relocated his domicile in Pennsylvania where he assumed several positions in government, before returning to Massachusetts to be elected United States Senator (1803-11) and Representative (1813-17). Pickering wrote from Pennsylvania (on April 7, 1783) a letter to Samuel Hodgdon in which he suggested that the Continental Congress purchase from the Indians a tract of land in the Old Northwest as a reward for officers of the army, whom he proposed as settlers. The heart of Pickering's communication concerned the Old Northwest, as a result of the Treaty of Paris (1783) ending the Revolution and establishing the sovereign new nation had become a Territory of the United States. He recommended immediate organized settlement of the Territory, with the proviso that "total exclusion of slavery form an essential and irrevocable part of the Constitution."[50]

Pickering's early proposal that abolitionism form the constitutive element in the Americanization of the Old Northwest did not come to fruition prior to the successive years during which the four states, claiming portions of the Territory, surrendered their claims to the United States--and thereby measurably strengthened the Federal Government: New York-1780, Virginia-1784, Massachusetts-1785, and Connecticut-1786. On March 11, 1784, the Continental Congress appointed Thomas Jeffer-son to chair the committee assigned to write the governance ordinances for the Northwest Territory. The committee returned with several including one on slavery that ignored Pickering's advice.

Jefferson proposed ordinances that were passed by the Continental Congress (on April 23, 1784), and remained operative in the thirteen "Disunited States" for three years--exclusive of his slave clause: "After the year 1800 of the Christian era there shall be neither slavery nor involuntary servitude in any of said States, otherwise than in punishment for crimes, whereof the party shall have been duly convicted." In a letter (April 25, 1784) to James Madison, Jefferson described the context in which his antislavery provision failed:

> The clause was lost by an individual vote only. Ten states were present. The four Eastern States, New York and Pennsylvania, were for the clause; New Jersey would have been for it, but there were but two members, and one of them was sick in his chamber. South Carolina, Maryland and Virginia voted against it. North Carolina was tied, as would have been Virginia, had not one of its delegates been sick in bed.[51]

Pickering communicated his response in a letter he forwarded to his fellow Federalist Rufus King (1755-1827)--currently a Massachusetts delegate, prior to relocating in New York where he was elected one of the state's first two United States Senators--on March 8, 1785:

> In looking over the act of Congress of the twenty-third April last, and the present report of an ordinance relative to these lands, I observe there is no provision made for ministers of the Gospel, nor even for schools and academies--the latter might have been brought into view; though after the admission of slavery, it was right to say nothing of Christianity. To suffer the continuance of slaves until they can be gradually emancipated, in those States where they are already overrun with them, may be pardonable, because unavoidable, without hazarding greater evils--but to introduce them into countries where none now exist can never by forgiven. For God's sake, then, let one more effort be made to prevent so terrible a calamity.[52]

Old Abolitionist Pickering understood why slavery might not be outlawed in the forthcoming Constitution, and he also knew that slavery would extend automatically to the Northwest Territory without a ratified contrary clause. On March 16, 1785, King submitted to Congress a resolution that excluded slavery from the Territory. But it was summarily rejected, as were two equally unconditional proslavery resolutions. King was not to be entirely denied, since he had worked on the draft of the Northwest Ordinance--and was largely responsible for its carefully drawn antislavery compromise that was adopted unanimously on July 13, 1787:

> There shall be neither slavery nor involuntary servitude in the said territory, otherwise than in punishment of crimes whereof the party shall have been duly convicted; provided always, that any person escaping into the same, from whom labor or service is lawfully claimed in any one of the original states, such fugitive may be lawfully reclaimed and conveyed to the person claiming his or her labor or service as aforesaid.

Complementarily, King and his compeer Old Abolitionist Puritans tried his best to keep the Constitution completely free of proslavery clauses. But they were outnumbered Federalists who preferred the Union to any alternative, and thus elected to accept the White Gentlemen's agreement to exclude Black folk from their private and parochial public compact. Certainly the South won more than it lost in the bargain. With its threat to secede from the "Disunited States"--before the Colonies could construct a Constitution the states could ratify and form the United States--the South had wrested a proslavery compromise.

The Constitution evolved a Union that turned on the "states' rights" pivotal point of law and conscience that appeared sharp enough to bear the weight of the right of the thirteen original colonies to the civil contract to determine the legitimate or illegitimate legal status of Black bondage in its sovereign state. Declaring the superimposition of dehumanization upon the Black race and the preemption of Black folk self-determination, as well as the preclusion of the Black male from the franchise and citizenship, among the legal "states' rights" effectively reduced *"the spirit"* of "76"--and *Declaration* "that all men are created equal"--to pro-White race/ethnic superhypocrisy and hyperexclusivity.

The Constitution legalized the cancellation of the color caste/captive individual and creation of the color caste/captive class, and the electorate ratified the compromise of Black-race essence in existence and Black existence in essence. Thereby the citizenry squarely established the government on the individual, the White race/ethnic male in sum and substance, and property that which Black slaves were in essence and manifestation.

As a rational and reasonable tradeoff for current concessions to the proslavery South, including ratifying a Constitution guaranteeing among the sovereign "states' rights" involuntary servitude forever--or as long as the White Gentlemen's Agreement is held sacrosanct and inviolable law and a conscience-bound compact as sacred as the Bible and Constitution--the North demanded and received a limitation on the extension of the international slavetrade as indubitably as the South lobbied for its maximum extension in order to insure there would be a sufficient internal supply to meet the demand through domestic progenitorship.

The compromise negotiated one planned for result, the Constitution-mandated proscription of the international slavetrade twenty years after ratification of the Constitution, and precipitated upon its realization the massive domestic slavetrade that antislavery architects neither intended nor anticipated (Article I, Section 9):

> The migration or importation of such persons as any of the States now existing shall think proper to admit shall not be prohibited by the Congress prior to the year one thousand eight hundred and eight, but a tax or duty may be imposed on such importation, not exceeding ten dollars for each person.

The fact that nearly all of the eighteen Congressional members present voted for the antislavery section of the Northwest Ordinance--save for the singular Abraham Yates (the younger) of New York--permitted revisionists to argue that an antislavery sentiment was dominant among the Southerners. The notion gains whatever credibility it deserves related matter of relative importance, that is, only eight (all slaveholding) colonies of the nine present approved the legislation--Massachusetts being the only represented colony to have abolished slavery--they were Georgia, South Carolina, North carolina, Virginia, Delaware, New York, Massachusetts, Pennsylvania, and Maryland.

Representatives of the Old Solid South, however, were not regenerate but politically astute. She was ably represented by professional politicians who refused to compromise their proslaveholding principle, not only made their point but made it stick, and having established their bottom line principle that they would not negotiate they were prepared to compromise negotiable values and interests. The slave labor-based Disunited States desired larger lands for their expansive plantations, and new markets for their cotton and other agricultural products. The agrarian political economy needed economic expansion far more than an additional political victory, and the real interests of the larger planter and small farmer in the regions seemed served best by the unrestricted opportunity to compete for the political power and people, economic lands and resource in the new Territory.

Disciplined reflection upon the decision-making dynamics at the inception of the republic, and a range of correlated current moral fiber and political economy parallels, dominated the approach of the New Abolitionists and saturated the studies of their serious Constitution students. They centered their sober analyses and searching interpretations on the ethical premises and principles as much as the practical ethical process and program promulgated by the profane and pious architects of the nation--who were noted sacred and secular scholars and statesmen no less than churchmen and non-churchmen lawyers and intellectuals as well as politicians. Their pondering of the perplexing Puritan patricians who compromised their fundamental principle, and the Anglican aristocrats who did not compromise their foundational principle, encompassed a fully developed appreciation of the difficulty compounded by complexity.

Finally the early New Abolitionists, who switched from anti-political to pro-political moralists, drew conclusions from their analysis and interpretation of the ample data. But somehow they managed to reach a consensus that was as critical as it was incredible. They evolved uniformly convinced that the abolition of slavery was the consensus will of the American majority at the emergence of the Union.

Immediatists bethought the moral movement that sacred and secular Old Abolitionist New Englanders directed in the civil power circles, and appeared similar both like and unlike the initiative Quaker Puritans exercised in the ecclesiastical spheres of the Religious Society of Friends, was undermined by the political maneuvers of master manipulators. Proabolitionists discovered and interpreted ample facts and figures to make this conspiracy theory plausible.

New Abolitionist churchmen/churchwomen, in their roles as researchers of the record, uncovered data disclosing the absence of a Protestant parson and parishioner as well as parish real presence or ecclesiastical power from the civil power decision-making circles within which slavery was abolished by constitutional convention in Vermont (1777) and by judicial ruling and citizenry ratification in Massachusetts (1780).

Alternatively, in the once pious Anglican Colonies and onetime pious Puritan Colonies' main rival region for the claim of being North America's first territory in which the original English fathers rooted the Anglo-American transplant, instead of constituted power and authority abolishing human bondage they enacted and enforced progressive to liberal at best but mainly permissive statutes granting a license solely to the select individual slavemaster electing to liberate his slave(s) or for pure private manumission.

Between instant Colony-wide abolition in two Northeastern emerging states, and the personal freedom of choice to manumitt or perpetuate slavery in perpetuity conditional policy opted for by the plantation-pervasive provinces, lawmakers wrote gradual manumission legislation extending over a variable number of years, applying to the whole evolving sovereign state, and commencing at different dates in Pennsylvania (1780), Connecticut and Rhode Island (1785), New York (1799), and New Jersey (1804).

During the 1780s, New Abolitionists either recalled and were reminded by surviving original proabolitionists or learned in their information amassing investigation, the Old Abolitionists thought that the spirit if not the letter of the Constitution-mandated law terminating legal international slavetrade also meant the cutoff point for slavery. But their idea and ideal apparently remained a minority interpretation which the majority of the electorate or the eltist strict constructionist either did not accept or honored in the breach.

Simultaneously, New Abolitionists rediscovered, in the early national period the manumission societies either spawned or sparked the enactment of gradual manumission legislation, and a major task-responsibility of the members was monitoring the progress and placing pressure on legislators to ensure the lawmakers met or shortened the abolition time schedule. These newly constituted original American antislavery associations com-menced with the Old Abolitionist societies in Pennsylvania (1775), New York (1785), and Delaware (1788). Primarily Protestant alliances of adults, they proliferated throughout the American landscape and were organized in nearly all the states--as far south as Virginia --by the 1790s, save for conspicuous exceptions like the Commonwealth of Massachusetts.

What partly explains without explaining away this absence of Old Abolitionism in the first abolitionist state of the original thirteen to become one of the United States entails the direct connection between Old Abolition Societies and the various manumission statutes enacted under the "states' rights" Article of the Constitution. In their preponderance, the initial Old Abolition Societies were formed in gradual manumission states with one of the prime missions being to serve as "watch dogs" for the public on their elected representative to insure the end of involuntary servitude would transpire with all deliberate speed on or before the date set in state statutes.

In this post-theoracy and pre-slavocracy first republican democracy decade,- compared to her sister slave labor-based states, the relatively liberal private manumission statutes in Virginia enabled the measurably few manumissionist and fewer Old Abolitionist Virginians to confer self-determination upon their color chattel property without challenging the proslavery system. The ancillary of this corollary involved the limitations that were place--though less for moral than for economic reasons--on foreign and domestic traffic in slaves in Maryland (1783) and in North Carolina (1787), where they were successively repealed in 1790 and 1803.

CELERITOUS CHARITY TO SLAVEHOLDERS

AND BRUTAL BENEVOLENCE TO SLAVES

Thus New Abolitionists were rediscovering, recovering, and revitalizing their solid ethical estate; sovereign state-wide broad and deep, long and pervasive, and poor/rich people-enriching Old Abolitionist true right and righteously fair and equitable roots; and demonstrable Vermont-leading/Massachusetts-following individual integrity and community character or sterling mind/body/soul both style and substance inheritance of radical, immediate, and universal abolition

--along with slow but sure and progressive abolition as a normative Northeastern legacy. This state realized hearty health and hope principle they understood comprehensively (why as well as) that the Puritan Founding Fathers compromised after they barely tried and fully failed to establish as the foundational premise of the Constitution created by the Continental Congress, and as their no less real for being odd and even peculiar Yankee sons and daughters they were determined not to make the same mistake of compromising the common universal human right principle.

Forthwith the New Abolitionists redoubled their efforts to actualize finally self-determination as the rule of right (rule of law) in the nascent (fifty years old) sovereign state Union of the old Disunited and new United States of America. Precisely because the rationalists ruled right rather than realism rules realistic, and realists content to make wrong right the real pernicious perfectionists who proved the truth of their posited axiom that the perfect is the enemy of the best possible, they exposed ethics as the simple and sole soul of society--and civilized society (conscious conscience-centered mind over matter individual and community co-existence) as not only the source and substance of positive law (justice) as well as its purpose but also the standard by which to consistently measure and constantly correct rational law and rulers.

New Abolitionists considered the Chistianity and civility criteria of civilization were met in their offering to to the citizenry of this fairness and equity litmus test of truth and justice and law and order. It was created by their highly informed and critical yet interlinked individual and community consciences. They formed a conscious higher collective conscience than either consensus or conventional law, and a wit and wisdom witness of competence and confidence as well as credibility and courage energized by heightened consciousness and common sense.

Due to their complete commitment to narrowing the great and growing gap between the American promise and performance, and coinstantaneously to cancelling the color caste/captive class contract and to making the American dream reality, New Abolitionists were denounced by conservatives and denigrated by realists who ruled them state-endangering revolutionary idealists at best and radicals at worst. Nevertheless, just as they thoroughly apprehended the problem of the people to be something more but not much more than their being arrayed power-keeping powerful and power-seeking powerless races, just so comprehensively they understood themselves to be realistic idealists challenging unrealistic realists and pragmatists to change from the self-deception inherent in revering reality they managed at once to create and to suit their preferred real interests and values.

Synchronically, Bacon was overreaching from the castle house of the "New Side" Evangelical Orthodoxy into the New Testament to preach a regressive antislavery doctrine. His love of positive law and the law of negative good ethics (deterrence-benevolence morality) led him to conflate these two profane and sacred legal-istic and narrow limits compatibles as if they were one.

This option was preferred to measuring the moral validity of social conservative rational law and ethics, produced in ecclesiastical and civil power sectors by the same reason-intensive minds, and determining their distinct values relative to the Christian agape-love ethic (virtue) and the principal secular ethic of justice (principle) with their capacity to attract and repel each other. He ruled as a "Consistent Calvinist" that biblical law and constitutional law were divinely instituted, compatible, and nearly interchangeable legislative legitimizations of the legal right and relative moral value of slavery. Being legitimated by positive, custom, and moral law, obedience to slavocracy statutes was a universal duty.

According to Bacon, on the presumption one possesses the correct interpretation of the New Testament that his "Rule of Scripture" and "Rule of Truth" guarantees, the rules and regulations of the "peculiar institution" did not need to be transcended by New Testament *agape*-love: conformance with the letter and spirit of which he understood to be the universal responsibility of each individual, and subsists of acting to advance the best interest of God, the neighbor-enemy, and oneself. Bacon raised obedience to the law of the church and state to the highest priority, and demoted the demanding obligation of *agape*-love (virtue), whereby the rule of law and the rule of deterrence-benevolence overrode virtue as the capsule daily principles of expediency that he preached and practiced in the public arena

From this narrow deterrence-benevolence surrogate for the power-generating love energizing justice Christian ethic, his logic directed him to declare that the New Testament condemned both the slave-breeding master and his pro-immediatism antagonist; while the gospel according to Bacon approved the "conscientiously and diligently" humane human bondage owner and the anti-slavery gradualist. His faulty premise failed him (ra-ther than his impeccable logic) because the restrictive covenant advocate of strict constructionism was rigidly committed to the literal law of love.

But love, he failed to duly note relative to his comprehension, is a spirit of obligation. Love is not subject to a contract as is duty, or to legal enforcement as is justice or principle. Love can no be a principle than it can be a law--since law is a rational tool for administering impartiality intentionally and appropriately. But law is as such necessarily approximate fairness and equity or justice. And law cannot be *agape*-love--that is, the will to virtue (**BEING RIGHT** and **GOOD**) or **BENEVOLENCE** (the nature of God).

Love is not a static or simple state but a dynamic and complex ethical relation between beings, as he knew but elected to act otherwise in the slavery question. The Christian love/power/justice ethic is the permanent process of coordinating relevant knowledge and values, as means to the ends of discovering and promoting the right and good--or best known possible interest of God, and therewith the neighbor and oneself.

Bacon fully grasped these great realities and cer-tainties but preferred pros-lavocrat priorities as the representative establishmentarian Protestant denominationalist. He declared his faith in Christian love-virtue--the ultimate standard of ethical thought and action--and promptly failed his own moral test. Certainly what he asserted constitutes the unity of *is* and *ought*--or the nature of truth as virtue--and cannot be the subject (because it is not the object) of law.

God is love, but neither love nor law is God--as Bacon nearly thought. Man's capacity for reason or law, and logic which is the essence of law, makes justice relatively correct rather than accurate--and grace or mercy a necessity that is no substitute for love, or advancing the right and the good. But in the constantly changing culture-created human condition, man's infinite imagination, irreversible reflectiveness, and inclination to engage in the manipulation of law (or logic which both serves law and is subject to limitless rationality) makes justice civil but difficult, and love indispensable but impossible as a rule. Yet justice and love are the efficient principle and sufficient virtue ying and yang to approaching the human right and good--insofar as they are engaged in mutual interpenetration.

Bacon argued, contrariwise, that an unjustified slaveowner as well as a slaveholder justified by faith in the righteousness of God could be justified by the right and righteous civil law and law of love or Christ--if the following conditions were met: (1) the slaveholder possessed a "legal power over the persons of these individuals," or legitimate "legal title to their services"; (2) the slaveowner, "for the welfare of those slaves," kept them in bondage to avoid their being sold "to the highest bidder"---in the aftermath of their emancipation and arrest by a sheriff; (3) the slavemaster neither "makes it a business to breed slaves for market" nor treats them "as if they were cattle"--but supplies their physical needs, "restrains their vice," and has them instructed "especially in the things of everlasting peace"; and (4) the slavebuyer purchases slaves neither for personal use nor profit but "to do them all the good he can."

Addressing his slavocrat brethren in the slavocracy, proslavocrat Bacon wrote to instruct them in the duty of the slavemaster in relation to slaves which he stated is to "educate them for liberty." And once the emancipated Black American bondman and bondwoman are

> competent to take care of themselves, you can put them in the way
> of earning a passage to Africa, or let them choose their own
> course to whatever country will open its doors to receive them.

Regarding the system of slavery, the slaveholder ought to "bear his testimony against it" vehemently, vociferously, and regularly; "promote its peaceful abolition"; and, beyond his preachments, set an example by emancipating his slaves and sending them

> where they will be free indeed, whether in Liberia or in Haiti,
> whether in the British West Indies or on the prairies of Illinois.

In other words, in the vision of Bacon, the disintegration of slavocracy will result only from the direct action of slavemasters in line with the foregoing general guidelines and particularly as each slaveowner commits himself to liberate, educate, deculturalized, denationalize, and deport the Black race--for such model attitudinal and behavioral modification "the consciences of his neighbors cannot resist."[53]

Contrapositive New Abolitionists attempted to improve upon the rediscovered Old Abolitionists, who came to life and to the light with the birth of the nation. Counteragent Bacon so revered the Old Abolitionist originals as the saints of law and order that he knew himself called to prove their enduring authority. Instead of receiving the New Abolitionists in the spirit of righteous indignation, with which they presented themselves to him, the symbol of Congregational Orthodoxy and Beecher's Colonizationist advisor measured New Abolitionists according to the letter of the law. They presented him with immediate abolition, accompanied by the clear and simple statement that there had been more than enough slavery. Bacon looked the gift horse in the mouth and refused it--complaining that proabolitionism was a total condemnation of each actor in the slavocracy system, as well as of each act of slavery.

Bacon grew accustomed to the role of ecclesiastical deterrence-benevolence dictator, desired no greater reward than to be credited with being the benevolent paternalist of the New Haven Black community, and developed into a master manipulator of the media and an expert in making central to the color caste/captive crisis issues that were was so trivial and peripheral they were entirely beside the point. And what appeared worse to the proabolitionists is that the best and brightest of Gurley's Colonizationist agents knew it as well as he articulated his Moral Reform bottom line: A slaveholder might well be an antislavery advocate or proslavery adversary in his heart.

His moral case for the greater virtue than vice of the Calvinist slavocrat turned on a nice point of law and reason. The private morality argument he propounded in parochial media for public consumption, together with the promise of puritanicalism which strained credulity in performance no less consistently than he extended logic beyond the facts and experience from the premise that deterrence-benevolence is a high principle, was of the greatest unimportance as an exercise in "sophistry" and of incalculable consequence as the proliferation of the great hypocrisy contemporary critics associated with Puritan Orthodoxy in all of its Congregational establishment varieties.

Bacon managed to ignore with impunity the equally elementary and critical point, to wit, slavocrat rulers of the slavocracy permitted no public criticism of the "peculiar institution"--and exceptions did not overturn but proved the rule. At once suspending judgment of intentions and guilt by association while holding the in-dividual and community responsible for the consequences of their actions, the New Abolitionists branded all voluntary attitudinal and behavioral affirmations of slavery unethical, uncivil, and unChristian.

Pro-Colonizationist Bacon harbored no doubt concerning the fact that the overwhelming majority of the anti-Colonizationists were Christians. These pro-immediatists hated the sin and not the sinner! But Bacon chose to ignore their major point; to reverse their priorities; and to place such extraordinary emphasis upon loving the slavocrat protector of his/her human bondage ownership rights and prerogatives--no less than his/her privilege and pleasure--until his antislavocracy judgments had the effect of approving and complimenting both the slavery systematizers and their system.

In his second article on the antislavery problem and solution that the Congregationalist *Spectator* journal of opinion published in 1833, entitled "The Abolition of Slavery," Bacon delineated the theme which three years later in her elitist *Essay* New York-native and Connecticut-reared Catherine Esther Beecher developed into state of the art "Connecticut Yankee" Puritan race discrimination. They acted on the shared judgment that the published ideas and ideals of the Black leadership class and representatives of the Black community were unworthy of serious consideration; whereas the fact Black folk were ninety-five percent opposed to the American Colonization Society he dearly loved was not the least important factor contributing to Bacon's so solidly silent and pervasive persuasion it was deafening. Persuaded and persuasive Bacon and Beecher certified in writing that even the class of the Black leadership corps were nothing more than mouthpieces for the Garrison organ their subscriptions kept alive.

Unlike Catherine Beecher, a representative voice of the Eastern cultural elite, negative antiblack white-ethnic virtue director Bacon was a power broker between Northern and Southern White men who had large responsibilities and authority. Yet, exactly in this pro-White race interests and anti-Black race values powerhouse role, the New Abolitionists' practice of the Puritan Piety public interest-advancing direct action ethic's positive antiblack white-ethnic virtue brought to light the anti-Black race interests of the master overt ACS agent. The Congregationalist model modern moralist asserted the equivalence of legal and moral right, and held out so strongly for legal rights as a higher priority than moral rights that he came close to affirming that a good man had a moral as well as a legal right to be wrong. And while the Calvinist legalist did not declare that what is legal is inerrantly ethical; Bacon did posit the legal right on the line with moral right.

Without second thoughts, Bacon argued adamantly the argument of the authorities. Captors of color captives are manifest rightness and goodness or justice, he contended, if only because it is legal for a Christian to be unrepentant "in the relation of overseer and governor to those whom the law has constituted slaves." As long as human bondage proprietorship is perpetuated conscientiously, decently, and gentlemanly, cessation from slaveownership is required by neither civility nor Christianity nor the Moral Law. He stated as a "true believer" that because the "states' rights" clause of the Constitution and therefore the republican democracy legitimates the slavocracy, the lawful violation of an involuntary slave's natural right is no more a crime than it is either immoral or a sin. Injustice, according to the logic of Bacon, is immediate and universal unconditional emancipation, that calls for discharging "the slave from all special guardianship and government, and his immediate investiture with the power of self-control"--especially in the context of "efforts now made at the south, by Christians of various denominations, for the thorough religious instruction of those held in bondage."

Actualizing deterrence-benevolence principles in the power circles of New England Congregationalism, and the national and international ACS, Bacon vigorously denied the existence of any universal categorical imperative or "duty of *immediate* emancipation." Coinstantaneously, he endorsed enthusiastically--as the governing rule for each slavemaster--the "*immediate* duty of *emancipation*." This nice nuance proabolitionists called demonstrable nonsense and defenders of Evangelical Puritan establishment congregations like Bacon declared "common sense."

Bacon singularly comforted as completely as he aided and abetted the anti-Black race forces--that scarcely needed his help as much as the Black powerless and defenseless the prince of the church patronized--when he made the centerpiece of his proclamation to the world the ideation that slavery, which is always wrong in principle, could be right in practice anywhere--though not always or everywhere at once. The right to practice slavery turned on the practice of the right--which revolved around the accurate application of the law and reason rather than the correct implementation of love and justice. On the one hand, Bacon was an insistent "Consistent Calvinist":

> To hold men as property, to claim them, and use them, and dispose
> of them, as things without personality, and without rights, is a sin,
> with which neither humanity nor religion can have compromise.[54]

On the other hand, he was confident the slavocracy could be converted from the slavocrat idea of democracy to his own divination of the republic:

> For there are hundreds of masters there, who are convinced already, and
> who act on the conviction, that they stand to their slaves, not in the
> relation of ownership over property, but in the relation of guardianship
> and government over men, intelligent, and invested by God of nature with
> the rights of humanity, yet ignorant, dependent, and, but for the master,

defenceless.[55]

The popularity of the ACS was real enough to darken his reason and cloud his vision; but that he was as honest to God and man as foolish consistency was the hallmark of his social ethics Bacon never doubted:

> Let the public sentiment of the country speak out for the emancipation of slaves, and for the abolition of slavery. This is the gradual abolition which we stand ready always to advocate...

Bacon was unprepared to admit he did not understand the question for which he provided the answer, because he was absolutely certainly he had the solution to the problem of slavery. By the power of "light and love" in the South, he avouched, breaking forth among the White pure pious and like minded pure profane friends of Black Protestants--the antislavery conviction may be made to spread, till, having first pervaded the churches there of every denomination, it shall become the strong conviction of the popular mind.

Then, predicted, the majesty of the people, speaking by distinct enactments, shall pronounce that the slaves are persons, having human rights, and, as such, subject to the law, and under its protection. In this imminent future the keystone of the mighty fabric of oppression will be removed and replaced by legislation that will initiate the abolition of slavery.[56]

MORAL UNION OF UNITARIAN AND
TRINITARIAN CONGREGATIONALISTS

By 1836, Bacon had found a kindred spirit in William Ellery Channing's Protestant *Emancipation* proclamation--notwithstanding his explicit "New Side" Calvinist criticism that the Unitarian's "Scriptural argument" argues from the "genius of Christianity, rather than from the inspired record of what Christianity is."

The New Haven pastor of the crystal cathedral of Trinitarian Congregationalism delighted in having his gradualist position confirmed by Channing--the Boston parson of the citadel of Unitarian Congregationalism:

> In regard to the means of removing slavery, he holds, that the best, safest, happiest remedy, is in the hands of the masters; that the institution of new relations between the master and the servant, without the master's full consent, though it may be far better than the perpetuity of the relations now existing, cannot but be attended with disaster; that while the recognition of the slave as a man entitled to the benefits of good government ought to be immediate, his emancipation must be a gradual process; that the slave ought to be trained for self-support, by being taught to labor under the impulse of other and manlier motives than mere terror of the lash, by seeing new privileges and honorable distinctions awarded to the honest and industrious; by being made to feel, that he has a family whose happiness depends on his industry, integrity and prudence, and by being imbued with the truths and motives of the Gospel of Christ. We need not say how entirely these views coincide with our own.[57]

The profound impression that Channing made upon his moral mind induced Bacon to moderate his own views of the proabolitionists. He proposed that in being "the occasion rather than the cause or source of the mischief," the "immediate abolitionists are only to a limited extent responsible for the excitement in the slaveholding States."

In the New Abolitionists' opposite motive and purpose the manager of reality managed to locate manipulatable means and opportunity for the very ACS that Garrison had condemned for its pretentions of being the antislavery association and caricatured the monstrous anathema of the antebellum age.

But to this Protestant power elite's popular philanthropy ACS agent Bacon remained wedded, specifically in his equally arguable and unmistkable America is the *White Man's Country* major implication--and single inference to be drawn from his article entitled "Slavery in Maryland" (1836):

> What, then, may we anticipate, as the destiny of the colored population of this country? If there are districts of this country, where the climate forbids the white man to labor, those districts will undoubtedly be inhabited by blacks. But in every other part, will not the white man be ultimately the laborer and the sole possessor? It is not for us to answer this question positively.[58]

Total White male dominance and Black male subdominance, if not absolute White race superiority and Black race inferiority, remained the affirmative action principle and equal policy Bacon promoted as late 1845, when he pressed post-Channing antislavery liberals and moderates to "try very hard" to remain engaged with conservatives who keep the faith of Channingesque-Emancipation and Baconesque-Colonization "true believer" antiabolitionists that their gradualism-specific Christian slavocrat ideal and idea of true slavemasters will out:

> I believe that thousands of the southern people are a great deal better than their laws are.

Strange as it may seem, Bacon demonstrated the convoluted thought and confusion or division of his mind and will when he credited White Protestant Anglo-Saxon slavocrat slaveholders with having not only principles but also the courage of their convictions and coinstantaneously refused to believe his Southern Christian brethren's word was their bond, to take them at their word or to accept their word and deeds at face value, and to admit they were what they claimed and the descriptive facts he quoted revealed:

> so insensible to the public opinion of the world as not to care what the world thinks of these laws of theirs.

Like Unitarian Congregationalist clergyman Channing and Presbyterian presbyter Beecher, Trinitarian Congregationalist parson Bacon, who distinguished himself as the "Consistent Calvinist" consensus worshipper and liberal conservative spokesman for "New Light" Orthodoxy and "New School" Reformed estabmentarians, continued to hold reasonable and relevant his rationalization and ratiocinative distinction--that followed in rationalistic revelation and reason and even reality but not in realism--

between the *power* of doing wrong which the law gives to the master as against the slave, and the *use* which the master makes of that power.

Bacon made the point stick even as the consistent Colonizationist denied that he was a poor prophet and an equally unreliable public ethicist. This evidence occurred one year after the formation of the Congregationalist Denomination, and before the once united Presbyterian Church divided (in 1837) into two ("New School" and "Old School" Northern-headquartered and Southern constituency-integrated) separate denominations divided again (in 1846)--as the "Old School" Church split into the Northern and Southern Presbyterian Denominations.

At this critical ecclesiastical Evangelical Prot-estant juncture, perforce the North and South cleavage of the Baptist, Methodist, and Presbyterian Denominations, Bacon decreed the existence of a "fraternal duty" that makes it (A) unconscionable to excommunicate "*slaveowners simply as such, and all churches which contain slaveholders*"; and (B) necessary to "discriminate" between the pro-White race interest and anti-Black race interest proslavery "*laws*"--that secular and sacred slavocrats enacted in the slavocracy--and the "individual *citizens* of those States."

Positive race laws and reasons ruled the Black male was not an individual (by definition a White race/ethnic male): a fact of life created by culture rather than nature, and existence legitimated in the Constitution and binding White Gentlemen's Agreement--negotiated in the American bid to out-Adam Adam or Original Sin and social contract.

Consequently, as Bacon reminded Calvinist congregants, the laws of his resident state and the slaveholding states determined Black inhabitants were not "individual citizens."

This cause correlated positively with the color caste/captive class effect Bacon fostered as late as 1845, namely his limited interest in promoting Black Connecticuters' legitimate claims and high regard in New Haven and boundless energy expended in extending high praise to White Southern Christian ladies and gentlemen he admired and respected. Bacon testified that he was more than "willing to treat" White Southerners as individuals (who were just like himself and unlike Black Southerners and Northerners the real representatives of the White race/ethnic groups) and "with all the courtesy and respect due to gentlemen and to American fellow-citizens."

His decision to respect most highly and reverently their time-honored *White Gentlemen's Agreement*, as a higher Christian commandment than the demanding equal membership and civil citizenship rights and responsibilities for their Black race cultural kin-group Christian mandate, can be explained but not explained away: Bacon was an ACS agent and thereby dedicated to the depopulation of the Black-race North American body.

Precisely due to this conscientious objection to biracial equalitarianism the Congregationalist spokesman cannot be excused for his color-conscious conscience, or for being like the ACS agencies he served as a field operator greater anti-Black race interests and values or the American problem promoters than solution solvers of the White male human bondage problem (Black male)--and Black male (White male)--that turned on the slavocracy system and its derivative Black body slavocrats (if not proslavocrats) desired and cherished so deeply it passed the litmus test of a fundamental need.

BACON'S APPROACH TO BLACK CALVINISTS
IN HISTORY AND IN HIS STORY

The minuscule positive and momentous negative contribution that Congregationalist Colonizationists and classic conservative Calvinists made as self-called traditionalists to the general welfare of antebellum Black Calvinists would be of no great importance were they not as powerful as they estimated themselves to be. Rather than reverence for unencumbered Black American life Bacon preferred to return the native North American Black race to what the presager determined to be their motherland, while in the fatherland his Black Christian cultural kin ("people of God") called their homeland he coveted a cultivated reputation as an internationalist. The color-conscious Calvinist made it perfectly clear to the Protestant public, for whom the credentialed card-carrying Colonizationist published, that he was far as from being against the color caste/captive class as he was from being color prejudiced:

> I could treat a gentlemanly Turk or Persian with
> courtesy and hospitality in my New England home.[59]

For perfectly intelligible reasons, this gratuitous effusion emitted by the proWhite race champion proved no more an indication of his rise above anti-Black race values than his advocacy of gradual abolitionism cancelled or counterbalanced the consequences of his complete commitment to replete depletion of the Black race in the North America.

Whether he professed or protested too much, his public attesting that he was entirely free and clear of color-intensive prejudice lucidly and concisely elucidated the negative realities in the positive relations between antiblack white-ethnic virtue and anti-Black race virtue--Calvinism and millennialism, Evangelicalism and colonizationism, and Puritanism and capitalism--the full range of which complementaries diverged and converged in reality and reached conscious crystallization in Connecticut.

Bacon did not cause the demanding pro-White race privilege and driving anti-Black race desire in which constraints he lived, moved, and found his being. Yet he bolstered "*the spirit*" from New Haven's First Church near Yale College, the two major institutions that formed the Calvinistical color caste/captive condition condemnation and class double election/damnation twin towering inferno signs and symbols (rather more conscious than style and substance); bid fair to out-Dante Dante's (1265-1321) *Divine Comedy* (1321) generally, and his Inferno particularly, in Evangelical Calvinist and Colonizationist productions that the faithful called the "*light to the nations*"; and emerged in the appearances as merged spiraling steeples of Ortho-doxy's wayward worldly saints's sons determined to complete the peculiar Puritan "*Errand into the Wilderness*" of North America.

But more than Bacon surmised, the strong and flexi-ble half of the powerful culture was by-passed by him as the Michigan native struggled to be engrafted with the *Corpus Christos* core of the inheritance corps or sons of the wayward worldly saints and sinners--who self-called themselves the "*seed* of Abraham"-- and succeeded in being ascribed status by Yankees who "inherited" status as well as identified with this least magnanimous descendants of Puritan New Englanders.

That he could respect a "Turk or Persian" as highly as a White ethnic immigrant, but could not grant the best interest of Black Calvinists equal re-spect, was scarely either an incidental or accidental occurrence. It was occasioned by good Yankee-Puritan economics as much as by solid Evangelical Calvinism. Following his theological education near the "Hub of the universe," Bacon journeyed from one "city on a hill" to another--from Boston to New Haven. He was a carrier--in his transplanted brain and heart--of a Puritan law enacted (following the precedents of fifteenth-century English statutes) in Mas-sachusetts (March 26, 1788) to suppress vagabonds and rogues, whom, one year after the Constitution was ratified, apparently Bay State lawmakers presumed Black folk to be:

> No person being an African or negro, other than a subject of the emperor of Morocco, or a citizen of some one of the United States, to be evidence by a certificate from the secretary of the State of which he shall be a citizen, shall tarry within this Commonwealth for a longer time than two months, and upon complaint...that said African or negro shall not depart as aforesaid, any justice of the peace...ten days after notice given him or her to depart as afore-said, shall commit the said person to any house of correction with-in the county, there to be kept to hard labor agreeably to the rules and order of said house...; and if upon trial at the said court it shall be made to appear that the said person has thus continued within the Commonwealth contrary to the tenor of this act, he or she shall be whipped not exceeding ten stripes, and ordered to de-part...; and if he or she shall not so depart, the same process shall be had, and punishment inflicted, and so *toties quoties*.[60]

Bacon migrated from Michigan as a Detroit emigrant to become a naturalized New Englander. During his Eastern establishmentarian developmental stages, in-clusive of New England culture assimilation and cul-tivation process, Bacon gradually syncretized consciously sacred traditional values and unconsciously learned secular "Massachusetts Yankee" and "Connecticut Yankee" color caste/ class attitudinal and behavioral patterns--which he acquired through formal edu-cation in Boston and professional experience in New Haven.

Thenceforth it was a natural progression paralleling his profession his e-volvement into a powerful hierarch--as well as influential spiritual and moral leader of five estates figures--to an antislavery proslavocrat proudly proclaiming publicly his moral embrace of Calvinist slavocrat slavemasters:

> I regard the people of those States as better than their laws--thousands of them a great deal better.

Evidently his embraced conventional wisdom emanated from first-hand ec-clesiastical bureaucracy and technocracy validating his certitude that the Southern Christian Cavalier types were the powerhouse complements of his Yan-kee Calvinist capitalist parishioners, and Protestant philanthropist fellow inter-locking directorates on the parochial boards and private corporations he served, and not the proslavocracy problem: unlike their nonobservant planter class com-rades whose partisan party political power he underestimated in his invention of a Southern Calvinist reform creative minority, he believed could direct the proslavocracy majority.

Doubtless Bacon knew equally precious little about the leadership of the planter class and the color caste/captive class doubtless. Exactly for this reason the ecclesiastical establishment leader regrettably failed to accord Calvinist clergy and lay leaders of the secular and sacred Black community the courtesy of his serious mind and respect they earned. Bacon left earnest and honest (if not always discerning) respect for the Black mind and message to his caricatured sensational New Abolitionists, who disclosed they had the common grace to make as much sense as news.

He knew the Old Abolitionist Societies were predominantly composed of Christians primarily led by Quaker ministers of the Religious Society of Friends --during their dominance of the antislavery movement prior to the rise of the pro-gradualist ACS and the bolt from the ACS of ex-Colonizationist converted pro-immediatist moralists. The division during democracy's slavocracy era between antiabolitionist Christian Colonizationists (who usurped the Protestant leadership of the antislavery movement from the Old Abolitionist Socieites) and the New Abolitionists who broke ranks with both pro-gradualism Societies, prior to the subsequent antislavery schism within a majority of the mainstream Evangelical denominations, was paralleled by the union between Northern White Christian clergymen enjoying considerable clout and Southern empathies that were stronger than their sympathy for Black brothers and sisters in Christ (they were never at a loss to declare).

When "Connecticut Yankee" Beecher left his native state to join forces with the "Massachusetts Yankee" Evangelical Calvinists in the "Hub of the universe" --at nearly the identical moment Bacon arrived in Connecticut from Massachusetts--they were carrying coals to Newcastle and practically passed each other on their way to and from Boston and New Haven.

In the critical perspective of Protestant American history, the instrumental Congregationalist clergyman Bacon and pivotal powerhouse Presbyter Beecher have been treated as luminaries. They were as fascinating as glowworms, equally striking and of incomparable illum-inative value in tracking the Evangelical Calvinist advance from Yankee Halfway Piety personal morals to Puritan Piety public interest ethics.

Since they represented antebellum traditions that gave institutional shape the death-enhancing chances and withheld substantive assistance in the form of structural support of life-enhancing chances from their Black race cultural kingroup, the firefly metaphor is misleading because it suggests that their leadership had relatively little or no lasting impact. They were, rather, live coals in the profane and sacred cultural system over which bare footed Black fugitives from legal injustice were forced to step from bondage to caste binds--far beyond their own appreciation but not beyond either the recognition or reach of the status quo perpetuating "Consistent Calvinists."

Bacon and Beecher were bountiful princes of Protestant philanthopy in the perception of persuaded parsons and parishioners. In appearances of the unpersuaded, they reposed and seemed to be exposed as the first among equals in the front ranks of principal powerhouses bound by boundless rigid principles; opposed to the true and real interests of slavery and the Black race alike; and predisposed, as a result of their anti-Black race values, to think their pro-gradualism/proslavocrat direction was not an antislavery zigzag but a straight line.

Antiabolitionist Beecher's sons, who were proabolitionists in the 1840s and 1850s, could not recover the Old- and New-Abolitionists' contracting/expanding

Black caste and bondage liberation ground their father lost to opportunity--that is, to inspire a social redeeming proabolitionist counterforce to the anti-Black race presence dominating the Congregational and Presbyterian denominations. The Congregationalist-Orthodoxy and Presbyterian-Reformed denominations far more their Baptist Calvinist cousin in the nation--and the either antislavery neutral or proslavery Protestant Episcopal Church--constituted the establishment American denominations.

They illustrated in their parochial forages their capacity to leap into the flow of history and expedite the liberation from dehumanization of Black Christians--at the very least--if not the resolution of slavery also. Power elite Protestants finally formally knew as certainly as they chose to ignore the hard fact that the decision to dissolve the slavocracy had been reached long before the Civil War.

Precisely put, veteran professional politicians and political realists of the embroiled Missouri Bill Congressional debate shared self-fulling prophecies as pragmatic United States Senators and Congressman who protected their different Northern and Southern political and economic: after bitter dispute surviving their contested and protested controversial Missouri Compromise that neither resolved nor buried but simply managed to make their conflict of interests barely tolerable and manageable, aggressive warriors predicted on the mid-antebellum record nothing short of forceful measures would solve published their prognostications, and conceded the coercive conclusion to be only a matter of time and question of method.

What accompanied the failure of power Protestants to learn this lesson of history was the advancement from the Missouri Compromise (reached through rank rancor and bargain as much rational reason) of crippling anti-Black race values that also appeared equally rife with cultural consequences and entirely lost on them. The American White race rule (segregation) and regulation (discrimination), evolving from the color caste/captive class condemnation custom law into positive law and rational rules, the intensive pro-White race/ethnic minorities' middle-class and upper-class rulers ruled in order, the positive and moral law, and the natural rights law of nature.

Every major denomination raised the rule from a parochial and profane culture-derived value to a national virtue. Indeed, Anglo-American Puritan and Anglican representatives of the English and British-ethnic peoples joined as fathers and sons of the "Old Families"--with their new immigrant cousins from the Continent--and informed Black folk in no uncertain terms their rule of law was the rational rule of the majority whose arbitrary will they had no choice but to live with.

They enforced this law and order of the land in and out of slavery, and during the late antebellum through the Reconstruction eras. It remained in force during the post-Reconstruction eras, when the maximized charitable allocations and contributions of Northern denominations peaked in evenhanded eleemosynary expenditures on and distribution among freedmen and cheek by jowl poor White ethnic Southerners; and Protestant power elite treated the anti-Black race values promoted as pro-White race/ethnic virtue their advocates as if lasting ancient color caste conditions were not in-dependent phenomena that pre-ceded and succeeded human bondage in the history of civilizations but mere ab-errations of modern (different by virtue of being distinct and unique) Black race-specific involuntary servitude.

This Puritan bequeathed Yankee bifurcation of reality correlated with the great man and powerful cultures approach to the study of history dominant learned Protestant intellectuals determined the correct methodological perspective and interpretation, and the discoveries the power elite cultural determiners failed to act upon.

Their results revealed that slavery was a history-long problem of human institutions, that the culture-created equally damaging and demanding anti-Black race values or common vice--and so-called virtue in the Occident and the Orient--was a mere mistake of undeveloped and underdeveloped or developing human beings and societies, and that these disvalues were far from a calculated error of deception cause and effect and near to being completely correctable by the enhanced human improvement and perfection capacities that modern moral man automatically advanced with his inevitable linear ethical progress.

ECCLESIASTICAL POWER POLITICS AND

ECONOMICS IN REPUBLICAN DEMOCRACY

American slavery for Northeast-based antebellum secular and religious intellectuals was (as it remains) a problem of White male power and authority relative to rational responsibility and reliability in the role of legitimate command and control leaders of the ecclesiastical and civil powers--although today it is a purely intellectual one.

The first New Abolitionists, who were Evangelical Protestants and liberal Unitarians preponderantly, exhibited at the birth of New Abolitionism (in 1830) a fully developed appreciation of the critical distinction that makes the difference between the Black American bondage and caste conditions appear an absolute rather than relative or different kind of dehumanization. By 1833, and the formation of the American Anti-Slavery Society they established that year as their national organization, New Abolitionists demanded the eradication of slavery and the color caste system and institution of biracial integration.

This trendy and transitory initial dual rational abolition of bondage and caste and implementation of biracial egalitarianism, through the instrumentation of radical rapid social structural change means and ends, constituted the distinctive factor in the difference the New Abolitionist equalitarians made. It complemented their immediate and unconditional universal aboli-tionism: the demonstrable proabolitionism that distin-guished New Abolitionist Societies from the pro-gradualist Old Abolitionist Societies, four decades later forming and competing ACS, and mid-1840s antislavery societies the denominations developed whose antiabolitionism shared value was their distinguished mark and featured negative antiblack white-ethnic virtue.

But the pro-immediatists were pressed by the pro-gradualist Northerners on one side--and the proslavery Northerners and Southerners on the other side--to compromise their dual abolition and integration principles. Modern moralists following Channing, and the Moral Reformers whom Beecher and Bacon led to support chief executive officer Gurley of the ACS, formed the consensus of the establishment denominations behind their leadership. This White race body of Christ and civility crusaders prided itself in being the rational alternative to the White ethnic crowd that turned into a mob.

The Protestant power elite presence added compelling force to the Beecherite and Baconesque and Channingesque champions' endeavors to persuade the a-bolition of anti-Black race values. The persuasive powers persuaded the preponderance of the New Abolitionists who forthwith evinced the persuasion

330   CONSTITUTION, CONSCIENCE, AND CALVINIST COMPROMISE

that eradication of human bondage might be accomplished immediately, but only by instant suppression of the demand for the elimination of the color caste class. Prior to this highly touted realistic reduction of idealism to realism, New Abolition was a dual objective crusade--equally like and different from the single-issue and single goal oriented precedents-establishing and pacesetting British Abolitionists.

Prior to and becoming one-dimensional abolitionists, as result of their expedient transition whose deliberate speed they accelerated after 1836, original two-dimensional New Abolitionism constituted the radical nature of the proabolitionists that the antiabolitionists feared and found so threatening they branded New Abolitionists real revolutionists. Due to mutual real interests and values, the sacred professors and trus-tees of private colleges and professional schools --whose force did nothing to impede the devolvement from two-dimensional to one-dimensional abolitionism--were joined by profane scholars.

Secular academics, nationally led by Harvard preceptors, were as unconcerned with the religious values shared by antislavery and proslavery activists as historians of religion were with elucidating the civil consequences of Black bondage. Indeed involuntary servitude was treated as a matter of the greatest unimportance by the cultural determiners, who, if concerned with anything remotely related to the problem of Black bondage dehumanization, were more interested in the theory of slavery than in the reality of anti-Black race values.

This traditional and transcendent English-American interest in keeping the color caste class statusless and in permanent pariah captivity, whose Bible and Constitution legitimated church and state law and enforced pro-White race values placed undue constraints on free Black Americans, hegemonic North America secular and religious scholars mostly preferred to circumvent and often misrepresented--together with the meaning of the largely Evangelical Protestant-observant minority of White proabolitionist adversaries of the antiabolitionist majority--to say little of paying no attention at all to the relevant thoughts and actions of Black New Abolitionists and Old Abolitionists.

Ignoring the instructive White and Black proabolitionists, an influential plurality of secular and religious intellectuals and students of nineteenth-century history concentrated nearly exclusively upon antislavery configurations: as if this one-dimensional criterion was the original standard of virtue (overwhelmingly Christian) New Abolitionists set for themselves, and thereby the singularity by which their contribution to the improvement of the human condition should be assessed. Hence they frequently obscured the dual abolition vision and great ambition of their subjects.

Their narrow focus reflected the comparative primary preference of historians in their preponderancy for the great man/woman theory of history, and the achievements of heroes and heroines rather than the accomplishments of heretics, whose logical approach resulted not only from the civilization enriching importance of power and prosperity producers but also in rendering the productive source of their social security and wealth as inconsequential as their enduring color caste dehumanization.

An additive factor solidifying the limited academic interest in the color caste and conscience cultural crisis was the fact that White New Abolitionists failed to sustain their own egalitarian resolve, as decisively as they succeeded in achieving the primary objective of the Old Abolitionists and preventing the American Colonizationists from realizing their Black race excludable from the fatherland of the Black body high principle, chief purpose and policy, and ultimate goal. Fundamentally, however, Beecher and Bacon, the Evangelical Calvinist princes of parochial-private-public institutional politics, orchestrated the Protestant establishment denominational forces whose forages into the color caste/captive cultural crisis constituted a more major than minor contributing cause of the reduced effect of New Abolitionism, and its retrogression of progressive binary abolitionism from a two-level liberation agency to a single-issue and special interest Anti-slavery Society.

As a consequence of this popular will to treat the correctable color caste class condition as an intractable outcast pariah existence in essence, free Black folk were the beneficiaries of neither either natural or democratic rights nor the Christian charity that benevolent paternalists extended to slaves, but the victims of their of their brutal benevolence whose deterrence-benevolence effectively delayed their access to freedom in liberty and realization of humanity dignity as effectually as it deterred the loss of chains binding their Black relatives in captivity.

In this matter of positive negation of Black folk interests, revolving around the capricious securing the assailability of the Northern color caste class so that the Black male could not meet the White male competition, White liberals engaged in extending the gap between their equalitarian promise and performance and demonstrated they even won in losing no more than face, which, of course, was precisely what Black players were disallowed who failed to compete successfully in the power politics and economics games White rulers designed and rigged with two sets of rules.

It is an indisputable fact that Beecher and Bacon developed the rules of this parochial power game as members of the ACS and especially the American Board of Commissioners for Foreign Missions. Through this ecumenical ecclesiastical eleemosynary enterprise primarily "New Side" Congregationalists together with "Old School" and "New School" Presbyterians, and secondarily the Reformed Dutch Church centering around Queen's (renamed) Rutgers College (1771), channeled their considerable charitable resources and missionary interests. Relative to this powerful church corporation, and the fast approaching turning point from their antiabolitionist dominance to proabolitionist hegemony of the antislavery movement--whose dramatic change in the theory and experience of reality Bacon realistically revealed in his descriptive and value judgment of "the collision between the Anti-Slavery Society and the American Board"--Bacon wrote an apology for the antiabolitionist American Board in a series of articles which the New York *Evangelist* published in 1846.

At this late date, and the climax point of his public defense of pro-gradualism, Bacon called instant liberation from human bondage an "erratic philosophy which has usurped the name of abolition." In a classic instance of the pot calling the kettle black, he censured pro-immediatists for engaging in "miserable, paltering, juggling sophism."

Evangelical Calvinist New Abolitionists were castigated by pro-Calvinist antiabolitionists for roundly and regularly impugning the motives of the Board; calling the benevolent enterprise the public defender of slavery; and declaring the bureaucracy slavocracy's not so secret admirer. For years the Board refused to state its position on slavery, but acquiesced under enormous and finally debated the antislavocracy/proslavocracy issue formally during the 1845 crisis in Congregationalism, from which antislavocrat/proslavocrat conflict of values sprang moderate proabolitionists in the previously overwhelmingly antiabolitionist denomination and its institutions.

What to the appearances made the debate between united and never divided Calvinist Congregationalist Churches of Christ civil, and quite possible, was the evasion of direct criticism of Southern White slaveholding interests.

The pro and con abolitionist arguments were precipi-tated when proabolitionists publicly berated the Board upon discovering the bureaucracy supported agents admitting to good standing in Orthodoxy converts to Calvinist Congregationalism, who remained slaveholders in their compound churches of Christ the missioners and ministers served in their posts on the boundaries of the Northeast and frontiers of the Northwest. English race and British ethnic missionaries of the Board, to Indian ethnic groups their Puritan fathers and Yankee brothers had driven onto the margins of the East and in the West, had received into Christian communion members of the captivated Cherokee and Choctaw nations who were themselves slavemasters and owners of Black bondage.

A committee of Congregationalist clergymen appointed by officers of the nascent Congregationalist Denomination to gather the facts, and make recommendations, reported its findings. The Reverend Amos Augustus Phelps (1805-47), who as an early immediatist and New England Anti-Slavery Society agent was a rare breed among Congregationalist clergymen, moved to amend the report to read that in the

> matter of instruction, admonition, and discipline, the Board would expect its missionaries and mission churches to treat slaveholding just as they would drunkenness, gaming, falsehood--[...wherefore] instruction is to be given against it by the missionaries, and admonition and discipline to be administered against it by them and the churches.

Bacon moved to amend the amendment so as to incorporate his characteristic Calvinist conservatism, that he promoted the wisdom of moderation in a crisis in Christian conscience, confidence, and credibility. He supported the commandment to condemn the sin of slavery but not the slavemaster. The Calvinist or Christian slaveowner *qua* slaveowner, Bacon contended, was necessarily involved in the sinful institution yet not a sinner but either a saint (hence necessarily not of it) or one of the select "Elect" (whence not necessarily of it) who might most certainly could be therein kept pure and undefiled. Bacon's alteration did not pass but induced further modifications. As a result, Bacon proclaimed himself the representative voice--and claimed a pyrrhic victory. A New York *Evangelist* reporter reported the donnybrook and Bacon later cited the churchman journalist to validate his own certification:

> Every individual of the Committee approved of the principles of Dr. Bacon's resolutions, but it was feared that to append them to the report would look too much like legislation, and might seem to ecclesiastical bodies as if the Board was trenching upon their proper province.[61]

The final report reflected Bacon's emphasis so satisfactorily that he was pleased to pronounce a benediction upon himself, to wit "my doctrine is sound" and "not in dispute," and to respond in the negative to the following query:

Whether the church has a right to go farther, and to demand of the master, under pain of excommunication, that he shall "at all hazards" dissolve the connection between himself and his slaves, shall divest himself of all power to govern or protect them, and shall leave them wholly and immediately to their own capacity of self-control, and to the tender mercies of a State that regards them as barbarians and as enemies.[62]

REVISED EVANGELICAL FAITH AND
ETHICS AND UNREVISED RACE VALUES

As his sole antislavery/proslavery defense, Bacon published details of his visitation on one good Christian "man's plantation"--where he experienced the "Great joy of the negroes at seeing their own master among them." This spontaneous welcome upon the return of the benevolent paternalist and expert civil disci-plinarian, celebrated for his rational human bondage management style and substance apropos his total command and control of the Black body system-- whom the chattel plantation property plainly preferred to the slaveholders who stood in his stead--Bacon could not relate as a preference for the lesser of two inevitable but equally unnecessary and intrinsic evils (slaveholding role models).

The masterful ratiocinator and rhetorician drew on his powers as a logician and used his first-hand field research data that recorded the preference of slaves for pleasure to pain (A) to disprove his antagonists whose facts and figures Bacon maintained were manipulated as evidence to prove their truth he proved their error, that bond men and women were always in a state of depression; (B) to function effectively as a self-serving indicator of his purported valid claim; and to bolster his contention concerning the human race or species (composed of human races and ethnic groups and individuals or beings), relative to human being (existence) and function (modes of self-enhancing and race-enhancing or self-defeating and race-defeating existence), that being human or good and right (the essence of existence) and an excellent slavemaster (function) are binary correspondences and not contraries.

Exactly because the advocate of antiabolitionism knows his proabolitionism adversaries sustain but he chooses not to conserve the crucial distinction between being and function, Bacon argues not only with (instead of the) facts but in lieu of the facts the arguments: Being a good human being and a good (civil and rational ruler if not also professional disciplinarian and people manager or efficiency expert) slavemaster (Bacon translates a good slavemaster is a good human being in principle and potential) is a natural relation--and even a just and right one--because non-cruelty is the mark of high Christianity and civility.

Bacon was scarely warranted in not only advancing as generalizable but also universalizable the natural relief and thanksgiving slaves on one plantation expressed in a most propitious moment blacks. Yet he founded it equally expedient and convenient to interconnect the presumably altogether surprising cheers of involuntary servitude-bound chattel property and "my friend's" "conscientious judgment" to prove the "effect of Christian principle on the mind of the master toward his slaves."

Accordingly, as Bacon interpreted and managed reality, "Christian principle" does not convict the slave-holder of the sin of slavery and demand immediate re-pentance basically because such radical re-thinking and action is a prescription for undermining domestic tranquility; and primarily because nature is an instinctive drive for freedom from slavery yet one that requires liberation from involuntary servitude to occur in accord with the natural laws of order. The thrust of Bacon's argument is that Christian principles turn a vulgar slaveholder and "Reprobate" slavemaster into an "Elect" and select White Christian gentleman, who engages human bondage and all other things decently and in order.

The Baconesque principle supports status quo slavocracy and democracy as a "Consistent Calvinist" predictably does equally persistently and selectively, who is not only justified by faith in the righteousness of God and reason but legitimated by the classic Calvinist conservative ethic whereby each and every civil order and authority is instituted by God. Indeed, since laws of God and man are preordained divine by Providence, and every authority is instituted by the Creator, the slave-based order is ruled righteous law order and nat-urally preferred to disorder.

Bacon's moral value and judgment is a perfect translation of traditional social conservative Puritan values, Calvinist sacred and secular social ethics, and classical Catholic civil teachings. French Catholic dissident John Calvin enacted into the ecclesiastical and civil law of Geneva the right and responsibility of the magistrate to use civil force to protect and defend the church; to ensure individual and community life and liberty; and to secure the domestic peace and as well as the national security.

Bacon argues in the era of Yankee democracy and Cavalier slavocracy, that the White individual "citizen" and "freeman" is the legitimate authority who therefore is warranted by the laws of God and man to the church and state powers to secure the good of the order and the prevention of revolution. He is as decisive as he is determined to make one thing perfectly clear: The asserted equivalence of the White ethnic individual and the constituent element of Calvinist (Presbyterian representative republican) democracy, capitalism, and Evangelicalism is cloaked or cloaks himself "in a magisterial capacity."

He enjoys rights and responsibilities that are inimical to the true and real interests of the Black race, whose members were (A) excluded by God and the Bible from being in power and authority, the concomitant natural need for and equal access to rights and responsibilities, of and the full complement of the fairness and equity agape-love/power/justice ethic; and (B) precluded by the Constitution and the citizenry from civil rights and civil liberties.

The "Christian principle" promulgated by Bacon does not awaken the free or slave Black female and male (A) to BEING--the essence of existence manifest in Her/His creation of the reason-bestowed and liberty-endowed as well as physical nature and her natural laws-granted and rights-conferred human spe-cies and each human be-ing; (B) to her/his God-given right to self-determination; and/or to (C) womanhood/manhood or the individual right and responsibility to act in self-defense and of-fense against foreign and domestic enemies who act to take or to exploit her husband or his wife and life.

Bacon's "Christian principle" is demonstrable deterrence-benevolence ethics; positive negation of moral power and political pressure as well physical force for the bondman/ bondwoman; negative good parsimonious and partial aid at best; and unfairness and inequity limited to ensuring the perfect obedience of human bondage in total conformance with the will of the White race/ethnic individual and community. They combine to comprise the constituent elements of the republican democracy, ethnic minorities who form the majority and the rule of law that normally translates the rule of the majority and majority rule, and the thesis and synthesis of "the spirit" of America produced by the positive negation of the Black man/woman antithesis.

Baconesque Christian principles purport to impel the observant slaveholder recognize those slaves as his brethren of the human race, who, though they may not be his equals in the eye of the state, are his equals at the tribunal of God.

Bacon chose to take his rational logic and word game play seriously; and elected not to face reality but to impose the ideal upon the real world through the use of selective descriptive facts as if they are actual facts. He appeared, at once, to pass for the mind of Calvinist faith and ethics; the Calvinist social ethics rule and its living proof--namely to prove the perfect is the enemy of the best possible; and to demonstrate conclusively (albeit unwittingly) the color caste/captive class condition to be the core problem of the relations between the corollary predominant power/status people and the ancillary subdominant powerless/statusless people in the sacred/secular civil and social sectors, and the conflict and competition inherent in pro-White race virtue advocates' perversion of negative-intensive antiblack white-ethnic virtue into anti-Black race virtue in public interest ethics.

The model traditionalist's solution to the color caste class cultural crisis in civil confidence entailed the admonition to pay no attention to negative anti-Black race virtue, and to accentuate negative antiblack white-ethnic virtue or positive pro-White race/ethnic virtue. It proved the quintessential answer of prototypical social conservative ethics. He struggled to dominate the middle ground--whose success he believed would result from sustaining full possession of the White race/ethnic positive and negative power poles.

Just as this chief objective was pressed the more evident it became his major goal was a lost cause, just so stridently Bacon advanced with absolute certainty his truth claim: White race existence is the presence of sufficient positive power and Black race existence is the absence of even negative power.

Bacon was totally for securing White race/ethnic interests and values, and against realizing slavery and Black-race interests and values. The prototypic Calvinist traditionalist was constitutionally incapable of grasping adequately his social ethics contradiction; and therefore he did not rise above the ordinary traditionalism--unlike the New Abolitionists whom the Old Abolitionist Quakers and pro-Colonizationist Calvinists opposed.

Bacon implied that to be human is to grow and develop the God-endowed, nature-structured, and culture-nurtured human being potential, that can be maximized best if not only through possessing freedom in liberty. This inference argued human existence and self-determination are synonymous and inextricable modes of being human and the converse of human bondage. Just as certainly for him as for many other compeer contemporaries, White being is the antithesis of Black being presumably because conventional wisdom dictated that they evolve from entirely different gene pools.

Yet Bacon directed neither moral principles nor practical thoughts and actions as corrective measures of what he confirmed (alternately negatively/unconsciously and positively/consciously) to be the heart of the color caste/captive issue: and of the credibility problem for professors of Christianity and civility who pronounce to the public that they can be trusted--and that their leadership can be relied upon by the people--because they possess an uncommon command of competence and courage, and enjoy more common sense than the common man. Whereupon his spiritual and moral power solution to the ecclesiastical and civil power crisis in civil faith and conscience proved unworkable because it failed to address the essential problems and possibilities of power politics:

> Christianity and the church recognize the slave as a man, an
> immortal spirit, a creature having rights, his master's equal before
> God.[63]

For Black bondage the proof of this Christian truth claim the antiabolitionist set forth as an idealistic and ultimate goal, to be reached in the long term
if not eternity, rather than as a realistic objective to be achieved in sum and
substance immediately in history. Bacon's technique of denying human being
equality and liberty and rights and responsibilities to the White and Black A-
merican alike, by affirming the spir-itual equality of each Black slave and White
master, revealed a relatively interesting faith and ethics theory of relativity and
rational exercise in absolutizing the relative--but what it hid was absolute.

This predeliberate White-class/Black-caste human being harmony omission and
spiritual being correspondence commission took the form of Church Militant and
Triumphant truth over error and moral power sufficient to check and balance
the *realpolitik* counterforce. His principle was advanced by the advocate of logical necessity or the virtue of necessity, and adversary of the necessity of virtue, and a convoluted and fatuous vehicle for deception born of necessity: it
was required to facilitate the pontificated corollary that the slave can enjoy
rights and manhood in the slavocracy, whose faulty premise and false promise
was exceeded in depth of deceit only by the Baconesque ancillary, to wit,
"Christianity and the church recognize" the free-born Black Northerner as "a
man" possessing ecclesiastical and civil "rights."

His misconstructions and misperceptions were frequently adjudged illusions by
proabolitionists, and exposed as delusions wherever they were tendered for
rigorous criticism. Yet they were arguable "true beliefs" that the exceptional
rationalist defended with tortuous logic or better rhetoric than reason, and
dangerous fantasies because the "true believer" attempted to live them in
reality.

Where the Black race's real interests are of serious concern, which they
never once were for Bacon, the seminal reason the kind and gentle hierarch is
an important representative figure--reflecting equally brilliantly and illuminat-
ingly the great enlightened host of Moral Reformers--is that the anti-Black race
interests-specific perpetrator's thesis was nearly as pernicious as any one sustained by a Northern opinion maker. Moreover, as Bacon delighted in confess-
ing, he deliberately perpetuated his hoax through articles published periodically
during several months in a journal "for the sake of speaking to thousands at
once."

Bacon's strict constructionist interpretation can be captured in a compressed
construct. He certified that in the Calvinist teachings the Black slave and the
White master are brothers--both "of a common humanity" and "in Christ"--who
share "thoughts and emotions, in experiences of infirmity and deliverance, in
joys and hopes, which place them on one level." Futhermore, as a direct result
of common Christian "faith and love," the master and the slave are "both alike
the servants of Christ and the freeman of the Lord."

This the apparent basis of Evangelical spiritual equalitarianism if not the
unique antislavery essence of Christianity for Protestant reformers. Christian
mutuality between master and slave, that Bacon did not extend to include the
Black-race migrant and White-ethnic immigrant labor groups, is engaged when a

"new feeling of respect and affection springs up in the mind of that master toward that servant."

When this transference occurs, religious instruction will be the instrumental outcome and automatically lead the "servants of Christian masters" to be the first to "rise gradually, but steadily, in the scale of intel-lectual and moral beings." He assured his readership that non-Christian slaveowners will find this parochial education--in lieu of private manumission--Christian initiative irresistible and fall in the line of march. Henceforth their slaves will be permitted slowly and deliberately but eventually to participate in the gradualism movement until "their brotherhood in the human family is more distinctly felt on all sides, and demands a more formal recognition."

Quite without indicating or even hinting at the secular and civil empowerment mechanism, facilitating the connective linkage between dynamic neutrality and stabilization and the progressive transition process toward radical change of the caste/captive condition, Bacon conjures up the millennial fantasy that by divine might overriding contrary human will and reason "the laws will chronicle the change, and will acknowledge the slave as a man." Bacon circumvented the pure profane and circled the pure pious diagnosis of the social cause and effect, and prescription of the cure. Predictably, the instrument of his mystical and mysterious reformation mystique was pure and simple church discipline in the slave states--where "the gospel has begun to be preached without pro-slavery or anti-slavery commentary."

This assertion was not the truth--but were it so the error would prove to be for Black folk another difficulty compounded by complexity. Yet it was solid social conservative neutral ethics, and the faith of Evangelical Protestant civil legal injustice-revering and obeying types. The dogma of faith and doctrinal ethics were translated alternately into theology and ideology, was parlayed by instrumental rationalists who believed they were subjective-free pure objective minds and vessels of divine will. They confronted Black folk and immersed themselves in the Bible without any race, ethnic, class, and cultural premises or prejudices; and encountered truth in their study of the Bible and the Constitution, wherein engaged and through the process of pure reason the self-revelation of the text unfolded.

Bacon was specific on this point and special matter for the "New Side" Congregationalist re-revision of the historical Calvinist doctrine of faith and ethics, regeneration or justification by faith in the righteousness of God and right reason, when he stated that the "effect the gospel produced in a mind regenerated by its power" is one of a pure "life in Christ and in the Spirit of God." Bacon predicted his projected progressive transformation from slavocracy to democracy would transpire over time and through time but in time and even momentarily.

But just how and why the absolute change from solid South Christian slavocracy and the Southern Way of Life could emerge he left for others to discern. As a visionary who regarded himself a prophet, it was enough for him to point to the obvious exceptions; to ignore the fact they normally neither undermine nor test but prove the rule conclusively; and to anoint them the general rule and new order.

His auditors and readers were made to understand that through entire confidence in him and his justification by faith, disciplined churches of "born again" Southern slaveholders would soon rise with a membership of masters who would treat their slaves as they would wish to be treated were they subjected to the same condition.

In summation, Bacon argued that in the "community we have supposed" "believing masters" "will be required by the church," through its supreme legislative and judicatory bodies, to treat slaves "as if they were hired servants, or apprentices, under the protection of the law."

ARCH-ESTABLISHMENTARIAN MOSES STUART'S PAROCHIAL POWER POLITICS THEOLOGY AND POLITICAL CLOUT IN CIVIL CIRCLES

What proslavocrat and antislavo-crat antagonists agreed was totally unrealistic Bacon declared manageable reality, and one so simple and clear as to be "obvious that in that community" (A) Christianity will infallibly, if gradually, reform the churches of the slaveholding populous, as well as quicken and guide its moral sense; (B) human sentiment, acknowledging the natural rights of slaves to self-determination, and asserting itself in legislation "cannot but be making progress"; and (C) Christianity, "thus administered through a disciplined church, will pervade the society and rout slavery--because Christian or church power alone and without civil power "civilizes," "humanizes," and is in essence love and goodwill or the light by which "slavery must decay and perish."[64]

Bacon provides extraordinary insight into the race and religion conscience and compromise of Yankee-Puritan Evangelical Calvinist establishmentarians by unwittingly setting them in grand relief. Nothing so much as depth is added to this perspective as a result of Congregationalist Bacon's special relation with Presbyterian Beecher. Recalling their interconnection in ecclesiastical bureaucratic power circles increases appreciation of the institutional power of anti-Black race values, that the bureaucrats and technocrats manipulated to oppose the public interest ethics Black clergymen-politician leaders published in several medias.

Beecher used the annual Connecticut and Massachusetts Consociation of the Churches of Christ to drive Black Americans further down the up stairs--whom he swore he was raising to new heights. An appreciation of Beecher--who was the peerless Protestant parson power organizer--is pertinent in this context, as the magnitude and range of his connection with men of influence among Orthodoxy was phenomenal.

A significant influential friend of Beecher, among the many, was the Reverend Moses Stuart (1780-1852): Nathaniel Taylor's predecessor as minister of First Church New Haven, in which role Taylor was succeeded by Bacon. Stuart was Bacon's professor of biblical theology, and the preceptor of Beecher's son, Edward Beecher. And Stuart, like Lyman Beecher and Taylor, was a disciple of Timothy Dwight. "Connecticut Yankee" Stuart was learned in Greek and Hebrew, a distinguished biblical theology scholar, and early professor (1812-52) at Andover Theological School (1808). His immediate successor was Harriet Beecher's husband, Calvin Ellis Stowe.

In his Congregationalist professorial chair, Stuart transmitted a revisionist Evangelical Calvinist faith and ethics that revolved around the following rational organizing principle he identified as the classical Protestant "Rule of truth": "The Scriptures are the *sufficient* and only rule of faith and practice."

At the height of his considerable rational powers, the end of his long career as a former partisan Federalist Party parson, and formidable public defender of the Calvinist tradition and offender of anti-Calvinists, and the turning point from antislavocracy/proslavocracy neutrality to war between the warriors for the competing interests of the Union and "states' rights" states, Stuart considered it "a sacred duty" to correlate the sacrosanct moral and legal laws of the Bible with the American republican democracy and slavocracy.

A model method messenger and moral medium, Stuart erupted with this message as a new motive, means, and opportunity, and published *Conscience and the Constitution* (1850) with the purpose of holding "before the world the declarations and doctrines of God' s eternal word."

Stuart earned the title chief Evangelical-Calvinist biblical theologian defending social conservative Orthodoxy. But in spite of the rationalist's herculean efforts to advance Orthodoxy and the Reformed tradition of Calvinism, Congregationalist/Presbyterian revolutionary biblical studies did not liberate White ethnic groups any more than they loosened or tightened, cut or untied, the caste/captive ties binding the Black race. During the forty-five years subsequent to his call to be the minister of the First Church of Christ in New Haven, Stuart reported in 1850, that he had renounced "all active pursuit of politics" and "never preached politics, or taught them, in public": without acknowledging his abandonment of power politics paralleled the demise of the Federalist Party he joined with Theodore and Timothy Dwight in supporting.

He also did not admit to promoting personal parochial values he desired to superimpose upon the public--in private communications with White Christian friends--as the nationally renowned polemicist of Orthodoxy, except when it served his cherished cause in the church and state political embroilment to selectively recall one response to a request for his expertise on political theology.

This singular occasion provided him with the opportunity to explicate clearly in a brief outline his appreciation of human bondage and interpretation of the proslavery Bible and antislavery Jesus of Nazareth: the Master Teacher whom Calvinists revered as "the righteousness of God." Stuart communicated his view in a formal reply to an inquiry he penned in a letter (April 10, 1837) to the Reverend Wilbur Fisk (1792-1839), the founder (1831) and first President of Connecticut Wesleyan University.

Fisk wrote a fellow Methodist clergyman, currently an active New Abolitionists, to advise him: "You have the ablest and those who are among the honestest men of this age, arrayed against you." For proof of his claim--in this Methodist Episcopal Church antislavery/proslavery controversy on eve of the division of the nationally united Methodist Denomination into separate and distinct Northern antislavocracy and Southern proslavocracy denominations--Arminian Fisk (one of the power elite Methodists for whom a mixture of Arminianism and Calvinism added efficiency to the sufficient *the method*) solicited support from Calvinist Stuart.

Fisk stated in writing that renowned biblical theologian Stuart, who earned his reputation as a New Testament faith specialist and represented himself as a Christian ethics expert, was his authority because he believed it to be inarguable that Stuart's credentials as a Christian scholar were exceeded in impeccableness only by his well-known "integrity of purpose" and "his unflinching regard for truth." Certain that conventional wisdom confirmed his judgment, Fisk requested Stuart's scholarly opinion regarding whether or not being both a Christian and a slavemaster was demonstrable error, immorality, and sin. Stuart responded that any equitable class and status or civil relations between Christian masters and slaves (who obviously occupied different stations) were abrogated "as a matter of course," since slaves were by the "good Old Book" required to "do their duty cheerfully."[65]

As the prelate to whom "Old Pope" Timothy Dwight passed the political power and authority miter that he at first put in and at last took out of mothballs, Stuart finally formed a political action committee. The sheer personality and will to power compelling force of the inspired one-man crusade, transmogrified a cult leader for the power priests, fashioned the formation of partisan parsons that he initiated two years before his death something more but not much more than a personality cult.

The Stuartian faith diverged sectarians engaged in ethics as a conscious clergy collective, converged as a charity converted into clout Christian company, and organized as charioteer contenders against caste challengers in a class war caused by their competition for the conscience of the civil community. They consolidated as a crusader caravan once the new consciousness consecrated as their centerpiece Stuart's sensational pontification: the Protestant *Emancipation* papal bull published by the pontiff elevated by "Old Pope" Dwight as an evenhanded antislavery and proslavery testament and protest entitled *Conscience and the Constitution.*

Essentially, Stuart wrote the partisan parson power politics piece to excite the Moral Majaority to defend Massachusetts Senator Daniel Webster (1782-1852) whom the moral minority arrested, charged, tried as a proslavocrat/proslavocracy protector of the real interests of the Southeast at the expense of the real interests of the Northeast. Webster deserved the credit he received from the conscience over class countermarching contemporaries, who claimed he earned the title Protestant Pilate as the primary publicist and pilot of the Fugitive Slave Act (1850). This controversial legislation compromised the principles of his constituents, the counterdemanding clan contended throughout the North for whom Webster's initiative was something more consequential than a concession to the South.

The Act, in addition to enacted severe penalties for free White men and women arrested as violators on the charge that at their hands slaves were permitted or assisted to make good their escape, mandated as the law and order of the land the slave-free sovereign states and "all good citizens" to be in conformance with Federal marshals and their deputies; to deliver protected fugitives from legal injustice when "commanded to aid and assist in the prompt and efficient execution of this law"; and to refrain from shielding runaways caught by slavecatchers.

Pursuant to parading in a public promise and performance his Protestantism will prevail posited premise, on which he pivoted to prove his political point-- that power is principle and principle is not only power but the power point and point of power--Stuart revived for revisionist "Consistent-Calvinist" culture conservatives the old strict constructionist interpretation of right as the rules and regulations ruled in order to secure social constancy rather than change in new cultural crisis by civil rulers ecclesiastical ruling elders.

In other words, Stuart restructured the cautious Bible-based and Constitution-grounded moral law of church and state that justified legal immorality; rendered ethical acts such as harboring fugitives that ethicists executed to end injustice unethical because they were illegal; and reverted to a rational defense of Old and New Testament slavery which the ratiocinator recommended as realistic rather than cruel and unusual punishment.

In the process, Stuart declared human bondage not the excellent but the expedient measure of the God-ordained Moral Law (and foundation of ecclesiastical law and civil law), church and state positive law, and legitimate government. Stuart expounded upon the fact that ancient Israel was at once a religious and a slave society.

In the course of his argumentation, he argued the arguments for the Mosaic law and/or the Deuteronomic Code being the Providence-permitted regulator of the ecclesiastical and civil powers of the Mosaic Dispensation and Kingdom of Israel. His critical points argued that (1) slavery was an ancient and therefore honorable rite; (2) only among the Jews "could the fugitive slave come to the knowledge and worship" of God; (3) Jewish law included recognized and enforceable if neither always realized nor enforced rights of slaves, and commanded Jewish slavemasters to be humane; (4) Jews possessed rights as slavebuyers, slavesellers, slave-traders, and slaveowners that involved holding as personal property Jewish and non-Jewish slaves; and (5) under Leviticus legislation reclamation of fug-itives "could be *lawfully* made."

The power point of the Stuartian morale and rationale proceeded from an obvious parallel: "Christianity is a *national* religion"--and the White "Southern master" resides in a state where "true Christianity" is observed by the overpowering majority of "our fellow citizens and brethren." It is most difficult to imagine that American Civil Religion could be stated more concisely or incisively.

Relative to this tale told by a rationalist warrior for Protestantism, White Americans are Christians or a monistic and not a pluralistic people. As one White Christian people Americans are the visible and indivisible mystical body of Christ civil body politic. The White secular and sacred American folk live under positive and moral laws God-instituted authorities legitimatize such as those established in the Constitution and Mosaic Law, crystallized in the Ten commandments, and enforced by the Dueteronomic legislative and juridical specifications.

From this pinnacle of his analysis, Stuart leaped not in being but to his slippery slope conclusion, to wit, since conscience binds the asserted equivalence of Christians and Americans to obey the Constitution and the Bible, therefore, they are as Northern and Southern brothers and sisters in Christ and the Union required to return a fugitive--even though Northerners "have reason enough to pity him." This proslavery and anti-Black race policy, proslavocrat Stuart argued, is mitigated by the fact that Northerners are "not in the least degree" responsible "for bad treatment of the slave," and in any case "we do *not* send back the refuge from the South to a *heathen* nation or tribe."

Stuart left every one with the capacity to follow a rational argument no reason to doubt that in the case of the Black-race cultural kin-group "we are one nation" does not apply: because the antiabolitionism advocate asserts, without fear contradiction, that not even his proabolitionist adversaries were so fatuous as to claim their Black contemporaries are "fellow-citizens and brethren," according to the law of the land and Moses (with whom Stuart confuses his own identity).

Straightaway, in the name of positive-limiting and negative-intensive antiblack white-ethnic virtue, Stuart advances Halfway Piety faith and ethics deterrence-benevolence to justify anti-Black race virtue--for establishment Trinitarian and Unitarian Congregationalists who were united in this value judgment. Exactly here the brilliant teacher--of powerhouse Calvinist-clergymen leaders for forty years--promulgates the dogma that being a Christian and a slavemaster has the sanction of Moses and national statutes that underpin the proslavery laws of slave states.

Evidently the pertinent point of the ruling elder legal scholar and authority on the positive law connection of the American Church and Constitution is made, perfectly clear, and sharp enough to beg the question, to wit, just who is the law giver and just who is the lawmaker or whether indeed they are one and the same ruler. What is neither a moot question or open to question is the e-qually evident fact that this posited axiom asserts the equivalence of the "Rule of Scipture" and the "Rule of Truth," the Moral Law of God and the Deuteronomic law of Moses, and the divine and civil "Rule of Law."

The New Testament Moses Stuart attests that his New Testament (A) is not the Bible but the continuum of the Old Testament; (B) originates with the Jew like Moses whom contemporaries chiefly called Jesus of Nazareth; (C) inheres in Jesus who emerges as ethical excellence less effectively when appreciated as the manifest essence in existence of *agape* than when approached as the commandment giver of the law-constricted Church constructed on the legal rules and regulations created for Christians to engage the Church and Civil powers by the Apostle Paul; and (D) transmits best the literal word rather "*the spirit*" of Jesus or the New Testament, that in turn is best translated not by the empirical and experiential method of being existentially engaged with the mind and message of the messenger but through substituting for this hermeneutical principle of interpretation the principal hermetical principle--that is, by making the mind of Paul the surrogate for the mind of Jesus and reading his legal mind to learn the original intent of *apape* mind of the New Testament.

Whence Stuart materializes as a strict constructionist who understands comprehensively the Christian claim that the absence occasioned the presence in history of *agape*, but a classic conservative Calvinist ethicist and narrow-scoped legal point interpreter for whom the original intent of the Moral Law of God is not the *agape* person and presence in existence but the Pauline rule that rules the Mosaic rules and regulations the law and order of God, nature, and man in civilization. The law established by the Old Testament Moses and the precedent followed by the New Testament Moses comprises the Stuartian gospel's basic premise, the essential point of whose keystone social ethics principle is that human bondage ownership cannot be a contradiction in terms of either Christianity or civility.

On this narrow point promulgated to mitigate the broad and deep meaning of the message delivered by the messenger who was stoned because the legalistic minds of his fellow descedants from the Mount Sinai law enactor (enforcer and expounder), Stuart certifies to Fisk that because the Bible legitimated the human bondage commercial enterprise so highly prized by slaveowning Jews and Christians throughout their history in the Orient and the Occident all known faithful Gentile and Semite American slavemasters "violated no sacred obligation in holding slaves, provided they should treat them in a Christian manner."

Beyond a shadow of doubt, Black-race kith and kin were in deeper trouble than they imagined after the master Christian preceptor of establishment ministers identified as identical twins the honorable human bondage "Christian manner" and Southern manner--as comple-ments of civil captors and manners whose evincement he declared the demonstrable White gentleman "Christian master." Moses Stuart linked these great realities and certainties which swore constituted the law of Moses--that Stuart affirmed the Apostle Paul appropriated but denied he superimposed to override the love of Christ--high civility and Christianity, and the truth of the Bible and the Church:

The Mosaic law does not authorize us to reject the claims of our fellow countrymen and citizens, for strayed or stolen property-- property authorized and guaranteed as such by Southern States to their respective citizens. These States are not *heathen*. We have acknowledged them as brethren and *fellow citizens* of the great community. A fugitive from them is not a fugitive from an idol- atrous and polytheistic people. And even if the Bible had neither said nor implied anything in relation to this whole matter, the sol- emn *compact* which we have made, before heaven and earth, to de- liver up fugitives when they are *men held to service* in the State from which they have fled, is enough to settle the question of le- gal right on the part of the master, whatever we may think of his claim when viewed in the light of Christianity.[66]

Stuart pronounced a divine benediction upon pro-White race interests and the White Gentlemen's Agreement (Constitution) he termed the "*compact*," en- tirely confident that Black folk were the only heathens and they, of course, had no rights.

Stuart was determined to leave no one to doubt he was responsible for his rational intentions and consequences, and thus restated the point to make it unmistakably transparent to any competent reader: The "Mosaic statute, which was the perpetual law of the Jews," permitted "an unlimited liberty to *pur- chase*, (not to steal), bond-men and bond-maids of the heathen around and out of Palestine."

Orthodoxy's major biblical scholar placed the full weight of his authority upon this exegesis, whose in-terpretation had the force law and like his eis- egesis argued that the *goyim* slaves of Jews were their "perpetual" and "*heritable* property."

Judgmental contemporaries could be excused for (A) understanding Stuart to imply that Black Christians remained the *goyim* of the descendants by faith and blood of the Puritan "chosen race of God," or heathens of other "Elect" and even "Reprobate" White Christians, whom White Anglo-Saxon Protestants were authorized by the Moral Law of God to enslave in perpetuity; (B) being caught unawares and captured entirely by surprised when he failed to evaluate the plight of Black slaves condemned to bondage in perpetuity in the light of the Jewish "poor brother slaves" whom Jewish masters were required by law to lib- erate every seven years and/or at the "Jubilee" (each fifty years); and (C) ac- ting as if they were certain perception is reality in the instance of Stuart who was fixed in their appearances as perversion of truth and justice.

Compared and contrasted to the "great Jewish legislator," Moses, Stuart ad- judged the New Abolitionist Evangelical Calvinists to be existence deficient of Christian "morals or religion": because they claim that "the ownership of slaves which heaven has given express leave to purchase, to be deemed a *crime* of the deepest dye." Stuart counterclaimed that if the immediatists were right, Moses was wrong; and God, who by the only inference reasonable men can draw from their implication sanctioned a crime He had forbidden in the Sixth Commandent, is an instance of self-contradiction.

In the Stuartian error of conception, perception, and deception, the Old Tes- tament proslavery Moral Law of God applied to St. Paul and to the New Testa- ment, and thus for Black American Christian slaves "it should suffice, that they are the Lord's *freemen*." Antiabolitionist Stuart was "Consistent Calvinist" puritanicalism in flesh and blood as he taught in Andover Theological School, an institution that refused admission to Black applicants, and preached in a denomination that closed its doors to their New Abolitionist defenders: who promoted abolition of the color caste/captive system and its replacement with biracial equalitarianism; whereas his cardinal New Testament rule, Stuart critically imposed and informed Black folk they had to live by, was a consummate proslavery doctrine.

The oppressed were to find in the Congregationalist denomination no basis for the Gospel's radical call for immediate liberation of the captives--"instantly free your slaves." But they were to discover the "Connecticut Yankee" leader of "Massachusetts Yankee" Congregationalists instructing them to hold dear the letter and spirit of the Gospel that he defined as the unity of "peace, of good order, of ready obedience where obedience is due, and of obligation to contentment with our lot, unless some peaceful way of changing it can be devised." The revised authorized version of "New Side" Calvinism and the Gospel, according to this scholarly authority, required obedience to the state whose legitimate "ground of national law"--together with the "constitutional compact" White Christian Gentlemen concluded because it served their real interests fully as much as it advanced their real values--removed all doubt concerning the validity of Black-race chattel identity, "question of property, or right of ownership." Deterrence-benevolence ethics and the Stuartian Moral Reform law and order argued that neither the Black fugitive nor the White citizen has the right of free choice and first refusal when faced with the slavehunter presenting his official papers, authorizing him to recapture the captive; all are bound by the Constitution whose White Gentlemen's Agreement is a higher authority than the Moral Law or the conscience.

Strict constructionist Stuart interpreted the sacred document as a static and inviolable one for Black race-specific human bondage property, whereby the Constitution, "in making him property," requires White citizens "to acknowledge as property" the enslaved Black race and each fugitive whom a state "has decided to be property."

Inarguably, this affirmation of perpetuated perpetual dehumanization in perpetuity as relatively right and instant universal self-determination as absolutely wrong in principle for Black folk answers the question put by Stuart: "How can one sovereignty usurp authority to decide for another?" The deliverance of the fugitive to an "inhabitant of another State," who has "a claim sanctioned by the law of that State," is not only commanded by the law but a *moral* or admonitory Christian duty" as well.[67]

Stuart ruled out or order and the unthinkable for Christians any suggestion of an appeal to conscience as "a higher law than the Constitution." The principled Calvinist equated the *"Christian* conscience" with St. Paul's "Christian conscience," that sent the slave Onesimus back to his master Philemon "for *conscience'* sake!" Paul, antebellum Stuartians were to proclaim on good authority, did not act out of "a conscience wholly *subjective*" or violate "a solemn compact"--as was pro-posed by William Lloyd Garrison, whom Stuart castigated as the New Abolitionists' "genius of slander, vituperation, and profaneness." The New Abolitionists' solid civility and good citizenship criterion for Christian residents of Massachusetts was absolute refusal to deliver a fugitive to the authorities, and total disobedience of the Fugitive Law. They interpreted it to be a statute conceived in sin and created by the politics of compromise in the body politic, whose diabolical compact tendered it beneath contempt and compliance tantamount to moral capitulation for the higher conscience of the informed Christian.

Traditional Calvinism revisionist Stuart found this interpretation too liberal for his progressive transformationism. He denounced to the public what the rule-revering ruling elder termed New Abolitionism's extra-biblical new measure, and proabolitionist proponents as bearers of "a truce-breaking, Paul-reproaching *conscience*." Stuart offered in the place of proabolitionism his antiabolitionism full faith and credit with his parochial prayer for the public: "The *CONSTITU-TION* in respect to fugitives held to service or labor *MUST* BE OBEYED."

It might be otherwise with White citizens and their real interests and values, but Black inhabitants were not citizens and evidenced a degree of difference so great as to be a different kind of American. Forthwith, the standard bearer of orthodox Halfway Piety's two-dimensional negative antiblack white-ethnic virtue and deterrence-benevolence ethic made anti-Black race virtue crystal clear: "*Gradual freedom* is the only possible practical measure" for ending slavery rationally, fairly, and peaceably.

In addition to gradual manumission, what also "must be a work of time"--as demonstrated by the thirty year-old ACS for the denaturalization and deportation of the American Black race--is the expansion and extension of the denationalization plan that requires dedication to "*colonize the blacks*" in a separate "Territory"; to assist Black native Americans in establishing "a government of their own"; and to locate and support White bureaucrats and technocrats satisfied to execute deterrence-benevolence ethics as "merely watchful guardians over their welfare and safety." Stuart was never more sincere and serious than when he concluded with his bifurcation of reality principle of biracial brotherhood and sisterhood: From the time Black expatriates and exported North Americans develop an independent state, but not before, "thenceforth we may be their friends and allies."

As leaders of establishment men and institutions, Bacon and Stuart were Beecher's cohorts. They spoke to and for Northeastern Congregationalist and Presbyterian denominations--as well as with leaders of other Calvinist and Arminian denominations. Trinitarian Congregationalist clergy, forming the consensus behind their initiative, increasingly exercised undue influence even in Unitarian Boston--that was exceeded only by their clout in economic and political affairs of church and state. Through their colleagues, friends, and students, they dominated if they did not command and control the social values of these Calvinist denominations, whose unmatchable fiscal resources and policies were directing lasting values and making an enduring difference that had greater public impact than the sister denominations' boasting a larger membership and popular following.

Stuart returned to his earlier role of partisan party power politics parson at the beginning of the end of Northern denominational divisions between pro-immediatists New Abolitionists and pro-gradualist American Colonizationists--and the end of the beginning of their unification as antislavocrat opponents of proslavocrat religious humanitarians and secular humanists. As late as the mid-1840s but certainly prior to the watershed Fugitive Slave Act, mainstream denominations were proslavery/antislavery neutral institutions emphasizing gradualism and private manumissions in cooperation with their Southern members, whose leadership as directors on the board of the ACS chief executive officer Gurley managed skillfully initially outnumbered Northerners.

Synchronously, Northern denominations--with the exception of the Protestant

Episcopal Church--switched from full support of the ACS as their antislavery auxiliary institution, and initiated sectarian antislavery societies, long after these establishmentarian leaders' competing nonestablishmentarian Evangelical New Abolitionist brethren had united and divided in the American Anti-Slavery Society.

Lyman Beecher already had more responsibilities than any ordinary Puritan powerhouse could be expected to fulfill adequately, but, he was nothing if not an exceptional Yankee figure, and to these demanding challenges he added a centrist role in the crisis over slavery. He could do so because behind, beside, and before him was the holy band that Stuart, Gurley, and helped him to organize to beat the competition.

4

FRIENDS OF FOES AS ENEMIES OF LYMAN BEECHER

Lyman Beecher advanced as a professional Protestant principles and practice generalist and Moral Reform specialist to become an original American Civil Religion theoretician and practitioner. His Continent continuum of classical conservative Catholic and Calvinist faith and ethics proclaimed securing the Church (the only medium of grace and salvation) and civil (the indispensable political economy rational instrument for protecting property and producing prosperity) powers a matter of stabilizing *status quo* social order, and of primary importance as the first and last foremost priority of the magistrate and citizen for guaranteeing ever-expanding not only survival growth and development but also the linear progress of proliferating Christianity and civility.

From this primary premise underpinning the prime social principle Beecher acted on the conclusion he drew from his analysis of society which dictated that the church and state are part of the problem and the solution to the color caste/captive cultural controversy. The Evangelical Calvinist evangelism and revivalism multi-media event in himself necessarily also approached the civil and Christian conscience crisis as an opportunistic mind-massaging messenger with a menacing message and mission.

In this mode and mood, Beecher appeared both like Moses Stuart--with whom he shared values--and unlike the academy-based and region-bound professor who engaged in occasional and highly selective class interests-protecting pursuits in church and state suits as an academic and an avocation.

Beecher distinguished himself as a professional ecclesiastical and civil affairs activist, an expert engaged in public interest-advancing ethics and action rather less precisely than therein attending the business of business and religion, and a powerhouse who scarcely shared power as effectively as he exerted private pressure and exercised parochial force.

Anti-Calvinist and pro-Calvinist critics discovered Beecher to be a challenging crusader for Calvinistical Christianity and civility, and middle-class morality and respectability. So far from being a mindless moral manipulator and motive in search of a method, and near to being the model modern master of morals and moralisms, Beecher joined motive, means, and opportunity not unlike Stuart, but differed from Stuart as a famous public figure who used his advantage to assist the expansion of color caste/captive-limiting collective class consciousness and conscience. This national upperdog presence proliferated during the antebellum era throughout the culture, took shape and form in reality as "*the spirit*" of White Protestants who bid fair to reverse the rising expectations of their underdog Black-race cultural kin-group,and largely succeeded in substituting their own liberty-delaying and opportunity-denying aspirations.

Since in spite of the potent and potential positive power of the powerful elite and negative power of the powerless Black masses, the substantial capacity for defiance of the profane and pious White Protestant friends and foes of Black folk was tested and strained in resistance so severely until even they could not escape scot free of the Second Great Awakening evangelism culture-impacting techniques Beecher pioneered, it was anything but surprising that

Black religious and secular brothers and sisters narrowly missed being eclipsed entirely by the storm of revivalism and its Moral Reformism calm center.

For the purposes of constructive Calvinist communication and conversion Beecher fashioned in his facile logic a complex revivalism strategy and evangelism tactic, whose most effective instrument was a highly proficient and efficient non-denial denial of universal salvation technical principle. This intricate and delicately balanced technique was designed to be applied by the Evangelical mind-changing professional personally and individually to each uninitiated or unregenerate, as if every willing soul was able to become a new "born again" being.

Whence the message of the revivalist translated personal regeneration of each individual in the universe was both necessary and possible. On this updated empirical rationalist psychology, religious humanism, and logical evangelism the revivalism of the Second Great Awakening turned in democracy and slavocracy; away from the largely local church-centered First Great Awakening revivalism Jonathan Edwards initiated; and toward both extra-church gathered meetings and a movement for the Moral Reformation of the whole society and world.

Beecher rationalized this radical reorientation from a pessimistic mundane worldview and relative unconcernment with human cultural institutions and civil order, yet hope empowered firm belief there existed no more exciting choice than the absolute concern with and total commitment to the establishment of the Kingdom of God (eternity) in history, toward optimistic involvement in direct moral change of society.

The partial return to John Calvin's real interest rather decided disinterest in church and state superstructures and infrastructures was a direct reaction to the political defeat of the Federalist Party and spiritual victory of the Second Great Awakening, as well as from an undefaced social conservative faith and ethics ground; a worldview supported by a hierarchical race-specific, ethnic-intensive, and class-consciousness Calvinist superiority complex; a Puritan race/ethnic ethic of uniformity; and an establishmentarian church and state related policy of coordinating religious-spiritual/moral and secular-politics/-economics components.

This partial retreat or reversal--from Edwardsean churchocracy for Christocracy to Dwightesque/Tayloresque/Beecheresque churchocracy for Christocracy and democracy/slavocracy--evolved during the color caste/captive cultural crisis from the Calvinist cultural conservative spiritual power and moral power principles. American pro-Calvinists rooted them in the millennialism-intensive faith and ethics that pre-destinarian Calvin contended was a corruption of the correct catholic *Institutes of the Christian Religion*, and Evangelical Calvinist Moral Reformers and social engineers managed preponderantly.

PARTISAN POLITICS ABANDONED FOR PAROCHIAL POLITICS

Beecher appeared full of himself and of zest, in command of his principles, and a preeminent Moral Reformer partly because his brain and will power matched his great ambition. He was held in high regard by his Connecticut sacred and profane political peers. Congregationalist clergy indicated their respect for the Presbyterian serving a Congregationalist congregation when they selected presbyter Beecher to preach the Annual Election Day Sermon (in 1826) "to the Legislature of Connecticut, at New Haven."

Later that year while still flush with success, fresh from recent moral reform victories, and armed with professional revivalistic strategic and tactical weapons, the Presbyterian warrior in Congregationalism--who had followed closely the successive Calvinist de-feats and divisions in Massachusetts with an eye to recouping the losses--invited a call to a new Evangelical mission he accepted, and promptly departed Litchfield to become the founding pastor (1826-32) of the Hanover Street Congregational Church in Boston.

Currently anti-Calvinists concentrated their conservatism in the continuum Charles Chauncy calcified as the leading Boston and Harvard clergyman, and chief critic of Jonathan Edwards of New Haven and Yale, who as an "Old Light" Calvinist nearly single-handedly limited the expansion of "New Light" Edwards' First Great Awakening initiative in "the Hub of the universe." Chauncy's theological liberal Calvinism survived with his Unitarian Congregationalist anti-Calvinist successors, whom pro-Calvinist challenged because they were in command and control of the power circles in the historic capital of Calvinist Puritan Orthodoxy, and restricted the flow of Second Great Awakening revivalism in Boston.

Theological liberal and social conservative Unitarian Congregationalists, who negotiated this vanquishment, doubtless believed their accomplishment to be anything but cost-prohibitive, Nevertheless, it was not a cost-free operation howbeit the case that the initiators of the division of the tradition into Unitarian and Trinitarian Congregationalism at once computed a cost/benefit analysis; were willing to pay the relatively high price for autonomous existence; and thought split into Calvinist faith and Puritan ethics was cost-effective.

In point of fact, the anti-Calvinist Congregationalists won the theological battle with the pro-Calvinist Congregationalists for the minds and hearts of proper Bostonians. But their victory was gained at the expense of a significant loss to involvement in power politics of the whole (liberal and conservative Congregationalist) Yankee/Puritan-clergy class. They beat a hasty retreat from the defeat and demise the Federalist Party suffered with the rise of the Democratic Party, that commenced with the nineteenth century.

By the end of Chauncy's life (whose death occurred in the year the Constitution was ratified) and the beginning of Beecher's career, direct action and interest in Puritan power politics waned among "Massachusetts Yankee" and waxed among "Connecticut Yankee" Congregationalist clergymen. Whereas in New Haven the secular and sacred "Connecticut Wits" were respectively led by Theodore and Timothy Dwight, in Boston the politics of Federalism evolved all but exclusively among the "Massachusetts Yankee" lawyers--the preponderance of whom could care less about nothing as much as being theological spokesmen.

Increasingly less sacred and more profane New England lawyers advanced as the lawmakers and professional politicians after their Federalist Party was out of power, while concomitantly their pro-Calvinist and anti-Calvinist clergymen preferred to public affairs and being public servants publicly prominent displays of private self-flagellation and parochial self-depreciation. Their expenditure of excessive energies in this extensive ecclesiastical engagement and exercise in exigency (futility rather than fidelity critics claimed) exposed disordered faith priorities and the missing link of serious social ethics, whose absence precipitated privation rather presence of the parson in power politics.

New England clergy were (A) equally enthusiastically and disproportionately engaged in theological controversy as pro-Calvinist and anti-Calvinist rival factions, and disengaged from submitting their candidacy in competitive public politics; (B) a divided class of theological liberals and conservatives united by common economic interests and political values; fierce friends of the Federalists and enemies of their secular humanist Democrat foes; (C) countermeasured by counteroffensive champions of Jeffersonian Democracy and "denounced by militant deists and neglected by genteel believers"; (D) evolving from convergence before and quantum leaping in divergence after the death of partisan Federalist Party parson *par excellence* Timothy Dwight; (E) self-defeated *realpolitik* defeatists--barely missed and easily displaced in the political process by their contemners; and (F) deterrence-benevolence deconstructionists dedicated to de-obligationism who refused to fight and to secure their true and real interests and values through stiff competition for the vote of the people, preferred to cut and run, and elected to switch from public to parochial politics.

Early national era hegemonic Federalist Party par-tisan parsons in Connecticut and Boston were counterparts of two theological liberal contemporaries of social conservative Chauncy, and forerunners of William Channing: the Reverend Jonathan Mayhew (1720-66), a militant Patriot, and the Reverend Jeremy Belknap (1744-98), an intellectual historian. Channing and fellow theological liberals and social conservatives who succeeded this trio of representative Boston determiners of Yankee values, and pacesetting guardians of the strengths and weaknesses of the powerful Puritan culture, despaired of politics.

Channing and company substituted an odd and even peculiar Yankee anti-political and moral power-only device. This mechanism for elitist ethicists was at best a deficient surrogate for virtue, and at worse a saturated self-serving vice of the latter day saints, and one revision whose reversion of the New England way was an instance of neither the necessity of virtue nor the virtue of necessity but so near to a flat contradiction of the tradition it appeared a counterfeit Puritan value born of Yankee pride and prejudice.

In truth and reality, Protestant moralists embraced church-confined and civil power-evading politics and irradiated the high value they placed on sharp conflict and stiff competition, on the one hand; their convincement that in translocating power politics from the public to the parochial sector that the politics of religion transmogrified the politics of compromise into the politics of morality, on the other hand; and, on yet another hand, their belief that they had secured simultaneously the high ground and elevated anti-political religion and apolitical moral power into a high ethical and publicly responsible social redeeming principle.

Forthwith, throughout the preponderance of the antebellum decades, establishmentarian Unitarian and Trinitarian Congregationalists presumed they were called and chosen as well as elected to be pure moralists; presupposed a moralist neither bends nor breaks nor compromises principles; and took it for granted that no self-respecting moral conquest-seeking clergy-men would stoop to conquer by participating in partisan party power politics as a candidate for elected office.

This value judgment was based on a conclusion they deduced from descriptive facts, whereby in their view it was axiomatic that religion is the art of the impossible (or implausible); politics is the art of the possible (or plausible); and, (primarily due to their deeming unworthy of their serious reflection the important fact that professional politicians understand that real interests and values are relatively impermanent and always negotiable but the permanent principles are appropriately compromised only in a crisis and even then only when they are no real alternatives), the profession of politics is anathema to the pure pious as well as risk-intensive for the pure profane, because a compromise of principles is at once never the correct choice (lesser of two evils) and the central business of professional politicians.[68]

Antebellum Moral Reformers substituted moral power for political power and --at the precise moment in history when these proslavocrats' antislavocrat challengers were at last counterbalancing slavocrat reactionaries--finally reentered as politics offensive agents the antislavocracy/proslavocracy cultural crisis too late with too little to be directive determinants rather than reactive neutrals.

Alternately recurring random and unpredictable Puritan-Yankee clerical engagement and disengagement in partisan politics commenced as abstention on principle with Jonathan Edwards' new churchocracy for Christocracy initiatives at the end of theocracy; ended with the birth of the republic and the Federalists; returned with the fall of the Federalist Party; and entered the gradual stages of termination, that ended with re-engagement in 1850, when antiabolitionist Moral Reformers formed their antislavery ACS--and/or the perfect parochial-private-public partnership model.

Direct action in the *realpolitik* conflict and competition arena emanated from the Evangelical and pro-political proabolitionists, who broke forth in vigorous reaction to the quasi-political pro-Colonizationists and their Moral Reform leaders--at the front and center of whose Evangelical establishmentarian pro-gradualism Lyman Beecher appeared as active as any Protestant powerhouse. The new mid-antebellum moral power plus political power phenomenon was developed and nurtured by the Manhattan-centered New Abolitionist rivals of the moral power-only proabolitionists, who followed the leadership of Boston-based William Garrison. Frustrated by the limited success of their prodigious antislavery endeavors, compared to the apparent absence of noticeable failures experienced by proslavocracy slavocrats in Congress, the innovative minority corps of proabolitionist New Yorkers and their friends in the East and the West turned to politics as the last, best hope for abolishing slavery peacefully.

Politics was the instrumental process of ecclesiastical power and authority, and therefore even in the realm of the art of the impossible the art of the possible was continuously practiced with consummate skill by church politicians. Denominational politics was the school in which pro-political New Abolitionists were nurtured, gained experience in stiff competition, and endured defeats inflicted by the normally victorious antiabolitionists at the helm of the ecclesiastical power apparatuses.

Unquestionably, they were quick studies who learned to follow the power politics analyses and conclusions formulated by expert church denominational politicians--whose selectively imposed rule of the majority by the ruling majority that establishment ruling elder Beecher-types advanced to its logical end--and to challenge the ecclesiastical locus of power within the institutions to focus upon the issue of slavery.

Given the opposition of the overwhelming American religious and secular majority to the small minority's goal of making the proscription of slavery the law and order of the land, their limited access to the denominational resources and power circles dominated by anti-abolitionist establishmentarians, and their scant political power connections and influence--as well as over-powering deficiency that was partially attributable to the delayed re-entrance of Evangelical Yankee-Puritans into rough and tumble American politics--it was as re-asonable as it was controversial for the New Abolitionists to exercise initiative and create the American Anti-Slavery Society, the Manhattanites to leave it to the Bostonians and form both the American and Foreign Anti-Slavery Society and their moral and partisan power politics Liberty Party.

New York New Abolitionists attempted to be effective power politics brokers by establishing the Liberty Party as an uncompromising, single-issue, and special-interest political bloc. They were convinced Constitution-legitimated human bondage was too serious a compromise of principle for politics as usual. But in the process of practicing their united idealism and realism principles in the civil realm to reform the Union, the idealists discovered they could not compete in the game of hardball politics played by the realists in charge of the American pragmatism and majority rule system.

Northern and Southern religious and secular politickers were committed to the two-party tradition so completely they joined as members of the rival Democratic Party and Federalist/Whig Party to condemn the antislavery Liberty Party as an Un-American third-party deviation from the tradition. Conventional wisdom impugned the common sense and character of the partisan Liberty Party parishioners and parsons by calling into question their motives, methods, and manners. Proabolitionist politickers' intense pressure enveloped difficulty that was compounded by complexity when the Evangelical Calvinist Liberty Party laity and clergy were chastised by rigid traditionalists for failing to be inflexible "Consistent Calvinists."

Traditionalist and nontraditionalist politics-limiting moralists acted confidently as if they were satisfied that the presence or absence of universal absolute and/or relative principles was irrelevant in the dehumanization versus self-determination crisis: precisely where what appears equally clear and significant is the inevitable and necessary conflict in human existence and competition of interests between high values such as life and happiness, class and caste, order and justice, peace and freedom, liberty and slavery, ethnicity and race, and *Conscience and the Constitution*.

Pro-political Evangelical moralists demonstrated a mature appreciation of the basic moral principles: life, goodness, rightness, honest, and individual liberty. Naturally, those activists who correctly understood these five ethical principles to be equally universal and permanent--but incorrectly believed their hierarchal order is fixed as herein set forth, and a different priority arrangement is an exception that does not confirm but overturns the rule--found their Liberty Party early experiment in the power politics system to be a disturbing but not an unsettling experience.

Once the leadership made the difference and clarified the distinguishing factors between permanently negotiable interests and values, permanent principles that are interchangeable in their order and should be compromised rarely and then carefully when necessary, and *agape*-love or the only absolute and true virtue--the always and everywhere at once applicable right and good--observant Protestants followed and after the pacesetting Liberty Party was "transubstantiated" joined the new antislavery political parties it helped to spawn.

As a consequence of the late antebellum partisan party power politics and participatory democracy engagement of Protestant pastors, parishioners, and parishes, an antislavocracy formation for securing Northern real interests and values expanded to divide institutions and the nation itself.

WARRIOR BEECHER'S ANTI-UNITARIAN
POLITICS AND EVANGELICAL WARFARE

When Beecher arrived in Boston, Calvinists as a bloc had long-since existed on the cultural margins, persisted on the periphery of civil politics, and been out of power. Orthodoxy's traditionalists survived on the boundaries of the power elite and at the center of city. They struggled and survived without an edge or a conservative presence possessing sufficient force to challenge liberal Puritan brethren at the helm of the ecclesiastical and civil powers, and the moderate Yankees on the edge of Calvinism, despair, and frustration.

The Presbyterian-Congregational federation comprised Evangelical Puritan preservationists and protectionists, whose cause Beecher made his own when he answered the call of these conservative Congregationalists and moved to Boston (A) to make his last stand in the heart of liberal Congregationalism to preserve the Evangelical Calvinist tradition; and to recover from progressive Puritans the balance of power commandeered by the cultural determinants. Amid this triangular rivalry, the return of the power once possessed by the Evangelical Calvinist Puritans to the Yankee Trinitarian Congregationalists was so compelling for these sons of the wayward worldly saints it reduced to a trivial matter any purist Puritan pride and prejudice or questions pertaining to Beecher being a Presbyterian pastor of a Boston Congregational church.

A quarter of a century before presbyter Beecher acceded to his last Congregationalist clerical office, Charles Chauncy's leadership of anti-millennialism and anti-Calvinism liberal theology in Boston and Harvard--that he developed to ensure there would exist nothing so great as distance between him and the E-vangelicalism of Jonathan Edwards of New Haven and Yale--had passed to the Reverend Henry Ware (1764-1845). His selection (1805) by the majority of liberals on the Harvard Board of Overseers to fill the new Hollis Professor of Divinity chair at Harvard galvanized their acrimonious dispute with the conservative and moderate minority and their constituency. Unitarian Congregationalists dominated the power positions in Boston and Harvard, but the Trinitarian congregations retained the plurality of Massachusetts Congregationalists.

The Congregationalist controversy created by Ware's election delayed his installment in the chair, contributed to the 1808-organization of Andover Theological Seminary, and precipitated the schism of liberal and moderate to conservative Puritan-Yankee Congregationalists into variously traditional and nontraditional Unitarian and Trinitarian Congregationalist churches, denominations, and seminaries. To this rapidly evolving process of division and diversity, Ware's appointment as professor of the newly founded Harvard Divinity School (1816) imparted irreversibility.

The initial reaction of Orthodoxy-defending Congregationalists was reorganize and to form Consociations of Trinitarians that excluded Unitarians. Contrapositively, the Unitarian Congregationalist Church embraced the minority of member ministers and churches who remained faithful to Christian symbols and rituals they cherished from the inherited and revered Trinitarian tradition, the singular one being the celebration of the Lord's Supper.

In their preponderancy, Unitarian Congregationalists sharply diverged from the Trinitarians as elitists who were equally persuaded by religious and secular humanism and opposed to Calvinistical doctrines and dogma. The precipitating causes dividing the grand American establishment denomination subsisted of the individual-centered proliferating Enlightenment rationalism that created new philosophies and theologies, logics and psychologies, and worldviews; the new industrial technology; and the expansive growth of a productive political economy engineered by exploding and fabulous wealth-generating industrial capitalism.

Inevitably in Boston, the hub of American Calvinist capitalists and Yankee capital owners and manager engineers of manufacturing companies who along with merchants were fast becoming Protestant philanthropists, distinctions of class and culture proceeded apace urban-suburban versus small town to rural different opportunities and upspringing conflicts of interests and values.

Nevertheless, these Yankees remained English/Puritan race representatives, whose Congregationalist divergences were complemented by uninterrupted convergences as social conservatives. They directed precious little disinterested goodwill toward actualizing the best interests of their Black race, albeit Black folk were as difficult to locate in their churches as they were impossible to miss in their civil residences.

Beecher had thoroughly studied the works of William Ellery Channing, and especially examined the Unitarian "creed," that issued forth from Channing's pivotal address entitled *Unitarian Christianity* (1819) which he delivered two years after the organization of the ACS. This stunning statement and surprising reversal of values had induced the Reverend Professor Leonard Woods (1744-1854) of Andover Theological School to write *Letters to Unitarians* (1820), that Ware answered in his *Letters to Trinitarians and Calvinists* (1820). Forward until the high intensity was exceeded in high anxiety by the malice-inciting Missouri Compromise, the raging faith-centered and ethics-innocent theological debate between Unitarian and Trinitarian Congregationalists extended the continuum of public interest ethics-consuming dogma and doctrine clashes competent and conscientious clergymen.

In the period of New England indifference to the color caste/captive class, and theological controversy-rife environment, the Woods-Ware faith-replete and ethics-deplete debate was as cogently reasoned faith as the relief it provides is remarkable when read against the background of the bitter argumentation in which it was framed. Woods argued a position that effectively mediated between Samuel Hopkins' theology (Hopkinsianism) and traditional Calvinism.

His posture provoked Nathaniel Taylor at Yale to comment that the arguments Woods of Andover directed against Ware of Harvard amounted to a retreat from the "New Side" advance of Calvinism Taylor was pioneering. The "architect" of the "New Haven Theology" Timothy Dwight developed to replace theology of Edwards and Hopkins--if not the revisionist of his puritanical moralism Lyman Beecher refined--Taylor was directing Yale Divinity School (1822) that had recently been established for him. Commencing with the rise of the slavocracy, Taylor finely honed a particular view of Calvinism in which he sought to provide a relevant model for revival theology "in the democratic ethos of Jacksonian America."

Beecher departed Connecticut for Boston fully confident that his skillful employment of "Taylorism" would vanquish the Unitarian Congregationalists, and enable him to reestablish the ecclesiastical and cultural hegemony of Orthodoxy, having left behind all traces of Hopkinsian theology. Old Abolitionist Samuel Hopkins' social ethics, however, that antiabolitionists Beecher and Taylor scarely ever seriously considered in relation to the Black race--except as Hopkinsianism supported their ACS sentiments--finally surfaced in the rational Puritan Christian Humanism philosophy and ethics of Channing, several years after countermarching Beecher left Massachusetts for Ohio.

Beecher appeared to be at once against immoral man and for his correction to perfection by protection moralisms and other moralistic measures.

In this posture and the appearances Beecher loomed the sharpest contrast imaginable to Channing: whose matching opposition to imperfect man and faith in moral man and his improvement seemed to be based on a fundamental belief in the linear progress of inextricably mutually fertile pure reason and pure ethics. The respective pluperfect Puritan advocates of perfect spiritual and secular morality were true believers in religion, whose commitment to its revelation and reason polar extremes preconditioned their different philosophical and theological purposes and confrontation over the correct interpretation and means to uncommon ultimate ends.

But Beecher and Channing were Puritans divided over church forms and civil fashions and united in state stability and public order first priorities, who there-fore did not clash upon Boston's turbulent antislavery seas and antiabolitionist waves of rationalizations against social structural changes--and *ipso facto* for *status quo* color caste/captive class continuation in cultural constraints.

Their common distrust and dislike of New Abolitionists, whom they disdained for channeling oceans of controversy from the docks to the main streets, was submerged by the soaring dogmatics contentiousness that was the cause of this effect scarcely surfacing from beneath the surface and Beecher and Channing slipping past each other on the slavery tidal waves like two slavetrading vessels, under the cover of darkness, following different legs of the triangular (Africa/West Indies/North America) Atlantic slavetrade route. Beecher centered a cultural criticism of the Unitarians upon what to his mind was their "pursuit of happiness" rather less than superfluity superficial superciliousness, whom he adjudged the "deadly foe" of true "human happiness" and the "general welfare" he sought to increase by whatever exacting moral means possible and necessary.

Unitarians were the power elite who naturally opposed Beecheresque Evangelical regenerative method for achieving the moral means and ends such as the social, political, and economic health and welfare of the common man, as solidly as they disparaged revivalistic preaching for "conviction and conversion" to a new being whose behavior followed suit.

The preponderance of predominantly upper middle-class and upper-class Channingesque/Unitarian Congregationalist consciences consciously counterpointing the middle miidle-class Beecheresque Trinitarian Congregationalist consciences strove for social stability and security enveloped by perfect peace and harmony, and resented their gentility being threatened by the aggressive tactics Beecher used to disturb Bostonians' tranquility.

But their efforts to curb his disquieting spirit succeeded only in persuading Beecher that he could not be faithful to Christ, benevolent to man, or true to himself short of leading the Trinitarian Congregationalist churches to "war" against the Unitarians.[69]

Warrior Beecher entered the fray fully armed with moralisms plus moralistic principles or "plowshares beaten into swords" (Joel 3:10). These mortal-wounding deadly weapons, of the moral war Beecher declared in the perceived immorality thicket of the Boston asphalt jungle, he wielded like guerrila warriors swing *machetes* to cut down the stubborn power proletariat and elite forming the massive resistance to his counterdemanding total abstention from draughts, card playing, theater going, and all the supple pleasures that were the delight of the masses and spice of life for cultivated culture determiners.

Beecher launched his class war against what he despised in order to check the culture-corrupting social style-pacesetting habits and fashion-dictating tastes of the upper-class, to conduct the national growth and development of mean middle-class manners and measures as well as mean, and to correct the appetite of the lower-class whom he feared formed a vulnerable and victimized group in imminent danger of descending to the under-class and joining there outcast color caste class. Beecher believed these leisure time activities did not inspire life-enhancing values, they were bad form and worse exercises in futility consisting of not only nerves heightening and/or calming drugs but also nervous system-numbing recreational narcotics, and that if not eradicated (or at least constrained and curbed severely) ordinary citizens would become addicted to these death-enhancing vices. He was confident that political, economic, and social conditions did not drive the unfairly utilized and rewarded laborers to seek relief in good cheer--where some lost, and others found, themselves in inebriation.

The better public moralist than public servant was not as such or in the moralistic religion business in a class by himself, which standard operating procedure entailed concentrating on not only the individual as the cause and effect of all problems and prospects but both the symptoms and ignoring the systematic and systemic cultural causes of enervating social effects such as community no less than personal poverty, ignorance, and disease. He elected join the vanguard of conventional wisdom as decisively as his counterintelligence discredited as error the truth that public problems were generated by unfair power elite enacted laws and social organization practices, inequitable capital sharing with labor the profits workers produced and distribution of economic goods and services, and superimposition by the authorities of political injustice.

Beecher proclaimed himself one "true believer" equally in affirmative action equal opportunity and justification by faith in reason. Having posited this prime premise and principle as a primary axiom, he asserted that undisciplined amusements were the demonstrable cause--rather than effect--of poor productivity in the private-sector industrial plants and the market-place and of poorer performance in the parochial and public sectors. Beecher seemed perfectly content to contend that pleasure-exciting and pain-deadening narcotics were nothing but self-defeating habits, leading for the addicted plurality to total dependency, and the precipitating factors resulting in daily discovered indecent public exposure throughout the common stratum of the body politic and other experienced embarrassing exercises of shameless exhibitionists, derelicts, and standard deviations from the norm of sobriety and propriety.

What is relevant and significant centers in the positive correlations between Beecher's complete abstinence answer to this White-ethnic issue and his total Black-race exclusion final religion solution to the race question, his choice of public problems to concentrate his full faith and credit in, and his acts of commission illuminating his acts of omission disclosing what he denies to be real butat he denies to be true or that reveal relative and hide absolute dehumanization. The reverse or color caste/captive class effect of Beecher's exemplary Moral Reform mind and message is the absence of White "Christian shame" in the presence of White Christian Northern repression and Southern oppression of their Black race male and female neighbors.

Precisely due to his civil order social reformation profession and expertise, Beecher's disinterest in the real interests of Black Calvinists may be explained as par for the norm of his age--but the judgmental moralisms and moralistic measures of expedience and convenience cannot be explained away as appropriate attitudinal and behavioral action based upon logical conclusions drawn from his classic Calvinist social conser-vative ethics-underpinned premises, principles, and analysis. Beecher and the Moral Reformers, in whose ranks he appeared the first among equals, rationalized their Evangelical Protestant prime priorities; justi-fied their personal and parochial primarily private-sector and individual-specific rather than either public and civil or social structural moral change policies, processes, and programs; disclosed a conscious color caste/captive class conservation motive, means, method, and opportunity.

Exclusive spiritual and moral power social conservatives further revealed, in their dispassionate determination to reform the nation, why they deliberately withheld their positive social redeeming reason, will, and power from correcting appropriately the natural cultural and therefore national problem of social un-fairness and inequity that power people perpetuated who asserted prerogatives, advanced privileges, and exercised rights and responsibilities to demand perma-nent Black bondage conditions; perpetual pariah caste existence; and progres-sive preemption of self-determination for the Black masses whom they denied equal access to opportunity.

At the same time they provided reasons why the privileged classes should own and trade or sell their real color chattel like their other interest-bearing and negotiable property, and argued effectively that neither Black race-essence nor Black bondage-existence possesses human rights or civil liberties that Chris-tianity and civility requires White slavemasters to respect, these impressive world redeemers focused their unmatched resources alternately on Foreign Mis-sion enterprises; Domestic Mission projects among White immigrants and Indian ethnics groups, whom they drove up against the wall of middle-class morality and respectability to squeeze the life out of their cultural values that were ob-jectionable to their sensibilities; and Evangelical revival and evangelism schemes whose excesses were as real as their successes.

Moral Reformer Protestant humanitarians decisively attacked the obvious symptoms of manifest public disorderliness, while insisting the negative social outcome was positively correlated with neither insufficient economic income or rationally designed faulty political structures and social systems nor immoral society and cultural values but only the unethical nature and function of the corrupt individual; and that change from an immoral to a moral citizen and community would occur only with the spiritual conversion of each individual. Undeniably, for the Moral Reformers, social problems were so clear and simple they seemed to emit no complexities that could withstand Evangelicalism and the evangelists' well-directed, sustained, and simple solution, that turned out to be for the color caste/captive class a "Consistent Calvinist" Hobson's choice ("that or none").

Operating under these Halfway Piety faith and ethics constraints and moral contrivances he ordained the "Good News," and answer to the "Bad News" he bore which proclaimed social disorder pervaded the birthplace of Puritan Piety, Beecher was no more surprised to discover himself under direct attack in Bos-ton than the messenger believed himself to be stoned because the Unitarians did not like the message he delivered:

> The Unitarians, with all their principles of toleration, were as real-
> ly a persecuting power while they had the ascendancy as ever ex-
> isted. Wives and daughters were forbidden to attend our meetings;
> and the whole weight of political, literary, and social influence was
> turned against us, and the lash of ridicule laid on without stint.[70]

Beecher appeared in Boston the perfect union of English Puritan race virtue and aggressive Scotch-Irish Presbyterian values; belligerence personified as he declared "war" on the Unitarian Congregationalists; and righteous right ruling no right to be wrong in pontificating that because he struggled to limit his crusade against anti-Calvinists to one for Christ and civility it was in intentions and consequences the equivalence of a "*just war*" rather than analogous to being a little bit pregnant. Beecher demonstrated the courage of his convictions when the warrior openly admitted his moral "war" means and ends in his letter of March 1, 1828:

> The time has come when the Lord Jesus Christ "expects every man to do his duty," and when nothing is required to give to error a final discomfiture, and to truth a permanent victory, but a united and simultaneous effort to rescue from perversion the doctrines and institutions of ours fathers, the fairest inheritance ever bestowed from Heaven upon men, and holding out to this nation and this world more prospective good than was ever committed to a merely human instrumentality.

> For a century or more there has been, as you know, a decline in evangelical doctrine and vital piety in this region; and so low did the pulse of life sink in this once holy city, that the enemy thought verily that the witnesses were slain, and began to divide the spoil. The college [Harvard] was given to Socinus, that he by its perverted funds and powerful influence, might corrupt the literature of the commonwealth and disciple all the cultivated intellect of the state, especially that which should be concerned in the formation and administration of law.[71]

In order to accomplish this incredible mission that matched his great ambition as evidently as it strained even his super powers, Beecher created a journal as his organ of communication which the "Puritan will" christened the *Spirit of the Pilgrims* (1828-33):

> Consultation had been as extensively as time and circumstances would allow, and but one sentiment and feeling prevails. We all seem to hear the voice from heaven saying, "Arise, shine, for thy light is come, and the glory of the Lord is risen upon thee." We dare not be disobedient. We only wish our brethren, and the churches, and friends of the institutions which are threatened by Unitarians, to respond to the call which we make upon them for their counsels, and prayers, and co-operation. The great point is to obtain readers, and for this we arc determined to send our ap-proved agents who can well explain our views and aid our union of efforts....

> > We wish to obtain in every town in this commonwealth the reading of the Spirit of the Pilgrims by a considerable number, so that its light may shine and its influence be felt.[72]

By this date, nearly two years after Beecher's initiated his no holds barred open warfare, the Uni-tarians' anger had turned to scorn. Beecher held the Unitarians accountable for errors of deception and conception. The prophet invited fear, threatened to strike terror in the hearts of his auditors who failed to heed his audacious claim, and denied his perspective was due to an error of perception when he alleged they "perverted majorities," and engaged in wholesale "plundering and blotting out the churches of the Pilgrims."

Beecher was determined to attain rational and rapid radical private cultural alteration of the individual, and parochial moral correction, rather than public structural social change. Achieving this primary purpose appeared to be his only public ethics message, and was so received by the Unitarians who could be forgiven for thinking awe or jealousy of their cultural elitism was the sole subject and object of his magnificent obsession. He directed his strong will against the power elite whenever and wherever he discovered them. From the point of view of critical charioteer champions and challengers, they seemed to his mind to be everywhere, on all "corners of the streets" of Boston, in contempt of the values while falsely "sounding the praise of our fathers and their institutions."

Beecher's message was inherent in his central method of accusing Unitarians of being irresponsible, yet responsible for the "degenerations" of the common people. This social corruption, Beecher charged, transpired because the class of Christian Bostonians chose to ignore the working class. Unitarians rejected out of hand both the messenger and the message they found unconscionable the newsmaker's disregard of toleration while appealing for toleration; blazoned news blaming them for the common people's disorderliness; and prescribed remedy for licentiousness intolerable.

Beecher evinced no empirically verifiable scientific diagnosis of the social disease he labeled rampant immorality, and the prescription he presented for its cure and prevention was equally suspect of being the superimposition of a patented formula. Beecher recommended absolute abstinence from selected and arbitrarily defined pain-inductive and harm-intensive pleasures, he ruled the bane of human existence, as the best ways and means to their complete banishment from the world.

BLACK CALVINISTS IN CONGREGATIONALIST CHURCHES

DURING LYMAN BEECHER'S PASTORATE OF ONE IN BOSTON

Beecher's success in the Hanover Street Church exceeded the evidence he cited such as his recollection that on "the first three Sabbaths the seats were free to all, and thronged above and below"--so that thereafter "they sold the pews." He could not believe the demonstration of success to leave open to question the virtue of the paragon of voluntarism, and found no difficulty in rationalizing the act of creating a class congregation that scarcely demolished the walls of segregation and doors of discrimination erected between poor White and poorer Black Bostonians. Beecher filled the vacuum of evangelistic preaching in Boston as he attracted a cross-section of observant and curious Bostonians to his church--by his exciting revival style and rational evangelism method of preaching--where "many that came to scoff remained to pray."

Among his other initial innovations, Beecher initiated a revival in Hanover Street Church. The first step in the professional revivalist's efficient technical method involved systematic and systemic sustained preaching for "awakenings and conversions." The second step in his evangelism strategy, following the sermon delivered to change minds wills, entailed the ingenious tactic of instituting an "inquiry meeting." The composition of his inventive instructional arrangement included ten separate and distinct classes, to which individuals were assigned according to their spiritual or moral "character and state." This proficient technique enabled Beecher to give seekers personal attention and "careful instruction." The "infidel and skeptical class" frequently required extended sessions in his home for the rationalists to work through their intellectual doubts, and differed sharply from the high intensity class consisting of persons of high anxiety who would "plead inability" to convert because they believed they could not be "born again":

> Many of these told me their ministers told them so. Now I rose into the field of metaphysics, and, instead of being simple, I became the philosopher, and began to form my language for purposes of discrimination and power.

Beecher's high rational and organized revival and evangelism program "never stopped for five years"--during which half decade he reported that "the numbers increased so fast it was overwhelming, so I kept a record"--and the final result of his impact upon his Calvinist cousins Beecher declared unprecedented in Boston, and proudly published as the complete vindication of his Evangelical form and function:

> The Baptists came to see what was going on, and pretty soon they began to revive. When I first set up evening meetings not a bell tingled; but, after a few weeks, not a bell that didn't tingle. The Unitarians at first scouted evening meetings: but Ware found his people going, and set up a meeting.[73]

Within a year of his arrival and bold experimental experiential Evangelicalism, novel successes for Trinitarian Congregationalism were experienced in Boston. For one, his second son and fourth child, the Reverend Edward Beecher (1803-95), accepted his election as pastor (1826-31) of the Park Street Congregational Church. For another, Evangelical Calvinist ministers were called to serve ten other churches. When reflected upon in the light of these developments, and his stronger logic and imagination than powers of prediction (determination and control) Beecher's 1838 prescription for the removal of Unitarians from power was not self-fulfilling prophecy but wishful thinking rooted in reason rather than reality:

> Under the influence of truth of the Holy Ghost a great attention is awakened to the subject of religion, and a public sentiment is formed and forming imminently favorable to free and fair discussion. We can now explain and assert our rights before a public that will hear and do us justice. We can uncover the deeds of darkness of past years to the wondering eye and the indignant heart of an honest community, whose confidence has been abused, and who can feel for our wrongs and indignities, and will not be partakers in other men's sins. The day of retribution now for a long time slumbereth not.
>
> All which is now needed is that the friends of religion and institutions of our fathers read, and understand, and feel, and act in unison for the defense of those liberties, civil and religious, which had well-nigh been taken away forever. All the great designs which God has to answer by planting our fathers here in this nation and

world depend, as I believe, on the efforts of this generation to
rescue their institutions from perversion, and restore them to their
native purity and glory. We have no sectarian views. file love all
who love our Lord Jesus Christ in sincerity and truth.[74]

By his own admission, Beecher had put the principles of his opponents to the
ultimate test. And for this reason he, of all men, should not have been surprised it was "two years before the leaders of the Unitarians began to change
their tactics and treat me gentlemanly."

At this height of Beecher's advancement of Halfway Piety faith and ethics in
Boston, a conscious color caste class incident occurred in the Park Street
Church, currently pastored by Edward Beecher, that revolved around what Har-
vey Newcomb later termed *The Negro Pew* (1837). The rational race and religion
realism related realistically to the legendary Connecticut anti-Black race values
that so permeated the bones of this "spirit of the Puritans." Realization of the
reality neither surprised nor shocked his sensibilities nor provoked Beecher, and
apparently confirmed the wisdom of his selective (uncharacteristic) caution that
easily could be misread as reserved for matters pertaining to Black folk: especially since his cost-effective approach to color caste/captive existence nearly
ended his career in a cloud of suspicion, rather than in the blaze of glory he
anticipated.

Lyman placed his body on the line with his expanding loyalty and dedication
to the anti-Black race interest-specific ACS, to make his private and public
individual moral values and social ethics perfectly consistent and unmistakable.
Edward Beecher, his second son, appeared not only embarrassed by his widely
publicized Congregationalist congregation's church-constructed "*colored curtain*"
but strengthened in his resolve: the experience heightened his growing antislavery conscience and consciousness of color caste/class segregation and discrimination.

In the aftermath of the test Congregationalism failed in this self-created
contest between Christian virtue and American Civil Religion race values, Edward found himself in sufficient difficulty with his congregation to make his
election to the office of President (1831-44) of Illinois College a welcome opportunity. During the ensuing period and some months following his relocation
in the West, Edward took a brave and bold antislavery stand in Illinois--nearby
Ohio where soon thereafter his father both migrated and proved unable to follow suit.[75]

This racist reason raged without inciting a race riot because it was so near
to routine racism in re-ligion. It occurred in 1830, the year after William Garrison bolted the ACS and approximately four years after Edward Beecher was
installed as pastor, after Frederick Brinsley, a Black Congregationalist, purchased a pew in Park Street Church. Brinsley and his family worshipped in their
newly owned pew the following Sunday morning under pastor Edward Beecher.

But when they returned for the afternoon service, lay officers of the
congregation called the authorities who dispatched a civil constable whom the
lay leaders ordered to remove the Brinsleys physically from their pew.

This police enforcement action was followed by a special session of the
Church, at which official meeting the overwhelming majority of the membership
voted to support the Prudential Committee's recommendation to nullify Brinsley's purchase.

In the same ecclesiastical and civil class action suit, Park Street officialdom authorized a classic Northern segregation and discrimination policy. It was translated into the following affirmative action for equal opportunity directive, Congregationalists-styled "separate but equal," that the chairman of the board of trustees, George Odiorne, set forth in the letter he addressed to Brinsley (March 6, 1830):

> Sir--The Prudential Committee of Park Street Church notify you not to occupy any pew on the lower floor of Park Street meeting-house on any Sabbath, or on any other day during the time of divine worship, after this date: and if you go there with such intent, you hazard the consequences. The pews in the upper galleries are at your service.[76]

Five or six subsequent meetings of the Prudential Committee were convened to determine the most felicitous way to keep Black congregants both segregated and in their place, before Park Street churchmen drafted a new pew clause to permanently install a refashioned "*colored curtain*" separating Black and White worshippers. Their enactment of unethical discrimination into ecclesiastical law matched for legal injustice the human bondage slavocracy order, became public knowledge, and deterred the overwhelming majority of self-respecting Black Bostonians from seeking in Park Street Church--and all other Congregationalist establishment churches--grace with status.

This parochial color caste/captive class-specific rule, that the ruling elders ruled Congregationalist law and order, was enacted to segregate the Black race; a high visibility sign and symbol, that evidenced the proliferating private-sector indiscriminate indifference to each individual and community part of the whole Black body; and an act of more substance than style that served the same public purpose as the civil "*Black codes*" lawmakers promulgated in the legislatures of the Northeast and Southeast, and the states and territories of the West.

Both the Park Street Church and the Massachusetts State "*Black codes*" compared favorably in intentions and consequences with the restrictive clause in the pew deeds utilized by the Rowe Street Baptist Church. In this Calvinist Boston church, pastored by the Reverend Baron Stowe, the faithful covenanted to covet only "respectable white persons"--who alone would be permitted to purchase church pews.[77]

In antebellum New England, positively odd and even peculiar either "Christian" and "Abolitionist" or "Christian and anti-Black race interest" proper Bostonians appeared a difference without a distinction. Equally evidently, Christian New Abolitionist advocates of egalitarianism who thought the institutional church was the one place where the great Northern emphasis upon the equality of souls and Christian brotherhood could be practiced as preached--apropos individual human beings enjoying spiritual and moral power--were rudely awakened from idealism by the realism these Calvinist Congregationalists and Baptists preferred. The pragmatism of the churchmen revealed the pervasive depth of social inequality in their local church law-sanctioned pernicious private customs.

This occurrence, during the year in which Garrison self-transfigured the original New Abolitionist and several months prior to the first issue of his *Liberation* journal, was a specific factor in the sequence of contributing color-intensive cultural elements resulting in Evangelical Boston New Abolitionists evolving in the plurality far less active in Evangelical churches than their New York counterparts, and far more determined not to expend excessive energy in attempting to decodify these anti-Black race ecclesiastical codifications.

Representatives of the American White-race majority (of White-ethnic minorities) managed with impunity to manifest in the churches of the establishment denominations real evil and error, the terror of "*the spirit*" inherent in Black race positive negation, and fortify the anti-hyperorthodox New Abolitionists. Religious racists added empirically verifiable validity to bi-racialists' condemnation of the highly conscious and hypocritical institutional anti-Black race values, that made the proslavocrat Evangelical Congregational denomination's subtle and/or unconscious support of Protestant slavocrats, and the slavocracy they coveted, equally unconscionable, intolerable, and unpardonable.

The first-hand experience plus the knowledge provided by ample facts and figures, the research and development cadre of New Abolitionists produced, created a sharp enough point to bear the weight of the Evangelical proabolitionists' critical conclusion. They asserted it was determinative that permissive and promiscuous proslavocrat establishmentarian Christians were active with their - slavocrat Southern brethren in the same infested political body politic, infectious and unclean spiritual body of Christ, and contagious immoral corporate body. Counterdemanding Northern Calvinist capitalists argued with equal logic, but less compelling force, that responsibility to God and man required them to secure and advance their capital investments in human bondage and the slave-based plantation economy; and to protect and expand these real economic interests, political priorities, and social values.

This adopted argument of Northeastern Christian capital Northern Protestant management copied and Catholic labor imitated. Among the analogous arguments the power elite and proletariat arranged to account for their adverse arrangement in relation to the powerless people precluded from the power politics and economics games, it argued the popular argument of the relatively powerful that their intention to be purely fiscal conservatives freed them of responsibility for the consequences of their rational thoughts and actions, including the exclusion of competitive Black males from the all-White male "pursuit of happiness" (or White ethnic individual-only Constitution-guaranteed opportunity to se-cure special interests and the general interest), open race to attain pleasure and profit, and positive competition for personal (individual) and private or parochial (race/ethnic community) as well as public prosperity, peace, and power.

Advancing the best interests of the Black race and the White race parts of the whole, and therefore the whole that is greater than the sum of its parts, was rejected for protecting the advantaged at the expense of the disadvantaged on the Machiavellian principle manipulated to suit the preferences of power, that is, selectively, what is good for the goose is good for the gander, good enough for the ganger, or not good for the gander. The odd and even peculiar power elite and proletariat bed-fellows reacted angrily upon discovering that their self-serving interests and market-generated values were not entirely lost on pro-immediatists.

Deterrence-benevolence rationalists responded by redoubling their efforts to prove they were benevolent paternalists and not brutal benevolence brutes. But anti-gradualist adversarsies of thes pro-gradualism advocates retorted that their kind dehumanization and gentle Black bondage power was no less absolute and absolutely corruptive for being administered through cruel and unusual mental rather than physical punishment of the body. In fact, they replied, being sincere and serious in intentions was completely irrelevant and beside the point given consequences--that is, Northern proslavocrats and Southern slavocrats were one in perpetuating involuntary servitude.

Rationalization of the natural right and spiritual righteous human bondage was a principle perpetrated upon the public, proabolitionists averred, and no less an error of deception for being orchestrated by anti-abolitionist Northern churchmen. Immediatists attested that its nature and function was exposed clearly by the ecclesiastical and civil anti-Black race codes, and the driving oppression churchmen-statesmen directed to repress the initiatives of Black self-liberationists.

What proabolitionists certified as co-equally absolute and relative as well as relevant was incontrovertible: Northeastern antiabolitionists' negotiated White Christian Gentlemen's agreements in church and state, whereby their Black race-regulating laws and rules, were at once legimatized by the legislated statutes of the sovereign states and churches and differed only in degree from those in the South. Racism and revelation made far more spurious than curious Christian and anti-Christian Northeasterners' specious pleas for respect of the rule of law in a government not of men but of laws, enacted by Northern proslavocrat and Southern slavocrat lawmakers elected to deny Black folk self-determination.

DEFENSIVE AND OFFENSIVE DOGMATICS

Beecher's "New School" theology was grounded in Dwightesque "New Haven" revisionism, updated and re-revised by incorporating "Taylorism," and translated Halfway Piety faith and deterrence-benevolence ethics when applied to the color caste/captive class civil issue. His strong suit was application of Yale theory and methodology, whose biblical and theological interpretations he refined imaginatively in his practical Evangelical mind.

This "Rule of Scripture" and "Rule of Truth" functioned as the utilitarian discipline of Beecher's penchant for reform, impetus of his will to power, and motive of his mission to remake the world with "Connecticut Yankee" notions. When the logical measures were implemented in the field of religion and race relations, they generated rational revelations and reasons so narrow-scoped until Beecher and his compeer Colonizationists provoked the provocative counter-culture ideas and ideals of Evangelical British and American Evangelical counter-traditionalists.

Emerging in North America as immediatist idealists dedicated to the abolition of slavery and anti-Black race virtue, these real power attracting rather than repelling Protestant foes of Beecher's proslavocrat and slavocrat friends were challenged and challenging. They discovered their capacity in conflict and competition with enemies of their Black friends, and constrained by their treasures of slavery and White ethnic interests--that were variously proclaimed national values.

As a figure of national prominence, Beecher expended considerable power and influence on Moral Reform causes. Whether he knew or whether he refused to accept reality, when subjected to a cost/benefit analysis and a needs/results test the calculations on balance read one way for the Beecherite Moral Reformers: The Beecher wing of the Moral Reform Movement produced positive possibilities for White Protestants, and the perfect prescription for perdition for Black Protestants. It initially diluted the trickle of concern for Black Calvinists in establishment denominations, diverted the power direction and directives of the Moral Majority moralists, and misguided the resources and values of the mainstream whereby they counterchecked the interests of Black folk.

Such reality tests were applied by the anti-Colonizationists, and their reasonable calculations led to perceive Beecher as the essential representative of the preponderant broad stream of historic establishment Protestant positive negation of the Black race. His New Abolitionist critics knew that anti-Black race values existed before and continued after their creative anti-slavery church minority finally leaped within the de-nominations, broke free of their antislavery/proslavery neutrality in the mid-antebellum decades without the consent of the official national bodies, and succeeded in provoking the crisis which ended in a catharsis of conscience.

Beecher's measurable moralisms and moralistic principles, however, did not begin and end in the contemptible leveling morality he was accused of promoting by Unitarians who counted themselves among the privileged few. He incited the caustic criticism when he taunted and labeled Unitarians the class for whom luxury was a state of being--much more than a style of living. They were members of the larger class in North America whose members appeared the pure imitation and sincere flattery of English upper-class life.

American philanthropic patricians in the Northeast and benevolent aristocrats in the Southeast joined with upwardly mobile middle-class merchants of enterprise to form new wealth-concentrated capital, who as the wealth-producing entrepreneurial and wealth-inherited social class were culturally conditioned by the capitalistic and free market-oriented free enterprise system to provide (A) jobs for the working-class--who were distinguished from the lower-class by their belief in work as a true virtue and engagement in productive profit-making ventures that combined to generate rising expectations; and (B) charity, especially from the overflowing portions of their superabundance, to the poor and needy underclass out of their bountifulness.

Beecher was best known to peers who respected him as the "father of more brains than any man in America," whether or not contemporaries knew as well that he was anything but a socialist hawk of a leveling morality. He was dedicated to a Puritan work ethic, a Calvinist capitalist wealth-accumulating ethic, and an Evangelical spiritual and moral cleansing ethic. His three-in-one ethic most certainly was not intended to pull down the well-endowed. It was formed and functioned to fa-cilitate ways and means to pull individual victims of misguidance out of the mire of disincentives onto the competitive field with incentives.

He was dedicated to elevate individuals so that with a new birth of vision they might become productive workers in the saving economy of God, and productive labor for capital in the political economy, and productive civil order stabilizing moral agents in the social economy. His social philosophy required the persistent existence of an underclass, a lower-class, a middle-class, and an upper-class; and complemented his theological deterrence-benevolence ethic that required the classes to be mutually productive. Puritan work and Yankee productivity for each class, he presumed had a place and sufficient common sense to know enough to stay in its place, was the indispensable necessity because only with more abundance could there develop greater benevolence to support Foreign Mission and Domestic Mission reformation movements.

In Beecher's reading of the Scriptures, "the Bible contemplates man as a moral agent, placed under law, and capable of obeying or disobeying." Directed by this perspective, and the understanding he was instituted by God and man one of the "guardians of public morals," by the time he left Boston for Cincinnati Beecher was sanguine that the Unitarians could unite with the Evangelicals in the Moral Reform Movement. But the power elite Unitarians whom Beecher provoked turned anti-Calvinist liberals, pressed the pro-Calvinist moderates and conservatives to the wall of consistency, and held the feet of the re-revisionists of Orthodoxy to the Calvinistical faith fire by making the reason and revelation ratiocinators accountable according to their strict constructionist interpretation of the Calvinist doctrine of infant damnation.

In the facile logic of litigious liberals who argued the arguments of the anti-Calvinist secular humanists to combat aggressive Calvinist conservatives and traditionalists, asserted that the infant damnation ancillary of the corollary *Original Sin* (or the *Fall of Man*) doctrine posits as axiomatic pragma the dogma the principal predetermination principle predestination selectively avow and disavow--namely that innocent children inherit Adam's Original Sin (free choice of self-interest over instead of along with God's interest), guilt, and responsibility.

It is arguable that contemporary anti-Calvinist secular humanists (and other challengers who distinguished between positive intentions and negative consequences) either/or both understood and could care less about the truth: The Calvinist doctrine of human being "total depravity" was set forth to magnify the magnificence of God--this is, not to damn man but to make the Creator (BEING RIGHT and GOOD GRACE and BENEVOLENCE) for the created cerebral creature the irresistible mode of being human.

It is inarguable that the Calvinistical predestination appeared to the antithesists not only "bad philosophy" and "worse theology" but the most "obscene psychology" and "pernicious sociology" ever created by the mind of man, and concluded the cause of the demonstrable dehumanization and human race-defeating effect inhered in the implicit premise and explicit principle of the predeterminationprocess of Providence--whereby the automatic transgenerational transmission of sin inerrantly follows from Adam's act.

The current result of the double jepoardy will of their Divine One (whom atheists called capacious caprice), contemporary incorrigible rigid dogmatists pontificated, is equally evident irreversible: Even children born "the Elect of God" but who die before they (the "called and chosen" few) accept their selection to be "the saints" are eternally damned.

They constitued a right and righteous inflexible fringe on the far right of centrist dogmatists--for whom grasping tightly and acting entirely on absolutely fixed in hierarchal priority (rather than firm but flexibly arranged permanent) principles were the essential elements of being a "true Christian" (or by definition of existence a high principled classic conservative "Consistent Calvinist" in essence and manifestation).

These rigorous and vigorous rationalists denied that double election entailed eternal salvation rather less than eternal double damnation in history and eternity for the majority of the Black race who were not Black Calvinists like the minority of the Black body during the antebellum era. But they affirmed that double election meant eternal salvation in history and eternal damnation in eternity for a precious few White "Elect" as well as White "Reprobate" compeers of Black Congregationalists.

The neither insecure nor unsecure power elite atheists (antitheists or agnostics) and theists united as anti-Calvinists reacted as if this pure and simple spurious hypothesis, and specious reasoned thesis, and poorly preached theory by an odd and peculiar couple of Calvinists that no one practiced or promoted as principle in actuality was a threat to their security, even though only a rare rationalist was unaware of the facts: in theory and experience the dogma of infant damnation was a narrow-scoped strict construction promulgated by Calvinists who revered consistency more highly than common sense, and that in reality applied to an imperceptible minority among the White majority.

What is of moment is that the power elite Protestant secular humanists and religious humanitarians expended excessive energy on these mere figments of the imagination--albeit the absence of fact and presence of fiction naturally generated friction between pro-Calvinist and anti-Calvinist fierce fighters for command and control of the power circles--compared to their current unconcernment with the condition of their color caste/captive contemporaries. Predestinarians offended the sensibilities of the sensible and sensitive cultural determiners. Yet their defensive offensive and offensive defensiveness and/or minor problem for more White elite than White proletarian power people proved a matter of pale significance compared to the perplexity compounded by complexity both parties to the conflict of interests were for Black free-born and slave-born native Americans.

In fact, predestination was a singular style and substance source of a powerful sign and symbol for the double jeopardy cause and effect superimposed by the sacred church and secular civil power and authority upon Black powerless indigenous North Americans as the precondition for their struggle and survival in the culture. Its enduring affects entailed lasting effects in not only myth and ritual but also history. Upspringing from Puritan-Yankee church and civil culture into American theory and experience in reality was the continuum of inescapable and irreversible double indemnity for White folk apropos double jepoardy for Black folk.

In sum and substance, the dogmatic pragmatists and pragmatic dogmatists united as the authorities at the helm of the ecclesiastical powers to bury their differences rather less precisely than razor-sharp racist reasons in the Black body. The religious and secular dogma and pragma of culture-long eternal caste if not bondage in perpetuity leaped from fiction into fact as the great reality of the idealists and realists.

Without doubt, White race pragmatists' promoted double damnation for the Black race in North America continuously had the positive force of law, the respect of profane and sacred professors of moral impartiality, and the greater sound than solid sense of equity emitted by the rule of law rulers--whose ways and means of evenhanded justice validated for the manipulative and manipulated the widely acclaimed White Protestant Christian Gentlemen'sfairness doctrine.

Few "Old Light" Orthodoxy and "Old School" Reformed traditions' defenders --and fewer "New Light" Congregationalists and "New School" Presbyterians-- chose to accept the inherent logic of this double election/double damnation doctrine as the litmus test of the "Consistent Calvinist."

However, hegemonic Unitarian and Trinitarian Congregationalists knew there abided defenders of what religious and secular humanists decried as a human being-defeating creed. These literalists would not retreat into silence but reiterated their reactions in the haunts of the respectable--hence the haunting specter surfaced in social spheres and soared in society.

Thus it was not simply a matter of Unitarians arguing the arguments to render their opponents ridiculous, and refusing to let pro-Calvinists off the hook.

A nearly endangered species of contemporary Calvinistic preachers surfaced who believed themselves called to preach this certainty, though seldom with the vividness of one zealot:

> Hell is paved with the skulls of infants one span long, and their
> parents look down upon them from Heaven, praising God for the
> justice of their damnation!

Beecher joined the Congregationalist anti-Calvinist and pro-Calvinist clerical debate on the merits of Calvinism in general and predestination in particular, between theological ("Old Light" Unitarian) radicals and ("New Light" Orthodoxy liberal and conservative) traditionalists who divided and united in distinguishing themselves from the Reformed "Old School" reactionaries, and as a moderate who bethought himself a liberal rational "Rule of Scripture" revering "New School" strict constructionist entered on the side of the re-revisionists. Harvard radicals rejected the "Rule of Scripture" hermeneutic that Princeton ("Old School" Presbyterian) reactionaries rigidly applied and Yale and Andover ("New Light" Congregationalists and "New School" Presbyterians) approached as a flexible interpretive principle.

Liberal, moderate, and conservative traditionalists committed to preserving Calvinism by revising the Orthodoxy tradition Puritan fathers bequeathed the Yankee sons, were not a body of uniformity but a party of diversity in unity and unity in diversity in the front ranks of whose leadership Taylor of Yale stood out as the first among equals. Taylor's admirers and adherents like Beecher accepted the logic of his hermeneutic, embraced it as a firm and fair real alternative to the rigid methodology, and affirmed it as utilitarian principle of interpretation.

Opponents of the "Rule of Scripture" and Calvinism castigated Taylor, characterized his defense of the tradition offensiveness, and called the "Taylorism" "Rule of Truth" a slippery slope rule of terrorism. Beecher understood the criticism of his "Consistent Calvinist" distinctive interpretive rational principle, constituting the distinguishing factor of his friends who made a difference as a different leadership faction among the scores of Calvinistical schools.

He apprehended but did not suffer gladly the compelling force of the power point made by the critics who combined forces whether they affirmed or disaffirmed the value of being permanently consistent in principles; located in the undead and unburied regretted but not forgotten legacy the defenseless inheritance of Puritan-Yankee Calvinism, whose friends were their worse enemies who refused to let the dead hand of bury its dead past; and concentrated their rational strength in exploiting the weakness of the rationalist re-revisionist Calvinists.

Beecher ascertained that, like the Stuartian "Rule of Scripture" Moses Stuart propounded at Andover Seminary, Taylor's "Rule of Truth" made it nearly impossible for the anti-Calvinist uninitiated in (the Yale *rite of passage*) "Taylorism" to avoid asserting the equivalence of literal interpretation and "Consistent Calvinism." He knew this Calvinistic vulnerableness that the revisionist rationalists resisted and reversed in reality existed in theory and experience as Calvinism's external and internal contradiction, as well as he knew that the sharp point pressed by anti-Calvinist logicians to ridicule the pro-Calvinists exposed rather than created out of whole cloth and imposed the predicament of predetermination and predestination.

Howbeit as ineradicable as the proslavery passages in the Bible and the Constitution, constituting the deadly force and weapons of proof-text wielding warriors for the defense of persecution, Beecher argued infant damnation like the perdition precondition of predestination had been was the subject of objective rational development pioneered by the "New School" New Haven Theology Taylor led, transmogrified and transcended by the overruling "Taylorism" principle, and ruled an error and out of order.

Beecher marshalled the evidence in his dispute with challengers who did not accept his rationalistic rhetoric on face value, and claimed it verified that his transubstantiation was a descriptive fact and not a uniquely self-serving value judgment. But given his candid and published public declaration of "war" on anti-Calvinists, and all is fair in war for the church and state instituted by God pontifical posture, the champion of Christianity and civility was in poor position to plead for principles and to demand respect for reason.

He was visibly unsettled and reacted viscerally to the shaking of his foundations by the Unitarians who persistently rejected out of his hand the proof that revisionists responsibly renounced infant damnation, and insisted on mean-spirited indecent public exposure of the explicable expletive to reveal the Calvinist "emperor has nothing on at all." Beecher denounced the denigration as "repulsive, distorted, false to the spirit of progress." Somehow he managed to forget conveniently the line he drew in the dirt upon issuing a call to arms against the Unitarians; and/or to contend cleverly but not successfully that he had declared a just war which, by definition, precludes the all is fair in love and war maxim.

The Unitarians' penetration of the Trinitarians' underbelly was so piercing that Beecher was impelled to gird up his "total depravity" loins, to take the offensive, to switch roles by first slipping out of his parson persecuter then into his pastor prosecutor robe and finally donning his litigator garb, and to serve as counsel to the defendant and the attorney-at-law in the trial of his client charged by the plantiff with mounting a defense for infants' damnation.

The ecclesiastical lawyer argued the arguments rather than the facts of the case. Whence litigator Beecher choose to contend that the Calvinistic damnation of infants is neither an essential nor a central but a rational doctrine "consisting chiefly, if not entirely, in the loss of that holy enjoyment in heaven for which their depravity disqualified them; and if they suffered a positive evil at all, it was of the very mildest kind."

As a Calvinist counselor in this controversy, Beecher materialized the demonstrable failure of pragmatic dogmatism and dogmatic pragmatism, howbeit the cultural consequences of his conscious intentions transmitted by rational thought and action he could no more correct in the current context appropriately than he could retract the results. Nonetheless, Beecher realized immediately after he perpetrated this serious self-styled "policy" that the statement he issued on the record was fraught with difficulties.

Delivered as part and parcel of the Puritan proselytism *Errand into the Wilderness* of urban-suburban and small city-rural New England, and the only Protestant power game in town, this gospel according to field marshal Beecher startled foes and stunned his friends. Friendly rival revivalists and Calvinist protectionists instantly reacted--in face-to-face relations where they hurled flat in his teeth their (that old dog won't hunt [preach or teach]) retort--and responded further by alternately chastizing and instructing and lecturing him on the facts of life that he ultimately admitted.

For example, Beecher's respected critical compeers recalled for the purpose of causing him to rethink and to change his mind their Calvinistical truth claim:

Parochial and private or personal values at once are public values and have public effects. They concluded with the implied assertion that the validity of these verifiable verities can no more be questioned than the probability that the social consequences of his inadequately examined principle and practice were the opposite of his intentions.

The rationalists and revisionists claimed to know the truth--and/or error, and thus it was not surprising that these ratiocinators reversed their race decision with regared to this religion rule and regulation upon being convinced that only the stubborn and/or stupid would abandon common sense to argue to the point of *reductio ad absurdum* the arguments of this inane consistency simply on principle or for the sake of being a "Consistent Calvinist."

The truth is, Calvinist brethern of the cloth declared to their competitive evangelist, the Beecher re-revisionist teaching is counterproductive: Because by modifying the Calvinist *Original Sin* dogma and pragma or doctrine in dispute so that "it respects the character and destiny of infants," Calvinist rationalists' revered Englightenment-derived Empirical Rationalism reviling strict constructionist interpretation of *Original Sin* "gives the enemy the advantage of the popular side," fixes "the hinge of controversy between the orthodox" and "unorthodox Calvinists," and divides rather than unites Orthodoxy.

The Reverend Asahal Nettleman (1783-1844), Beecher's solid soldier friend and perhaps his superior as a pure revivalist, fellow "Connecticut Yankee" renowned for his professional success in producing converts, and measurably more consistent Edwardsean than post-Edwardsean in his commitment to conversion as the work of the infusion of the Holy Spirit by God alone, appraised Beecher's "policy" and declared it unconditional surrender:

> With all my love and respect for Beecher I must say that neither my judgment, nor conscience, nor heart can acquiesce, and I can go with you no further. Whatever you may say about infants, for one, I do solemnly believe that God views and treats them in all respects, just as he would do if they were sinners.[78]

Nettleton offered an alternative to the fatuous strategy that made Evangelical Calvinism--the rational evangelism organizing principle uniting in Orthodoxy moderate and conservative Trinitarian Congregationalists--the hinge of their controversy with the Unitarian Congregationalists:

> Why not take this ground with Unitarians? We feel no concern for old Calvinism. Let them dispute it as they please; we feel bound to make no defense. Come home to the evangelical system now taught in New England. Meet us, if at all, on our own avowed principles, or we shall have nothing to say.[79]

Beecher had a problem on his hands with this good strategy and better tactic that Nettleton advised and counseled while at ease in Zion, and from relative insulation and isolation in Connecticut where he resided throughout his illustrious career as a competent and competitive evangelist. Whether indeed Beecher believed Nettleton's advice was a luxury he could afford, or whether he considered it an alternative he could refuse with impunity, he had moved his ministry to Boston in order to conquer Unitarians by conquest or any means necessary and possible.

PARALLEL EXPANSION OF AGGRESSIVE
CHURCHOCRACY AND SLAVOCRACY

"Taylorism" also underpinned Beecher's confidence in an evangelism that would cleanse both the individual soul and the whole society. Directing a one hundred and eighty degree move from traditional Orthodoxy and Reformed Calvinism, Nathaniel Taylor opposed irreversible and predestined double election/ damnation. Taylor's "New Light" opposition to rigid predestination persisted in conflict with "Old Light" Congregationalist traditionalists and "Old School" Presbyterians. In the debate among the Calvinists, Beecher revised his position to state that with regard to Original Sin the "grand dispute with liberals should be, not respecting innate, but total depravity."

Whether or not he believed in "total depravity" as either/or both the condition of a plurality of the human race and one no less true of the human race as a rule for including human being exceptions who neither disprove nor improve but prove the rule, Taylor was decisive in his faith and ethics principal principle, namely, "sin is sinning" and/or both the natural result of the capacity to choose self-interest over other-regarding interest and the power of choice.

Taylor argued that freedom of choice is--like or the faculty of reason--a permanent human condition; choos-ing the good or evil in each situation determines the moral (virtue) or immoral (sin) nature of each existential choice; and, therefore, sin is always possible but never necessary. From this ratiocinative analysis and conclusion he calculated that each individual both can and does choose to do good or evil, to improve or to default, in every human predicament; the human being is a free, rational, moral, and knowledge-oriented individual who both is capable of choice and actually always chooses the right or the wrong; and, therefore, s/he is responsible.

The rigid "New Light"/"Old Light" Congregationalists and inflexible "New School"/"Old School" Presbyterians responded viscerally and vigorously verbally. They stated flatly that Taylor's interpretation proved he opposed the dogma of "casually necessary" Original Sin. Edwards had taught this fundamental Western Catholic doctrine, and Taylor updated, refined, and corrected the dogma to achieve its correct correlation with new epistemological methodologies generated by exploding empirical rationalism theories.

Instead of asserting a causal or genetic connection with eponymous Adam, Taylor asserted that Original Sin (individual self-interest served before or instead of God-interest) is the universal human experience. It is arguable that in the process of developing "Taylorism" to supercede the Edwardseanism, Hopkinsianism, and Dwightesque ethic, Taylor's ethic turned on the individual and turned up an individualism informed by the White ethnic individual constituent element of Calvinism, capitalism, and democratic republicanism (secular humanism); eliminated the dynamic mysticism component of Edwards' system; fashioned drastically revised version of Edwardsean/Hopkinsian/Dwightesque millennialism dogma, resulting in a doctrine that was marginal at best rather than the central core organizing principle; and retained the essential regeneration experience and "born again" principle of direct encounter with the *mysterium tremendum et fascinan.*

Taylor advanced an interpretive principle that set him in intellectual competition with compeer Congregationalist theologian Leonard Wood, who generated from his Andover Seminary post near Boston an interest in preserving the theoretical purity of Boston-centered "Old Light" Congregationalism that Harvard theological liberals appropriated and modified; and the Edwards/Hopkins' "New Light" modification of the Calvinist Puritan tradition. The ethic that Taylor struggled to make a utilitarian functional instrument of faith in the age of Jacksonian democracy was fashioned to correct Wood, and to counterbalance the Reverend Henry Ware (1764-1845) and his son Henry Ware: the father and son theological liberals who focused on the present and future relevance of Yankee-Puritan ethical Congregationalism.

Consistent with the majority of mainstream theologians in the classical Western Christian and American Evangelical Calvinist traditions, Taylor was a stronger faith than ethics thinker. The evidence of Taylor's conservative parochial and public morality inheres in the negative good major principle and positive good minor principle critical components of his ethics.

This limits-revering narrow focus-concentrating ethic of "Taylorism" irradiates in his famous theological dictum: The individual possesses freedom of choice or "power to the contrary." This negative good and negative power ethic was a utilizable utilitarian principle, and one that functioned effactually to facilitate the purposes of evangelists like Beecher and Nettleton as well as Taylor himself: whose legitimacy as Evangelical Calvinist revivalists lay in limiting the revivals they led to the confines of establishment or leastwise approved local churches.

The negative "power to the contrary" moral rule formed a power tool of incalculable instrumental value. It provided the peer evangelism professionals with a rational conversion philosophical principle, policy, and process; a psychological method, means, and measure; and a private/parochial/public ethics-limits firm and sharp but flexible instrument for inducing and controlling the appropriate attitudinal and behavioral modification. From the negative "power to the contrary" point of securing confidence, and eliminating all fear of flying, flailing, or failing, Beecher could confront any foe of faith with irrepressible arrogance and fortitude--energized by the fusion of absolute faith in God, the Bible, and reason. "Taylorism" added certainty to his "truth claims," competence, and courage that vanquished all doubts and any second thoughts.

Beecher and his Evangelical Calvinist evangelist brethren were fortified with all the requisites of a modern evangelism crusade. The revivalists appeared the absence of doubt and presence of assurance, as they confronted the sinner in (and with) the knowledge that if he was willing he was able to be reborn to a new way of life. They stressed the infinite gap between God's moral law and man's moral will, until the potential convert felt the point and discovered relief from the tension in the experience of spiritual conflict and conciliation. The unsuspecting sinner (or suspected derelict) was seared spiritually with the impression that the divine/human connection could be made easily and permanently; and furnished with the moral provision for concretely knowing, securing, and improving constantly the experience of being a new person.

The "born again" being was defined as a reborn spiritual power and moral power person, who, due to these new or renewed capacities, abstained from every vice and gave himself to promoting virtue: in ways provided by the evangelist or approved by the church. In this positive and negative implementation of antiblack white-ethnic virtue, the moral will was subjected to the Moral Law of God, which, revivalists certified, legitimates because God institutes constituted civil authority. The Moral Law also authorizes moral activity--but only the moral action that is sanctioned by the rules of social custom, the mores of culture, and the legal statutes of church and state.

This methodical individual-specific, north of slavery, broad spiritual and narrow moral power evangelism was developed by Halfway Piety practitioners especially for White ethnic emigrants and immigrants. Conversely stated, while systematic evangelism was mutually adaptable to the cross-sectional interests of White folk, it was not specifically directed for or against Black folk originally in the pre-slavocracy Northeast. In this regard they were quite unlike the current White ethnic evangelists who were the only Protestant preachers permitted in the slavocracy--where White and Black Southerners resided cheek by jowl in biracial communities but segregated functional spaces and places overwhelmingly.

Between the 1770s and the 1840s, the Black race was excluded from Congregationalists' order of priorities. Complementarily, prior to the referendum era, Black Calvinists and Arminians as well as Anglicans normally appeared in the legislative sessions of the major Evan-gelical denominations only as an item on the addendum agenda.

In the process of building national churches, the unrestricted interchange between evangelism and Moral Reform frequently connected as the live wire of moralism. With great temerity, Moral Reformers demanded universal compliance with the one right and uniform good of each individual they presumed to know. Upper-class citizens, and far more of the upper and middle than lower middle-class White Americans, were in a position to dismiss the moralisms summarily-- as doctrinaire values unworthy of being dignified by giving them serious consideration. However, the White ethnic great unwashed--who were the majority in popular Evangelical religion, if not the populous, and frequently in conflict with Black competitors--found evangelism a socially useful cultural phenomenon they could regard or disregard at will.

Moralisms-intensive and negative-specific antiblack white-ethnic virtue, in the antebellum decades, most certainly remained a standard of ethical conduct that masterful Yankee-Puritans and White Evangelical ruling elders in the North, and master and overseer rulers in the South, were perfectly willing and able to accept or reject at will; to apply or not apply to themselves when expedient and convenient; and to develop from a permissible to a mandated exacting principle for White folk to preach in their role as Black race-specific benevolent and malevolent paternalists: and for Black folk to practice.

In this English race-master/British ethnic-overseer versus Black slavedriver/Black slave masses system, demonstrable black Devil/evil and immorality driving antiblack white-ethnic virtue functioned as self-luminous moral reason; self-justifying indispensable moral power; and self-revelation of the benign and malign neglect relative effect of White Evangelicals' affectionate regard for Black folk, and professed genuine concern for their spiritual health and social welfare.

Throughout the antebellum age, the church- and state-legitimated Northern and Southern Evangelicalism-empowered evangelists engaged Black folk with similar messages and methods--apropos their primary interest in the future in eternity and secondary interest in the future in history of their Black race; different purposes; and disparate minds superimposing diametrically opposite social intentions and public consequences.

The Black race-specific first and last as well as foremost concern of Evangelicalism-advancing Southern Moral Reformers was to save Black folk for their New World slavocracy; and that of compeer Northern world redeemers was to save Black Americans for Africa and the Black Africans. While their goals emitted a difference in degree so great they amounted to a different kind of objec-

tive in history, proslavocrat and sla-vocrat evangelists were determined to secure eternal salvation; and, therefore, through time and over time, they were
committed to saving Black folk in time in this world for the world to come.

Given the mutually fertile yet mutually exclusive and impossible to unite
ultimate authority of reason for secular humanists, and of revelation for the
religious humanitarians, the Northern and Southern Evangelical parties to the
conflict and competition loomed large in the appearances of the non-churchmen
as walking contradictions. The image occurred as a result of Evangelicals proclaiming they managed to effect a tension-free union of the polar criterions of
truth, and specific shared values of Halfway Piety faith and morality such as
their negative good deterrence-benevolence ethic.

Hence it comes as no surprise to discover, after taking the crusaders for
church and state stability, that White Evangelical powerhouses either could save
the world from Black folk or save this world but could not save both: because
"Taylorism" and other rational forms of the Evangelical Calvinist gospel of
double salvation required the whole Black race to be saved, but the double
election scheme delivered Black bondage and color caste double damnation.

In the conflict of principles and internal contradiction, Evangelical Moral
Reformers, the heart and soul of the voluntary nature and function of the body
of churches forming the American mainstream denominations, demoted authentic
Puritan Piety and promoted the Halfway Piety moralism-intensive anti-Black race
virtue alternative. Henceforth, Protestant powerhouses were bound and determined to make Black poor underlings, and powerless victims of the arbitrary powerful adversary, pay for the solutions to the problems created by the rich White
majority.

RIVAL REVIVALISTS AND ANTISLAVERY ALTERNATIVES

These choices were elected while encountering the visible and indivisible
body of Black folk, who were no more invisible to the world saviours and crisis
managers in Beecher' s day than they were imperceptible in the decades dominated by the original Puritan and subsequent Yankee Evangelical Moral Majority.

As a result of moral power and religious opportunity, these reverence for
revelation distinguishable wayward worldly saints differed from the reason
revering secular humanist minority--in control of politics--who promised Black
folk rewards and punishments, but never imparted hope in either history or
eternity.

Beecher proudly proclaimed publicly his pledge of allegiance to the Northern/
Southern-based, politics-replete, and Evangelicalism-pervasive ACS, the major
American parochial-private-public and multinational corporation that Gurley, his
fellow Northern presbyter, administered so ably. They were distinguished by
their unchanging affirmation of the ASC from former Colonizationists who were
a distinct minority. Standing out among the Beecher and Gurley antislavery
competitors as sometime Colonizationists were Unitarian convert to Evangelical
Presbyterianism, Lewis Tappan; and the Old Abolitionist Quaker, the Reverend
Benjamin Lundy (1789-1839).

Lundy's offer of employment initiated the process in which Colonizationist
William Lloyd Garrison moved from Massachusetts to Maryland to begin his professional career as a full-time antislavery journalist. After two years, Garrison
returned to Boston the original New Abolitionist--where he attended Beecher's
church before he departed despairing of the presbyter's cost-accounting ap-

proach to slavery.

Equally different from Friend Lundy and the near-Reverend Theodore Dwight Weld--the friend and associate of Colonizationists but non-member of the Society--and unlike these onetime ACS fellow travelers, Beecher was a permanent supporter but not an active agent of the body. He did not follow Leonard Bacon and become one of the official agencies of the Society for his own dramatic reasons.

Nevertheless, he embraced the Society's existence as the manifest essence of anti-Black race interest increasingly firmly with each indirect and direct criticism of the organization. Beecher's cross-town nemesis, Channing, was a critic who refused to join the ASC, and onetime associates Tappan and Garrison departed the ACS to become two of the Society's major opposition agencies. Beecher's Moral Reformer rivals were complemented by his revivalist competitor, the Reverend Charles Grandison Finney (1792-1875): a nontraditionalist, rationalist, and unconventional Presbyterian evangelist. Like the Reverend George Whitefield (1714-70), the First Great Awakening peerless preacher and friend of Jonathan Edwards, and unlike Lyman Beecher and the strictly local church-centered Evangelical Calvinist revivalists, evangelist Finney initially preached to save sinners in any place and space--and at any time; and not simply for the purpose of keeping churches lively, filled to capacity, and increasing the millennial majority through growing enrollments.

The equal of Beecher as an empirical rationalist psychologist, and innovative experimental experientialist evangelist, Finney developed the revivalistic "protracted meeting" into the state of the art. Following his revival sermon night after night, for upwards of a week and frequently longer, convicted and convinced saints and sinners were propelled from their seats forward where they merged at "anxious bench": not merely to confess their sins but largely to profess their "born again" experience expressly through public prayer, praise, and testimony.

Finney enjoyed extraordinary success as an evangelist, evolved into a controversial legend in his own time, and appeared larger than life in the perception of Beecher and Nettleton. Thus, in 1827, at New Lebanon, New York, they conferred with other traditional Calvinist Evangelicals to clarify their solid common ground and differences with Finney's approach to revivalism. Specifically, they met to dissociate united Reformed/Orthodoxy's middle-class, respectable, and local congregation-limited revivalism from Finneyite unchurched-concentrated or masses-centered, mass media-oriented, and maverick techniques-enveloped popular evangelism.

Finney, the "father of modern evangelism," stood out as the revivalist who insisted that the sinner, upon conversion, demonstrate his new being through direct involvement in a work of public consequence. In his system, a sinner was converted to increase the "interests of God's Kingdom" on earth: rather than to overreach from delight in eternal salvation in history from damnation in eternity to reveling in escaping reality by focusing on new and future rewards in heaven. Christians, urged Finney, "have no separate interests" in the civil sector from those of the non-Christians, where each "born again" new being should "*aim at being useful in the highest degree possible*."

Finney's most famous converts, in promise and performance, were the brothers Arthur and Lewis Tappan--and Theodore Weld. As the leader of the Manhattan Calvinist capitalist Protestant philanthropists, Arthur Tappan rented the Chatham Street Theater in New York City as a worship center for Finney; supported him at the Second Free Presbyterian Church; and aided him at Oberlin College--where Finney first served as professor (1835), prior to his election as its President (1851-66). Basically a natural social conservative, but a more firm and flexible than rigid one, his personal antislavery thoughts and actions were one cut above Old Abolitionism and below New Abolitionism.

As neither a reactionary nor a radical but moderate conservative standard deviation from the norm of proabolitionism, he lagged far behind his convert Weld. In spite of being a reluctant immediatist, Finney's "revivals were a powerful force in the rising antislavery impulse." Doubtless this proabolitionist identity rendered him suspect for antiabolitionist Beecher. But he did not require this clearly harbored suspicion to be drawn into the antislavocrat/proslavocrat fray as a counter-force to Finney: his currently despised antagonist but later compatible Presbyterian brother of the cloth.

BEECHER'S SINGLE CATEGORY FOR BLACK CHRISTIAN MALES

Beecher by contrast was a typical Evangelical social conservative. Being a masterful model of this traditionalist mode, his customary cavalier disregard of the Black race could be set aside on occasion if it suited his paternalistic purposes, and it was appropriate and circumspect to do so. These cost-conscious criteria were exemplified in Boston on June 5, 1830, when, one year before the death of the Reverend Richard Allen (1760-1831), the founder and first Bishop (1816-31) of the African Methodist Episcopal Church (1816), Beecher preached for a conference of the A.M.E. Denomination at the request of the Reverend Morris Brown (1770-1849)--the second A.M.E. Bishop (1828-49):

I preached for the Methodist Society of coloured people last Sabbath afternoon, at the invitation of their bishop. They had a Conference, with fifty preachers present from different parts of the Union, and four from Haiti. Two thousand blacks present. All a surface of black heads, wedged in a solid mass almost. I came down to them and upon them in a way which made them cry "Amen! amen!" "True! true! " "That's good! that's good!" "That's preaching!" and clap hands, and jump up, etc.

Two hundred came forward and subscribed a pledge of entire abstinence which I wrote for them--the largest Temperance Society, I believe, ever organized at once, and promising to carry it through all the colored families of the land. About as much good, *I guess*, as ever I did in so short a time.[80]

Commencing six months later, and continuing for several years thereafter, Black Northeasterners were the major subscribers to Pro-Temperance Garrison's *Liberator* (January 1, 1831). Without their early subscriptions, the New Abolitionist Garrisonian journal of thought either would not have survived or would have sustained an anemic existence at best. Synchronically, they comprised the largest single body of converts to Moral Reformer Beecher's Temperance movement.

Forward from Garrison's defection from the ACS, Temperance, the central and universal Protestant Moral Reform concern, was nearly the only ethical perspective Beecher and Garrison shared: after Beecher condemned the White and Black New Abolitionists' pro-immediatism as the opiate of Black people, while he declared Black decision-makers' affirmative action on behalf of his

Temperance/pre-Prohibition crusade a healthy and wise exercise of leadership. In Beecher's methodical process, and implementation of his myopic and bifurcated compartmentalization of race and religion classes, Black folk were located in laughter, fixed in pomp and circumstance, and then provided with the elixir of moralism: not as a supplement to but as the mean substitute for grace. The theological evils of the day ("causing error to flourish and truth to decline") for Beecher, and his fellow Calvinist crusaders--existing in direct opposition to the "doctrines of the reformation and the needs of the evangelical character"--were antinomianism, Arminianism, heresy, and infidelity.

With regard to attracting and holding Beecher's positive concern, and eliciting his action beyond mere ameliorative response, the Black race could not light a candle to these spiritual curses of darkness. As a result, acceptance of the Black race could hardly be part and parcel of the "great and glorious" "cause" of revivals: temperance, public charities, and missions. Beecher believed these new, Evangelical-inspired, confident and cooperative religious forces were "all moving the right way"--to vanquish the foes of the new age. Black folk existed as a divisive entity, disrupting the unity for victory that Beecher's cohorts had worked strenuously and at length to achieve.

What proved a matter of not only the least social insignificance to the important mind of Beecher but of such little interest as to be neither an interesting subject nor even an object of his normally boundless curiosity was the peculiar condition of Black people, who, like the race itself, were briefly noted in his diary or filed under strange and unusual topics. The ACS made perfectly intelligible in its articles of incorporation just why Black American human bondage and caste-bound free persons were rarely--yet even then equally selectively and seldom--adequately appreciated as individuals; always viewed as an inextricable part of the collective community; and considered of the greatest unimportance as an indivisible member of the at once invisible and visible pariah class.

The Black race being for the Northern pure pious and pure profane power elite a powerless, harmless, and unnecessary nuisance in the body politic: to be flicked off or driven away like some unwelcome pest that Mother Nature produces for her own as often human species harmful as helpful mechanistic functions. Regardless of this actuality, Black folk existence in essence and manifestation persisted as the irrepressible powerful Protestant protest if not positive negation of White Christian Gentlemen's Agreements; White Protestant Northern Moral Reformers' and Southern governor redeemers' priorities; and pro-White race/ethnic-exclusive real interests and values.

Demonstrable negative (as opposed to positive) power countercharging power elite emerged propellers of negative (rather than positive) good deterrence-benevolence ethics. Outcast Black presence proceeded apace these powerhouses analogous to a flash point. The Black body's potential for interrupting the linear progress of moral and immoral White man and society was reflected in the leadership of the Evangelical World Alliance, who decreed the Black race the Devil incarnate; the evil and immoral anathema; and the evincement of invincible ignorance rather than the *cause célèbre*. Alternating between subtle and silent, violent and vicious, attitudinal and behavioral modification superimpositions, this leadership class resisted and resented absolutely their asserted equivalence of the Black race and the cause and effect deterring the upward and onward mission of their God, Church, and Yankee/Cavalier people.

Cavalier real interests in their Black chattel property counterbalanced

Yankee Black race obsolescence and banishment real values, of course. The alternation meant that indigenous North American Black people could not be eliminated as a group; a select "Elect" part of the whole body might be deported; it was necessary to settle for a compromise of principles intrinsic to the Halfway Piety faith and deterrence-benevolence ethic; selective means-ends constructive engagement inclusive of righteous non-observance of the free-born and freed or self-liberated Black leadership class, whom Black parishioners elected parsons and selected their clergymen-politician representatives; and it was sufficient or expedient and convenient if not efficient to neutralize the pervasive negative power of Black folk.

JOHN STEWART: PIONEER BLACK MISSIONARY

New England isolation and insulation may have been a contributing cause to the peculiar Puritan social effect throughout the society and affect upon "*the spirit*" and soul of the American conscience, including the Yankee failure to communicate in the commonwealth with their color caste class cultural kith and kin. This widespread and persistent norm of "Consistent Calvinists" was made conspicuous by the exceptions who confirmed the suspicions as solidly as they proved the rule.

But even while Congregationalism remained essentially region-bound until the mid-1840s, ministers and missionaries managed to take seriously Indian ethnics in the region and boundaries of the New England borders. Yet Evangelical Orthodoxy-Reformed establishmentarians studiously avoided, when they were unable to totally ignore, their independent-minded, counter-ethic persuaded, and corrective action-determined Black ministerial brethren.

It followed from this Calvinist Puritan revelation and reason in reality that it was within the peerless perspective and prodigious depth perception range, but beyond the narrow-focused public ethics-interest scope, of the fully informed and knowledgeable hierocrats at the helm of the Congregational/Presbyterian Union to appreciate the Reverend John Stewart (1786-1822), to say little of his Indian-reared, Black interpreter, Jonathan Poynter. Stewart was one free-born native--son of free Black Virginians--whom even pioneer Puritan explorers in the West for the New England Churches of Christ may have missed because he was a competitive contemporary and convert to Methodism.

They passed by--on the other side--of the presence no doubt due only in part to his Arminianism and their Calvinism persisting as a conflict of interests, as well as of faith and ethics, and Stuart's being the self-appointed (1816) founding missionary to the Wynandotte Indians of Sandusky, Ohio.

Public servant Cotton Mather promoted John Eliot as the model authentic Puritan Piety saint, and Jonathan Edwards memorialized David Brainerd as the wayward worldly saint standard of Halfway Piety. Stewart emerged in the age of the post-Edwardseans a pioneer missionary in the West whose lot "was one of *poverty*, persecution, and extreme adversity." Both like and unlike the Arminian Methodist brethren he joined, and Beecher along with other Calvinist sons of the wayward worldly saints fought as if they were so far from being either heroes or heroines they were close to being heretics, Stuart materialized as the methodical medium is the message who was denied the credit he deserved for his missionary prowess. Just as certainly as he was given little benefit of the doubt--and less notice as a man of worth, and of the Black race--[81] just so positively Beecher and his brethren in the West could give ample reasons for ignoring Stewart.

But there emerged in their ranks, as the first among equals in the class of Black clergymen-politicians, the Reverend Lemuel Haynes (1753-1833). Haynes was the unavoidable West Hartford, Connecticut native, son born to a Black father and a White mother, and clergyman who married (in 1783) an English/ Puritan race woman: "Connecticut Yankee" Bessie Babbit of certain Piety and education.

One of the Black Patriots who survived those who made the supreme sacrifice, and also like Presbyterian presbyter John Chavis a Calvinist clergyman, after fighting in Revolution War--to secure liberty and justice for all White males--Haynes evolved as one Congregationalist clergyman cast in caste called and chosen by class congregations to be the parson of their parishes. His career consisted of serving exclusively as the pastor of several successive all-White churches in the Northeast.

The Black-race biculturalist and biracialist by birth and marriage, together with his White race/ethnic-specific wife, pastored in Vermont--where he was employed initially by the Connecticut Missionary Society, (in 1804), and later by the Vermont Missionary Society (in 1814); Granville, New York (in 1822); and Torrington, Connecticut, his first pastorate from which post he preached (to White Calvinists only) throughout Connecticut.

Perchance Haynes was born too late to become a New Abolitionist--as he died in the year the New Abolitionist American Anti-Slavery Society was organized, whose formation transpired several months after the British Abolition Act was passed. But he was not born too early to be an anti-slavery proponent. An Old Abolitionist, Haynes shared with antiabolitionist "Connecticut Yankee" Beecher the same state of mind rather less precisely than the identical state birthplace and place of ministry.

No New England Calvinist clergyman was ignorant of Haynes' ecclesiastical fame and fortune after his traditional Evangelical Calvinist faith defending sermon on *Universal Salvation* (1805)--challenging the Universalist (separate and distinct offshoot of the Unitarian Congregationalist) doctrine espoused by the Reverend Hosea Ballou (1791-1852)--was printed, discussed, and distributed widely.

Synchronous Black Presbyterian-presbyter examples also might have served as models to deter Beecher from placing his establishment institutional authority behind the publicly proclaimed anti-Black race interestspecific ACS. The significant advance of New Abolitionism over Old Abolitionism and gradualism achieved by maverick Presbyterians who refused to acquiesce to either the "New School" or the "Old School" Presbyterian denomination--and whose ecclesiastical slow social change resolutions Lyman Beecher successfully short-circuited in the church power circles--was directed by proabolitionist Northerners in New York, and Southerners relocated in Southern Ohio and centered in the Chillicothe Presbytery.

The Chillicothe, Ohio Presbytery was dominated by Southerners who were equally attracted and propelled to the region by their antislavery sentiments, which were so unwelcome in the antebellum slaveholding localities. Manumitting slaves to the ACS was an exception to the near-rigid law (proscribing the liberation of human bondage) slave states normally permitted the influential affluential slavocrats.

Compared to this standard deviation from solid South law and order, concomitantly advanced in the sharpest imaginable contrast to (but not in conflict) with the "peculiar institution" an even more instructive sharp variable. In the slavocracy, where loyalty and honor to the system mandated the preemption of proabolitionist thoughts no less than pro-immediatist actions from civil discourse as well as the civil realm and therefore the ecclesiastical sector also, the far more parochial- and private- than public-antislavery (gradualism) was at once permitted and severely (almost exclusively) restricted to the Quaker-dominated regions.

Non-Quaker admirers of the conscience Quakers called Friends the "birthright" antislavery people. Friends were well-known for their post-Revolution era discretion and peace-seeking principles. But few understood their ranks included a minority of slavemasters and proslavocrats committed to the slavocracy. They cele-brated by most moralist direct actionists as a slave-free majority possessing no slaves to liberate--and as more sincere antislavery idealists than serious abolitionist realists, who could be trusted to be law and order abiding citizens.

While under this umbrella of protection sociable and social-minded Quakers gave no umbrage and joined Black Conductors and Passengers as Stationmasters, along the not-so-secret and yet not-so-open Underground Railroad, Evangelical Southern slaveowners and onetime slavemaster converts to manumissionism (and/or antislavery Protestants) were preponderantly moderates; without church or state support; aware their individual acts of manumission, permitted during the liberal manumission era in the South, would not be tolerated by the slavocracy regime; certain their Moral Reformer values could not change the system slavocrats commanded and controlled; and idealists turned realists who faced reality which forced them to bend, break, or to brook exile.

JOHN GLOUCESTER: EX-SLAVE MANUMITTED TO PIONEER

THE PHILADELPHIA COLORED PRESBYTERIAN CHURCH

The Reverend Gideon Blackburn (1772-1838) was one stellar Southern Ohio presbyter with whom Beecher worked closely in the state, prior to the period when Blackburn gained fame as the Presbyterian apostle to the Cherokee Indians. A relocated Southerner, Blackburn once sold two slaves he deemed incorrigibles. But under the progressive revelation of the ACS he freed others for emigration to Liberia. Earlier in his career, Blackburn had been a member of the Union Tennessee Presbytery, at which time one of his slaves came to the attention of the Reverend Archibald Alexander (1771-1851). Venerated as a Princeton Theological Seminary professor, Alexander had founded the Philadelphia Presbyterian Evangelical Society (1807)--whose mission included projects of relief for the "truly needy" approximately one thousand Black Philadelphians.[82]

The Reverend John Gloucester (1776-1822), one of Blackburn's slaves whom he set free, apparently re-ceived some instruction under his master, was recommended to Alexander to be a missionary in Philadelphia. Alexander--who later regretted having previously sold two slaves (whom he placed on the market because they broke his rules)--manumitted Gloucester for the purpose of fulfilling the Philadelphia Presbyterian mission. The task-responsibility involved proselytizing efforts in the Quaker city, but whose Calvinist sectarian forages were viewed by Black clergymen as competition in conflict with the pioneers of the self-generated and autonomous Black churches.

First among the rival originals issued forth Mother Bethel African Methodist Episcopal Church, which Richard Allen formed when he led Bethelites out of White ethnic-dominated St. George's Methodist Church: the original citadel of the Methodist Episcopal Church, that had established itself as a denomination upon severance of official ties with the Church of England in her 1784 organizing conference. Gloucester's second stiff competitor was St. Thomas' Episcopal Church, the first Black Episcopal church in America, that Absalom Jones founded after leaving St. George's with Richard Allen. Jones was the first Black Episcopal priest, whereby established his credentials as either the reversionist to the Anglican mother Church of Methodists or the Episcopal convert from Methodism.

Gloucester's licensure was approved, but not granted by the General Assembly of the Presbyterian Church (in 1807)--the year he founded in the City of Brotherly Love America's First African Presbyterian Church. The delay in his ordination occurred because the Philadelphia Presbytery determined that Blackburn's Presbytery in Tennessee should officially license and ordain Gloucester, which it did in 1810. The initial separate Black Presbyterian congregation began with twenty-two members; increased to one hundred twenty-three, when it was formally received into the Philadelphia Presbytery (in 1811); and grew to three hundred at the height of Gloucester's fifteen-year ministry. His effectiveness was hampered not only by stiff Black Methodist and Episcopalian competition, but also by the considerable amount of time he spent away from the African Church in his effort to earn the $1,500 required to purchase his enslaved wife and four children.[83]

PATRIOT JOHN CHAVIS: BLACK PRESBYTERIAN

SOUTHERNER-EDUCATOR OF WHITE SOUTHERNERS

Gloucester may not have impressed Beecher sufficiently to offset the Puritan-Connecticut anti-Black race values, which harm-intensive persuasions the Presbyterian connection with the ACS expanded rather than contracted sharply. But his complete confidence in deculturating and deporting the Black race to Liberia, and indifference to the desperate need of Black slave and free Calvinists, could have been easily questioned had he taken seriously the Reverend John Chavis (c.1763-1838): most probably born free near Oxford, North Carolina, and the first Black Presbyterian missionary whom Presbyterians commissioned in the South.

Following his service as a soldier in the Revolutionary War, Patriot Chavis was a sponsored student at the College of New Jersey (1746)--renamed Princeton University (1896)--where he reputedly studied privately for the ministry with President John Witherspoon. Prior to the Revolution, Witherspoon had consented to instruct the Newport, Rhode Island Black Congregationalist congregants of Samuel Hopkins and Ezra Stiles, whom their parsons encouraged and sent to the College to be trained as their missionaries and colonizationists to Black West (not Black or White South) African ethnics.

Reputedly, as well, Calvinist Chavis was formally enrolled in Washington Academy (Washington and Lee University), during the late 1790s. However this remarkable man grew in knowledge and wisdom, he was licensed to preach, the documents record, by the Lexington, Virginia Presbytery--and related to several presbyteries in Virginia as a missionary to Black Southerners. In this capacity, as a role model clergyman-missionary for the North and South united one and only Presbyterian denomination in the United States, Chavis annually reported to the Presbyterian General Assembly (during the years 1801-08) and was better known than respected by Beecher as one of the brethren of the cloth.

Several years later, during the pre-slavocracy era when public schools did not exist in the Cotton Kingdom and he was permitted to function as a professional Kingdom of God builder, Chavis returned to his native state of North Carolina where he was welcomed not only in his parochial office as presbyter, missionary, and supply preacher to Black and White congregations but especially in his new vocation as a private academy preceptor.

This Black-race distinct *tour de force* distinguished himself as a productive principal and practitioner of Protestant principles as indisputably as his biracial, dual professional, and sacred experience as well as secular experiment was unique to the Old South.

But Chavis's astonishing White race/ethnic and Black-race class barriers overjumping--rather more precisely than bridging--solo performance was neither surprising nor shocking because (A) he was a classic case of the ex-ception not either overturning or testing but confirming the rule; (B) his noteworthy act of creation occurred in the early national era prior to republican democracy's slavocracy, and during the Independence-lingering (spirit of universal liberty-sustained) period when not only slave states passed liberal private manumission statutes, but, similar and dissimilar to synchronical Northern slaveowners, earnest and honest freedom revering Southern slavemasters were Old Abolitionists and manumissionists, among whom were remarkable slaveholders who released immediately and unconditionally and without demanding further compensation their two or ten and in some instances hundreds of slaves; (C) random and odd or inconsistent and arbitrary more exactly than capricious harmonious trans-legal relations between Black and White Southerners in the "peculiar institution" persisted, as benevolent paternalists exercised the prerogatives of privilege to break the anti-Black race-specific laws they mandated when it served their real interests and advanced their real values to do so; and (D) as elsewhere generally throughout the South, and particularly in Virginia, laws in North Carolina were one thing--and their observance by independent-minded Quaker Puritan English race (and Scotch-Irish or Welsh Calvinist British-ethnic) representatives another thing.

Like and different from pre-Independence era immigrant Presbyterians and emigrant Friends in the Cotton Kingdom dominated by the Anglican theocracy, the pre-Revolution Arminian minority and Calvinist majority of Northern and Southern Baptists not only violently violated the ecclesiastical space and civil rules Anglican establishmentarians instituted, but, managing as the pure pious Freedom Fighters in the Revolution to construct a cooperative and corrective connective linkage with the pure pious and Deist Virginian aristocrats like Thomas Jefferson and James Madison, they succeeded in changing the laws to secure religious freedom and liberty of conscience.

As certainly as they were united in the Union and one and undivided in exercising freedom of choice selectively, the call of White Southerners for the uniform enforcement of the Fugitive Slave Act and "states's rights" in the slave and free states, and the total obedience to church and state authorities response White Northerners emitted primarily as a demanding cry for absolute conformance with law and order, New Abolitionists broke forth as one third of the nineteenth century passed to denounce to the public a compact between hypocrisy and duplicity. But the Anglican-Cavalier two sets of rules of interpretation and application for compliance with the law was a difficulty compounded by complexity--such as the fact that exceptionalism was also a Puritan-Yankee law.

Of course, the turning point for Chavis and the South was the uniform turn of the slave states from a flexible Cotton Kingdom to a rigid slavocracy. The nature and meaning, form and function of the slavocracy reached the stage of crystallization during the crucial two-year rancorous debate in Congress which ended with the Missouri Compromise (1822). This incredible turn of events occurred four decades after the White Gentlemen's Agreement establishing the Union resulted in Northeasterners compromising their principles; dra-matized the different Northern and Southern real values and conflicts of real interests, and so extensively until the Northern Old Abolitionist vanishing breed and en-dangered species rediscovered their principles in the throes of death and dying as a class, and made them their last will and testament following a forty year-long quietus; and precipitated Denmark Vesey's insurrection (1822) in Charleston, South Carolina--the rebellion that effectively sealed Chavis' fate in North Caro-lina.

Following upon the heels of pro-White race North Carolina lawmakers "de-claring that rape committed by a black on a white shall be punished with death," in their 1823 legislative enactment, anti-Black race reaction mushroomed instantly with the slavocracy into sacrosanct folkways and inviolable morays. Whereupon White men and women were constrained from being standard devia-tions from the norm; dissuaded from being exceptional individuals; prevented from allowing a Black performer to be either an exceptional or an individual; and prohibited from permitting White and Black power and authority, command and control, dominant and subordinate or superior and inferior role model re-versals to continue.

The 1830 North Carolina statute that declared the "marriage of a free negro with a white to be void" impacted Chavis negatively and disproportionately with far less deadly force than the "*Black Code*" prescribed that year "*to prevent all persons from teaching slaves to read or write; the use of figures excepted.*" Nevertheless, the essential fact and critical point withstands nice nuances and fine points developed to adorn the virtue and obscure the vice of benevolent proslavocrat paternalists. It is not only that anti-Black race laws were enacted for the convenience of the White race/ethnic male class but fundamentally that men with connections circumvented with impunity those they determined incon-venient.

However, even power brokers who made law and obeyed or disobeyed laws at will discovered their personal privileges and prerogatives were narrowed after the near-Reverend Nat Turner's insurrection (1831). In the same year that Turner demonstrated he was a self-determinationist, and as a direct reaction seeking to prevent the proliferation of his self-liberation model, the North Carolina legislature mandated a law to regulate enslaved and free Black North Carolinians. The statute rescinded the fifty year-old custom law granting a license to be at liberty, preach at will, and organize self-controlled autonomous churches to Black preachers authorized by their White master or employer. This "*Black code,*" reflecting the slavocracy-wide end of Black race independent church life and beginning of White-ethnic total command and control of Black congregations, was promulgated largely because exhorter Turner and other in-surrectionists were ministers of the Word.

In the aftermath of the Vesey insurrectionists, the Orange County, North Carolina Presbytery heard Chavis' protest against being preempted from equal access to opportunity, earning a livelihood, meeting the competition, and employing his professional skills. The presbyters promptly ruled that the state

law barring Chavis from preaching had to be obeyed by the church. White citizens' fear of insurrections was so extensive in the slavocracy that none of his
previous beneficiaries came to his defense.

Ironically, before being barred from preaching publicly to White and Black
Southern Presbyterians and it became positive law, Chavis had violated with
impunity the unenforced custom law against teaching Black folk to read.

Prior to the overpowering acts of 1831 that resulted in the irreversible permanent termination of his 1808-commencing integrated ministry and schools,
Chavis established a two-track private academy in North Carolina that functioned effectually as a college preparatory school. He taught sons of the planter
class in the daytime and charged sufficient tuition rates whereby, effectively,
howbeit unbeknown to them, his White pupils subsidized his Black students he
instructed for free or a lesser fee in the evenings. Chavis' curriculum emphasized classical studies--including Greek, Latin, English and mathematics--and his
competence in the classics enabled him to prepare for college many sons of a-
ristocrats from "Wake, Granville, Chatham, and Orange counties" who became
men of prominence:

> His pupils included Archibald and John Henderson, sons of North
> Carolina's Chief Justice. Two pupils, Charles Manly and Abraham
> Rencher, became governors of North Carolina and New Mexico,
> respectively. Rencher and Willie P. Mangum became congressmen:
> Rencher also was a diplomat. Other pupils became physicians,
> lawyers, ministers, and professors. Chavis reputedly ran the best
> college preparatory schools in North Carolina.[84]

BEECHER'S STELLAR SOUTHERN BLACK PRESBYTERIAN

CLERGYMEN PEERS AND CRITICS IN THE NORTH

Irrespective of all of his accomplishments as an Evangelical Presbyterian
clergyman, no doubt, for Beecher, Chavis remained nothing but a Black man
whom he found more of a curiosity than a luminary. The onetime Federalist
Party partisan parson and admirer of Thomas Jefferson reached this value
judgment from his own rational analysis and conclusion drawn from reasons that
correlated with those causing Jefferson to associate with diminished capacity
Black inventors like Benjamin Banneker (1731-1806): the free-born Maryland
native and Black scientist whom President (1789-97) George Washington (1732-
99) appointed (in 1791) an assistant surveyor to the architects developing
Washington, D.C. into the nation's capitol; and who, as the first Black Presidential appointee, wrote Vice President Jefferson in an August, 1791 letter to plead
with "you and all others"--who deny the "universal Father" endows Black like
"all other men" with "a natural right to our freedoms" and "the same faculties"
--"to wean yourselves from those narrow prejudices."

The color caste/captive values shared by Beecher and Jefferson illuminate
the presbyter's inestimable resources that he likewise employed effectively, and
to undermine rather than to undergird the positive potential and possibilities of
the Black race that Chavis and Banneker in their creative contributions to
White and Black Americans demonstrated.

Several other Presbyterian (ex-slave or free-born) men of the cloth he ought
to have engaged and appreciated but could not respect and therefore was unable
to learn from were exemplary Calvinists: the Reverend Samuel Eli Cornish

(1790-1859) whom New York Evangelical proabolitionists heeded, and whose idea for a Black college in New Haven Simeon Jocelyn developed and Arthur Tappan funded before Connecticut Yankees forced them to cease and desist; the Reverend Henry Highland Garnet (1815-82), who proclaimed to the slaves "Let your motto be resistance!"; the Reverend James William Charles Pennington (1809-70), who, while legally a slave, published in England *The Fugitive Blacksmith or Events in the History of James. W. C. Pennington, Pastor of A Presbyterian Church in New York, Formerly a Slave in the State of Maryland* (1849), and upon whom the University of Heidelberg conferred the honorary D.D. degree; and the Reverend Theodore Wright (17971847), the first Black graduate (in 1828) of Princeton Theological Seminary (1812).

First-hand experience color caste churchmen added to Beecher's second-hand knowledge of these celebrated fellow clergymen, who were seeking to minister to a people in dire straits with limited resources, either did not occur or occasion Beecher to examine his premises, to rethink his principles, and to reverse his priorities that included supporting their enemies whose agents and agencies were engaged in blocking their endeavors. White and Black proabolitionists' anti-denationalization advisement, and antiabolitionist Beecher's procolonizationist deportation solution to the problem of slavery and freedom in liberty, intersected in the ecclesiastical and civil power struggles where they met and drew a line in the dirt.

The conflict and competition did not but could and should have alerted the power broker to his harm and their hurt, and compelled the powerhouse existing at real advantage and without risk to expend a modicum of the expanding resources at his command in healing--rather than in wounding--the disadvantaged.

The so deep and permanent as to be a nonnegotiable difference between Black Presbyterian clergymen for self-determination and against dehumanization, and Beecher's deculturalization, denaturalization, and deportation critical imposition, could have been contemplated in his irreversible reflectiveness relatively objectively rather than only absolutely subjectively--and shifted easily from positive negation of immediate and unconditional universal abolition into neutral--had he respected his Black peers. The failure to do so early, decisively, and in time, did not cancel his capacity to make a mid-course correction or require him to be automatically indifferent to their visible and viable alternative presence--which he could escape only through callous disregard. By not aiding the Black Presbyterian-clerical leadership in need, while privately organizing parochially on behalf of his personal friends--who were their public enemies--Beecher was hardly a brother in deed.

He most certainly was not a failure to communicate either/or both the arrogance of power and the power of arrogance. They issued forth in his paternalistic approach to Black men of vigorous mind, rarely differed from his patronizing view of the fettered slaves or unlettered free Black Northerners and Southerners, and certified an anti-Black race interest-specific heart and soul of a color-conscious high class and low caste professor.

SOUTHERN ABOLITIONIST JOHN RANKIN AND EASTERN ANTIABOLITIONIST LYMAN BEECHER IN THE WEST

Anti-Black race interest was an alternating un-conscious, preconscious, and conscious persuasion Beecher preferred to being persuaded by Black men of mark, whereas, synchronously, there were White Southern Calvinist brethren relocated with him in Ohio who tolled the bell he could not but hear--and might well have heeded. He generally held Southern White men in high regard--and especially if they were men of Evan-gelical persuasion and large influence. Apparently, they did not need be doubly endowed with sacred and secular power so as to be his equal; one or the other was sufficient to suspend his disesteem.

Arriving before him in the West was the nonpareil pioneer Presbyterian Missionary in Tennessee--an exile from systemic slavery--the Reverend Samuel Doak. Doak became so convinced of the iniquity and inequity of slavery that he freed his slaves, sent them to live in Ohio rather than in Liberia, and demonstrated in his decision a conscience countermanding the consensus ethos in the Presbyterian denomination and her surrogate antislavery ACS.

Advancing a social redeeming ethnic, Doak transmitted his antislavery ideals to the men he trained for the ministry. They became the leadership corps of the Ohio Presbyterian New Abolitionist, who, along with the New York City revolving Presbyterian proabolitionists, formed East-West coordinates of the Manhattan-centered wing of the American Anti-Slavery Society. Gideon Blackburn was a singular one among the many Southerners whom Doak prepared for the ordination as a Presbyterian Elder.

Chief among Doak's able social ethics students was his son-in-law, who as a social ethicist joined the company who challenged by constantly shaking the fundamental faith ground and ethics foundation of their Denomination--and held in highest esteem by non-Presbyterian New Abolitionist crusaders--the Reverend John Rankin (1793-1886). Rankin pastored several churches in Tennessee and Kentucky--and there formed Old Abolitionist societies--before moving to become the minister (1822-66) of the Ripley and Strait-Creek, Ohio Presbyterian Churches. Shortly after his settlement, his brother, Thomas, a merchant in Virginia, communicated to him in a letter that he had purchased slaves for profit and pleasure. John Rankin formally responded in Letters on American Slavery (1833) that were originally addressed to his brother in 1824.

The correspondence, along with his persistent prow-ess that was consistent with his development from a pro-manumissionist and Old Abolitionist into a New Abolitionist, earned his reputation as "the Martin Luther of the antislavery movement." Rankin's private letters thoroughly impressed Garrison, who had them published as a book in the volume entitled Letters in 1833. They were published on the East Coast following Theodore Dwight Weld's initial Western field investigation for the American Anti-slavery Society--and involvement with the precursor of immediatism in the districts of Ohio.

Rankin's work, published in several editions, was widely read after Rankin began to lecture (in 1836) for the American Anti-Slavery Society. His agency began the year after Charles Grandison Finney wrote his seminal Lectures on Revivalism (1835)--"indisputably the most powerful theoretical statement of the significance of the titanic enterprise."[85] Unlike her antiabolitionist father, proabolitionist Rankin's heroics on behalf of fugitive slaves in Ohio provided the New Abolitionist model for Cincinnati resident (1832-50) Harriet Beecher Stowe's Uncle Tom's Cabin (1852).

RANKIN'S COLOR CASTE/CAPTIVE CLASS

THEORY AND EXPERIENCE IN REALITY

Rankin's early and profound antislavery statement was at once incisive and concise. It was also written with grace sufficient to meet the cultivated manners Lyman Beecher relished so thoroughly that he delighted in rejecting Garrison's message because he despised his method. Rankin set in print and published in the parochial media for the public to read and heed the private counsel and advice he communicated to his brother. Thuswise John Rankin wrote for the correct Chrisitianity and civility and/or Calvinistical right race and religion relations record that Thomas Rankin was "a mistaken brother, who had manifested to me a kind and generous heart"--and "claims my strongest sympathy."

The distinguishable distinctive feature in Rankin's writing was his clear understanding of anti-Black race values, the depth of which Beecher--and the antiabolitionist forces in the Northeast which he headed, even while residing in the West--should not have underestimated, however debatable the cause and effect espoused by Rankin, the Old South born, bred, and reared captor reborn liberator of captives:[86]

> Their color is very different from our own. This leads many to conclude that Heaven has expressly marked them out for servitude; and when the mind once settles upon such a conclusion, it is completely fortified against the strongest arguments the reason can suggest, or the mind of man invent. In the Bible...you will find that the blackness of the African is not the terrible mark of Cain, nor the direful effects of Noah's curse, but the mark of a scorching sun. "*Looke not upon me because I am black because the sun hath made me the keeper of the Vineyard.*" Canticles I;6. In this passage the Creator of the Church of Christ evidently speaks of himself under the figure of an Ethiopian, on whom the sun looked with such intensity as changed his color, and so rendered him the object of hatred to the rest of mankind, who with himself originally thus marked them out for servitude. But how false, how ungenerous, how unreasonable is such a conclusion.[87]

The Evangelical Protestants forming the majority of the not born but made original New Abolitionists were essentially neither born nor bred Old Abolitionists; born after the death of the preponderancy of the Old Abolitionists who formed the clerical leadership class; and united in confirming the transformation of Rankin from an Old Abolitionist to a New Abolitionist, and identifying him as the missing link between Old Abolitionism and New Abolitionist.

Garrison and the Tappan brothers, the rational organizing decision-makers of the Boston and New York halves of the American Anti-Slavery Society, both led and followed Garrisonians and Tappanites in the East in citing Rankin as their model modern moral man in the West; moral measure medium and/or the moral (ways and means-ends) method is the message messenger; authorized version of true spiritual and moral power apropos his conversion in the proslavery world to the antislavery archetype; and as their ideal and idea of a true and real White Christian Southern gentlemen, while conferring upon him the title New Abolitionist apostle and apostle to the New Abolitionists apostle for being as well as raising the standard of the public interest-advancing direct actionist Protestant social ethicist.

Proabolitionist Northerners and Southerners treated Rankin as the representative realistic and responsible Southerner, realized hope of the South in the West, and promise of a future in the slavocracy. Immediatism enveloped a creative minority whom religion and race relations revolutionists expected to generated a conscience heightened majority of Southerners, and the precious few immediatist engaged in myth and reality experiences were dearly loved and liked Christian social ethics signs and symbols.

Garrisonians and Tappanites at once certified and validated Rankin's AAS *bona fides*. Weld avouched his immediatism credentials were the empirically verifiable and vindicated binary principles of abolitionism and equalitarianism: the equalitarian meaning and value of whose experimental and experiential nature and function he defined and demonstrated in the process of binding as one ethical right and good the abolition of slavery and anti-Black race values. What they found to be particularly significant and relevant was his profound grasp of anti-Black race desire.

Instantly upon joining the AAS Rankin became the immediatists' conscious conscience, informed mind and will, and therefore creditable witness for the defense of Black self-determination--and/or the prosecution of the White dehumanization offensive. Contemporary co-horts certified his character who insisted he inspired confidence, demonstrated courage and credibility and claimed he deserved to be credited for being reliable as well as credible. Enthusiastic AAS supporters of Rankin were excited by his rational reflection and relevant social structural change action leadership style and substance. They cited for certification of his color caste/bondage condition constructive engagement/disengagement the direct actionist's instructive comparative class and culture analysis of the negative function and positive dysfunction of race-conscious religion in the antebellum East and West, North and South, and church and state.

New Abolitionists' lavished their high praise on Rankin's treatment of right and righteous crusaders for Christ and color caste/captive civility as "bad faith" passing for "good faith"; the heart and soul of pro-White race/ethnic folk religion; idol worship and adored idolatry whose "true believers" castigate as treason all questions of the sanctity of their idols; and "*the spirit*" driving the White ethnic will over mind to secure Constitution-legalized individual rights holding hostage community responsibility enlightened interest. Proabolitionists especially appreciated his descriptive facts and value judgment, that were verifiably garnered from his analytical methodology and critical conclusion; and the constructive engagement/disengagement corrective action he recommended for the transformation of the positive harm-intended religion of the superior White race and inferior Black race.

They applauded as Rankin argued the case for change from color caste parochial and private self-serving individual values to enlightened public interest-advancing ethics. Their cheers were clamorous when he concluded Christian and civil conversion from exploitation and exclusion to equity and egalitarianism can be achieved by citizens determining to be engaged in moving from critical ethical reflection and re-thinking through real repentance to reconciliation: but not by reason alone, because different premises can support disparate equally correct personal logics and truth claims no less than real wrongs as righteous rights, as well as solidify as collective conscious advancing in direct competition and conflict truth and error or democracy and slavocracy as equally right and good governmental arrangements.

Moreover, proabolitionists coincidentally compared and contrasted Beecher and Rankin in their perception is reality perspective. Therein, predictably, Rankin emerged the distinctive presbyter color-conscious conscience distinction who confirmed their suspicions, to wit, the different antislavery intentions and consequences Beecher engendered made a significant difference to the antebellum past, present, and future possibilities of the color class/bondage class. In their admittedly partially subjective rather than purely objective rational judgment, Beecher's equally functional and dysfunctional individual-specific spir-itual and Moral Reform revivalism featured parochial values-enhancing evangelism, and evolved as state of the art private interests-securing and public good-limiting Evangelicalism.

Contradistinguishingly, Rankin's counterdemanding ecclesiastical and civil motive and purpose developed a church and state related social redeeming connection between Evangelicalism and individual regeneration--that is, a positive ethical connective linkage between Evangelicalism and universal immediate and unconditional abolition. Garrison, a moral absolutist of the first rank, argued there is no way to moral and nonviolent abolition: moral and nonviolent abolition is the way, the truth, and the light. He spontaneously embraced the Rankin approach instantly upon discovering his life and work, and misestimated the Evangelical Calvinist social ethicist.

In addition to asserting the equivalence of *agape*-love and virtue and making this sacred value his ethical norm--as well as the criterion of the worth of the highest secular principle of justice in each moral decision situation--Rankin preached and practiced the five universal and permanent principles (life-liberty, goodness, justice, honesty, and individual freedom); approached the complex set of high ethics as flexible-interchangeable parts of the whole virtue-principles system; and arranged the principles carefully and skillfully in a rational and firm hierarchal order rather than in a fixed priority. But Garrison inevitably misconstrued him to be a moralist exactly like himself, a high principled ethicist who stuck to the inflexible order of his principles and therefore became stuck in his rigid order.

Contrapositively, secular and religious rationalist critics of Rankinesque radicalism found it impossible or counter-productive to call into question his motives; and possible or necessary to quarrel with his methodological analysis and conclusions. Rankin's convincement of the generalizable and even universalizable value of his sweeping proabolitionist generalizations and interpretations of the facts left him prey to the preying antiabolitionists, who focused their narrow-scoped rather than broad-gauged limits-revering ethics on the simplicities to obscure the complexities of the *Conscience and Constitution* color caste/captive cultural crisis issue.

CLASSIC CALVINIST CHIAROSCURIST RANKIN

(COMPLEMENTARY OF COTTON, MATHER, AND EDWARDS)

In the process of being engaged like John Cotton, Cotton Mather, and Jonathan Edwards in extending the American Puritan-specific classic Calvinist chiaroscuro continuum--but as a different kind of color-intensive chiaroscurist--Rankin proved a better social ethics practitioner than theoretician when he published his assertions: (A) "Black skin" is neither the "peculiar mark of heaven's displeasure" nor empirical "evidence that he who wears it is doomed by the Creator to endless servitude" but simply "the effect of climate"; and (B) "color and degradation" are synonymous with anti-Black race demands and chattel slavery. Whereunto, instead of church and state united moral and political power priorities being the fundamental and enduring dehumanization sources, color-intensive caste and economic profit are the cause of color-specific human bondage. In short, both race superiority and slavery arise singly from "the love of gain" because the root of all evil "has a most blinding influence upon the mind."

As a direct result of developing theory and experience amassed as an active presbyter in the Presbyterian denomination, whose Reformed tradition affirmed capital and grace to be equivalences and met Orthodoxy's competition as the Church of the Calvinist capitalists, Rankin understood capitalism-intensive secular and sectarian Americans making the love of money and real interests--like the acquisition of profits and the accumulation of wealth--their highest value to be the root of the private and public color caste/captive ethical error and evil: "The love of gain is the polluted fountain" that is always and everywhere "found to accommodate itself to hue peculiar to that Country or climate."

Consistent with his appreciation of the new economic realism, promoted by natural law and natural rights Protestant powerhouse managers of reality, the idealist proposed an alternative to viewing the color caste/captive class as an intractable cultural given for consid-eration by the Protestant philanthropists. Whereon he pressed, as "an established law of nature" and practical principle for moral social rule, the ethical corollary "that it is much easier to communicate a stain than to purge it away." English race and British ethnic penetrators of the African race, and progenitors of their deethnicized Black race-only North American indigenous cultural and genetic kin-group, his concluding ancillary argued, certainly know and ought to act in line with the knowledge that blackness is a natural (nature-specific) result of existence for generations "under a tropical sun" that is not "in our climate, bleached white in two or three."

Rankin's proabolitionist advocates and antiabolitionist adversaries evinced in their antagonistic positions protagonist Rankin's arguable logic, that matched for compelling force the power of his principle and principal point--that its, at bottom the race and religion issue of Bible-authorized caste and bondage is a problem of "*the spirit*."

Whether they liked it or not, the antislavocracy proslavocracy proponents demonstrated that Rankin nearly hit upon but just missed the distinguishing factor in the two-dimensional issue of color: AntiBlack race virtue is pro-White race/ethnic values-protectionists organized in individual and institutional opposition to pro-Black race real interests and values; exacerbated by color and slavery; grounded in "*the spirit*" of culture that is equally based in and confirmed by the Bible and the Constitution, moral and positive law, cultural experience and knowledge, and history; and advanced as a matter of rational belief and faith that rationalists may approve or disapprove of at will.

Anti-Black race virtue is a vice, and a national treasure device for White race and ethnic folk as certainly as for Black folk race essence precedes and succeeds existence. It can be proved or disproved conclusively nearly as rarely as it can be proved and disproved successively--that is, so sufficiently as to efficiently remove the extrinsic anti-Black race values phenomenon of private belief or personal religion from its intrinsic cultural dynamic.

Rankin is concerned in the *Letters*, friends like Garrison and Weld attest, to project his hope that crusaders for positive antiblack white-ethnic virtue will overpower warriors for negative antiblack white-ethnic virtue and its perversion as anti-Black race virtue:

> The Africans are the children of our common mother: let us not be angry with them because the sun hath looked upon them; the change of complexion ought never to break the ties of humanity.

Unlike the real reasons and easily rationalized excuses Beecher believed justified his patented complaint against Garrison, no rancor existed in Rankin's reason and revelation here or elsewhere which Beecher could manipulate reasonably: either to write off his Presbyterian brother as offensive or to defend sending his Black Presbyterian clergymen brethren off to Africa. Contradistinctively, in these *Letters* from the antislavocrat presbyter to his slavocrat and lay Presbyterian brother, Rankin is an affirmative action White Southerner inviting another White Southerner to negotiate a new White Southern Christian Gentlemen's Agreement. The operative common consent and assent line in the Christian and civil contract Rankin constructed constituted the paradigmatic affirmative action equal opportunity prayer: Since God has created "of one blood all nations of men, wherever, and whenever

> we find a man, let us treat him as a brother without regard to his color; let our kindness sooth his sorrows and cheer his heart."[88]

Rankin left no reasonable reader to doubt his thorough apprehension of the slavocracy, which he termed a slavery system based on the Black bondage body underpinning real estate and other real economic interests: sustaining and sustained by real political values; real social values; and good White male and female Christians who own Black men and women they treasure and use as negotiable chattel property or collateral like cattle. Being good men and women and *"true believers"* who harbor no doubt that advancing their real interests in human bondage serves their best interests, Christian slavemasters, Rankin challenged his Calvinist slaveowning brother to believe,

> often argue according to what they suppose to be right: though naturally honest as other men, they are pressed on the side of injustice by the weight of interest,

because, once driving real interest

> takes full possession of the heart, the strongest faculties yield to its influence.

Concurrently Beecher's antiabolitionist arguments left the implication that he expected anyone who followed his logic to draw a singular inference, to wit, that he thought because he could explain why capital investors in and exploiters of human bondage equate their love of gold as well as greed and gore with grace and goodness that he *ipso facto* (1) explained away the ethical error; (2) changed the unconscionable to the tolerable by calling irrepressible real interests ravages of the Black body either natural and therefore reasonable and manageable or expedient and convenient; and/or (3) made the desired the desirable or the preferred the preferable, and the wrong the right.

Rankin's proabolitionist principle demonstrated he knew to be true what Beecher's antiabolitionist denied--namely, that human beings are endowed by the Creator with liberty and reason as self-evidently as involuntary servitude is explicitly inimical to the performance of "social and relative duties" because, being dehumanization in essence and manifestation, human bondage robs a man of himself and induces ignorance, immorality, unchastity, and dishonor.

What is still a more serious evil, it interferes with the divine
prerogative over man, and robs the Almighty of the service which
is due him.[89]

CHARLES JONES: ESTABLISHMENT PRESBYTERIANS'

ROLE MODEL SLAVEHOLDER AND MISSIONARY TO SLAVES

Negative antiblack white-ethnic virtue overreaches precipitated Beecher's
advancement of anti-Black race values. Beecher could have made positive
antiblack white-ethnic virtue an overriding moral principle, and reached the
ethical high ground Rankin stood on to promote pro-Black race interests from
the low ground of anti-Black race demands. Instead, he chose contempt for the
laws of logic and culture in his endeavor to make the exception the rule--that
is, the exceptional White slavemaster the rule.

Arguably either/or both unwilling and unable to be evenhanded in his race
relations, because he was congenitally deficient in nothing so much as motive,
nevertheless, Beecher commanded sufficient reason and opportunity to have
made a comparable attempt to make the equally well known exceptional Black
Christian the general rule for Black folk. This selective ethical commission and
omission was of a piece with and followed from the fact that he could accept
neither the Black Calvinists in White Presbyterian religion nor the White Calvinists in what he perceived as the black religion of New Abolitionism.

An arguable set of reasons for the patrician "Connecticut Yankee's"
complete rejection of contemporary White Presbyterians who strove to respect
their Black clerical brethren entailed Beecher's preference for (A) aristocrats
committed to stabilizing the social values; (B) the current ecclesiastical and
civil law and order; and (C) the culture-specific arrangement of superior and
inferior races, ethnic groups, and classes.

He admired men of means and especially the plurality who being conservatives (whether only protectors of their real interests or whether also cultivated
culture values-conservatationists and physical universe preservationist) naturally
strove to sustain the *status quo*, partly because he believed that *nobility* is *virtue* (genetically transmitted either relative or absolute rightness and goodness)--
whose manifest essence in existence the ethicist declared his inherited select
"Elect" Puritan race and saints of God genius and gene (or "*seed*" of Abraham).

Virtue, he argued from silence, is first and foremost primarily inherent in
inherited genes, but second and secondarily ascribed or achieved through
acquired class and property.

Contrapositively, Beecher appeared poorly prepared to doubt conventional
wisdom whose headmen presumed the propertyless he knew to be the powerless
were offspring of a different gene pool; genetically diminished in capacity and
congenitally deficient in wisdom; and virtue-free, as a consequence of being
culture-deprived entities devoid of both class and property as well as intellectual substance.

Beecher identified in his three-volume published *Work* (1852-53) paramount
patricians and aristocrats whose opinions and values he trusted implicitly. The
Reverend Charles Colcock Jones (1804-63) was one mem-ber of the Princeton-
dominated "Old School" Presbyterian General Assembly whom the presbyter leader in the rival Yale-centered "New School" Presbyterian apparently admired no
less than he respected John Caldwell Calhoun or embraced enthusiastically the

slaveholding members of his Northern "New School" Church.

A native of Georgia, and student of Moses Stuart at Andover Seminary prior to transferring to and graduating from Princeton Seminary, presbyter Jones organized the Association for the Religious Instruction of Negroes in his native community of Liberty County, Georgia. A master planter (major plantation owner of a large number of slaves) and masterful disciplinarian, whose mastery of a productive and wealth-producing plantation plus professional people management skills matched his social engineering expertise, Jones integrated his church and civil powers and implemented these profane and religious capacities in his distinctive sectarianism.

Being a model private, parochial, and public powerhouse proved his distinguishing feature that set him apart from sacred and secular slavocrats.

What made the genius of Jefferson possible as a national presence also was the critical cultural that enabled the distinctive Jones factor to make a difference, namely, his productive and profitable human bondage. Jones' color chattel made it feasible for him to labor for his Presbyterian Church without pay during the years 1831-41, after he received an official commission as a Presbyterian Missionary (1833-48).

At this point in his private and parochial public servant role, Jones determined a change in pace was in order. He applied for and obtained a two year leave of absence; accepted his appointment as a Columbia Seminary professor (1848-50); returned to the national headquarters of the Old School Reformed Denomination as a Church bureaucrat and technocrat, and the original Secretary 1850-53) of the Presbyterian Board of Domestic Missions; and resigned from the office due to poor health, and retired to his slave plantation.

The slavocracy had long since driven the liberal manumissionists from the planter class centers of power, and forced the moderate manumissionist clergy to keep silent or to become slavocrats. In this context, during his professional career, planter Jones was the overseer in charge of the national office through which "Old School" Presbyterian Denomination ministered to slaves; and emerged one of the strong voices of the best spirit the slavocracy would listen to--and allow to speak with unbridled tongue.

Jones was impressive as the demonstrable deterrence-benevolence benevolent paternalist exemplar, command and control churchman, and efficiency expert for the ecclesiastical and civil powers. As a wealth-producing and wealth-accumulating plantation master, and educated clergyman-slaveowner with national clout, Jones clearly flourished in Georgia as the bare essence of civility as a powerhouse state-authorized governor redeemer and church politician.

The quintessential bureaucrat theoretician and technocrat technician understood himself to be one of the many called and few chosen professionals who elected the vocation of exercising spiritual and moral power and authority over the slave thousands. Girding up his loins that were composed of indomitable will and robust reason enveloped by indefatigable energy, the progressive transformationist volunteered to direct the "Old School" and Princeton-centered Presbyterian gen-eral Assembly's domestic mission to the slaves. In the process, he developed and implemented the Church's Black folk-specific deterrence-benevolence principle and constructive engagement policy.

Doubtless grateful for his "election" to eternal salvation from damnation throughout terrestrial and extraterrestrial existence, Jones dedicated himself to systematic and systemic Calvinist double election/double damnation indoctrination of Black bondage, as a brutal benevolence benevolent paternalist: who was duty, honor, and loyalty personified, and therefore bound to determine the destiny of the Black race in history and eternity.

He was in power and authority during the beginning of the end of the antebellum era, when the Presbyterian power elite in the free states no longer preferred to permit the ACS to perform their antislavery task-responsibility; and Presbyterian slavocrats found the ACS deportation of Black bondage a contraction rather than expansion of their real interests, and the leadership selected him to check the absence of the Black body and guarantee the pleasurable and profitable Black presence. Jones won the admiration of his Northern Calvinist capitalist clergy-brethren and their Protestant philanthropist parishioners.

They gave him *carte blanche* but not a blank check, whereby his free reign to venture at will was unaccompanied by adequate monetary, material, and personnel support.

Jones knew every powerhouse Calvinist interested in the religious-specific moral manipulation, instruction, and direction of Black folk; corresponded with most of the influential Presbyterian Moral Reformers; and communicated clearly his domestic mission to human bondage:

> We believe that their moral and religious condition is such as that they may justly be considered the Heathen of this Christian country, and will bear comparison with Heathen in any country of the world."[90]

As persuasive in this parochial principle, private precept, and public example as the persuaded of the positive value of his caste/captive possessions and Calvinist condition was rich and famous, Jones took full advantage of his opportunity to speak with, to, and for his class.

Perforce the great slavemaster's mastery of empirical rationalism-rooted Calvinist conversionist psychology, initiative in this sectarian task-responsibility was evidenced in the philosophical theologian's patented advancement of his posited Black caste and White class incentives-inducing and disincentives-deterring grand principle of impartiality.

Purported Jonesesque evenhandedness proved better dogma than pragma, and expanded from theology into ideology as the proslavocracy disciplinarian developed subtle but powerful rational constraints. In a ying and yang promise and performance, he checked the life- and liberty-loving drives of his slaves, and balanced the act of preemption by enticing his fellow slaveholders to imitate his attitudinal and behavioral modification formula.

Jones argued the case for slaveowners' employing Evangelical Calvinist religion to indoctrinate their slaves by appealing to self-serving interests; guaranteeing greater benefits than liabilities would occur from the efficient expenditure of the affordable disposable resources required to achieve the objective; and asserting his double bottom line.

The first one subsisted of his personal certification that his progressive Presbyterian process and program--for the actualization of appropriate Christian master and slave relationships--were cost-effective rather than cost-prohibitive principles. And the second one insured the slavocrats' minor investment in Christianity and civility, entailing the affordable and manageable commitment of the limited resources necessary to inculcate efficient reward and punishment moralisms, would pay major dividends. The assets over the liabilities the Jonesesque cost/benefit calculation generated included relatively perfect plantation producers and productive slaves; self-acting Black race conformity and conformance with ecclesiastical and civil law and order; and domestic peace and safety.

Jones proved a worthy successor in the long line of color-intensive and clever "Consistent Calvinist" strategists and tacticians, whose Black-race analysis, prediction, and control mechanism was not one whit less real and portentous for being a more pretentious than scientific device. The macro and micro social engineer managed reality, and to manipulate vulnerable Black folk to affirm cheerful obedience to instituted legal injustice and immoral men in an unethical society. His total command and control management style maximized efficiency and minimized costs systematically and systemically. Jones' utilitarian operation required segregated worship to work effectively. Whence the spiritual-moral nature and nurture specialist publicly applauded subjectively, and appraised objectively, the "separate and unequal" principal Northern and Southern race and religion principle and practice:

> The galleries or back seats on the lower floor, of white churches, are generally appropriated to the negroes, when it can be done with convenience to the whites. Where it cannot be done conveniently, the negroes who attend must catch the Gospel as it escapes by the doors and windows.[91]

A past master of totality and detail, as thoroughly statistically informed and reliable as he was organized to beat the Devil, Jones was an alert bureau chief concerned to ensure his agency attained its fair share relative to the other agencies competing for the resources allocated to the Domestic Mission by the "Old School" Presbyterian bureaucracy. Whereupon he published data garnered from his fact finding mission throughout the slavocracy, where he discovered that the combined total from all the Evangelical Protestant denominations of only twelve White missionaries to Black Southerners compared favorably to the single Presbyterian church among the sum total of five churches that the Protestant denominations constructed for their Black Southern constituents.

While his far more generous Northern than Southern supporters were clamoring for domestic Christianization in lieu of foreign Colonization, as neither the best nor the best possible but the most probable good housekeeping measure, Jones estimated that five per cent of the Black people in the slave states were regular worshippers in the aggregate of Southern White Protestant churches. White lay and clerical members of the rapidly region-expanding Methodist Episcopal Church fielded more missionaries to slaves than any other antebellum denomination, and enjoyed their largest constituency in the South.

Such also certainly was the case no less with the democracy era-organized Protestant Episcopal Church than with theocracy era-dominant Church of England, from whose womb sprang the dynamic duo American Episcopal and Methodist Episcopal Church. Baptists were currently reversing their pre-slavocracy and early national era initiative, when they distinguished themselves from Evangelical sectarian rivals by ordaining many more Black men than their proselytizing competitors.

This Baptist performance was quite in accordance with (as much as in spite of) the custom and civil laws they managed, manipulated, and mandated as regularly as they honored them in the breech.

Presbyterians were far less engaged in innovative biracial leadership in the

South during the decades of the new nation--those between Independence and the Missouri Compromise--than their Baptist Calvinist cousins. But as the antebellum age advanced, Presbyterian law and order Christians proceeded apace. Representative parochial and private plantation masters and overseers refused on principle to violently violate neither the Black body nor the Black space but primarily only the instituted laws of church and state.

Thus, as naturally as day precedes and succeeds night, presbyters declining to ordain Black Presbyterians in the slavocracy followed willy-nilly in truth and reality.

For similar late theocracy and early democracy as well as mid-slavocracy more compelling interests than values, inclusive of the high priority of existing in compliance with ecclesiastical law, leaders of the Reformed tradition not only excluded Black folk from developing in their White-race dominated denomination but coinstantaneously precluded the development of Black-race Presbyterians in the South--like White-ethnic immigrants--from dependence through independence to interdependence via forming autonomous color caste/captive congregations.

Consequently, Black converts to the Reformed faith and order, desirous of obtaining spiritual and moral power in public worship, were left to implore pure pious and pure profane masters who were frequently enough proponents of different persuasions; pursuing pleasure instead of Christian joy or happiness; and in the business of making profits instead of saving souls.

Following the immoral mandates of the proslavery Moral Law of the church and positive law of the state, rather than the secular principle of justice and the sacred rule of *agape*-love, the classical Calvinist continuum advanced which the traditionalists selectively elected and validated; swore was the will of God revealed in the Bible, and especially in the Apostle Paul's preponderancy of law overriding love and liberty writings; and claimed the most effectual ways and means for cost-conscious Christians to engage the slavocracy creatively.

These great realities and certainties were precipitating reasons why the superior "Old School" General Assembly wing of the Presbyterian establishment left the ministry to slaves in the hands of Jones, their overruling overlord agent. A masterful rhetorician and logician, yet equally charismatic chief executive officer of private and parochial plantations, Jones exuded the charm and wit and exuberant humor traits so characteristic of the White Southern Christian gentlemen. These strong character traits were among the reasons that he was far more effective in gaining support in principle from the Northern Elders than from the planter class, and the owners of fewer slaves than the patrician.

Directly as a result of the class of Presbyterian slavocrats being exactly engaged in the City of God and Man, as the exemplary Protestant for church and state united rather than either separated or divided ecclesiastical and civil powers in soulcraft and statecraft on the one hand, and, on the other hand, relatively against theocracy and meritocracy and absolutely for both sacred Christocracy and churchocracy and secular democracy and slavocracy, Jones makes crystal clear traditional Calvinists' cost-conscious concernment with and compromise of their dearly loved color-intensive conscience, Constitution, and "Colored" folk. Specifically, when speaking of Black brothers and sisters in the body of Christ as distinguished from the body politic, Jones proclaims proudly and publicly "we separate entirely their *moral* and their *civil* condition."

Jones made this principle point stick so solidly it became a slavocrat premise for proslavocrat Beecher's antiabolitionist premise, and the measure of his Moral Reform promise and performance. Jones was a warrior for the Reformed "Old

School" tradition "New School" crusader Beecher challenged on its merits. Thus it is arguable that at best Jones at best was Beecher's formidable friend and foe rather than hero. Nevertheless, the "Connecticut Yankee" passed for the conservative mind of the Eastern establishment in the West, where Beecher vociferously defended what the Georgia Presbyterian stood for and rallied to his side. This configuration occurred most dramatically in 1835, two years before the schism divided the united Presbyterian Church into Northern and Southern divisions.

Beecher raced to the media to denounce to the public and publish for the record precisely why his parochial and private pro-gradualism was an evidentiary difference in degree so great from pro-immediatism it proved a different kind of antislavery motive, message, means, and ends--just after Jones rushed to judgment and defiance of the proabolitionists:

> The abolitionists have no more right to use the Liberty of the Press, or of free discussion to the destruction of the lives and property of the Southern people, than they have to use their guns or swords.[92]

The New Abolitionists were located solely in the North, and numerically overwhelmingly but not only Northerners: because Southern direct actionist Old Abolitionists and onetime slaveholders emerging into manumissionists, and evolving antislavery gradualists and immediatists, were driven out of the slave states by the slavocrats in charge of the slavocracy. To the antislavocrat collective mind of this Northern and Southern creative minority, their proabolitionism was validated as the beautiful truth by the proliferating facts and figures generated by the mushrooming Beecher and Jones types.

Forward from the mid-1830s, these antiabolitionists' solid slavocrat South truth claims were lodged in the appearances as errors of deception. Therein Jones was perceived as indulging himself in the most extreme form of self-serving protest. Moreover, through his active support of the Southeasterner, the Northeastener provided the smoking gun that confirmed their suspicions. It validated the fairness and equity of applying to him the value judgment that a critical contemporary issued in another context, where he asserted that Beecher had "long racked and harrowed the people."

BLACK-RACE VALUE ECLIPSED BY BRITISH
ETHNICS' ARRIVAL, REVIVAL, AND UTILITY

Beecher and his fellow Evangelical Calvinist establishmentarian spiritual and moral power reformer advocates and adversaries of "Taylorism" proved they were in total command and control of "power to the contrary." This was especially evident as they turned down the positive and turned up the negative dynamic of antiblack white-ethnic virtue to perfect their politics of anti-Black race interests. No tears of sorrow were shed for the Black condition, since rationalists were efficiency experts who reasoned that any sympathy reflecting upturning empathy, guilt transformed into grace, and serious repentance (or rethinking) emitted a counter-productive expenditure of energy, that excited nothing so little as possibilities or so great as optimism-depleting pessimism.

The great White Christian hope Evangelical Protestants sought to protect as the highest priority was not the moral secular and civil issue of cultural crisis.

Millennium-intensive colonization, proselytization, and missionization were the invaluable means to the ultimate end. They generated the sacred and sectarian spiritual growth industry, and brought "tears of joy" to the eyes of the faithful upon hearing reports of successes Foreign Missions and the revival, reform, and charity Domestic Mission.

Like Jonathan Edwards, a century and a Great Awakening earlier, Beecher a-bandoned participatory theocracy and democrat for participatory Christocracy and churchocracy. This reversal of values from early doctrinaire Federalism occurred with the simultaneously declining significance of the Federalist Party and the inclining repercussion of the millennialism-pervasive Second Great Awakening.

In this period of the American culture-created sustained and dynamic society both spawned and spanning spiritualization, sincere Evangelical Christians approached the imminent arrival of the eminent Kingdom of God so seriously it appeared an idea whose time had come. This incredible recurring religious revivial and turn of events phenomenon, best known to history as the Second Great Awakening, produced no right race and religion relations moral power but generated boundless spirituality so endlessly exciting that it not only filled the spiritual power vacuum but also nearly consumed the color caste/captive condition conscious conscience and change capacities of American Civil Religion.

The Protestant power people--who built a parochial dam to hold and to harness productively this kinetic ethical energy generated by the Protestant powerless and powerful in private and public sectors--directed this moral power to secure their secular and religious both individual and social ethics preferred priorities, that excluded expressly all effectual concern with the class over caste question. Jonesque and Beecherite types made their professional reputations in the aftermath of this sensational period, whose resources churchmen were employ-ing to institutionalize Protestant religion and denominations in America. They guided the evangelized who believed that they were approaching the boundary of history and eternity, on the verge of welcoming in cultural time and space the millennium (or one thousand year reign prior to the return to the world slaves and slavemasters made of Jesus as the Christ of faith and ethics), and due to witness momentarily the spiritual (to which they added) moral transformation of the world surfacing initially in North America (if not New England as Edwards thought). Precisely in this vision Puritan Piety disappeared as Halfway Piety churchocracy for Christocracy faith, and deterrence-benevolence ethics. materialized.

Between the Halfway Piety Edwards initiated and Beecher revised, Evangeliical Puritan/Yankee Calvinists' concernment with advancing the best interest of their Black race emerged from recurring cycles of progression and retrogression. It was attended on a par at the comparative level of importance Black folk were as a body for the New Englanders forming the generations between slave-owner-governor John Winthrop (slaveholder-clergyman John Cotton) and slave-buyer-clergyman Cotton Mather. Slavemasters Cotton Mather and Jonathan Edwards elected not to speak out against human bondage, unlike slaveholding and nonslaveholding contemporaries who protested involuntary servitude; failed to distinguish themselves as ethical giants from moral dwarfs; and succeeded in tolerating and paying little heed to the Black race, the rule of indifference to the Black race's interests, and the Black exception to the rule.

Significant but far from sufficient change through-out North America was the cultural continuum for the color caste/captive class from theocracy to democracy into the slavocracy. The Black race's English-British race/ethnic and Puritan-Anglican religion progenitors in mid-antebellum America, no less than their Yankee and Cavalier procreators, were better benevolent pa-ternalists and deterrence-benevolence generators than parents.

These antebellum color-conscious and color-conscienceless prodigious sires pretended to be color-blind, and that this height of hypocrisy was the height of civility. They advanced their aims under the cover of this mythomania because they preferred (A) to ac-cepting the work of their loins to work miracles--that included manipulating the custom laws of culture to make their Black offspring vanish (in social reality but not in either nature or truth) through sleight of hand acts of banishment; and (B) to manage reality by implementing their fantasies in actuality, and living in the illusion their visible and indivisible multi-colored progenies were invisible. Due to these no more or less than hypernormal priorities, their opportunity for constructive, peaceful, and gradual social redemption of their dominated Black race kith and kin had passed long before Beecher's crusade.

But this irreclaimable cause, and lesson that seemed to be entirely lost on Beecher, was not the fundamental reason why in his role as a public ethicist he loomed large as a remarkable study in borderline benign and malign neglect of the Black race--rather than in "*amazing grace.*" Unlike Edwards, whose "*Apocalyptic Vision*" and doctrine of imminent millennialism excluded all mundane pursuits of territorial expansionism and serious interest in other civil affairs, Beecher grounded his politics of religion ultimate vision and millennarian ultimate end in the Calvinist religion of capitalism, church and state order, and the politics of power. He endeavored to actualize these concerns on the Frontier, where he bid fair to unite White Christian nationalism and anti-Black race values.

In spite of being a peerless parochial and power politics protestant and professor of the politics of perception, Beecher appeared to the apperceptive Evangelical proabolitionists alternately a White and Black folk sacred and secular common good-securing--or civil order and culture redeeming and advancing--public interest ethic step behind, an ecclesiastical step ahead, and in spiritual step with his time.

Fastened in direct encounters of the third kind with the *mysterium tremendum*, that was the fascinating fashionable fashion of his middle-class kith and times, Beecher combined the theory he mastered in the East and the experience he learned in the West with progressive reason and revelation to fabricate a driving progressive transformationist rational organizing principle.

He formulated this up-to-date Calvinist instrument of individual conversion and social conservative change for logicians and rhetoricians, sharing his view of history and the physical universe, to direct his dream of the triumph of the spiritual over the material world toward gradual actualization and full realization.

This sacred and secular or churchocracy and democracy uniting utilitarian instrument of American Civil Religion, and empowering his version of realized eschatology or hope and vision of ultimate reality, facilitated the successful integration of church-millennialism and state-nationalism with the pure pious and profane spirit of the Frontier.

The Frontier spirit's "*rugged individualism*" dominant style and substance obtained structural cultural shape throughout the Territory; secured form as the flesh and blood folkways and morays ethos demanding emigrants and immigrants evidenced always and every-where at once; and, since nothing of *"the spirit"* or the literal letter of this ethnic rule was lost in the interpretation published in Illinois by Abraham Lincoln of Kentucky--who was not only born and reared but moved nearby the Ohio border line from the border state Mid-West section where the Lyman Beecher ménage relocated--acquired credibility after it was literally yet perfectly translated by Lincoln. His free translation communicated clearly asserted "this is a White-ethnic man's country."

The Reverend James McGready (1758-1817), an awe-inspiring Scotch-Irish and Reformed Church revivalist, located and prevailed on the Frontier prior to the arrival on the boundary between the East and the West and the North and the South of evangelist Beecher with his instrumental method and functional system. A British-ethnic immigrant and Presbyterian leader in the Second Great Awakening that crystallized with the critical role he played in the Cane Ridge, Kentucky revival (1801), presbyter McGready was celebrated for his central Calvinist Evangelical leadership that was not unlike the centermost presence in the First Great Awakening of English transmigrant George Whitefield and the Calvinist Anglican's Congregationalist host who concentrated mind, Jonathan Edwards.

Cane Ridge spontaneously spawned the first great camp meeting and therewith set the precedent that became the hallmark of revivalism on the Frontier, whose spiritual stirrings reverberated back and forth between the West and the East--throughout the Second Great Awakening--and precipitated the unpolished model of the open field and tent revival to which Evangelical evangelism Finney contributed sophisticated rational style and substance, spiritual and moral motive and methodology, and form and function.

In democracy's emerging slavocracy and mobocracy, the South and North not identical twin cultures wherein mob psychology and herd instinct vyed with *"the spirit"* of the *"rugged individual,"* a White-ethnic crowd turned into a crusade estimated at between ten and twenty-five thousand Presbyterian, Baptist, and Methodist emigrants and immigrants was initially attracted to Cane Ridge, and became engaged in the unusual albeit not entirely unparalleled spiritual outpouring in Kentucky.

Whether or not totally possessed for six or seven days, they gave full and free expression to their feelings in unrestrained and excessively emotional screams, shouts, jerks, runs, jumps, laughs, barks, grunts, singing, and prostrations. Similar but usually far less extreme expressions and forms of these un-pre-cedented psychological attitudinal and behavioral mod-ification patterns became the norm of mainstream Evan-gelical churches, throughout the region and nation dur-ing the succeeding sixty years.

This second religious revolution seemed subsequently to concentrate the mind of secular humanists challenged by religious humanitarians, who turned pure profane protestors of the pure pious professors. These pseudo-scientific social scientists transmogrified White-ethnic spiritual strivings; transposed and translocated the transmutation as the entirely unique, separate, and distinct spirituality of the Black folk only; and published their researched and developed findings that argued what they believed and proved conclusively: pure and simple Black race-specific spirituality is the manifest bare essence of Black folk existence, empirically verifiable rare marks of the Black body's too emotional nature and child-like stature, and evidence of the color caste/captive class' atypical diminished capacity.

What may be far less transparent than it appears evident is the extent to which the Second Great Awakening-inspired heightened spirituality elevated faith (parochial dogma) far above ethics (public pragma), and its consuming capacity contributed to the change in the social conscience's content and concentration and *ipso facto* of the course of consciousness in the cultural color caste/captive class crisis. Concurrent with the Cane Ridge connection and nexus if not correlation to the changing prospects and possibilities of authentic Puritan Piety public interest-ethics, Samuel Hopkins was ending his long life and celebrated Old Abolitionist career in Newport; William Channing was leaving Newport and Harvard to commence his stellar professional role in Boston; Samuel Doak was leaving the South and freeing his slaves in the West; and Lyman Beecher was beginning to combine individual spiritual and moral conversion and to rationalize the proliferating Moral Reform Movement.

Prior to this mid-antebellum through post-Reconstruction denigration of Black religious and secular thought and action, whose intensification the inspired critical imposition of pseudo-science organized and rationalized successfully, the Second Great Awakening originated in the East.

In this American stronghold of pure reason and revelation, revivalism was no less intense than evangelism in the West but noticeably less acrobatic.

Contrapositively, in this section and others, Second Great Awakening inciting and exciting Evangelicalism produced disproportionately more so-cietal value than the First Awakening.

The difference entailed the addition to the spiritual sensation of a more serious and intense moral-specific individual conversion and improvement in (not only or merely the parochial and private but especially) the public sector factor. This moral intensity advanced the philosophical theological and psychological empirical experiential experiments Jonathan Edwards developed as a dual subjective observant and objective participant observer. Development of the Edwardsean spiritual system involved the significant Finney refinements of the rational techniques pioneered by Timothy Dwight and his students, such as Beecher, Taylor, and Nettleton--who confined their revival experiments to the confines of the local churches and congregations.

In New England, the Awakening generated a spirit of self-sacrifice rather less precisely than affordable generous charity. Abundant benevolence was neither the forte nor characteristic of need-blind New Englanders, who from the Puritan-Anglican settlement through the First Great Awakening were so niggardly in their voluntary contributions to society redeeming causes that their social redeemers were forced to secure operational funds from the fiscal grant and aid liberal English-race and Scotch-Irish philanthropists in the British Isles.

Second Great Awakening-generated increased American ecclesiastical annual giving. It was concentrated in sectarian spiritual and moral societies concerned with both parochial and public redemption, and normally channeled through church circles in allotments that accorded with the moral reforms that denominational bureaucrats and technocrats determined to be high priorities. The universally accessible records report the evidentiary fact that the overwhelming preponderance of the Protestant denominations' gifts and grants were directed primarily to procure the rapid growth and expansion of developing Foreign and Domestic churches and missions, ministers and missionaries engaged in ecclesiastical enterprises, Moral Reform societies and eleemosynary institutions, and other religious humanitarian organizations such as sectarian seminaries and colleges.

Selectively competing and cooperating nontraditionalist parsons and parishioners often were anti-denominationalists because they conceived the hierocrats of the national Churches ruling as if they were the Protestant peers of their own perceived perilous Catholic vicar of Christ and higher authority than conscience (requiring obedience in any conflict of moral truth claims), projected the future rulers would be the elected among the current ecclesiarchs in the hierarchy headed by the past and present Roman Catholic and Protestant establishmentarian pope types, and pointed out that their suspicions and fears were confirmed by the positive parallels between the Catholic and Pres-byterian central church governments governed by the devotees of the Vatican and followers of "Old Pope Timothy Dwight."

Frequently emerging counter-culture leaders in the front ranks of the conventional wisdom counteractant people of God were nonconformist evangelists in the East. They formed a counterintelligence operation to counterbalance the church and state conflict of interests between liberty-preempted Black Calvinists and the preemptive strike of Black folk freedom, perpetuated by the aggressive and permissive or neutral and indifferent protectors of Orthodoxy and Reformed denominations. These counterintelligence agents counseled each reborn and regenerate professor of the Protestant Evangelical faith once delivered to the saints to examine his/her individual conscience, and to raise in tandem his/ her individual and social consciousness sufficiently to be irresistibly and irreversibly engaged in confronting conservative church and state representatives on the one hand, and, on the other hand, in causing the ecclesiastical and civil powers to reverse the direction of their leadership in the color caste/captive class crisis.

As a result of the dynamic Evangelical force generated by the two-way spiritual and moral power, produced all along the points of the spectrum and places across the landscape as a result of the interconnections between the Eastern activation and Western reactivation poles of the Second Awakening, revivalism became the innovative American pattern for church growth and denominational expansion on the Frontier.

Due to its natural elective affinity between charismatic leadership and spontaneous followership, Evangelicalism radiated and endured as a prime source of the greater numerical membership if not vitality the Arminian Methodists and Baptists enjoyed relative to their Calvinist Presbyterian cousins. Presbyters in the rival Reformed "New School" and "Old School" Denominations challenged the stiff competition, and especially strongly as the first Evangelical Churches to place higher education uppermost among their proselytizing priorities in the West--and second only to organizing and sustaining local congregations. In this mode and mood presbyters instituted in the West the Eastern establishment directive that evangelism serve Presbyterians' educational priorities rather than as their surrogate.

Presbyterians expanded in the West as the proxy for the Congregationalist churches. They chose, until the mid-1840s, to confine their central existence within the boundaries of New England, managed this exception to the rule for hyperexclusive Yankee reasons, and proved rather than improved the rule in this odd way to complete the peculiar Puritan "*Errand into the Wilderness*" of North America. This Yankee performance and interpretation of the Puritan promise clearly was no more predetermined than it was either dictated by or in violation of the division of labor implicit in their Congregationalist/Presbyterian Plan of Union.

However, their White Gentlemen's Agreement included an informal Reformed-Orthodoxy territorial arrangement but formal understanding whereby New England would remain the major purview of the Congregationalists--while the Frontiers of the South and West would be proselytized for the alliance by the Presbyterian Denomination.

The Presbyterian advance appeared less extensive on the Frontier than either party to the ecclesiastical compact expected; and far less successful than they hoped and anticipated that the Reformed Church would be in capturing the South and West for the presumed one and only true faith and ethics; the authentic Church (extending the Congregational Churches) of Christ and Reformed and Orthodoxy religion; and the establishment of the Kingdom of Christ. British-ethnic Presbyterians' equally selective and subtle suggestion that they were the inheritors of the Puritan Piety faith and ethics bequeathed by the English/Puritan race of saints and chosen people, and Scotch-Irish directors of Jonathan Edwards's Halfway Piety millennialism faith and deterrence-bene-volence ethics, was at most a minor matter relative to a major reason why the Presbyterian-Congregationalist claim to be the revised authorized standard version of genuine Christianity received an enthusiastic welcome among the middle class, and met with popular resistance in the White-ethnic lower class and Black-race under class.

The critical factor in the measurable limitation of the Reformed Church was their boasted distinction consisting of the high academic education and professional qualification tests Presbyterianism required theologues (as well as standards of comprehensive knowledge of Presbyterian polity and ecclesiology no less than theology set for the less formally trained churchmen seeking ordination in the Reformed Church) to pass in order to become fully credentialed presbyters. These strong strictures, along with a highly structured central church government organized to establish and to direct a national Church, severely curbed natural raw talent no less than individual charisma, restricted community and congregational spontaneity, and limited local options.

Presbyterian formal education rather less than such high standards as high scores on academic achievement tests, plus the rational organization apropos central command and control power and authority, combined with stiff discipline and ordination rituals to consolidate more formidable demands than those imposed upon the common people by the Methodist Arminian (majority and Calvinist minority) and Baptist Calvinist (dominant and Arminian subdominant) Denominations. These competitive Evangelical ecclesiastical powers sprouted everywhere and produced on the Frontier untrained charismatic Methodists and Baptists who heard and followed what they testified to be an inspired divine leading to vocation, and gathered a community who spontaneously accepted their call to preach the Gospel, whereas rival (mono Calvinist rather than duo Arminian and Calvinist) Presbyterians were discovered selectively located and properly propagated.

THE WESTERN INITIATIVES OF BEECHER AND

WELD UNDERWRITTEN BY ARTHUR TAPPAN

Nevertheless, the promise of authentic Puritan Piety no more faltered entirely than either the Puritan *Errand into the Wilderness* or the Halfway Piety millennarian faith and deterrence-benevolence ethics of Jonathan Edwards failed to unfold with Presbyterians on the Western Frontier. They appeared to be fulfilled for some advocates and aborted for their adversaries by men like Lyman Beecher. The "Connecticut Yankee" did not state that he was attracted from

404 CONSTITUTION, CONSCIENCE, AND CALVINIST COMPROMISE

Boston to the Frontier as an opportunist seeking fun, fame, and fortune. Yet, like many other men equally determined to take advantage of opportunity but graced with less perception and wisdom, he was no less earnest than he was honestly called by (and naturally attracted to) God, gold, and glory.

Beecher was not in a state of despair but frustrated by the exacting constraints cultural determiners imposed that limited his possibilities and potential in Boston. This experience with conventional wisdom in-creased his receptivity to rational reflection upon the comparative freedom to make a new world on the Frontier. Committed to completing the mission of the select "Elect" of God, the Yankee son of the wayward worldly saints conceived the West to be an exciting choice in the process of carefully calculating the opportunities and risks of the wide open Western status as well as spaces and places; evaluating its boundless liberty and rule of men confused with absolute license and limited order constrained by excessive licentiousness and lawlessness; weighing the benefits and liabilities; and reaching the conclusion from his analysis that--unlike earlier generations of saints and sinners who were not so well-equipped and thus less fortunate--he possessed the intellectual and fiscal resources to realize the Puritan dream and Evangelical vision on the hard ground of reality.

Beecher appeared to eyewitnesses and history clearly in his element orbiting the Union as her original American Civil Religion professional; parochial partisan parson and president no less than professor and protestant for the selective divergence and convergence of church and state; and often imitated as frequently approached but unsurpassed standard deviation from the norm Cotton Mather crystallized as North America's first public servant. The masterful rationalist, spiritual and moral power master, naturally was drawn to the arguable reasons expert idealists and professional realists invoke to legitimatize their rational and arbitrary plans and programs. These recyclyed ratiocinations routinely revolve around the principle and policy whose process entails protecting rationalizations perforce embracing one or more of the standard three kinds of error, namely, the error of conception (logic or reason), perception (natural/cultivated intelligence or physical nature), and deception (ethical or moral).

Utilizing this measure, mode and mood, Beecher elected to elucidate the praiseworthy arguments for accepting the western mission in his testament describing his call and response to the West; and not to publish his blameworthy hidden persuasions. The latter included the spurious moral notions underpinning his belief in an absolutely structured yet relatively fluid White race-high/ethnic-low class and outcast color-caste hierarchy, and social system organized around intractable White race dominance and superiority over Black race subdominance less precicely than subordination and inferiority.

Beecher materialized in the appearances of his apperceptive contemporary critics self-possessed and/or full of himself (essentially neither furtive fury nor solid stolidity nor sound sense but indignation and vindicativeness of the right confused with righteous vindication), rational justification perforce the fusion of moral war powers and moral power principles justifed by faith in the righteousness (Jesus Christ) of God, and ample spiritual and legal knowledge driven by the compelling force in church and civil life of logic and law rational power.

They knew or quickly discovered that he departed Boston buoyed by "Taylorism"; the "New Divinity" interpretation of faith and the new ethics of the "New Haven Theology"; and Calvinistic capitalism religion. Perchance paralleling his being in the vanguard and bucking trends for his own dramatic purposes, Beecher declared only (but not all of) his sincere and serious intentions and pretensions in his *Plea for the West* (1832).

Momentous momentum in his moment and this monumental movement west of the American people and culture, co-equally engaged and engineered over and through as well as in and on time, Beecher materialized as, at once, the evincement of up-to-date Calvinist justification by faith-ethics in the righteousness of God and the right inherent in the right man or the asserted equivalence of right reason/revelation and philosophy/theology; the marvelous model modern moralist; and the premier pioneer prophet and practitioner of the principal Evangelical Protestant principle of perfection.

Beecher clearly appeared in actually to be called by divine true interest and enticed by human real interests to go West--as a mature and prominent leader at the top of his form--no less definitely than he was solicited to fill the Cincinnati post as the first prexy of the "New School" Presbyterians' newly created Lane Theological Seminary. His instant hesitation and decline of the initial offer doubtless emanated more from rational reasons, or less from any resentment resulting from reflection upon the fact that he was not only the second choice but that his arch rival, Charles Grandison Finney, was the first firm choice of Arthur Tappan (1786-1865): the Manhattan-relocated "Massachusetts-Yankee," Evangelical Presbyterian-Congregationalist, and philanthropic millionaire merchant--whose brothers were prominent Boston businessmen and churchmen, active Moral Reformer acquaintances of Beecher, and in a position to advise and counsel their brother regarding Beecher's credentials and recommendations as well as to serve as mediators and emissaries.

Refusing to take Beecher's no for an answer, Tappan persisted in his pursuit and finally presented Beecher with a second proposal. It subsisted of a guaranteed annual salary of $60,000, that was a fabulous figure Beecher could not refuse. Straightaway, he acquiesced to the wishes of his benefactor and acceded in the office of President (1832-50) of Lane Seminary. And he quickly coupled his academic selection with his election as minister (1833-43) of Cincinnati's Second Presbyterian Church.

Arguably the Calvinist capitalist gained the "Consistent Calvinist" cleric's attention by appealing to his fundamental interests and ultimate interest. Beecher's Cincinnati initiative was excited by major incentives that reduced the real disincentives to manageable problems he believed could be turned into opportunities. Forthwith the "Connecticut Yankee" Puritan host in himself, in his own inimitable way, filled the two offices of pastor and teacher normally held in the Puritan tradition by two clergymen like, for example, Harvard President Increase and Cotton Mather, the father and son co-ministers, or Solomon Stoddard and Jonathan Edwards, the grandfather and grandson co-pastors.

Further complementing many of the Presbyterian's Congregationalist Calvinist forefathers who were outstanding Protestants and strong partisans in the politics of church and state, *vis-á-vis* his particularization of the tradition's historic millennial theological dogma and anti-Roman Catholic Church ideological pragma, Beecher was moved both like them by the challenge of "saving the west from the Pope" and unlike them also by respect for the memory of Protestant "pope" Timothy Dwight.

Located in the slave-free state of Ohio (1802) on the border of slaveholding Kentucky, Cincinnati was settled with their Black-race free and fugitive migrants by the dominant new White-ethnic immigrants and old White-race emigrants--divided between proslavery and antislavery sentiments. A decade after the ratification of the Constitution, Northeasterners and Southeasterners arrived in the first Old Northwest Territory and established Chillicothe as the original capitol of Ohio. Concurrent with the founding of Columbus as Ohio's permanent capitol (1816), and her rapidly expanding population following the birth of the slavocracy (c.1822), a statistically significant number of Eastern establishment secular and sacred culture representatives populated and dominated the state.

The relocated sacred and profane power elite not only contributed ra tional ecclesiastical and civil law and order to Ohio's antislavocrat and proslavocrat volatile social mixture, but, primarily as emissaries of pure pious and pure profane civility on one level and, on the other level, proselytizers for the aggressive sectarian denominations, these agents and agencies of Evangelical Protestantism added rationalization to the anti-Catholic prejudices they carried from the East to the West. Advancement of Protestant majorities and opposition to Catholic minorities emerged with class and caste preferences as principal principles and priorities of power and authority Protestants that left the powerful powerless to dominate the organization of the unorganized but nascent spirit of nativism, "white supremacy," anti-Semitism, and anti-Catholicism.

Upspringing as "the spirit" of White folk forming the culture on the previously unsettled plain, the phenomena sporadically spread spontaneously with the rapidly proliferating White Protestant ethnic types' varieties of violent violations of the Black body and space. In sum and substance, the antiabolitionist acts of the intensive White ethnic minorities were excited by proslavocracy values primarily; and only secondarily by either real or imagined more dreaded than feared insurrections before their formation of the Know-Nothing movement in the 1840s, and the Ku Klux Klan in the 1860s. Liberal, moderate, and conservative Evangelical Calvinist establishmentarians (like the preponderance of all other ethnic Americans and their religions) were united as one in the protection of the anti-Black race interests-specific tradition.

These traditionalists formed an antiabolitionist preeminence in all the Evangelical Protestant denominations, whose social conservative hegemony was not relinquished until Northern real interests and values were perceived by the power elite to be in nonnegotiable conflict with Southern real interests and values. This reality made the few serious establishmentarian religious humanitarians who took exception to the proslavocrat rule of law remarkable in fact and deed.

Emboldened by conventional wisdom, whose headmost men embraced custom folkways and morays with high praise, Beecher acquiesced to the anti-Black race interest-specific common lore and ecclesiastical and civil positive law; discovered himself to his entire surprise in not only sudden conflict and combative competition but also the sharpest imaginable contrast with Theodore Weld--his student and fellow "Connecticut Yankee"--who honored the proslavery church and state law in the breach; and proclaimed he had captured the high ground with high principles.

(Given this context, Beecher and Weld as the representative antiabolitionist and proabolitionist principals revealed that even though they usually but not always bracketed the complex color caste issue and concentrated in their controversy on the problem of slavery--howbeit a major but not the only significant anti-Black race interest phenomenon--it was the audacious leadership of the minority and not the will of the Protestant establishment majority that permits agreement between historical reality and its translation in the following present-day assessment.

Specifically, when set in the perspective of history, this solidly scholarly revisionist interpretation of positive social change apparently argues as truth the error that attitudes towards the Black race were overturned in the 1830s or the 1960s. It arguably reduces to insignificance the Northern versus Southern real interests factor, redounding to profound Black race respect rather less than securing real interests through violence: whereby it appears to suggest incorrectly that abolition was neither cherished by the majority as an instance of the necessity of virtue nor comparable for the plurality to the Civil War (the virtue of necessity). Consequently, the corollary implies erroneously that in the twentieth century anti-Black race reality has been defeated by desegregation, from which one is left to infer the ancillary is positive acceptance of the Black race:

> In the 1830s there occurred a remarkable change, almost a revolution, in the nation's attitude toward the slavery in its midst. The transition which took place in this decade can only be compared to the transformation in American race relations during the 1960s. Inert pronouncements like that of the Presbyterians in 1818 or those of the many Southern antislavery organizations became acutely relevant. Slumbering acceptances awoke as existential realities; silence, indecision, or mere lip service became increasingly rare, both North and South.[93]

If the antebellum South was part of the "nation," it is difficult to understand how the unchanging slavocracy relates to this interpretation of history. But the importance of this value judgment inheres less in its being an instructive instance of a descriptive fact passing for a bare fact and more in the clue that it provides to the capacity of anti-Black race desire to endure.)

SOCIAL MODERATE CHARLES FINNEY'S

CONVERTS TURNED POWER POLITICS AGENTS

By the time the near-Reverend Theodore Dwight Weld (1803-95) emerged as Beecher's student and nemesis at Lane Seminary, he had evolved into the New Abolitionist son of his Old Abolitionist and "Old Light" father--a younger contemporary of proabolitionist Samuel Hopkins and antiabolitionist Timothy Dwight, and comparatively liberal social and theological Connecticut Congregationalist clergyman: the Reverend Ludovicus Weld (1766-1845). Theodore Weld was also the great-great-grandson of New England clergymen, whose Calvinist Puritan heritage included a direct line of descent from the Pierpont and Edwards through the Dwight families.

A Congregationalist "*born again*" a *new being* in Christ, Weld was reborn and/or regenerated (in 1825) by Presbyterian Charles Grandison Finney while a student at Hamilton College. Following this college revival experience, Finney successfully recruited him as one of the assistant revivalists in the Finneyite "holy band." In this role, Weld joined another recent Finney convert who also became Weld's educational sponsor and New Abolitionist cohort: the near-Reverend Charles Stuart (1783?-1865), a Jamaica-born English Creole who emigrated to New York after retiring as a British Army officer.

In 1827, supported in part by the gracious gifts and grants Stuart contributed to secure his post-college professional education, Weld began his theological studies as one of the first theologue matriculants in Oneida Institute: the experimental seminary founded that year at Whitesborough, New York by Presbyterian evangelist George Washington Gale, who conducted the revival in which Finney was converted, for the ministerial training of the young men Finney converted, inspired, and led to follow his evangelist calling and vocation. Weld emerged the leader of the Oneida student body, developed into a forceful Temperance lecturer, and, because Temperance remained the central Moral Reform commitment in which antiabolitionism and proabolitionism divided Evangelical Protestants were united, shared the pro-Temperance passion with firm foes and friends such as Lyman Beecher, William Lloyd Garrison, and Arthur and Lewis Tappan.

During Weld's brief period of study at Oneida Institute before he changed his mind, and decided to complete his academic training for a career as a professional clergyman in another institution, near the close of 1820s and end of Old Abolitionists' leadership of the antislavery movement and beginning of New Abolitionism, Stuart sailed to England to join the English Evangelicals who led the British Abolition movement for the eradication of slavery in his native British West Indies. Stuart wrote theologue Weld regularly to keep him fully informed concerning the partisan party power politics principles and pressure employed by English Abolitionists, and to prod him to expand his Moral Reform commitments to include antislavery activities. Concurrently, Old Abolitionist Benjamin Lundy successfully attracted Colonizationist William Garrison to full-time work in the antislavery movement.

At this pivotal point of parsons and parishioners returning to the classic Catholic and Calvinist practice from the current Protestant non-practice of principles to secure the public (and thereby the private and parochial) interest, Yankee New Englanders recovered their pure Puritan Piety fathers' Old Abolitionist "*Spirit of '76*," endeavored to wrest hegemony of the antislavery movement from Old Abolitionism and American Colonizationism in the process of turning from gradualism and Colonizationism to creating New Abolitionism, and exercised leadership by forming the pro-immediatism consensus behind their initiative.

Synchronously, the two sons of Lewis Tappan who were enrolled at Oneida Institute introduced student leader Weld to their father and uncle Arthur Tappan prior to the formal Beecher and Tappan nexus. As a direct result of this New York connection of a different social ethics kind and quality of "Connecticut Yankee" and "Massachusetts Yankees," an extraordinary parochial sphere-energized and private sector-instrumentalized public sector-restructuring relationship developed between Weld and Lewis and Arthur Tappan. Demonstrable pure pious promise and performance, they distinguished themselves in their agencies by diverging from Halfway Piety deterrence-benevolence ethics and converging as the developers of the underdeveloped potential and promise of authentic Puritan Piety's public interest-enhancing direct action ethics.

In brief, their unique social ethics formation ad-vanced the national growth of New Abolitionism--as the radical alternative to Old Abolitionism and American Colonizationism--so distinctively its constructive con-tribution was second in significance only to Garrison's pioneering initiative.[94]

The Garrisonian moral one-dimensional and Tappanite moral/political two-dimensional Christian ethics evolved as uncommon Yankee Evangelical interpretations of their common New England inheritance, to wit, the Puritan-Calvinist bifurcation of reality. Genuine Puritan Piety public interest ethics reached their zenith at close of the theocracy in the life and work of public servant Cotton

Mather. During this period of his frustration with the reversal in fortune of Calvinist Puritans in Massachusetts, the Religious Society of Friends dominated the legislature of the Province of Pennsylvania.

Mather's long and productive life ended two decades before the French and Indian War, waged on the border of the Province governed by the Quaker economic, political, and theological competitors of the Calvinist mercantilist merchants (emerging capitalists) and captors of color captives, whom, during the last years of his public servant role, he solicited as former foes and new-found fast friends to engage in conciliation and cooperation rather than conflict as a Quaker and Calinist Puritan alliance against anti-church lawyers emerging in command and control of the Commonwealth.

During these hostilities, that despite his prophetic powers Mather probably neither predicted nor anticipated, White ethnic immigrants in Western Pennsylvania demanded that the lawmaker Friends, in power and authority at the helm of the Pennsylvania Province Legislature, provide a militia for their defense and security; the Quakers denied the request and refused to engage in war efforts; and the Friends elected to abandon power politics as a collective body forever, because they chose not to compromise and preferred to practice their nonviolence and peace principles. Twenty years earlier, during his final years, Mather proposed unsuccessfully a power politics alliance between the Calvinist Puritan and Quaker Puritan traditions.

One hundred years later, during which decades the Quaker Puritan switch from power politics to a pure moral influence style of civil leadership appeared an irreversible principle to the conscious Christian conscience, Garrison endeavored to cancel the Calvinist Puritan militant politics and military tradition with his superimposition on the antislavery movement of a no less real for being an unconscious poor imitation of the Mather initiative. A Calvinist Baptist "Massachusetts Yankee," Garrison adopted and adapted in Boston the Quaker Puritan moral power-only faith and ethics.

Tappan transferred from his Boston-based "Massachusetts Yankee" Puritan Piety with his translocation in New York, following the Congregational/Presbyterian Plan of Union. This confederation for the advancement in democracy of the Calvinist Puritan ecclesiastical and civil culture rather than theocracy entailed the alliance of English-race and British-ethnic aggressive political competitors and military warriors. Drawing on these diametrically opposite and primary rather than secondary dimensions of the Puritan Piety inheritance and Matherean public power politics legacy, Tappan, who was forced by the absence of Congregational churches in New York to affiliate with Presbyterian congregations, united representatives of Calvinism's Northern Orthodoxy and Southern Reformed traditions in moral and political power church and state experiments and experiences.

Primarily as a result of these critical culture factors, Garrison attracted more Northeastern religious and secular intellectuals and less sacred and profane power politics Southerners and Northerners than did Tappan. Due particularly to their coordinated Boston and Manhattan experimental ethical expositions and forages throughout the Northern settlements, the antiabolitionists forming the majority of the White-only electorate in the body politic experienced the emergence in the 1830s of a creative minority of Black and White proabolitionists.

In this upspringing biracial countermovement sprang forth a statistically significant number of White ethnic Southerners and Northerners. They were formed and informed by equally different and mixed motives as well as competing legitimate claims and conflicting interests, which, complementing the arrangement of their principles, these Evangelical Moral Reformers prioritized in an either rigid or firm but flexible political, economic, legal, social, and religious hierarchal order.

The biracial proabolitionists who followed the centralized New York leadership enveloped a merger of Northern and Southern Evangelicals on the Frontier--whose initial antislavery mission was concentrated in the regions outside the old establishment Puritan and Anglican Eastern reserves. As a result of this design rather than happenstance, the antislavery movement was most popular on the Frontier; its populace formed the majority of this minority; and the dictatorship of this proletariat was the Evangelical Protestant elite corps of Southern politics-intensive former slaveholders and resourceful Eastern Calvinist ethicists and capitalists.

"*True believers*" clearly were not born but made by a compelling force--especially those best characterized as the Calvinist concentration who combined in their life and experience the Southern ex-slavemasters' expert knowledge of the human experimentation nature and function of the "peculiar institution"; of the recent slaveholding statutes of New York (a slave state until 1827); and of the current direct involvement of White and Black liberators with fugitives from legal injustice. These diverse and complex relations resulted in Easterners' asserted equivalence of human bondage and dehumanization effectually being the evincement of solid theory and experience in reality.

Moreover, and in addition to the speeches delivered on the antislavery circuit by agents of the Massachusetts Anti-Slavery Society, antiabolitionist evangelists fired the plain people's antislavery consciousness in the revivals they conducted in the West, and Western Pennsylvania and New York, where their searing moral fervor became infectious and the contagious ethical conscience leaped state and territorial boundaries to affect consciousness across sovereign body lines.

Synchronical pro-Colonizationist and other antiabolitionist types of antislavery establishmentarians, who remained in 1830 and for fifteen years after this year of the great division neither Old Abolitionists nor New Abolitionists, constituted the power and authority bureaucrats and directorates in total command and control of the Presbyterian and Congregationalist denominations, as well as the technocrats whom the pro-immediatist churchmen in the West viewed with healthy disrespect. As a consequence, New Abolitionist Evangelical Calvinist churchmen were forced to create both extra-ecclesiastical and new religious humanitarian proabolitionist institutions outside of their denominations; to work with independent-minded parsons and parishioners as well as parishes; and to compete with the powerful denominational superstructures and infrastructures.

ARTHUR TAPPAN SPEARHEADS CHARLES

FINNEY'S FINANCIAL UNDERWRITERS

Presbyterian evangelist Finney moved his Western New York-focused revival campaign to New York City in 1830, where he converted from birthright to "born again" Evangelical Congregationalists Arthur and Lewis Tappan: two Northampton, Massachusetts-born, New York-based, and Manhattan Presbytery-affiliated mercantilists turned capitalists. Finney won the Tappan brothers over immediately and as completely as he was excluded from the establishment Presbyterian churches, organs of communication, and journals of opinion.

Responding to the refusal of the Presbytery to publish the theological thoughts Finney propounded, Arthur Tappan created and funded the *New York Evangelist* (1830-43) to provide a voice for Finney's ideas and ideals. The first editor of the Evangelical paper was the Reverend Joshua Leavitt (1794-1873), who had recently completed his professional training as a member of Nathaniel William Taylor's first Yale Divinity School graduating class. Leavitt's advocacy of unorthodox evangelist Finney's anti-"Taylorism" dogma and pragma, "New Haven Theology" counteracting Evangelicalism, and nontraditional coupling of Evangelical Calvinist faith and social ethics provoked Taylor to indict Finneyism as the "portentous union between the New Divinity and the New Measures."

But "the accumulation of property for selfish purposes is repugnant to the gospel" moral principle that Finney taught, Leavitt caught and published in the *Evangelist*. It appeared to triumph in the Tappans, Taylor's objections to the contrary notwithstanding, and to be on its face an Evangelical social ethics advance over Taylor's "power to the Contrary." The Tappans turned the practice of Finney's ethical principle into their imaginative and solid benevolence vocation, and in the process bound New York Calvinist capitalists in an "association of gentlemen" committed to address the social problems of the poor White-ethnic immigrants and needy Black-race emigrants.

Quite unlike Beecher who coveted the pews purchased in Park Street Church, these Manhattan Protestant philanthropists acted as if they realized their membership in wealthy Northeastern churches--primarily financed by the fortunate few who owned pews--was at once the prerogative of privilege; the *rite of passage* ritual resulting in parochial exclusion no less clearly than it was an exercise of the private right of freedom of association; and the preemptive strike from participation in the body of Christ of the body politic exercised by the body corporate. Tappan led the sensible to be increasingly sensitive to the fact that their public works of charity and parochial acts of discrimination raised the standards of the church and community rather less solidly than the barriers to Christianity and civility.

Tappan was convinced by the commissioned studies of the urban condition that the poor condition of the teaming thousands of new and poor White-ethnic immigrants and emigrants streaming into the cities was due to the absence of nurture rather than to a deficient nature. He became convinced and encouraged in his convincement by Finney--who converted a goodly number of new Americans--that labor required capital to provide structures that would enable the working-class to obtain consistent and constant spiritual and moral power disciplinary exercises, and increase their opportunity to earn a livelihood. But there existed no institutional churches in which the lowerclass could feel welcome,or that addressed their specific needs.

The Tappans reflected on the problem and opportunity and reached the conclusion that a free and open church, unrestrained by Presbyterian polity and policy, was necessary if significant numbers of the unchurched were to be churched. Their innovative church extension proposal and design for a experiment in Christian living was presented and accepted for debate on its merits by the Manhattan presbyters. A plurality of the New York Presbytery delegates rose above the standards and sustained opposition, voted to accept the motion urging the normal rule for forming a local congregation be suspended, and authorized the Tappans to organize the First Presbyterian Free Church.

This historic decision, whereby the Presbytery initiated the free church movement in New York, was made an even more extraordinary innovative devel-

opment by the fact that in this exciting act of creation money did not speak--
and only pure ethics talked principle into taking a walk for practice. Nevertheless, it was perfectly natural and understandable why Presbyterian officialdom
elected not to make this flexible church experiment and exception a rule, or at
least a model for the development of Black Presbyterian churches and churchmen in the nation.

Finney was the candidate of choice for the Tappans who chose not to accept
their invitation, and recommended a Presbyterian evangelist from his Western
New York revival stronghold to be the first minister of the First Presbyterian
Free Church--The Reverend Joel Parker (1799-1873). The success which followed
during the months and years after Parker's (June 27, 1830) initial Sunday morning worship service inspired the Tappans' larger vision. They determined to secure in the heart of New York City a dual purpose edifice: with an auditorium
large enough to function as a house of worship in which the attracted body of
the "20-25,000 strangers" disembarking in Manhattan each year would feel welcome, and also as an assembly hall to house adequately the annual meetings of
the American Anti-Slavery Society and other benevolent societies.

Manhattan Presbyterian churches and the philanthropic "association of gentlemen" jointly committed resources to fund this project. As a result, located and
leased as the headquarters of their philanthropic endeavors the Chatham Street
Theater. The congregation that formed there (in 1832) selected field evangelist
Finney who accepted their election and relocated from Western New York to be
their settled minister: as Parker answered the call (tendered to and refused by
Weld) to pastor (1832-37) the First Presbyterian Church in New Orleans. Chatham Street Theater was replaced as the worship center for the First Presbyterian Free Church by Broadway Tabernacle--"the largest Protestant house of worship in the country"--which the Tappan largess "built for Finney." A parochial
and private corporate center, Broadway Tabernacle functioned effectively as
"the capitol of the new empire of expanding benevolence" in the new North
American financial capital.[95]

THE BLACK COLLEGE IDEA OF SAMUEL CORNISH,
SIMEON JOCELYN, AND ARTHUR TAPPAN

In 1828, several years before he built Broadway Temple for Finney and Lane
Seminary for Beecher, Arthur Tappan purchased an expansive summer home in
Connecticut--that was situated immediately adjacent to Nathaniel Taylor's New
Haven residence. During his leisure time in this recreational domicile, Tappan
related regularly with Simeon Smith Jocelyn--the Manhattan-headquartered Congregational Home Missionary Society's urban missionary to free Black New Ha-
venites.

Currently the White minister of the all-Black Temple Street (renamed Dexter
Avenue) Congregational Church, that Tappan frequented, Jocelyn articulated a
plan for the advancement of Black Americans in New Haven and throughout the
United States. Acting upon the idea advanced (in 1827) by Samuel Eli Cornish--
his Black Presbyterian ministerial colleague, and New York-located newspaper
editor--Jocelyn proposed the establishment of a Black college in New Haven
with high academic standards.[96]

Arthur Tappan purchased the acreage; pledged a substantial amount toward
the construction of the build-ings; and secured commitments from Yale professors who agreed to form the organizing core of the projected faculty. This plan

for Black folk improvement originating in the mind of an able Black minister--
who as a progressive advanced in liberalism years ahead of most White and
Black contemporaries--was developed to prove conclusively their mental abilities
to citizens who preferred to identity Black Americans with diminished capacity;
to demonstrate further their well-known intellectual capabilities and denied opportunities for learning; and to provide an institution organized and supported
with sufficient resources to train and develop them for productive and competitive existence as free men in North America.

Co-equally noteworthy is the truth that this Black college model was developed by Black and White pro-abolitionists as their answer to antiabolitionists
who opposed New Abolitionism; preferred to argue the clever canard that universal liberation from human bondage would result in releasing Black bondmen
in a society unprepared to accommodate their demands for equal access to opportunity; and were unwilling to commit the resources necessary to prepare
Black me for fair competitive engagement and equal citizenship rights and responsibilities, prerogatives and privileges, and civil liberties. The biracial trinity
also proposed the Black college as an alternative to the ACS's deculturalization,
denationalization, and deportation express plan and purpose for educating Black
Americans.

The promotion of the Black college radical proposal illuminates the change
from moderation negotiated by Lewis and Arthur Tappan, who were committed
to gradual abolition when they were converted to Finneyite Evangelical Calvinism. Prior to the Finneyite experience, Arthur Tappan had been the equal of
Gerrit Smith as a financial contributor to the ACS. Lewis Tappan shared in the
policy formulations of the Tappan mercantile and reform enterprises, that he
also shaped skillfully as the business manager of their enterprise after 1828.
Blessed with uncommon Christianity and civility sen-sitivity no less than
integrity and managerial ability, he enjoyed the role of chief executive action
officer for his brother who functioned as the chairman of the board; the complete confidence of his brother which his competence, courage, and common
sense earned; and the self-imposed task-responsibility of shouldering the onerous
burdens, taking charge of the daily details and implementing the decisions and
commitments made by his brother, whereby Lewis relieved the pressure and
physical pain Arthur Tappan suffered from constant headaches.

Following the Tappans' initial personal encounter with fellow former Colonizationist Garrison in 1830, and the moral conscience's recently reached new
consciousness peak he shared during his week-long visit as the private guest of
Arthur in his Manhattan home, their personal rendezvous with destiny and experience of being conducted by him through the stages of moral conversion
from gradualism to immediatism was evidenced by Lewis Tappan's perfect translation of Garrisonianism, in his description of the ACS as "a piece of malignant
jesuitry," that he published for private and parochial consumption to benefit the
public.

BENJAMIN LUNDY'S INFLUENCE WITH LYMAN BEECHER,
WILLIAM CHANNING, AND WILLIAM GARRISON

The William Lloyd Garrison (1805-79) with whom the Tappan shared values
was an impressive birthright "Massachusetts Yankee" Moral Reformer, both
engaged in the Temperance Moral Reform mission and disengaged from the Old
Abolition movement not unlike "Connecticut Yankee" Theodore Weld, before his

self-conversion persuaded him to leap from American Colonizationism to New Abolitionism.

Garrison did not complete the high school curriculum--or receive a diploma in his home town of Newburyport, Massachusetts--but the teenager began his self-education for his future career as a professional writer while employed by the community's newspaper as a printer's apprentice for the Newburyport *Herald*. Garrison subsequently founded the *Free Press* (a short-lived periodical); initially moved his residence to Boston in 1825, one year before Lyman Beecher arrived as pastor of Hanover Street Church; served as a journeyman printer at the Boston *Recorder*; co-edited (in 1827) the *National Philanthropist*--a Baptist periodical reputed to be the first American publication singularly devoted to Temperance Reform (achieved as a result of total abstinence from alcohol production and consumption); and departed Massachusetts for Vermont in 1828, to became editor of the Bennington *Journal of the Times*.

He returned to Boston later that year, as a member of the ACS, to deliver the July 4th annual address for the ACS's branch, the Massachusetts Colonization Society. On this occasion, and again in November, Garrison listened to the employment offer tendered to him by the Reverend Benjamin Lundy (1789-1838): the peer-respected gradualist Old Abolitionist New Jersey native and Religious Society of Friends elder, national spokesman for the pro-gradualist Quakers, an organizer of the anti-slavery Union Humane Society (1815).

Lundy promoted among non-Quakers the old Quaker-abolitionist private manumission persuasion and process or parochial promise and performance for the national removal of slavery by the secular and profane public. Protestants setting free their personal slaves in defiance of the slavocracy laws forbidding manumission as a matter of conscience and prerogative of the privileged was positive lawbreaking; approved to precipitate positive lawmaking by these neither outlaws nor lawless but positive moral lawmakers and lawbreakers who were bound rather less by the ecclesiastical and civil as well as the moral law (*agape*-love/power/justice whose quintessence is helping the helpless to help themselves by advancing the needs of perforce serving not the sabbath but the poor before the powerful) and rather more by either moral principles (moral rules and regulations) and/or both the law of logic and the logic of law and order; and justified heightened consciousness and higher conscience partially by the prototypical principle of inviolable private property rights taking priority than sacrosanct public (eminent domain) rights in any conflict and competition that falls short of special interests threatening the general interest (proceeding from the premise that the public good is best expanded by securing the private interest).

Friends did not corner the moral market but turned from antiabolitionism and proabolitionism to middle-of-the-road gradualism on this antebellum corner, established by the Northern proslavocrat and Southern slavocrat elected and appointed legitimate authorities in command and control of the Three Branches of Government. Precisely there in the capital of the nation and the sovereign states, chiefly lawyers, emerging and expanding in power and authority as so far from moralists and near to ruling class (Yankee and Cavalier sons of the Northeastern Puritan patrician and Southeastern Anglican aristocrat English) rulers of the rules, ruled the rule of law follows and takes precedence; set logic over *love* to facilitate by the force of reason their arguable posited axiom that the legal is never lethal injustice but always the law and order or intrinisic duty because it is both explicit justice and implicit right; and stuck a feather in their cap and called it Yankee Doodle Dandy.

Gradualism seemed sane and safe in this situation and thus sound sense to the solid state and society servants for a civil culture and church. It leaped from the minds of sons of the Quaker Puritan fathers who had outlawed holders of human bondage in their one American Friends Church, after they relinquished power in the French and Indian War before they elected neither to participate in the War for Independence from England or the Continental Congresses but chose to becoming founding fathers of abolitionism rather than Founding Fathers of the nation, and of the Calvinist Puritan fathers who abolished slavery in their civil commonwealths and not Churches of Christ in New England (albeit the Yankee Church followed the state as uniformly as the Cavalier Church).

Singularly significant social consequences stemmed from establishmentarian pro-gradualism springing forth as the primary antislavery principle as well as private and public way to abolition currently preferred by the slave-free Religious Society of Friends--and adopted as the official position of Stated Quaker Meetings. The Religious Society of Friends continued as the first and only national denominational body to affirm the private manumission/gradual abolition principle as a parochial rule and recommended public policy. Howbeit explainable as a pragmatic expedience and convenience principle, an odd and even peculiar promise and performance if neither a compromise of consciousness nor a contradiction in terms of conscience Friends, and a moral precept and process taken exception to in thought and practice by slaveholding Quakers in the slavocracy--and other one-time faithful followers of their founding father (the Reverend George Fox [1624-91])--who no longer either were Friends or remained in good standing in Quaker Stated Meetings.

Just as Friends established Old Abolitionism as the basic principle to secure basic decency and dignity in civilization, and self-determination as the elementary constituent element and criterion of Christianity and civility, just so effectually their not civil or public but parochial and private manumission American standard of ethical excellence was raised by the Reverend John Woolman (1720-72). A New Jersey Quaker and Friends elder who died prematurely--due to contracting a virus and its externally induced deficiency in his immune system, nearly two decades before the birth in the same state of Lundy (his disciple)--Woolman was the proabolitionism major moral measure and model conscience for the American Friends. He also who wrote the book on antislavery affirmative action or the manumission-specific type of Quaker abolitionism, in the new testament of faith and social ethics gospel according to Woolman entitled Some Considerations on Keeping Negroes (1754).

Woolman's Quaker Puritan private-parochial-public good and interest expanding ethics either illuminated or eclipsed the touchstone of Calvinist Puritan Halfway Piety deterrencebenevolence ethics, that his contempo-rary Jonathan Edwards wrote in 1755 and his survivors published posthumously as A Dissertation Concerning the Nature of True Virtue (1765). Compared to anti-slaveholding Woolman and slaveholding Edwards, when juxtaposed as the Quaker Puritan and Calvinist Puritan neither matched pair nor identical twin moralist models, Lundy appeared a study in contrasts as a consistent manumissionist Old Abolitionist, persistent antiabolitionist, and insistent Colonizationist.[97]

As an enterprising agent for the Old Abolitionist Societies, Lundy traveled throughout the United States maintaining established Societies for the private and public manumission of human bondage, and encouraging the organization of new ones. On one of his many missions Lundy traveled through New England generally and to Massachusetts particularly. In the Bay State no Old Abolitionist Society existed (besides two student societies) and only a branch of the ACS was organized by churchmen to extend its different purposes and consequences. Besides enjoying peer respect for his charitable contributions in this avocation, his reputation as a professional journalist preceded him.

Also the founder of the Baltimore-based Genius of Universal Emancipation (1821-35), Lundy hoped to attract Boston subscribers to this periodical that he published at his own expense and was distinguished for being America's currently only (if not first) antislavery newspaper. By the Fall of 1828, Lundy had failed to locate Bostonians willing and able to organize an Old Abolition Society and succeeded in persuading editor Garrison to join his Baltimore antislavery press.

A man of very modest physical stature and beauty, Lundy emerged the dynamo antislavery Friend and the not so radical heir to John Woolman: the greatest American Quaker Old Abolitionist traveling preceptor, preacher, and prophet. Woolman stood out as the exemplar among equals, such as Anthony Benezet, who contributed able peer pressure assistance that enabled him to complete the historic Quaker Puritan antislavery mission. This ethics-specific continuum paralleled the diametrically opposite faith-specific Calvinist Puritan Errand into the Wilderness of North America. Largely due to the consequences of Woolman's leadership of the Quakers' Religious Society of Friends-exclusive anti-slavery social ethics, the Quaker Church as a national Denomination foreswore involvement by Friends in any positive proslavery engagement (be it to secure commercial profit or private property) as inimical to the spiritual and moral truth principles of Christianity, civility, and Quaker Stated Meetings.

In the post-Independence period Northeasterners organized Old Abolitionist Societies as eternal vigilance political pressure associations for private public interest guardians and public good guaranteeing citizens, to ensure the enactment and enforcement of state-mandated gradual manumission statutes by reluctant and Machiavellian commonwealth legislatures that required monitoring to legislate the general will; to encourage through unification and joint efforts with allied Societies the liberation of slaves in Southern states, where private-only manumission laws were enacted in lieu of and to prevent a movement among the citizenry for state abolition; and to add to positive negation of bondage positive attraction and assistance of free and freed Black inhabitants.

Coinstantaneously, at the commencement of the slavocracy era, slavocrats were redoubling their efforts to eliminate eventual abolition from the realm of the thinkable, to which end they rescinded the early national era liberal private manumission laws in the "peculiar institution."

In this era Lundy, and Old Abolitionists who shared his approach to abolition, effectively redefined the parochial-intensive Quaker principle of private-specific manumission as the equivalence of gradual but total abandonment of slavery. He recommended the manumission point--which seemed to be as efficient and effective a civil power policy in the Northeast as it was an effectual Quaker ecclesiastical principle. Lundy even pressed the rule of private manumission upon the other Protestant denominations with an idealism that refused to respect the transparent realism emitted in the direct opposite manumission laws being enacted in democracy and slavocracy, and the competition between Northern and Southern churchmen enveloped by increasingly intense conflicts of interests and values.

Understandably, Lundy implicitly denied the charge subsequently leveled by

Garrison--that he essentially stretched out of shape and nearly beyond recognition Woolman's pure pious spiritual and moral power religious rule. But this was public effect whose parochial cause Garrison concluded correlated positively with Lundy's essays to add to his recommended private manumission way to e-rase involuntary servitude the convenient and expedient antiabolitionist motive, and pro-Colonizationist means and ends.

Lundy fostered an alliance between the Old Abolitionist Societies and the American Colonization Society, and thereby argued the ACS's economic, political, and theological final solution was an equally ethical, pragmatic, and feasible color caste/captive class cancellation critical imposition. However, he heard the original, unassailable, and irre-futable American critique of the Colonization Society from the voice of the Black people he knew personally, and all color caste cultural crisis-conscious consciences knew at least by reputation.

This social ethical analysis and conclusion issued forth from the mass meeting of the Black body in Philadelphia, that the universally well-known Bishop Richard Allen called and hosted there in Mother Bethel African Methodist Episcopal Church, who ratified the moral thought and action of the Black religious leadership class. They rejected the solicitation of the ACS agents who implored them to support the formation of the institution, and made their objection official and formal when the class of the Black leadership corps published their public protest and parochial-intensive power politics statement condemning the ACS as pro-White race interest and anti-Black race interest Society during the month of January 1817, just a few days after the incorporation of the ACS.

In response to the declaration of the ACS as anathema and its total repudiation by Black people, and the leaders they selected their spokesmen, Lundy modified his procolonization program. Instead of deporting the Black race directly to Africa only, he recommended to White Protestants that they promote and underwrite the territorial segregation of Black from White Americans in Texas, Mexico, or Liberia.

He emerged a national conductor and conduit of the positive racial separation principle posited and rationalized by Moral Reformers, who argued that extra-territorial "separate but equal" proved the one and only way the Black race could obtain self-determination, political participation and representation, and independent self-government. Lundy was an effectual national instrument of this flexible removal plan who exerted potent pressure to achieve its goal.

Like his progenitor Friends' eighteenth-century interruption of Church of England worship services in the Anglican theocracy to protest for religious freedom, they asserted was purely nonviolent because it was non-physical coercion, Lundy and his Quaker company preferred to call political protest through pressure politics and persuasion pure influence; declared it peaceful change and termed their non-space violent violation leverage; and managed, both as a virtue of necessity and out of necessity, to distinguish their politics of pressure from the force generated in the exercise of partisan party power politics by fiat, that decreed they had opted out of stiff political competition and conflict to avoid compromise.

It is of some relevance to the matter at hand that Ralph Gurley and friends of the ACS he administered, such as Lyman Beecher and Leonard Bacon, were open to Lundy's modification scheme because it did not alter fundamentally their Africa-deportation arrangement.

What is significant entails the Black-race positive negation influence Lundy's peace initiative extended. In his role as a roving Moral Reform presence with influential and affluent friends throughout the nation, Lundy superimposed the notion that the ACS formed effectively a corollary of the Old Abolition Societies and not an ancillary of White Nationalism.

The ACS Lundy embraced Black brothers of the cloth asserted is by definition of its nature and purpose Black-race excludable existence, and therefore White Nationalism in essence and manifestation. In the mind of Black archetypes the ACS persisted as the bare essence White Nationalism and thus it constituted the efficient cause and effect of Black Nationalism.

Alternatively the deconstruction of the Black vanguard stated that the Society was a precipitating factor in the sharp rise of random and cyclically recurring Black Emigrationism--or the White race/ethnic-directed Society's Black-race alternative. It is best known as Black folk territorial, economic, political, religious, and cultural Black Nationalism.

In the aftermath of the failure of the Black Equalitarians to end the White Nationalism idea and ideal of the ACS before it was born, or to ensure that it was declared brain dead on arrival, following the massive mass meeting Richard Allen convened in January 1817 and the success of the ACS' Black race excludable design, Black Emigrationism (Nationalism) broke forth in a Black minority at once opposed vehemently by the Black majority.

But, truth to tell, the Black parties to the conflict of racial separation and integration united in opposition to the ACS that the White Protestant denominations established as their antislavery national representative.

Establishmentarian denominationalists were determined to direct resources to their Black race only for the purpose of advancing the acceleration of the Black body to Africa (or perchance an alternative territory beyond the United States).

A walking repository of the foreign and domestic slavemaster-escaping and slavecatcher-eluding fugitives, exuding loyalty and honor to pro-White race values and anti-Black race interests during his 1828 New England tour, Lundy reported his ecumenical ministerial meeting with Lyman Beecher and seven other clergymen was the coup d'état of his Boston sojourn:

> I visited the Boston clergy, and finally got eight of them, belonging to various sects. Such an occurrence, it was said, was seldom, if ever before known in the town. The eight clergymen all cordially approved of my object, and each of them cheerfully subscribed to my paper, in order to encour-age, by their example, the members of their several congregations to take it...William L. Garrison, who sat in the room and wit-nessed our proceedings, also expressed approbation of my doctrines.[98]

Lundy's moderate morality presence and dominating the middle ground performance appeared state of the art middle-of-the-road Moral Reform means-ends. This posture enabled the Old Abolitionist to attract the ACS clergy who embraced him as a centrist statesman rather than as either a value-neutral or value-free balancer of the proslavocrat and antislavocrat polar extremes. The traditionalist pastors instinctively understood that his "object" and "doctrines" affirmed the ethical efficacy reactionary pro-Colonizationism which they misconstrued the radical end through gradual means destabilization of the "domestic slavetrade" organization.

Lundy was approached as the presence of mystery and mystique, and peer reverence increased as the self-revelation of spiritual power revealed his character and credibility: his personal and public confrontation of slavetraders resulted in his being both assaulted in Baltimore and able to turn the problem into an opportunity to witness for peace and order achieved through moral power.

Fifty three year-old Beecher and twenty three-year old Garrison not only were seated together and riveted in rapt attention as they heard and heeded Lundy (yet entered and departed this Boston parson and parishioner mutual admiration body neither Old Abolitionists nor antiabolitionists) but also respected each other as antislavery Evangelical Calvinists, pro-Temperance Moral Reformers, and American Colonizationists.

These shared values plus Garrison's recollection of Beecher being engaged with Lundy in this Boston churchmen antislavery strategy session were drawn on two years later, and provided young Garrison with better hope than reason to think the elder Beecher also had no fear of flying from reactionaryism to radicalism.

In spite of Garrison's great perspective and depth perception, that were normally reliable whenever his moral mind and iron will engaged his photographic memory in irreversible reflectiveness, apparently Garrison failed and Beecher flatly refused to appreciate early enough what made the remarkable difference in their conscious intentionalist and consequentialist social consciences that were informing and being informed by their Evangelical Calvinist Protestant parochial and private and public ethics, and resulting in a difference in degree so great as to form a different kind of moral virtue and vice device.

The critical factors were neither their generation gap nor their disparate "Connecticut Yankee" and "Massachusetts Yankee" identities nor either class conflict or religious/secular profession occupational competition but the autonomous Baptist independent individual rule and the Presbyterian rule of ruling elders--that is, systematic and systemic protectionism established to conserve and preserve the Reformed tradition; ecclesiastical and academic "Old School" or "New School"; and independent and interdependent individual and community system of central church government rule of law and order.

As decisively as Beecher and Garrison turned from firm friends to fierce foes, Beecher positively held Lundy in the very highest esteem throughout the rest of his life.

Dissimilar from the surging submerged differences that would soon surface and leave Beecher and Garrison awash with mutual contempt, Beecher's admiration for Lundy soared and survived a sharp difference between the permanent gradualists.

Lundy approved and promoted for Old Abolitionist Societies the following antiabolitionist principle and practice--currently proliferating among a Protestant minority in the West and espoused by the Tennessee Manumission Society (1825)--that combined a radical educational policy with the liberal policy of open admission to slavemasters. Lundy published this new condition--that apparently the Bee-cherite establishmentarians could not condone--in the Genius.

The rigid right rule of amelioration ruling elders ruled the bottom line law of gradual abolitionism was indicative of the factors contributing to the 1837 schism in the Presbyterian Denomination, as well as of the complementary conflicts of proslavocracy and anti-slavocracy interests and regulations over which the Evangelical denominations would divide and establish Northern and Southern denominations within less than fifteen years:

420 CONSTITUTION, CONSCIENCE, AND CALVINIST COMPROMISE

Resolved, that all *slaveholding members* of the Manumission Society, who shall hereafter refuse or neglect to educate their slaves, so far as it is practicable, be excommunicated, and no longer considered members of this Society.[99]

The difference between the gradualism (the gradual abolitionism New Abolitionist declared a contradiction in terms) espoused by the antiabolitionist representatives of the two different (Quaker and Calvinist) faith and ethics traditions was the implicit moral and spiritual power distinction Lundy made explicit. Lundy clearly held churchmen to the high standard of moral performance according to the promise of pure pious perfection, and that he was more tolerant than other Old Abolitionists of the non-churchmen whose pure profane criterion he perceived to be a comparatively low standard seemed as natural as it was explainable.

Beecher advanced the Calvinist Puritan tradition Congregationalists dominated in New England. It entailed the preclusion from the churches of Orthodoxy serious wrestling with the antislavery/proslavery issue, since abolition or manumission was officially determined to be a purely civil rather than ecclesiastical matter, and the business of the state and not a church affair. Contradistinctively, Lundy was reflecting and rejecting or reversing his tradition, when applying to the 1830s slavocracy and democracy secular society and civil powers the 1770s Quaker theocracy and ecclesiastical power enacted and enforced Religious Society of Friends law and order that ruled slaveholders could not be members in good standing within Quaker Stated Meetings.

In truth the apparent absolute rule inherent in the asserted equivalence of Christian and nonslaveholder offended and forced the disaffection of relatively few Friends, essentially united rather than divided the plurality of establishment Quakers, whereas, after 1837, it divided rather than united the major Evangelical denominations who followed the Presbyterians in suffering the division of their body of Christ.

The churches separated because they disagreed over the precise explication of the profane principles of reason and justice (fairness and equity); the appropriateness of connecting the sacred and secular correlations as well as the correct interpretation of the catholic premises of agape-love and liberty (self-determination and "you will know the truth, and the truth will make you free" in body, mind, and soul); and the compromise of principles implicit in the above cited acceptance of "slaveholding members" in Christian churches who were committed to educating slaves and to keeping them in human bondage. The compromise of Christian conscience followed from insisting this criterion of Christian value did not fail to approach the standard of high Christianity and civility that commenced with ceasing and desisting from being engaged in dehumanization.

The preponderance of Massachusetts Trinitarian and Unitarian Congregationalist parsons, parishioners, and parishes managed to divide on principle in matters of religious and secular reason as a result of their different profane philosophy and sacred theology premises and interpretations, and ritual and ecclesiology preferences and priorities; to unite to protect their Puritan heritage against all foreign and domestic enemies as the peerless powerhouse Yankees and Protestant force in the Commonwealth; and to abide as the least active and effective Old Abolitionists in the Union.

ment and rule of indiscriminate indifference was neither tested nor overturned but confirmed by the exception, whom William College undergraduates and Andover Seminary theologues proved to be who organized and sustained on their academic campuses the only Old Abolitionist Societies in the state.

The absence in Massachusetts of a Congregationalist churchmen-led Old Abolitionist Society was a missing link in the national chain of Old Abolitionist Societies Lundy labored in vain to locate and connect. Abolition-free Bay State parishes, parsons and parishioners, ensued from neither rational design nor an accident of history nor positive failure in society but the direct cause of effect was the success produced by the powerful culture and people. The result was the end of a commonwealth beginning with her electorate exercising their sovereign "states' rights," demonstrating a collective consciousness' fully developed appreciation of the difference and connection between the moral Constitution and ethical conscience, and creating a citizenry-ratified constitution proscribing slavery and entering the Union as the first slave-free state.

This praiseworthy performance subsisted of blameless performers establishing the public good on the universal categorical imperative ethical principle. Just as indubitably as these Yankee Puritans succeeded, just so irrefutably they failed to achieve the goal of leaving Massachusetts insulated and isolated from slavemasters and slavehunters, and their slaves and fugitives from legal injustice. What the Massachusetts act of abolition created besides liberation included different church and state possibilities and prospects, and therefore responsibilities, for turning enduring color caste/captive problems into opportunities.

Leaving aside the permanent and pervasive color caste value in the White-race status v. White-ethnic class social system, Massachusetts people's perfectly executed strike of involuntary servitude at once precluded human bondage legitimacy from the secular and civil power sphere, and preempted the growth and development of rational relevant reflection and action on questions of human bondage (dehumanization) and liberation (self-determination) in the ecclesiastical power realm.

Four decades after the Old Abolitionist secular and civil Massachusetts authorities proclaimed the Commonwealth the first abolitionist sovereign state in the United States, and their establishment of negative good rather than positive good both the world-class standard of the common good and good enough for Black Massachusetts people, Yankee Congregationalist clergy awakened from their long and deep conscience-frozen state to discover the "peculiar institution" had not contracted as predicted by Old Abolitionist Puritan clergymen but expanded as neither expected nor anticipated since their passing as a class (by 1810).

Forthwith they paid their respects by leaving Old Abolitionism to rest in peace alongside the dead and buried Old Abolitionist parsons; arranged their anti-slavery/proslavery ambivalence around the antiabolitionist rational organizing principle; and authorized the formation of the ACS to function as their gradualism surrogate for Orthodoxy's immediatism tradition bequeathed by Old Abolitionist parsons.

Presbyterian and Congregationalist ecclesiastical bureaucrats, parochial academy administrators, and clerical technocrats moved as interlocking directorates to establish the ACS as a formal body politic, body corporate, and body of Christ; to institute the ACS as the official antislavery organ of the Evangelical denominations; and to fashion millennial-missionary-evangelistic coordinates to facilitate the para-church means and ends of the Society. The purported chief objective of the ACS was to arrange and guide the orderly and peaceful end of slavery, and the Colonizationists guaranteed these coordinates were the most efficient mechanisms available to achieve this sufficient aim.

In actuality, however, ACS agency director Gurley and his agents used these Evangelical instruments most effectively to downgrade the universal liberation and self-determination centermost concernment of the antislavery cause from an end in itself to a means for realizing the Evangelical World Alliance's conversion of the whole earth goal.

Ergo overriding the best known possible right and good interest of the Black race, the ACS focused on Christianizing-Civilizing-Colonizing Black American people. Coinstantaneously, Colonizationists concentrated on transforming human bondage from the Black chattel property of the slavocracy into Evangelical means for the White churchocracy and Christocracy to achieve the Protestant end perforce the establishment of the Kingdom of God--whose actualization they certified would be advanced through Black-race Americans' conversion of the Black-ethnic groups on the African Continent.

Overreaching to further Black race-only Americans for Africa--and to foil Africa for the Black-ethnic Africans--White Protestants expended enormous energy endlessly escaping evil and repeating distinctly all of the three distinct kinds of error: the error of conception, deception, and perception.

Lundy understood the eight clergymen he engaged in their private Boston conference considered the ACS an extension of the Presbyterian, Congregationalist, Episcopal, and Methodist denominations. In his dual role as an emissary of two competing and predominantly Protestant antislavery organizations--the Evangelical sacred/sectarian ACS and the nontraditional and nonsectarian Old Abolitionist Societies--Lundy set in perspective the absence of a Massachusetts Old Abolitionist Society, if he did not surprise the dedicated Colonizationists who believed the ACS was the unmatched and unmatchable antislavery organization, when he apprized them of the viable impressive number of Old Abolitionist Societies existing elsewhere throughout the North and the South.

They were particularly receptive as Lundy shared the latest information he compiled from the most recent national conference of Old Abolitionist Societies, that had convened in the City of Brotherly Love the previous year. One official delegate to this 1827 Old Abolition Convention in Philadelphia estimated that-- excluding "ten or twelve societies in Illinois"--a majority of the Old Abolitionist Societies were located in the Quaker sections of the slaveholding states. And while Lundy was unable to provide the documentation for these statistics and calculations, he assured the Boston churchmen that the facts and figures printed in the national conference's published report reflected his first-hand knowledge and experience as a field consultant.

Since these Northeastern clergy met with Southeastern members of their denominations and the ACS during their annual conventions, they were far less astounded to learn an antislavery minority survived in the slavocracy than delighted to have their high hopes for the ACS reinforced by the information Lundy shared. His data included specific findings and details such as that White Southerners--within the Quaker-peopled pockets of the slavocracy and on the northern and western edges of the Cotton Kingdom--comprised the majority of subscribers to the Genius. Nevertheless, Lundy entered and departed Massachusetts without discovering a clerical leader interested in organizing for Bay State citizens an Old Abolitionist Society complement of the two student Societies.

Thus while his Old Abolition and American Colonization alliance for progress message and method inspired traditionalists to adjust their dogmatic faith and pragmatic ethics priorities relative to their pro-Colonizationist commitments, Lundy was unable to augment the number of Old Abolitionist Societies in the United States:

> The Massachusetts, Rhode Island, and New York 4 **societies** and 300 **members** differ decisively from the respect societies and members in Eastern Pennsylvania 4,-400; Western Pennsylvania 12,-- 500; Delaware 2,--100; Maryland 11,--500; District of Columbia 2,--100; Virginia 8,--250; Ohio 4,--300; Kentucky 8,--200; Tennessee 25,--1,000; and North Carolina 50,--3,000: A total of 130 societies and 6625 members, exclusive of Illinois. Of the 130 societies, 106 were located in slaveholding states.[100]

Lundy enjoyed influence with his Boston hosts, who fairly represented the preponderance of New England establishment divines. His positive affect included providing information plus interpretation that made the receptive Protestant priests of protectionism a little wiser, but this increased knowledge leading to decreasing ignorance and heightening awareness was counterbalanced by the net effect of leaving the clergy essentially centrists oscillating just to the right of or on dead center.

They remained totally committed conservatives who were dedicated to furthering their own religious humanitarian designs; completely satisfied a direct correspondence existed between the truth and their truth; insisting on being identified as socially responsible traditionalists no less than the vanguard theological and social progressive transformationist Trinitarian Congregationalists; and thoroughly comfortable being primarily concerned with their prerogatives and privileges.

Given their published diaries containing experience-informed personal analyses and conclusions drawn regarding the caste/captive versus class/freedom crisis of conscience and confidence in the state of liberty and justice for all, antebellum contemporaries did not find Lundy and other visitors from across the nation and abroad failures to communicate, especially when they reported their reflections on being perplexed and puzzled by the conscientious clerical New Englanders' choice of social concerns and commitments.

Foreign explorers of North America who followed the premier European and American comparative cultures analyst Alexis de Tocqueville (1805-59), whose penned penetrating analyses and conclusions drawn were published in his celebrated disquisition on Democracy in America (1835), and native investigators like Lundy whose forages across the land of the free and into the home of the brave were initiated to induce cultural change, recorded being especially amused and amazed to discover these rational professional Protestant parsons at once divided over Calvinist dogma, united as official guardians of the two centuries-old Commonwealth's folkways and morays, and committed to prove the virtues of Calvinism; to propound the values of Puritanism; and to improve the morals of Yankees.

What the uninitiated adjudged far less great grace than great gall and grit took actual shape and form in reality as an unsettling experience especially for the pure pious and pure profane inhabitants, who were not among the "Elect" of

God or the select of man. Pure profane (secular humanist) lawyers protested pure pious (religious humanitarian) lawyers engaged as ecclesiastical and civil lawmakers (legislators) peculiarly potently but not uniquely.

They were particularly prone to dismiss the neither decisive nor insignificant permanent power amassed and perpetuated by the philosophical theologians due expressly also to their experience with them in history and current culture, as well as to the truth that they despised parsons on principle and deplored their past performance both in public power politics and as public servants--whether more or less than they detested their present power politics principal persuasion and purpose contemporaries discovered it was most difficult to determine.

Partly as a result of these power paradoxes, Protestant profane and pious partition principals and principles propagated over time and through time, and evolved out of an implicit White Gentlemen's Agreement an explicit division of labor in time or tacit toleration of all but hermetically sealed compartmentalization: whose arrangement of professionals set profane politicians in charge of public politics and pious parsons paid with state taxes dispensed by these legislative authorities to promote Puritan public and parochial rule of law and work-ethic principles in the private sector.

Thus it was neither natural nor inevitable but perfectly understandable why secular-humanist challenging religious-humanitarian culture critics, and convinced of the conclusions drawn from their alternative cerebral cultural critiques, could not appreciate the fact that these New England Halfway Piety faith and ethics experts--in their moral power role as efficient deterrence-benevolence ethicists that they exchanged for political power partnership--were as easily energized by as they were expressly enamored of positive power-producing puritanical moralisms.

Parsons were neither able nor willing to admit they made a mistake when as a conscious clerical class they entered into this civil compact with politicians, and especially since the ecclesiastical lawyers agreed to absent themselves from participation as professionals in partisan party power politics. Democracy's slavocracy and this gross error and profound misjudgment procceeded apace throughout the plurality of the antebellum decades, even though the appercep-tive among the establishment professional parsons whether temporary or permanent residents rationalized their passion for apolitical puritanicalism with impeccable logic and arguable principles based on erroneous premises.

Specifically, power elite Protestants did not abandon reason when they leaped to the moral mountain's moralisms-specific slippery slope--which they commenced negotiating with complete confidence because the comfortable were comforted by the belief that moralisms provided the perfect answer to the perplexity, and expended their security-seeking energies in essaying to advance pure and simple solutions to social difficulties compounded by cultural complexities.

Members of the "Old New England Families," and other natives of the region, were themselves unevenly fascinated and divided by their Massachusetts State tax-supported clergy. Bostonians encountered parsons on the public streets deeply disturbed by disturbers of their peace, and who appeared so shaken that they simultaneously collared these deviants from their standard preferences and demanded that they renounce their evil desires and ways at once.

Hence the class of educated evangelists abided in the appearances of their critics, who certified that perception is reality, as a universally empirically verifiable example of misplaced Puritan Piety public interest-enhancing faith and ethics; and classic in-stance of more obstinate than "Consistent Calvinists" insisting on their self-seduced misreckoned priorities.

In reality, Deterrence-benevolence or Halfway Piety ethics-superimposing Congregationalist clergy were unable to produce constructive cultural change in the Black caste/captive and White class/liberty system because they failed to relate appropriately the relevant agape-love/power/justice generating dynamics of authentic Puritan Piety faith and ethics in the private conscience, parochial consensus, and public consciousness crisis.

Successive Calvinist church, college, and seminary professors and the intellectuals they trained not only struck terror in the souls of Black folk and horror in the hearts of White folk but they posited their positive (negation ethics) error as the proof of the truth (they claimed) in the heads of evil minds. And posthaste, in full command and control of rational power and authority, preeminent parochial-academic and private-corporation as well as public-sector and establishment-ecclesiastical divines converged as trend-setter vicars of divine right and righteousness whose pontifications proclaimed that their dynamic connections and simple truth overrode profound truth and relations between personal faith and social ethics.

Their reasoned intentions and consequences resulted in upper-class and middle-class churchmen giving priority to rational charity--or deterrence-benevolence and negative moralisms--and theological clarity.

The charged Calvinist capitalists whose power to propose and dispose was exposed in their exercise of executive privilege, and who were converted Protestant philanthropists, preponderantly pioneered positive parochial-intensive and private-related humanitarian programs and institutions, on the one side, avoided the abolition of slavery and anti-Black race interests on the other side, and, on yet another side, definitively voided pro-Black race interests by the same decisive margin they voted the endeavors to effect the abolition of color caste and bondage conditions demonstrable instances of social sin and evil.

SELF-CONVERSION TO NEW ABOLITIONISM

CALVINIST BAPTIST WILLIAM GARRISON

In addition to being New England's major modern moralist model, pacesetter Garrison proved a prime example of the Calvinist Puritan propensity Evangelical Yankees manipulated to manage complexity with simplicity. These moral exemplars accomplished this sophisticated feat by moving subtly and shrewdly from faith and ethics to either faith as ethics or ethics as faith. Specifically, in reacting swiftly to the true religion authorized by the denominational protectionists, who set Halfway Piety beliefs and deterrence-benevolence morality or sectarian special interests above the right and good general interest, Garrison reduced to one the dual moral and political power parochial/private/public-interest expanding coordinates of authentic Puritan Piety, in the process of driving pure pious public faith beneath pure pious parochial morality to secure pure profane private principles.

No less effectually, earnest and honest Garrison transposed the nearly identical twin faith and ethics constituent elements of great religions by turning morality into his ultimate religion. He was so concerned to secure ethics in faith that he developed an ultimate faith in ethics, and made the ethical principles of man the test of faith instead of faith or the righteousness of God the test of human principles and practices. Extending the logic of this mood and mode, Garrison reversed the Calvinist rationalistic-specific justification rule of faith before, over, and above ethics. Garrison engaged in this exercise in futility because he found Halfway Piety right and good limiting rather than expanding faith and ethics. Therefore, Garrison believed it to be repulsive to e-quate with moral truth the law of faith first, last, foremost, and always preceding and succeeding as well as often supplanting ethics.

In this reversal of faith and ethics premises and norms, principles and processes, and means and ends, Garrison fused religious and secular values and con-fused profane rules of logic with sacred regulations of morals. Nonetheless, as a direct result of virtually dismissing as invincible ignorance the standards of Yankee establishmentarianism, he nearly escaped the moral morasses secular humanist and religious humanitarian determiners of culture dictated as the conditions of Christianity and civility and terms of their agreement--whose com-promise of principle connective linkage subsisted of elevating cultivated public neutrality as the operative ethical form and function in controversial issues of social consequence.

Garrison clearly advanced as a New England Protestant phenomenon only in part because he was an Evangelical moralist whose native intelligence and informal education fostered not only profound understanding without formal learning, but also reason and revelation in the form of sheer puritanical moralism. These brilliant logical and rhetorical skills, inflexible moral principles, and exciting personal integrity formed the complex personality and strong character traits that first attracted and then repelled Lundy. But Lundy was far from being unique in failing to discover the secret of Garrison's complete confidence and conscience, combative spirit and iron will, and courage of his convictions.

Garrison was not a Halfway Piety Moral Reformer like Lyman Beecher, and other "Connecticut Yankee" prototypes with whom the antipodean "Massachusetts Yankee" moralist united as a pro-Temperance principled Protestant and divided as a revolutionist.

Conversely, Garrison was an archetype atypical Puritan Piety ethicist. He defected from the partisan party power politics portion as decisively as he tolerated the spiritual segment, and aggressively advanced the moral power component, of the right and good expanding Puritan Piety ethic: entailing the three-dimensional power-intensive parochial, private, public individual and community rights and responsibilities. The Evangelical body, mind, and soul of his rational moral thought survived his resignation from active churchmanship. The nerve of this church verve Garrison exposed in his innovative translation of millennialism and perfectionism, and translocation of these instant subjective means and ultimate objective ends of conversion-specific Calvinist faith to his universal and unconditional immediatism Calvinist ethic.

As with this Yankee son of wayward worldly saints, genuine Puritan Piety was partially developed and undeveloped as well as developing no less obviously than it was underdeveloped in the life and works of its representative originator John Cotton and his paradigmatic successor Cotton Mather. Their exercise of church and state political power and authority proved the command and control factor distinguishing them from John Eliot, the consensus model Puritan saint and counterintelligence agent. As the Black-race bondage liberator, Garrison is correctly correlated with Eliot's millennarian central rational organizing principle far less positively than with his Evangelical outreach to the Algonquin Indian ethnics.

Cotton and his grandson Mather standardized Puritan Piety as the rational and regenerated parochial individual and community united personal faith and private and public ethics engaged in coordinated action to advance the general interest, community welfare wealth and health, and common right and good. And Garrison also contributed distinction to this tradition in ways that were similar and dissimilar to these pioneers.

Masterful mystical and magical men of mystique, whose mastery of reason exceeded their great ambition, they were equally autocratic and committed to church and state harmonized politics as the necessary power conflict and competition managing instrument of civil and religious moral law and order.

As audacious and arrogant as their pretentions and intentions were impossible, nevertheless, the idealists were realists who affirmed secular politics for its own sake. They accepted civil politics, like civil power and militia force, as the indispensable human governance arrangement, and the best one for guaranteeing the security of the church: whose ultimate purpose, they assumed, is not to form the perfect society but to be the ground on which the millennium surfaces, and after a thousand years the Kingdom of God is established with the Second Coming of Christ.

While Cotton and Mather were spiritual, moral, and political power-driving Puritan Piety ethicists, Eliot accepted all three constituent elements of the ethic but concentrated his extraordinary rational thought and action in the first two force fields of the magnetic ethic: as the personal agent/emissary of the church and state or public and parochial private professional minister-missionary-educator to the Natick Indians. Garrison disengaged the third dimension and in his positive negation of power politics evolved into a powerhouse, yet odd and even peculiar Calvinist Puritan Piety ethicist.

Arguably not born a Puritan Piety ethicist but a self-made one, Garrison revealed (A) himself to be an authentic heir in the direct line of the great tradition, in the process of developing and expanding the continuum he extended; (B) emerged a Yankee son of the wayward worldly saints who was neither the equal nor a perfect match of the Puritan saints but just as great a public servant; and (C) distinguished himself both as the two-dimensional Puritan Piety ethicist (anti-political public servant), and from the three-dimensional and pro-political Cotton and Mather and the two-dimensional and apolitical Eliot.

In this light, the pro-White race religion and race essence and of Halfway Piety deterrence-benevolence faith and ethics and ethicists is the sharpest imaginable contrast to the public interest-advancing distinctive constituent element of authentic Puritan Piety faith and ethics. It formed the critical virtue-drawing and vice-driving device employed by the principal Puritan seventeen-century and Yankee eighteenth-century Evangelical Calvinist ethicists--and their identical not negative good only but also positive good and right public interest-advancement direct action and objective but different means to this end.

Existing according to this definition as the definitive Puritan Piety public servant ethicist, in spite of his anti-political proclivity being the distinction separating him from the in-and-of-this-world and the-other-world pro-political Mather and apolitical Eliot, Garrison was neither a Halfway Piety faith and ethics ethicist nor one approaching the secular and civil order as the realm of the greatest unimportance like Jonathan Edwards.

Unlike profane and sacred society-engaged fellow Calvinist millennialists Cotton and Mather and even Eliot, Edwards, the pioneer Halfway Piety ethicist, was a deterrence-benevolence ethics expert; a sectarian single issue and special interest director of the churchocracy for Christocracy; a revolutionary seeking to superimpose upon history the solution of eternity; and the ultimate millennium revolution's peerless partisan party power politics parson.

Like and nearly concurrent with the Quaker Puritans--but due to entirely different motives and purposes from those driving these peace-loving masterful mercantilist rivals of the war-permissive Calvinist Puritans, who were fast becoming Calvinist capitalists--Edwards withdrew any lingering serious concernment with profane partisan party power politics.

Dissimilar from the Quakers, whose commitment to reform of the culture was not diminished when they chose to replace power politics with the force produced between the generation of pressure and exercise of influence, Edwards created Halfway Piety deterrence-benevolence faith and ethics; turned from theocracy to churchocracy; and shifted from human reformation to divine transformation of the civil order.

When set in the perspective of Edwards' relentless reversal of Calvinist Puritan secular interests and values, and their rudimentary removal and replacement by ideal ones, Garrison's restricted version of genuine Puritan Piety appears equally real and conspicuous albeit a far less radical deviation from the norm.

Garrison remained a rigid theological and social conservative only as a doctrinaire legalist warrior for several of the few secular and civil social questions traditionalist Evangelical Protestant Moral Reformers elect to attack. They are facilitated in this selective engagement and disengagement by a facile nondenial denial of their characteristic tendency to assert as truth the error that morality cannot be legislated but must be either inculcated or indoctrinated. But for those issues they determine to be of ultimate importance and neither their spiritual force nor moral power can resolve to their satisfaction, they demand a law to enforce their final solution because they consider their selective individual and community rights and responsibilities decision-making matters too serious to be left to freedom of choice.

Garrison did not suffer gladly the antiabolitionist executionists of his citizens arrest. At once ruling themselves in order, the conventional social and poli-tical wisdom, and nothing but the collective community conscience--without serious objection from capital, management and/or labor--proslavocrat Northern and Southern brothers and sisters in Christ, Congress, the college and the corporation arrested Garrison with impunity. The arbitrary approached the vulnerable and preferred the charge that his diminished Christianity and civility capacity was positively dangerous.

These vigilance committees proclaimed his deficiencies were prominently paraded in his daily indecent public exposure of private and parochial power people's obscene and even pernicious claim--namely, that their superior race and religion was evident in their ownership of human bondage, and imparted the right to violently and viciously violate the Black body, space, and race. He was tried forthwith for being a nontraditionalist by representatives of his cost-conscious contemporaries, who formed an ecclesiastical and civil traditionalist judge and jury of his peers.

It was far less ironic that Garrison failed his accusers' major social conservative litmus tests than it was paradoxical that these law and order crusaders for the peace and stability of the status quo at any price missed--or refused because they were deficient of the capacity to admit--a singular fact: Garrison either passed one minor test or for a strict constructionist reversion to the re-revisionist Jonathan Edwards-type of Halfway Piety deterrence-benevolence perfectionist moralist. Howbeit these counteroffensive moralists were his bettors at minding their manners and misconstruing these minor matters both measures of and major moral standards, Garrison was not only their match as a master of moralisms but their equal as a moral force who demanded uniformity and conformity.

In the process of disturbing the peace of the Commonwealth and the tranquility of the Union, Garrison disclosed his unsurpassed undue reverence for absolute and rigidly ordered principles, instead of not only universal and firm but also flexibly interchangeable permanent principles. He confused the five omnipresent but neither omniscient nor omnipotent principles with *agape*-love-- or the always and everywhere at once ap-plicable one and only true virtue--in his struggle to avoid the presumed vice of relative values.

While the hero and heretic endeavored to evade his self-determined equivalence of absolute principle and virtue device, by riding the principles and values horns through the middle of the dilemma, he did not escape scot free but leaped to the slippery slope of certainty, where, emitting more high intensity than high anxiety in an exercise of futility, the survivor was reported by his Black and White enemies to be expending his vigor absolutizing the relative and relativizing the absolute.

This character trait of the benevolent paternalist, which he shared with Yankee and Cavalier masters of the color caste/captive class, Garrison displayed specifically in his pontifications on morals and other questions of style rather than substance--that his religious humanitarian and secular humanist opponents termed matters of personal preference. Conversely, he and his fellow Protestant moralists comprehensively understood their peculiar passionate penchants in fashion to be taste-specific values or disvalues. But with equal total apprehension of their intentions and the consequences of their action, the Moral Reformers transformed their White middle-class preferences from concerns of choice in the civil culture into laws of nature and universal principles.

Transmitted customs translated culture laws conducive to absolute certainty that shaped their propensity to be free of doubt or full of certitude that they possessed the absolute truth as they were convinced the United States is God's country, and the Protestant principality they were set in charge of to secure the establishment of the Kingdom of Christ. High-principled monocrats persisted after theocracy their futuristic monocracy as the real alternative to either democracy or slavocracy and insisted that everyone follow their monochromatic morals. They proliferated as stability-fixated and security-conscious mono moralists who not only feared risks but especially did not like the odds against the people in their plurality choosing to obey their commandments.

First and foremost among these Garrisonian critical impositions upon the civil order were principled Prot-estants' public good-impacting anti-politics and pro-Temperance rules and regulations for religious and secular citizens.

Calvinist Baptist Garrison and the Evangelical Con-gregationalists sustained Edwards' perversion of the three-dimensional Puritan Piety ethic when they spurned the partisan party power politics central dynamic of Puritan Piety faith and ethics. Garrison was born too late to experience what his elder contemporaries who were onetime fierce Federalist Party partisan parsons selectively failed as a conscious clergy class and collective conscious to recall. It was that irrespective of the saints' failure to be impartial and fair power politicians-- and/or political power being neither the soul nor the sole purpose of the powerful Puritan culture--ecclesiastical and civil politics were vital secular and sacred rational organizing arrangements of the Puritan Commonwealth. Nevertheless, Garrison deserved the peer respect he received and earned for his promise and performance during a long and useful life of practicing the principles he preached. He was credited for being credible as the counter-culture conscience; not only committed and competent but also efficacious; and primarily engaged in opening the closed American mind and society his fundamentally quodlibetic and sometime formidable friends and foes appeared bent on closing.

Garrison's quixotic natural connection and unnatural disconnection with the sacred and secular Puritan Piety faith and ethics norm, and its intensive deterrence-benevolence and religious-specific Halfway Piety standard deviation, enabled him to transcend ambivalence; to recognize and to engage ambiguity successfully more often than unsuccessfully; to risk error and mistakes in order to turn problems from difficulties into opportunities; and to advance from a disadvantage into a strategic and tactical advantage his selective engagement and disengagement of the pure pious and pure profane.

In brief, instead of being short-circuited, Garrison's fragile and fragmented genuine Puritan Piety public ethics connective linkage was firm enough to form a Yankee conduit for the positive error/evil-repelling and positive good/right-attracting compelling force of antiblack white-ethnic virtue, and to fasten it to the individual and community right and good New England norm of the special and general interest.

Once the young professional journalist sprang forth a mature Yankee, his fully developed Puritan connection functioned effectively (1) to manage with old idealism and modern realism the new social reality; (2) to re-cover after his first serious encounter with the color caste/captive phenomenon and, after being caught unawares and taken entirely by surprise, to redirect the adrenalin flow from excitement to zeal; (3) and to con-duct the shocks of consciousness to the American national, regional, state, and local centers of culture and conscience created--currently and unexpectedly--by the international extension to and rapid expansion within North America of the world-class and Evangelical-headed British Abolition Society.

The transfiguration of Garrison was as dramatic as Samuel Hopkins' transubstantiation overnight from a "Connecticut Yankee" slavemaster and "Consistent Calvinist" clergyman to the archetype Old Abolitionist Puritan. Hopkins' transformation transpired upon moving his mission from Great Barrington, Massachusetts, and awakening to discover the Black masses in the New England slavetrade capital of Newport, Rhode Island. "Massachusetts Yankee" Garrison embarked slave-free Boston, disembarked in the domestic slavetrade port of Baltimore, and discovered himself face to face with the absence of the Massachusetts Body of Liberty in the presence of a massive body of human bondage.

This sudden exposure to slavocrats in their domestic slavetrade port was experienced as such an incredible turn of events it produced a profound sense of absolute right and wrong, and the immediate experience of absolute good and evil. The culture of Baltimore appeared so charged with color captives and concerned to create an atmospheric condition conducive to securing a state of stable dehumanization that it initially shocked the young Yankee and newcomer to the slavocracy--and then enlivened his development of the Puritan Piety faith and ethics connection into the live ethical wire.

Demonstrable antislavery high energy, Garrison transformed antiabolitionist negative good into pro-abolitionist positive good possibilities. The new force was

generated from Garrison's counter-culture move from direct connection to disconnection with the Colonizationism charioteers cherished, formation of the
missing secular and religious link to Massachusetts Old Abolitionism, and resolution to actualize fully and permanently in the immediate future of the sovereign
state the past and present partially realized hope of universal liberty.

Garrison moved swiftly as a dedicated ACS member and made rapid strides
from gradualism to immediatism after his ship docked in the domestic slavetrading port of Maryland, and he located a domicile in slaveholding Baltimore,
eleven years before the fugitive slave Frederick Bailey escaped from the city to
New Bedford, Massachusetts: to become the Massachusetts Anti-Slavery Society
lecturer that Garrison hired (in 1841), and known both to history and Garrison
as Frederick Douglass (c.1817-95). Once a Maryland resident, and a twenty-four
year-old professional colleague and neophyte religious student of forty year-old
Lundy, Garrison surfaced as a quick study under the tutelage of the publisher
of the Baltimore *Genius*.

Lundy's Quaker Puritan nonpolitical and nonviolent principles were new ideas
and ideals for Garrison, who, albeit a Baptist, was nurtured in the contrapositive Evangelical-Calvinist Puritan tradition. As distinguished from a religious
transformation and/or eccles-iastical transposition, his experimental experiential
education in the teachings of the Religious Society of Friends was a spiritual
lesson. And it was one that so far from being entirely lost on Garrison produced an experience in which he underwent a moral power conversion.

Garrison departed Lundy's more Friendly persuasion than Friends' indoctrination sessions with precious few indelible surfacial marks to show that he had
learned but rejected Quaker ideological class values and spiritual practices. An-
tithetically, Friends' philosophical premises and theological principles left a deep
and lasting impression on Garrison.

In truth, the pro-political Protestant opponents of the anti-political paradox
acted as if his existence in their appearances corresponded at once with reality
and their perception that embracing these great Quaker realities and certainties
should have raised serious doubts in his mind, and/or left Garrison in a state of
animated tension. In point of fact, the encounters between pro-political Manhat-
tanite and an anti-Poli-tical Bostonian proabolitionists made it perfectly clear
Garrison was conscious existence in conflict and competition with his Evangelical-Calvinist Puritan tradition's positive engagement of not only spiritual and
moral but also political and military power.

Contradistinctively, it is arguable that he was less aware of being a direct
actionist engaged in striving to elude self-defeating ethical self-contradiction--
that appeared as transparent as it was inherent in affirming the Quaker Puritan
influence style, as a process for his highly esteemed rational and radical rapid
social structural change means and end, while denying the Calvinist Puritan
legitimate claims of just war and pragmatic power politics.

The predestinarian thesis of Orthodoxy and antiwar antithesis of Friends
were dynamic dialectics of Yankee Garrison's Puritan moral power synthesis
(Calvinist/Baptist-religious liberty and Quaker-freedom of conscience). The un-
questioned and questionable values en-ergizing the synergy generated the dynamics of moral power, love, and justice driving his unassailable logic past the
overriding Old Abolitionism preferred by re-vered Old Abolitionist Lundy; the
overreaching antiabo-litionism of Lyman Beecher, who managed reality with
moral reason and revelation and to pass for the mind of Yankee conventional
wisdom in spite of promoting the principles of expedience and convenience and

thereby being a contradiction in terms of Puritan Piety Old Abolitionists; and the overbearing pro-Colonizationism.

Garrison evolved into a prophet not entirely without honor in his native state. Precisely there the dematerialized universal and categorical imperative ethic materialized with the transmogrified model modern moralist who appeared to declare his the moral motive, means, and measure the only morality, and as the moral medium and method is the message messenger to the mediators of middle-class morality and respectability. Power Protestants stoned him on principle and sight because they did not like the message; they loathed the messenger; and they detested his method.

Being the revitalized reembodiment of the original Moral Majority and positive negation of the moral majority of one distinguished the moralists, and convinced their numerical majority relative to his measurable numerical minority translated majority rule of morality they protested the Garrisonian truth claim-- there is no way to the moral means-end, the moral means-ends is the way--on the grounds that the direct actionist was one perfectionist who refused to adore both the abstract power points preferred by political thereoticians and technicians and their concrete hypothetical questions and answers.

Their primed and pumped poison pen was filled with the plain and plump well of ink flowing from the Garrison press, and of resentment for his ideas set in print and published in his paper where the *Liberator* seldom failed to adorn the color captive/caste tale of the church and state united and to point the moral.

These principal Protestant protectionists and eyewitnesses to history in the making, preferred patience, process, and perservance to the demand for less continuity and constancy and more change and correction directed by the counter-culture conscience. They revealed in their recorded contempt, and charges of recklessness leveled at the counterdemanding conscioussness, that Garrison was an unyielding "*true believer*" in moral perfection, who, being bent on maximizing his and minimizing their direct action intentions and consequences in the civil sector, combined the individual plus community social conscience of Puritan Piety public interest-promoting ethicists; the rigid theology and morality of   "Consistent Calvinists"; and the ideology of doctrinaire secular humanists with far more empirical rational theory than experience in reality.

Garrison's identifiable adversaries and advocates of judicial restraint were more curious than concerned to discover the critical connection between the old Puritan public servants and this new Yankee Evangelical Calvinist who astounded himself and left his contemporaries more alarmed than alerted, when, destitute and incarcerated for failing to compromise his principles in a community concerned with the productive capicity of their profit-making color chattel property and minding one's manners, he awakened suddenly to find himself a "born-again" to a new morality and a reborn new moral being. He arose self-transformed from an antislavery liberal into a proabolitionist radical; no longer divided in mind and will and one body and soul united by a different moral motive and purpose; and resolved to know, to be, and to do the right and good.

If fifty year-old William Ellery Channing neither elected nor was prepared to place his twenty-five year-old Boston rival for the title of the moral conscience of the nation in the appropriate perspective at the commencement of the 1830s, Channing demonstrated con-clusively a decade later that he was entirely able (if not completely willing) to appreciate Garrison as the New Abolitionist existence preceding essence in this fourth dimension of moral meaning, and a Yankee updated version of Puritan Old Abolitionist Samuel Hopkins.

While seeking at the end of the 1820s and his so-journ to fulfill the promise and mission of the saints in a personalized and solo performance, a task-responsibility transpiring during the Yankee's peculiar Puritan "*Errand into the Wilderness*" of Baltimore, Garrison looked askance at Lundy as if he were a Friend who had lost the "*Golden Rule*" Quaker-conscience and gained a new consciousness as a master of Aristotelian "*Golden Mean*" ethics: centered in the moral principle of moderation adopted by Protestant protectionists who reviled-revolution or revered risk-free reformation and preferred to secure the middle between the extremes of ethical excellence and mediocrity. Lundy rose in his vision as a moralist who majored in minor relief as the moral war measure and alternative to violent war amidst an immoral war ini-tiated by immoral warriors; and one whose all deliberate speed middle-of-the-road morals guided by mild manners and directing conservative means led to the reactionary continuity rather than radical end of slavery.

Garrison drew the conclusion from his analysis of his sometime spiritual and moral mentor that Lundy supported unwittingly the face-saving manners real values and peace-keeping profits real interests high priorities of the principled proslavocrats, as he engaged and encouraged enthusiastically in the common cause of gradualism Colonizationists whose establishmentarian hierarchal arrangement Lundy could neither deter nor accept. Garrison determined ACS churchmen managed to promote this realism overriding idealism as the Protestant standard of enlightened self-interest morality because the gifted rhetoricians and capacious rationalists were able as skillful logicians to elevate the prudential rule (or ethic) of expedience and convenience into the highest ethical principle for antiabolitionists.

Within a few months of Garrison's arrival in Maryland, the new investigative reporter for the *Genius* discovered in the Baltimore port a Northern domestic slavetrader-owned cargo of human bondage, researched the port authority records and found that the slave-trading ship's owner was a Calvinist capitalist or Yankee son of Puritan mercantilists from his own home town of Newburyport, Massachusetts, and learned that the entrepreneur authorized the Northern captain of his vessel to load the purchased slaves at Baltimore and transport them to the New Orleans slave market.

The extensive domestic slavetrade entailed the investment of Northern capital in Southern planters' plantations and chattel property, whose free labor-dependent industrial capitalism and slave labor-grounded agrarianism was a productive partnership that guaranteed the permanent loss of liberty fate of the slave class and gain of an expanding profit margin for Northeastern and Southeastern businessmen. Garrison's initial first-hand knowledge of this ordinary business was a stunning experience that left him more perplexed than confused or confounded.

Synchronously recovering from the shock and discovering the power point of his Puritan Piety ethic, and specifically its elemental positive error-driving antiblack white-ethnic virtue, Lundy's new associate (1829-30) wrote his first proabolitionist piece for the *Genius*.

Garrison's published *exposé* appeared the complete condemnation of the subject, vilification of the villains, and *Muckraking* precedent setting piece. It also would become his trademark in a famous career during which an army of admirers affectionately called Garrison their special *enfant terrible*. Garrisonians reported that his enemies were legion who preferred to deny his charge they promoted anti-Black race interests, to countercharge him with proliferating reckless incriminations, and to label him the *bête noire*.

To be candid, the major purpose and chief objective of his Calvinist state of mind was to win friends and influence foes to make, keep, and improve humankind-enhancing promises and performances. Constant and consistent challenge to change was considered the best way, and uncompromising principles the best means to achieve the goal of improving the human condition.

Garrison's values and role reversal process and progress proceeded apace his provocative and even provoking certainty that either the end justifies the means or nothing does, and permanent placement of substance above style.

Although the Garrison factor produced solid as opposed to easy answers and quick fix solutions, Garrisonianisms were no less plausible and praiseworthy for being radical rational reality management premises and principles, policy and process procedures, and programs and practices.

These radical and rapid rational structural change forms and functions formulated by master moralist Garrison constituted, for the aggressive Moral Reformer adversaries of the assertive advocate, the positive proof they claimed argued their case: Garrison relocated from Baltimore and returned to reappear in Boston a revolutionary whose management of reality was a failure exceeded only by his success as a manager of crisis, change, ambiguity.

Garrisonian factors were not sweeping generalizations but generalizable and even universalizable egalitarian means-ends. His equalitarianism materialized as controversial types of problem solving axioms for ubiquitous millennarian perfectionists who offered guaranteed certainty to the madding crowd, and massive presence seeking greater spiritual security rather more than searching to secure righteousness.

Perfection marketing millennialists' driving power hunger need, matching a voracious appetite for simple remedies to intractable issues, was evidenced in their boundless intolerance for leaders failing to generate and supply the demand; and insistence upon nothing less than a painless way through the cultural maze of difficulty compounded by complexity.

Garrison emerged with authentic Puritan Piety's power and authority norm, positive evil-propelling antiblack white-ethnic virtue rational organizing principle, and direct action standard operating procedure that entailed deploying words like bullets to destroy the determinative enemy of principle. What concentrated the mind was the David versus Goliath reappearance in the Boston of the original muckraking journalist, as the Bay State native hurled flat in the teeth of the slavocracy his synergetic sacred and secular Puritan Piety ethic-generated principles.

This moral anathema projectile not only took shape and form in flight, but upon hitting the targeted subject the objective word turned into a rejected object that the offensive-minded offended defendant and plaintiff returned with the force of a boomerang.

Thuswise, the Yankee's Evangelical Calvinist-Puritan disclosure in Baltimore reaped the whirlwind that redounded to him a small reward and a great punishment.

Garrison's exposé failed to change the minds of Bay State proslavocrats who preferred charges with the Baltimore slavocrats that resulted in his criminal indictment--for disturbing the peace and inciting Black Baltimoreans to insurrection--and a civil suit for libel.

Completely certain he was entirely warranted by the First Amendment to exercise his rights as a professional journalist, safe and secure as a citizen enjoying civil liberties and civil rights protected by Yankee independence and Puritan-Massachusetts sovereignty no less than the freedom of speech and the press guarantees of the Union, Garrison strode confidently as a resident of the liberty-limiting slavocracy that had elevated "states' rights" above the Bill of Rights.

The brash New Englander and young muckraking reporter stood out inevitably in the slaveholding and slavetrading city as the last man in the world to believe he had better hope than reason to think he could take the "*peculiar institution*" seriously as a critical cancer on the body politic and be a public spokesman for massive moral surgical removal of the culture *malaise*-conducing growth within a regime that had silenced or expelled nearly the entire class of native manumissionists (who advocated slavocracy-wide manumission), save the respectable and respected capitalist Quakers whom slavocrats apparently protected--as if they constituted an endangered species--and certainly tolerated.

In an exercise in decision-making that had the effect of disabusing Garrison of his illusions, the Northeasterner was convicted--on both charges by Southeasterners whom he was informed formed a jury of his peers--and sentenced by the judge. Clearly far from despairing and desperate but nearly frustrated and destitute of sufficient finances and friends to obtain release from his imprisonment, Garrison served a term of seven weeks in jail before Lundy's appeal on his behalf was successful. Lundy communicated the Baltimore plight of Garrison to Arthur Tappan, his "Massachusetts Yankee" Puritan brother in Manhattan, who, without prior personal acquaintance with the fellow Colonizationist, paid the young editor's fine in April, 1830.

During his confinement, when he had nothing but time to read back editions of the *Genius,* Garrison developed a rational scenario and connection to the antislavery continuum and reasoned his way from Old Abolitionism (immediatism redefined by Quaker leadership gradualism) through Colonizationism (antiabolitionism) and Old Abolitionism (original immediatism) to New Abolitionism. In the August 25, 1827 issue of the *Genius*, notice was given of Immediate, Not Gradual Abolition (1824)--a pamphlet written and published in the British Isles by a female English Abolitionist seven years before she died a Protestant publicist, Elizabeth Heyrich (1769-1831).

GARRISON'S CONVERSION OF THE TAPPANS

FROM COLONIZATIONISM TO ABOLITIONISM

Besides the immediatists in the Old Abolitionist Societies, who were increasingly becoming gradualists with the growth and development of the expansionist antislavery ACS, and the English in the British Abolition line of immediatism that was unbroken from the inception of the British Abolition Society several years prior to the American Revolution, Samuel Doak, John Rankin, and George Bourne were also engaged immediatists before Garrison converted from Colonizationism and gradualism to immediatism and became the original New Abolitionist and competitor of the Ralph Gurley antislavery agency. But the Baltimore jail-incarcerated New England Baptist and editor was not fully aware of these White ethnic Calvinist cousins, and other Southern Presbyterian ministers, whose experience in being driven from the slavocracy for their antislavery principles he would soon share.

To restate the essential point apropos a free translation, in which nothing of the letter or spirit is lost but translates literally and figuratively the truth in reality, Garrison, in his Baltimore cell, self-generated New Abolitionism and emerged the first New Abolitionist who possessed no real alternative to taking his leave of both Old Abolitionist Lundy and Baltimore.

Garrison journeyed from the Baltimore jail directly to New York City home of Arthur Tappan, the benefactor of Lyman Beecher and Charles Finley as well as other White and Black Americans, to greet him in the flesh for the first time and to thank him personally for his generosity. He remained in Arthur Tappan's home for a week, which was more than enough time for the original New Abolitionist to make the Tappan brothers his first converts to New Abolitionism.

CHANNING AND BEECHER REJECT GARRISON'S

PLEA FOR THEIR ABOLITION LEADERSHIP

Operating under Garrison's influence, Arthur Tappan began to question seriously his involvement in the ACS. Garrison moved Tappan from shock toward revelation of the ACS's deceptive nature by pointing up its inconsistency in the matter of Temperance--which the onetime American Colonizationists both espoused as moralists, rather than as "pussyfoots." Tappan did not immediately withdraw his formal support. But resigned after six months of inquiry and reflection led him to the conclusion that the ACS flatly refused to divest the profits of "demon rum" generated by the Liberian enterprise.

Garrison first entered and departed Tappan's home in 1830. Straightaway he returned to Boston, which served as the permanent base of his antislavery operations during the last twenty-five years of his remarkable professional career. Soon after his arrival, one of his initial acts on behalf of the new movement was to ad-dress private letters to Massachusetts establishment clergymen (including William Channing and Lyman Beecher) and lawmakers (like Jeremiah Mason and Daniel Webster), whom he had previously known personally or by reputation and who were reputedly the moral conscience of New England. He appealed to these Yankee religious and secular powerhouses to take the lead in forming the society he planned to be the first American antislavery organization to advance New Abolitionism.

Channing had yet to declare in public his personal commitment to antiabolitionism and the principle of individual-only moral reform, let alone to make up his mind on this volatile issue. His Congregationalist antagonist and fellow antiabolitionist, Lyman Beecher, had been unequivocal regarding Moral Reform programs and practices, but he remained an unrepentant member of the ACS.

Channing, Beecher, and Garrison joined the other New England religious leaders in the 1828 Boston con-ference Lundy addressed; but only Garrison among the linear moral progress proponents had advanced beyond the Old Abolitionist gradualism espoused by the highly respected Quaker minister. Instead of anti-Colonizationist Garrison appreciating he was depreciating in value for Beecher and Channing, and deprecated as a traitor and spoiler of a good cause and name.

When Garrison asked Beecher to meet with a small group forming the New England Anti-Slavery Society in Boston, Beecher's response was a definite "No, I have too many irons in the fire already."[101] Later in the year that he returned to Boston, during the month of October (1830) Garrison gave a series of three anti-ACS lectures at Julien Hall in Boston. His auditors includ-ed

Lyman Beecher who, shortly thereafter, denounced the "few foolish whites" advocating proabolitionism.

GEORGE BOURNE: PRO-BLACK RACE
INTEREST PROMOTING ENGLISH IMMIGRANT

On January 1, 1831, Garrison published the initial issue of the *Liberator*. In New York, within several months of the *Liberator's* first edition, the Tappans contacted Theodore Weld at Oneida Institute regarding the fact finding body they commissioned to assess the prospects of organizing a New Abolitionist New York Anti-Slavery Society, and invited him to join the exploratory discussion with Lewis Tappan, Joshua Leavitt, Simeon Jocelyn, the Reverend William Goodell (1792-1878)--the more reluctant than ambivalent Temperance reformer--and George Bourne. An immigrant from the British Isles, Bourne distinguished himself from Garrison as the first White ethnic American pro-immediatist to publish his analysis and to promote publicly anti-Colonizationism.

Save for the Tappan brothers, who as lay leaders both inspired and financed many Congregationalist and Presbyterian clergy together with other selected Protestant leaders and institutions, these initial New York explorers of a real alternative to the ACS were Evangelical Calvinist clergymen--the exception being theologue Weld, who was currently preparing for the profession.

Garrison acknowledged an "early and large indebtedness" to the Reverend George Bourne (1780-1845) for his comprehensive grasp of the "sinfulness of slavery," and unreserved commitment to "immediate and unconditioned emancipation," as Lyman Beecher confessed his apprehension of both principles. Born in Westbury, England several years after the origin of the British Abolition Society, Bourne transplanted Evangelical English Abolitionism when he landed in America (c.1805).

Bourne disembarked at Baltimore where, like Garrison, he was first employed in journalism. Unlike Ga-rison, who remained the strange Evangelical Calvinist as the lay preacher of radical moral repentance and conversion to immediatism, Bourne became a Presbyterian exhorter, beginning in Virginia (c.1809). In 1812, he was admitted to the Lexington Presbytery (that earlier had licensed the Black missionary, John Chavis), and ordained an elder and minister of the South River Presbyterian Church.

In a paper delivered at the 1815 Presbyterian Gen-eral Assembly, Bourne requested an interpretation of the Presbyterian ecclesiastical law as to whether it conferred on or whether it withheld from slaveholders all the rights and privileges granted to each member of the Presbyterian Church. He translated the deflective response to mean Reformed Church law had evolved from positive negation to positive tolerance of slaveholding membership.

Being effectively silent on the subject of the contradiction in the body of Christ, inherent in the conflict of Christian conscience and captivity, Bourne determined church law followed state law to be in conformance and permissive of the practice, and el-evated custom law into revered positive ecclesiastical and civil law.

Whereupon Bourne promptly and pointedly condemned the denominational rule as an anti-Christian regulation. Upon returning to his church, the presbyter was met by congregation up in arms over his challenge of the regional custom law governing church and civil laws--and demanding his dismissal as pastor of their South River Presbyterian Church. Their wishes were the command of the Lexington Presbytery, that the presbyters executed in September without objection.

Whereas Garrison would be sued for libel in a civil court fifteen years later, Bourne was charged with slander by his Presbytery and tried by an ecclesiastical court of peers. He was convicted of the crime of refusing to name the Virginia Presbyterians who, he declared, were slaveholders--and thus in violation of Christian principles.

Present at his trial (December, 1815) were four of the thirteen presbyter members of the Presbytery--and four lay elders: including the Reverend John David Paxton (1784-1868), then of Norfolk, who eight years later manumitted his slaves. On this occasion, Paxton was a witness for the prosecution, whose body Bourne associated with the Star Chamber of his roots, castigated as a rationale for uncivil persecution, and ac-cepted for the sake of righteousness.

BEECHER'S SACRED COW GORED BY BOURNE

The trial ended with Bourne being defrocked by the Presbytery. But the 1817 General Assembly ruled that the procedures lacked due process--and ordered a retrial. The Presbytery retried Bourne (in April, 1818) and reaffirmed its previous decision. It was sustained later that year by the General Assembly. These judgments were reached without the countenance of Bourne, who believed a charade rather than a fair hearing was the best he could hope for in either judicatory.[102]

As an official delegate to the 1818 General Assembly of the nation-wide united Presbyterian Church, Lyman Beecher heard the reading of Bourne's dismissal as presbytery from the Presbyterian Church. If nothing else, Beecher learned from the Bourne episode a valuable lesson in the virtue of the manly art of self-defense. Arguably the experience prepared him for the Reformed Church charges he would meet and defeat handily seventeen years later.

Beecher also respectfully heard and adhered to the denomination's position on slavery. The 1815 General Assembly had opposed the foreign and domestic slavetrade, even though only the slavetraders engaged in the international (not the domestic) slavetrade were in violation of the Constitution. But the 1818 Assembly that convened one year after the organization of the ACS as a pro-Colonization body, opposed evenhandedly aggressive proslavery and antislavery proponents, and admonished Northern Presbyterians to withhold judgment of Southern slaveholders. The Assembly counseled members from the North to initiate a policy of constructive engagement with their slavocrat brothers and sisters from the South; advised them to advance a fully developed appreciation of Southern pro-Colonizationists' good faith efforts to end slavery quickly and safely as a harbinger of future slavocracy-wide manumission; and instructed the brethren to abandon Old Abolitionism and even the intense encouragement of private manumission as the plague upon the North and the South, as well as upon the masters and the slaves.

All good Presbyterians were exhorted to Christianize their Black bondage; to treat their color chattel as kindly as their cattle property and without cruelty; and to support fully the ACS presbyter Gurley directed, as a Northern-Southern Confederation of Christians and churches in its original design, development, and expansion.

Mainstream Evangelical denominations functioned ecumenically to form the ACS as the antislavery organization of the Protestant establishment churches, when they finally followed the manumission societies-evolving and nonsectarian-

Christian Old Abolitionist Societies into the pro-gradualism movement the ACS dominated for thirteen years: before the New Abolitionists bolted from the ACS and created the AAS, as counter-establishment Evangelical pro-immediatist challengers of both the ACS and Old Abolition rival manumission organizations. The ACS was appreciated as a formidable tri-dimen-sional parochial-private-public, Christianization-Civilization-Colonization, Evangelicalization-proselytization-missionization, and spiritual-moral-political power organization. Breaking away from the ACS were the Evangelical insurgents, who called into question its secular and sacred virtues by labeling them vices of a patently low order of moral, democratic, and Christian values. New Abolitionists evidenced a different motive and purpose, that sprung from the depth perception of dehumanization extended by an alternative self-determination perspective from which they viewed reality.

Their worldview was evidenced in the New Abolitionist leaders who understood the fatal flaw of their Old Abolitionist Puritan-Anglican fathers, and procreators of their Black race-only cultural kinsfolk. It subsisted of, by turns, the willingness of the Independence era exemplars of the proabolitionist North and refusal of the antiabolitionist South to compromise their principles; the Puritan-Anglican Northerners being too quick to compromise their principles in order to form the Union with their equally principled English Cavalier-Anglican cousins; and the Founding Fathers rationalizing as enlightened self-interest and true interests the self-serving protection of real interests apropos promoting color class/bondage class dehumanization and preempting self-determination.

GARRISON'S RADICAL ANTI-COLONIZATIONISM

REIFICATION IN A CONTEMPORARY RETROSPECTIVE

New Abolitionists asserted the universally empirically verifiable facts argued the case that the intentions and consequences of the parties to the White Gentlemen's Agreement were revealed in the ratification of convenience and expedience; a Constitution of great good for White race/ethnic folk and great harm for their Black-race folk; and a color-conscious caste/captive versus class/status social system for the advantage of White (as well as other ethnic) males and disadvantage of Black males.

Pro-immediatists were idealists and realists who knew the difference between inevitable and necessary compromise, appreciated the distinction between arbitrary rational and the rational art of compromise, and believed the free choice in exercising the preferred option and electing absolute rather than the relative compromise of Black existence and essence was primarily the result of neither inevitability nor necessity but of a critical failure of nerve.

This New Abolitionist notion evolved from a lingering suspicion that new primary and secondary data confirmed, and immediatists advanced into an argument for idealism in a world of realism that realists secured for the status quo. In time, over time, and through time this radical perspective and interpretation of history and current reality crystallized as the reason why New Abolitionists held Colonizationists suspect. It also explained why they refused to consider the ACS anything less than a rational organization of evil, error, and terror: or anything more than a proslavocrat institution organized for the rational compromise of human liberty and freedom principles, that natural morality, secular democratic rules, and Christian ethics declare nearly devoid of public redeeming value.

To be truthful, American Colonizationists and New Abolitionists were not united but divided by the term, antislavery, a phrase they used in common and their uncommon opposition to slavery--without shared meaning, values, and interests. The positive good feature by which the biracial New Abolitionist leadership distinguished themselves, and the distinctive setting them apart from the negative good revering monoracial American Colonizationist leadership, was their respect for the real interests and values--ideas and ideals--of Black and White New Abolitionists who were mutually engaged as part of the solution as well as the problem.

The insulated White Protestant elite in power and authority isolated Garrison whom they rendered *persona non grata* the instant after the new New Abolitionist concluded his Boston anti-Colonizationism lectures. He ended critical analysis by denouncing to the public the ACS a pernicious and mean-spirited invention of good Christian men, who did not intend to be demeaning; and the extension of establishment religion, whose priority of commitments could hardly be other than dehumanizing. Only under the aegis of the unassailable ideals of virtuous men in command of eleemosynary institutions, ex-Colonizationist Garrison attested, could the ACS be portrayed as the positive negation of evil and absence of harm, and the presence of disinterested will to the good.

Garrison quickly discovered that explaining the Society comprehensively was easy but it was difficult to gain an audience willing to listen. He adjusted to reality and treated the Colonizationism subject and object of his contempt as a capricious and rapine power, which, wholly under holy auspices, thoroughly violated the Christian humanitarian and secular humanist spirit. He commanded the complete and over-whelming facts and figures, in a comprehensive deep and broad perspective and fair but searching pre-deconstructionist analysis, that argued his overpowering case for the rapid and radical abolition of the ACS.

Garrison proved stunningly smart as he developed his impeccable logic, overpowering rational theory, and incontrovertible first-hand experience in the ACS experiment in better living in Africa than America for the North America indigenous and native Black race. And what gave compelling force to his righteous indignation and moral fury was the converted soul of White folk, so far from resentment and jealousy and near to embarrassment and guilt over having been a member of the ACS, that Garrison revealed in a public act of repentance and re-thinking seeking forgiveness of through reconciliation with Black folk.

His despisement turned to scorn as he caricatured the ACS an obscene continuum of the Yankee-Puritan Calvinist establishment; the official organ of ecclesiastical power apropos the visible and divisible device of vice rather than virtue; and the institutionalization of pro-White race virtue perforce the radical demotion of the positive pole and elevation of the negative pole of antiblack white-ethnic virtue, and its perversion into anti-Black race virtue.

In this active unconscious role, consciously ac-claimed without White "Christian shame" or cost to holiness, the ACS fashioned the fashionable secular and sacred rationalization of pro-White race values into a formidable religious defense and offense to beat the profane competition in the race for moral power and authority.

Forthwith, driven by the Protestant will to power and hegemony in the universe no less than the driving need to demonstrate superiority over civil power, the highly motivated and very competitive Evangelical World Alliance ecclesiastical power launched an aggressive offensive against the Black-race body, and, invoking as their legitimate claim to truth and reason the Moral Law of the no less Holy Bible for being a proslavery and anti-Black race interest-specific *sacred document*, automatically extended universal credibility to the letter of the positive law created by "*the spirit of '76*" and the demonstrably pervasively religious and secular as well as sacrosanct and inviolable civil Constitution that made the Black race excludable in law, principle, and fact.

Garrison understood the past and present doubtless more comprehensively than the future sensibilities that deem spurious all honest respect for the Black race. He reflected on the color caste/captive rule ruled in order by ruling elders among the Puritan and Anglican fathers and their Yankee and Cavalier sons, whose personal exercise of force in public and private or parochial sectors was the definition and standard of power or the capacity to realize the will.

He concluded that specious reasoning alone could deny that the Protestant power elite's directed intentions and consequences were realized in uniting the invisible members of the Black race-only group in one visible and indivisible Black body. Garrison demonstrated conclusively that his descriptive facts of potent procreators' value judgments corresponded with the actual facts even his hostile host of enemies admitted it was nonsense to argue with, when he did not instruct specialists in the subject of their expertise but reminded the race and religion experts in subtle references of what from this distance may be far less obvious than it appeared to Garrison's auditors.

The pertinent point he implied was sharp enough to bear the weight of the inference he left the persuaded to draw from the conclusions he pressed upon the public: The irreversible change in physical nature and civil condition cultural effect and cause of the elite who dictate the values of the society results in the fact that each White race/ethnic person can be an individual, and the individual is the constituent ele-ment of American civil democracy and Evangelical Protestantism, but no Black person can be an individual because each member of the Black race-only group finds identity finally in his/her race only, and is irremovably bound in the double damnation bind.

According to the logic of Garrison's argument, who not only inferred but also referred his peers to their first-hand experience to document the point alluded to in lieu overstating the obvious, every Black American proves the well-known Black race-specific essence precedes and succeeds existence rule by being admitted exceptions because they are exceptional performers.

It is relevant whether he affirmed or denied the truth of disclosed by his social observation, to wit, each Black existence must prove that s/he is an exception to the general rule--or that they s/he can be and is selectively accepted as a so-called individual by either the White power elite class or individual.

Not one of Garrison's challengers or colleagues needed to be told that the exceptional White race/ethnic-individual who accepts the exceptional Black exception to the rule does nothing so little as to mitigate normative disregard for the Black race entity. No known pro-Colonizationist or antiabolitionist--to say little of a proabolitionist--doubted that the Black-race pariah cast existence in essence at once is inherent and persists differently in each Black existence in reality; wherein reality the repeatedly regularly or irregularly recurring phenomenon alternately submerges, surges, surfaces, soars, and survives in standard deviation from the norm functions and relations.

Antislavery and proslavery Bostonians not only continuously designed and carried out experimental individual and commissioned collective systematic and systemic comparative culture social ethics analyses but consistently acted in line with the conclusions dictated by their rational constructions.

Ensuing therefrom, these independent-minded sub-jective and objective public ethics analysts reached from their diverse perspectives unanimity regarding the critical color-intensive and race-specific constituent elements underpinning "*the spirit*" of Anglo-American culture--or soul of the United States: whose self-evident unique and distinct yet dynamic and spontaneous multi-ethnic societal nature and function they computed to be neither either underived or nature-derived nor divinely ordained but basically formed by and informing the intermixture of original and newcomer ethnic immigrants and émigrés from the Occident and Orient along with their native-born descendants.

Their radical analysis and conclusion affirmed these foundational mores, upspringing from historic class roots as fundamental cultural correspondences and contradictions, exist and consist of two mutually exclusive and near instinctive cultural realities, primarily transplanted from the British Isles and the European Continent but peculiarly nurtured and developed in North America.

(1) A fully developed appreciation of the mutually fertile nature of the human races comprising the human species; and, regarding the asserted equivalence of natural virtue and respect comprising the quality of worth distinguishing the human from all other species. (2) An inclination either to presume their preferred superior/inferior hierarchal social order and transparent arrangement of White ethnic/race inclusion and Black race-specific preclusion to be a rational occurrence produced automatically by not their selective culture critical imposition but by the natural selection process, whereby human races and their complemental ethnic groups as well as supplemental classes are unequally endowed with absolute and relative quantities of natural virtue-respect; and to proclaim the bare essence of the true nature and only purpose of human being groups and individuals to be manifested in the existence in honest and intimate consanguine relationships of the highest virtue-inherited (or ascribed) and therefore best ethnic individuals.

Proabolitionists proposed as the ancillary of this corollary the equally native sense that respect cannot pertain to Black and White encounters of the same kind. Normally when biracial honorable public and private liaisons are encountered in the urban-suburban imaginations and excursions of metropolitan residents, avouched the counter-culture public ethicists, they break forth from the cultural conceptions instantly translated demonstrable bestiality: where they existed in the perceptions of the precursor Darwinists and Creationists juxtaposed with biracial progenies, whose acts of creation appeared both in reality and to be exceeded in repulsiveness only by the so revolting as to be unthinkable if imaginable idea of a scientist fertilizing the sperm of a man with the egg of another primate.

The distinctive contribution of the biracial critics of conventional ethics was their insistence that this perverse Americanization of social reality developed out of the identical religious and secular cultural forces that created the ACS. Moreover, they averred, anti-Black race values were extended and not countered effectively by these agents of middle-class morality and respectability because the contrary evidence was considered inadmissable.

The elementary emotional significance of this American character trait can be seen, Garrison avowed, in the widely read published statements and imitated public testaments of Presbyter Lyman Beecher. Therein, contended Garrison, Beecher's declared priority principles and values underpinned a low tolerance for not only a value-free society but primarily for disorder that for Black and

White Calvinists resulted, by turns, in a high tolerance for involuntary servitude in perpetuity; the reduction of liberty from an absolute second only to life as a universal principle to the level of a relative value beneath the high principles of order and stability apropos the equivalence of value-neutral existence in human bondage; and the rationalization of the dispute between high churchmen over whether the Christian Church should support either the slavocrats or both the antislavocrats and the proslavocrats.

Antiabolitionist Beecherite types argued as if the enslavement of the entire Black race was not to be compared with either the slavery of a single White ethnic or with the freedom of the White race. When pressed by proabolitionist Garrisonian/Tappanite types to defend suppression of self-determination for their Black race cultural kinsfolk, Northern proslavocrats argued that slavery was a temporary inconvenience that Christian spiritual equality made tolerable.

Moreover, Garrison proved the power of their reason was their command of the logic of deception when he followed their argument to its conclusion: Black and White Americans are equal in the sense that in principle (as evident in its rare evenhanded practice) individual members of each group could be indentured servants.

He understood as well as these Protestants, who out-Pilate Pilate as pilots of protectionism, that they argued the arguments because the facts and figures revealed the truth and consequences: only members of the Black race were compelled to be perpetual slaves, and defined in the Constitution three-fifths human; only White ethnic males were granted civil liberties and rights, or neither slaves nor either free-born or freed Black Northern and Southern males could be citizens.

In order to impart the religious basis of this demeaning nature informing the ACS, Garrison accepted the risks entailed in challenging the establishmentarian Protestants with an anti-Colonizationist thesis and pro-Colonizationist antithesis he developed into a proabolitionist synthesis. He appeared a radical to the reactionaries, who, like the moderates and conservatives, failed to join him in reflecting upon the roots of the color caste/captive pride and prejudice they proclaimed a measure of principle. Anglo-Americans are Christians in their preponderancy, Garrison posited as an axiom, who were in their colonial commencement dominated by the hierarchical religious caste and hyperexclusive social class of competing English gentlemen at the helm of the equally different and real Anglican-Puritan, Quaker-Puritan, and Calvinist-Puritan theocracies.

Garrison's authentic Evangelical Calvinist progenitors, and quasi-adopted Quaker-Puritan forefather settlers, included observant and nonobservant polar extremes, and increasing varieties in between, who evolved into one English-race/British-ethnic people with two minds regarding Black Americans--divided by a will energized respectively by positive versus negative antiblack white-ethnic virtue, whose perversion into a color caste/captive vice produced a rational device for the generation of anti-Black race values.

Unlike the Middle Colonies proprietor William Penn, who owned and settled followers of George Fox in New Jersey and Pennsylvania where the slavemaster's Religious Society of Friends descendants severed their slavery ties and sealed their caste connections, in New England where the hegemonic "chosen people" struggled to advance from "presumptive" toward "real" Puritan saints-- while their Southern brethren cavalierly accepted their English-Anglican status--color caste and bondage substance matching symbolism resulted from their dialectic style of opposing impure deeds and persons.

Control of Puritan race impurity and Puritan religion impiety was an Evangelical Calvinist commandment, and antiblack white-ethnic virtue methodical measure, informed by the Puritan secular and sacred principal principle, to wit, the practice of Puritan Piety and profane paternalism.

The matter of pertinence at this turning point in Garrison's irreversible reflectiveness breaks forth from the light generated by his sharp comparisons and contrasts of the radical continuity and discontinuity between the seventeenth- and nineteenth-century vari-ations on the theme of Calvinist rationalization of bondage. Throughout these centuries random recycling and recurring racism reasons and revelations resulted in the maladroit transformation of slavery from pure malevolence to a benevolence rule of truth, whose Westtern Civilization proslavery for the unfortunate in the Occident and Orient, antislavery for White European Christians, and proslavery for Black African Christians on the Continent and the New World race and religion reversal of values competitive Catholic and Calvinist Christians wherever the expansive European powers extended their rule.

Both the wayward worldly saints at the helm of the Puritan Confederacy and their Yankee sons directing the ACS claimed their collective class corres-pondence with the color caste/captive class was sanctioned by the biblical law precedents. Upon the Old Testament promulgated statues, primarily derived from neither ecclesiastical nor civil legislative enactments but from the decisions of magistrates and jurists, John Cotton based *Moses His Judicals*. Cotton's Bible-rooted theocracy law book was selectively included in the superceding Massachusetts Body of Liberties, which positive law evolved and formed the ground for the Massachusetts Constitution that abolished slavery. Vermont was the first Colony to eradicate Black bondage, and Massachusetts was second but the first abolition state to join the Union.

But the original Calvinist Puritan legalists were litigators who as lawmakers enacted and enforced laws that survived revisions and reversals by secular and civil lawyers. In a word, after the secular state (but not the Christian Church) of Massachusetts (following Vermont) abolished involuntary servitude, the hierocrats reverted to the law and order of the theocrats and not only supported the "*states' rights*" article of the Constitution but re-revised the Cottonesque arguments as ecclesiarchs in charge of the ACS.

Their Moral Law of Moses in direct correspondence with justification by faith in the righteousness of God (Jesus Christ) and the ethics of human bondage, informing the justice principle underpinning Christianity and civility together with ecclesiastical and civil law, remained the standard of Moral Reform traditionalists that equally high-principled nontraditionalist moralist Garrison tested and overturned with a counteroffensive criterion of public virtue and vice.

ENDURING POWER AND LASTING VALUE

OF THE CAIN AND CANAAN-HAM CURSES

In the process, Garrison also disclosed the existence of individuals whose rational thoughts and actions were not always but often superior to the laws of church and state on the one hand, and, on the other hand, hardly meant these higher conscience actors expressed the will of the authorities or that of the people that the ecclesiastical, civil, and custom laws of the republican democracy embodied.

Garrison elected not to explicate the historical and current theoretical premises and applied principles of psychology, philosophy, and theology of either the Old Abolitionist Puritan Founding Fathers or their Yankee New Abolitionist sons. Instead of explaining either the cause and effect relation or the relative moral values of the former and the absolute ethical principles of the latter, Garrison chose to concentrate on elucidating the meaning of both the *White Gentlemen's Agreement* and their compromise of principles for the ante-bellum decades, by means of amassing massive data and propounding descriptive facts and value judgments.

He addressed moralists who approached secular and sacred history and reality through profane philosophical and religious theological constructs, guided by empirical rationalist logic and psychology. They did not require instruction in the great realities and certainties, so much as understanding of the truth and consequences of their acts of omission and commission, Garrison bethought, and left them to draw their own macro and micro ecclesiastical and civil power connections.

Proabolitionists and antiabolitionists understood comprehensively the Enlightenment underpinned superstructure and infrastructure of Calvinist capitalism no less than of the complemental Calvinist crusade for worldwide Christianity, civility, and Colonizationist hegemony. Evangelical World Alliance proslavocrat adversaries of the antislavocrats were pro-Colonizationist advocates who also evinced better reason to deny than to doubt what transpired in the New World and for the first time in history (that human civilizations and their record of human bondage nearly parallel).

Antiblack white-ethnic virtue was systematically rationalized and transubstantiated anti-Black race virtue by their pro-White race virtue agents, and Calvin-ists foremost among the bibliolatrous North-American Protestants--for whom the enslavement of White Christian people was even more unthinkable than it was for Roman Catholic adherents. In this transmutation process, African multi-ethics were outlawed by the English and British who embraced the African ethnics to create the deethnicized Black American race.

The new people and indigenous North Americans were promptly condemned to perpetual slavery, and legally proclaimed property, whose condition was the inevitable and automatic result of their progenitors choosing to reject the race they created, denominated black, and declared heathen. Concurrently, of course, no thinking Euro-American would label either an Eastern Christian or one converted by the African West Coast European slavetrade a heathen: to say little of the faithful African ethnic members of the historic Ethiopian Coptic Church, who survived the earlier and continuing rival East Africa Coast slavetrade and proselytization engineered by the so-called "infidel" Arabs.

The New World sectarians who universally proselytized at the same time they caricatured Black African (and not the concurrently South Africa emigrating White) ethnics one visible and indivisible body of heathens proved they lacked the capacity to admit (as incontrovertibly as they demonstrated conclusively) that the Black-race they deethnicized and deculturalized the progenitors recreated their cultural kin-group; and their non-denial denial of kith and kin was a Western Christian propensity rather than a unique proclivity of settlers and immigrants from the British Isles. What constituted the distinctive feature of English Christian color caste/captive positive negation was their biblical "Rule of Truth," that in these race-intensive matters became positive civil and church law.

North American Puritan-Anglicans were unequaled pontificators of the hypothesis defining Black brothers and sisters the shadowy figures of God, whom their Bible revealed determined to be good for nothing but inhuman use and human consumption. The antediluvian and dishonorable history of human bondage and caste systems advanced long before and after the birth of Christianity. Yet compared and contrasted with the fifteenth-century Western Christian inception and conception of Black African ethnic enslavement, the sixteenth-century Protestant biblically-grounded right and good of the arbitrary exploiting the vulnerable color bondage/caste class was so different in degree as to amount to a difference in kind of dehumanization.

It turned on capacious parochial authority and arbitrary public power uniting to sustain the legitimate claim of securing the real interests and values of church and state powers', and their private entrepreneurs. In short, to an extent unrealized in past or present slavery-pervasive societies like the competing Arab/Moslem slavetrade cultures, the peerless profit-making motive and means as well as opportunity of Cal-vinist capitalism-propelled Protestant over Western Catholic African slavery, advanced each free market and free enterprise Protestant state into a pure and simple wealth-producing and wealth-accumulating slave-based political economy: Irresistible Calvinist capitalism and the Puritan work ethic made the exception the rule whereby instead of a means to an end--such as a protectionist political and military device designed and executed to defend the national security--slavery became an end in itself.

The English Bible reading people understood their affirmation of slavery to be disinterested will to the good of Black African ethnic groups, based on three biblical pillars. This Calvinist justification by faith in the righteousness of God and righteous reason redounded to full faith and credit in the sacred and secular legal system of justice, and conformance with the proslavery rule of law instituted by divine and human power meant that perchance even Godless anti-Calvinist proslavocrats like law and order God-fearing Calvinists might be either right in what they affirm and wrong in what they deny or err in their interpretation of the "Rule of Truth" and "Rule of Scripture": but they could not be in grievous error even though their sincere and serious intentions and consequences resulted in harm-intensive effects, as long as they were earnest and honest in their beliefs. Thus the sincerely wrong Evangelical-Calvinist Puritan fathers and their Yankee sons were right and righteous because they harbored no doubt they were justified by faith in their predestinarian truth claims:

(A) The black mark of Cain functioned effectively as the indelible sign and symbol of the deepest diabolical dye and intractable transgenerational genetic sin or rebellion against God. The Blackness phenomenon was the perceived presence of absolute evil and/or absence of relative good whose essence was predestined to survive the flood on Noah's ark--that housed all existence created and preserved by God--in the person of Noah's Black son Ham, through whom positive error entered the world of human beings at the second commencement of history.

(B) The ineradicable Old Testament canon's Mosaic Law reveals the divine double damnation of Black folk, in transcribing the blessing God visited upon Noah and his three sons or eponymous human race per-sonages Japeth (European), Shem (Semite), and Ham (African)--

who therefore could not be cursed--and the curse God visited on Ham's son Canaan and his descendants, who were stricken black and remanded to slavery in perpetuity for the unspeakable acts of (AIDS-like contagious) sexual deviance Ham perpetrated on the ark.

(c) The positive negation the Israelite sons of Shem and "chosen people of God" inflicted upon the Black-race Canaanite sons of Ham and heathen anathema of God, is as divinely ordered as the Jews are themselves the enemies of God.

Centuries-old Old Testament and New Testament myths and mysteries evidently sustained sufficient reason and revelation for the Gentile-Japeth and Semite-Shem sons of Noah to justify ensconcing their Ham/Canaan-African brother in the permanent Western condition of involuntary servitude; during which four centuries-long color bondage/caste ordeal pro-White race advocates, of the divine right of human bondage and will to punish Black folk, advanced Black African slavery as a high principle, that fed upon and confirmed the righteousness of the prior and more potent anti-Black race virtue.

This popular God-ordained color caste/captive mind-set, and pervasive Christian translation of Old Testa-ment myths, was deeply mined and finely honed in North America by English Enlightenment rationalists who were without peer as a Bible reading, oriented, and directed Puritan people. Old and New England managers of reality were masters of mystery and magic as well as of enterprise. Given their masterful rise as the "Elect" saints called to appropriate for themselves the Jewish "chosen people of God" state of superior grace, their mastery of the Puritan will to antiblack white-ethnic virtue, and the ancient Jewish Ham/Canaan myth of anti-Black race virtue, it followed as naturally in their logic and life that immediately upon usurping the land Native Americans highly prized they found these color caste/captive principles to be the truth of the Bible and experience. Precisely in this spiritual and moral no less than political power connection and disconnection, myth became the one reality for a doctrinaire people of *The Book*.

The power elite Puritan-Anglican reborn English-American Calvinist "seed of Abraham" not only were birthright superiority complexes, and asserted the universe-wide supremacy of their derivative ethnicity and faith to out-Anglo Anglo "true believers" in the superior English race and Anglican religion, but the select "Elect of God" could no more be fairly accused of either flouting or flaunting the composite superior Evangelical-Calvinist religion and Puritan race axiom these potent procreators superimposed upon their designed inferior Black-race progeny than there abided any reasonable doubt pro-White race and anti-Black race Puritan pride and prejudice flourished in the popular imagination: partly because preferred color-specific bondage/caste pariah existence was subtlety developed by sophisticated power people, throughout the Evangelical Calvinist evolvement into "real saints" from English-British/Anglican-Puritan "presumptive sinners" in the New World.

So far from color-blind and near to color-conscious persuasions of the equally persuaded and persuasive, upspringing from no less real for being either hidden or unexamined premises and embraced natural laws and rights issuing forth as positive principles of color-intensive race and religion priorities of privilege, anti-Black race values were nurtured in the philosophical ideologies and theo-

448   CONSTITUTION, CONSCIENCE, AND CALVINIST COMPROMISE

logical doctrines advanced by scholarly chiaroscurists from John Cotton through Cotton Mather to Jonathan Edwards.

Necessarily, therefore, between Samuel Hopkins whose professional career encompassed the First and Second Great Awakening, and Lyman Beecher who was born at end of the First and developed into the paradigmatic figure in the Second Great Awakening, these shared values found rational interpreters in post-theocracy Evangelicalism--the common religion of the new nation--among the principal protectionists of the race and preservationists of the religious tradition.

A DECONSTRUCTIONIST INTERPRETATION

OF GARRISON'S NEGATIVE COLONIZATIONISM

Garrison and Beecher most certainly apprehended this wide-ranging social ethical background, and did not set the ACS in this broad perspective. They preferred to argue the effects rather than the causes as the paradigmatic respective prosecutor of its "Bad News" and litigator for the defense of its "Good News." Instead of their differences, the warriors set an edge as sharp and as deadly as a *machete* on their "Bad Faith" offensive principles and buried them deep into each other's body of beliefs. Since they drew on their credentials as sometime active *bona fide* members of the ACS, the adversaries found it sufficient to advo-cate their rival constituents' competing certification of the ACS's ultimate value and disvalue. It is the case, nonetheless, that the positive ethical evil, political error, economic outrage, and social terror the ACS or-chestrated are best interpreted and realized clearest through the retrogradation of pro-Colonizationists' hidden agendas.

When the three-dimensional spiritual, political, and moral power centermost constituent elements of Puritan Piety are distinguished, and focus is limited for purposes of summation to its spiritual power component, the double bottom line of historic Puritan Piety subsisted of being "born again" or a "new being," and the driving doctrine of millennialism--that made rebirth not only a compelling experience but a matter of ultimate concern. The sacred coordinate plus its correspondent secular culture coordinate formed an efficient ecclesiastical and civil power device, which functioned effectively to squeeze the life of the Black outcaste fastened between the lower-class and middle-class pro-White race/ethnic virtue direct actionists.

The cause and effect of their fool-proof and text-proof Bible-based, elimination of positive and accen-tuation of negative antiblack white-ethnic virtue was its perversion into anti-Black race values. These intentionalist moralists and progressive transformationists were equipped to produce this textbook interpretation and literal "Word made flesh" translation expressly by their expert direction of an overactive millennial theology and untrammeled *Great Chain of Being* social conservative philosophy. As a consequence of the equal utilitarian direction of the identical command and control of reason and revelation, the Puritan settlers' sacred and secular culture solidly worked for White and against Black Calvinists.

Neither necessarily nor inevitably but equally obviously and understandably, expedience and convenience were rationalized means of protecting their preferences and privileges. Straightforwardly, their church and state color-conscious law and order rules and regulations were inflicted upon Black New Englanders to oppress their psyche; break their body; and repress their spirit. Ironically,

White Christian English gentlemen were, in their central bearing, nothing if not professors of the grace of repentance. Still, in the matter of demonstrating grace, graciousness, and gratitude by way of demanding full respect for their Black race and advancing the best interests of Black kith and kin, the preponderancy of Puritan-Anglican slavemasters preferred their invincible ignorance or indiscriminate indifference as unquestionably as they remained unchangeable in their heart, mind, and will.

Contrapositively, reasonable men discovered no reason to doubt Puritan slaveholders were more merciful than vicious in vitiating the character of Black bondage. Slaveowners exercising their capacity which that consisted of sacred and secular power, rooted in a spiritual and material nature, Puritan professionals were equally rich and famous Bible-reading rationalists. Indeed, their very identity was tied to independent-minded interpretations of the Scriptures, that they honored and obeyed as the sufficient moral guide and rule for their large capacities and opportunities--whose capaciousness they were determined to realize regardless of cost. What arguably did nothing to mitigate the awesome cultural clout of the pure pious and masterful powerhouse Puritans was their positive correlation and feedback between their capacious capacities, total belief in themselves, and complete confidence that they were Providence's peculiar people--that is, the one and only class of called, "chosen," and confirmed saints.

It was far less the destiny than the fate of Black slaves to serve these irrepressible powerhouses, and irreversible forces of rational compulsion. A measure of the irresistible force the Puritan slavemasters exercised in the state of grace is revealed in these potent procreators' capacity to preempt their Black property of "power to the contrary," while insisting they possessed both free choice and free will.

Perforce this driving Puritan bifurcation of reality, secular and sacred inextricably interlinked ecclesiastical and civil power parsons and parishioners persisted in their determination to reconcile two mutually exclusive universalizable imperatives--the Scripture rule of absolute slave obedience to the master, and the profane law of self-determination. In the process of exposing their Evangelical Calvinist fairness and justice principle, or justification by faith in the righteousness of the election to double damnation in history and eternity of their color caste/captive class, the saints and sinners revealed their hidden colonization persuasion--wherein the entire complexity of the pure pious and pure profane Puritan faith and ethics culture came to a head in double jeopardy. It can be elucidated sufficiently to make this interpretive point clear (if not stick) in a brief construct:

(1) Western White Christian men comprised the superior human race and religion, whose *creme de la creme* were respectively Englishmen and Puritan faith.

(2) Roman Catholics were devils who cor-rupted Christian truth, whose pope was the antiChrist whom the Puritans hated on a par with the Spaniards they castigated in the "Black Legend."

(3) Puritans were the new "chosen people" God called to convert humankind to the true Christianity of Evangelical Calvinism, to replace the Jews who misunderstood their calling and refused to

become Christians--at the same time prophetic millennarian literature projected a statistically number of Jews would convert before the new age, whose conversion would be the sign of the impending new aeon.

(4) The New World was the "New Israel" God had granted the Puritans for their preparation as saints, whose purpose was to be the light that would bring the nations to salvation.

(5) The Bible, whose Old and New Testaments proved Catholics and Jews to be in error and without rights--like the heathen who were in ignorance--also disclosed the millennium as the revealed purpose and design of God's will to rule triumphantly, imminently upon earth.

(6) The Bible visited a double curse upon Black-ethnic Africans, specifically in the Old Testament but particulary in the extant exegeses and eisegeses or the interpretative extra-bibical critiques through which scholarly process the meaning of the text for the faithful is transmitted to each generation of observant Jews and Christians. Therein they were left the ignorant heathen whom God created *black* (whereby they left Spaniards tainted if not stained) and condemned to slavery, (the legal enterprise Jews and Gentiles vied to dominate after the commencement of the Christian era until the rise of the infidel Moslems, whose seventh century-emerging slavetrading hegemony in Black Africa redounded to Englishmen in the sixteen century); but the *Book* also provided for their ultimate salvation in post-history eternity, after the fall of the Roman Catholic "Beast" and the conversion of the Jews.

(7) Colonizationism was approved by the Scriptures, and the Bible authorized the Puritans to complete their "*Errand into the Wilderness*" of North America through appropriating the land required by the Native American culture confining Indians to reservations. Puritans enjoyed the warrant of Scripture for their aggressive pursuit of anti-Black race values and anti-Black race interests, discovered in the Bible far less broad or more narrow anti-Indian race interests sanctions, and liked Indian ethnics--whom they desired to bring to their cultural light and saving truth--as certainly as reminiscence of the centuries-long and worldwide successful Christian rejection operations launched by Jews concentrated the minds of imperialistic Puritans as the Indians engaged in massive resistance of overt and covert Puritan deculturalization schemes.

(8) The primary millennial purpose and objective along with its Evangelical message and missionary method, originally checked and frustrated during the initial settlement period by the Indian counteroffensives and problematics of developing a viable mercantilistic political economy, were finally untracked in the work of the first great practitioner of millennialism, and Puritan missionary to the Indians, John Eliot. He earned the honor of consensus Puritan

saint conferred upon him by grateful peers and his younger contemporary and biographer, Cotton Mather, when in a brilliant *tour
de force* he eased simultaneously the Puritan guilt of stealing the
birthright of the Jews and the land of the Indians.

(9) Eliot reached the conclusion--following his personal biblical exegesis and eisegesis and conncurrent communication with complemental doctrinaire millennarians and Evangelical-Calvinist rationalists on the Continent, who were developing there and disseminating
throughout Europe and America their millennial hypotheses--that
the Natick and Algonquian Indian ethnics in Massachusetts were not
the heathen like the color captive class that he ignored appeared
to their Puritan captors. On the contrary, in his supersessionism,
(Calvinist Puritans have replaced Jews as the "chosen people" of
God), Indian ethnics were discovered by Eliot to be Jews in the
New World, to wit, the lost-found Ten Tribes of Israel.

(10) Forthwith Eliot directed the colonization of the relatively few
seduced Indians on Massachusetts reservations. Colonizationism was
not merely an expedient policy and program for protecting the deethnicized and deculturalized "praying Indian" converts to Evangelical Calvinism from preying anti-Calvinist Indian and White ethnics.
Complementarily, colonization of the Indians was decreed an imperative strategic and tactical process for creating through the host
body of Evangelical-Calvinist Indian Jews for Jesus the first Church
of God, and space in which the imminent millennium would surface
and reign for one thousand years prior to the establishment of the
Kingdom of Christ. In brief, the New England Native Americans
Eliot converted from Indian ethnics to Christian sectarians were
projected as the front line millennarians who would save the world
and White Christians. This convincement of Evangelical Calvinists
followed from their dogma and pragma, namely that the millennium
epoch--of ten centuries-long preparation for the establishment of
the Kingdom of God on earth--would transpire after the conversion
of the Jews--whom Eliot certified his Indian churchmen were.

This pure reason-created ultimate colonization form and function and demonstrated the enduring political power of rational myth and symbol, no less unmistakably than Eliot's work of supererogation among the Indians placed him
atop the Puritan pantheon of saints. Inevitably, of course, the Eliot program for
com-pleting the peculiar Puritan *"Errand into the Wilderness"* was a mission
impossible that failed its contest with reality. Yet the lesson was lost on the
most creative millennialists the tradition produced. First among these equals was
Jonathan Edwards, the great Puritan Calvinist philosophical theologian, for
whom like Eliot Black slave and free-born Americans were of far less moment
than they were for Benjamin Franklin--the other "great eighteenth-century Puritan-Calvinist mind"--who was known more for his pragmatic morality than for
his dogmatic theology.

Edwards emerged with commanding reason that he directed in the defense of
the universal value of both pure pious Puritanism and millennialism. In the process he passed for the mind of New England Evangelical Calvinism, yet institu-

ted Halfway Piety as the substitute for Puritan Piety. He declared that pure pious presence rather than sacred and secular civil Puritan Piety was the Evangelical Calvinist Puritan message, and that it failed to be heard and acted upon rightly because the church was attempting to do the work of the state.

In his vision of reality, power politics and economics were transitory forms of order and survival, yet the civil power of the magistrate remained for (Calvin in Geneva and) Edwards in Massachusetts indispensable means for protecting the churchocracy from the legion of foreign and domestic assailants, and guaranteeing it can fulfill its Christocracy-securing mission. Edwards argued the task of the church was to be the means of grace enabling the Holy Spirit to convert sinners; to become an ever-expanding community of the regenerate; and to develop as the reliable dynamic entrance point for the millennium. What convinced the preeminent rationalist of imminent millennialism, as the overriding reality, was the outbreak of revival phenomena during the First Great Awakening.

Thus it is arguable that Jonathan Edwards, the sometime missionary to the Indians, evolved into the prototypical Puritan-Yankee Calvinist link between the colonialism, colonizationism, and Christianization major missions of the saints. His liberating mind established the legitimate claim to virtue of millennialism, brilliantly rationalized the value of revivals, and guaranteed the millennial end and evangelism-revivalism means would become the way of the "New School" and "New Light" revisionists and protectionists of traditional Orthodoxy. In his role as the nonpareil First Great Awakening New England revivalist, Edwards struggled to advance the interest of the Kingdom of God through securing the radical renewal of the individual. His rational intentions and consequences were in line with his narrow-scoped method and largely achieved ends; whereby personal and private Halfway Piety faith and ethics were expanded and Puritan Piety public interest-advancing political, social, and economic faith and ethics were diminished.

It is arguable, at the very least, that Edwards' relative rather than absolute equation of disinterested will to the good and indiscriminate indifference to secular and civil public ethics occurred because he thought social issues were amenable to a single and simple solution (millennarianism); or could not be so nearly intractable difficulties compounded by complexities as to mitigate the power of the individual in an imperfect world. Whether or not his rational thoughts and actions were relevant omissions and commissions perforce foreign and domestic affairs of the post-theocracy and pre-democracy Commonwealth of Massachusetts, it is inarguable that his public-limiting Halfway Piety faith and ethics had significant future social consequences. Howbeit a result of design or accident, it was scarcely incidental that his rational influence was weighted toward social conservative establishmentarianism.

Moreover, his logical defense of revivalism and millennialism also proved a methodical boon to future defenders of their (and his) own status quo. Appropriation of Edwardsean social conservative values was especially consequential in the nineteenth century, when revivalism and evangelism were joined with imperialistic missionization and colonization by establishment people, for remote control of the heathen at home and abroad. Of course it made a difference that millennialism was no longer either imminent or a matter of eminence for the powerhouse Calvinist capitalist Yankee sons of the wayward worldly saints. The difference was revealed in the distinction sustained by the Puritan fusion of evangelism-revivalism and millennialism.

It comprised the distinguishing factor that allowed Edwards' social conservatism to be uncritically acclaimed the height of Puritan sublimity. However, in spite of his uncommon idealism and mysticism, Edwards' Halfway Piety moral values served to reinforce Yankee "*true believers*" who claimed Puritans (like the ancient Greeks they honored more than they adored) bequeathed to them the world-class social order.

The relevant point is neither to assign blame nor to affix deniability nor to deny responsibility, since the rationale Edwards provided Halfway Piety revivalism and millennialism was remodeled but not razed in the Second Great Awakening. "New Light" and "New School" Evangelicalism enlivened congregants as well the nascent Denominations that were experiencing unusual growth, and captivated the interest of the local churches, precisely at a time when Evangelicalism augmented democracy's political and economic extensions of slavocracy. Concurrently, as the improvers of Edwards' Halfway Piety in the early national era, the post-Edwardseans' analysis of what Edwards expressly entitled *The Nature of True Virtue concluded it to be in essence* Orthodoxy's manifest deterrence-benevolence destiny.

As a result of holding Beecher's feet to the fire, Garrison disclosed the true nature and meaning of Half-way Piety faith and deterrence-benevolence morality to be transparent and transposed charity, whose proliferating form and function was evident in the enlarged eleemosynary role in the church and state played the "Robert Baron" Yankee merchants, industrialists, and financiers turned Protestant philanthropists. The advent of this unprecedented New England benevolence, and presumed Puritan bare essence, selective Calvinist capitalists partially attributed to Edwards' single and slim but gem of a social ethics volume wherein he defined ethics as the *Nature of True Virtue or Benevolence.*

In truth, as evidenced by this Yankee Evangelical Calvinist charity, Puritan benevolence was a comparatively late development.

The source of the support for missionaries to the Indians John Eliot and Jonathan Edwards leaves no reasonable doubt concerning this singular fact: Puritan fathers and Yankee sons had not been the generous givers but the grateful recipients of Evangelical British benevolence in American missions for nearly two hundred years; established few precedents in the missionary, colonization, and Moral Reform religious humanitarian spheres; and followed primarily pacesetting leaders of the English Anglican and Independent traditions and other British churchmen.

Samuel Hopkins, Edwards' brightest student, best friend, first biographer, and most faithful Anglophile, initially elevated Edwards' classic Puritan Calvinist ethics, set forth in his text on *The Nature of True Virtue,* when the Edwardsean translated Edward's theory in experience and reality as the Hopkinsian "New Divinity" moral principle and practice. Hopkinsianism was studied and studiously ignored by Beecher of Yale, and appreciated near the end of his career by Channing of Harvard. Hopkins' liberal disinterested benevolence ethic, and conservative social philosophy, were uniquely combined in his person. As a result, he took the color-caste Black presence seriously, and the former slavemaster converted to become Orthodoxy's first clerical Old Abolitionist. He carried few Calvinists with him in the first direction and many in the second direction. In point of fact, few nineteenth-century establishment clergymen approached and fewer raised the "Old Abolitionism" standard Hopkins established in the eighteenth century.

Nevertheless, it was not his Old Abolitionism and "New Divinity" spirit--

whose secular and sacred dynamics he extended into the nineteenth century-that made the Edwardsean a live moral wire and connection between crusading post-Edwardseans' transformation of negative-only antiblack white-ethnic virtue into anti-Black race interests. Hopkins was as advanced a theological and social liberal as any establishment Puritan Calvinist, doctrinaire millennialist, and partisan Federalist Party parson. As such, his interest in liberating Black bondage immediately and unconditionally universally was not equaled--let alone exceeded--by any peer parson or parishioner in Orthodoxy.

Yet, the historic Puritan bifurcation of reality, and the superiority complex perforce Puritan superior race and religion, constituted inherited cultural values that determined that Hopkins would also become a conduit in the proslavery antislavery controversy for the Black race positive negation propensity of Evangelical Calvinism. This error of conception and error of perception led as often as not to the error of deception, because its idealism-optimism and realism-pessimism social ethics principles were grounded in social conservatism, and, when in the course of dynamic conflict and competition they were caught in crisis, the tendency was to revert to conservatism and executing a reservation or colonization type of preemptive strike preservationism; to reverse the press from progression to regression; to defer to proslavery and pro-White race/ethnic priorities; and/or to give way to stubborn benevolent paternalism.

As the crystallizer of this reservation/colonization tradition, (whose outcome contradicted his spirit but conduplicated his rational plan as the law of Gospel order), Hopkins fathered the Black race-specific colonization movement and mission enterprise, that subsequently became the official American church and state response to the Black race. He formulated his pioneering preemptive program a quarter of a century before the first American missionary society was organized in Connecticut (1798), and the formal alliance of the Presbyterian-Congregationalist Plan of Union (1801).

Fifty years after Hopkins' foreign and domestic parochial blueprint, his successor brethren in the Orthodoxy and Reformed Calvinist traditions consolidated their national benevolence enterprises in the American Home Missionary Society (1826). The establishment Society exported "eastern culture" to White and Indian ethnics in the West but not to the South during the antebellum era--and thus evenhandedly withheld their resources from the English race and British ethnic slavemasters, and their free and enslaved Black Calvinist and other Evangelical Protestant brothers and sisters. The only antebellum Southern beneficiaries of the Puritan largess were fellow members of the Congregationalist and Presbyterian yoked churches and bureaucracies, including the Colonizationists who were waning rather than waxing at least as rapidly as the slavocracy was ascending and slaves were being bred.

The ascension and expansion of the new constellation of fabulously wealthy Northeasterners corresponded to the revolutionary change from a mercantilist to a capitalist economy; the new technology advanced by the industrial revolution and financed through industrial capitalism; the outbreak of secular humanism energized by competing realism and optimism values; and the eruption of the Second Great Awakening with its outpouring of religious humanitarian idealism.

At this moment of sacred and secular focalization of social structural change means and ends, and turning point from a predominantly agrarian to a hegemonic manufacturing political economy, Second Great Awakening Evangelical fervor and idealization merged as the dual spiritual and moral power energies harnessed by Samuel John Mills, Jr., who was born in 1783 and died in 1818, and several classmates at Williams College. The undergraduates took refuge from a downpour, where, after being hit by spiritual lightning, they lit the Evangelical "Haystack Prayer Meeting" (1806)--in which they warmed to the call to become missionaries. Professional preparation began at nearby Andover Seminary, where Mills and a company of students organized what the Congregational General Associations of Massachusetts and Connecticut incorporated (and controlled following consolidation with the Presbyterians) as the American Board of Commissioners for Foreign Missions (1810).

Mills desired to be among the original American foreign missionaries, where the American Board's first class was headed by Adoniram Judson and Luther Rice and sent (in 1812) to India. But fragile health prevented Mills from realizing his foreign mission ambition, and he turned his energies to domestic missions. Returning from an assignment in the West for the Board of Commissioners, at the juncture in history when antislavery ideas and ideals and idealists were as scare as hens' teeth in New England, Mills relocated and continued his theological studies at Princeton Seminary--during which period the theologue founded a school for Black Northeasterners in Parsippany, New Jersey. Subsequently, learning from his father of the Samuel Hopkins' essentially dead and buried and certainly forgotten African colonization scheme, the "Connecticut Yankee" Congregationalist in New Jersey shared Hopkins' stratagem with the Reverend (1795) Robert Finley (1772-1817): a Princeton-born (College of New Jersey renamed) Princeton-graduate (1787), and Presbyterian-ordained (1795) brother of the cloth, who was serving as minister and headmaster of a school for boys in Basking Ridge, New Jersey.[103]

On February 14, 1816, Finley communicated the gist of his updated version of the Hopkinsian Black-race deportation program in a letter to John P. Mumford:

> The longer I live to see the wretchedness of men, the more I ad-mire the virtue of those who devise, and with patient sacrifice labor to execute plans for the relief of the wretched. On this subject the state of the free blacks has very much oppressed my mind. Their number increases greatly, and their wretchedness too it appears to me. Everything connected with their con-dition, including their color, is against them; nor is there much prospect that their state can ever be greatly ameliorated, while they shall continue among us. Could not the rich and benevolent devise means to form a colony in some part of *Africa* similar to the one at *Sierra Leone*...? Ought not Congress to be petitioned to grant them a district in a good climate....? Our fathers brought them here, and we are bound, if possible to repair the injuries inflicted by our fathers. Could they be sent to Africa, a three-fold benefit would arise. We should be cleared of them;--we should send to Africa a population partially ci-vilized and christianized for its benefit; --our blacks themselves would be put in a better situation.[104]

Contemporaries who were less familiar with the writings of the two architects of colonizationism than William Ellery Channing, could be appreciated if after reading their letters they reported a sense of *déjà vu* and an imperceptible difference between Finley's analysis and conclusion in this communication and those penned by Samuel Hopkins--who had died thirteen years earlier. Hopkins was more of an intellectual and less of an organization man and chief executive officer type than Finley, which was one of the several crucial reasons why the successful rational design he developed and Ezra Stiles supported failed for lack of support, on the eve of the American Revolution and during the early national years.

Hopkins' imaginative plot for sending the free Black indigenous North American race to Africa as missionary colonists finally became attractive to Northeastern and Southeastern Calvinists, as well as other Evangelical Protestants. The positive response from the establishment occurred as a result of two among other essential factors: conceivably secondarily because of the superior administrative gifts and managerial skills Finley demonstrated even more impressively than Mills; and doubtless primarily because the 1808 law mandating the proscription of the international slavetrade, by order of the Constitution, resulted not as New Englanders anticipated in the contraction of slavery but in the unanticipated expansion of domestic breeding and slavetrading.

Finley managed nearly instantly to excite sufficient interest in his findings to warrant calling a meeting at Princeton to explore the possibilities and impossibilities inherent in his projected race and religion prospective. By late 1816, the project appeared so meritorious to Calvinist capital, management, and clergy until Finley was able to organize a national colonization society--that church and corporation officers publicly pledged to underwrite in cooperation with clandestine commitment of funding from United States treasury by the majority leader of the Congress.

The grand machination found favor with the Speaker of the House, and Presbyterian layman, Representative Henry Clay of Kentucky: a relocated native Virginian who served as the Society's first vice-president, and presided over the December 21, 1816 meeting in the Halls of Congress. A constitution was hammered out but could not be finalized and ratified by the delegates before the end of the year.

Thus the organizing convention remained in session until January 1, 1817, when the parties to the color and colonization conflict of interest elected officers of *The American Society for Colonizing the Free People of Color of the United States.*

Founder Finley acceded to the office of President the University of Georgia the previous year and died in the year the Society was chartered. The ACS played a key role in the founding of Liberia, and served as its trustee for fifty years after Mills died on the return leg following his forage into Africa to select the settlement site of Liberia. George Washington's Virginia-born nephew and executor of his estate, Associate Justice of the United States Supreme Court (1798) Bushrod Washington (1762-1829), was a founding member and the Society's first president. Including Justice Washington, twelve of the initial seventeen vice-presidents were native Southerners; and each one of the original twelve managers was a slaveholder.

The City of Brotherly Love was the mecca for Black Northerners during the period and for the same reasons she was the home of the first liberation from bondage Black denomination, Continental Congresses, Constitution Convention, capitol, bank, and cultural center of the nation. Given the proximity of the Philadelphia to the relocated capitol in Washington, D.C., where the Society was founded, and her well-known Black leadership class, during the months of the Society's planning stage the all-White directors naturally solicited Black Philadelphians to cooperate with the emerging model perfect private-parochial-public partnership institution. Learning of its mandate, the Black elite corps of leaders summarily rejected the Society out of hand as an anti-Black race interest instrument of interlocking directorates of the church, corporation, and Congress bureaucracies.

Consequently, upon discovering that instead of their advice and counsel being heeded, by the power elite who insisted they were forming the organization to serve the best known right and good interests of Black folk and the establishment created the ACS, the Black leaders counterreplied within days of the ACS's incorporation. Organized by Bishop Richard Allen, and convened in Mother Bethel African Methodist Episcopal Church of Philadelphia, the massive protest convention of the Black masses and middle-class--who previously elected their parsons and currently selected them their political representatives--unanimously supported their spokesmen's denouncement to the public of the philanthropic organization as a deterrence-benevolence denationalization, deculturalization, and deportation enterprise. No one who listened doubted they passed, without objection, the consensus value judgment that ACS existence was the manifest essence of the error of conception, perception, and deception.

Speaking for themselves, long before any White person or body presumed to speak for them, Black leaders set themselves squarely in opposition to the Halfway Piety faith and deterrence-benevolence ethics line of the establishment --and an unbroken continuum wrought by Edwards, Hopkins, Beecher, Finley, and the slaveholding Christian congregants. It is a commonplace that bene-ficiaries of power and privilege preponderantly oppose measures capable of overturning their vested interests. Applying the self-defense moral principle and practice in this context, the question concerning just whose real interests and values proslavocrat gradualists as well as slaveholding Southern Colonizationists were protecting can be answered readily. When the question is addressed to nonslaveholding but proslavocrat Northerners, the problem is far more complex and therefore the answer is exceedingly elusive and difficult to state with entire confidence.

Obviously not the proslavocracy moral majority but the moral minority of White Southerners were sympathizers with Finley's transformation of Hopkins' pet pilot project from a dysfunctional to a functional private-parochial-public institution. They were also founding members and spokesmen for the Society, that was founded by Christian idealists who were convinced that they were the only realists. Their highest praise was extended to the last of the three successive Chief Executives from Virginia particularly, and the Administration of President (1817-25) James Monroe (1758-1831) generally, when in an act of appreciation for whose support the ACS named the capital of Liberia, Monrovia. Perspective it is added by recalling that the Society's annual meeting (February 19, 1825) met in the "Supreme Court Room of the Capitol"--with another Virginian in attendance, Chief Justice (1801-35) John Marshall (1755-1835).[105]

The pertinent point is that reality set in when the Southern Christian gentlemen-dominated ACS discovered they could not finance their Black race "back to Africa," and determined that a singular reason among others was the fact that the Southeastern aristocrats in power and authority in the Cotton Kingdom were far less wealthy than the Northeastern "Robber Barons" turned Protestant philanthropists and Calvinist capitalist captains of industry. Thus the ACS turned the controls over to the Calvinist capitalists, who selected as their professional manager and chief executive officer (1822-64) presbyter Ralph Randolph Gurley.

During the twenty years between the ratification of the Constitution

(1788)--that made slaves property and slavery the rule of law--and the 1808 act prohibiting the international slavetrade, private manumissions decreased rather than increased in the South. Idealists and realists who at their peril failed to take the cotton gin plantation economy revitalizing machine and the proslavery warriors seriously, generally were so sanguine until this private and personal moral promise and performance was presumed to reflect the enlightened spirit of unrepresentative Southern aristocrats and plebeians. It was widely presupposed in the North that these benevolent paternalists sanctioned and led the preferred stable and peaceful or progressive transformationist way of Christianity and civility to secure the eventual end of the "peculiar institution."

Southern interest in the ACS for the expatriation of free Black Americans was guaranteed by the full faith and credit in the ACS reputedly extended by Thomas Jefferson--the supreme spokesman for the South--after his conflict with the Federalists and sharp attack upon the Federalist Party partisan parsons, who did not appreciate the criticism. Publishing a testament that could pass for a perfect imitation or translation of Samuel Hopkins' rational program, Jefferson summarized his procolonizationism in a letter he addressed to John Lynn (dated January 21, 1811) six years before the ACS was organized:

> You have asked my opinion on the proposition of Mrs. Mifflin, to take measures for procuring, on the coast of Africa, an establishment to which the people of color of these States might, from time to time, be colonized, under the auspices of different governments. Having long ago made up my mind on this subject, I have no hesitation in saying that I have ever thought it the most desirable measure which could be adopted, for gradually drawing off this part of our population, most advantageously for themselves as well as for us. Going from a country possessing all the useful arts, they might be the means of transplanting them among the inhabitants of Africa, and would thus carry back to the country of their origin, the seeds of civilization which might render their sojournment and sufferings here a blessing in the end to that country.
>
> I received, in the first year of my coming into the administration of the General Government, a letter from the Governor of Virginia, (Colonel Monroe,) consulting me, at the request of the legislature of the State, on the means of procuring some such asylum, to which these people might be occasionally sent. I proposed to him the establishment of Sierra Leone, to which a private company in England had already colonized a number of negroes, and particularly the fugitives from these States during the Revolutionary War; and at the same time suggested, if this could not be obtained, some of the Portuguese possessions in South America, as next most desirable. The subsequent legislature approving these ideas, I wrote, the ensuing year, 1802, to Mr. King, our Minister in London, to endeavor to negotiate with the Sierra Leone company a reception of such of these people as might be colonized thither. He opened a correspondence with Mr. Wedderburne and Mr. Thornton, secretaries of the company, on the subject, and in 1803, I received through Mr. King the result, which was that the colony was going on, but in a languishing condition; that the funds of the company were

likely to fail, as they received no returns of profit to keep them up: that they were therefore in treaty with their government to take the establishment off their hands; but that in no event should they be willing to receive more of these people from the United States, as it was exactly that portion of their settlers which had gone from hence, which, by their idleness and turbulence, had kept the settlement in constant danger of dissolution, which could not have been prevented but for the aid of the Maroon negroes from the West Indies, who were more industrious and orderly than the others, and supported the authority of the government and its laws. I think I learned afterwards that the British government had taken the colony into its own hands, and I believe it still exists. The effort which I made with Portugal, to claim an establishment for them within their claims in South America, proved also abortive.

You inquire further, whether I would use my endeavors to procure for such an establishment security against violence from other powers, and particularly from France? Certainly, I shall be willing to do anything I can to give it effect and safety. But I am but a private individual, and could only use endeavors with private individuals: whereas, the National Government can address themselves at once to those of Europe to obtain the desired security, and will unquestionably be ready to exert its influence with those nations for an object so benevolent in itself, and so important to a great portion of its constituents. Indeed, nothing is more to be wished than that the United States would themselves undertake to make such an establishment on the coast of Africa. Exclusive of motives of humanity, the commercial advantages to be derived from it might repay all its expenses. But for this, the national mind is not yet prepared. It may perhaps be doubted whether many of these people would voluntarily consent to such an exchange of situation, and very certain that few of those advanced to a certain age in habits of slavery, would be capable of self-government. This should not, however, discourage the experiment, nor the early trial of it; and the proposition should be made with all the prudent cautions and attentions requisite to reconcile it to the interests, the safety and the prejudices of all parties.[106]

Reality dictated to the Colonizationists the value of awareness of the economic burden of the slaves; personal commitments to slaves; religious interests in final purification rites; and moral judgment aided by external and internal reflection; the expectation that politically abolition was inevitable. These factors of realism, alone and in combination with nearly as many motives as can be humanly imagined, all impacted upon the discerning Southerners as the official date for ending the slavetrade approached.

There abided some general consciousness, if not pressure, among the sensible that a change was in the offing. But beyond liberal laws for private manumission, proslavery did not decline in the South--its significance inclined with the invention of the cotton gin and the foundation which give rise to the expansionist slavocracy.

During the period of their loyal and faithful membership in the ACS, Garrison and Beecher were undistinguished from the Moral Majority who were confused concerning the South's economic development and its portent since the Revolution. At the very least, competitive political economy measures seemed to fasten proslavocrats in a cross-fire of Northern industrialization and Southern slavocracy. In this state of prudential pragmatism and ambiguity, as the Southeast held more slaves than the Northeast, and upheld the all-purpose slavocracy, an elite Southern minority discovered they could afford to withdraw from the slavocracy some support in favor of Colonizationism. After the formation of the ACS, Colonizationists developed as "the larger force in the antislavery movement"--between 1808 and 1831--and beat their competition who quickly discovered they could not compete with the Evangelical Protestant denominations-backed ACS. Thus entered into precipitous decline even strong Old Abolitionist Societies such as those formed in Kentucky (1808), Tennessee and Maryland (1815), and in North Carolina (1816).[107]

Alternatively stated, the combination of Democrat Jefferson's 1803 Louisiana Purchase (over the objections of the New England Federalists), with its extension of slavery in selected parts of the new national acquisition, together with the increase of economic profits made possible by the unholy combination of man and the cotton gin machine, were factors accelerating the rapid rise of the real interests and values of the Northeastern capitalists and politicians, and their emergence in the antislavocracy/proslavocracy issue of power and wealth. Where once the Old Abolitionists (for whom slavery was a religious and moral issue) of the North and the South tacitly agreed that freedom and slavery--like good and evil, virtue and vice--were incompatibles, this compromise of principles spirit gave way to slavocracy as the new Southern economic priority--and concern to extend slavery.

Concurrent with this triumph of the Southern expanse, her resident pro-Colonizationist antislavery idealists tried to snatch private manumission from the Jaws of defeat through a magnanimous public gesture. But the ACS they created and supported for this purpose, in part, fundamentally functioned to expel free Blacks Americans: whom the dominant and aggressive Southern expansionists considered (in the light of the 1801 Haitian Revolution, which encouraged Napoleon to sell his Louisiana territory to Jefferson) potential insurrectionists.

Agents of the Gurley-directed ACS did not accept the clear, consistent, and constant critically analyzed political and economic implications of its Black race excludable mission. They were rationalized as unfortunate but incidental consequences of little moment--compared with the larger good of the philanthropic missionary resettlement enterprise. Sending free Black Americans to Africa--by paying all their expenses, and providing seed money--argued for White Colonizationists that Black Colonizationists journeyed to Africa voluntarily because they were not physically forced but only psychologically coerced to choose between this Church-Congress-Corporation pattern of economic and political relief and none. The ACS affirmed heralded expatriation as the safe, sane, humane, moral, and Christian way of expurgation, that at once served the best interests of White and Black people alike.

In spite or because of the clear and present descriptive facts and value judgment Anti-Colonizationist Garrison published, Colonizationists did not understand themselves to be the foil to economics and politics of slavocracy--or the spoilers of the hoped for abolition, and the dream of liberty in freedom with dignity that Black men sought to realize. The ACS agencies from Gurley through Beecher to Bacon did not believe the Black race should be enslaved. These angels of mercy also did not believe the American Black race should or could compete with the White race--even if provided with the opportunity they were convinced was beyond contemplation. They would not expend their resources in aiding Black folk to improve their lot as free persons in the United States.

Overriding countermarching anti-Colonizationist Garrison types, pro-Colonizationist Beecherite types argued praiseworthy rather than blameworthy initiative was evidenced in their predeliberate rejection of deniability and acceptance of responsibility for piloting the systematic and systemic exclusion of the Black body from the White body politic, body corporate, and body of Christ; advanced banishment as their principal principle and practice or deterrence-benevolence end justifying their Christian charity enterprise means; and, as the surrogate value for freedom in liberty they insisted Black folk accept who countercharged their true and real interests were served only by securing selfdetermination in their native land, promoted the critical imposition of permanent exile and émigré existence upon Black folk as the last, best hope of the Black African ethnic-deethnicized and/or Black race-only group their English-race/British-ethnic progenitors created, denominated black, and refused to accept.

Clearly, Anglo-American Colonizationists displayed the height of egotism when they unwittingly imitated the Founding Fathers, who at the birth of the nation simultaneously committed what passed for Original Sin and proved the truth and consequences in reality of the myth--that is, instead of enhancing the human condition through making, keeping, and improving agreements, they aspired to improve upon the Creator's promise and performance. But even Providence is unable to achieve the objective Colonizationists superimposed upon the color caste/captive class. In a word, as long as either and/or both history and human existence abides God is unable to drive the Devil out of His world!

Contrapositively, no less real predestinarians and dangerous predeterminationists for being equally obvious deterrence-benevolence quintessence and demonstrable constructive engagement antecedence, pro-White race/ethnic Colonizationists, by turns, denied individual harm-intensive and community self-defeating consequences were entailed in their positive negation of their kith and kin; affirmed the direct opposite of destructive dehumanization to be the equivalence of disinterested will to the good and constructive disengagement from their Black-race progeny; and bid fair not only to rebuff both the Original Creator's creatures and their recreations but also to out-God God who could not repel permanently from His presence either His "Elect" or "Reprobate."